Lecture Notes of the Institute
for Computer Sciences, Social Informatics
and Telecommunications Engineering 165

More information about this series at http://www.springer.com/series/8197

Phan Cong Vinh · Vangalur Alagar (Eds.)

Context-Aware Systems and Applications

4th International Conference, ICCASA 2015
Vung Tau, Vietnam, November 26–27, 2015
Revised Selected Papers

 Springer

Editors
Phan Cong Vinh
Nguyen Tat Thanh University
Ho Chi Minh City
Vietnam

Vangalur Alagar
Concordia University
Montréal, QC
Canada

ISSN 1867-8211 ISSN 1867-822X (electronic)
Lecture Notes of the Institute for Computer Sciences, Social Informatics
and Telecommunications Engineering
ISBN 978-3-319-29235-9 ISBN 978-3-319-29236-6 (eBook)
DOI 10.1007/978-3-319-29236-6

Library of Congress Control Number: 2015960419

Printed on acid-free paper

This Springer imprint is published by SpringerNature
The registered company is Springer International Publishing AG Switzerland

Preface

ICCASA 2015, an international scientific conference for research in the field of context-aware computing and communication, was held during November 26–27, 2015, in Vung Tau City, Vietnam. The aim of the conference was to provide an internationally respected forum for scientific research on the technologies and applications of context-aware computing and communication. This conference provided an excellent opportunity for researchers to discuss modern approaches and techniques for context-aware systems and their applications. The proceedings of ICCASA 2015 are published by Springer in the Lecture Notes of the Institute for Computer Sciences, Social Informatics and Telecommunications Engineering series (LNICST; indexed by DBLP, EI, Google Scholar, Scopus, Thomson ISI).

For this fourth edition, repeating the success of previous years, the Program Committee received over 100 submissions from 15 countries and each paper was reviewed by at least three experts. We chose 42 papers after intensive discussions held among the Program Committee members. We appreciate the excellent reviews and lively discussions of the Program Committee members and external reviewers in the review process. This year we chose three prominent invited speakers: Prof. Vangalur Alagar from Concordia University, Canada; Prof. Chintan Bhatt from Charotar University of Science and Technology, India; and Prof. Phan Cong Vinh from Nguyen Tat Thanh University, Vietnam.

ICCASA 2015 was jointly organized by The European Alliance for Innovation (EAI), Ba Ria-Vung Tau University (BVU), and Nguyen Tat Thanh University (NTTU). This conference could not have been organized without the strong support of the staff members of these three organizations. We would especially like to thank Prof. Imrich Chlamtac (University of Trento and Create-NET), Anna Horvathova (EAI), and Ivana Allen (EAI) for their great help in organizing the conference. We also appreciate the gentle guidance and help from Prof. Nguyen Manh Hung, Chairman and Rector of NTTU, and Dr. Nguyen Thi Chim Lang, Rector of BVU.

November 2015

Phan Cong Vinh
Vangalur Alagar

Organization

Steering Committee

Imrich Chlamtac   Create-Net, Italy (Chair)
Phan Cong Vinh   Nguyen Tat Thanh University, Vietnam
Thanos Vasilakos   Kuwait University

Honorary General Chair

Nguyen Manh Hung   Nguyen Tat Thanh University, Vietnam

General Co-chairs

Phan Cong Vinh   Nguyen Tat Thanh University, Vietnam
Nguyen Thi Chim Lang   Ba Ria-Vung Tau University, Vietnam

TPC Co-chairs

Truong My Dung   Ba Ria-Vung Tau University, Vietnam
Nguyen Thanh Tung   Ha Noi Vietnam National University, Vietnam

Technical Program Track Leaders

Phan Ngoc Hoang   Ba Ria-Vung Tau University, Vietnam
Bui Thi Thu Trang   Ba Ria-Vung Tau University, Vietnam
Vangalur Alagar   Concordia University, Canada

Workshop Chair

Emil Vassev   University of Limerick, Ireland

Publication Co-chairs

Vu Van Dong   Ba Ria-Vung Tau University, Vietnam
Nguyen Kim Quoc   Nguyen Tat Thanh University, Vietnam

Local Arrangements Co-chairs

Ngo Van Luoc	Ba Ria-Vung Tau University, Vietnam
Nguyen Thi Cam Van	Ba Ria-Vung Tau University, Vietnam
Nhu Van Duong	Ba Ria-Vung Tau University, Vietnam
Do Nguyen Anh Thu	Nguyen Tat Thanh University, Vietnam

Marketing and Publicity Co-chairs

Hoang Ngoc Thanh	Ba Ria-Vung Tau University, Vietnam
Nguyen Thanh Binh	Ho Chi Minh City University of Technology, Vietnam

Website Co-chairs

Hoang Ngoc Thanh	Ba Ria-Vung Tau University, Vietnam
Thai Thi Thanh Thao	Nguyen Tat Thanh University, Vietnam

Sponsorship and Exhibits Co-chairs

Nguyen Phan Cuong	Ba Ria-Vung Tau University, Vietnam
Do Nguyen Anh Thu	Nguyen Tat Thanh University, Vietnam

Panels and Keynotes Co-chairs

Nguyen Thi Cam Van	Ba Ria-Vung Tau University, Vietnam
Phan Cong Vinh	Nguyen Tat Thanh University, Vietnam

Demos and Tutorials Chair

Bach Long Giang	Nguyen Tat Thanh University, Vietnam

Posters Co-chairs

Vu Van Dong	Ba Ria-Vung Tau University, Vietnam
Thai Thi Thanh Thao	Nguyen Tat Thanh University, Vietnam

Industry Forum Co-chairs

Truong My Dung	Ba Ria-Vung Tau University, Vietnam
Tran Thi Nhu Thuy	Nguyen Tat Thanh University, Vietnam

Special Sessions Chair

Phan Cong Vinh	Nguyen Tat Thanh University, Vietnam

Conference Coordinator

Anna Horvathova   European Alliance for Innovation

Technical Program Committee

Abdur Rakib	The University of Nottingham, UK
Aniruddha Bhattacharjya	Narasaraopeta Engineering College, India
Areerat Songsakulwattana	Rangsit University, Thailand
Asad Masood Khattak	Kyung Hee University, South Korea
Ashad Kabir	Swinburne University of Technology, Australia
Ashish Khare	University of Allahabad, India
Athar Sethi	Universiti Teknologi PETRONAS, Malaysia
Charu Gandhi	Jaypee Institute of Information Technology, India
Chien-Chih Yu	National Chengchi University, Taiwan
Chintan Bhatt	Charotar University of Science and Technology, India
David Sundaram	The University of Auckland, New Zealand
Dinh Duc Anh Vu	University of Information Technology - HCMVNU, Vietnam
Duong Tuan Anh	Ho Chi Minh City University of Technology - HCMVNU, Vietnam
Dzati Athiar Ramli	Universiti Sains Malaysia, Malaysia
François Siewe	De Montfort University, UK
Gabrielle Peko	The University of Auckland, New Zealand
Giacomo Cabri	University of Modena and Reggio Emilia, Italy
Govardhan Aliseri	Jawaharlal Nehru Technological University Hyderabad, India
Hoang Huu Hanh	Hue University, Vietnam
Huynh Quyet-Thang	Hanoi University of Science and Technology, Vietnam
Huynh Trung Hieu	Ho Chi Minh City University of Industry, Vietnam
Huynh Xuan Hiep	Can Tho University, Vietnam
Ichiro Satoh	National Institute of Informatics, Japan
Issam Damaj	The American University of Kuwait, Kuwait
Jamus Collier	University of Bremen, Germany
Krishna Asawa	Jaypee Institute of Information Technology, India
Kurt Geihs	University of Kassel, Germany
Ly Quoc Ngoc	Ho Chi Minh City University of Science - HCMVNU, Vietnam
Manmeet Mahinderjit Singh	Universiti Sains Malaysia, Malaysia
Moeiz Miraoui	University of Quebec, Canada
Mubarak Mohammad	Concordia University, Canada
Muhammad Fahad Khan	Federal Urdu University of Arts, Science and Technology, Pakistan

Contents

Products and Coproducts of Autonomic Systems

Phan Cong Vinh[✉]

Faculty of Information Technology, Nguyen Tat Thanh University (NTTU),
300A Nguyen Tat Thanh Street, Ward 13, District 4, HCM City, Vietnam
pcvinh@ntt.edu.vn

Abstract. Self-* is widely considered as a foundation for autonomic computing. The notion of autonomic systems (ASs) and self-* serves as a basis on which to build our intuition about category of ASs in general. In this paper we will specify ASs and self-* and then move on to consider products and coproducts of ASs. All of this material is taken as an investigation of our category, the category of ASs, which we call **AS**.

Keywords: Autonomic computing · Autonomic systems · Coproduct · Product · Self-*

1   Introduction

Autonomic computing (AC) imitates and simulates the natural intelligence possessed by the human autonomic nervous system using generic computers. This indicates that the nature of software in AC is the simulation and embodiment of human behaviors, and the extension of human capability, reachability, persistency, memory, and information processing speed. AC was first proposed by IBM in 2001 where it is defined as

> "*Autonomic computing is an approach to self-managed computing systems with a minimum of human interference. The term derives from the body's autonomic nervous system, which controls key functions without conscious awareness or involvement*" [1].

AC in our recent investigations [2–6] is generally described as self-*. Formally, let self-* be the set of self-_'s. Each self-_ to be an element in self-* is called a *self-* facet*. That is,

$$\text{self-*} = \{\text{self-}\_ \mid \text{self-}\_ \text{ is a self-* facet}\} \tag{1}$$

We see that self-CHOP is composed of four self-* facets of self-configuration, self-healing, self-optimization and self-protection. Hence, self-CHOP is a subset of self-*. That is, self-CHOP = {self-configuration, self-healing, self-optimization, self-protection} ⊂ self-*. Every self-* facet must satisfy some certain criteria, so-called *self-* properties*.

© ICST Institute for Computer Sciences, Social Informatics and Telecommunications Engineering 2016
P.C. Vinh and V. Alagar (Eds.): ICCASA 2015, LNICST 165, pp. 1–9, 2016.
DOI: 10.1007/978-3-319-29236-6_1

In its AC manifesto, IBM proposed eight facets setting forth an AS known as *self-awareness, self-configuration, self-optimization, self-maintenance, self-protection (security and integrity), self-adaptation, self-resource- allocation* and *open-standard-based* [1]. In other words, consciousness (self-awareness) and non-imperative (goal-driven) behaviors are the main features of autonomic systems (ASs).

In this paper we will specify ASs and self-* and then move on to consider products and coproducts of ASs. All of this material is taken as an investigation of our category, the category of ASs, which we call **AS**.

2   Outline

In the paper, we attempt to make the presentation as self-contained as possible, although familiarity with the notion of self-* in ASs is assumed. Acquaintance with the associated notion of algebraic language is useful for recognizing the results, but is almost everywhere not strictly necessary.

The rest of this paper is organized as follows: Sect. 3 presents the notion of autonomic systems (ASs). In Sect. 4, self-* actions in ASs are specified, products and coproducts of ASs are considered. Finally, a short summary is given in Sect. 5.

3   Autonomic Systems (ASs)

We can think of an AS as a collection of states $x \in AS$, each of which is recognizable as being in AS and such that for each pair of named states $x, y \in AS$ we can tell if $x = y$ or not. The symbol $\oslash$ denotes the AS with no states.

If AS_1 and AS_2 are ASs, we say that AS_1 is a sub-system of AS_2, and write $AS_1 \subseteq AS_2$, if every state of AS_1 is a state of AS_2. Checking the definition, we see that for any system AS, we have sub-systems $\oslash \subseteq AS$ and $AS \subseteq AS$.

We can use system-builder notation to denote sub-systems. For example the autonomic system can be written $\{x \in AS \mid x \text{ is a state of AS}\}$.

The symbol $\exists$ means "there exists". So we can write the autonomic system as $\{x \in AS \mid \exists y \text{ is a final state such that } self\text{-}*action(x) = y\}$

The symbol $\exists!$ means "there exists a unique". So the statement "$\exists! x \in AS$ is an initial state" means that there is one and only one state to be a start one, that is, the state of the autonomic system before any self-* action is processed.

Finally, the symbol $\forall$ means "for all". So the statement "$\forall x \in AS \ \exists y \in AS$ such that $self\text{-}* \ action(x) = y$" means that for every state of autonomic system there is the next one.

In the paper, we use the $\overset{def}{=}$ notation "$AS_1 \overset{def}{=} AS_2$" to mean something like "define AS_1 to be AS_2". That is, a $\overset{def}{=}$ declaration is not denoting a fact of nature (like $1 + 2 = 3$), but our formal notation. It just so happens that the notation above, such as Self-CHOP $\overset{def}{=}$ {self-configuration, self-healing, self-optimization, self-protection}, is a widely-held choice.

4   Products and Coproducts of Autonomic Systems

If AS and AS' are sets of autonomic system states, then a self-*action *self-*action* from AS to AS', denoted *self-*action*: $AS \to AS'$, is a mapping that sends each state $x \in AS$ to a state of AS', denoted *self-*action*$(x) \in AS'$. We call AS the domain of *self-*action* and we call AS' the codomain of *self-*action*.

Note that the symbol AS', read "AS-prime", has nothing to do with calculus or derivatives. It is simply notation that we use to name a symbol that is suggested as being somehow like AS. This suggestion of consanguinity between AS and AS' is meant only as an aid for human cognition, and not as part of the mathematics. For every state $x \in AS$, there is exactly one arrow emanating from x, but for a state $y \in AS'$, there can be several arrows pointing to y, or there can be no arrows pointing to y.

Suppose that $AS' \subseteq AS$ is a sub-system. Then we can consider the self-* action $AS' \to AS$ given by sending every state of AS' to "itself" as a state of AS. For example if $AS = \{a, b, c, d, e, f\}$ and $AS' = .\{b, d, e\}$ then $AS' \subseteq AS$ and we turn that into the self-* action $AS' \to AS$ given by $b \mapsto b, d \mapsto d, e \mapsto e$. This kind of arrow, $\mapsto$, is read aloud as "maps to". A self-* action *self-*action*: $AS \to AS'$ means a rule for assigning to each state $x \in AS$ a state *self-*action*$(x) \in AS'$. We say that "x maps to *self-*action*(x)" and write $x \mapsto$ *self-*action*(x).

As a matter of notation, we can sometimes say something like the following: Let *self-*action*: $AS' \subseteq AS$ be a sub-system. Here we are making clear that AS' is a sub-system of AS, but that *self-*action* is the name of the associated self-* action.

Given a self-* action *self-*action*: $AS \to AS'$, the states of AS' that have at least one arrow pointing to them are said to be in the image of *self-*action*; that is we have

$$\mathrm{im}(\textit{self-*action}) \stackrel{def}{=} \{y \in AS' \mid \exists x \in AS \text{ such that } \textit{self-*action}(x) = y\} \quad (2)$$

Given *self-*action*: $AS \to AS'$ and *self-*action'* : $AS' \to AS''$, where the codomain of *self-*action* is the same set of autonomic system states as the domain of *self-*action'* (namely AS'), we say that *self-*action* and *self-*action'* are composable

$$AS \xrightarrow{\textit{self-*action}} AS' \xrightarrow{\textit{self-*action}'} AS''$$

The composition of *self-*action* and *self-*action'* is denoted by *self-*action'* $\circ$ *self-*action*: $AS \to AS''$.

We write $\mathrm{Hom}_{\mathbf{AS}}(AS, AS')$ to denote the set of *self-*actions* $AS \to AS'$. Two self-* actions *self-*action, self-*action'* : $AS \to AS'$ are equal if and only if for every state $x \in AS$ we have *self-*action*$(x) = $ *self-*action'*(x).

We define the identity *self-*action* on AS, denoted $id_{AS} : AS \to AS$, to be the self-* action such that for all $x \in AS$ we have $id_{AS}(x) = x$.

A *self-*action*: $AS \to AS'$ is called an *isomorphism*, denoted *self-*action*: $AS \overset{\cong}{\to} AS'$, if there exists a self-* action *self-*action'* : $AS' \to AS$ such that *self-*action'* $\circ$ *self-*action*$= id_{AS}$ and *self-*action* $\circ$ *self-*action'* $= id_{AS'}$. We also say that *self-*action* is *invertible* and we say that *self-*action'* is the *inverse* of *self-*action*. If there exists an isomorphism $AS \overset{\cong}{\to} AS'$ we say that AS and AS' are isomorphic autonomic systems and may write $AS \cong AS'$.

Proposition 1. *The following facts hold about isomorphism.*

1. *Any autonomic system AS is isomorphic to itself; i.e. there exists an isomorphism $AS \overset{\cong}{\to} AS$.*
2. *For any autonomic systems AS and AS', if AS is isomorphic to AS' then AS' is isomorphic to AS.*
3. *For any autonomic systems AS, AS' and AS'', if AS is isomorphic to AS' and AS' is isomorphic to AS'' then AS is isomorphic to AS''.*

Proof:

1. The identity self-* action $id_{AS} : AS \to AS$ is invertible; its inverse is id_{AS} because $id_{AS} \circ id_{AS} = id_{AS}$.
2. If *self-*action*: $AS \to AS'$ is invertible with inverse *self-*action'* : $AS' \to AS$ then *self-*action'* is an isomorphism with inverse *self-*action*.
3. If *self-*action*: $AS \to AS'$ and $\widehat{self\text{-}*action} : AS' \to AS''$ are each invertible with inverses *self-*action'* : $AS' \to AS$ and $\widehat{self\text{-}*action}' : AS'' \to AS'$ then the following calculations show that $\widehat{self\text{-}*action} \circ self\text{-}*action$ is invertible with inverse $self\text{-}*action' \circ \widehat{self\text{-}*action}'$:

$$(\widehat{self\text{-}*action} \circ self\text{-}*action) \circ (self\text{-}*action' \circ \widehat{self\text{-}*action}') =$$
$$\widehat{self\text{-}*action} \circ (self\text{-}*action \circ self\text{-}*action') \circ \widehat{self\text{-}*action}' =$$
$$\widehat{self\text{-}*action} \circ id_{AS'} \circ \widehat{self\text{-}*action}' = \widehat{self\text{-}*action} \circ \widehat{self\text{-}*action}' = id_{AS''}$$

and

$$(self\text{-}*action' \circ \widehat{self\text{-}*action}') \circ (\widehat{self\text{-}*action} \circ self\text{-}*action) =$$
$$self\text{-}*action' \circ (\widehat{self\text{-}*action}' \circ \widehat{self\text{-}*action}) \circ self\text{-}*action =$$
$$self\text{-}*action' \circ id_{AS'} \circ self\text{-}*action = self\text{-}*action' \circ self\text{-}*action = id_{AS}$$

Q.E.D.

For any natural number $n \in \mathbb{N}$, define a set $\underline{n} = \{1, 2, \dots, n\}$. So, in particular, $\underline{0} = \varnothing$. A function $f : \underline{n} \to AS$ can be written as a sequence $f = (f(1), f(2), \dots, f(n))$. We say that AS has cardinality n, denoted $\mid AS \mid = n$ if there exists an isomorphism $AS \cong \underline{n}$. If there exists some $n \in \mathbb{N}$ such that AS has cardinality n then we say that AS is finite. Otherwise, we say that AS is infinite and write $\mid AS \mid \geq \infty$.

Proposition 2. *Suppose that AS and AS' are finite. If there is an isomorphism of autonomic systems $f : AS \to AS'$ then the two autonomic systems have the same cardinality, $\mid AS \mid = \mid AS' \mid$.*

Proof: Suppose that $f : AS \to AS'$ is an isomorphism. If there exists natural numbers $m, n \in \mathbb{N}$ and isomorphisms $\alpha : \underline{m} \overset{\cong}{\to} AS$ and $\beta : \underline{n} \overset{\cong}{\to} AS'$ then

$$\underline{m} \overset{\alpha}{\to} AS \overset{f}{\to} AS' \overset{\beta^{-1}}{\to} \underline{n}$$

is an isomorphism. We can prove by induction that the sets $\underline{m}$ and $\underline{n}$ are isomorphic if and only if $m = n$.   Q.E.D.

Consider the following diagram:

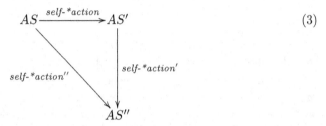

(3)

We say this is a diagram of autonomic systems if each of AS, AS', AS'' is an autonomic system and each of *self-*action, self-*action', self-*action''* is a self-* action. We say this diagram commutes if *self-*action'∘ self-*action = self-*action''*. In this case we refer to it as a commutative triangle of autonomic systems. Diagram (3) is considered to be the same diagram as each of the following:

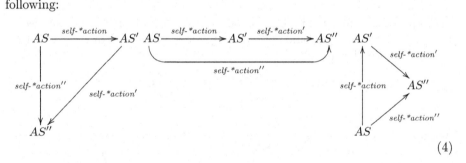

(4)

Consider the following picture:

$$AS \xrightarrow{\text{self-*action}} AS'$$

(5)

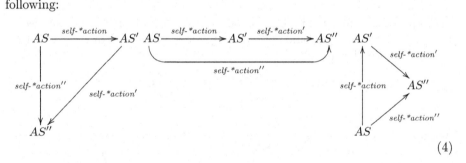

We say this is a diagram of autonomic systems if each of AS, AS', AS'', AS''' is an autonomic system and each of *self-*action, self-*action', self-*action''*, *self-*action'''* is a self-* action. We say this diagram commutes if *self-*action'* ∘ *self-*action = self-*action'''* ∘ *self-*action''*. In this case we refer to it as a commutative square of autonomic systems.

Let AS and AS' be autonomic systems. The product of AS and AS', denoted $AS \times AS'$, is defined as the autonomic system of ordered pairs (x, y) where states of $x \in AS$ and $y \in AS'$. Symbolically, $AS \times AS' = \{(x, y) | x \in AS, y \in AS'\}$. There are two natural projection actions of self-* to be *self-*action*$_1$: $AS \times AS' \to AS$ and *self-*action*$_2$: $AS \times AS' \to AS'$

$$AS \times AS' \tag{6}$$

$$\text{self-*action}_1 \qquad \text{self-*action}_2$$

$$AS \qquad\qquad AS'$$

For illustration, suppose that $\{a, b, c\}$ are states in AS and $\{d, e\}$ in AS', the states are happening in such autonomic systems. Thus, AS and AS', which are running concurrently, can be specified by $AS|AS' \overset{def}{=} \{(a|d), (a|e), (b|d), (b|e), (c|d), (c|e)\}$. Note that the symbol "|" is used to denote concurrency of states existing at the same time. We define self-* actions as $disable(d, e)$ and $disable(a, b, c)$ to be able to drop out relevant states.

$$\{(a|d), (a|e), (b|d), (b|e), (c|d), (c|e)\} \tag{7}$$

$$disable(d,e) \qquad\qquad disable(a,b,c)$$

$$\{a, b, c\} \qquad\qquad\qquad \{d, e\}$$

It is possible to take the product of more than two autonomic systems as well. For example, if AS_1, AS_2, and AS_3 are autonomic systems then $AS_1|AS_2|AS_3$ is the system of triples,

$$AS_1|AS_2|AS_3 \overset{def}{=} \{(a|b|c)|a \in AS_1, b \in AS_2, c \in AS_3\}$$

Proposition 3. *Let AS and AS' be autonomic systems. For any autonomic system AS'' and actions self-*action$_3$: $AS'' \to AS$ and self-*action$_4$: $AS'' \to AS'$, there exists a unique action $AS'' \to AS \times AS'$ such that the following diagram commutes*

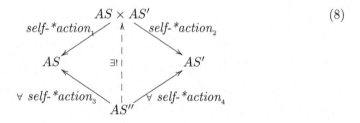

$$\tag{8}$$

We might write the unique action as

$$\langle \textit{self-*action}_3, \textit{self-*action}_4 \rangle : AS'' \rightarrow AS \times AS'$$

Proof: Suppose given *self-*action*$_3$ and *self-*action*$_4$ as above. To provide an action $z : AS'' \rightarrow AS \times AS'$ is equivalent to providing a state $z(a) \in AS \times AS'$ for each $a \in AS''$. We need such an action for which *self-*action*$_1 \circ z = \textit{self-}$*action*$_3$ and *self-*action*$_2 \circ z = \textit{self-*action}_4$. A state of $AS \times AS'$ is an ordered pair (x, y), and we can use $z(a) = (x, y)$ if and only if $x = \textit{self-*action}_1(x, y) = \textit{self-*action}_3(a)$ and $y = \textit{self-*action}_2(x, y) = \textit{self-*action}_4(a)$. So it is necessary and sufficient to define

$$\langle \textit{self-*action}_3, \textit{self-*action}_4 \rangle \overset{def}{=} (\textit{self-*action}_3(a), \textit{self-*action}_4(a))$$

for all $a \in AS''$.　　　　　　　　　　　　　　　　　　　　Q.E.D.

Given autonomic systems AS, AS', and AS'', and actions *self-*action*$_3$: $AS'' \rightarrow AS$ and *self-*action*$_4 : AS'' \rightarrow AS'$, there is a unique action $AS'' \rightarrow AS \times AS'$ that commutes with *self-*action*$_3$ and *self-*action*$_4$. We call it the *induced action* $AS'' \rightarrow AS \times AS'$, meaning the one that arises in light of *self-*action*$_3$ and *self-*action*$_4$.

For example, as mentioned above autonomic systems $AS = \{a, b, c\}$, $AS' = \{d, e\}$ and $AS|AS' \overset{def}{=} \{(a|d), (a|e), (b|d), (b|e), (c|d), (c|e)\}$. For an autonomic system $AS'' = \varnothing$, which stops running, we define self-* actions as $enable(d, e)$ and $enable(a, b, c)$ to be able to add further relevant states. Then there exists a unique action

$$enable((a|d), (a|e), (b|d), (b|e), (c|d), (c|e))$$

such that the following diagram commutes

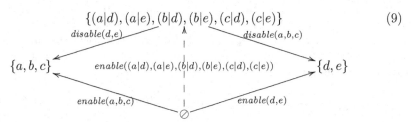

$$\{(a|d), (a|e), (b|d), (b|e), (c|d), (c|e)\} \qquad\qquad (9)$$

Let AS and AS' be autonomic systems. The coproduct of AS and AS', denoted $AS \sqcup AS'$, is defined as the "disjoint union" of AS and AS', i.e. the autonomic system for which a state is either a state of AS or a state of AS'. If something is a state of both AS and AS' then we include both copies, and distinguish between them, in $AS \sqcup AS'$. There are two natural inclusion actions *self-*action*$_1 : AS \rightarrow AS \sqcup AS'$ and *self-*action*$_2 : AS' \rightarrow AS \sqcup AS'$.

$$AS \qquad\qquad\qquad AS' \qquad\qquad (10)$$
$$\textit{self-*action}_1 \quad \textit{self-*action}_2$$
$$AS \sqcup AS'$$

For illustration, suppose that $\{a, b, c\}$ are states in autonomic system AS and $\{d, e\}$ in AS'. Thus, $AS \sqcup AS'$, which is disjoint union, can be specified by $AS \sqcup AS' \overset{def}{=} \{a, b, c, d, e, \}$. We define self-* actions as $ensable(d, e)$ and $enable(a, b, c)$ to be able to add further relevant states.

$$
\begin{array}{ccc}
\{a, b, c\} & & \{d, e\} \\
& \searrow \; enable(d,e) \qquad enable(a,b,c) \; \swarrow & \\
& \{a, b, c, d, e\} &
\end{array} \tag{11}
$$

Proposition 4. *Let AS and AS' be autonomic systems. For any autonomic system AS'' and actions self-*$action_3 : AS \to AS''$ and self-*$action_4 : AS' \to AS''$, there exists a unique action $AS \sqcup AS' \to AS''$ such that the following diagram commutes*

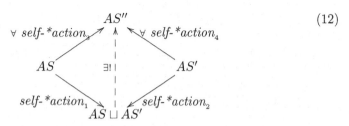 (12)

We might write the unique action as

$$[self\text{-}^*action_3, self\text{-}^*action_4] : AS \sqcup AS' \to AS''$$

Proof: Suppose given self-*$action_3$, self-*$action_4$ as above. To provide an action $z : AS \sqcup AS' \to AS''$ is equivalent to providing a state self-*$action_3(m) \in AS''$ is for each $m \in AS \sqcup AS'$. We need such an action such that $z \circ$ self-*$action_1 = $ self-*$action_3$ and $z \circ$ self-*$action_2 = $ self-*$action_4$. But each state $m \in AS \sqcup AS'$ is either of the form self-*$action_1 x$ or self-*$action_2 y$, and cannot be of both forms. So we assign

$$
[self\text{-}^*action_3, self\text{-}^*action_4](m) = \begin{cases} self\text{-}^*action_3(x) & \text{if } m = self\text{-}^*action_1 x \\ self\text{-}^*action_4(y) & \text{if } m = self\text{-}^*action_2 y \end{cases} \tag{13}
$$

This assignment is necessary and sufficient to make all relevant diagrams commute.   Q.E.D.

For example, as mentioned above autonomic systems $AS = \{a, b, c\}$, $AS' = \{d, e\}$ and $AS \sqcup AS' \overset{def}{=} \{a, b, c, d, e\}$. For an autonomic system $AS'' = \oslash$, which stops running, we define self-* actions as $disable(d, e)$ and $disable(a, b, c)$ to drop out relevant states. Then there exists a unique action $disable(a, b, c, d, e)$ such that the following diagram commutes

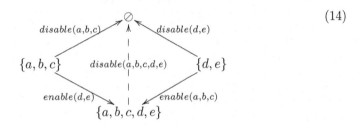

$$(14)$$

5 Conclusions

The paper is a reference material for readers who already have a basic understanding of self-* in ASs and are now ready to consider products and coproducts of ASs using algebraic language. Algebraic specification is presented in a straightforward fashion by discussing in detail the necessary components and briefly touching on the more advanced components.

Acknowledgements. Thank you to NTTU (Nguyen Tat Thanh University, Vietnam) for the constant support of our work which culminated in the publication of this paper. As always, we are deeply indebted to the anonymous reviewers for their helpful comments and valuable suggestions which have contributed to the final preparation of the paper.

References

1. IBM. Autonomic Computing Manifesto (2001). http://www.research.ibm.com/autonomic/
2. Vinh, P.C.: Formal aspects of self-* in autonomic networked computing systems. In: Zhang, Y., Yang, L.T., Denko, M.K. (eds.) Autonomic Computing and Networking, pp. 381–410. Springer, US (2009)
3. Vinh, P.C.: Toward formalized autonomic networking. Mob. Netw. Appl. **19**(5), 598–607 (2014). doi:10.1007/s11036-014-0521-z
4. Vinh, P.C.: Concurrency of self-* in autonomic systems. Future Gener. Comput. Syst. **56**, 140–152 (2015). doi:10.1016/j.future.2015.04.017
5. Vinh, P.C.: Algebraically autonomic computing. Mob. Netw. Appl. (2016). doi:10.1007/s11036-015-0615-2
6. Vinh, P.C., Tung, N.T.: Coalgebraic aspects of context-awareness. Mob. Netw. Appl. **18**(3), 391–397 (2013). doi:10.1007/s11036-012-0404-0

Finite Limits and Colimits
in Autonomic Systems

Phan Cong Vinh$^{(\boxtimes)}$

Faculty of Information Technology, Nguyen Tat Thanh University (NTTU),
300A Nguyen Tat Thanh Street, Ward 13, District 4, HCM City, Vietnam
pcvinh@ntt.edu.vn

Abstract. Self-* is widely considered as a foundation for autonomic computing. The notion of autonomic systems (ASs) and self-* serves as a basis on which to build our intuition about category of ASs in general. In this paper we will specify ASs and self-* and then move on to consider finite limits and colimits in ASs. All of this material is taken as an investigation of our category, the category of ASs, which we call **AS**.

Keywords: Autonomic computing · Autonomic systems · Coequalizer · Colimit · Equalizer · Limit · Pullback · Pushout · Self-* · Span

1 Introduction

Autonomic computing (AC) imitates and simulates the natural intelligence possessed by the human autonomic nervous system using generic computers. This indicates that the nature of software in AC is the simulation and embodiment of human behaviors, and the extension of human capability, reachability, persistency, memory, and information processing speed. AC was first proposed by IBM in 2001 where it is defined as

> "*Autonomic computing is an approach to self-managed computing systems with a minimum of human interference. The term derives from the body's autonomic nervous system, which controls key functions without conscious awareness or involvement*" [1].

AC in our recent investigations [2–5,7] is generally described as self-*. Formally, let self-* be the set of self-_'s. Each self-_ to be an element in self-* is called a *self-* facet*. That is,

$$\text{self-*} = \{\text{self-\_} \mid \text{self-\_ is a self-* facet}\} \tag{1}$$

We see that self-CHOP is composed of four self-* facets of self-configuration, self-healing, self-optimization and self-protection. Hence, self-CHOP is a subset of self-*. That is, self-CHOP = {self-configuration, self-healing, self-optimization, self-protection} ⊂ self-*. Every self-* facet must satisfy some certain criteria, so-called *self-* properties*.

© ICST Institute for Computer Sciences, Social Informatics and Telecommunications Engineering 2016
P.C. Vinh and V. Alagar (Eds.): ICCASA 2015, LNICST 165, pp. 10–20, 2016.
DOI: 10.1007/978-3-319-29236-6_2

In its AC manifesto, IBM proposed eight facets setting forth an AS known as *self-awareness, self-configuration, self-optimization, self-maintenance, self-protection (security and integrity), self-adaptation, self-resource- allocation* and *open-standard-based* [1]. In other words, consciousness (self-awareness) and non-imperative (goal-driven) behaviors are the main features of autonomic systems (ASs).

In this paper we will specify ASs and self-* and then move on to consider finite limits and colimits in ASs. All of this material is taken as an investigation of our category, the category of ASs, which we call **AS**.

2 Outline

In the paper, we attempt to make the presentation as self-contained as possible, although familiarity with the notion of self-* in ASs is assumed. Acquaintance with the associated notion of algebraic language is useful for recognizing the results, but is almost everywhere not strictly necessary.

The rest of this paper is organized as follows: Sect. 3 presents some basic concepts to support consideration of limits and colimits in autonomic systems (ASs). In Sect. 4, we consider some finte limits such as pullbacks of ASs, spans on ASs and equalizers of self-*. In Sect. 5, we consider some finte colimits such as pushouts of ASs and coequalizers of self-*. Finally, a short summary is given in Sect. 6.

3 Basic Concepts

We can think of an AS as a collection of states $x \in AS$, each of which is recognizable as being in AS and such that for each pair of named states $x, y \in AS$ we can tell if $x = y$ or not. The symbol $\oslash$ denotes the AS with no states.

If AS_1 and AS_2 are ASs, we say that AS_1 is a sub-system of AS_2, and write $AS_1 \subseteq AS_2$, if every state of AS_1 is a state of AS_2. Checking the definition, we see that for any system AS, we have sub-systems $\oslash \subseteq AS$ and $AS \subseteq AS$.

We can use system-builder notation to denote sub-systems. For example the autonomic system can be written $\{x \in AS \mid x \text{ is a state of AS}\}$.

The symbol $\exists$ means "there exists". So we can write the autonomic system as $\{x \in AS \mid \exists y \text{ is a final state such that } self\text{-}*action(x) = y\}$

The symbol $\exists!$ means "there exists a unique". So the statement "$\exists! x \in AS$ is an initial state" means that there is one and only one state to be a start one, that is, the state of the autonomic system before any self-* action is processed.

Finally, the symbol $\forall$ means "for all". So the statement "$\forall x \in AS \; \exists y \in AS$ such that $self\text{-}* \; action(x) = y$" means that for every state of autonomic system there is the next one.

In the paper, we use the $\overset{def}{=}$ notation "$AS_1 \overset{def}{=} AS_2$" to mean something like "define AS_1 to be AS_2". That is, a $\overset{def}{=}$ declaration is not denoting a fact of nature (like $1 + 2 = 3$), but our formal notation. It just so happens that the notation above, such as Self-CHOP $\overset{def}{=}$ {self-configuration, self-healing, self-optimization, self-protection}, is a widely-held choice.

If AS and AS' are sets of autonomic system states, then a self-* action $self$-$*action$ from AS to AS', denoted $self$-$*action$: $AS \rightarrow AS'$, is a mapping that sends each state $x \in AS$ to a state of AS', denoted $self$-$*action(x) \in AS'$. We call AS the domain of $self$-$*action$ and we call AS' the codomain of $self$-$*action$.

Note that the symbol AS', read "AS-prime", has nothing to do with calculus or derivatives. It is simply notation that we use to name a symbol that is suggested as being somehow like AS. This suggestion of consanguinity between AS and AS' is meant only as an aid for human cognition, and not as part of the mathematics. For every state $x \in AS$, there is exactly one arrow emanating from x, but for a state $y \in AS'$, there can be several arrows pointing to y, or there can be no arrows pointing to y.

Suppose that $AS' \subseteq AS$ is a sub-system. Then we can consider the self-* action $AS' \rightarrow AS$ given by sending every state of AS' to "itself" as a state of AS. For example if $AS = \{a, b, c, d, e, f\}$ and $AS' = \{b, d, e\}$ then $AS' \subseteq AS$ and we turn that into the self-* action $AS' \rightarrow AS$ given by $b \mapsto b, d \mapsto d, e \mapsto e$. This kind of arrow, $\mapsto$, is read aloud as "maps to". A self-* action $self$-$*action$: $AS \rightarrow AS'$ means a rule for assigning to each state $x \in AS$ a state $self$-$*action(x) \in AS'$. We say that "x maps to $self$-$*action(x)$" and write $x \mapsto self$-$*action\ (x)$.

As a matter of notation, we can sometimes say something like the following: Let $self$-$*action$: $AS' \subseteq AS$ be a sub-system. Here we are making clear that AS' is a sub-system of AS, but that $self$-$*action$ is the name of the associated self-* action.

Given a self-* action $self$-$*action$: $AS \rightarrow AS'$, the states of AS' that have at least one arrow pointing to them are said to be in the image of $self$-$*action$; that is we have

$$\mathrm{im}(self\text{-}*action) \overset{def}{=} \{y \in AS' \mid \exists x \in AS \text{ such that } self\text{-}*action(x) = y\} \quad (2)$$

Given $self$-$*action$: $AS \rightarrow AS'$ and $self$-$*action'$: $AS' \rightarrow AS''$, where the codomain of $self$-$*action$ is the same set of autonomic system states as the domain of $self$-$*action'$ (namely AS'), we say that $self$-$*action$ and $self$-$*action'$ are composable

$$AS \xrightarrow{self\text{-}*action} AS' \xrightarrow{self\text{-}*action'} AS''$$

The composition of $self$-$*action$ and $self$-$*action'$ is denoted by $self$-$*action' \circ self$-$*action$: $AS \rightarrow AS''$.

We define the identity $self$-$*action$ on AS, denoted $id_{AS} : AS \rightarrow AS$, to be the self-* action such that for all $x \in AS$ we have $id_{AS}(x) = x$.

A $self$-$*action$: $AS \rightarrow AS'$ is called an $isomorphism$, denoted $self$-$*action$: $AS \overset{\cong}{\rightarrow} AS'$, if there exists a self-* action $self$-$*action'$: $AS' \rightarrow AS$ such that $self$-$*action' \circ self$-$*action = id_{AS}$ and $self$-$*action \circ self$-$*action' = id_{AS'}$. We also say that $self$-$*action$ is $invertible$ and we say that $self$-$*action'$ is the $inverse$

of *self-*action*. If there exists an isomorphism $AS \xrightarrow{\cong} AS'$ we say that AS and AS' are isomorphic autonomic systems and may write $AS \cong AS'$.

Consider the following diagram:

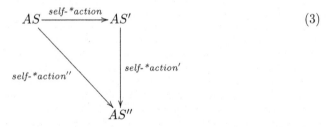

$$(3)$$

We say this is a diagram of autonomic systems if each of AS, AS', AS'' is an autonomic system and each of *self-*action, self-*action', self-*action''* is a self-* action. We say this diagram commutes if *self-*action' $\circ$ self-*action = self-*action''*. In this case we refer to it as a commutative triangle of autonomic systems. Diagram (3) is considered to be the same diagram as each of the following:

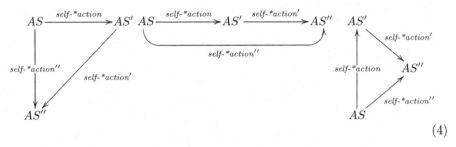

$$(4)$$

Consider the following picture:

$$AS \xrightarrow{self\text{-}*action} AS' \qquad (5)$$

$$\begin{array}{ccc}
AS & \xrightarrow{self\text{-}*action} & AS' \\
\big\downarrow{\scriptstyle self\text{-}*action''} & & \big\downarrow{\scriptstyle self\text{-}*action'} \\
AS'' & \xrightarrow{self\text{-}*action'''} & AS'''
\end{array}$$

We say this is a diagram of autonomic systems if each of AS, AS', AS'', AS''' is an autonomic system and each of *self-*action, self-*action', self-*action''*, *self-*action'''* is a self-* action. We say this diagram commutes if *self-*action' $\circ$ self-*action = self-*action''' $\circ$ self-*action''*. In this case we refer to it as a commutative square of autonomic systems.

4 Finite Limits in Autonomic Systems

In this section, we consider what are called limits of variously-shaped diagrams of ASs.

4.1   Pullbacks of Autonomic Systems

Suppose given the diagram of ASs and self-*actions below.

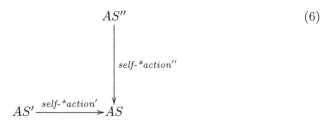

$$AS'' \qquad (6)$$

$$\downarrow \; self\text{-}*action''$$

$$AS' \xrightarrow{\; self\text{-}*action' \;} AS$$

Its fiber product is the AS

$$AS' \times_{AS} AS'' \stackrel{def}{=} \{(x,w,y)\,|\,self\text{-}*action'(x) = w = self\text{-}*action''(y)\}$$

There are obvious projections $self\text{-}*action_1 : AS' \times_{AS} AS'' \to AS'$ and $self\text{-}*action_2 : AS' \times_{AS} AS'' \to AS''$. Note that if $AS''' = AS' \times_{AS} AS''$ then the following diagram commutes

$$AS''' \xrightarrow{\; self\text{-}*action_2 \;} AS'' \qquad (7)$$

$$\big\downarrow \scriptstyle self\text{-}*action_1 \qquad \lrcorner \qquad \big\downarrow \scriptstyle self\text{-}*action''$$

$$AS' \xrightarrow{\; self\text{-}*action' \;} AS$$

Given the setup of diagram (7) we come to the pullback of AS' and AS'' over AS to be any AS''' for which we have an isomorphism $AS''' \stackrel{\cong}{\to} AS' \times_{AS} AS''$. The corner symbol "$\lrcorner$" in diagram (7) indicates that AS''' is the pullback.

Some may prefer to denote this fiber product by $self\text{-}*action' \times_{AS} self\text{-}*action''$ rather than $AS' \times_{AS} AS''$. The former is mathematically better notation, but human-readability is often enhanced by the latter, which is also more common in the literature. We use whichever is more convenient.

Suppose given the diagram of ASs and self-actions as in (8).

$$AS'' \qquad (8)$$

$$\downarrow \; self\text{-}*action_4$$

$$AS' \xrightarrow{\; self\text{-}*action_3 \;} AS$$

For any AS''' and commutative solid arrow diagram as in (9). In other words, $self\text{-}*action_1 : AS''' \to AS'$ and $self\text{-}*action_2 : AS''' \to AS''$ such that

$self\text{-}^*action_3 \circ self\text{-}^*action_1 = self\text{-}^*action_4 \circ self\text{-}^*action_2$ there exists a unique arrow

$$< self\text{-}^*action_1, self\text{-}^*action_1 >_{AS}: AS''' \to AS' \times_{AS} AS''$$

making everything commute. In other words,

$$self\text{-}^*action_1 = self\text{-}^*action' \circ < self\text{-}^*action_1, self\text{-}^*action_1 >_{AS}$$

and

$$self\text{-}^*action_2 = self\text{-}^*action'' \circ < self\text{-}^*action_1, self\text{-}^*action_1 >_{AS}$$

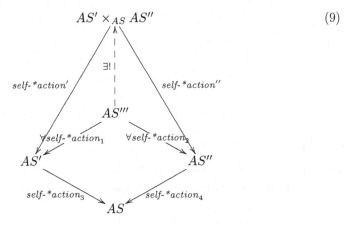 (9)

Consider the diagram drawn in (10), which includes a left-hand square, a right-hand square, and a big rectangle

$$AS'_1 \xrightarrow{self\text{-}^*action_1} AS'_2 \xrightarrow{self\text{-}^*action_2} AS'_3$$ (10)

with vertical arrows $self\text{-}^*action_3$, $self\text{-}^*action_4$, $self\text{-}^*action_5$ and bottom row

$$AS_1 \xrightarrow{self\text{-}^*action_6} AS_2 \xrightarrow{self\text{-}^*action_7} AS_3$$

If $AS'_2 \cong AS_2 \times_{AS_3} AS'_3$ then the right-hand square is a pullback. The right-hand square has a corner symbol indicating that $AS'_2 \cong AS_2 \times_{AS_3} AS'_3$ is a pullback. But the corner symbol on the left might be indicating that the left-hand square is a pullback, or the big rectangle is a pullback. Thus, If $AS'_2 \cong AS_2 \times_{AS_3} AS'_3$ then the left-hand square is a pullback if and only if the big rectangle is.

Consider the diagram drawn in (11)

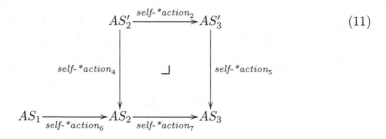

$$(11)$$

where $AS'_2 \cong AS_2 \times_{AS_3} AS'_3$ is a pullback. Then there is an isomorphism

$$AS_1 \times_{AS_2} AS'_2 \cong AS_1 \times_{AS_3} AS'_3$$

In other words,

$$AS_1 \times_{AS_2} (AS_2 \times_{AS_3} AS'_3) \cong AS_1 \times_{AS_3} AS'_3$$

4.2 Spans on Autonomic Systems

Consider AS_1 and AS_2, a span on AS_1 and AS_2 is an AS together with self-* actions $self\text{-}*action_1 : AS \to AS_1$ and $self\text{-}*action_2 : AS \to AS_2$.

$$
\begin{array}{c}
AS \\
\swarrow \quad \searrow \\
AS_1 \qquad AS_2
\end{array}
\qquad (12)
$$

Let AS_1, AS_2, and AS_3 be autonomic systems, and let

$$AS_1 \overset{self\text{-}*action_1}{\longleftarrow} AS' \overset{self\text{-}*action_2}{\longrightarrow} AS_2$$

and

$$AS_2 \overset{self\text{-}*action_3}{\longleftarrow} AS'' \overset{self\text{-}*action_4}{\longrightarrow} AS_3$$

be spans. Their composite span is given by the fiber product $AS' \times_{AS_2} AS''$ as in the diagram (13):

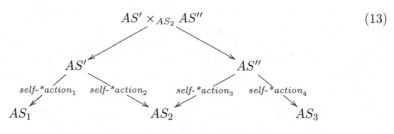

$$(13)$$

If there is a span as $AS_1 \leftarrow AS \rightarrow AS_2$ then by the universal property of products [6], we have a unique map $AS \overset{\exists!}{\rightarrow} AS_1 \times AS_2$.

If there are two spans as $AS_1 \leftarrow AS' \rightarrow AS_2$ and $AS_1 \leftarrow AS'' \rightarrow AS_2$. We can take the disjoint union $AS' \sqcup AS''$ and by the universal property of coproducts, we have a unique span $AS_1 \leftarrow AS' \sqcup AS'' \rightarrow AS_2$ making the diagram (14) commute.

$$(14)$$

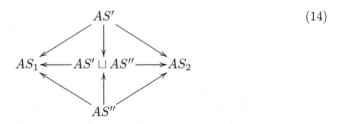

Given a span $AS_1 \overset{self\text{-}^*action_1}{\leftarrow} AS \overset{self\text{-}^*action_2}{\rightarrow} AS_2$, we can draw a bipartite graph with each state of AS_1 drawn as a dot on the left, each state of AS_2 drawn as a dot on the right, and each state a in AS drawn as an arrow connecting vertex $self\text{-}^*action_1(a)$ on the left to vertex $self\text{-}^*action_2(a)$ on the right.

4.3   Equalizers of Self-*

Suppose given two parallel self-* actions

$$AS_1 \underset{self\text{-}^*action_2}{\overset{self\text{-}^*action_1}{\rightrightarrows}} AS_2$$

The equalizer of $self\text{-}^*action_1$ and $self\text{-}^*action_2$ is the commutative diagram in (15),

$$Eq(self\text{-}^*action_1, self\text{-}^*action_2) \overset{p}{\longrightarrow} AS_1 \underset{self\text{-}^*action_2}{\overset{self\text{-}^*action_1}{\rightrightarrows}} AS_2$$

$$(15)$$

where we define

$$Eq(self\text{-}^*action_1, self\text{-}^*action_2) \overset{def}{=} \{a \in AS_1 \mid self\text{-}^*action_1(a) = self\text{-}^*action_2(a)\}$$

and where p is the canonical inclusion

5   Finite Colimits in Autonomic Systems

We consider several types of finite colimits to obtain some intuition about them, without formally defining them yet.

5.1   Pushouts of Autonomic Systems

Suppose given the diagram (16) of ASs and self-* actions below:

$$AS \xrightarrow{\;self\text{-}*action_2\;} AS_2 \tag{16}$$

$$\downarrow {self\text{-}*action_1}$$

$$AS_1$$

Its fiber sum, denoted $AS_1 \sqcup_{AS} AS_2$, is defined as the quotient of $AS_1 \sqcup AS \sqcup AS_2$ by the equivalence relation $\sim$ generated by $a \sim self\text{-}*action_1(a)$ and $a \sim self\text{-}*action_2(a)$ for all states a in AS. In other words,

$$AS_1 \sqcup_{AS} AS_2 \overset{def}{=} (AS_1 \sqcup AS \sqcup AS_2)/\sim$$

where $\forall a \in AS, a \sim self\text{-}*action_1(a)$ and $a \sim self\text{-}*action_2(a)$

There are obvious inclusions $self\text{-}*action_3 : AS_1 \rightarrow AS_1 \sqcup_{AS} AS_2$ and $self\text{-}*action_4 : AS_2 \rightarrow AS_1 \sqcup_{AS} AS_2$. Note that if $AS_3 = AS_1 \sqcup_{AS} AS_2$ then the diagram (17) commutes.

$$AS \xrightarrow{\;self\text{-}*action_2\;} AS_2 \tag{17}$$

$$self\text{-}*action_1 \downarrow \qquad \ulcorner \qquad \downarrow self\text{-}*action_4$$

$$AS_1 \xrightarrow[self\text{-}*action_3]{} AS_3$$

Given the setup of diagram (17), we define the pushout of AS_1 and AS_2 over AS to be any autonomic system AS_3 for which we have an isomorphism $AS_3 \xrightarrow{\cong} AS_1 \sqcup_{AS} AS_2$. The corner symbol "$\ulcorner$" in diagram (17) indicates that AS_3 is the pushout.

For diagram (16), For any autonomic system AS_3 and commutative solid arrow diagram in (18). In other words, self-* actions $self\text{-}*action_3 : AS_1 \rightarrow AS_3$ and $self\text{-}*action_4 : AS_2 \rightarrow AS_3$ such that $self\text{-}*action_3 \circ self\text{-}*action_1 = self\text{-}*action_4 \circ self\text{-}*action_2$, there exists a unique arrow

$$\ll self\text{-}*action_3, self\text{-}*action_4 \gg : AS_1 \sqcup_{AS} AS_2 \rightarrow AS_3$$

making everything commute. In other words,

$$self\text{-}*action_3 = \ll self\text{-}*action_3, self\text{-}*action_4 \gg \circ self\text{-}*action'$$

and
$$self\text{-}^*action_4 = \ll self\text{-}^*action_3, self\text{-}^*action_4 \gg \circ self\text{-}^*action''$$

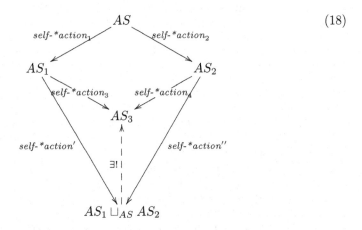

(18)

5.2   Coequalizers of Self-*

Suppose given two parallel self-* actions

$$AS_1 \underset{self\text{-}^*action_2}{\overset{self\text{-}^*action_1}{\rightrightarrows}} AS_2$$

The coequalizer of $self\text{-}^*action_1$ and $self\text{-}^*action_2$ is the commutative diagram in (19),

$$AS_1 \underset{self\text{-}^*action_2}{\overset{self\text{-}^*action_1}{\rightrightarrows}} AS_2 \overset{q}{\longrightarrow} Coeq(self\text{-}^*action_1, self\text{-}^*action_2)$$

(19)

where we define the coequalizer of $self\text{-}^*action_1$ and $self\text{-}^*action_2$ is the quotient of AS_2 by the equivalence relation generated by

$$\{(self\text{-}^*action_1(a), self\text{-}^*action_2(a)) | a \in AS_1\} \subseteq AS_2 \times AS_2$$

In other words,

$$Coeq(self\text{-}^*action_1, self\text{-}^*action_2) \overset{def}{=} AS_2 / self\text{-}^*action_1(a) \sim self\text{-}^*action_2(a)$$

6   Conclusions

The paper is a reference material for readers who already have a basic understanding of self-* in ASs and are now ready to consider finite limits and colimits in ASs using algebraic language. Algebraic specification is presented in a straightforward fashion by discussing in detail the necessary components and briefly touching on the more advanced components.

Acknowledgements. Thank you to NTTU (Nguyen Tat Thanh University, Vietnam) for the constant support of our work which culminated in the publication of this paper. As always, we are deeply indebted to the anonymous reviewers for their helpful comments and valuable suggestions which have contributed to the final preparation of the paper.

References

1. IBM. Autonomic Computing Manifesto (2001). http://www.research.ibm.com/autonomic/
2. Vinh, P.C.: Formal aspects of self-* in autonomic networked computing systems. In: Zhang, Y., Yang, L.T., Denko, M.K. (eds.) Autonomic Computing and Networking, pp. 381–410. Springer, US (2009)
3. Vinh, P.C.: Toward formalized autonomic networking. Mob. Netw. Appl. **19**(5), 598–607 (2014). doi:10.1007/s11036-014-0521-z
4. Vinh, P.C.: Concurrency of self-* in autonomic systems. Future Gener. Comput. Syst. **56**, 140–152 (2015). doi:10.1016/j.future.2015.04.017
5. Vinh, P.C.: Algebraically autonomic computing. Mob. Netw. Appl. (2016). doi:10.1007/s11036-015-0615-2
6. Vinh, P.C.: Products and coproducts of autonomic systems. In: Vinh, P.C., Alagar, V. (eds.) ICCASA 2015. LNICST, vol. 165, pp. 1–9. Springer, Heidelberg (2016)
7. Vinh, P.C., Tung, N.T.: Coalgebraic aspects of context-awareness. Mob. Netw. Appl. **18**(3), 391–397 (2013). doi:10.1007/s11036-012-0404-0

A Context-Aware Healthcare Architecture for the Elderly

Tolulope Peter Oyekanmi$^{(\boxtimes)}$, Nhat Nguyen, and Vangalur Alagar

Concordia University, Montreal, Canada
{t_oyekan,duyn_ngu,alagar}@encs.concordia.ca

Abstract. In order to provide dependable healthcare services for the elderly, it is necessary to have a patient-centric system in which service automation dominates through the use of context-awareness. Healthcare service automation has the virtues to overcome the disadvantages arising from the disabilities that are inherent in the elderly population, physically challenged, and those who live in remote areas. In order that patients trust the healthcare services provided by the system, the creation of healthcare services must be founded on accurate model of patients, and must be delivered by experts through dependable medical devices and secure channels. Motivated by this goal, we propose a healthcare architecture based on a generic Context Awareness Framework (CAF) adapted to the elderly. The automation aspects of healthcare services based on this architecture are discussed.

Keywords: Health care · Elderly population profiles · Context awareness · Healthcare model · Healthcare determinants

1 Introduction

A survey in US [1] has revealed that most US citizens believe that old age actually starts at age 68, with some of them pegging it at as high as 74. In 2012, the population of the elderly made up 11 % of the world's population and was projected to reach 22 % by 2050, with 68 % of the world's population over 80 living in Asia and Latin America and the Caribbean [2]. At the moment, one in six Europeans can be regarded as elderly [3]. It is estimated that by 2020, China will have 230 million elderly people, thereby making it the largest population of elderly worldwide, while India will come next with about 158 million old people [4]. This study also asserts that by the year 2030, the number of people aged 18 across the world will be lower than the ones over age 65, with the number of those aged 85 and above being 8.5 million [5]. From these reports it is evident that the proportion of care givers to the elderly will be decreasing, while the cost of giving care for the elderly will be increasing. An effective solution to this problem is 'healthcare service automation', which can provide services whenever and wherever they are demanded. It can maximize the health

This research is supported by Discovery Grants Program, NSERC, Canada.

© ICST Institute for Computer Sciences, Social Informatics and Telecommunications Engineering 2016
P.C. Vinh and V. Alagar (Eds.): ICCASA 2015, LNICST 165, pp. 21–30, 2016.
DOI: 10.1007/978-3-319-29236-6_3

service utilization and minimize service cost. In this paper, we have focused on creating a context-aware architecture for implementing healthcare system from bottom up.

We have chosen to focus on the elderly due to the numerous vulnerabilities and healthcare needs they face, especially personal care in daily living which could range from taking care of personal hygiene to feeding themselves. When an elderly person's nutritional requirements are not met, it could result in malnutrition and degrading health conditions [6]. A health condition that can result out of poor nutrition is diabetes which has been found to lead to higher rates of premature death. Stroke is a common illness that can coexist with diabetes [7]. Since sedentary lifestyle, social isolation, loneliness, or depression can lead to malnourishment, and depression medications can also change how nutrients are absorbed or how food tastes, caring the dietary needs of elderly is paramount. For the chronically ill elderly, for example those suffering from arthritis [8] who also have a recurring episode of osteoarthritis [8], care needs to be given in multiple dimensions. It has been reported that about 20 % of those who are 55 years and older experience mental disorders such as anxiety disorders, severe cognitive impairment and mood disorders which are not part of normal aging [9]. Mental illness is very difficult to address as many seniors are either unwilling or unable to report their situations. Most elderly people lack knowledge about the causes or symptoms behind their health problems and assume their health problems are simply due to their aging [10]. A survey [4] has revealed that 96.0 % of the elderly have never utilized any of the geriatric welfare services because of lack of awareness. Elderly also go through physical, psychological and financial vulnerabilities [11], become dependent on others which exposes them to societal dangers [12] such physical and psychological assaults, and financial exploitation [13]. The different vulnerable situations and the health conditions discussed above can be related to specific contexts thereby creating a need for context-aware solutions.

1.1   Context Awareness

Context is very important to our day-to-day living. It is how we interpret and interact with the environment. For example, we use context to sense and react to cases of impending danger. However, this innate ability does not automatically translate when we interact with computer systems. While it is easy for a health provider to interpret the current health condition of a patient, a computer system needs to be modeled in such a way that it makes use of certain tag values in making relevant and accurate decisions.

Context can be defined as any information that can be used to characterize the situation of an event [14]. A situation occurs when multiple entities around an event are assigned values. In ubiquitous computing context is regarded as any circumstance or condition surrounding a user that is considered relevant to the interaction between the user and the ubiquitous computing environment [15]. Therefore, a context-aware healthcare architecture intends to make use of the situations around a patient to make better decisions with the overall goal of improving the patient's health conditions.

A context-aware healthcare system makes use of sensors to perceive context and actuators to realize its decisions. Sensors are entities that provide measurable responses to changes in a system's environment. Example include hardware devices such as GPS Sensor [16]. Actuators usually work by subscribing to events and getting instructions included in the event [17]. For example, an *Emergency Service* can request to be notified when an elderly patient requires such services.

The paper is organized as follows: We briefly survey the current technology-based solutions in Sect. 2. We provide a brief introduction to context awareness concepts in Sect. 1.1. Following that we present the entity model of our proposed healthcare architecture in Sect. 3. In Sect. 4, the healthcare architecture is discussed. We conclude the paper in Sect. 5 with remarks on our ongoing work in a prototype implementation and testing of the healthcare architecture.

2   Related Systems

We first review a few existing context-aware healthcare architectures for the elderly. Next we comment on their inadequacies in meeting the daily care and protection of the elderly.

University of Rochester, Georgia Tech, Massachusetts Institute of Technology (MIT) and TIAX, LLC all have smart living projects where they combine context-aware and ubiquitous sensing, computer vision-based monitoring and acoustic tracking through the use of infrared sensors and video cameras in laboratories in order to monitor health information for long periods of time [18]. Another wearable sensor-based mobile healthcare system that reads context-based information such as motion and location of an elderly is *CarePredict* [19]. *CarePredict* transmits data through wireless communication service to remote servers from where experts can examine the information in order to detect any acute deviation, such as restless sleep patterns and changes in eating patterns of the elderly which can then be isolated and investigated further. In addition, *Codeblue* developed by University of Harvard is a healthcare system heavily reliant on context awareness [20]. *Guardian Angel Service*, developed for the Symbian OS platforms, provides active context-aware monitoring for medical stakeholders about elderly facing chronic conditions [21]. It uses context-aware sensors to read vital signs like heart rate and skin temperature in order to help the patient avoid hazardous health conditions. *CareMerge* is an enterprise mobile healthcare system that helps provide real time information about the health of the elderly to their healthcare providers and family [22]. It offers communication with and notification to family members, tracking and sharing of health information and automatic reminders. *Virtual Health Pet* system, developed in Brazil with Java Micro Edition (J2ME) technology, sends out alarm to remind the elderly on medication, as well as alerting emergency services. *GetMyRx* system attempts to simplify the administrative task behind the elderly people in getting their prescriptions [23]. It involves scanning and sending of paper prescriptions with name and address of the patient to a local pharmacy for delivery.

Fig. 1. Entity model

Doctors are also able to send prescriptions directly to pharmacies from the comfort of their offices. *Chinese Aged Diabetic Assistant*, developed by Microsoft in China, is a smart-phone-based support system for elderly diabetics patients that provides recommendations and guidelines for patients in taking insulin and oral medications. *Mobile HIV/AIDS Support* assists healthcare workers in rendering quality services in the developing world by providing reliable medical information for use while the health staff are in the field. *EpiSurveyor* is an easy to use open source software developed by Washington-based non-profit software company *DataDyne* that helps in the creation and sharing of surveys for development of policies by healthcare authorities.

From the above review above it is clear that the current systems are more advantageous to the medical staff than to patients. Most elderly patients lack skills to interact with many current mobile healthcare systems, because the systems do not provide easy to use interfaces. In spite of some of the advantages they offer to patients, an elderly patient may have to use more than one system depending upon her medical situation. Moreover, collectively they do not adequately address the daily health needs and the vulnerabilities of the elderly.

3   Entity Model

In this section, we present the entity model of our healthcare architecture. Below is an informal explanation of the entities shown in Fig. 1.

- *Elderly Home (EH)*: The entity *Elderly Home* represents a smart physical accommodation for elderly people where they are managed and monitored by primary caregivers through the use of sensors. An elderly can be under multiple care givers in a particular elderly home, since a caregiver might just be responsible for a particular type of health condition and an elderly can have multiple health conditions. Electronic communication in the Elderly Home is often done through a mobile terminal which is simply a mobile device such as a phone or personal display assistant that has an application running on its operating system acting as a hub to record the data coming in from all the sensors and actuators. It usually stores temporary information in a local database and then sends data to the Cloud Cyberspace through network technologies, such as 3G and WLAN over Hypertext Transfer Protocol (HTTP).

- *Cloud Cyberspace (CC)*: The *Cloud Cyberspace* represents the server where all incoming medical information from the elderly home will be received, stored, and made available to healthcare service providers. It is usually installed at the hospital or a wireless service provider when the system is expected to share patient's personal health information with multiple clients. It runs a web server such as Apache and IIS which is used for processing and persisting data usually in a database like MySQL or SQL Server. The Cloud Cyberspace (CC) also analyzes medical information for predefined states and executes the corresponding response as stated by the healthcare providers. For example, a doctor might specify to alert emergencies services through email when the blood pressure of an elderly has remained above a safe level for some period of time.
- *Service Providers (SP)*: *Service Providers* represents the generic actuators in the system that provide healthcare services to patients. A variety of actuator types may exist in the system. Actuators receive instructions from the *Cloud Cyberspace (CC)* and then execute them. A good example is "a pharmacist actuator" acting on a drug delivery request. Entities like government health agencies, health insurance companies, and medical research groups that are not directly involved in the treatment of the patient can make use of the information to provide other services to the patient.

4   Architectural Design

Figure 2 shows the detailed design of our architecture. We specialize it based on the Generic Context Awareness Framework in [16] to a detailed architectural design for elderly healthcare applications with focus on fulfilling the healthcare needs of such patients. The architecture is discussed in details below:

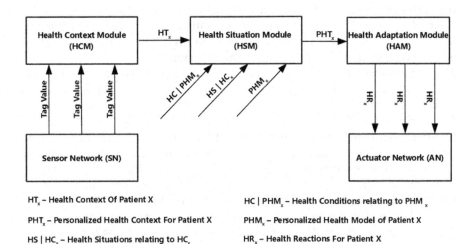

Fig. 2. Detailed architectural design

4.1 Basic Concepts

In this section, we present basic healthcare terminologies that we used in our design.

- *Health Determinants (HD)*: By *Health Determinants*, we refer to factors that affect the health of an individual. These factors can be used to create a personalized health model for that patient, thereby assist in making decisions that will ultimately lead to the improvement of the patient's health status. A patient's health model can further be enhanced by including his desired privacy policies. Examples of *Health Determinants* include biological, environmental and physiological factors. Health determinants can be represented as either atomic or tuples or a collection of atoms and tuples where an atomic representation refers to a tag-value pair with specific data types and units. The values can be monitored initially, at specific intervals or even continuously especially when they are critical to the health of the patient. An example is heart rate.
- *Health Conditions (HC)*: The term *Health Condition* refers to the medical diagnosis of a patient done by healthcare professionals. For example, based on the medical tests, a patient's health condition may be determined as 'depression' or 'dementia'. It is important to note that a patient can have multiple health conditions and can also be at risk of developing additional health conditions that can result from one or more of existing health conditions. We intend to categorize health conditions in terms of the health determinants that can be monitored to assess a patient's health progress over a period of time.
- *Health Context (HT)*: We use the term *Health Context* to denote the continuous monitoring through sensors that is being done for each patient taking into consideration time and other useful information that can be useful in making better decisions. It is important to constantly evaluate a patient's *Health Context* in order to derive the appropriate current *Health Situation* existing for the patient's *Health Condition* and ultimately execute the appropriate adaptations for that patient in an intelligent manner.
- *Health Situations (HS)*: We use *Health Situations* to represent states of interest to the healthcare application in our architecture. Usually, for each health condition, there will be a certain set of health situations that are important for consideration. For example, the *High* health situation is realized when a patient diagnosed with a *diabetic* health condition records a blood sugar level of 10.5 mmol or above. *Health Situations* can have relations between each other. For example, an *Emergency* situation usually follows a *Danger* situation. It is important to note that *Health Situations* are constructed by the medical experts, based on medical knowledge and clinical experience. As such, a health situation is domain-dependent and context-sensitive.
- *Personalized Health Context (PHT)*: We use *Personalized Health Context* to represent the the complete information set that can be used to perform adaptations by the system. This set consists of the current and past relevant *Health*

Contexts, the *Health Conditions* of the patient, the current *Health Situations* for the patient based on the current *Health Contexts* and the personalized health model for that patient.

- *Health Adaptation (HA)*: *Health Adaptation* is the set of predefined execution plans usually provided by healthcare experts for a patient taking account of each health situations that can occur for that patient as well as the patient's context history and personalized health model. Our architecture considers past histories of context to cater for cases where a particular context might need to occur for a number of times before its associated *Health Adaptation* can be triggered. An example of a *Health Adaptation* is sending an email to emergency ambulance services to pick up a dementia patient who is currently experience a health situation indicative that he or she is lost.

4.2 Architecture Modules

In section, we present information about the modules in our architecture.

- *Sensor Network (SN)*: The *Sensor Network* is the combination of sensors with the sole purpose of measuring entity tag values. In the healthcare field, sensors are usually wearable or implanted photoelectric and connected in a star topology through wires and short-range wireless techniques such as IEEE 802.15.1/Bluetooth or IEEE 802.15.4/ZigBee, or a combination of the two [24]. Each sensor acquires data, converts it into an electrical signal and amplifies it for communication with other modules for interpretation. For example, a diabetic patient can require different sensors to measure his or her glucose level and body mass index continuously.
- *Health Context Module (HCM)*: The *Health Context Module* is responsible for the generation and validation of health context based on the aggregated tag values from sensors. For each tag value, there is an expected range of values that can be regarded as valid which is known as the input range for that parameter. For example, the input range of a temperature sensor could be between -30 and 100 degrees Celsius. The *Health Context Module* is responsible for filtering out values outside the input ranges of these sensors. Different sensors in the *Sensor Network* might also be responsible for monitoring the same tag value. An example is the case study of a patient whose location is required to be continuously monitored. The tag value of the location can either be determined using a GPS sensor or any other sensor with Internet Protocol (IP) reporting capabilities. The *Health Context Module* is then responsible for picking the most accurate and relevant value from the numerous available tag values.
- *Health Situation Module (HSM)*: The *Health Situation Module* is responsible for generating *Personalized Health Context* of the patient being monitored. When the health context comes in from the *Health Context Module*, the *Health Situation Module* searches for the personalized health model for a patient with the associated *Health Conditions*. The *Health Situation Module* then uses the health context to fetch the appropriate *Health Situations* corresponding to the

Health Conditions for that patient. This information is then forwarded to the *Health Adaptation Module* as the *Personalized Health Context.*

- *Health Adaptation Module (HAM)*: The *Health Adaptation Module* is responsible for generating the appropriate *Health Adaptations* or *Health Reactions* and picking the right actuators relevant to the chosen reactions. The privacy policies provided by the patient in the healthcare model is also used here to restrict how much information is made available to the actuator. This module is also responsible for logging adaptations as feedback in order to improve the personalized health model for the patient later.
- *Actuator Network (AN)*: The *Actuator Network* is a network of actuators similar to the *Sensor Network*. An actuator is a device to convert an electrical control signal to a physical action, and constitutes the mechanism by which an agent acts upon the physical environment [25]. Actuators could also be software-based [16]. In healthcare, a good example of an actuator is an insulin pump that can receive an instruction to either increase or decrease its rate of flow. In our architecture, most of the actuators are human. For example, caregivers, doctors and pharmacists can use certain devices that are part of the architecture for providing better healthcare services to the patient.

5   Conclusion

This paper has proposed a context-aware architecture that can be used for constructing a smart living system for the elderly. We have established the various population profiles, health needs and vulnerabilities of elderly people in order to establish why we need this architecture, which was specifically adapted for old people. We also surveyed existing health care systems and architectures for elderly people. We developed an entity model for the architecture and discussed a detailed architectural design.

Currently, we are working on developing the set of health determinants, situations and contexts for several health conditions such as dementia and care giving for lonely depressed elderly people. We are investigating data and communication security issues along with patient's privacy concerns that are necessary for mobile healthcare applications. We will integrate security and privacy policies in the architecture that we have developed and implement a prototype of the system.

References

1. World Health Organization. Definition of an older or elderly person (2015). http://www.who.int/healthinfo/survey/ageingdefnolder/en/ (accessed 29 January 2015)
2. Hope, P., Bamford, S., Beales, S., Brett, K., Kneale, D., Macdonnell, M., McKeon, A.: Creating sustainable health and care systems in ageing societies, Technical report, Ageing Societies Working Group (2012). Accessed 29 January 2015
3. The Economist Intelligence Unit Limited. Healthcare strategies for an ageing society, Technical report, Economist Intelligence Unit (2009). Accessed 29 January 2015

4. Goel, P., Garg, S., Singh, J., Bhatnagar, M., Chopra, H., Bajpai, S., et al.: Unmet needs of the elderly in a rural population of Meerut. Indian J. Commun. Med. **28**, 165–166 (2003)
5. David, M.: The changing elderly population and future health care needs. J. Urban Health **76**(1), 24–38 (1999)
6. Nutrition for older persons. http://www.who.int/nutrition/topics/ageing/en/index1.html. (accessed 29 January 2015)
7. Guidelines for improving the care of the older person with diabetes mellitus (2003)
8. Peat, G., McCarney, R., Croft, P.: Knee pain and osteoarthritis in older adults: a review of community burden and current use of primary health care. Ann. Rheum. Dis. **60**(2), 91–97 (2001)
9. US Department of Health and Human Services and others, Older adults and mental health: Issues and opportunities. Rockville, MD: Author (2001)
10. David, B., Alistair, T.: Community care of vulnerable older people: cause for concern. Br. J. Gen. Pract. **63**(615), 549–550 (2013)
11. Claudette, D.: Aboriginal Elder Abuse in Canada. Aboriginal Healing Foundation Ottawa, Canada (2002)
12. Lauren, F., Deana, B., Chien-Chih, L., Samuel, B., Joseph, B.: Frail elderly as disaster victims: emergency management strategies. Prehospital Disaster Med. **17**, 67–74 (2002)
13. Tueth, M.: Exposing financial exploitation of impaired elderly persons. Am. J. Geriatr. Psychiatry **8**(2), 104–111 (2000). (accessed 29 January 2015)
14. Abowd, G.D., Dey, A.K.: Towards a better understanding of context and context-awareness. In: Gellersen, H.-W. (ed.) HUC 1999. LNCS, vol. 1707, pp. 304–307. Springer, Heidelberg (1999)
15. Ranganathan, A., Campbell, R.H.: An infrastructure for context-awareness based on first order logic. Pers. Ubiquit. Comput. **7**(6), 353–364 (2003)
16. Alagar, V.S., Mohammad, M., Wan, K., Hnaide, S.A.: A framework for developing context-aware systems. EAI Endorsed Trans. Context-aware Syst. Appl. **1**, 1–26 (2014)
17. Ricquebourg, V., Durand, D., Menga, D., Marine, B., Delahoche, L., Loge, C., Jolly-Desodt, A.-M.: Context inferring in the smart home: an swrl approach. In: 21st International Conference on Advanced Information Networking and Applications Workshops, AINAW 2007, vol. 2, pp. 290–295. IEEE (2007)
18. Wood, A.D., Stankovic, J., Virone, G., Selavo, L., He, Z., Cao, Q., Doan, T., Wu, Y., Fang, L., Stoleru, R., et al.: Context-aware wireless sensor networks for assisted living and residential monitoring. IEEE Netw. **22**(4), 26–33 (2008)
19. Care predict – empowering independent living for seniors. http://carepredict.com/ (accessed 29 January 2015)
20. Malan, D., Fulford-Jones, T., Welsh, M., Moulton, S.: Codeblue: an ad hoc sensor network infrastructure for emergency medical care. In: International Workshop on Wearable and Implantable Body Sensor Networks, vol. 5 (2004)
21. Maria, P., Katerina, T., Evangelos, B., Taxiarchis, T.: Mobile phone application to support the elderly. Int. J. Cyber Soc. Educ. **6**(1), 51–56 (2013)
22. Care coordination and communication software for senior care – caremerge. http://www.caremerge.com/ (accessed 29 January 2015)
23. Getmyrx delivered free today. https://www.getmyrx.com/ (accessed 29 January 2015)

24. Ramon, M., Jaime, D., Xavier, P.: Security specification and implementation for mobile e-health services. In: 2004 IEEE International Conference on e-Technology, e-Commerce and e-Service, EEE 2004, pp. 241–248. IEEE (2004)
25. Wireless sensor and actor networks (wsan). http://www.ece.gatech.edu/research/labs/bwn/actors/ (accessed 25 July 2015)

Snapcab: Urban Scale Context-Aware Smart Transport Using Adaptive Context Tries

Alistair Morris[1]([✉]), Constantinos Patsakis[2], Vinny Cahill[1],
and Mélanie Bouroche[1]

[1] Distributed Systems Group, Trinity College Dublin, Dublin, Ireland
morrisa5@tcd.ie
[2] Department of Informatics, University of Piraeus, Piraeus, Greece

Abstract. Traffic gridlock has become a very familiar scene in cities due to the inefficiencies of existing transport systems. Context-aware dispatch has the potential to solve such congestion problems. Thus, this paper addresses the problem of realising large scale real-time taxi dispatch with service guarantees on road networks. Such a system requires the dynamic matching of travel requests made by passengers with appropriate taxis. Crucially this must occur while also ensuring the satisfaction of all waiting or travel times constraints. Results gained from simulations show that a novel approach, based on Adaptive Context Tries (ACT), provides fast response times, bounded complexity and thus scalability.

1 Introduction

A real-time taxi dispatch system attempts to solve the problem of matching taxis with passengers, hence avoiding taxis having to drive around looking for fares [1,2]. Potential passengers send travel requests, which include a *start* and an *end*, that respectively denote where a passenger wants to be picked up and dropped off. Recent research has extended the problem to support the concept of *ride sharing* between passengers to further increase efficiency of taxis [3,4].

Each request made by a passenger can contain two constraints: a *waiting time*, that defines the latest time a passenger wants to picked up by, and a *travel time*, that establishes the acceptable extra diversion time from the shortest duration for a given journey between a *start* and an *end*. In order to accept a request a taxi must satisfy all constraints; not only those of the newly encountered request, but also the requests it has committed to for all previous passengers [1].

However, providing such a dynamic taxi dispatch system at an urban scale presents a non-trivial problem. It involves a real-time matching algorithm that can quickly determine the best taxi that can satisfy an incoming request from a large set of choices [5]. Context-awareness offers one potential solution [1], but traditional context-aware middleware solutions using flooding, gossip or overlay based dissemination algorithms cannot scale due to their overhead [6,7].

In this paper, we show that Adaptive Context Tries (ACT) [6] can efficiently disseminate context and enable the distribution of previously-accepted travel

© ICST Institute for Computer Sciences, Social Informatics and Telecommunications Engineering 2016
P.C. Vinh and V. Alagar (Eds.): ICCASA 2015, LNICST 165, pp. 31–40, 2016.
DOI: 10.1007/978-3-319-29236-6_4

requests, organised as a itinerary for each taxi. When a new request arrives, our system searches the trie to determine the best match, if any, and assign the request to the nearest taxi that can honour all its constraints. Note that this means the itineraries obtained are not guaranteed to be optimal but workable.

In the following: Sect. 2 provides an overview of traditional optimisation algorithms that solve related problems and argues for an alternative approach. Section 3 provides first a more formal problem definition and introduces our method, with some optimisations presented in Sect. 4. In Sect. 5 we experimentally compare our method to its points and the paper concludes with some ideas for future work in Sect. 6.

2   Related Work

Previous research mainly focuses on a single vehicle and a static scenario where a system knows the set of requests ahead of time [4,5,8]. However, this cannot provide a realistic approach in context-aware taxi dispatch problem at an urban-scale. Notably, earlier work highlights that this constitutes an NP-hard problem and therefore can only be solved for small sizes [9]. To address this, recent work proposes the use of context driven dynamic programming algorithms [10]. Hence, the processing of travel requests in real time becomes the main issue [11], as for any new request, the travel itinerary of each taxi, based on previously-assigned travel requests, needs to be processed. Crucially this means that only taxis at a distance smaller than a threshold w from the start can satisfy the waiting time constraint. This limits the amount of taxis considered. At this point a system could naively use brute-force to find the taxis which could accommodate the request. This requires the enumeration for all permutations and then checking whether the constraints are met. However, the complexity of this approach is exponential which means that it does not provide a scalable solution.

The *branch-and-bound* algorithm provides a more efficient method that systematically enumerates all candidate itineraries and organises them in an itinerary tree. It then estimates a lower bound of each partially constructed itinerary and stops building candidate itineraries with lower bounds greater than the known best solution [12]. Again, this approach can only solve small-scale problems as it also has exponential complexity in terms of response time [13].

Mixed integer programming presents an alternative approach [10,14]. This reduces the problem to finding the maximum/minimum of a linear function of non-negative variables subject to constraints expressed as linear equalities or inequalities. Although it is conceptually simple, many researchers state that the NP-hard set also contains this approach [15] so it also cannot scale.

3   Adaptive Context Tries (ACT)

This section first formalises the Real-Time Context-Aware Taxi Dispatch problem and it introduces the ACT structure that can maintain as well as update any calculations performed up-to-now and use them effectively when passengers issue new travel requests [6]. To deal with the highlighted challenges, our idea is based on a simple observation: A new legal itinerary accommodating a new request can be derived by extending any already existing current travel itinerary.

Based on this observation, the ACT-based solution to the taxi dispatch problem uses the following method: Firstly, it stores a legal travel itinerary for each taxi in a prefix tree (trie) structure at all times [6]. When a new request is received, the system checks if it can extend any travel itinerary to handle the new request. This method provides a promising approach because its incremental nature removes many redundant computations. Therefore, a system does not need to fully recompute an optimal legal travel itinerary for each new request, providing a non-optimal yet workable real-time approach. This outperforms current state of the art methods based on traditional unfeasible optimisation algorithms.

3.1   Formal Problem Definition

We consider a road network $G = \{V, E, W\}$ consisting of a vertex set V and an edge set E. Each edge $(u, v) \in E$ $(u, v \in V)$ has a weight $W(u, v)$ which indicates the travel time from (u) to (v), which is assumed to be a constant value.

Given two points s and e in the road network, a route π between them forms a vertex sequence $(v_0, v_1, \cdots, v_k)$, where (v_i, v_{i+1}) denotes an edge in E, $v_0 = s$, and $v_k = e$. The route cost $W(\pi) = \sum W(v_i, v_{i+1})$ denotes the sum of each edge cost $W(v_i, v_{i+1})$ along the route. Thus, the shortest route cost $\delta(s, e)$ describes the minimal cost for routes available from s to e, this gives $\delta(s, e) = \min_\pi W(\pi)$.

Definition 1 (Travel Request). *A travel request tr across a road network $G = \{V, E, W\}$ takes the form of a quadruplet (s, e, t, τ), where $s \in V$ is the start, $e \in V$ the end, $t \in \mathbb{R}_+^*$ is the maximal waiting time and $\tau \in \mathbb{R}_+^*$ denotes a travel time for any extra diversion time in a travel. This bounds the overall distance from s to e to $(1 + \tau)\delta(s, e)$.*

For each travel request $tr_i = \{s_i, e_i, t, \tau\}$ and a given taxi, r_i denotes the taxi's location. A sequence of $3x$ points can describe a general *travel itinerary* for a taxi with x travel requests: $(p_1, p_2, \cdots, x_{3x})$ as an point p_j in the sequence denotes either a *start* (s_i), an *end* (e_i), or travel request point (r_i). Furthermore, this paper assumes that a taxi takes shortest route when moving between any two consecutive points in the travel itinerary p_i and p_{i+1}.

Thus, the *travel cost* between any two points (p_i, p_j) in the travel itinerary $\delta_T(p_i, p_j)$ becomes $\delta_T(p_i, p_j) = \delta(p_i, p_{i+1}) + \delta(p_{i+1, i+2}) + \cdots + \delta(p_{j-1}, p_j)$ and the overall travel cost $\delta_T(p_1, p_{3x})$. Figure 1 illustrates this for four travel requests.

Fig. 1. A travel itinerary that contains the travel starting point s_i, a travel ending point e_i and taxi location r_i when request of travel tr_i arrives.

However, not all travel itineraries can meet the service quality guarantees for each individual travel request. Hence, we must define a *legal travel itinerary*:

Definition 2 (Legal Travel Itinerary). *A legal travel itinerary I for a travel request set $T_R = \{tr_1, tr_2, \ldots, tr_m\}$ must satisfy three conditions for any tr_i:*

1. **Order of events**: *Let $p_{i1} = r_i$, $p_{i2} = s_i$, and $p_{i3} = e_i$, then, $i_1 < i_2 < i_3$, i.e., the requesting point must happen before the pickup point, etc.*
2. **Waiting time**: *The time to travel from the taxi's location to the start can never exceed the waiting time constraint, i.e., $\delta_T(r_i, s_i) \leq t$*
3. **Travel time**: *The actual travel time from the start to the end $\delta_T(s_i, e_i)$ should be at most $(1 + \tau)\delta(s_i, e_i)$.*

To finally define the *Real-Time Context-Aware Taxi Dispatch* problem we need to provide one more definition to take into account multiple travel requests:

Definition 3 (Aggregated Legal Travel Itinerary). *Assuming at time t, there are x travel requests allocated to a given taxi; let $(p_1, p_2, \cdots, p_{3x})$ denote the current legal travel itinerary. For a new travel request tr_{m+1}, the aggregated legal travel itinerary contains any legal travel itineraries $(p'_1, p'_2, \cdots, p'_{3x+3})$ that satisfy $p'_j = p_j$ for $j \leq i$, and $p'_{i+1} = r_{x+1}$.*

Thus, we can define the **Real-Time Context-Aware Taxi Dispatch** as:

Definition 4 (Problem Definition). *Given a set of taxis, a set of previously-allocated requests and a new request $tr = (s, e, t, \tau)$, find the taxi that minimises the travel cost from s to e at that time, in its aggregated legal travel itinerary.*

Note that due to subsequent request allocation, a taxi may not minimise the travel cost of those already accepted, but it will *always* satisfy all constraints.

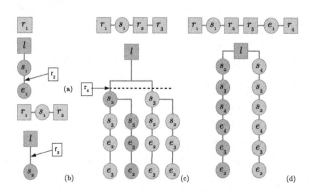

Fig. 2. Adaptive Context Trie (ACT) for travel itineraries. Darkened/red route indicates the selected itinerary to be executed. The dark circled/red travels denoted completed travel requests (Color figure online).

3.2   Trie Structure

ACT stores a travel itinerary for each taxi by associating a key to each itinerary point p. That key is used to store the next itinerary point. A virtual network structure orchestrates the storage of key-context value pairs by assigning keys to different points; the point will store the values for all the keys for which it is responsible. Thus, ACT specifies how keys are assigned to points, and how a point can access context for a given key by first locating the point responsible for that key. In short, this enables ACT to preform urban scale context dissemination method across all points, both for passengers and taxis [6]. Specifically a system uses ACT to maintain all legal travel requests with respect to the taxi's location. Eventually, as the taxi moves, a part of the itinerary becomes obsolete. Thus we need ℓ to track the current position of a taxi and root of its trie.

For a given t and τ, Fig. 2 illustrates the ACT structure corresponding to the complete travel itinerary and context stored across peers in Fig. 1. The darkened/red route represents the selected itinerary that the taxi will execute. Initially, for the first travel request, only one legal travel itinerary exists as shown in Fig. 2(a). When the second request arrives, the taxi has finished with the first passenger. If the taxi accepts the new request it can only perform one option, as it will first pick up the second passenger, but it has the flexibility to accept other travels if needed. This means, for now at least, that the taxi must take the route (ℓ, e_1, s_2, e_2), to drop off the first passenger and pick up the second.

However, on its way to pick up the second passenger, the third request arrives. The taxi now may either pick up the second passenger or the third one. Assuming that the taxi decides to move along the shortest route $(\ell, s_2, s_3, e_3, e_2)$. It then drives to pick up the second passenger and the fourth request arrives the entire right sub-trie of r_3 in Fig. 1(c) becomes inactive. Thus advantageously:

Corollary 1 (Legal Itineraries during Mobility). *When a taxi reaches a new pickup location or drop off location in the travel itinerary, then the taxi only follows legal itineraries which contain unfinished travels and share the same prefix in ACT. The taxi can safely ignore and exclude all the other itineraries.*

3.3   Processing a New Travel Request

When processing a new travel request containing (r_k, s_k, e_k) we assume that the taxi has already an ACT containing all legal itineraries of unfinished travels. Now, it needs to extend all legal itineraries in the prefix trie to a new legal itinerary to include it, if possible. To deal with the new request, it first focuses on the start s_k and then the end e_k. Essentially, a system needs to scan this trie to determine where s_k can be inserted.

All itineraries that share the same prefix from ℓ, the *root* of a trie with respect to the current location of the taxi, to the inserted edge will be added into the trie. Then, we append e_k after s_k in the new trie. Furthermore, if the system can append s_k or e_k at a given location forming an edge in this trie, then the system must find out which travel itineraries containing that edge with an additional point will be invalid and will be excluded. This introduces two problems: (a) How to determine at which edge the system can insert s_k or e_k, in addition to: (b) How to quickly delete any invalid travel itineraries that now exist.

Inserting Start Location: Here a system must know whether it should first insert s_k and then e_k afterwards. To insert s_k in a trie edge, e.g. (p_i, p_{i+1}), it must handle the following cases: (a) only when the distance from the current location to the pickup location s_i satisfies $\delta_T(l, s_i) = \delta(l, p_1) + \delta(p_1, p_2) + \cdots + \delta(p_i, s_k) \leq w$, then it can insert s_k; (b) the additional travel time introduced by the diversion to s_k may make some existing travel itinerary invalid in the sub-trie containing this trie edge (p_i, p_{i+1}), i.e. $\delta(p_i, s_k) + \delta(s_k, p_{i+1}) - \delta(p_i, p_{i+1})$ should not be too large. It should now exclude these from the sub-trie to ensure: $\delta_T(\ell, s_k) \leq w$. Thus, the shortest distance from the current location to the pickup location s_k has a value less than w given a itinerary from ℓ to p_j.

As ACT enables a search across peers starting from the root ℓ to generate all the candidate edges (p_i, p_{i+1}) to insert s_k it can handle condition (b): the explicit maintaining and checking of constraints for each travel request in the sub-trie of the point p_i provides a straightforward way to erase itineraries.

Furthermore, only a single criterion needs to be tested: if the taxi has not picked up the passenger, then ACT can test the pickup waiting time constraint $[r_j, s_j, w]$; once the taxi picks up the passenger, ACT can check the travel constraint $[s_j, e_j, \tau]$. Thus, at any given point, ACT can enable a system to simply partition the "active" passengers into two sets: A that records those passengers who need to be picked up and B that records the on-board passengers who need to be dropped off. When a new location is reached, it moves passengers from A to B and/or remove passengers from B. For travel j in A, the system tests the first criteria: $[r_j, s_j, w]$ and in B, tests the second one: $[s_j, e_j, \tau]$. Therefore, for the sub-trie rooted at p_i, a system can first generate these two sets A and B and then, when it inserts s_k, however it also needs to test each condition associated with the sets A and B.

Algorithm 1. Insert points (from a travel request) pseudo-code

---

Require: root (taxi location) ℓ, request points $P = (p_1, x_2, ...)$, at current depth *depth*
  if $feasible(l, x_1, depth + \delta(\ell, x_1))$ **then**
    $fail = 0$, $n = create(\ell, x_1)$ {Copy feasible child branches beneath n}
    for all c such that edge (ℓ, c) exists **do**
      $copy(n, \{c\}, \delta(n, c) + \delta(n, c) - \delta(\ell, c))$ {If copy fails, $fail = 1$}
    end for{Insert remaining request points to n}
    if $fail = 0$ and $|P| > 1$ **then** {Detour now begins negative as no p_2 yet}
      $insert(n, \{x_2, ...\}, -\delta(p_1, x_2))$ {If insert fails, $fail = 1$}
    end if{Now insert request points into children}
    for all c such that edge (ℓ, c) exists **do**
      $insert(c, P, diversion + \delta(\ell, c))$ {If insert fails, exclude (ℓ, c)}
    end for
    if $fail = 0$ **then**
      Add edge (ℓ, n)
    else if No points c with edge (ℓ, c) exist **then**
      Insert fails! {We have an unfeasible sub-trie}
    end if
  else
    Insert fails! {We have an unfeasible sub-trie}
  end if

Algorithm 1 implements this described recursive insertion of a new request $tr_k = (s_k, e_k)$ into ACT. This insertion occurs using a call, $insert(l, \{s_k, e_k\}, 0)$. The call to $feasible(parent, point, diversion)$ determines if it can feasibly insert a *point* as a child under a *parent* leaf in the discovered itinerary to always ensure an legal aggregate travel itinerary.

The $copy(to, from, diversion)$ function recursively copies points from a set of leaves in the trie, $from$, to the target, to. Here, tolerance of the root's (ℓ's) children in $insert$ is implemented through calling $feasible$ with a $diversion$.

Figure 3 shows how to insert the pickup location s_4 into an existing trie. First s_4 will be inserted directly below ℓ. Then, the branch with root at s_3 will be copied underneath this new s_4 point, forming a trie of $(\ell, s_4, s_3, ((e_2, e_3), (e_3, e_2)))$. Assuming the unfeasible route $(\ell, s_4, s_3, e_3, e_2)$; then, a system should exclude the branch from this trie until we reach s_3, when it has an alternate feasible route $(\ell, s_3, s_4, e_3, e_2)$. This deletion occurs in the *copy* function, which will succeed because s_4 falls along at least one feasible route as shown in Fig. 3(b).

Then, the insertion algorithm moves down to s_3 and attempts to insert the pickup location. This forms two routes: $(\ell, s_3, s_4, e_2, e_3)$ and $(\ell, s_3, s_4, e_3, e_2)$, as a result of the insertion between s_3 and e_3 and between s_3 and e_2 as Fig. 3(c) shows. Suppose inserting s_4 between e_2 and e_3 or between e_3 and e_2 is unfeasible, then, this case is shown in Fig. 3(d). To complete the insert, a system now tries to insert e_4 in the sub-tries that start at s_4 following the insert operation.

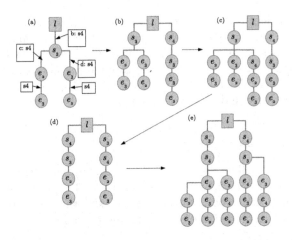

Fig. 3. Trie Insertion. The insertion of s_3 into each edge using ACT.

4   Cluster-Based Optimisation

Although the ACT approach is promising, the exponential explosion of the size of the trie when there are multiple start or end locations close to each other is not avoided. For example, if a taxi has 6 starting points in spatial proximity around similar time e.g. a large park or university campus, any permutation of the starts may result in a legal itinerary. So $6! = 720$ possibilities exist.

The following **clustering algorithm** deals with this situation. When the system inserts a starting point s_k to an edge (p_i, p_{i+1}), we check if $\delta(p_{p+i}, s_k) \leq \mu$, where μ denotes a small number. If so, ACT inserts s_k into the point of p_{i+1}. s_k and the system can treat p_{i+1} as one *cluster* in the trie and it can choose an arbitrary itinerary among the points in a cluster. When the cluster contains more than one point, the newly inserted point needs to be within μ of all the other points in the cluster. A similar procedure can be done for the end points and the mixture of starting and ending points. Once a system combines the cluster with any point, it will stop trying to insert it to any other edges using ACT (Fig. 4).

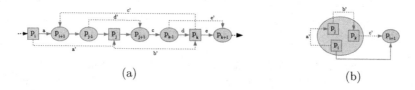

(a)　　　　　　　　　　　(b)

Fig. 4. p_i, p_j, and p_k in one cluster. Black lines: optimal itinerary S_o. We can convert S_o by connecting p_i, p_j, p_k consecutively first and then thread the other locations (represented by circles). The itinerary has a bounded cost.

Assuming sufficiently large travel times with all possible itineraries: For a travel request set T_R, let S_o define the optimal itinerary. Suppose there exists a cluster c among the start and end locations of T_R. This cluster-based method chooses an arbitrary itinerary S_c that goes through the points of the cluster in a consecutive manner. The following can then crucially prove that the bounded cost of S_c, which clearly indicates a feasible approach:

Theorem 1. $cost(S_c) \leq cost(S_o) + 2(x+1) \times \mu$ where x denotes the number of points in the cluster without considering constraints.

Because after ACT builds the whole trie, a system can select the shortest itinerary with cluster $cost(S_c) \leq cost(S_o) + 2(x+1) \times \mu$. However, when the constraints of points of the best itinerary are relaxed, the corresponding cluster-based itinerary can also depend on the following theorem:

Theorem 2. $cost(S_c) \leq cost(S_o) + 2(x+1) \times \mu$ where x defines the number of points in the cluster when constraints of all points in $S_o > x\mu$.

5   Simulation Results

To compare our proposed method with its points we have made extensive simulation experiments. The implementation of the ACT approach [6] was used directly as a Java library, while for the traditional optimisation algorithms and mixed integer programming methods we used MATLAB's (R2014b build) Optimisation Toolbox. The experiments were conducted on an Intel i7-2600 SMP-based GNU/Linux computer using the v4.1 kernel and OpenJDK v1.6.

Figure 5a compares the waiting time for a taxi as exhibited by the ACT approach with branch and bound, brute-force and mixed integer optimisation algorithms as the number of travel requests increase with a fixed number of 2^{10} taxis. Notably although traditional algorithms cannot continue processing as the problem sizes become too large, ACT can scale to higher capacities in terms of response time. This also confirms our hypothesis that situations where a large number of passengers wish to depart from a single point infer the biggest issue for capacity. ACT through clustering combines such points in a trie to provide an urban-scalable approach. Figure 5b shows the time complexity of each algorithm to further highlight these observations. This also demonstrates the workability of non-optimal taxi dispatch against traditional optimisation algorithms.

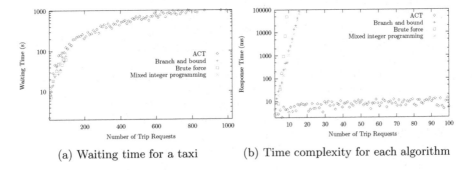

(a) Waiting time for a taxi   (b) Time complexity for each algorithm

Fig. 5. A comparison of ACT against existing approaches (see related work)

6 Conclusion and Future Work

This paper formulates and proposes an ACT-based approach with a cluster-based optimisation to match real-time travel requests to taxis in a road network to realise efficient context-aware taxi dispatch while ensuring all conditions of a given travel request are met. Our proposed solution might not find the best solution but it provides an acceptable solution efficiently. It also clearly outperforms current state of the art optimisation-based solutions, as shown by large scale experiments. Future work will consider the uncertainty issues in scheduling [16] as this will likely form a major road block in achieving scalable context-aware transport systems. It will also include a more complete analysis of the cluster-based optimisation and provide the full proofs to the relevant theorems to further outline the soundness of the cluster-based optimisation and investigate how the inevitable privacy issues could be tackled in such frameworks.

References

1. Smirnov, A., Levashova, T., Shilov, N., Kashevnik, A.: Context-aware decision support in dynamic environments: theoretical and technological foundations. In: Obaidat, M.S., Koziel, S., Kacprzyk, J., Leifsson, L., Ören, T. (eds.) Simulation and Modeling Methodologies, Technologies and Applications. Advances in Intelligent Systems and Computing, vol. 319, pp. 3–20. Springer, Heidelberg (2015)
2. Hwang, R.H., Hsueh, Y.L., Chen, Y.T.: An effective taxi recommender system based on a spatio-temporal factor analysis model. Inf. Sci. **314**, 28–40 (2015)
3. Zhang, D., He, T., Liu, Y., Lin, S., Stankovic, J., et al.: A carpooling recommendation system for taxicab services. IEEE Trans. Emerg. Top. Comput. **2**, 254–266 (2014)
4. He, W., Hwang, K., Li, D.: Intelligent carpool routing for urban ridesharing by mining gps trajectories. IEEE Trans. Intell. Transp. Syst. **15**, 2286–2296 (2014)
5. Dong, H., Zhang, X., Dong, Y., Chen, C., Rao, F.: Recommend a profitable cruising route for taxi drivers. In: 2014 IEEE 17th International Conference on Intelligent Transportation Systems (ITSC), pp. 2003–2008. IEEE (2014)
6. Morris, A., Patsakis, C., Dragone, M., Manzoor, A., Cahill, V., Bouroche, M.: Urban scale context dissemination in the internet of things: challenge accepted. In: 9th International Conference on Next Generation Mobile Applications, Services and Technologies. IEEE (2015)
7. Morris, A., Bouroche, M., Cahill, V.: Urban scale dissemination in mobile pervasive computing environments. PECCS **2014**, 18 (2014)
8. del Carmen Rodríguez-Hernández, M., Ilarri, S.: Towards a context-aware mobile recommendation architecture. In: Awan, I., Younas, M., Franch, X., Quer, C. (eds.) MobiWIS 2014. LNCS, vol. 8640, pp. 56–70. Springer, Heidelberg (2014)
9. Schmidt, M., Schöbel, A.: Timetabling with passenger routing. OR Spectrum **37**, 75–97 (2015)
10. Gacias, B., Meunier, F.: Design and operation for an electric taxi fleet. OR Spectrum **37**, 171–194 (2015)
11. Qu, M., Zhu, H., Liu, J., Liu, G., Xiong, H.: A cost-effective recommender system for taxi drivers. In: Proceedings of the 20th ACM SIGKDD International Conference on Knowledge Discovery and Data Mining, pp. 45–54. ACM (2014)
12. Hu, T.Y., Chang, C.P.: A revised branch-and-price algorithm for dial-a-ride problems with the consideration of time-dependent travel cost. J. Adv. Transp. (2014)
13. Nisse, N., Mazauric, D., Coudert, D.: Experimental evaluation of a branch and bound algorithm for computing pathwidth. In: Gudmundsson, J., Katajainen, J. (eds.) SEA 2014. LNCS, vol. 8504, pp. 46–58. Springer, Heidelberg (2014)
14. Rais, A., Alvelos, F., Carvalho, M.S.: New mixed integer-programming model for the pickup-and-delivery problem with transshipment. Eur. J. Oper. Res. **235**, 530–539 (2014)
15. Bonami, P., Kilinç, M., Linderoth, J.: Algorithms and software for convex mixed integer nonlinear programs. In: Lee, J., Leyffer, S. (eds.) Mixed Integer Nonlinear Programming. The IMA Volumes in Mathematics and its Applications, vol. 154, pp. 1–39. Springer, Heidelberg (2012)
16. Cats, O., Gkioulou, Z.: Modeling the impacts of public transport reliability and travel information on passengers waiting-time uncertainty. EURO J. Transp. Logistics, 1–24 (2015)

Sound Waves Gesture Recognition for Human-Computer Interaction

Nguyen Dang Binh[(✉)]

Hue University of Sciences, 77 Nguyen Hue, Hue city, Vietnam
ndbinh@hueuni.edu.vn

Abstract. Gestures, a natural language of humans, provide an intuitive and effortless interface for communication with the computers. However, the achievements do not satisfy researcher's demands because of the complexity and instability of human gestures. We propose a new method to recognize gestures from sound waves. The main contribution of this paper is to recognize gestures based on the analysis of short-time Fourier transforms (STFT) using the Doppler effect to sense gestures. To do this, we generate an inaudible tone, which gets frequency-shifted when it reflects off moving objects like the hand. We measure this shift with the microphone to infer various gestures. Experimenting method and evaluating results by using the hand gestures of many different people to browse applications such as website, document and images in the browser on the computers in the classroom and library environment for accurate results. In addition, we describe the phenomena and recognition algorithm, demonstrate a variety of gestures, and present an informal evaluation on the robustness of this approach across Laptop device and people.

Keywords: In-air gesture sensing · Doppler effect · Interaction technique

1 Introduction

Gesture recognition is very useful for automation. Gesture is becoming a common means, as technology trends in the management and control interfaces. Gesture recognition based on the variation in sound waves frequency domain approach is a sound wave sensors utilize computer speakers and microphone. It has the advantage of not being affected by light, as the technical language recognition in images, video, voice. For example, the Microsoft's SoundWave and University of Washington [7] or Acoustic Doppler Sonar (ADS) [2]. Currently, this problem is continuing to develop applications, e.g., a gesture recognition system that leverages wireless signals to enable whole-home sensing and recognition of human gestures [6] and bringing gesture to all device [1]. Basically, the gesture recognition systems using more than one characteristic, using machine learning models Hidden markov models, Support vector machine to recognize gestures are really complex and restrict much of the processing speed of the system. We present a method of recognizing the gesture by dividing the energy levels of short-time Fourier transforms and using Doppler effect to recognize gestures. This method conducted discrete signal on the frequency domain with time into the signal frame of

© ICST Institute for Computer Sciences, Social Informatics and Telecommunications Engineering 2016
P.C. Vinh and V. Alagar (Eds.): ICCASA 2015, LNICST 165, pp. 41–50, 2016.
DOI: 10.1007/978-3-319-29236-6_5

equal length and continue dividing the energy level briefly on each frame signal sequentially. Also, the analysis of energy levels in a short time each signal frame allows detection of noise and remove signal preprocessing steps for reliable results and somewhat reduce the fees charged math. Energy function in short-time been researched much in image recognition, speech recognition [5, 8]. We are inspired by the Doppler effect, the effect of Doppler is used to detect sound waves, voice, gestures [2–4, 7] (Fig. 1).

Fig. 1. An illustration of hand gesture recognition via sound waves used to control applications on laptop.

The paper is organized as follows. In Sect. 2 we review the main ideas, which build the sound waves gestures recognition system. A method that combines the Doppler effect is based on the division of power levels short-time Fourier transforms to recognize gestures. In Sect. 3 presents empirical evaluation results in sound waves gesture recognition. Finally, we summarize and conclude the paper in Sect. 4.

2   Sound Waves Gestures Recognition System

The system of sound waves gestures recognition and controls often include: signal sound waves acquisition, features extraction, finally classify, recognize and control interfaces. General diagram of gesture recognition system is shown on Fig. 2 sound waves uses existing speakers on commodity devices to generate tones between 18–22 kHz, which are inaudible. We then use the existing microphones on these same devices to pick up the reflected signal and estimate motion and gesture through the observed frequency shifts.

Sound Waves Acquisition: Use the built-in microphone on your computer to capture sound wave signal of gesture Doppler effect to change when it has changeable of the location of the two sources of waves.

Features Extraction: Typical short time energy is extracted Windowing choose soon step of Fourier transforms in a short time (STFT). Sound waves gestures and noise classification: positive and negative energy based on the distribution of energy levels in the short time-frequency domain to classify gestures and noise Doppler effect.

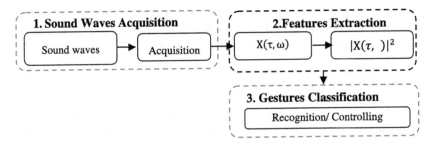

Fig. 2. The diagram of the basic stages of gestures recognition systems and controlling.

Gesture Recognition and Controlling: The user selected control functions, through the state classification system gestures to recognize gestures that execute commands from the controlling interface application browsers use.

2.1 Sound Waves Acquisition Based on Doppler Effect

In our approach, the computer speakers act as a broadcast source, microphone as receiver. Speakers will continuously emit a signal whose frequency from 18 kHz–22 kHz constant (adjusted by the user), although the sound waves can operate outside our scope but consistent over the range from 18 kHz–22 kHz because matching most hardware devices on the computer and we do not need higher frequencies to sense gestures in the air [2, 7, 10]. Then, use the built-in microphone on the device to capture and digitize signals through the recording (sampling frequency is 44.1 kHz) signal observed Doppler principle. It is a combination of two separate effects induced by two sound wave sources (hand moves and speakers), frequency will increase as the hand observer moving closer to the computer and will decrease when the hand moves away. The principle is the Doppler frequency shift of sound waves obtained in microphone (f_r) upon the relative shift of position with hands in the air compared with the computer speakers. The relationship between observed frequency f_r and emitted frequency f_t is given by

$$f_r = f_t \cdot \left(\frac{c + v}{c - v} \right)$$

where f_r is perceived frequency at microphone; f_t is original frequency from speaker; c is the velocity of sound waves in the air (speed of sound in air) and v is the velocity of hand in air; if hand is moving towards the source then positive

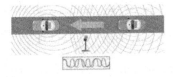

Fig. 3. Description of the Doppler effect is obtained at the microphone for two waves approach each sources.

(and negative in the other direction). Any motion nearby computer (about 1 m depending on speed), integrated microphone in your computer will obtain the frequency shift of the reflected Doppler effect (Fig. 3).

2.2   Features Extraction

In fact, the gesture moves continuously in a certain period of time and often not consistent between the times the performance (in speed, direction and time travel) and depending on the user (Campaign airborne sound transmission speed of 343 m/s, speed hand gestures about 0.25 m/s–4 m/s) [10]. Another factor, the acquisition of sound waves from the moving gesture greatly affected by noise (interference) available or random existence in their surroundings (as a hardware device or operating emitted program that uses active sound created). Therefore, the signal processing and extracting features selected to recognize what is a gesture or environmental noise in the frequency domain is really complex.

Windows of Signal: Signal in the short period of time can see the signal is relatively stable and unchanged over time. For a signal of gesture, this can be done by windowing of a signal x(n) into an unbroken chain of sequential x(t) window, t = 1,2,... T call is the signal frame. The selection window Hamming [7], for discrete signals into the signal frame (with sample points in 2048) we considered suitable for the energy spectrum will be concentrated in the middle of the frame signal:

$$w[n] = \begin{cases} 0.54 - 0.46 \cos\left(\frac{2\pi n}{N}\right) & \text{with } 0 \le n \le N \\ 0 & \text{otherwise} \end{cases}$$

where n is the number of samples on a window (n is an even number), N is the number of signal frames. Featured short time energy. Energy shortly is determined by calculating the average of the total area of the sample (sample) single in each frame. With a window ends at the mth sample, short time energy function E(m) (Fig. 4):

$$E(m) = \sum_{-\infty}^{\infty} [x(n)\, w(m-n)]^2$$

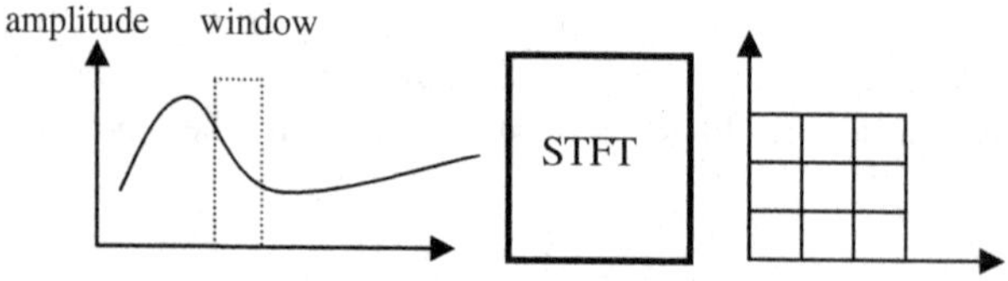

Fig. 4. Description of STFT.

Frequency signals emitted from the hand gestures or environmental noise signal is not stopped (non-stationary signals) means a periodic signal over time. Energy analysis shortly after each frame signal is unstable, or no detailed process of moving gesture or noise already exist or appear at random. So we continue discrete signal on each frame (framing) using short-time Fourier transforms.

$$\text{STFT}\{x(t)\}(\tau, \omega) \equiv X(\tau, \omega) = \sum_{-\infty}^{\infty} x(t)\,\omega(t - \tau)e^{-j\omega t}$$

$$\text{spectrogram}\{x(t)\}(\tau, \omega) \equiv |X(\tau, \omega)|^2 \equiv |\text{STFT}(\tau, \omega)|^2$$

where, $x(t)$ is the signal to change at time t ($1 \leq t \leq \tau$), $X(\tau, \omega)$ represents the phase and amplitude of the signal in time and frequency. Spectral energy distribution function is the result of the transformation process STFT, featured short time energy is calculated after each step sliding window (windowing) of STFT:

$$\text{Energy} = \sum_{t_i}^{t_{i+1}} x^2(t) = x^2(t_i) + x^2(t_{i+1})$$

in which energy is featured in short time, $x^2(t_i)$ is the energy spectrum signals in frame t_i ($1 \leq i \leq N$) (Fig. 5).

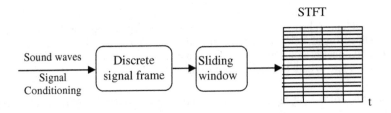

Fig. 5. Describe the process selected feature extraction.

2.3 Gestures Classification

In this paper, we limit the waving gesture (palms facing the computer, limit the distance in 1 m depending on the speed of movement of the hand than the computer and audio hardware of the computer) move from top-down "up to down", from right to left "right to left" is called the "state" move closer or move away from the computer including gestures moving from left to right "left to right", from bottom to top "down to up". The moving gesture is shown clearly in Fig. 6.

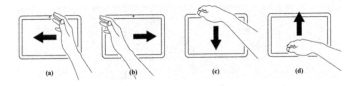

Fig. 6. The hand gestures. (a) and (b) is approaching "Coming". (b) and (d) is carried away "Leaving".

The idea of gestures classification is based on the transformation of the energy of the positive or negative on the frequency domain (oy axis is frequency-domain, time-domain is the ox axis) through the distribution of energy levels Shortly after wave change on every frame STFT signal Doppler effect principle. When there is not any movement, short time energy to wave signal emitted from the speakers (whose frequency is cf) called threshold (ethrd) will remain unchanged. When a gesture is moving towards or away from it a short time energy component increased or decreased distribution around the threshold of the Doppler principle. We call the energy increase in the short period of time is positive energy (pose) similar to the energy reduction (nege) is negative energy (this is why we calculated the energy function for the amount of the short time period after the sliding window step change STFT).

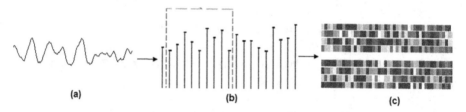

Fig. 7. Distribution of share positive/negative energy. (a) the signal of gesture has been digitized. (b) The modified signal STFT using Hamming window. (c) The distribution of the energy of negative/positive energy around the threshold when motions are shown colored boxes with value increases from white to dark blue (Color figure online).

The analysis of the energy positive or negative in scope (range) of the near threshold energy level (cf − oy ≤ range ≤ cf + range) is not specific to the "state" moving gesture hand because it changes so fast around the threshold. In this case, may be due to the noise of the hardware or the program that uses sound triggers. We are interested in the

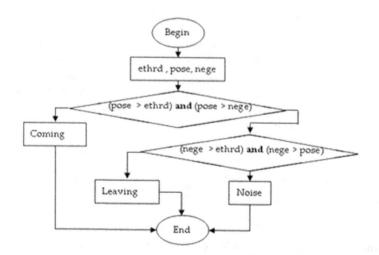

Fig. 8. Flowchart gestures classifier algorithm and noise.

range (oy < cf − range and oy > cf + range) to change the energy section briefly relatively clear than the threshold to classify gestures into advanced classes closer "Coming" or move away from the "Leaving". Similarly, in a range (extrange) larger (oy < cf − extrange and oy > cf + extrange) existence of the energy available to a positive or negative than the threshold, then it is sure to be noise "Noise "which is not the state of motion of hand gestures, because it is not fast enough to spread the energy distribution around the threshold (Figs. 7 and 8).

Algorithm 1: Classification algorithm for gesture and noise

Input: Feature vectors are extracted from short time energy function of the sound
       waves.
Output: one of 5 Classes gesture:
        "Coming" = {go down; translated into left},
        "Leaving" = {go up on; translated to right},
        "Noise" = {other cases}.
Methods:
1. Browse the energy levels in the frequency domain (oy <cf - range and oy> cf + range) to calculate the input parameters (ethrd, pose, nege) by the following formula:

$$\text{Energy} = \sum_{t_i}^{t_{i+1}} x^2(t) = x^2(t_i) + x^2(t_{i+1})$$

2. Comparison of the parameters are calculated in step 1 with the threshold to classify gestures to the state of motion "Coming", "Leaving", or "Noise".
3. **End.**

2.4 Gesture Recognition and Control Application Interface

We built a system to recognition and control the selection gesture function using virtual keys to browse applications include: Browse the document horizontally, browsing the document vertically, transforming a document page, scroll up or scroll down the document page by user selection options virtual keys in Fig. 9. When a moving gesture of waving at a computer, the system will classify it into class gesture "Coming" (approached), including two gestures: "shift to the left" and "go down" (the celebration only (a) and (c) in Fig. 6) or belonging to the class "Leaving" (moved away) include gesture "translated to" and "go down" (the gesture (b) and (d) in Fig. 9).

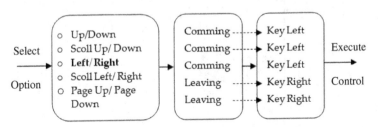

Fig. 9. Select functional diagram of the control system.

Through the selection of options to browse virtual key document by the gesture was introduced, the system will accurately recognize either gesture in each class from which execute control commands instead of interact directly with the computer keyboard or mouse.

3   Experiment and Results

In this section we focus on the construction of the experimental program identifiable sound waves hand gestures to control a laptop computer. With applications built, I show the results, evaluate the effectiveness and applicability of the method was developed. Since then outlined the limitations of the method and the innovative direction to develop better applications.

3.1   Sound Waves Gesture Recognition System

The aim to build the application as a motion recognition system of the laptop based on sounder speaker and microphone. That's touch less sensor can recognize movement of the hand. Users can use gestures to control programs like Flip Slide PPT, moving in the photo browser, browse PDF documents, Word, Excel, or surf websites … This app is similar to sound waves Microsoft is researching how to handle it but completely different. The system is operating on sound waves at 18 kHz–22 kHz frequency and can be adjusted in the user interface. Some techniques are built in the programming make the results reliable recognition, including short time Fourier transforms, Doppler effect, gesture recognition algorithm, the human voice and recognize ambient noise, as well as enhanced recognition algorithms strong identity.

3.2   Environmental Construction and Operation of the Application

Application is installed on Microsoft Visual C++ environment, so it may or fine on computers using Windows operating systems understand. Application allows to run on

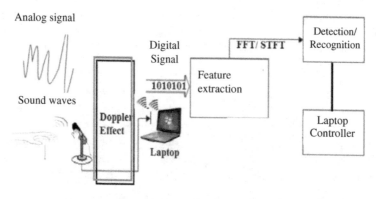

Fig. 10. Our sound waves gesture recognition system for controlling applications on Laptop.

any laptop computers have integrated at least a microphone and speakers. The application uses sound waves to the use of the day or night absolutely not affect other applications that use the camera identification. The application uses the built-in microphone and speakers on the laptop computer so the gap between users and computers in applications is only 0.7 m, the closer the distance, the higher the accuracy (Fig. 10).

3.3 Experimental Results

We conduct empirical methods in place (environment) calm, considered easy to recognize gestures such as a library or a quiet place. In these locations, usually at survival signals emitted sound waves or less random noise existed available to affect the classification process and recognize gestures. At the same time, we also experimentally in noisy places such as classroom, locations are often available randomly or other source of sound waves that are not only caused by. Through noisy places or quiet, we evaluate the effectiveness of methods for environmental use. Also, in both quiet environments (library) and noisy (classrooms) for many different users to assess the impact (in terms of speed, direction of movement) of the election different only for the method. To review the stability and effectiveness of the methods implemented, we use a number of different types of computers. The computers operate in different modes but (allowing applications to run simultaneously in multiple time difference) to control a number of applications such as web surfing, browse PDF documents, PPT slides, or browse Photos in the browser application using four hand gestures were introduced instead of using direct or mouse navigation keys on the keyboard. By aggregating data in the evaluation method mentioned above, we found that the method can recognize gestures resulting noise and very reliable. The experimental results are we averaged in each gestures shown in Table 1.

Table 1. The average percentage of four gesture recognition.

Environment experiment	Results percentage ratio of gestures recognition controller			
	Control move up	Control go down	Control shift to the left	Control shift to the right
In the classroom	80.7 %	74.6 %	82.4 %	73.5 %
In the library	89.3 %	77.7 %	88.1 %	79.9 %

Through the development, implementation and evaluation methods, we found that the analysis of the short-time energy levels through the energy of positive/negative reflects well the movement of the hand gestures on the frequency domain with time. Beside eliminate the impact of environmental noise interference. The method focuses on a specific analysis of energy that no combination with many other features, it kind of makes findings is somewhat restricted compared with other methods. In addition, the energy spectrum analysis only considered the basic hand gestures through two states approaching and moving away. The more complex gestures have not been considered in the energy spectral features shortly.

4   Conclusion

We have presented a novel sound waves gestures recognition system. The basic idea is to recognize gestures based on the analysis of short-time Fourier transforms (STFT). Our method that combines the Doppler effect and the division of power levels short-time Fourier transforms on the frequency domain to recognize gestures. The method is based on a single feature to recognize gestures and noise removal of ambient devices make cost in terms of computation and processing improved somewhat. Also, the method also shows the simplicity and ease application deployment for leverage spacious sound hardware often built on the device from which the cost price is minimized. Next time, we will research and development towards detection and gesture control completely automatic no longer depend on the selection of the control functions of the user. Using machine learning models (HMM, SVM) based on the energy characteristic short time to train and discovered many more gestures. The use of filters and sound waves combine this method with other methods of detecting gestures from images through the camera in a system to improve the accuracy and detect multiple complex gestures.

References

1. Bryce, K., Vamsi, T., Shym, G.: Bringing gesture recognition to all devices. In: NSDI, April 2014
2. Kalgaonkar, K., Raj, B.: Ultrasonic doppler sensor for speaker recognition, acoustics, speech and signal processing. In: ICASSP (2008)
3. Kalgaonkar, K., Raj, B.: Ultrasonic doppler sensor for voice activity detection. IEEE Sig. Process. Lett. **10**, 754–757 (2007)
4. Kalgaonkar, K., Raj, B.: One-handed gesture recognition using ultrasonic doppler sonar. In: Proceedings of IEEE Acoustics, Speech and Signal Processing (2009)
5. Liu, D., Tian, J., Yang, B., Sun, J.: Time-frequency analysis based motor fault detection using deconvolutive STFT spectrogram. J. Convergence Inf. Technol. (JCIT) **7**, 1–6 (2012)
6. Pu, Q., Gupta, S., Gollakota, S., Patel, S.: Whole-home gesture recognition using wireless signals. In: Proceedings of the 19th Annual International Conference on Mobile Computing and Networking (2013)
7. Pu, Q., Gupta, S., Gollakota, S., Patel, S.: Soundwave: using the doppler effect to sense gestures. In: Proceedings of the 2012 ACM Annual Conference on Human Factors in Computing Systems (2012)
8. Chikkerur, S., Govindaraju, V., Cartwright, A.N.: Fingerprint image enhancement using STFT analysis. In: Singh, S., Singh, M., Apte, C., Perner, P. (eds.) ICAPR 2005. LNCS, vol. 3687, pp. 20–29. Springer, Heidelberg (2005)
9. Tarzia, S.P., Dick, R.P., Dinda, P.A., Memik, G.: Sonar-based measurement of user presence and attention. In: Proceedings of ACM UbiComp (2009)
10. Xin, L., Kang, L., Dong, C.L.: A sound-based gesture recognition technology designed for mobile platform. J. Inf. Comput. Sci. **12**, 985–991 (2015)

Context-Based Classifier Grids Learning for Object Detection in Surveillance Systems

Dang Binh Nguyen[(✉)]

Hue University of Sciences,
77 Nguyen Hue Street, Hue City, Vietnam
ndbinh@hueuni.edu.vn

Abstract. We propose a new method to adaptive object detector is to incorporate the scene specific information without human intervention to reach the goal of fully autonomous surveillance where the focus is on developing adaptive approaches for object detection from single and multiple stationary cameras that are able to incorporate unlabeled information using different types of context in order to collect scene specific samples from both, the background and the object class over time. The main contributions of this paper tackle the question of how to incorporate prior knowledge or scene specific information in an unsupervised manner. Thus, the goal of this work is to increase the recall of scene-specific classifiers while preserving their accuracy and speed. In particular, we introduce a co-training strategy for classifier grids using a robust on-line learner. The system runs at 24 h per day and 7 days per week with 24 frames per second on consumer hardware. Our evaluation show high accuracy on both synthetic and real test sets. We achieve state of the art in our comparisons with related work and in the experimental results these benefits are demonstrated on different publicly available surveillance benchmark data sets.

Keywords: Context-based learning · Classifier grids · Object detection · Online learning

1 Introduction

Robust learning interactive object detection has applications including surveillance intelligence systems, computer vision, gaming, human-computer interaction, security, and even health-care. One main challenge of incorporating unlabeled information is to preserve the long-term robustness of object detection, which is a major requirement for real-world applications. With the increasing number of surveillance cameras the need for autonomous visual surveillance systems is increasing tremendously. One of the first steps towards autonomous visual surveillance is object detection. The main focus of this research is on object detection from static cameras with specific emphasis on the applicability to real-world environments. To deal with changing environmental conditions which usually occur in real-world environments an adaptive object detector is required. To ensure robust object detection without the need for human intervention we develop different approaches which allow for robustly incorporating scene specific information. Context could help to limit appearance changes and thus scaling down the

© ICST Institute for Computer Sciences, Social Informatics and Telecommunications Engineering 2016
P.C. Vinh and V. Alagar (Eds.): ICCASA 2015, LNICST 165, pp. 51–61, 2016.
DOI: 10.1007/978-3-319-29236-6_6

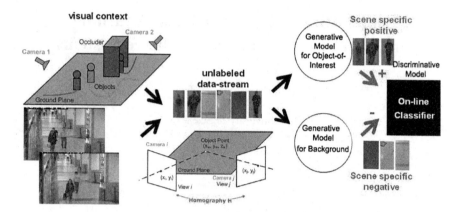

Fig. 1. Proposed approach of context-based classifier grids. 3D Context: A homography, maps a point on the ground plane from one view to another. The unlabeled large data-stream is analyzed and scene specific positive and negative samples are collected for continuously updating the classifiers, i.e. a local grid detector and using various types of context.

training set. It is well known that context plays a very important role, e.g., exactly the same image patch can be interpreted very differently depending on its embedding in the world [21].

A generic object detector tries Fig. 1. Having access to a large data-stream and using various types of context (e.g., scene knowledge) our approach continuously updates an specific object detector. to solve just the ill-posed problem of detecting the object of a class in any context [22]. Hence, generic detectors often fail in real world scenarios. In many application scenarios the detection problem would be far simpler. For example, in a 24/7 surveillance scenario the camera is often static and focuses always on one and the same scene. Further, there is a continuous data stream providing a huge amount of (unlabeled) data which should be explored for (i) improving detection results as well as (ii) speeding up the detection process. One simple way to benefit from the static camera is to incorporate information about the particular scene (e.g., using a ground plane to limit the size of persons). However, such information usually helps only to reduce the number of false alarms (e.g., [10]). In order to increase also the detection rate, on-line methods adapting to a particular scene have been investigated (e.g., [18]). These methods focus on solving the object detection task in the particular scene and take advantage from the continuous incoming data stream. In fact, these approaches use context (scene knowledge) already in the training process and not just as post-processing. Therefore, on-line unsupervised learning methods are usually used to continuously adapt the model. The main problem, however, is to robustly include the new unlabeled data. If the data is wrongly interpreted, the performance of the detector will be reduced. In other words, the detector might drift and would end in an unreliable state. The most prominent approach is to apply a sliding window technique [6–8, 16]. Each area of the image of a certain image is tested whether it is consistent with a previous estimate model or not, and finally all the images matching the notice results. Typically, the goal of this approach is to develop a general model in which can be applied to all possible scenarios, and the problem of detecting various objects [7, 8, 12]. However if trained from a very large number of training samples for the detection of common objects ("broad application") often fail in specific situations. Because not all change, especially for coverage negative (e.g., all objects can be the background image), can be obtained results with performance and low accuracy. Assuming a fixed camera, which is a reasonable constraint for most applications, using information specific circumstances may help reduce the number of objects are detected [10]. To further improve the results of the classification of the classification on the specific object can be applied, designed to solve a specific task (for example, detecting objects for a set specific). In fact, the training of classification needs few training data is necessary and for a specific problem which we often better for accuracy and efficiency [13, 18, 19]. The method of detecting objects using traditional models and use the sliding window search object [1–5] then it is usually done coaching a single classification used to detect or identify the object on the whole picture. Therefore, the model of offline learning will encounter the following problems: Firstly, to establish a classification in the offline model of traditional learning (such as SVM, Boosting, neural networks,…) collective training samples must be prepared in advance, can call sample data is big problem depending on the application (several thousand samples). This makes labor expensive and time consuming sample preparation. Additionally due to the sample preparation prior to the application on the new scene to detect objects they can not promote efficiency, want effective it must retrain for new or updated models added adapt the template in this new context. Thus to access online learning. Secondly, after the training is completed the classification exam to detect objects, the classification must perform a search greed from above, from left to right, with all positions and different size search of objects not only on the current image frame in which the entire frame sequence of images. Thus, the complexity of the detection object will increase. Thirdly, usually to extract characterizing select training samples, the system only uses a specific method chosen only deduct certain to form. Therefore, can choose specific extraction method suitable for this kind of data, but may not be the best fit with other data types and in many different problems, but mostly for a particular problem dirty. Characteristics such as geometry, movement of objects, objects change shape, color, texture, and features can quickly calculate matching problem in real time. Therefore, the research to be able to use multiple methods to detect specific selected data in the same form and thus allows the selection of a specific type best characterized of the sort used for system is a matter of concern and this is the approach in this research. In this research, we used 03 extracted choose specific methods wavelet Haar, a local binary pattern, and chart directions simultaneously and choose Gradient method to suit each school model in which the estimated error the smallest model selected. Finally, a problem encountered in the detection methods and update the wrong object is detected errors and omissions objects here's the problem is many researchers focus on finding solutions to improve the ratio object detection system. The approach of this paper is also aimed and basic goals and overcome these drawbacks. Therefore, we develop different approaches that allow incorporating scene specific information for object detection and tracking in static camera setups. This allows adapting to specific scenes, which is beneficial in both single and multiple camera setups.

The rest of the paper is structured as follows. First, in Sect. 2, we mention issues related research recently. Next, we consider the idea of learning classifier grids in

Sect. 3. We give an empirical evaluation of the approach experimental evaluation and results in Sect. 4. Finally, we summarize and conclude the research in Sect. 5.

2 Related Works

To improve the strength of classification and continue to reduce the number of training samples of a classification adaptive use online learning algorithms can be applied [11, 16, 18]. Therefore, the system can adapt to the environmental changes (e.g. change of light conditions) and changes without the need to handle by the original model. In fact, in this way the complexity of the problem is reduced and the classification can be more effective training. The adaptive system has a drawback: the new data has not been labeled will be included in a model has been built. This approach typically self trained [14, 17], training and [4, 13], semi-supervised learning [8] or the app itself sample data generated during training [16]. The semi-supervised method, often used by combining the information given and explores new models from available data to form a set of classification. Self-training method or training Frequent synchronization constraints theory of constraints can not be guaranteed in practice or is based on the feedback of the current classification, classification results both unnecessary trust. The classification more effectively avoid the above problems can be trained to use the classification grid [9, 20]. In contrast with sliding window technique, in which a classifier can be quantified with different positions on the image, the main idea of the classification grid is coaching the separate classification for each different location of image. Thus, the complexity of the classification task was handled by a single classification so complexity is significantly reduced. Each classification is only able to distinguish the object to be detected from the background in a particular location in the image. Using the classification system online that can adapt to changing environmental conditions, further reducing the complexity of the classification. Adaptive approach, in general, enjoy problem affecting lost or missing information, for example, due to wrong system update start learning something completely different performance degradation of classification. To avoid this problem in the classification grid [20] have adopted strategies fixed update. Special sampler for updating the classification grid is generated from the corresponding area of the image, while positive samples are trained before and immobilized. This updated strategy to ensure stability in the long run, that is classified is not degraded. In fact, the classification has been chosen the wrong sample labeling update may restore a certain amount of time, this problem we call the short term lost. This could be the case if an object remains in the same place in a longer period of time determined in advance and background information used as samples of audio classes. In this research, we solve the problem of missing object detection in continuous data sequence by combining information temporarily and replace the updated strategy fixed by an adaptive combination between sets classification has been chosen in advance as an initial knowledge of the classification grid adapted, using the classifier is trained beforehand to verify the model before performing the update for each classification unit in net. The experimental results clearly show the benefits of the proposed approach. Especially considering approaches have no moving object can be significantly better handling, increased both in terms of both accuracy and performance of the classifier.

3 Classifier Grids Learning

The main challenge of adaptive object detectors is to incorporate scene specific unlabeled information, which allows for adapting the detector to new environmental conditions in a robust manner without human intervention. In the following, we review the ideas of classifier grids and learning, which build the base for the proposed approach.

(a)   (b)

Fig. 2. Classifier Grids. (a) The main idea of classifier grids follows the divide and conquer principle. The image is divided into highly overlapping grid elements (regions), where each grid element. (b) The classifier grids on the left side are updated using labels generated by a second independent co-trained classifier evaluated on the background subtracted image.

3.1 Classifier Grids

The main concept of classifier grids [9] is to sample an input image by using a highly overlapping grid, where each grid element i ($i = 1,..., N$) corresponds to one classifier C_i. This is illustrated in Fig. 2. To reduce the number of classifiers within the classifier grid the ground-plane is pre-estimated. Thus, the classification task that has to be handled by one classifier C_i can be drastically reduced, i.e., discriminating the background of the specific grid element from the object-of-interest. To further reduce the classifiers' complexity and to increase the adaptively, on-line learning methods can be applied, where the updates are generated by fixed rules. For positively updating a grid classifier C_i a fixed pool of positive samples is used; the negative updates are generated directly from the image patches corresponding to a grid element. In general, for estimating the grid classifiers any on-line learning algorithm can be applied, however, on-line boosting has proven to be a considerable trade-off between speed and accuracy [15]. The goal of classifier grids is to further reduce the complexity of the task by training a separate classifier for each position within the image. Using a separate classifier for each position within the image significantly simplifies the problem. In this way, classifier grids follow the, in computer science well-established, divide and conquer paradigm, where the problem is broken down until the sub-problems become simple enough. Afterwards, the solutions to the sub-problems are combined to solve the original problem. Classifier grids divide each input image into a highly overlapping set of grid elements (regions), where each of the grid elements corresponds to one sub-problem of the whole object detection problem which is solved by a separate classifier. This is visualized in Fig. 3(a). The classifiers within the classifier grid can profit from simplifying the problem to discriminate between the object of interest and the background at one specific location within the image. The reduces variability at one specific location within the image allows for using less complex and compact on-line classifiers, which can be evaluated and updated efficiently and further reduces the number of false alarms. Hence, in contrast to standard sliding window approaches which have to evaluate different scales at every position in the image, the use of scale information can significantly reduce the number of classifiers within the classifier grid. The number of classifiers within the classifier grid can be defined by an overlap parameter. There is always a trade-off between run-time and performance of the classifier grid object detector.

3.2   Learning for Classifier Grids

During the initial stage our system is trained in a co-training manner as shown in Fig. 3. Given n grid classifiers $\mathbf{G_j}$ operating on gray level image patches $\mathbf{X_j}$ and one compact classifier C operating in a sliding window manner on background subtracted images $\mathbf{B}$. To start co-training, the classifiers $\mathbf{G_j}$ as well as the classifier C are initialized with the same off-line trained classifier (see Algorithm 1). The classifiers within the classifier grid $\mathbf{G_j}$ and the classifier C operating on the background subtracted images co-train each other. A confident classification (no matter if positive or negative) of a classifier $\mathbf{G_j}$ is used to update the classifier C with the background subtracted representation at position $\mathbf{j}$. Vice versa, a confident classification of classifier C at position j generates an update for classifier $\mathbf{G_j}$. The off-line trained prior information already capturing the generic information causes a small number of updates to be sufficient to adapt the classifiers to a new scene. The update procedure during the initialization for a specific grid element $\mathbf{j}$ is summarized in Algorithm 1.

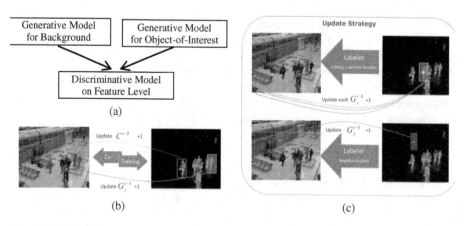

Fig. 3. (a) The grid-based classifiers can be interpreted as a combination of two generative models, one describing the back ground and one describing the object of interest, which are combined to a discriminative model at feature level by linking off-line and on-line boosting. (b) Co-grid initialization stage: the grid classifiers on the left side are co-trained with an independent classifier operating on the background subtracted image on the right side. (c) Co-grid detection stage: the classifier C is used as an oracle to perform positive as well as negative updates of the classifiers within the classifier grid. Positive updates are spread to all classifiers in the grid whereas negative updates are performed for a particular classifiers in grid.

Detection Stage: After the initial stage, as described above, the classifier C operating on the background subtracted images is no longer updated and is applied as an oracle to generate new positive and negative samples as illustrated in Fig. 3. In combination with our robust learning algorithm this oracle can now be to replace the fixed update rules. Moreover, we perform negative updates for the classifiers G_j only if they are necessary, i.e., if the scene is changing. Even if the oracle classifier C has a low recall, the precision is very high. Thus, only very valuable patches are used to update the classifier G_j, which leads to an increasing performance of the classifiers within the classifier grid. In particular, a confident positive classification result of classifier C at position j generates an update for all classifier G_j, $j = 1,..., n$ in the classifier grid. In this way new scene specific positive samples are disseminated over the whole classifier grid. Negative updates are performed for classifiers G_j if there is no corresponding detection reported at this position for classifier C. The update procedure during the detection phase for a specific grid element j is summarized in Algorithm 2.

Algorithm 1: Co-Grid Initialization
Input:
   grid-classifier G_j^{t-1}
   co-trained classifier C^{t-1}
   patch corresponding to grid-element X_j
   background subtracted patch B_j
Output: grid-classifier G_j^t and classifier C^t
Method:
1. **if** $C^{t-1}(B_j) > \theta$ **then** update(G_j^{t-1}, X_j, +1)
2. **else if** $C^{t-1}(B_j) < -\theta$ **then** update(G_j^{t-1}, X_j, -1)
3. **end if**
4. **if** $G_j^{t-1}(X_j) > \theta$ **then** update(C^{t-1}, B_j, +1)
5. **else if** $G_j^{t-1}(X_j) < -\theta$ **then** update(C^{t-1}, B_j, -1)
6. **end if**

Algorithm 2: Co-Grid Update
Input:
   grid-classifier G_j^{t-1}
   co-trained classifier C
   patch corresponding to grid-element X_j
   background subtracted patch B_j
Output: grid-classifier G_j^t
Method:
1. **if** $C(B_j) > \theta$ **then**
2. $\forall_j$: update(G_j^{t-1}, X_j, +1)
3. **end if**
4. **if** $C(B_j) < -\theta$ **then**
5.   update(G_j^{t-1}, X_j, -1)
6. **end if**

4 Experimental Evaluation and Results

In the following, we demonstrate our approach on different publicly available datasets for multi-camera person detection. We first describe our experimental setup and evaluation methods used and then evaluate our approach on two different datasets. To demonstrate the benefits of the proposed approach, we conducted two experiments (person object). We selected some of the data is publicly available for research to quantify the results to conduct experiments. From these experiments the benefits of the proposed approach is obvious. For the experiment of detecting pedestrians, we use the classification of 20 of selectors, each selector has 10 weak classifiers. For detecting person experiment we used the classification of 50 of selectors. each selector has 30 weak classifiers. When the classification we use simple decision tree than on the response characteristics Haar- like. To increase the solidity of the negative samples updates, we collected four background images overlap activities four different time periods.

4.1   PETS Dataset

In this experiment, we used a series of publicized PETS 2006 data includes 308 frames (720 × 576 pixels), including 1,714 pedestrians. We compare our approach with other advanced methods, namely the object model deformation Felzenszwalb et al. in 2008 (FS) [7] and the approach chart of Dalal Gradients and Triggs 2005 (DT) [5]. Both methods use fixed classifier was trained offline and is based on the sliding window technique. In addition, we compare our approached at classifier grids and compare with the approach of Roth et al. in 2009 (CG) [20]. The results of the Pet dataset is shown in Fig. 4 and Table 1. Illustrated object detection is shown in Fig. 6(a).

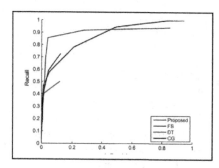

Fig. 4. Recall-precision of Pet dataset.

Table 1. The Recall and Precision Comparison

Methods	Comparison		
	Recall	Precision	F-Measure
Felzenszwalb and el.	0.74	0.89	0.79
Dalal and Triggs	0.51	0.88	0.66
Roth and el.	0.80	0.81	0.80
Our proposed	0.88	0.99	0.92

4.2   CAVIAR Dataset

Datasets Caviar show a corridor in a shopping center from two different angles. First corner side of the corridor, the second corner of the face directly. Because we are interested in the process of discovering who the percentage change should we focus on first dataset. Data may or JPEG and MPEG resolution is 384 × 288. For our experiment, we choose a fairly complex data set to assess the ShopAssistant2cor because it contains a large number of pedestrians (e.g. 1265). There are 370 frames with size 384 × 128 image. To conduct experiments with the approach based on the classification of cells in the data sets Caviar, the following parameters are initialized: the image size: 32 × 64. The selectors used to train online for classifiers is: 10. Number of weak classifier of a selector is 20. The results of the Caviar dataset is shown in Fig. 5 and Table 2. Again it can be seen that the detection adaptive grid (CG-OOL) better than the generic object detection (HOG-DT and DPM-FS), especially Recall. Results illustrated object detection is shown in Fig. 6(b).

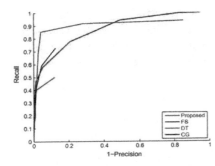

Fig. 5. Recall-precision of Caviar dataset

Table 2. The Recall and Precision Comparison

Methods	Comparison		
	Recall	Precision	F-Measure
Felzenszwalb and el.	0.62	0.90	0.74
Dalal and Triggs	0.41	0.91	0.57
Roth and el.	0.78	0.87	0.82
Our proposed	0.92	0.93	0.92

      (a)   (b)

Fig. 6. (a) Illustrative detection results of person detector for the Pet Sequence. (b) Illustrative detection results of person detector for the Caviar Sequence.

5 Conclusion

We developed a approaches to incorporate this information based on the idea of classifier grids. Classifier grids divide the input image into highly overlapping grid elements, where each grid element contains its own classifier. Based on the idea of classifier grids learning strategies. To allow for incorporating both, scene specific object information as well as scene specific background information we propose a co-training related approach for the classifier grids, i.e., classifier co-grid. In combination with our robust learning algorithm this allows for incorporating unlabeled information from the scene but still preserving the reliable labeled information. This approached aim to preserve long-term stability, which is given by either using specific update strategies or by using our robust learning algorithm. We demonstrate the long-term stability of the proposed approaches empirically by evaluating them on a real-world surveillance scenario, where a corridor in a public building is monitored over one week and object detection is performed. Even though the whole approach is updated without supervision, the robustness is preserved. The experimental results, demonstrating against the problem with different objects, clearly shows that very good results detected with high precision, while ensuring that it can perform online, adapting with many environmental and drifting problem detection system for short-term performance improvements explicit.

References

1. Agarwal, S., Awan, A., Roth, D.: Learning to detect objects in images via a sparse, part-based representation. IEEE Trans. Pattern Anal. Mach. Intell. **26**(11), 1475–1490 (2004)
2. Andrews, S., Tsochantaridis, I., Hofmann, T.: Support vector machines for multiple-instance learning. In: Advances in NIPS, pp. 561–568 (2003)
3. Babenko, B., Yang, M.-H., Belongie, S.: Visual tracking with online multiple instance learning. In: IEEE Conference on CVPR (2009)
4. Blum, Mitchell, T.: Combining labeled and unlabeled data with co-training. In: Proceedings of Conference on Computational Learning Theory, pp. 92–100 (1998)
5. Dalal, N., Triggs, B.: Histograms of oriented gradients for human detection. In: IEEE Conference on CVPR, vol. I. pp. 886–893 (2005)
6. Viola, P., Platt, J.C., Zhang, C.: Multiple instance boosting for object detection. In: Advances in Neural Information Processing Systems, pp. 1417–1426 (2005)
7. Felzenszwalb, P., McAllester, D., Ramanan, D.: A discriminatively trained, multiscale, deformable part model. In: IEEE Conference on CVPR (2008)
8. Goldberg, B., Li, M., Zhu, X.: Online manifold regularization: a new learning setting and empirical study. In: Proceeding on European Conference on Machine Learning and Knowledge Discovery in Databases, vol. I, pp. 393–407 (2008)
9. Grabner, H., Roth, P.M., Bischof, H.: Is pedestrian detection really a hard task?. In: Proceeding of IEEE Workshop on Performance Evaluation of Tracking and Surveillance (2007)
10. Hoiem, D., Efros, A.A., Hebert, M.: Putting objects in perspective. In: Proceeding of IEEE Conference on Computer Vision and Pattern Recognition, vol. II, pp. 2137–2144 (2006)
11. Javed, O., Ali, S., Shah, M.: Online detection and classification of moving objects using progressively improving detectors. In: Proceeding of IEEE Conference on CVPR, vol. I, pp. 696–701 (2005)
12. Leibe, B., Leonardis, A., Schiele, B.: Robust object detection with interleaved categorization and segmentation. Int. J. Comput. Vis. **77**(1–3), 259–289 (2008)
13. Levin, P., Viola, Freund, Y.: Unsupervised improvement of visual detectors using co-training. In: Proceedings of ICCV, vol. I, pp. 626–633 (2003)
14. Li, L.J., Wang, G., Fei-Fei, L.: Optimol: automatic online picture collection via incremental model learning. In: Proceeding of IEEE Conference on CVPR, pp. 1–8 (2007)
15. Grabner, H., Bischof, H.: On-line boosting and vision. In: Proceedings of IEEE Conference on Computer Vision and Pattern Recognition, vol. I, pp. 260–267 (2006)
16. Nair, V., Clark, J.J.: An unsupervised, online learning framework for moving object detection. In: Proceedings of IEEE Conference on CVPR, vol. II, pp. 317–324 (2004)
17. Rosenberg, C., Hebert, M., Schneiderman, H.: Semi-supervised self-training of object detection models. In: IEEE Workshop on Applications of Computer Vision, pp. 29–36 (2005)

18. Wu, B., Nevatia, R.: Improving part based object detection by unsupervised, online boosting. In: Proceedings of IEEE Conference on CVPR, pp. 1–8 (2007)
19. Roth, P.M., Grabner, H., Skočaj, D., Bischof, H., Leonardis, A.: On-line conservative learning for person detection. In: Proceedings of IEEE International Workshop on Visual Surveillance and Performance Evaluation of Tracking and Surveillance, pp. 223–230 (2005)
20. Roth, P.M., Sternig, S., Grabner, H., Bischof, H.: Classifier grids for robust adaptive object detection. In: Procceding of IEEE Conference on CVPR (2009)
21. Torralba, A.: Contextual priming for object detection. IJCV **53**(2), 169–191 (2003)
22. Koller, D., Heitz, G.: Learning spatial context: using stuff to find things. In: Forsyth, D., Torr, P., Zisserman, A. (eds.) ECCV 2008, Part I. LNCS, vol. 5302, pp. 30–43. Springer, Heidelberg (2008)

Using the Cumulative Sum Algorithm Against Distributed Denial of Service Attacks in Internet of Things

Pheeha Machaka[1](✉), Andre McDonald[1], Fulufhelo Nelwamondo[1], and Antoine Bagula[2]

[1] Council for Scientific and Industrial Research, Modelling and Digital Science, Meiring Naude Rd, Pretoria 0184, South Africa
{PMachaka, AMcdonald, FNelwamondo}@csir.co.za
pheeham@gmail.com
[2] University of the Western Cape, Robert Sobukwe Road, Bellville 7535, South Africa
BBagula@uwc.ac.za

Abstract. The paper presents the threats that are present in Internet of Things (IoT) systems and how they can be used to perpetuate a large scale DDoS attack. The paper investigates how the Cumulative Sum (CUSUM) algorithm can be used to detect a DDoS attack originating from an IoT system, and how the performance of the algorithm is affected by its tuning parameters and various network attack intensities. The performance of the algorithm is measured against the trade-off between the algorithm's detection rate, false alarm and detection delay. The performance results are analysed and discussed and avenues for future work are provided.

Keywords: Anomaly detection · Internet of things · Change detection · Distributed denial of service · TCP SYN flooding · Cumulative sum · Intrusion detection

1 Introduction

The recent advances in Information Communications Technology (ICT) have led to a new era called the Internet of Things (IoT). In this paradigm, many of the objects (or things) that surround our living environment will be connected to the Internet or another network in one form or another. The services and applications provided by these technologies may include smart electricity meter reading, intelligent transportation, stock exchanges monitoring and health monitoring [1].

IoT allows everyday use objects like the smartphones, smart-TV, smart-fridge and many other smart devices to be connected to the Internet. This trend will keep on growing as more objects gain the means and capacity to directly interface with the Internet. The use of these services and devices will result in enormous amounts of data being generated by these inter-connected devices. This data needs to be stored, processed and presented in a seamless, efficient, and easily interpretable form [1]. Of most importance is the security and privacy of the services provided by these technologies

© ICST Institute for Computer Sciences, Social Informatics and Telecommunications Engineering 2016
P.C. Vinh and V. Alagar (Eds.): ICCASA 2015, LNICST 165, pp. 62–72, 2016.
DOI: 10.1007/978-3-319-29236-6_7

that ensures the confidentiality, integrity and authenticity of the data in IoT. This is because each device and service is susceptible to abuse by attackers. Therefore the escalated use of IoT raises several security vulnerabilities [2].

The vulnerabilities and concerns that are present in IoT are due to the characteristics that make up the IoT architecture. The one concern is the increased population of objects; this presents an opportunity for attackers to use them as an army of zombies to carry out a large scale attack [1]. Another concern is the ubiquity, mobility and interoperability of IoT systems. The ubiquity and physical distribution of IoT devices provides a window of opportunity for attackers to gain physical access and get closer to the target system [2]. The IoT system's increased mobility and interoperability intensifies the threat of IoT systems such that the attacker may gain access to the system and institute infected devices into the system in order to further jeopardise the system and evade detection of a large scale attack [1].

The IoT system presents an opportunity for attackers to launch a large scale Distributed Denial of Service (DDoS). A DDoS attack is a malicious attempt by an attacker to disrupt the online services of a service provider to make it unavailable to its legitimate users. This may lead to disgruntled service consumers and major financial losses; it may also lead to losses in an organization's intellectual property which in turn affects the long term competitiveness of businesses and governments in industrial and military espionage incidents [1]. It is therefore important that organizations and governments deploy methods and techniques that will help them to accurately and reliably detect the onset and occurrence of the DDoS attacks.

This paper investigates the performance of the CUSUM algorithm against a DDoS attack. The paper also investigates the trade-off between the algorithm's detection rate, false alarm and detection delay. The paper seeks to further investigate how the performance of the algorithm is affected by the tuning parameters and how various network attack intensity affect its performance.

The remainder of the paper is organised as follows: In Sect. 2 a brief review of a DDoS flooding attack and related work is provided. Section 3 discusses the research and experiment design while Sects. 4 and 5 presents and discusses the results obtained from the experiments.

2 Background and Related Work

An attacker uses DDoS attacks in order to prevent legitimate users from accessing the service of a provider. The attacker does this through the use of an attack that streams multiple illegitimate requests to the victim, e.g. a High-Rate Flooding (HRF) attack. There have been various classifications of DDoS attacks in the literature [3–8], however the focus of this paper will be on the malicious and widely used TCP SYN flooding attack.

2.1 TCP SYN Flooding Attack

A TCP SYN flooding attack is an example of a network layer flooding attack, and it is one of the most common and powerful flooding methods. It exploits the vulnerabilities of the TCP three-way handshake. In a normal TCP connection, the client initiates the connection by sending a SYN packet to the server, as a way of requesting a connection. Upon receiving the connection request, the server will open a connection session and respond with a SYN_ACK packet; by doing this the server stores details of the requested TCP connection in the memory stack and allocates resources to this open session. The connection remains in a half-open state, i.e. the SYN_RECVD state. To complete the three-way handshake with the server, the client will need to confirm the connection and respond with an ACK packet. The server will then check the memory stack for an existing connection request, and the TCP connection will be moved from the SYN_RECVD state to ESTABLISHED state. If there is no ACK packet sent within a specific period of time, the connection will timeout and therefore releasing the allocated resources [5, 8, 9].

In a TCP SYN flooding attack, the attacker streams large volumes of SYN packets towards the victim server. A vulnerable IoT system can be used for this purpose. These packets normally contain spoofed IP addresses, i.e. IP addresses that are non-existent or are not utilised. TCP SYN floods can also be launched using compromised machines with legitimate IP addresses, however the machines need to be configured in such a way that it does not respond or acknowledge a SYN_ACK packet from the victim server. In this way the server will not receive any ACK packet from the clients for the 'half-open' connection request. During the high rate flooding attack, and for a period of time, the server will maintain a large volume of incomplete three-way handshake and allocates resource towards the fictitious connection requests. The server will gather more fictitious requests and eventually exhaust its resources. This will prevent new requests, including legitimate client requests, from being further processed by the server [5, 8, 9].

2.2 Anomaly and Change Detection Algorithms

In the event of a DDoS attack, abrupt changes in observed network traffic can be observed. Similarly, an abrupt change in statistical properties of detection features can be observed. Thus, the problem of anomaly detection can be constructed as change point detection problem [10, 11]. The aim of change detection techniques are to help detect a change in statistical properties of observed network traffic with minimal detection delay and false positive rate [12]. The approach first starts by applying filter to the traffic data by desired features and arraigning the data into a time series data. For change detection, if there was a DDoS attack at time λ, the time series will show a significant statistical change around or at a time greater than λ [13].

Detecting changes in statistical properties of observed network traffic has been studied extensively and applied in various fields like image processing, network traffic and financial analysis. There are a number of techniques that are used for change detection and amongst them the most common technique used for the detection of DDoS attacks is the Cumulative Sum (CUSUM) algorithm [14].

2.3   Cumulative Sum (CUSUM) Algorithm

Several variants of the CUSUM algorithm were first introduced by Page in [15]. The CUSUM algorithm is based on hypothesis testing and was developed for independent and identically distributed random variables $\{y_i\}$. In the approach, an abrupt change occurring at any time can be modeled using two hypotheses, θ_0 and θ_1. The first hypothesis θ_1 represents the statistical distribution before the abrupt change occurring; and the second hypothesis θ_2 represents the statistical distribution after the abrupt change has occurred. The test for signaling a change is based on the log-likelihood ratio S_n.

$$S_n = \sum s_i$$

Where,

$$s_i = \ln \frac{P_{\theta_1}(y_i)}{P_{\theta_2}(y_i)}$$

According to Siris et al. [9]. the typical behavior of the log-likelihood ratio S_n includes a negative divergence before an abrupt change and a positive divergence after the change. Therefore, the relevant information for detecting a change lies in the difference between the value of the log-likelihood ratio and its current minimum value [12]. The alarm condition for the CUSUM algorithm takes the form:

If $g_n \geq h$ (h is a threshold parameter) then signal alarm at time n;

$$\text{where } g_n = S_n - m_n \tag{1}$$

and

$$m_n = \min_{1 \leq j \leq n} S_j. \tag{2}$$

In the above equations, it is assumed that $\{y_i\}$ are independent Gaussian random variables with known variance σ^2 and mean μ_0 and μ_1 represents the mean before and after the abrupt change, respectively. Accordingly, $\theta_0 = N(\mu_0, \sigma^2)$ and $\theta_1 = N(\mu_1, \sigma^2)$. Following an application of various calculations, Basseville et al. [12] implemented the following CUSUM algorithm:

$$g_n = \left[g_{n-1} + \frac{\mu_0 - \mu_1}{\sigma^2} \left(y_n - \frac{\mu_1 + \mu_0}{2} \right) \right]^+ \tag{3}$$

The above algorithm was adapted and applied to the problem of detecting SYN flooding attacks. This algorithm was applied as follows [9]:

$$\tilde{x}_n = x_n - \bar{\mu}_{n-1} \tag{4}$$

where x_n represents the number of SYN packets in the n-th time interval, and $\bar{\mu}_n$ represents the estimated mean rate at time n. The estimates mean rate is computed using an exponentially weighted moving average as follows:

$$\bar{\mu}_n = \beta \bar{\mu}_{n-1} + (1 - \beta) x_n \tag{5}$$

where β is the exponentially weighted moving average (EWMA) factor.

The mean value of $\tilde{x}_n$ prior to a change is zero, therefore the mean in (3) is $\mu_0 = 0$. The mean traffic rate after a change cannot be known in advance. It can therefore be estimated with $\alpha \bar{\mu}_n$, were α is an amplitude percentage parameter. The parameter equates to the most likely percentage increase of the mean rate after an attack has occurred. For purposes of detecting SYN flood attacks, the algorithm in (3) has been adapted to:

$$g_n = \left[g_{n-1} + \frac{\alpha \bar{\mu}_{n-1}}{\sigma^2} \left(x_n - \bar{\mu}_{n-1} - \frac{\alpha \bar{\mu}_{n-1}}{2} \right) \right]^+ \tag{6}$$

In the CUSUM algorithm, the tuning parameters are the amplitude factor, α, the Weighting factor, β, and the CUSUM algorithm threshold, h.

2.4   Related Work

The CUSUM technique has been applied to various problems including DDoS detection. It calculates the cumulative sum of difference between actual and expected values of a sequence, the CUSUM value. This value is compared to a threshold value (an upper bound). A CUSUM value greater than the upper bound threshold indicates a change in statistical properties in the observed network traffic time series values.

There are a number of variations of the CUSUM technique, and Tartakovsky et al. [10] proposed fully-sequential and batch-sequential algorithms. They are both non-parametric variations of the CUSUM techniques adapted to detecting changes in multiple bins. The algorithms were found to be self-learning, which enables them to adapt to various network loads and usage patterns. They also allow for the detection of attacks with a small average delay for a given false-alarm rate and they are compu-tationally feasible and thus can be implemented online.

Bo et al. [16] also used an algorithm which is a variation of the CUSUM technique to enable quick detection of worm attack incidents. In their experiments they observed the computer's degree of connection to estimate the CUSUM score. It was concluded that the algorithm could detect new attacks fast and effectively.

There has been various combination of the CUSUM technique with other detection techniques. For example, Dainotti et al. [17] used a combination of the adaptive threshold, Continuous Wavelet Transform (CWT) and the CUSUM technique to detect volume based attacks. In this proposed techniques, two detection engines were used. An anomaly will be detected by the first stage detection engine will detect an anomaly, and an alarm is sent to the second stage detection engine (based on CWT) which refines the detection in order to avoid high number of false alarms.

Siris et al. [9] proposed and investigated a change point detection algorithm, which is also based on the CUSUM technique. The algorithm revealed robust performance over various attack types, it was computationally feasible and not computationally expensive. Wang et al. [18] also proposed an algorithm which is a variation of the

CUSUM technique on an application for detecting DDoS attacks. Protocol behaviors of TCP SYN – FIN (RST) pairs where used to make detections. The experiment results revealed that the algorithm had a low detection delays and high detection accuracy.

3   The Research Design

The experiments were conducted using actual network traffic data from the MIT Lincoln Laboratory, the DARPA intrusion detection dataset. The data contains trace data taken during a day of network activity. The experiment considered trace data where there was significant traffic activity. Therefore trace data between the times 08h00–19h00 were considered, and thus an 11 h period of real network packets was used for experiments.

To allow for investigations of the algorithm's performance across different types of attack characteristics, the attacks were generated synthetically to simulate an IoT system. They were generated as a homogenous Poisson process with independent and exponentially distributed delays between packet arrivals. The synthetically generated attack was designed to last for 300 s (5 min) over 30 time intervals (using a 10 s time interval). To consider all possible attack combinations within the 11 h network packet trace, each 5 min window was injected with attack data in separate runs of the experiments.

In these experiments we consider and simulate two types of attack characteristics: high intensity and low intensity attacks. Low intensity attacks are those attacks whose intensity increases gradually. In these experiments we considered the case of a low intensity attack to be an attack that, within the 5 min attack interval, has its mean amplitude to be 50 % above the actual attack free traffic's mean rate. High intensity attack are those attacks whose intensity increases abruptly and reach a peak amplitude within one time interval. High intensity attacks were considered to be attacks that are 250 % higher than the peak rate within the 5 min attack interval.

4   Results and Discussions

These experiments were investigating the performance of the CUSUM algorithm for both low and high intensity attacks, testing the following: (1) the effect, on detection-rate, of the amplitude factor α, tuning parameter; (2) the effect, on detection rate, of the weighting factor β, tuning parameter; (3) the trade-off between detection rate and the false positive rate; (4) the trade-off between the detection rate and detection delay. The result and discussion from the experiments are expanded in the sub-sections that follow.

4.1   The Effect of the Amplitude Factor (α)

In this section the effect of the amplitude factor (α) on the detection rate and the false positive rate is investigated. In this part of the experiments, the value of the weighting factor was held constant β = 0.8; the CUSUM amplitude factor *h* = 3; while the amplitude factor was varied between [0.05; 1.0].

The Fig. 1 depicts the results of the experiments. From the Fig. 1(a) it can be observed that for low rate attacks, the detection algorithm yields a detection rate between 0 % – 81 % and a false positive between 0 % – 7 % for values of 0 < α ≤ 0.5.

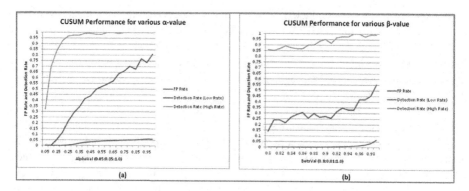

Fig. 1. Detection rate and False Alarm rate for (a) varied amplitude factor value (α); and (b) varied Weighting factor (β), for both Low rate attacks and High rate attacks.

From the Fig. 1(a), it can be observed that for high rate attacks and values of 0 < α ≤ 0.95, the detection algorithm yields a 32 % – 100 % detection rate while having a false positive rate between 0 % – 6 %. The above experiment signifies that when the value of the amplitude factor increases, the values of the detection rate and the false positive rate also increases.

4.2   The Effect of the Weighting Factor (β)

In this section the effect of the value of the Weighting factor (β) on the detection rate and the false positive rate is investigated. In this part of the experiments, the value of the amplitude factor was made constant α = 0.5; the CUSUM amplitude factor *h* = 3; while the value of the Weighting factor (β) was varied between [0.80; 1.0].

From the Fig. 1(b) it can be observed that the performance of the detection algorithm was poor. For low rate attacks, the algorithm had a detection rate between 14 %-56 %; while the false positive rate was between 0 % - 7 %. For high rate attacks, shown by Fig. 1(b), the detection rate was between 85 % and 100 %; In this experiment, the CUSUM algorithm reached a 100 % detection rate for values of β ≥ 0.95. However, the higher detection rate was accompanied by an increased false positive rate. Therefore there is a trade-off between a higher detection rate and an increased false positive rate.

4.3   Trade-off Between False Positive Rate and Detection Rate

In this set of experiments we were investigating the trade-off between false positive rate and detection rate. The values for the tuning parameters were as follows: the amplitude factor $\alpha = 0.5$; the Weighting factor $\beta = 0.98$. The CUSUM amplitude factor h was varied from 1 to 10.

Figure 2 displays the Receiver operating curves for the experiments, where each point corresponds to a different value of h. Good operating points on the graph are those points that are closer to the upper-left corner of the graph. Figure 2(a) shows results for the experiments simulating low rate attacks. In the case of low rate attacks, an increase in the algorithm's detection accuracy was accompanied by a sharp increase in the false alarm rate. Therefore higher detection accuracy will also result in a higher false alarm rate. This is a performance that is not desired in a detection algorithm. Therefore the CUSUM algorithm did not perform very well for cases of low rate attacks.

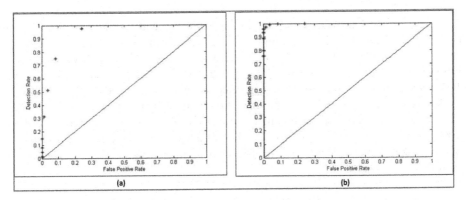

Fig. 2. Receiver Operating Curves for trade-off between FP Rate and Detection Rate for (a) low rate attacks and (b) high rate attacks.

Figure 2(b) depicts the performance of the CUSUM algorithm in the case of high rate attacks simulation. Most of the operating points are closer to the upper-left corner of the graph. This is also indicative that for a higher detection rate there is a slight increase in the false alarm rate. This is an improved algorithm performance when compared with the low rate attack simulations.

4.4   Trade-off Between Detection Rate and Detection Delay

In the next set of experiments we further analyzed the trade-off between detection rate and detection delay. The results are shown in Fig. 3 below. Detection delay in this case is the average time taken by the algorithm to successfully detect an attack, from the onset of that attack. Each point corresponds to a pair of detection rate and average detection delay. The values for the tuning parameters were as follows: the amplitude factor $\alpha = 0.5$; the Weighting factor $\beta = 0.98$. The value of the amplitude factor h was varied from 1-10.

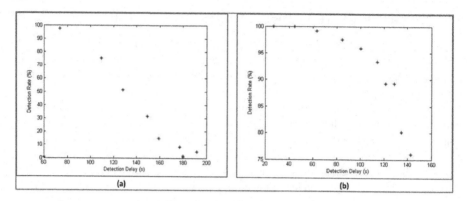

Fig. 3. Graph displaying the trade-off between Detection Rate and average Detection Delay for (a) low rate attacks and (b) high rate attacks.

Figure 3(a) depicts the trade-off between detection rate and average detection delay performance of the CUSUM algorithm for low rate attack simulations. From the graph it can be observed that as the detection rate decreases, the accompanying detection delay increases. From the simulation with low rate attacks, the CUSUM failed to reach a 100 % detection rate, but the best average detection delay was just below 80 s (73.3 s).

Figure 3(b) displays results for the simulations with high rate attacks. The algorithm had an improved performance for high rate attacks. For a 100 % detection rate the average detection delays was at 26.94 s and 44.71 s for varying h-values. It can also be observed that for lower detection rate performance the average detection delay also increases.

5   Conclusions

This paper described, analyzed and discussed how the CUSUM algorithm can be used for detecting DDoS attacks in an IoT system. The simulation experiments investigated how the performance of the algorithm is affected by the tuning parameters (α, β and h). These were efforts to find optimal parameter tuning for best CUSUM algorithm performance. It also investigated the trade-off between detection rate and false positive rate, as well as detection rate and average detection delay. Furthermore, the experiments were conducted on real network traffic data with synthetically generated attack data with two levels of attack intensity (i.e. low rate and high rate attacks).

In these experiments it was found that optimal CUSUM parameter tuning for this network traffic was: $\alpha = 0.5$, $\beta = 0.98$ and $h = 3$. Furthermore, it was found that the CUSUM algorithm performs well for high rate attacks, however its performance subsides for low rate attacks. This further confirms the findings by the authors in [9].

Ongoing research work will include performance comparison of the CUSUM with other anomaly detection algorithm, similar to the work of authors in [19–23]. Another avenue for future work is the development of change detection algorithms that perform well under various attack characteristics and intensity.

References

1. Uckelmann, D., Harrison, M., Michahelles, F.: An architectural approach towards the future internet of things. In: Architecting the Internet of Things (2011)
2. Weber, R.H.: Internet of things-new security and privacy challenges. Comput. Law Secur. Rev. **26**(1), 23–30 (2010)
3. Douligeris, C., Mitrokotsa, A.: DDoS attacks and defense mechanisms: classification and state-of-the-art. Comput. Netw. **44**(5), 643–666 (2004)
4. Mirkovic, J., Reiher, P.: A taxonomy of DDoS attack and DDoS defense mechanisms. ACM SIGCOMM Comput. Commun. Rev. **34**(2), 39–53 (2004)
5. Zargar, S.T., Joshi, J., Tipper, D.: A survey of defense mechanisms against distributed denial of service (DDoS) flooding attacks. IEEE Commun. Surv. Tutorials **15**(4), 2046–2069 (2013)
6. Lazarevic, A., Kumar, V., Srivastava, J.: Intrusion detection: a survey. In: Managing Cyber Threats (2005)
7. Bhattacharyya, D.K., Kalita, J.K.: Network Anomaly Detection A Machine Learning Perspective. CRC Press, Boca Raton (2013)
8. Zhou, C.V., Leckie, C., Karunasekera, S.: A survey of coordinated attacks and collaborative intrusion detection. Comput. Secur. **29**(1), 124–140 (2010)
9. Siris, V.A., Papagalou, F.: Application of anomaly detection algorithms for detecting SYN flooding attacks. Comput. Commun. **29**(9), 1433–1442 (2006)
10. Tartakovsky, A.G., Rozovskii, B.L., Blazek, R.B., Kim, H.: A novel approach to detection of intrusions in computer networks via adaptive sequential and batch-sequential change-point detection methods. IEEE Trans. Signal Process. **54**(9), 3372–3382 (2006)
11. Tartakovsky, A.G., Polunchenko, A.S., Sokolov, G.: Efficient computer network anomaly detection by change point detection methods. IEEE J. Sel. Top. Sign. Process. **7**(1), 4–11 (2013)
12. Basseville, M., Nikiforov, I.V.: Detection of Abrupt Changes: Theory and Application, vol. 104. Prentice Hall, Englewood Cliffs (1993)
13. Poor, H.V., Hadjiliadis, O.: Quickest Detection, vol. 40. Cambridge University Press, New York (2009)
14. Carl, G., Kesidis, G., Brooks, R.R., Rai, S.: Denial-of-service attack-detection techniques. IEEE Internet Comput. **10**(1), 82–89 (2006)
15. Page, E.: Continuous inspection schemes. Biometrika **41**, 100–115 (1954)
16. Bo, C., Fang, B., Yun, X.: A new approach for early detection of internet worms based on connection degree. In: Proceedings of 2005 International Conference on Machine Learning and Cybernetics (2005)
17. Dainotti, A., Pescapé, A., Ventre, G.: Wavelet-based detection of DoS attacks. In: Global Telecommunications Conference, GLOBECOM 2006. IEEE (2006)
18. Wang, H., Zhang, D., Shin, K.G.: Detecting SYN flooding attacks. In: Proceedings of Twenty-First Annual Joint Conference of the IEEE Computer and Communications Societies INFOCOM 2002, IEEE (2002). doi:10.1109/INFCOM.2002.1019404
19. Machaka, P., Bagula, A., De Wet, N.: A highly scalable monitoring tool for wi-fi networks. In: 2012 IEEE 1st International Symposium on Wireless Systems (IDAACS-SWS) (2012)
20. Machaka, P., Bagula, A.: An investigation of scalable anomaly detection techniques for a large network of wi-fi hotspots. In: Jung, J.J., Badica, C., Kiss, A. (eds.) INFOSCALE 2014. LNICST, vol. 139. Springer, Heidelberg (2014). doi:10.1007/978-3-319-16868-5

21. Tran, D.Q., Nguyen, M.H.: Drought monitoring: a performance investigation of three machine learning techniques. In: Vinh, P.C., Alagar, V., Vassev, E., Khare, A. (eds.) ICCASA 2013. LNICST, vol. 128, pp. 47–56. Springer, Heidelberg (2014)
22. Bagula, A., Machaka, P., Mabande, T.: Monitoring of a large Wi-Fi hotspots network: performance investigation of soft computing techniques. In: Hart, E., Timmis, J., Mitchell, P., Nakamo, T., Dabiri, F. (eds.) BIONETICS 2011. LNICST, vol. 103, pp. 155–162. Springer, Heidelberg (2012)
23. Bagula, A., Machaka, P.: Preemptive performance monitoring of a large network of Wi-Fi Hotspots: an artificial immune system. In: Masip-Bruin, X., Verchere, D., Tsaoussidis, V., Yannuzzi, M. (eds.) WWIC 2011. LNCS, vol. 6649, pp. 494–504. Springer, Heidelberg (2011)

Memory Resource Estimation of Component-Based Systems

Trinh Dong Nguyen$^{(\boxtimes)}$

HPU, Haiphong, Vietnam
dongnt@hpu.edu.vn

Abstract. Traditional relational interface theory focuses on expressing functional aspects of software components. We extend the theory by adding resource specification to reason for the quality of composite components in terms of resource efficiency. For practical application, we instantiate interface using automata and present algorithms to check if a component system met the predefined resource requirements. In particular, we can answer if a component can be plugged into an environment of whether it is a refinement of another component.

Keywords: Estimation of memory resources · Resource estimation component-based systems · Model compositions · Interface based designs · Interface compositions

1 Introduction

Estimating resources of component-based systems is one of the important issues in software engineering. The estimation covers many features in a system such as memory resources, time resources, and the others in which the estimation of memory is addressed. The memory resource identification of component-based systems aims for forecasting memory resource of a system that consumes in operating. It then calculates supreme memory resources of a system, whether they satisfy the system's requirement. In particular, those can be fulfilled in design phase. This is important in utilization of resources in the embedded system whose the memory optimization is always considered. Hence, how do estimate memory resources of a component-based system in design phase? The problem will be solved in the next sections.

The first, the paper extends the relational interface [6] and timed design in [1] for memory constraints. Components in a system are described by relational interfaces with memory design constraints. Hence, they are composed together depending on plugable, refinement, parallel and sequential operations to construct complex systems. The second, the paper calculates the memory resource which is used in an interface, and predicts memory resources for pluggable, refinement, parallel and sequential compositions. The third, the paper proposes algorithms to estimate the memory resources for above items within a system. By using this theory, the estimation of memory resources of a component-based

© ICST Institute for Computer Sciences, Social Informatics and Telecommunications Engineering 2016
P.C. Vinh and V. Alagar (Eds.): ICCASA 2015, LNICST 165, pp. 73–82, 2016.
DOI: 10.1007/978-3-319-29236-6_8

system can be implemented effectively. This estimation can be done at the earliest stage of a system development.

In general, the aim of this paper uses the memory resource design pattern with memory resource constraints for specifying component-based systems and estimating memory resources. Especially, the proposed algorithms in this paper can estimate memory resource of a component-based system in design phase.

The paper is organized as follows: The next section is related works. Section 3 describes the specification of components by interfaces with their environment, and modeling them by finite automata. Simultaneously, this section also introduces to the pluggable, refinement, parallel and sequential composition of those automata. Section 4 estimates memory resources for automaton interface, pluggability of automata interfaces, composition of automata interfaces, and proposes algorithms to compute those resources. The last section is the conclusion of our paper.

2   Related Work

Interface theory is one of promise approaches for component-based system in which relational interface emerges as most efficiency method [6]. However, this approach has just captured the relation between input and output sets of components in terms of first-order logic, and other properties have not addressed such as memory resources property, timed property, etc. D.V. Hung et al. use the UTP notation to denote timed design pattern in [1]. Those signatures are concise, easy to depict components in a system. However, the authors use for specifying time feature purpose.

In the memory resource estimation, recently, A.V. Fioukov et al. introduced a method to calculate the static properties of an architecture depending on a framework in which estimating memory resource was one of aspects, and this work based on the source codes [3]. The authors used two approaches bottom-up and top-down algorithm to predict memory size and to evaluate static properties of components, the contribution has only applied to *Koala Component Model* [2,3]. Johan Muskens and Michel Chaudron proposed an approach to predict resources of a system in run-time based on scenario. However, this method cannot apply for interface based design [5]. Merijn de Jonge et al. proposed a method to estimate the resource of a system in run-time. This proposal focus on evaluation of memory resource relying on modeling behaviors of a component by sequence of messages, and called scenarios [4].

In general, all above works consider various aspects of systems and specific applications such as *Koala Component Model, Robocop*, but they do not formalize a general theory for component-based systems. Furthermore, memory resources cannot predict in early state of the software development.

3   Interface and Interface Modeling

3.1   Memory Resource Design

A component supplies services to its environment, it invades memory resources within a system. Therefore, a component consumes memory resource depending on the variables size and what kind of services for which it provides. In this part, the paper uses a notion *memory resource design*, denoted μ. Let X be a set of input ports, Y be a set of output ports, C be upper bound memory resources of an interface that stores the memory size value of an interface at a specific run-time.

Definition 1 (Memory Resource Design). *A memory resource design is of the form $\mu = p \vdash (R, C)$, where p is a guard over input set X, called precondition, R is a first-order logic formula, depicts the relation between X and Y and called post-condition, and C is an upper bound memory resource.*

This Definition depicts that a *memory resource design* as an atomic constraint in an interface. For an assignment $\mathcal{V}$ over X, the values satisfy precondition p will activate the interface and give values that also satisfy post-condition R at output ports Y. In the software evolutionary context, a *memory resource design* can be replaced by the other provided that the new one supplies better services and using fewer resources than the original one. The refinement of two memory resource designs is defined as follows:

Definition 2 (Memory Design Refinement). *Given two memory resource designs $\mu = p \vdash (R, C)$ and $\mu' = p' \vdash (R', C')$, μ is said to be a refinement of μ', denoted as $\mu \sqsubseteq \mu'$ iff $p' \Rightarrow p$, $R \Rightarrow R'$, and $C \leq C'$. When $\mu \sqsubseteq \mu'$ and $\mu' \sqsubseteq \mu$ we say μ and μ' are equivalent.*

Let $\mathbb{N}$ be the set of natural numbers, an assignment over $X \cup Y$ is a pair $(\mathcal{V}, t)$, denoted as γ and called a computation step, where $\mathcal{V}$ is an assignment over variables in $X \cup Y$, and t is a memory capacity using for the $\mathcal{V}$, $t \in \mathbb{N}$. The γ is a computation step of an interface iff γ satisfies a memory resource design $\mu = p \vdash (R, C)$ in that interface, signified $(\mathcal{V}, t) \models \mu$, iff $\mathcal{V}|_X \models p$, $\mathcal{V} \models R$ and $sizeof(t) \leq C$, where $\mathcal{V}|_X$ is an assignment on variables X, and $sizeof(t)$ is the capacity of memory. If for all $p \equiv false$, no computation step γ can satisfy μ. Considering two pairs $(\mathcal{V}, t)$ and $(\mathcal{V}', t')$, the $(\mathcal{V}, t)$ is equal to $(\mathcal{V}', t')$ iff $\mathcal{V} = \mathcal{V}'$ and $sizeof(t) = sizeof(t')$. Given any equivalent γ, γ' and a memory resource design μ, this only holds that $\gamma \models \mu$ if and only if $\gamma' \models \mu$. A computation step $\gamma = (\mathcal{V}, t)$ is said to be before a computation step $\gamma' = (\mathcal{V}', t')$, in other words, γ' is after γ. Given a sequence of consecutive computation step $s = (\gamma_1 \ldots \gamma_n)$, where $n \in \mathbb{N}$, for all $i \in n$ such that γ_{i+1} is after γ_i to be called a state.

Let $\mathcal{S}(X, Y)$ denote the set of all states, $\mathcal{M}(X, Y)$ denote the set of all *memory resource designs* over the set of $(X \cup Y)$. A relational interface with memory constraint is defined as follows:

Definition 3 (Interface). *A relational interface with memory resources is a triple $\mathcal{I} = \langle X, Y, \xi \rangle$, $X \cap Y = \varnothing$, $\xi : \mathcal{S}(X, Y) \twoheadrightarrow \mathcal{M}(X, Y)$ satisfying the formula $\xi(s) = \mu$. If $s = \epsilon$ implies $\xi(s) = \mu_0$, where ϵ is an initial state, and μ_0 is a memory resource design corresponding to initial state. In the contrary, let s be a sequence of $(\gamma_1 \gamma_2 \ldots \gamma_n)$, if $\xi(\gamma_1 \gamma_2 \ldots \gamma_n)$ is defined, then $\xi(\gamma_1 \gamma_2 \ldots \gamma_{n-1}) = \mu_{n-1}$ is also defined, and $\gamma_n \models \mu_{n-1}$. When $\xi(s)$ is defined, s is said a reachable state of $\mathcal{I}$. Let $\mathcal{R}(\mathcal{I})$ denote the set of all reachable states of interface $\mathcal{I}$.*

Example 1. This example illustrates a relational interface.

$$\mathcal{I} = \langle \{x\}, \{y\}, \{(x \geq 80 \wedge x \leq 260) \vdash (x \geq 80 \wedge x \leq 260 \wedge y = 220, 9)\} \rangle$$

This interface describes a component that has only one input port $\{x\}$, one output port $\{y\}$ and ξ guarantees that if $x \geq 80 \wedge x \leq 260$ then y always is equal to 220. The number 9 indicates that the interface consumes at most 9 memory units.

An interface is activated if it is plugged to its environments. Those environments supply resources to interfaces such as data, memory resources, etc. No all behaviors of an interface is implemented, but only behaviors satisfy conditions of the environment. Suppose a sequence of behaviors $(\mathcal{V}_1, t_1)(\mathcal{V}_2, t_2) \ldots (\mathcal{V}_m, t_m)$, where $\mathcal{V}_i$ is an assignment over $(X \cup Y)$, $t_i \in \mathbb{N}$, t_i is a current memory capacity at computation step i^{th}, $t_1 = 0$. An environment gives an assignment over input variables X of an interface by $\mathcal{V}_i|_X$ and expects values at output variables $\mathcal{V}_i|_Y$. Therefore, the assignment $\mathcal{V}_i$ consumes a memory capacity that is stored in variable t, where $sizeof(t_i) \leq C_i$. Let $\mathcal{P}(X, Y)$ be the set of all computation step sequences on (X, Y) of an environment.

Definition 4 (Environment). *An environment is a triple $E = \langle X, Y, \delta \rangle$, where $\delta : \mathcal{P}(X, Y) \nrightarrow \mathcal{M}(X, Y)$. E is defined as $\mathcal{I}$ excepts the sequence $w = (w_1 w_2 \ldots w_n)$ to be an interaction of E with $\mathcal{I}$. The w is said to be a reachable state of environment E. Let $\Pi(E)$ denote the set of all reachable states of environment E.*

3.2   Interface and Environment Modeling

The behaviors of an interface are infinite, therefore an interface $\mathcal{I} = \langle X, Y, \xi \rangle$, where ξ is a partial function from infinite set $\mathcal{S}(X, Y)$ to the set $\mathcal{M}(X, Y)$ need to be finitely represented. This part describes a method to represent interfaces and environments by label automata.

Definition 5 (Labeled Automata). *A labeled automaton M is a tuple $M = \langle Q, X, Y, q_0, T, l_s, l_t \rangle$, where Q is a finite set of locations, X and Y are sets of input and output ports, respectively, and $X \cap Y = \varnothing$, $q_0 \in Q$ is an initial state of M, $T \subseteq Q \times Q$ is a set of transitions, l_s and l_t are labeling functions. The labeling functions $l_s : Q \rightarrow \mathcal{M}(X, Y)$ associates each location in M with a memory resource design, and $l_t : T \rightarrow \mathcal{F}(X \cup Y)$ associates each transition in T with a guard formula. For any two different transitions (q, q') and (q, q''), the formula $l_t(q, q'') \wedge l_t(q, q') \Rightarrow false$ in order to make M deterministic.*

Hence, how to use a labeled automaton presents the behaviors of an interface. Let $\mathcal{A}(X \cup Y)$ be the set of all computation steps over $(X \cup Y)$. Suppose an assignment $\mathcal{V}_i$ in one of any sequences belonging to $\mathcal{A}(X \cup Y)$, i.e., $\mathcal{V}_i \in \mathcal{A}(X \cup Y)$, $i \leq n$. The assignment $\mathcal{V}_i$ inputs a set of values to input ports X and expects a set of values at output ports Y. This assignment has to satisfy one of memory resource designs that are available in an interface. Let $f : \mathcal{A}(X \cup Y)^* \nrightarrow \mathcal{M}(X \cup Y)$, i.e., M represents the partial function f. The labeled automaton M depicts partial function f as follows: For the initial state ϵ, $f(\epsilon) = l_s(q_0)$, i.e., ϵ leads M to q_0, and for any sequence $s \in \mathcal{A}(X \cup Y)^*$, if $f(s) = p \vdash (R, C)$ then s leads M to location q. According to the Definition 5, at current time there is at most one location q' such that $\mathcal{V} \models l_t(q, q')$. Therefore, an automaton describes an interface is defined as follows:

Definition 6 (Automata Interface). *A labeled automaton M is a description of an interface $\mathcal{I}$, and the interface $\mathcal{I}$ becomes an automaton interface iff for any sequence $(\mathcal{V}_1, t_1), \ldots, (\mathcal{V}_k, t_k)$ in labeled automaton M such that $(k \geq 0$, and the case $k = 0$ corresponds to the state $\epsilon)$, the value $\xi((\mathcal{V}_1, t_1), \ldots, (\mathcal{V}_k, t_k))$ is defined exactly when $f(\mathcal{V}_1, \ldots, \mathcal{V}_k)$ is defined and $\xi((\mathcal{V}_1, t_1), \ldots, (\mathcal{V}_k, t_1)) = f(\mathcal{V}_1, \ldots, \mathcal{V}_k)$ provided that $sizeof(t_i) \leq C_i$, where $f(\mathcal{V}_1, \ldots, \mathcal{V}_i) = p_i \vdash (R_i, C_i)$, $i \in n$.*

In order to use M describing an environment. The labeled automaton M gets over all sequence of behaviors of an environment such that satisfying all requirements of the environment. Given a sequence $(\mathcal{V}_1, t_1)(\mathcal{V}_2, t_2) \ldots (\mathcal{V}_n, t_n)$, for each $(\mathcal{V}_i, t_i)$, $i \leq n$, the function δ always is defined, i.e., labeling function l_s mounts a label corresponding to a location within automaton M. The $\delta((\mathcal{V}_1, t_1) \ldots (\mathcal{V}_k, t_k)) = p \vdash (R, C)$ iff there is a derivation $q_0 \xrightarrow{(\mathcal{V}_0, t_0)} \ldots \xrightarrow{(\mathcal{V}_{k-1}, t_{k-1})} q_k$ in automaton M such that $l_s(q_k) = p \vdash (R, C)$, and $\mathcal{V}_i \models p_{i-1} \wedge R_{i-1}$, where $l_s(q_{i-1}) = p_{i-1} \vdash (R_{i-1}, C_{i-1})$, $i = 1, \ldots, k - 1$. All the derivations in automaton M are distinct sequences.

Definition 7 (Automata Environment). *A labeled automaton M is a description of Environment $E = \langle X, Y, \delta \rangle$ and environment E becomes an automata environment iff for any sequence $(\mathcal{V}_1, t_1), \ldots, (\mathcal{V}_k, t_k)$ in labeled automaton M such that $(k \geq 0$, and the case $k = 0$ corresponds to the state $\epsilon)$, the sequence $\delta((\mathcal{V}_1, t_1), \ldots, (\mathcal{V}_k, t_k))$ is defined exactly when $f(\mathcal{V}_i, \ldots, \mathcal{V}_k)$ is defined and $\delta((\mathcal{V}_1, t_1), \ldots, (\mathcal{V}_k, t_1)) = f(\mathcal{V}_1, \ldots, \mathcal{V}_k)$ provided that $sizeof(t_i) \leq C_i$, where $f(\mathcal{V}_1, \ldots, \mathcal{V}_i) = p_i \vdash (R_i, C_i)$, $i \in n$.*

3.3 Automata Interface Composition

This section considers three operations which are pluggable, parallel and sequential compositions. Given $\mathcal{I}, \mathcal{I}', E$ represented by $M = \langle Q, X, Y, q_0, T, l_s, l_t \rangle$, $M' = \langle Q', X', Y', q_0', T', l_s', l_t' \rangle$, and $M^e = \langle Q^e, X^e, Y^e, q_0^e, T^e, l_s^e, l_t^e \rangle$, resp. $\mathcal{I}$ and $\mathcal{I}'$ compose together in parallel, denoted $\mathcal{I} \| \mathcal{I}'$. $\mathcal{I}$ and $\mathcal{I}'$ compose together in sequence, denoted $\mathcal{I}._\theta \mathcal{I}'$, and the interface $\mathcal{I}$ plugs to E, denoted $\mathcal{I} \circ\!\!-\!\!\circ E$. Given the automata interface $\mathcal{I}$ and the automata environment E, a sequence $(\mathcal{V}_1, t_1), (\mathcal{V}_2, t_2), \ldots, (\mathcal{V}_n, t_n)$ of environment E, and a set of memory resource designs $\mathcal{M}$ with $\mu \in \mathcal{M}$. For any an assignment $\mathcal{V}_i$, $i \in n$, the automaton E offers a set of values over X that satisfies p_{i-1} to the automaton $\mathcal{I}$, and expects results Y by $\mathcal{V}_i$ from the interface, and the outputs satisfies the post-condition R_{i-1}. i.e., $\mathcal{V}_i \models p_{i-1} \wedge R_{i-1}$. When E invokes $\mathcal{I}$, a protocol is created between

E and $\mathcal{I}$, this means that the specification of automaton interface $\mathcal{I}$ satisfies the requirement of automaton environment E at anytime in the process of interaction. Let μ be a memory resource design of $\mathcal{I}$, and μ^e be a memory resource design of E. For any computation step $(\mathcal{V}_i, t_i)$ is assigned from the E to the $\mathcal{I}$, the $(\mathcal{V}_i, t_i) \models \mu_{i-1}^e \wedge \mu_{i-1}$, i.e., the formulas $p_{i-1}^e \Rightarrow p_{i-1}$ and $p_{i-1}^e \wedge R_{i-1} \Rightarrow R_{i-1}^e$ hold. The memory resource uses for a computation step of the environment and the interface to be calculated as follows: Let $C_{\circ\!-\!\circ}$ be an upper bound memory resource of $\mathcal{I} \circ\!-\!\circ E$, the supreme memory $C_{\circ\!-\!\circ} = C + C^e$.

Definition 8 (Pluggability). *Given $\mathcal{I}$ is represented by M and E is represented by M^e. The $\mathcal{I}$ is pluggable to the E, denoted $\mathcal{I} \circ\!-\!\circ E$, iff $X = X^e$, $Y = Y^e$ and the following conditions are satisfied:*

1. *Let $\delta(\epsilon) = p_0^e \vdash (R_0^e, C_0^e)$ and $\xi(\epsilon) = p_0 \vdash (R_0, C_0)$, where ϵ is an initial state of both E and $\mathcal{I}$. Then, $p_0^e \Rightarrow p_0$, $p_0^e \wedge R_0 \Rightarrow R_0^e$. For any $\mathcal{V}_1$ such that $\mathcal{V}_1 \models p_0^e \wedge R_0$, if $\delta(\mathcal{V}_1, t_1^e)$ is defined then $\xi(\mathcal{V}_1, t_1)$ is also defined, and the pair $(\mathcal{V}_1, t_1)$ is called reachable state of $\mathcal{I} \circ\!-\!\circ E$. The memory constraints for state ϵ is defined as follows: The $C_{\circ\!-\!\circ_0} = C_0^e + C_0$.*
2. *Let $n \in \mathbb{N}, n \geq 1$ and let $w_n = (\mathcal{V}_1, t_1^e), \ldots, (\mathcal{V}_n, t_n^e)$ be an interaction behavior sequence of E with $\mathcal{I}$, and $s_n = (\mathcal{V}_1, t_1)...(\mathcal{V}_n, t_n)$ be a computation sequence of $\mathcal{I}$ interacts with E. Furthermore, let $\delta(w_n) = p_n^e \vdash (R_n^e, C_n^e)$ and $\xi(s_n) = p_n \vdash (R_n, C_n)$, then, $p_n^e \Rightarrow p_n$, $p_n^e \wedge R_n \Rightarrow R_n^e$. For any $\mathcal{V}_{n+1}$ such that $\mathcal{V}_{n+1} \models p_n^e \wedge R_n$, if $w_{n+1} = (\mathcal{V}_1, t_1^e), \ldots, (\mathcal{V}_n, t_n^e)(\mathcal{V}_{n+1}, t_{n+1}^e)$ is a reachable state of E, then $s_{n+1} = (\mathcal{V}_1, t_1), \ldots, (\mathcal{V}_n, t_n)(\mathcal{V}_{n+1}, t_{n+1})$ is also a reachable state of $\mathcal{I}$, and s_{n+1} is called a reachable state of $\mathcal{I}$ w.r.t. w_{n+1} while w_{n+1} is called a behavior of E w.r.t. $\mathcal{I}$. The memory constraints for reachable state (w_{n+1}, s_{n+1}) is defined as follows: The upper bound memory is $C_{\circ\!-\!\circ_{n+1}} = C_{n+1}^e + C_{n+1}$.*

For any pair $(\mathcal{V}_i, t_i^e)$ in a reachable behavior $w = (\mathcal{V}_1, t_1^e)(\mathcal{V}_2, t_2^e), \ldots, (\mathcal{V}_n, t_n^e)$ of E is expendable, then it makes the state $s = (\mathcal{V}_1, t_1)(\mathcal{V}_2, t_2), \ldots, (\mathcal{V}_n, t_n)$ of the interface $\mathcal{I}$ is also expendable.

Definition 9 (Parallel Composition). *Given two automata interfaces $\mathcal{I}, \mathcal{I}'$ represented by labeled automata M, M' respectively, such that $(X \cup Y) \cap (X' \cup Y') = \varnothing$. The parallel composition $\mathcal{I}\|\mathcal{I}' = \langle X \cup X', Y \cup Y', \xi'' \rangle$, where $\xi'' : S(X \cup X', Y \cup Y') \nrightarrow M(X \cup X', Y \cup Y')$. Suppose $s = (\mathcal{V}_1, t_1'')...(\mathcal{V}_n, t_n'')$, $s \in S(X \cup X', Y \cup Y')$, $\xi''(s)$ is defined as follows:*

- $\xi((\mathcal{V}_1|_{X \cup Y}, t_1), \ldots, (\mathcal{V}_n|_{X \cup Y}, t_n)) = p \vdash (R, C)$, *and*
- $\xi'((\mathcal{V}_1|_{X' \cup Y'}, t_1'), \ldots, (\mathcal{V}_n|_{X' \cup Y'}, t_n')) = p' \vdash (R', C')$,

where $\mathcal{V}_i|_{X \cup Y}$ and $\mathcal{V}_i|_{X' \cup Y'}$ are the restriction of $\mathcal{V}_i$ over $X \cup Y$ and $X' \cup Y'$, $i \in n$, respectively. $\xi''(s) = p \wedge p' \vdash (R \wedge R', C + C')$ and t_n'' satisfies that $sizeof(t_n'') \leq C + C'$.

For the sequential connection, given two automata interfaces $\mathcal{I}, \mathcal{I}'$ such that an input of the second connects to only one output of the first and $(X \cup Y) \cap (X' \cup Y') = \varnothing$. A connection from $\mathcal{I}$ to $\mathcal{I}'$ is a set of pairs $\theta \subseteq Y \times X'$ that satisfies $\forall (y, x), (y', x') \in \theta.(x = x' \Rightarrow y = y')$. Let $X_\theta = \{x \in X' | \exists y \in Y.(y, x) \in \theta\}$. An assignment $\mathcal{V}$ over $(X \cup X' \cup Y \cup Y')$ passes through a connection θ by an assignment $\mathcal{V}_\theta$ over $((X \cup X') \setminus X_\theta) \cup Y \cup Y'$ such that $\mathcal{V}_\theta|_{((X \cup X') \setminus X_\theta) \cup Y \cup Y'} = \mathcal{V}|_{((X \cup X') \setminus X_\theta) \cup Y \cup Y'}$, and for $x \in X_\theta$ then $\mathcal{V}_\theta(x) = \mathcal{V}(y)$, where y is the unique element in Y and $(y, x) \in \theta$. Therefore $l_\theta = \bigwedge_{(y,x) \in \theta}(x = y)$.

Definition 10 (Sequential Composition). *Let $\mathcal{I}, \mathcal{I}'$ be represented by M, M' respectively, such that $(X \cup Y) \cap (X' \cup Y') = \varnothing$. A sequential composition of $\mathcal{I}$ and $\mathcal{I}'$ w.r.t connection θ, denoted by $\mathcal{I}._\theta\mathcal{I}'$ is an automaton interface $\mathcal{I}'' = \langle X'', Y'', \xi'' \rangle$, where $X'' = (X \cup X') \setminus X_\theta$, $Y'' = Y \cup Y'$. For $s = (\mathcal{V}_1, t_1''), \ldots, (\mathcal{V}_n, t_n'') \in \mathcal{S}(X'', Y'')$, $\xi''(s)$ is defined iff the both formulas $\xi((\mathcal{V}_{\theta 1}|_{X \cup Y}, t_1), \ldots, (\mathcal{V}_{\theta n}|_{X \cup Y}, t_n)) = p \vdash (R, C)$ and $\xi'((\mathcal{V}_{\theta 1}|_{X' \cup Y'}, t_1'), \ldots, (\mathcal{V}_{\theta n}|_{X' \cup Y'}, t_n')) = p' \vdash (R', C')$ are defined, and then $\xi''(s) = p \wedge \exists Y.(R \wedge p' \wedge l_\theta) \vdash (R \wedge R' \wedge l_\theta \wedge p', max(C, C'))$ and t_n'' satisfies that $sizeof(t_n'') \leq max(C, C')$.*

4   Estimating Memory Resources

In this section, we introduce a method to calculate the memory resources of an interface. Given a *memory resource design* $\mu = p \vdash (R, C)$, we can estimate the memory resource that is consumed when the interface was enabled. Therefore, memory resource in a given automaton interface $\mathcal{I}$ can be computed as follows: The supreme memory resource of an interface, denoted $U = max(C_i)$, $i \in n$.

Lemma 1. *The memory resource consumption of $\mathcal{I}$ has estimated based on the memory resource designs in $\mathcal{I}$.*

The algorithm is illustrated below computing the maximum lower bound and upper bound memory capacity of an interface.

Algorithm 1. The memory resource estimation for an automaton interface

---
    Input: Automata interface $\mathcal{I}$
    Output: The memory resource consumption of an automaton interface
1 **begin**
2 | $MaxUpperbound \leftarrow 0.$
3 | **foreach** $\mu \in \mathcal{M}$ **do**
4 | | $MaxUpperbound \leftarrow Max(MaxUpperbound, \mu.C)$
5 | **end**
6 | **return** $MaxUpperbound$
7 **end**

Lemma 2. *Given $\mathcal{I}$ and E, the memory resource consumption for pluggable operation has been estimated iff the $\mathcal{I}$ plugs to the E.*

Algorithm 2. Get memory resource consumption for $\mathcal{I}$ plugs to E.

Input: $M = \langle Q, X, Y, q_0, T, l_s, l_t \rangle$ and $M^e = \langle Q^e, X^e, Y^e, q_0^e, T^e, l_s^e, l_t^e \rangle$.
Output: Memory consumption of $\mathcal{I} \multimap E$

1 **begin**
2   Let $f \subseteq Q^e \times Q$, $f \leftarrow \{(q_0^e, q_0)\}$ and (q_0^e, q_0) be unmarked.
3   **while** *(true)* **do**
4   **if** $GetAllMarked(f) = true$ **then**
5   return true
6   **else**
7             $CurrentElement \leftarrow GetUnmarked((q^e, q) \in f))$
8   let $l_s(q) = p \vdash (R, C)$ and $l_s'(q') = p' \vdash (R', C')$.
9             $q_{next}^e List \leftarrow GetReachableE(Q^e)$ such that $F_{(q^e, q_{next}^e)} := p^e \wedge R \wedge l_t^e(q^e, q_{next}^e)$ is satisfiable.
10            $q_{next} List \leftarrow GetReachableI(q_{next}^e List)$ such that $(q, q_{next}) \in T$ and $l_t(q, q_{next}) \wedge F_{(q^e, q_{next}^e)}$ is satisfiable.
11   **if** $(F_{(q^e, q_{next}^e)} \Rightarrow \bigvee_{q_{next} \in q_{next} List} l_t(q, q_{next})) = false$ **then**
12   return false
13   **else**
14                $f \leftarrow (q_{next}^e, q_{next})$ for any $q_{next} \in q_{next} List$
15   **end**
16   **end**
17   **end**
18     $Max \leftarrow GetMaxMemoryResourceConstraint(f)$
19   **return** Max
20 **end**

In parallel composition, given two automata interfaces $\mathcal{I} = \langle X, Y, \xi \rangle$ and $\mathcal{I}' = \langle X', Y', \xi' \rangle$. The automaton interface $\mathcal{I} || \mathcal{I}'$ is a triple $\langle X \cup X', Y \cup Y', \xi'' \rangle$. According to Definition 9, if $\mathcal{I} || \mathcal{I}'$ implements in a system, it consumes a memory resource depending on a pair of μ, μ' for which an assignment over *input/output* of $\mathcal{I} || \mathcal{I}'$ satisfies μ, μ', i.e. $\mathcal{V}(X \cup X', Y \cup Y') \models \xi''$, where $\mu \in \mathcal{M}$ and $\mu' \in \mathcal{M}'$.

Lemma 3. *Given $\mathcal{I}, \mathcal{I}'$. The memory resource consumption for parallel operation has been estimated iff automaton interface $\mathcal{I}$ composes with $\mathcal{I}'$ in parallel.*

Algorithm 3. The computation of memory constraint in Parallel

---

Input: $M = \langle Q, X, Y, q_0, T, l_s, l_t \rangle$ and $M' = \langle Q', X', Y', q_0', T', l_s', l_t' \rangle$.
Output: Memory capacity in Max variable.

1 **begin**
2   Let $f \subseteq Q' \times Q$, $f \leftarrow \{(q_0', q_0)\}$ and (q_0', q_0) is unmarked.
3   **while** *(true)* **do**
4   **if** $GetAllMarked(f) = true$ **then**
5   return true
6   **else**
7             $CurrentElement \leftarrow GetUnmarked((q', q) \in f)$
8   let $l_s(q) = p \vdash (R, C)$ and $l_s'(q') = p' \vdash (R', C')$.
9             $p_{next}' List \leftarrow GetReachableI'(Q')$
10            $p_{next} List \leftarrow GetReachableI(Q)$
11            $F_{(q_{next}, q_{next}')} := p \wedge p' \Rightarrow R \wedge R'$
12   **if** $(F_{(q_{next}, q_{next}')} = false)$ **then**
13   return false
14   **else**
15                $f \leftarrow (q_{next}, q_{next}')$ for any $q_{next}' \in p_{next}' List$
16   **end**
17   **end**
18   **end**
19     $Max \leftarrow GetMaxMemoryResourceConstraint(f)$
20   **return** Max
21 **end**

Similar to the parallel composition, the following result computes the memory constraint for sequential compositional operation.

Lemma 4. *Given $\mathcal{I}, \mathcal{I}'$. The memory resource consumption for sequential operation has estimated iff automaton interface $\mathcal{I}$ composes with $\mathcal{I}'$ in sequence.*

To bring the result to the practice, the paper introduces Algorithm 4 to calculate the memory resource for the interface sequential compositions.

Algorithm 4. The computation of memory resource constraint in sequential composition

Input: $M = \langle Q, X, Y, q_0, T, l_s, l_t \rangle$ and $M' = \langle Q', X', Y', q_0', T', l_s', l_t' \rangle$.
Output: Memory capacity in Max variable.

begin
  Let $f \subseteq Q' \times Q$, $f \leftarrow \{(q_0', q_0)\}$ and (q_0', q_0) is unmarked.
  while *(true)* **do**
    if *GetAllMarked(f)= true* **then**
      return true
    else
      $CurrentElement \leftarrow GetUnmarked((q', q) \in f))$
      let $l_s(q) = p \vdash (R, C)$ and $l_s'(q') = p' \vdash (R', C')$.
      $p'_{next}List \leftarrow GetReachable\mathcal{I}'(Q')$
      $p_{next}List \leftarrow GetReachable\mathcal{I}(Q)$
      $F_{(q_{next}, q'_{next})} : := p \wedge \exists Y.(R \wedge p' \wedge l_\theta) \vdash (R \wedge R' \wedge l_\theta \wedge p')$
      if $(F_{(q_{next}, q'_{next})} = false)$ **then**
        return false
      else
        $f \leftarrow (q_{next}, q'_{next})$ for any $q'_{next} \in p'_{next}List$
      end
    end
  end
  $Max \leftarrow GetMaxMemoryResourceConstraint(f)$
  return Max
end

Theorem 1. *The memory resource consumption of a component-based system has estimated iff the systems are constructed by pluggable, parallel and sequential composition of relational interfaces with memory design resources.*

5 Conclusion

The paper carries out a sequential works, from specification and modeling component-based systems by memory resource designs to the construction algorithms in order to estimate memory resources of a component-based system. The paper extends relational interfaces and timed design for estimating memory resource purpose. The memory resource design, which has supreme memory, is an atomic element in an interface, from which we use memory resource design constructing interfaces and environments. The paper also uses labeled automata to model interfaces and environments, and considers some their operations. Using this model, some operations of component-based system are considered such as, refinement, pluggability and compositions. The combination of an interface with its environment and interfaces with the others have made an utilizable method to deal with the specification and modeling problem in estimation of memory resources. Depending on the models, the paper proposes some algorithms to calculate memory resources in the cases of pluggability and composition. According to the approach in this paper, others resources can be specified and be forecast in early stage of the system design.

References

1. Dang Van, H., Truong, H.: Modeling and specification of real-time interfaces with UTP. In: Liu, Z., Woodcock, J., Zhu, H. (eds.) Theories of Programming and Formal Methods. LNCS, vol. 8051, pp. 136–150. Springer, Heidelberg (2013)
2. Eskenazi, E., Fioukov, A., Hammer, D., Chaudron, M.: Estimation of static memory consumption for systems built from source code components. In: 9th IEEE Conference and Workshops on Engineering of Computer-Based Systems (2002)
3. Fioukov, A.V., Eskenazi, E.M., Hammer, D.K., Chaudron, M.R.V.: Evaluation of static properties for component-based architectures. In: Proceedings of 28th EUROMICRO Conference, Component-based Software Engineering Track, pp. 33–39. IEEE Computer Society Press (2002)
4. Jonge, M.D., Muskens, J., Chaudron, M.: Scenario-based prediction of run-time resource consumption in component-based software systems. In: Proceedings of the 6th ICSE Workshop on Component-based Software Engineering, CBSE6. IEEE (2003)
5. Muskens, J., Chaudron, M.R.V.: Prediction of run-time resource consumption in multi-task component-based software systems. In: Crnković, I., Stafford, J.A., Schmidt, H.W., Wallnau, K. (eds.) CBSE 2004. LNCS, vol. 3054, pp. 162–177. Springer, Heidelberg (2004)
6. Tripakis, S., Lickly, B., Henzinger, T.A., Lee, E.A.: On relational interfaces. In: Chakraborty, S., Halbwachs, N. (eds.) EMSOFT, pp. 67–76. ACM, New York (2009)

Context-Aware Approach
for Determining the Threshold Price
in Name-Your-Own-Price Channels

Asanga Nimalasena[⊠] and Vladimir Getov

Faculty of Science and Technology, University of Westminster,
115 New Cavendish Street, London W1W 6UW, UK
{a.nimalasena,v.s.getov}@westminster.ac.uk

Abstract. Key feature of a context-aware application is the ability to adapt based on the change of context. Two approaches that are widely used in this regard are the context-action pair mapping where developers match an action to execute for a particular context change and the adaptive learning where a context-aware application refines its action over time based on the preceding action's outcome. Both these approaches have limitation which makes them unsuitable in situations where a context-aware application has to deal with unknown context changes. In this paper we propose a framework where adaptation is carried out via concurrent multi-action evaluation of a dynamically created action space. This dynamic creation of the action space eliminates the need for relying on the developers to create context-action pairs and the concurrent multi-action evaluation reduces the adaptation time as opposed to the iterative approach used by adaptive learning techniques. Using our reference implementation of the framework we show how it could be used to dynamically determine the threshold price in an e-commerce system which uses the name-your-own-price (NYOP) strategy.

Keywords: Context-aware systems · Self-adaptation · Multi-action evaluation

1 Introduction

Context-aware systems react to changes in the perceived environment so that computing output is best suited to the current context. Generally, the context-aware systems are associated with mobility and applications related to mobile devices. This is mainly due to the fact that context changes are most likely encountered in mobile devices when these devices navigate through various contexts [1] as opposed to stationary devices where context data is often acquired through sensors.

But this is a narrow view of the context domain as there are many definitions as to what is a context. Context has been defined by location [2], location combined with behavior [3] or encompassing multitude of factors such as the definition given by Dey [4]: "Context is any information that can be used to characterize the situation of an entity. An entity is a person, place, or object that is considered relevant to the interaction between a user and an application, including the user and the application themselves". This definition makes no assumption about the mobility of devices and

© ICST Institute for Computer Sciences, Social Informatics and Telecommunications Engineering 2016
P.C. Vinh and V. Alagar (Eds.): ICCASA 2015, LNICST 165, pp. 83–93, 2016.
DOI: 10.1007/978-3-319-29236-6_9

leaves to the context-aware system developers to decide what constitutes a context in their application. The adopted approach allows differentiating the operation environment from context based on potentiality and relevance [5]. Context-aware systems react to a context change by executing an action, while what action to execute is determined by the context inference. A context-aware application does context inference on the basis of the so-called 5W1H (Where, When, What, Who, Why, How) factors [6]. Expanding on this, context-aware applications look at the who's, where's, when's and what's (that is, what the user is doing) of entities and use this information to determine why the situation is occurring [7]. But it is not actually the application that determines why a situation is occurring, but the designer of the application. This means the designer has to capture the domain knowledge and input it to the system. This dependency on application designer to capture the context changes introduces inaccurate contexts and inflexible context definitions [8]. Moreover the context inference would fail if the system encounters a context which the designer did not foresee.

The self-learning and self-adapting methods are employed to overcome the aforementioned limitations. They use an iterative approach to find the best possible action when the system encounters an unknown context. If an action executed as a result of unknown context change is not the optimal then an error-feedback-loop-based correction mechanisms are employed to further refine the action. This process is iterated until the gap between the expected and the actual outcome is reduced or eliminated. However, when there are large numbers of actions to evaluate, the time to find the best action increases resulting in late system reaction to a context change.

This paper proposes a context-aware framework which concurrently executes and evaluates multiple actions from a dynamically created action space when an unknown context is encountered. The proposed framework overcomes the problems in the iterative approach of the self-adapting system and having to rely on application developers to encompass all possible contexts and context changes.

The rest of the paper is organized as follows. Section 2 reviews related work on context and self-adapting context-aware models. Section 3 gives a description of the proposed framework and Sect. 4 describes the implementation of the proposed framework for a NYOP channel. Section 5 presents experimental results of the implementation. Finally, the paper concludes with Sect. 6 which summarizes the findings from the evaluation and outlines directions for future work.

2 Related Work

Based on the association between contexts change and the resulting action(s) the existing context models could be loosely classified as *single context – single action* models and *single context – multiple action* models. The simplest model is the *single context – single action* model most commonly used for smart physical environments [9–11]. In practice, these types of models acquire sensory data from one or more devices (hard sensing) and act on other devices or make state changes that bring optimal result for the current context change. Due to the close association between this model and the physical hardware each context has one and only one precise action. This context-action pairing is built into the context-aware system by the application developers by considering all possible context changes the system is likely to encounter. A generic framework has been proposed [12], which allows system developers to formally define the adaptation to context changes based on system policies. However, this dependency on system developers could result in inaccurate and inflexible context definitions. He et al. [13] provide an example of a smart plant-watering context-aware system. One of the context values considered is the ambient temperature. However, if due to some freaky weather pattern an unusual temperature is encountered by the system which system developers had not foreseen, then the context inference would fail and the system would be unable to act on the perceived context change. A customizable context model which enables customization by the developers in order to recognize more context changes is presented in [14]. Other work makes use of a central repository of context knowledge that is periodically updated [15], but the drawback of having to depend on the system developers is still there.

The self-adapting and self-learning context-aware models are used to overcome these limitations arising from having to depend on the system developers to foresee all context changes. These models could be summarized as single context – multiple actions model. When an unknown context is encountered the system would execute sequence of actions iteratively with feedback loop base learning to self-adapt. A self-adapting algorithm which implements the resource, actors and policy triples (RAP model) is presented in [16] which use a closed feedback loop for adaptation. In [17] a formal method for incremental context awareness is proposed based breadth-monotonic model and depth-monotonic model. A self-adapting context with the use of context edges (a context edge is the border between two contexts) and context spaces is proposed on [18]. The model is based on Q-Learning with a feedback loop which finds the optimal action for each state by the reward it receives from the environment for actions taken in that state. Other self-adapting techniques used by context-aware system includes using case base reasoning to address domain specific problems and incomplete data sets [19] and try to address the lack of domain knowledge through self-adaption. Similarly, the approach described in [20] uses fuzzy sets to allow imperfection in context that is being sensed.

Though not from the context-aware domain, another commonly used autonomic adaptation model is IBM's MAPE-K (Monitor, Analyze, Plan, Execute, and Knowledge) loop reference model [21]. The components of the MAPE-K loop could be superimposed into the three main areas of sensing, inference and action of a context-aware application. However, a MAPE-K loop still depends on the system developers to formulate the event-condition-action (ECA) rules for self-adaptation [22] which makes it unsuitable for situation where unknown context could be encountered. ECA knowledge comes from human experts or other methods such as concept utility [23], Bayesian techniques [24] or reinforcement learning [25] which suffers from poor scalability when large number of ECA state changes exists.

A problem with these feedback-based models is that when the system consists of a large action space the amount of time needed to execute and evaluate each action iteratively keeps increasing and the overall time taken to find the best possible action could become unacceptably long. A context-aware application developed on the basis of soft sensing of social media [26, 27] data provides a different model to that of the feedback-loop-based self-adapting models described earlier. The focus in these models is towards context inference and ontology-based reasoning models are employed to achieve context-aware adaptation in them.

3 Proposed Context-aware Framework

The two primary goals of the context-aware framework that we propose are to reduce the dependency on system developers to capture and input all possible context changes and to eliminate the need for a feedback loop base iterative approach for self-learning/self-adapting. With the proposed framework the system developers are expected to setup few base parameters and input any domain knowledge or past experience they have of the application domain into a knowledge base. But this is not expected to be extensive as the system is expected to expand its knowledge base dynamically. As iterative approach becomes unfeasible when there's a large action space to evaluate, the framework proposes a concurrent multi-action evaluation approach where action space is executed and evaluated in a single pass reducing the time for adaptation.

The proposed framework consists of three systems, namely the context system, the inference system and the actions system. These three systems encompass the main characteristics of a self-adapting context-aware system, which are sensing, actuators (actions) and inference/self-adapting. Figure 1 shows a high-level diagram of the proposed framework and system components.

The primary objective of the context system is context sensing and acquisition. How the context sensing happens is implementation specific and could be either hard sensing or soft sensing. The framework assumes that context space is a heterogeneous where context values are acquired from various sources. As a result of the heterogeneous context space the system could acquire wide variety of context values in different

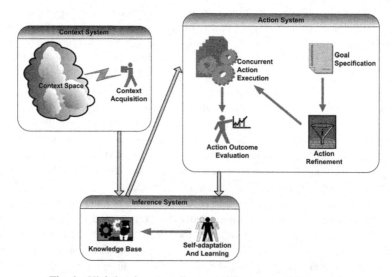

Fig. 1. High level system diagram of the proposed framework

units of measurement. Context acquisition is expected to transform these heterogeneous context value types in different measurement units into single unit of measurement allowing comparison of contexts. This context comparison is used in the action system to find the closest known context to an unknown context.

The inference system consists of a knowledge base and a self-adaption/learning mechanism. When a context change is sensed the context inference is carried out querying the knowledge base to identify if the new context values are known. If the new context is inferred to be unknown then the action system is invoked. The other component in the inference system is the self-adaptation and learning mechanism which updates the knowledge base and adapt the context-aware application based on the outcome from the action system. The knowledge base could be modelled in many different ways such as semantic representation of context [28]. The use of ontology to represent context has the added benefit of leveraging inherent inference capabilities that comes with ontology classifications.

The action system is responsible for concurrent action execution and evaluation when an unknown context is encountered. The goals of the action system are to reduce the number of required actions qualifying for evaluation and to complete the action execution and evaluation in a single pass as opposed to iterative manner. To achieve this first goal the action system uses goal specification and action refinement. The goal specification defines the extremities of the variable parameter used to build the action space. This is different to existing goal driven approaches to self-adaptation [29] which are based on rules created by the system developers. These extremities are denoted as G_{lo} and G_{hi} and are considered elements of the configuration parameter space which are used to differentiate one action from another.

$$(G_{lo}, G_{hi}) \in \{ \text{ configuration parameter space} \}$$

The action refinement limits what action qualifies to be in the action space thus reducing the action space size. Without the limiting effects of the action refinement the context-aware system would have to experiment on every value between G_{lo} and G_{hi} which would be a resource and time intensive endeavor. The action limiting process starts by identifying from the knowledge base, the context that is closest to the unknown context. The closeness is measured by the difference of the context values. If more than one context is found to be the closest then the priority of each context is considered. The configuration parameter setting of this known context is used to device the initial action. This is denoted as A_k and defined as a function of the configuration parameter configuration of the closest known action

$$\text{Initial action} = A_k(\text{configuration}_k)$$

The framework introduces three parameters for the dynamic creation of the action space. They are the lower bound expansion range denoted by p which specifies number of actions to define in the direction of G_{lo}. The upper bound expansion range denoted by q specifies the number of actions to define in the direction of G_{hi} and finally the distance between each configuration parameter denoted by Δ. These three parameters and the goal specification are the only inputs that depend on system developers, effectively eliminating the need to identify all possible context changes. Having defined these, all the actions (action space) that needed to be executed and evaluated to find the best course of action for unknown context could be defined as a union of three action sets.

$$
\begin{aligned}
\text{Action space} = \{ \; & A_k(\text{configuration}_k) \; \cup \\
& A_p(\text{configuration}_p) \; \cup \\
& A_q(\text{configuration}_q) \\
& | \;\; p = \{1 .. n\}, n > 0, \; q = \{1 .. m\}, m > 0, \\
& \text{configuration}_k - p\Delta \geq G_{lo}, \\
& \text{configuration}_k + q\Delta \leq G_{hi}, \\
& \Delta > 0 \\
\}
\end{aligned}
$$

The defined actions are then executed concurrently in a private workbench. The private workbench ensures that configuration changes in each action under evaluation is opaque to and does not affect the current state of the system. As all actions are executed concurrently the outcome of each action is known at the same time, as opposed to iterative approach where the analysis of results has to be delayed until all actions have finished. This concurrent action evaluation is somewhat similar to the optimizing technique used in particle swarm optimization (PSO) [30] where each particle is a possible solution. However, one key difference between PSO and our action space is that in PSO the particles must update their velocity and position relative to the particle with the global optimal after each iteration. In our proposed framework each action is a candidate to be a global optimal and to evaluate the problem space independent of each other.

The final phase of the action system is the outcome evaluation. The evaluation criteria for choosing the action that results in the highest benefit depends on the domain in which the context-aware system is implemented. Thus, the best action to execute (and its configuration parameter) as a result of the unknown context change could be formally defined as

$$
\begin{aligned}
\text{configuration}_{best} = \{ \; & \\
& \forall \text{ configuration}_i \in \{\text{action space configurations}\} \\
& \exists \; A_i(\text{configuration}_i): \text{Maximum}(\text{Benfit}(A_i)) \\
\}
\end{aligned}
$$

Once the best setting for the configuration parameter is known for the unknown context it could be used to update the knowledge base so the context-aware system recognizes this context in the future (learning and adaptation). Figure 2 shows the information flow for known context detection and unknown context detection. $C_1 - C_4$ in Fig. 2 represents context considered relevant to the interaction between a user and an application.

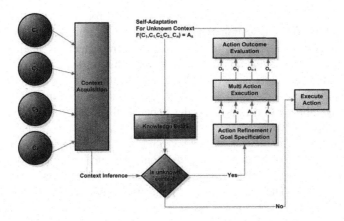

Fig. 2. Information flow for known and unknown context detection

4 Context-aware Framework Implementation for NYOP Channels

The proposed context-aware framework was implemented for a use case where an hotelier sells rooms through a NYOP channel. The NYOP operates by allowing buyers to bid for an item on a perceived value rather than based on the actual value set by the seller. The seller has an internal threshold price hidden from the buyers which he considers to be the minimum value for a bid in order to successfully complete the transaction. For our experiments we do not employ any such NYOP strategies [31]. Instead, each value is considered as an individual bid and not as a subsequent bid part of a bidding transaction. If the hotelier decides to accept or reject a bid solely based on its value, then he will not have the fluidity to react to the demand uncertainty that occurs due to the change in context. A context-aware approach is beneficial in this case, instead of having one threshold price T the context-aware NYOP system could be set up multiple threshold price $T_1...T_n$. Bids will be evaluated against all threshold prices in real time and results evaluated to find out which threshold price results in highest yield (T_{Max}). Once the highest yielding threshold price is identified, the e-commerce system is adapted to use it to evaluate all bids under current context.

We have developed a scenario where a new event has been planned near the vicinity of the hotel and there is no historical data or knowledge to rely on to set a threshold price which would give a high yield. We define this as an unknown context based on the definition given earlier on [4] as the hotelier is unaware of the threshold price to use in this situation (context) to optimize the interaction between buyer and seller. The context space was modelled with three soft sensed contexts, which are current occupancy (source: internal reservation database), event location, event type (extracted from social media. i.e. Twitter feed). Taking the NYOP threshold price as the configuration parameter, the formal modeling of the proposed context-aware frame-work was instantiated with the following values. Goal specification (G_{lo}, G_{hi}) = (210, 350). In essence, the goal specification is a sub-range of the entire application value range. For example, if the universe of prices for a hotel room is considered, it could vary between $0 (100 % discounted) – millions of dollars (based on luxury). But for this particular hotelier such a large value range is irrelevant. His interest lies in a smaller range of values so that accepted bids do not result in loss or high price resulting in low conversions and unsold rooms. Action refinement values $(p, q, \Delta) = (2, 2, 15)$. Initial action (closest known context action) = A (250). As stated earlier G_{lo}, G_{hi}, p, q, Δ are the only inputs from the system developer to the system and initial action is retrieved from the knowledge base.

The evaluation criterion was set to threshold price with highest number of successful bids. It is possible that some bids would be successful in more than one threshold. In such cases the bid would be considered successful only in the highest threshold it exceeds. The context-aware application was developed as a Java web application and deployed in Tomcat application container which ran on a server with 12 GB RAM, 2.0 GHz Intel quad core processor and 500 GB SAS disks running on RedHat Linux 6.4. The knowledge base was modelled using Java implementation of Protégé OWL API. We devised two test cases for the evaluation. One test case simulates an unknown context in which the majority of bid values are lower than the threshold value of the closest known context. If the hotelier does not lower the threshold price to capture the bids, he will lose out under the current context. The second test case simulates an unknown context under which the majority of bid values are considerably higher than the threshold price. Under this context the hotelier can increase the threshold price to gain a higher yield. This is a NYOP strategy that encourages higher bidding values. Though we make no assumption about the bidding strategies we include this test case for the completeness of the evaluation, to test the suitability of the framework works for both cases.

5   Experiments and Results

Two sets of bid values were generated for each of the test case (1000 values each) using a normal distribution function where mean values are 237.50 and 268.50 for lower and higher bid value test cases. The control test was defined as using the closest known context threshold price to evaluate the bid values while in the unknown context (non-adaptive system). The bid submissions were emulated using JMeter's http requests. The action space, created dynamically based on the $(G_{lo}, G_{hi}, p, q, \Delta)$ resulted in 5 actions to be concurrently executed and evaluated. These are denoted as A(220), A(235), A(250), A(265) and A(280) in the Figs. 3 and 4 below.

In this unknown context, Fig. 3 shows the majority of successful bids which have occurred in the action that had a threshold value of 235. The hotelier could associate the current unknown context with the threshold value of 235, thus effectively evolving the system to recognize the current unknown context in the future. We know that this conclusion is correct as we have generated the bid values using a normal distribution with a mean value of 237.50. For the second test case shown in Fig. 4, the majority of successful bids have occurred in the action that had a threshold value of 265. We know that this is true because the bid values generated under the normal distribution had a mean value of 268.50. In both cases, if the hotelier has decided to stay with the closest

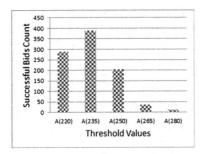
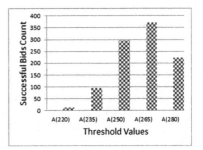

Fig. 3. Context resulting in lower bid values   **Fig. 4.** Context resulting in higher bids values

known context's threshold price, the successful bid count would have been less than the one achieved by the context-aware adaptive approach.

6 Conclusion

In this paper, we proposed a context-aware framework which reduces the dependency on system developers to capture all possible context changes and eliminate the feed-back loop base approach to self-adaption. We have listed the generic framework structure and presented the formal model that underpins it. An implementation of the proposed framework was completed for the NYOP scenario. The experimental results from the tests have shown that the framework concurrent multi-action evaluation approach could correctly identifying the best course of action for the unknown context and is able to evolve the system, thus being able to recognizing more contexts over time. Though we implemented the framework for NYOP channel case study, we believe the framework could be easily used in many other domains such as a context-aware approach to experiment-based performance tuning.

References

1. Using Apache Hadoop* for Context-Aware Recommender Systems, Intel Corporation White paper (2014). http://intel.ly/1nRRoUZ
2. Schilit, B.N., Theimer, M.M.: Disseminating active map information to mobile hosts. IEEE Network **8**(5), 22–32 (1994)
3. Brown, P.J., Bovey, J.D., Chen, X.: Context-aware applications: from the laboratory to the marketplace. IEEE Pers. Commun. **4**(5), 58–64 (1997)
4. Dey, A.K.: Understanding and using context. Pers. Ubiquit. Comput. **5**, 4–7 (2001)
5. Roman, G., Julien, C., Payton, J.: Modeling adaptive behaviors in context UNITY. Theoret. Comput. Sci. **376**, 185–204 (2007)

6. Ko, K.-E., Sim, K.-B.: Development of context aware system based on Bayesian network driven context reasoning method and ontology context modeling. In: Proceedings of the International. Conference on Control, Automation and Systems (ICCAS). pp. 2309–2313 (2008)

7. Madhusudanan, J., Selvakumar, A., Sudha, R.: Frame work for context aware applications. In: Proceedings of the International Conference on Computing Communication and Networking Technologies, pp. 1–4 (2010)

8. Lee, H., Lee, S.: Decision supporting approach under uncertainty for feature-oriented adaptive system. In: 2nd User Centered Design and Adaptive Systems (COMPSACW) (2015)

9. Al-Rabiaah, S., Al-Muhtadi, J.: Context-aware security framework for smart spaces. In: Innovative Mobile and Internet Services in Ubiquitous Computing, pp. 580–584 (2012)

10. Wu, C., Weng, M., Lu, C., Fu, C.: Hierarchical generalized context inference or context-aware smart homes. In: Intelligent Robots and Systems (IROS), pp. 5227–5232 (2012)

11. Gupta, A., Pandey, O.J., Shukla, M., Dadhich, A., Ingle, A., Gawande, P.: Towards context-aware smart mechatronics networks: integrating swarm intelligence and ambient intelligence. In: Issues and Challenges in Intelligent Computing Techniques, pp. 64–69 (2014)

12. Alagar, V., Mohammad, M., Kaiyu, W., Hnaide, S.A.: A framework for developing context-aware systems. Trans. Context-aware Syst. Appl. ICST 1(1), 1–26 (2014). (Springer)

13. He, J., Zhang, Y., Huang, G., Cao, J.: A smart web service based on the context of things. ACM Trans. Internet Technol. 11(3), 13:1–13:23 (2012)

14. Yu, L., Wang, Z., Huang, Y., Chen, S.: Building customizable context-aware systems. In: 2011 International Joint Conference on Service Sciences (IJCSS), pp. 252–256 (2011)

15. Chang, J., Na, S., Yoon, M.: Intelligent context-aware system architecture in pervasive computing environment. In: Parallel and Distributed Processing with Applications, pp. 745–750 (2008)

16. Cioara, T., Anghel, I., Salomie, I., Dinsoreanu, M., Copil, G., Moldovan, D.: A self-adapting algorithm for context aware systems. In: Proceedings of 9th Roedunet International Conference (RoEduNet), pp. 374–379 (2010)

17. Loke, S.W.: Incremental awareness and compositionality: a design philosophy for context-aware pervasive systems. Pervasive Mobile Comput. 6(2), 239–253 (2010)

18. O'Connor, N., Cunningham, R., Cahill, V.: Self-adapting context definition. In: Proceedings of the 1st International Conference on Self-Adaptive and Self-Organizing Systems (SASO 2007), pp. 336–339 (2007)

19. Nwiabu, N., Allison, I., Holt, P., Lowit, P., Oyeneyin, B.: Situation awareness in context-aware case-based decision support. In: Conference on Cognitive Methods in Situation Awareness and Decision Support (CogSIMA), pp. 9–16 (2011)

20. Anagnostopoulos, C., Hadjiefthymiades, S.: Advanced inference in situation-aware computing. Part A Syst. Hum. 39(5), 1108–1115 (2009)

21. An architectural blueprint for autonomic computing, IBM Corp. http://ibm.co/1IP7TvG

22. Huebscher, M.C., McCann, J.A.: A survey of autonomic computing—degrees, models and applications. ACM Comput. Surv. (CSUR) 40(3), 1–28 (2008)

23. Bhola, S., Astley, M., Saccone, R., Ward, M.: Utility-aware resource allocation in an event processing system. In: International Conference on Autonomic Computing, p. 55 (2006)

24. Guo, H.: A Bayesian approach for autonomic algorithm selection. In Proceedings of the IJCAI Workshop on AI and Autonomic Computing: Developing a Research Agenda for Self-Managing Computer Systems (2003)

25. Sutton, R.S., Barto, A.G.: Reinforcement Learning: An Introduction. MIT Press, Cambridge (1998)
26. Derczynski, L.R.A., Yang, B., Jensen, C.S.: Towards context-aware search and analysis on social media data. In: 16th International Conference on Extending Database Technology, pp. 137–142 (2013)
27. Hu, X., Li, X., Ngai, E.C.-H., Leung, V.C.M., Kruchten, P.: Multidimensional context-aware social network architecture for mobile crowd sensing. IEEE Commun. Mag. 52(6), 78–87 (2014)
28. Ejigu, D., Scuturici, M., Brunie, L.: Semantic approach to context management and reasoning in ubiquitous context-aware systems. In: Proceedings of ICDIM (2007)
29. Salehie, M., Tahvildari, L.: Towards a goal-driven approach to action selection in self-adaptive software. Softw. Pract. Experience 42(2), 211–233 (2011)
30. Qi, B., Shen, F.: Performance Comparison of Partical Swarm Optimization Variant Models. In: Information Technology: New Generations (ITNG), pp. 575–580 (2014)
31. Hinz, O., Hann, I., Spann, M.: Price discrimination in e- commerce? An examination of dynamic pricing in name-your-own price markets. Mis Q. 35(1), 81–98 (2011)

Travel Destination Recommendation Based on Probabilistic Spatio-temporal Inference

Chang Choi[1($\boxtimes$)], Junho Choi[2], Htet Myet Lynn[1], and Pankoo Kim[1]

[1] Department of Computer Engineering, Chosun University, 375 Seoseok-dong,
Dong-gu, Gwangju, Republic of Korea
enduranceaura@gmail.com, htetmyet@gmail.com,
pkkim@chosun.ac.kr
[2] Division of Undeclared Majors, Chosun University,
375 Seoseok-dong, Dong-gu, Gwangju, Republic of Korea
xdman@chosun.ac.kr

Abstract. Recently, a lot of users are increasing for searching travel information through smart devices such as, tourist attractions, accommodation, entertainment, local gourmet food and so on. A general method for recommendation system has a data sparseness and the first rate problem. This problem can be solved by ontology and inference rules. In this paper, we propose the travel destination recommendation using Markov Logic Networks based on probabilistic spatio-temporal inference. The most inference engines determine simply if there is a result from inference or not. However, probabilistic inference methods have emerged and classified problems that cannot be defined easily in the probabilistic way, which provides better results.

Keywords: Recommendation system · Ontology · Markov Logic Networks

1 Introduction

The information retrieval for travel destination has become commonplace through smart devices due to the development of IT technology. A travel destination is the most important factor and travel information is consists of tourist attractions, accommodation, entertainment, local gourmet food. Many researches have been studied about travel destination recommendation using personalized information based on user preference. Also, there have been studied the recommendation method using social data [1]. A lot of recommendation systems are built to use the historical data and the profile file. Generally, the collaboration filtering algorithm is used in recommendation system but this approach will suffer from the problem of data sparseness and the first rate problem. Another method is the content based recommendation method. This method provides recommendation for users by comparing the representation content in list. However, content based recommendation method is needed more effort on extraction of content list [2]. This problem can be solved by ontology and inference rules.

In this paper, we propose the travel destination recommendation using Markov Logic Networks based on probabilistic spatio-temporal inference. The travel ontology

© ICST Institute for Computer Sciences, Social Informatics and Telecommunications Engineering 2016
P.C. Vinh and V. Alagar (Eds.): ICCASA 2015, LNICST 165, pp. 94–100, 2016.
DOI: 10.1007/978-3-319-29236-6_10

building used our previous work between object movement information and vocabulary based on spatio-temporal relation. In this case, spatio-temporal relation consist of temporal relation depending on the passage of time, directional relation depending on changes of object movement direction, changes of object size relation, topological relation depending on changes of object movement position, and velocity relation using concept relations between topology models. To this end, ontology building part defines the inference rules using proposed spatio-temporal relation and the use of Markov Logic Networks (MLNs) for probabilistic reasoning [3]. Travel Destination information is consists of accommodation, restaurant, activities and so on in Jeju (located in the Southern Korea, is famous for a volcanic Island) [9].

2 Previous Work

2.1 Travel Destination Recommendation

This proposal has been extended from the previous intelligent recommendation system architecture based on travel ontology [2] in order to give efficient recommendations to the tourists throughout their trip without getting any help from travel agency. The system's ontology used the tourist attraction places, available hotels and sight-seeing spots in Jeju Island in Korea. According to those properties and relationships of the ontology, the system provides the most relevant information and destinations upon what the user needs [10, 11]. The previous travel recommendation system architecture consists of three parts. Firstly, the metadata which holds the user information such as user's preference profile and transaction must be collected since most of the recommendation systems are depending on the stored records of what the users have been gone or what the users have visited, and the record of their feedbacks for the places they visited. Secondly, the information repository of ontology for the recommendation system takes place which was built based on the information in Jeju. Finally, the recommendation agent preserves the visualization of recommendation service to the user on AIMap.

2.2 Probabilistic Spatio-temporal Inference

The proposed probabilistic spatio-temporal inference using spatio-temporal relation and MLN for probabilistic reasoning [3], which is used to detect the motion of moving object in previous work, will be applied to build travel ontology. The method indicates the object movement in a vocabulary form as high-level information according to the specific relations such as temporal relation which relies on the passage of time, directional relation which depends on the object movement direction, object size relation, velocity relation depending on the changes in speed of moving object, and topological relation relies object movement position. The proposed spatio-temporal relation used Markov Logic Networks for inference rules to obtain the probabilistic reasoning.

The integration of temporal flow with factors of spatial characteristics; temporal relation of object, directional relation, size relation of the object and velocity relation, is the ideal of the spatio-temporal relation model. The model can be expressed based on the movement of the object which coordinates are defined as top, bottom, left and right. The rules of topology between the objects can be drawn in inference rules and the movement of object has 13 rules for each Y-coordinate and X-coordinate respectively. Thus, the spatio-temporal relations are classified to the total of 241 models. All those movements can be classified as "equal", "inside", "cover", "overlap", "meet", "disjoint", "covered-by", and "contains", according to M.J. Egenhofer's proposal. The ontology was built to seek the object relation patterns for sharing and distributing as training set. Eventually, the verified probabilistic inference of the object relation was executed to verify spatio-temporal relation.

3   The Method of Travel Destination Recommendation

3.1   Extended Jeju Travel Ontology

In this paper, Jeju travel ontology is extended from previous Jeju travel ontology [2]. Domain and related classes of extended ontology can be seen in Table 1.

Table 1. Extended Jeju travel ontology

Domain	Classes
Travel Type	Experience activity, Leisure Sports, Healing/Natural Recreation Forest
Accommodation	Hotel, Resort/Condominium, Pension, Motel, Tourist home, Guest house
Restaurant	Korean food, Japanese food, Chinese food, Western food, Local food, Vegetarian
Location Information	Jeju City, Western Jeju City, Eastern Jeju City, Seogwipo, Western Seogwipo, Eastern Seogwipo, Hallasan National Park
Travel Member	Family, Couple, Single, Friend, Team
Shopping	Local specialty market, Traditional Market, Duty-free shop

According to Table 1, the information for Travel Type Domain is collected from the previous Jeju travel ontology, while the other domains and classes are newly extended into the system. More importantly, the location information domain plays as an essential role in travel destination recommendation and it consists of 6 regions such as, Jeju City, Western Jeju City, Eastern Jeju City, Seogwipo, Western Seogwipo and Eastern Seogwipo. Figure 1 indicates seven regions of Location Information.

The proposed travel destination recommendation system provides a different weight according to the regions based on user's current location. But the Travel member domain contains five categories such as Family, Couple, Single, Friend, and Team. By discriminating the type of traveler group, the recommendation system should offer more accurate suggestions to the travelers. For instance, the museum of Sex & Health is an inappropriate place to visit in Jeju for a group of family members. The Shopping domain consists of three different types such as Local specialty market, Traditional Market, Duty-free shop.

Fig. 1. Classification of location information

3.2 Probabilistic Spatio-temporal Inference

MLN is a language for probabilistic inference that is based on first-order logic and probability model for artificial intelligence. This is expressed in the form of first-order logic [4]. In addition, MLN is used to express semantic method using Markov network and provide logic and probability-based inference [5]. MC-SAT [6], which is used in the MLN, is algorithm that performs learning based on Markov Chain Monte Carlo Algorithms. The algorithm enables extracting sample at a specific stage before clarifying difference in weight value within margin of error where such extracted sample can be accepted, which facilitates classification [7]. Actually, it is necessary to transform description logic rules, which are defined in ontology, to the form of first-order logic for applying of the MLN [3]. Table 2 shows transformation of Description Logic Rules to First-order Logic.

Table 2. Transformation of description logic rules to first-order logic

Description logic	First-order logic
SubClassOf (equal, equal)	$\forall x$: equal(x) => equal(x)
ClassAssertion (spatio-temporal relation, topological relation)	Spatio-temporal relation (topological relation)

Table 3 shows the rules for inference based on Probabilistic Spatio-temporal Inference. According to the table, X, Y and Z are sets of our instances and properties for inference in the extended Jeju travel ontology. Set X is the list of locations of Location Information domain which consists of 7 different regions from Jeju. And Set Y is Travel Member domain consisting of 5 different types as we mentioned in Sect. 3.1. Finally, Set Z is the most common travel destinations in Jeju and it consists of 115 places.

For Rules for inference, there are basically four rules in to distinguish and to predict the definition of destination recommendation system [12]. If the domain of Location Information (X) intersects with Travel Member (Y), the suggestion definition will be

Table 3. Rules for probabilistic spatio-temporal inference

Rules for Inference

Definition

X = { Jeju City, Western Jeju City, Eastern Jeju City, Seogwipo, Western Seogwipo, Eastern Seogwipo, Hallasan National Park }

Y = { Family, Couple, Single, Friend, Team }

Z = { Banglimwon, Drama World, Aqua Planet Jeju, World Seashell Museum, Bonte Museum, Nexon Computer Museum, The Museum of Sex & Health in Jeju, ...} 115 cases

Rules

$\forall$X,Y : Location(X) $\wedge$ Travel_Member(Y) $\rightarrow$ Preference_1(X,Y)

$\forall$X,Z : Location(X) $\wedge$ Travel_Destination(Z) $\rightarrow$ Preference_2(X,Z)

$\forall$Y,Z : Travel_Member(Y) $\wedge$ Travel_Destination(Z) $\rightarrow$ Preference_3(Y,Z)

$\forall$X,Y,Z : Preference_1(X,Y) $\wedge$ Preference_2(X,Z) $\wedge$ Preference_3(Y,Z)
$\rightarrow$ Recommendation(X,Y,Z)

Preference_1, while the Location Information domain (X) intersects with Travel Destination (Z), the system will produce a suggestion as Preference_2. Moreover, if Travel Member domain (Y) intersects with Travel Destination (Z), the system will produces Preference_3 for the definition. On the other hand, preference 1, 2 and 3 intersect with each other together, the prediction definition will be Recommendation (X,Y,Z).

4   Experiment and Evaluation

In general, inference for ontology is performed by using ontology inference engine. There are a variety of inference engines such as Jena, FOWL, Pellet, and Fact++. These inference engines simply determine whether there is a result from inference or not. Recently, probabilistic inference methods such as the MLNs have emerged and classified problems that cannot be defined easily in the probabilistic way, which provides better results. Against this background, this paper intends to use probabilistic inference method with use of the MLNs, rather than the existing ontology inference engine, for conduction of experiment [2].

This proposal evaluates the inference results of travel destination recommendation which is slightly similar to Disaster Information Sharing system [8]. In experiment, Scenario is as follows: (1) User's current location information assumes staying in Eastern Seogwipo. (2) Also, user is alone and he wants to search travel destination. Totally, travel destination consists of 115 cases and some of the experimental results are shown in Table 4.

Table 4 shows the probabilistic results depending on weight values and probabilistic results is values between 1.0 and 0.5. When inference result exists in Table 4, result value is higher than around 0.5 because the sampling value p = 0.500000. It means that the first probability value is 0.5. In order to obtain result from learning, the test was performed 1000 times.

In Table 4, the place is Eastern Seogwipo between case number 1 and case number 7. And the place is neighborhood Eastern Seogwipo between case number 7 and case number 11. According to the results, the performance is satisfactory.

Table 4. Experiment results for travel destination recommendation

No.	Probabilistic result	Place
1	0.629	Seongsang Ilchulbong
2	0.627	Seopjikoji
3	0.626	Micheon Cave
4	0.623	Seongeup Folk Village
5	0.621	Jeju Horse Park
6	0.619	Jeju Land ATV
7	0.619	Jeju Folk Village
8	0.570	Jeju National Museum
9	0.567	Jeju April 3rd Peace Park
10	0.563	Seokbujak Museum
11	0.562	Jeongbang Waterfalls
…	…	…

5   Conclusion

This proposed method for travel destination recommendation system has been extended from the previous proposal in order to provide the travelers with more accurate suggestions to the closet and relevant destination from user's current location and to improve the travelling experience at ease. In this paper, the travel destination recommendation system is extended by using Markov Logic Networks based on probabilistic spatio-temporal inference. The extended travel ontology is built from our previous work. In building ontology section, we define the inference rules using proposed spatio-temporal relation and the use of Markov Logic Networks (MLNs) for probabilistic reasoning. Our future study will be focusing on extending of travel information domain and improving the suggestion accuracy with weight values.

Acknowledgment. This work was supported by Basic Science Research Program through the National Research Foundation of Korea (NRF) funded by the Ministry of Education (No. 2013R1A1A2A10011667) and Basic Science Research Program through the National Research Foundation of Korea (NRF) funded by the Ministry of Science, ICT & Future Planning (2015R1C1A1A02037515)

References

1. Choi, J., Choi, C., Lee, E., Kim, P.: A Markov logic network based social relation inference for personalized social search. In: Kim, S.-W., Trawiński, B., Camacho, D. (eds.) New Research in Multimedia and Internet Systems. SCI, vol. 572, pp. 195–202. Springer, Heidelberg (2014)
2. Choi, C et al.: Travel ontology for intelligent recommendation system. In: Third Asia International Conference on Modelling and Simulation, pp. 637–642. IEEE (2009)
3. Choi, C., et al.: Probabilistic spatio-temporal inference for motion event understanding. Neurocomputing **122**, 24–32 (2013)
4. de Oliveira, P.C.: Probabilistic reasoning in the semantic web using Markov logic. M.Sc. Thesis (2009)
5. Richardson, M., Domingos, P.: Markov logic networks. Mach. Learn. **62**, 107–136 (2006)
6. Domingos, P., Lowd, D.: Markov Logic: an Interface Layer for Artificial Intelligence, pp. 1–155. Morgan and Claypool, USA (2009)
7. Alchemy Open Source AI. http://alchemy.cs.washington.edu/
8. Ishida, T., Takahagi, K., Uchida, N., Shibata, Y.: Proposal of the disaster information sharing system for the disaster countermeasures headquarters. IT Convergence Pract. (INPRA) **2**(3), 34–54 (2014)
9. Jose, I., Jose, S., Ju, J., Dios, D., Zangroniz, R., Pastor, J.M.: WebServices Integration on an RFID-Based Tracking System for Urban Transportation Monitoring. IT Convergence Pract. (INPRA) **1**(4), 1–23 (2013)
10. Agrafiotis, I., Legg, P., Goldsmith, M., Creese, S.: Towards a user and role-based sequential behavioural analysis tool for insider threat detection. J. Internet Serv. Inf. Secur. (JISIS) **4**(4), 127–137 (2014)
11. Than, C., Han, S.: Improving recommender systems by incorporating similarity, trust and reputation. J. Internet Serv. Inf. Secur. (JISIS) **4**(1), 64–76 (2014)
12. Kim, M., Seo, J., Noh, S., Han, S.: Reliable social trust management with mitigating sparsity problem. J. Wireless Mobile Netw. Ubiquitous Comput. Dependable Appl. **1**(1), 86–97 (2010)

MBTI-Based Collaborative Recommendation System: A Case Study of Webtoon Contents

Myeong-Yeon Yi, O-Joun Lee$^{(\boxtimes)}$, and Jason J. Jung

School of Computer Science and Engineering, Chung-Ang University,
Heunseok-Dong, Seoul 156-756, South Korea
{dalaetm, concerto34, j3ung}@cau.ac.kr

Abstract. A large number of Webtoon contents has caused difficulties on finding relevant Webtoons for users. Thereby, an efficient recommendation services are needed. However, since the existing recommendation method (e.g. collaborative filtering) has two fundamental problems: (i.e., data sparsity and scalability problem), it has difficulties with reflecting users' personality. In this paper, we propose the MBTI-CF method to solve these problems and to involve users' personality by building personality-based neighborhood using MBTI. In order to verify the efficiency of the proposed method, we conducted statistical testing by user survey (anonymous users have rated set of the pre-selected Webtoon contents). Three experimental results have shown that MBTI-CF provides improvement in terms of the data sparsity problem and the scalability problem and offers more stable performance.

Keywords: Webtoon · Recommendation · MBTI (Myers-Briggs Type Indicator) · Collaborative filtering

1 Introduction

Webtoon[1] is digital comic contents published on the web. With the emergence of smart devices, the Webtoon has been the most popular digital contents in South Korea and actively reproduced in various media like movies, dramas and so on. The amount of the Webtoons is huge and increasing rapidly. For example, in 2014, the number of Webtoons in Naver recorded 520 while it is released in 2004, later than Yahoo! Korea's "Cartoon Sae-sang" (in 2002), and Daum's "Manhwa sok Sae-sang" (in 2003). Webtoon Platform corp. TapasMedia recorded about 21,500 Webtoons in 2014, its first year. It is getting more difficult for users to find relevant Webtoons since the number of the Webtoons is growing rapidly. Hence, an efficient recommendation service is needed.

There are three major approaches to recommend digital contents: content-based filtering, demographic filtering and collaborative filtering. The Content-based filtering and the demographic filtering require external data that are difficult to get. However, the collaborative filtering can work without external data. Moreover, it performs higher performance than others [1]. Therefore, we propose recommendation system for the webtoon using collaborative filtering.

---

[1] Webtoon is also known as web comics, online comics, internet comics.

© ICST Institute for Computer Sciences, Social Informatics and Telecommunications Engineering 2016
P.C. Vinh and V. Alagar (Eds.): ICCASA 2015, LNICST 165, pp. 101–110, 2016.
DOI: 10.1007/978-3-319-29236-6_11

Two major problems of collaborative filtering are data sparsity problem and scalability problem [2, 15]. The data Sparsity problem occurs when a rating matrix is sparse. The rating matrix can be sparse in many situations such as cold-start problem, new-user, new-item problem (when a new user or item has entered in the system). Since the user has not rated or purchased items or the item has not been rated yet, it is difficult to find a group of similar users or items. In other word, the lack of rating history causes the data sparsity [3].

The scalability problem occurs when the number of users or items grows. Dealing with the scalability problem is important because the numbers of the users and the items are extremely large in the real world. Since the existing CF algorithms have to estimate the similarities of every users and items, they suffer serious scalability problem.

Another issue of the existing recommendation systems is that they have difficulties with reflecting users' personalities. We need to develop a new approach to extract users' personalities and reflect them on the recommendation system. There were some studies suggesting personality-based recommendation system [4, 17]. They used *Big Five Factor personality model* (Big Five) to solve the data sparsity problem of the collaborative filtering. However, the scalability problem, one of the collaborative filtering's major problems, remained unsolved.

In this paper, we propose to use *Myers-Briggs Type Indicator* (MBTI) to understand users' personalities and to solve the major two problems of the collaborative filtering. The MBTI is a psychometric questionnaire to measure psychological preference. There are four bipolar discontinuous scales which are implied in Jung's theory that humans experience the world by the four major principles - sensation, intuition, feeling, and thinking [6]. The MBTI categorize people in 16 types by an abbreviation of the four initial letters of each of their four type of preferences. For example, people who are extraverted and prefer sensing, thinking and judgment will be categorized to ESTJ type.

The remainder of this paper is organized as follows. In Sect. 2, we provide a brief overview of related works. Section 3 explains the procedure of the proposed method. In Sect. 4, three experiments evaluate the improvement and the performance by comparing the result of the proposed method with that of the existing method. In Sect. 5, we draw a conclusion that provides a summary of the proposed method and future work.

2   Related Work

2.1   Existing Recommendation Systems for the Webtoon

There have been no precedent study of recommendation Systems for the Webtoon. The recommendation services that the existing webtoon service platforms are providing are limited to using content-based filtering and demographic filtering or so on. For example, there are platforms provided by Naver, Daum and so on [14]. They recommend the Webtoons which are preferred by users with common age and gender or which are in same genre that the user preferred.

However, the content-based filtering works based on a description of the content or the users' choices made in the past. The demographic filtering suppose that the users with common personal attributes like age and gender will also have common preferences [12]. Therefore, the content-based filtering and the demographic filtering cannot give high-performance recommendations if the system has not enough external information [11]. The collaborative filtering, however, analyzes the users' ratings without much external information of a specific domain. Since the Webtoons are multimedia contents, we propose recommendation system using the collaborative filtering.

2.2 Recommendation System Based on Personality Information

Personality of human consists of two parts. One is consistent behavior patterns and the other is intrapersonal processes [7]. The previous researches have shown that the personality is highly related to the preferences and tastes [9]. In other words, people with similar personality would have similar behavior patterns and preferences. Hence, we can predict a person's preference of items by investigating users' purchased items or preferences whose personalities are similar to the person.

Recommendation System Based on the Big Five. There are studies on collaborative filtering recommendation systems that use personality information to group similar users [4, 17]. They apply the Big Five, the widely used personality model within psychology. The Big Five is a hierarchical model of personality traits with five factors [5]. However, since the Big Five measures personality traits on a dimensional scale, they had to estimate similarities between all users. Thus, the scalability problem had grown worse as a result of using the Big Five.

To solve the scalability problem, we propose to use the MBTI. The MBTI is leading academic model of personality with the Big Five. On the contrary to the Big Five, the MBTI is typological so that we can categorize users to 16 types. Since we make personality-based neighborhood group by using MBTI, we do not have to estimate all similarities between all the users. Thus, we can relieve the scalability problem.

Recommendation System Based on MBTI. Song et al. proposed recommendation system based on collaborative filtering using emotional word selection and the MBTI. They conducted experiments to show that the users with the same MBTI type will select similar emotional words and have similar movie preference [8]. In the experiments, they selected several movies and extracted emotional words for subjective evaluation on the movies. Then, they classified subjects by the MBTI and encouraged them to select the emotional words on each movie and to evaluate the rating for each movie.

As a result of the experiments, the subjects with the same MBTI type had choose similar emotional words and rated similarly except for extremely popular movies. Finally, they drew a conclusion that the users with the same MBTI type have similar emotions and preferences on the same movie. Thus, it is reasonable to use the MBTI to recommend the movies. Since the Webtoons are narrative contents like the movies, we propose a new approach to use the MBTI to recommend the Webtoons.

3   MBTI-Based Collaborative Filtering

The collaborative filtering using the Big Five Factor personality model has been already proposed. It has solved the data sparsity problem by building personality-based neighborhoods using the Big Five. However, the Big Five measures personality traits on a dimensional scale so recommendation system using the Big Five had to estimate similarities between all users. Thus, the scalability problem, one of the collaborative filtering's major problem, had grown worse. Therefore, we need to develop a new approach to relieve the collaborative filtering's fundamental problems.

The MBTI-based Collaborative Filtering (MBTI-CF) can solve the data sparsity by building neighborhoods using the MBTI. In contrast with the Big Five, the MBTI is typological so users can be categorized into 16 types. Since the MBTI-CF makes the personality-based neighborhood group by using the MBTI, we do not have to estimate all similarities between all users. Thus, we can relieve the scalability problem. And by using the psychometric questionnaire MBTI, we can make recommendation system reflecting users' personalities.

The proposed method consists of three major parts.

(1) Normalizing ratings and Grouping users by the MBTI: we normalize ratings to unify the standard of ratings, and identify neighborhoods of the user using the MBTI.
(2) Computing Similarities between users in a neighborhood: we compute similarities between users using vector cosine similarity.
(3) Estimating Prediction of user-preference: we estimate prediction of user-preference by computing weighted average of all the ratings for the item.

3.1   Normalizing Ratings and Grouping Users by MBTI

Standard points and measure of the rating scores vary across users, we need to unify the standard of the ratings. Therefore, newly-arrived ratings are normalized by the Gaussian Probability Model. This step is formulated as

$$preR_{u,n} = \frac{F_{u,n} - \overrightarrow{F_u}}{\sigma(F_u)} \tag{1}$$

where $F_{u,n}$ represents a newly-arrived rating that user u rated for item n, $\overrightarrow{F_u}$ and $\sigma(F_u)$ are the average and standard deviation of the historical ratings rated by the user u respectively. $preR_{u,n}$ indicates the preprocessed rating of which standard is unified. After normalizing ratings, we identify a neighborhood of the new user by using the MBTI.

3.2   Computing Similarities Between Users in Neighborhood

We have to estimate all similarities between the users with the same neighborhood before we make a prediction of the preference.

In order to estimate the similarities, we adopted the vector cosine similarity, which compares two users' ratings by the cosine of the angle between the users' corresponding rating vectors [13]. The vector cosine similarity between user u_i and u_j is given by

$$w_{u_i, u_j} = \cos(\overrightarrow{u_i}, \overrightarrow{u_j}) = \frac{\overrightarrow{u_i} \cdot \overrightarrow{u_j}}{\|\overrightarrow{u_i}\| * \|\overrightarrow{u_j}\|} \tag{2}$$

where u_i is i-th user, u_j is j-th user, then $\overrightarrow{u_i}$ is vectors consist of rating by the user u_i and $\overrightarrow{u_j}$ is the vectors consist of rating by the user u_j. And "·" denotes the dot-product of the two vectors [2]. If R is the $n \times m$ user-rating matrix, then the similarity between two users u_i and u_j is defined as the cosine of the n dimensional rating vectors corresponding to the i-th and j-th row of the matrix R.

3.3 Estimating Prediction of User-Preference

In Sect. 3.2, the similarity matrix between the users is created. Each component of the matrix has a similarity between the users, and the similarities are measured by using the vector cosine similarity.

To make a prediction of the preference on an item i for active user a, a weighted average of all the ratings on that item is given by

$$P_{a,i} = \bar{r}_a + \frac{\sum_{u \in U}(r_{u,i} - \bar{r}_u) \cdot w_{a,u}}{\sum_{u \in U}|w_{a,u}|} \tag{3}$$

where $\bar{r}_a$ and $\bar{r}_u$ indicate the average ratings of all the items that the user a and user u rated. $w_{a,u}$ is the weight between the user a and user u that we estimated in the Sect. 3.3. The summation is over all the users $u \in U$ who have rated the item i. Finally, we can predict $P_{a,i}$, which is the preference on the item for the user [2].

4 Experimental Results and Analysis

This section presents three experiments that aim to verify improvement of the proposed method on three different foci: performance, robustness for the data sparsity and robustness for the scalability [10]. In the first experiment, we compared performance of the MBTI-CF with that of the CF. In the second experiment, the improvement of the robustness for the data sparsity is verified. We verify the improvement of new-user problem which is one of the major situations in that the data sparsity occurs. In the third experiment, the improvement of the robustness for the scalability is verified by comparing a time complexity of MBTI-CF with that of CF.

4.1   Experimental Environment

In order to collect Webtoons ratings, we conducted a survey of anonymous users by Google docs. The questionnaire we distributed is shown in Table 1.

Table 1. Average, standard deviation and range of MAE of CF and MBTI-CF.

	Question	Choices
1	What is your MBTI type?	ISTJ, ISTP, ISFJ, ISFP, INFJ, INTJ, INFP, INTP, ESTP, ESFP ESTJ, ESFJ, ENFP, ENTP, ENFJ, ENTJ
2	What is your gender?	Male, Female
3	What age group are you in?	~ 10, 10 ~ 19, 20 ~ 29, 30 ~ 39, 40 ~ 49, 50 ~
4	What method do you mostly use to read Webtoons?	Smartphone, PC, Tablet PC, Comic book,
5	What Webtoon service platform do you mainly use? (Pick two of them)	Naver, Daum, Lezhin Comics, Toptoon, Olleh Market, Nate, Kakao Page, Yahoo, etc.
6	Give ratings to these 20 Webtoons.	1 ~ 10

For question 6, we selected 20 Webtoons which are popular in different genre. We finally have obtained 90 of survey replies.

4.2   Performance Evaluation

In order to evaluate the performance, we compared Mean Absolute Error (MAE) of the MBTI-CF with that of the CF. The MAE is the most widely used measure of prediction error of the CF [2]. It is an average of the absolute deviation between a predicted rating and a real rating for the items. The MAE is formulated as

$$\text{MAE} = \frac{\sum_{i=1}^{N} |r_i - p_i|}{N}, \tag{4}$$

where N is the number of items, and p_i and r_i represent the prediction of preference and the real rating of i-th item. A lower MAE value means better prediction performance.

Evaluation of performance was conducted as followings. First, we predicted users' preferences of items using the MBTI-CF and the CF. Second, we measured MAE of the two methods and compared MAE of the two methods.

As shown in Table 2, the MBTI-CF presents more stable performance than the CF but shows a slight lower performance on average performance. The MBTI-CF shows an improvement of 70.88 % over the given standard deviation and 50.96 % over the given range. The MBTI-CF shows lower performance of 9.58 % over the given average.

The results show that the performance of the MBTI-CF is more stable but less accurate than that of the existing CF.

Table 2. Average, standard deviation and range of MAE of CF and MBTI-CF

	CF	MBTI-CF	Improvement
Average	0.678	0.743	−9.58 %
S.D.	0.261	0.076	70.88 %
Range	1.042	0.511	50.96 %

4.3 Dealing with Data Sparsity

To verify the improvement of the robustness against the data sparsity, we investigated the improvement of the new-user problem which is one of the major situation that the data sparsity occurs.

The CF cannot recommend items to a new user since there is not enough user's historical rating. However, the MBTI-CF can estimate the new user's prediction of preferences on the items by assuming that the new user has the same weight to other users in neighborhood.

To evaluate the performance of the MBTI-CF on the new-user problem, we compared the MAEs under two circumstances, when the data of the user exist and when the user is a new user. Figure 1 shows MAEs for each circumstance classified by MBTI types and averages of them. Table 3 shows the average, standard deviation, and range of the MAE for the two circumstances.

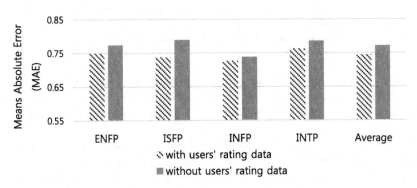

Fig. 1. MAE of each MBTI type and average

Table 3. Average, standard deviation and range of MAE when data exist and when the user is new user.

	With users' rating data	Without users' rating data
Average	0.743	0.772
S.D.	0.076	0.078
Range	0.511	0.523

The results in Fig. 1 indicate the MBTI-CF performs similarly whether the data of the user exist or not. The increase of average of MAE is 3.80 % when the user is the new user.

As shown in Table 3, the stability of the performance has slightly reduced. The standard deviation and range of MAEs when the user is new user had increased 2.63 % and 2.34 % in percentage, respectively.

Observing the results, we can claim that the performance of the MBTI-CF is stable whether the user is new or not

4.4   Improvement of the Scalability

To verify the improvement of the scalability, we compared time complexity of MBTI-CF with that of CF. Let U be a set of n users and I a set of m items and k a size of the neighborhood.

The collaborative filtering procedure is composed of 3 major parts: estimating similarity, grouping the similar users and predicting the preference of the item. The computation complexity of a user similarities to other users is $O(nm)$ as explained below:

```
uₐ : a particular user
For each user uᵢ
    For the set of m items that have been co-rated by
    user uₐ and uᵢ
            Compute similarity between uₐ and uᵢ
```

In order to group the similar users, we have to find k users who are most similar to the user to build a neighborhood. The computation complexity of grouping the similar users is $O(n)$ since we have to find k users which have maximum similarity to the user in n users.

The computation complexity of predicting the preference of the item is $O(k)$ since we have to compute weighted average of 1 items for k users.

The most expensive computation of the classic CF is the computation of the user-to-user similarities [16]. Since the MBTI-CF builds 16 neighborhoods by MBTI types, we don't have to estimate the user similarities of all the users to group the similar users. We have to estimate similarities between the user and the users in the neighborhood. The average neighborhood size will be $\frac{n}{16}$. Thus, the computation complexity of the user similarities to the other users reduced in 1 over 16. The computation complexity of predicting preference of the item is $O(k)$ since we have to compute weighted average of 1 items for k users.

Since the MBTI-CF does not have to estimate the user similarities of all the users, the computation of user-to-user similarities is reduced linearly. Therefore, building the neighborhood using the MBTI improves the scalability.

4.5 Result Analysis

The results of the experiments show that the scalability problem in the existing CF is relieved in the MBTI-CF. Also, the performance of the MBTI-CF is more stable than that of the existing CF. But the performance of the MBTI-CF is less accurate than that of the classic CF.

This is because there was a tradeoff between the accuracy and the scalability. Grouping users by the MBTI could exclude a user who rated most similarly to the user from the neighborhood. However, the scalability is improved since the number of similarities that has to be computed is reduced.

The result of the second experiment shows that the performance of the MBTI-CF is stable whether the user is the new user or not. Since we can identify the new user's neighborhood by his MBTI type, we can solve the data sparsity problem.

5 Conclusion

A large number of the Webtoon contents has caused difficulties to find relevant Webtoons for users. Thus, we need a systematic process to recommend the users a suitable Webtoon. We propose recommendation system using collaborative filtering since collaborative filtering works without external data and performs high performance. However the collaborative filtering has two fundamental problems: the data sparsity problem, the scalability problem. In addition, the existing recommendation systems for the Webtoons have difficulties with reflecting users' personality.

In this paper, we proposed the MBTI-CF to solve the data sparsity problem and the scalability problem by building personality-based neighborhood using the MBTI personality type. Also, the MBTI-CF reflects users' personalities.

In order to verify the improvement of the proposed method, we conducted survey of anonymous internet users to collect Webtoons ratings. The three experiments have shown that MBTI-CF provides improvement in terms of the data sparsity problem and the scalability problem. Also, the proposed method offers more stable performance.

In the future work, we will conduct testing of the proposed method with more datasets and understand further about the performance of the MBTI-CF. The MBTI-CF presents a more stable performance than the existing CF, but shows a slight lower performance on average performance. Therefore, we will find solutions to improve the performance of the MBTI-CF.

Acknowledgments. This research was supported by the MSIP (Ministry of Science, ICT and Future Planning), Korea, under the ITRC (Information Technology Research Center) support program (IITP-2015-H8501-15-1018) supervised by the IITP (Institute for Information & communications Technology Promotion). Also, this work was supported by the National Research Foundation of Korea (NRF) grant funded by the Korea government (MSIP) (NRF-2014R1A2A2A05007154).

References

1. Adomavicius, G., Tuzhilin, A.: Toward the next generation of recommender systems: a survey of the state of-the-art and possible extensions. IEEE Trans. Knowl. Data Eng. **17**(6), 734–749 (2005)
2. Su, X., Khoshgoftaar, T.M.: A survey of collaborative filtering techniques. Adv. Artif. Intell. **2009**, 1–19 (2009). Article ID 421425, Hindawi
3. Billsus, D., Pazzani, M.J.: Learning collaborative information filters. In: Proceedings of the 15th International Conference on Machine Learning, vol. 98, pp. 46–54 (1998)
4. Tkalčič, M., Kunaver, M., Tasič, J., Košir, A.: Personality based user similarity measure for a collaborative recommender system. In: Proceedings of the 5th Workshop on Emotion in Human-Computer Interaction-Real World Challenges, pp. 30–37 (2009)
5. Gosling, S.D., Rentfrow, P.J., Swann Jr., W.B.: A very brief measure of the Big-Five personality domains. J. Res. Pers. **37**(6), 504–528 (2003)
6. Harasym, P.H., Leong, E.J., Juschka, B.B., Lucier, G.E., Lorcheider, F.L.: Myers-briggs psychological type and achievement in anatomy and physiology. Am. J. Physiol. **268**(6 pt. 3), S61–S65 (1995)
7. Burger, J.M.: Personality, 7th edn. Thomson/Wadsworth, Belmont (2008)
8. Kim, H.-G., Namgoong, H., Eune, J., Song, M.: A proposed movie recommendation method using emotional word selection. In: Ozok, A., Zaphiris, P. (eds.) OCSC 2009. LNCS, vol. 5621, pp. 525–534. Springer, Heidelberg (2009)
9. Rentfrow, P.J., Gosling, S.D.: The do re mi's of everyday life: the structure and personality correlates of music preferences. J. Pers. Soc. Psychol. **84**(6), 1236–1256 (2003)
10. Herlocker, J.L., Konstan, J.A., Terveen, L.G., Riedl, J.T.: Evaluating collaborative filtering recommender systems. ACM Trans. Inf. Syst. **22**(1), 5–53 (2004)
11. Pazzani, M.J., Billsus, D.: Content-based recommendation systems. In: Brusilovsky, P., Kobsa, A., Nejdl, W. (eds.) Adaptive Web 2007. LNCS, vol. 4321, pp. 325–341. Springer, Heidelberg (2007)
12. Pazzani, M.J.: A framework for collaborative, content-based and demographic filtering. Artif. Intell. Rev. **13**(5–6), 393–408 (1999)
13. Breese, J.S., Heckerman, D., Kadie, C.: Empirical analysis of predictive algorithms for collaborative filtering. In: Proceedings of the 14th Conference on Uncertainty in Artificial Intelligence, pp. 43–52 (1998)
14. Naver Webtoon. http://comic.naver.com/webtoon/weekday.nhn
15. Lee, O.-J., Jung, J.J., You, E.-S.: Predictive clustering for performance stability in collaborative filtering techniques. In: Proceedings of 2nd IEEE International Conference on Cybernetics, CYBCONF 2015, Gdynia, Poland, pp. 24–26 (2015)
16. Rousidis, I., Plexousakis, D., Theoharopoulos, E., Papagelis, M.: Incremental collaborative filtering for highly-scalable recommendation algorithms. In: Hacid, M.-S., Murray, N.V., Raś, Z.W., Tsumoto, S. (eds.) ISMIS 2005. LNCS (LNAI), vol. 3488, pp. 553–561. Springer, Heidelberg (2005)
17. Hu, R., Pu, P.: Enhancing collaborative filtering systems with personality information. In: RecSys 2011, Proceedings of the Fifth ACM Conference on Recommender Systems, pp. 197–204 (2011)

Social Affinity-Based Group Recommender System

Minsung Hong[1], Jason J. Jung[1]([⊠]), and Minchang Lee[2]

[1] Department of Computer Engineering, Chung-Ang University,
Heukseok, Seoul 156-756, South Korea
minsung.holdtime@gmail.com, j2jung@gmail.com
[2] Division of Public Administration and Welfare, Chosun University,
Gwangju, Republic of Korea
savio@chosun.ac.kr

Abstract. Information collected from the social network is recently used to improve a performance of recommender systems to an individual user or a group. During selecting the items among the group members, the relationships (e.g., position, dependency, and the strength of the social ties) often has an important role than the individual preference in the group. Hence, we propose a novel recommendation method based on social affinity between two users. This recommendation method consists of (*i*) the similarity calculation between movies based on weighted feature, (*ii*) the generation of initial affinity network graph, and (*iii*) the computation of user's affinity to group based on the graph. Experimental results on synthetic dataset show that our proposed method can discover social affinities efficiently.

Keywords: Social affinity · Similarity · Weighted features · Group recommender system

1 Introduction

In this work, we focus on social interactions among users. People often resort to friends in their social networks for advice before purchasing a product or consuming a service [1]. The information collected from the social network is recently used to improve a performance of recommender systems to an individual user or a group.

Since these studies do not consider the real situations, we want to show a typical scenario. Suppose that there are two couples who try to select the best movies for watching. While the first couple has usually chosen the movies which a girl friend has preferred, the second couple has selected the movies which both have preferred as much as possible. Thus, during selecting the items among the group members, the relationships (e.g., position, dependency, and the strength of the social ties) often has an important role than the individual preference in the group.

© ICST Institute for Computer Sciences, Social Informatics and Telecommunications Engineering 2016
P.C. Vinh and V. Alagar (Eds.): ICCASA 2015, LNICST 165, pp. 111–121, 2016.
DOI: 10.1007/978-3-319-29236-6_12

Hence, we propose the novel recommendation method based on social affinity between two users. Particularly, the similarity calculation among items, weight of item feature based on TF-IDF, and the graph based method are exploited to get the affinities among users who have not watched the movie together.

2   Related Work

Online social networks present new opportunities as to further improve the accuracy of recommender systems. In real life, people often resort to friends in their social networks for advice before purchasing a product or consuming a service [1]. Hence, some systems use the social information such as trust, and relation between users to improve the performance of recommender systems. Yang et al. [2] focused the "Friends Circles" which refines the domain-oblivious "Friends" concept. To influence the multiple domain specific, they proposed circle-based recommender system using the trust circles. Ma at el. introduced a Social recommendation (SoRec) model to adapted the social trust in recommender system in [3]. They used the directional concepts which are defined as an out degree (i.e., the number of users who a target user follows/trusts) and an in degree (i.e., the number of users who follow/trust target user). Jamali and Ester proposed a matrix factorization based approach for recommendation in social networks [4]. They incorporated the mechanism of trust propagation into a social model. For this mechanism, the model extracts a transitivity of trust in social network, as the dependence of a user on the direct neighbors. It can propagate to make a user's feature vector dependent on possibly all users in the network with decaying weights for more distant users.

Most work on recommender systems focus on the recommendation items to individual users. For instance, they may select a book for a particular user to read based on a model of that users preferences in the past [5]. However, we should consider the recommendation to group in many real recommendations such as a music of gym or health center, a TV program sequence for family, a travel destination with friends, and a good restaurant for colleagues to have a lunch, and so on. Some researches focused the aggregation of the individual preferences or other information for group. Masthoff [6] summarized eleven aggregation strategies of the individual user's likes and dislikes inspired by social choice theory, such as average, multiplicative, least miserty, fairness, and so on. Amer-Yahia et al. [7] proposed a recommender that aggregates preference of members based on member's relevance to create the recommendation for group. Then, they analyzed the preference disagreements between pairs of individuals and employed to rank the recommended list. Additionally, Kim et al. [8] taken into account both the effectiveness and the satisfaction of individual members to group recommendation. Their system generates a recommended book list and removes an irrelevant items in order to improve satisfaction of individual members. Finally, Quijano-Sanchez et al. [9] adopted the users' personality in the group and the trust of connections among members as the factors which improve a prediction accuracy of group's rating.

However, these recommender systems do not consider important factor which is called "affinity" such as position, leverage, and relationship in real world, like previous mention. In other words, it is the affinity of users about group. Furthermore, these need the preference of individual users to aggregate into group's preference. While, our method use item's features and history instead of it to calculate the affinity between two users. Also, this method can get the affinity based on graph, even though users had not watched the movie together.

3 Measuring Social Affinity Between Two Users

In this section, we describe the initial social affinity calculation to generate the social affinity network graph. It is divided by the calculation of the weighted feature to similarity, computation of the movie similarity, and the generation of affinity between two users based on the movie similarity.

3.1 Movie Features and Preprocessing

Before the similarity calculation, we account the used movie features in this paper. Debnath et al. [10] defined the distance of the 13 movie features which are served by IMDB[1]. Also, they analyzed the importance degree of features to choose the movie by users based on a linear regression equations. However, they supposed that a director feature has one people and equally applied the analysis results to all users. In case of both "Dumb and Dumber To" and "Crazy, Stupid, Love.", these movies had two directors. Besides, the same value inappropriate to all users. Therefore, we need to modify the features as following Table 1. Also, we have to use the novel weight calculation method which differently creates the weights according to users based on the basic idea of TF-IDF. In this paper, we use the 7 features such as release, rating, director, genre, leading actor, country, and leading actor, country, language (note that used rating is collected by the IMDB and the leading actors extracted from the Naver movie[2]).

To analysis the similarity between movies, many methods are studied. We adopt the Jaccard's, Overlap coefficient, and Euclidean distance as the similarity measure. We need to transform the feature values into terms, because former two methods use a common ground between two set, we use the TF-IDF to create the weight of each feature, and we avoid a duplication among features (e.g., D_Seth MacFarlane, LA_Seth MacFarlane). Also, we apply prior Table 1 to the Euclidean distance.

3.2 Weighted Feature Based on TF-IDF

Above-mentioned weighted features which is studied by Debnath is not perfect to users group in aspects of personalization. Hence, we propose the method which

---

[1] IMDB, http://www.imdb.com
[2] NAVER MOVIE, http://movie.naver.com/

Table 1. Features used in movie recommendation

Feature	Type	Cardinality	Distance measure
Release	Year	YYYY	$(300 - |Y_1 - Y_2|)/300$
Rating	Float	$(0 - 10)$	$(10 - |R_1 - R_2|)/10$
Director	$(String)^*$	$(< name >)^*$	$(|D_1 \cap D_2|)/D_{max}$
Genre	$(String)^*$	$(< genre >)^*$	$(|G_1 \cap G_2|)/G_{max}$
Leading actor	$(String)^*$	$(< name >)^*$	$(|LA_1 \cap LA_2|)/LA_{max}$
Country	$(String)^*$	$(< country >)^*$	$(|C_1 \cap C_2|)/C_{max}$
Language	$(String)^*$	$(< language >)^*$	$(|L_1 \cap L_2|)/L_{max}$

calculate the weight of feature based on TF-IDF. The TFIDF, short for term
frequency inverse document frequency, is a numerical statistic that is intended
to reflect how important a word is to a document in a collection or corpus. The
term frequency express the importance degree in a target document. While, the
inverse document frequency is a measure of how much information the word
provides, that is, whether the term is common or rare across all documents [11].
To use it in creation of feature's weight, we need some basic defines and setting.

Target document(d) is a set of the feature values about movies which are seen
together by both users.
Document set(D) represent the sets of the feature values of movies which are
watched by each users.
Term(t) appear terms (the feature value of movies) in the *Target document*(d).

Next, we describe the proposed weight calculation method using prior example which is the movie history between "Fames" and "John". In this case, the d
and t is an enumeration of the feature values both "Interstellar" with "The Wolf
of Wall Street" movie and the it's terms, respectively. Also, the D include the
movies ("Inception", "The Dark Knight", "Dumb and Dumber To", "Ted", "The
Mask", and "Crazy, Stupid, Love.") as documents. We use the "raw frequency"
as TF weighting scheme and TF-IDF integration method as Definition 1. The
different with basic TF-IDF is square of the TF part. The document which is
set by use in this domain is different with normal documents, because it is a list
of feature value. Therefore, the count of term in the document d is very small.
However, if the movies which is watched together between two users have the
same feature values, it have to deal with as very importance point to them. To
reflect this actual state, we adopt the square of TF in this study. Also, λ_i is
normalization constant of each feature. This weight is combined with coefficient
(or distance) of each feature to calculate the similarity between two movies.

Definition 1 (TF-IDF for Feature Weight). *Let $d \in D$ and $f \in Feature$,
given term $t \in d$. The weight between two users based on TF-IDF is defined as
follows:*

$$tf(t,d) = f_{t,d}, \quad idf(t,D) = log\frac{N}{1 + |\{d \in D : t \in d\}|}, \tag{1}$$

$$tf\_idf(t,d,D) = tf(t,d)^2 \times idf(t,D), \tag{2}$$

$$weight(James, John) = \lambda_f \times tf\_idf(t,d,D). \tag{3}$$

3.3   Movie Similarity Based on the Weighted Feature

Previously, we refer to the used the similarity calculation methods between two movies such as Jaccard's coefficient, Overlap coefficient, Euclidean distance. In this chapter, we respectively show these process through one part in prior movie history.

Jaccard's and Overlap create the similarity based on a common attribute like Definition 2. Also, Euclidean method uses the definitions in Table 1. These methods are applied to *each feature* as Definition 3. In the next section, this similarity is altered to the affinity between two users.

Definition 2 (Jaccard's and Overlap coefficient). *The similarity using the Jaccard's and Overlap coefficient between two movies is defined as follows:*

$$jaccrard(a,b) = \frac{N_{a \cap b}}{N_{a \cup b}}, \tag{4}$$

$$overlap(a,b) = \frac{N_{a \cap b}}{Min(N_a, N_b)}, \tag{5}$$

$$Euclidean(a,b) = Distance(a,b) \quad in \ the \ Table \ 1. \tag{6}$$

Definition 3 (Similarity between two movies). *Let $d \in D$, the w_f, s_f are the weight based on TF-IDF and the similarity which is obtained by Jaccard's coefficient (or Overlap, Euclidean), respectively. Also, the f is 7 as the number of the features. The similarity between two movies is integrated with weight by definition as follows:*

$$Similarity(w_f, s_f) = \sum w_f \times s_f, \quad f \in Features. \tag{7}$$

3.4   Social Affinity Based on Movie Similarity

Until now, we calculate the similarity through six methods used both the similarity measures such as Jaccard's, Overlap coefficient, and Euclidean Distance with the weighted features. The social information in our recommender system is the affinity between two users in case of the view movie together them. To adopt it in recommendation, we need to transform the similarities as the affinities between two users int Definition 4.

Definition 4 (Affinity between two users). *Let user A and B is the target users. Also, the k of MA and the l of MB appear the movie lists which are watched by user A and B, respectively. The m of MC expresses the list of movies which are viewed by them together. In this case, the affinity between A and B is created by the similarity which is obtained in presence as follows (we mark the Definition 3 into sim() and affinity() into affi() by the limitation of length):*

$$affi(A, B) = \begin{cases} \dfrac{\sum_{i,j=1}^{i=k,j=m} sim(MA_i,MC_j)/k}{\sum_{i,j=1}^{i=k,j=m} sim(MA_i,MC_j)/k + \sum_{i,j=1}^{i=l,j=m} sim(MB_i,MC_j)/l} & if\ m \neq 0, \\ 0.5 & if\ m = 0. \end{cases}$$

$$(8)$$

4   Exploiting Social Affinity Graph to Group Recommendation

In this section, we account the recommendation of group through the request. Firstly, we introduce the calculation of social affinity between two users based on the social affinity graph. Then, the computation of the user's social affinity to group. Finally, we show the process of the proposed SAGRS.

4.1   Social Affinity Between Two Users on the Network Graph

Several existing work try to improve the performance of recommender system based on social information. Jiaming and Wesley [12] proved the effect of "Immediate Friend" (i.e., the friends who are directly connected in social network) and "Distant Friend" (i.e., the friends who have the indirect connection such as two or three hop in social network) in recommendation. Ma et al. applied the concepts "Follower" and "Leader" in recommender system [3]. In this paper, we reflect these concepts to generate the affinity between two users who watch the movie together or not.

1. Proposed affinity has the direction between two users as the concept "Follower" and "Leader",
2. The multiple hop include the "Immediate friend" and "Distance friend" in the social affinity network.

To describe a using reason of this concept, a simple scenario is shown as follows:

"Robert" and "John" had watched the movies with "Patricia" and "James", respectively. In this case, "James" can look for advice by "Robert" and "John" to see the movie with "Patricia".

That is, user can refer the hints of his/her friends to the preference of target user, even though he/she doesn't have experience which look the movie together.

To understand this situation, we add some suppositions into this scenario. When "James" watch with "John", he has a effect to "John", and "John" has the similar affinity with "Patricia". Besides, "James" has alike influence with "Robert", and "Robert" has a big leverage to "Patricia". In this case, we can expect that the affinity of "James" is bigger than "Patricia". Likewise, we can obtain the information about the affinity from indirect connection, even though between user are not directly connected. To consider this point into recommendation, we express the affinity among users into graph. The vertex of graph appears the user, and it's edges have direction as the affinity of user pair. Also, "James" is indirectly connected with "Patricia" and this connection is called "two hop". Then, the affinity between two users is calculated by Definition 5. It is comprised of the creation of affinity and normalization.

Definition 5 (Affinity Formula for Recommendation). *Let H is the maximum number of indirect connection in the affinity network graph, and P is the number of path in each hop such as one hop, two hop, three hop. The affinity for recommendation is defined as follows:*

$$affinity(A, B) = affi(A, B) + \sum_{h=2}^{H}\sum_{p=1}^{P}(product(aff_1, ..., aff_h)/P), \quad (9)$$

$$Affinity(A, B) = \frac{affinity(A, B)}{affinity(A, B) + affinity(B, A)}. \quad (10)$$

We can get the "Affinity" between "James" and "Patricia" using the Affinities of indirect connections (i.e., two hop about "James, John, and Patricia" and "James, Robert, and Patricia", three hop about "James, Mary, Michael, and Patricia". This affinity is calculated by the follows formula.

In the affinity, First term express the initial affinity about direct connection, and Second and third term appear the indirect connection as two and three hop, respectively. Particularly, Second term which is a multiply between two affinities regular bigger than third which is a product of three values, because the rage of used figures less than or equal to 1. It can be larger an influence of near connection than a far connection.

4.2   Social Affinity of the Users to Group

Until now, we explain the generation of initial affinity graph based on the affinity between two users who had watched the movie together. Additionally, we introduce the calculation of the affinity between users who had not watched the movie together based on the indirect connection in the affinity graph. We note that It use the values in the initial affinity graph. To answer our third research question, from now on we describe the member's affinity computation method to group which has three or more users. For this method, we use the case of the group which has members such as *James, John, Patricia,* and *Robert*. It appears the affinities which are calculated by the indirect connection among group members. Also, the affinities nearby an user express the affinities of the user about the others.

In this case, we can consider several methods which get the affinity of users to group such as average, product, and so on. However, the information of high affinity can dilute in the integration methods. Therefore, we adopt the maximum method which used the largest value as the user's affinity about the group which is processed as follows:

1. a maximum affinity and an applicable user is found,
2. the affinities relate to the user is removed,
3. process 1, 2 are repeated before a final user,
4. the affinity of the final user is allocated as the affinity about an user of the previous step,
5. all affinities are normalized to group.

"Robert" who has large affinities about the others has higher affinity to group than other users as 0.333. While, In the case of the "John" and "Patricia", they relatively have low affinity to group. It show the propriety of our method in the example. Until now, we get the affinity of users to group based on the affinity between users. In next section, we explain the proposed SAGRS based on the previous definitions.

4.3   Recommendation Based on the Social Affinity

The SAGRS is comprised of three parts:

1. In the case of the input users movie history, this information is transformed and saved to database in the preprocessing step. The transformation makes the terms about the feature values of the movies to calculate the weighted based similarity. The values is served by IMDB and Naver movie. We skip the detail description of this part, because it is explained in Sect. 3.
2. Initial affinity graph is generated based on the user's movie history. It not influences in the aspects of the recommendation time, because it can be processed in idle time. Alike the preprocessing part, it is introduced in Sect. 3. Therefore, we show the simple order of this part.
3. In the recommendation part, the movie list is generated to recommendation through the request of users. Firstly, the affinities of the users who are belong to the request group are computed by the initial affinity graph. Secondly, the affinities of users to group are created by these. Finally, these are applied the recommendation for the group. It's detail context is described in the next section.

Social Affinity Based Group Movie Recommendation. The first, second part are process in the idle time. While, third part is started by the recommendation request of the users. This structure makes to reduce the response time of recommendation. From now on, we explain the steps of third part as:

1. The users who request the movie list are found in the graph.
2. The affinities of the pair users in the group are calculated by indirect connection in the graph.
3. The affinities of each user are computed about the group.
4. The movie lists are created by similarity to each user.
5. The user's affinities are integrated with the similarities of the movie lists as values to one movie list.
6. The list is ranked by the unified values, and a top n movies are recommended to the group.

Because the others are described in the previous sections, we want to explain steps 4, 5, and 6. Firstly, the movie lists for each user are obtained by the similarity of the overlap coefficient between the user's movie history and the novel movies, because the similarity of overlap properly expresses the affinity between two users than the others. Then, the product of movie similarities and the affinity of user are unified as one movie list to the top N movie recommendation.

5   Experiment

To evaluate the proposed SAGRS, we create the virtual users and movie history in this section. Firstly, the users are divided by three groups (i.e., group A is very certain, group B is certain, and group C is uncertain) based on the degree of obviousness. Hence, we generate the 18 users and distribute users into three groups. Also, the characteristics of users who belong to group A and B are set. The 100 movies of which the feature information is collected from the IMDB and the Naver movie as the 7 features such as release, rating, director, genre, leading actor, country, and language. Then, these are allocated as 7 to 10 movies into per user, because the movie which are watched together is overlap. Also, we use the graph which are made by the virtual movie history. The users of the group A are appeared by black circle and white name as a vertex in the graph. The users of the group B, C are expressed by the gray circle and the white circle as black name, respectively. The average and standard deviation of the virtual data result among group A, B, C are shown in Table 2. In this result, the proposed method which use the affinity between users is effective, because it is natural as our setting (i.e., the affinity of the group A bigger than group B, the group B larger than the group C).

Table 2. The affinities of the result among groups

Groups	Average of affinity	Groups	Average of affinity	Standard deviation
A to B	0.531	B to A	0.469	0.022
B to C	0.580	C to B	0.420	0.035
A to C	0.584	C to A	0.416	0.055

6   Conclusions and Future Work

The existing works adopted the friends information of user in online social networks to recommender system. In this paper, we propose the method which use the affinity between users based on the movie watching history among users. Besides, it can operate without the user's rating or other profile information. Also, we show the validation of the method using the virtual users and movie watching history.

However, the limitations of this study are as follows:

1. We need to test on the more large user set instead of the only 18 users.
2. We have to create the virtual network which reflect the real world based on the normal theory such as scale-free network, small wold network, and random network.
3. The various networks based on the theories are tested about the range of the used indirect connection (i.e., mutiple hop) in the aspects of the data sparsity.
4. Above all, our method needs the revaluation using the survey of user, because the experiment is progressed on the virtual data which are the users and movie history of three group based on the degree of obviousness.

Hence, we plan to construct the real system which connect to $Facebook^3$ based on the proposed SAGRS. Through the it's service, we can analyze the performance of the our system such as satisfaction, usefulness, response time, and so on.

Acknowledgement. This research was supported by the MSIP (Ministry of Science, ICT and Future Planning), Korea, under the ITRC (Information Technology Research Center) support program (IITP-2015-H8501-15-1018) supervised by the IITP (Institute for Information &communications Technology Promotion). Also, this work was supported by the National Research Foundation of Korea (NRF) grant funded by the Korea government (MSIP) (NRF-2014R1A2A2A05007154). Also, this research was supported by SW Master's course of hiring contract Program grant funded by the Ministry of Science, ICT and Future Planning (H0116-15-1013).

References

1. Yang, X., Guo, Y., Liu, Y., Steck, H.: A survey of collaborative filtering based social recommender systems. Comput. Commun. **41**, 1–10 (2014)
2. Yang, X., Steck, H., Liu, Y.: Circle-based recommendation in online social networks. In: Yang, Q., Agarwal, D., Pei, J., (eds.) KDD, pp. 1267–1275. ACM (2012)
3. Ma, H., Yang, H., Lyu, M.R., King, I.: Sorec: social recommendation using probabilistic matrix factorization. In: Shanahan, J.G., Amer-Yahia, S., Manolescu, I., Zhang, Y., Evans, D.A., Kolcz, A., Choi, K.S., Chowdhury, A., (eds.) CIKM, pp. 931–940. ACM (2008)
4. Jamali, M., Ester, M.: A matrix factorization technique with trust propagation for recommendation in social networks. In: Amatriain, X., Torrens, M., Resnick, P., Zanker, M., (eds.) RecSys, pp. 135–142. ACM (2010)

---

[3] Facebook, https://www.facebook.com/

5. Masthoff, J.: Group recommender systems: combining individual models. In: Ricci, F., Rokach, L., Shapira, B., Kantor, P.B. (eds.) Recommender Systems Handbook, pp. 677–702. Springer, US (2011)
6. Masthoff, J.: Group modeling: selecting a sequence of television items to suit a group of viewers. User Model. User-Adapt. Inter. **14**(1), 37–85 (2004)
7. Amer-Yahia, S., Roy, S.B., Chawla, A., Das, G., Yu, C.: Group recommendation: semantics and efficiency. PVLDB **2**(1), 754–765 (2009)
8. Kim, J.K., Kim, H.K., Oh, H.Y., Ryu, Y.U.: A group recommendation system for online communities. Int. J. Inf. Manage. **30**(3), 212–219 (2010)
9. Sánchez, L.Q., Recio-García, J.A., Díaz-Agudo, B., Jiménez-Díaz, G.: Social factors in group recommender systems. ACM TIST **4**(1), 8 (2013)
10. Debnath, S., Ganguly, N., Mitra, P.: Feature weighting in content based recommendation system using social network analysis. In: Huai, J., Chen, R., Hon, H.W., Liu, Y., Ma, W.Y., Tomkins, A., Zhang, X., (eds.) WWW, pp. 1041–1042. ACM (2008)
11. Wikipedia: Tf-idf. https://en.wikipedia.org/wiki/Tf
12. He, J., Chu, W.W.: A social network-based recommender system (SNRS). In: Memon, N., Xu, J.J., Hicks, D.L., Chen, H. (eds.) Data Mining for Social Network Data. Annals of Information Systems, vol. 12, pp. 47–74. Springer, US (2010)

Context-Based Traffic Recommendation System

Khac-Hoai Nam Bui[1], Xuan Hau Pham[2(✉)], Jason J. Jung[1(✉)], O-Joun Lee[1], and Min-Sung Hong[1]

[1] Chung-Ang University, Dongjak-gu, Seoul, Korea
hoainam.bk2012@gmail.com, j2jung@gmail.com, concerto9203@gmail.com,
minsung.holdtime@gmail.com
[2] QuangBinh University, Dong Hoi, Quang Binh, Vietnam
pxhauqbu@gmail.com

Abstract. In this paper, we propose a new traffic system recommendation based on support real-time flows in highly unpredictable sensor network environments. The approach system is real-time recommendation system which meet various demands of users. The proposed algorithm include two phases. First phase is proposed to deal with the real-time problem. By this way, the drivers are able to transfer on the way with the shortest-time. For second phase, a research algorithm based on Depth First Search (DFS) algorithm will recommend the paths which meet demands of drivers based their context such as the paths with include the famous landscapes or the paths where they can find out good restaurants for their break while driving.

Keywords: Recommendation system · Sensor network · DFS algorithm

1 Introduction

With growth rate of world population, vehicular traffic is also increasing tremendously, especially in urban areas. This result affects directly to economies, human health, and environment because of huge traffic congestion. An effective solution is necessary to deal with this vehicular traffic problem. Wireless sensor network (WSN) based intelligent transportation systems (ITS) have emerged as an effective technology for management vehicular traffic since their low cost, flexibility of deployment and ease to maintains. There have been many studies on WSN technology to improve the circulation of vehicles. In [1], it has provided an innovative Wireless Sensor Network for traffic safety measurements. Liang [2] has used WSN to detect traffic flow. The simulation shows that the sensor nodes provide average detection rate of above 90 percent. On other hands, some papers focus on using sensor to monitor vehicular traffic. In [3], Li, X. et al. indicate that Vehicle-based sensor can be used for traffic monitoring. The performance evaluation shows that traffic congestion will be reduced.

Recommendation System is proposed as one of the effective solutions for traffic management. Recommendation systems are a subclass of information filtering system that seek to predict the 'rating' or 'preference' that a user would give to an item [4]. It has become extremely common in recent years, and are

© ICST Institute for Computer Sciences, Social Informatics and Telecommunications Engineering 2016
P.C. Vinh and V. Alagar (Eds.): ICCASA 2015, LNICST 165, pp. 122–131, 2016.
DOI: 10.1007/978-3-319-29236-6_13

applied in a variety of applications. The most popular ones are probably movies, music, news, books, research articles, search queries, social tags, and products in general... In [5], Phanich et al. introduced a Food Recommendation System (FRS) which recommend the proper substituted foods in the context of nutrition and food characteristic. For the music application, Soo-Hyun et al. in [6] proposed a new recommendation system for public places based on sensor network, the system will play a music which best matches the current situation such as the number of people, season, weather and time in public places. Otherwise, there have been some studies using recommendation system to deal with traffic problem. Wang, H. et al. in [7] developed a real-time route recommendation system. They indicated that using route recommendation system can not help control traffic jam since it always recommend the same route for users while traffic flow are always changing. Recommendation Systems are designed broadly in tourism. Long, L. et al. in [8] is also proposed a novel recommendation system to provide self-drive tourist with real-time personalized route recommendation. Meehan et al. in [9] proposed context-aware intelligent recommendation system for tourism, their system is a hybrid based recommendation approach made up of collaborative filtering, content based recommendation and demographic profiling. Otherwise, Patcharee and Anongnart in [10] presented the personalized recommendation system for e-tourism by using statistic technique base on Bayes Theorem to analyze user behaviors and recommend trips to specific users.

In this paper, we propose a traffic recommendation system based on wireless sensor network for users who want to find out a suitable path to theirs destination. There have been some studies using recommendation system for traffic traveling problem, but they do not focus on traffic congestion. In this paper, the approach system is a real-time system, this thing not only recommend for users the paths to save their time but also meet theirs demand at that time since drivers are not always want to find a short-path, sometimes they want to enjoy theirs travel during driving. The proposed recommendation system works based on contexts of vehicular traffic. In this paper, we assume the context that the drivers on the road network usually prefer to transfer on the paths with the shortest-time, famous landscapes and good restaurants... The approach system will recommend the paths which include the most place names with taking as little time as possible for users.

The main contributions of this paper include: (1) The proposed system based on wireless sensor network which are flexible deployment and ease to management. (2) Since the proposed system is a real-time system, it is able to control traffic jam as well as recommend for users the best routes. (3) The proposed system is not only provide for users the shortest-time paths to save their time but also recommend for them the suitable paths to make their routes become more interesting based on their favorite. The remaining parts of this paper are organized as follows. In Sect. 2, The system architecture of the proposed system is presented. The detailed algorithms of the approach system are proposed in Sect. 3. We make a discussion by give out an example to evaluate the effectiveness of our system in Sect. 4. Finally, we conclude this paper as well as point out some problems for future work in the last section.

2   System Architecture

This section describes the architecture of proposed traffic recommendation system based on wireless sensor network. The architecture of system is shown in the Fig. 1. As shown in the figure, the proposed system includes Road Network which created by many nodes and edges between nodes in the map, a Host Server analysis information and recommend lists for users. The process of proposed system works as follows: User will send request to Host Server, and then Host Server collects information from the request of user and data of Road Map to analysis and return back a suitable recommendation list to user.

Road Network consists sensor nodes which located in cars and sensor nodes which located fixedly in the public places where people coming and going frequently. As shown in Fig. 2, Road Network consists nodes which presented as sensor nodes and edges which are distance between two nodes. The sensor nodes can be located in public places which up to the specification geography of each areas, they may be located in popular places such as place names or famous restaurants... and they all are managed by Host Server. When user send request, sensor node which located in car transmit sensed information (the destination, the latitude and longitude of the car..), sink node collects and transmit sensed information to Host Server. By this way, Host Server collects all sensed information to find out the suitable paths by proposed recommendation algorithms.

The proposed algorithm is real-time recommendation system, it can be solved the problem which finding the shortest path between nodes. Since traffic flow is always changed every time, the shortest distance sometimes is not the shortest time, it is up to the traffic congestion at that time. The system will recommend the shortest time for user based on their speed and distance from source to

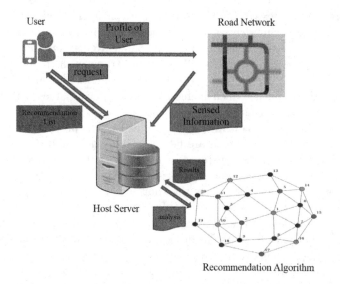

Fig. 1. System architecture

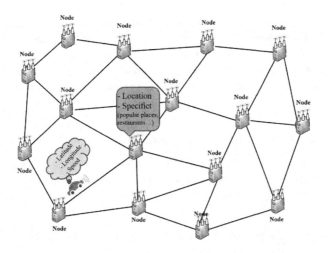

Fig. 2. Road network

destination of user. Moreover, drivers sometimes do not want to the shortest time paths. In some cases, they like to drive on the path which include famous landscapes or they want to enjoy their meal in a good restaurant for their break during driving. The proposed algorithm will recommend the suitable path based on the context of traffic network. Since the road network is developed based on sensor network, we can see the sensor network structure as the graph structure which the vertexes are nodes, the edges are the links of two neighboring nodes. By this way, the recommendation algorithm is transform to graph coloring algorithm. Detail of the proposed algorithm will be introduced in next section.

3   The Proposed Algorithm for Context-Based Traffic Recommendation System

To solve with the approach problem, the proposed system is divided into two phases. First phase is proposed to estimate the time to drive between two nodes to deal with real-time problem. Second phase is the recommendation algorithm to recommend the paths from source to destination which meet user's demands based on their context.

3.1   Phase 1: Estimate the Time Between Two Nodes

Since traffic flow is always changing, the shortest distance is not mean we can reach the destination with shortest time. By this way, in first phase, we estimate the time to transfer between nodes. The time to move from node A to node B (in case there is an edge between Node A and Node B) can be calculated as:

$$t_{A,B} = \frac{s_{A,B}}{v_{A,B}} \tag{1}$$

in Eq. (1), s is the distance between node A and node B, v is the average speed of vehicular traffic transferring on the way from node A to node B at that time. Thus, we are able to estimate the total time that the drivers need to take from source to destination for their route. It is noticeable that if the traffic flow is high, the average speed of vehicles will be low, so it takes more time to transfer from node A to node B.

3.2 Phase 2: Recommendation Algorithm

In this phase, we propose the algorithm to recommend the suitable paths for users. The outputs are different based on the contexts of vehicular traffic on the road network.

Data: Source S; Destination D, Adjacency Matrix A, Set of Node N.
Result: Set of Paths P from S to D
initialization;
if $S==D$ **then**
| Print Path (P[S]); // Print out the path from S to D
else
  marked S; // marked the Node S we already passed
  for *each U of set N* **do**
    if $U \in A_S$ **then**
      if *U is not marked* **then**
        marked U;
        Put U in P; //get node U in the path
        Recall DFS(U,A,D); // recursion method
        Unmarked U; //unmarked for Node U
        Put U out P;
      end
    end
  end
end

Algorithm 1. Search Algorithm

The process of the proposed algorithm is given as follows: (1) first, we transform the system model into undirected graph G(N,E) with N is set of Nodes and E is set of Edges between neighboring nodes. The weigh of edge between two neighboring nodes is the time that we computed in Eq. (1). (2) in second step, we based on Depth-First Search (DFS) algorithm to find out the paths from Source S to Destination D as shown in Algorithm 1, A is Adjacency Matrix of network which are computed based on sensed information from sensor nodes. (3) the system will collect and analysis information from results of Phase 1 and Algorithm 1 to compute and synthesize the paths as much as possible from Source to Destination of user (detail in Algorithm 2). (4) Based on context of users, the system will return back the recommendation list of paths for user (Algorithm 3).

Data: Set of Paths P from S to D
Set of Time T between 2 node
R, L the set of specific of Nodes
Result: List Data of Paths P
initialization;
Rr[]; Ll[];
for *each p of P* **do**
 | **for** *each V of p* **do**
  | | Totaltime = TV + TV+1 ; **if** $V \in R$ **then**
  | | | put $V \in Rr$;
  | | **else**
  | | | **if** $V \in L$ **then**
  | | | | Put $V \in Ll$;
  | | | **end**
  | | **end**
 | **end**
end

Algorithm 2. The data of paths from Source to Destination

Data: Set of Paths P from S to D
Set of Time T between 2 node
t,r,l are contexts of users
Result: List Data of Paths P
initialization;
for *each path p of paths P* **do**
 | **if** $p \in t$ **then**
  | | **if** $p \in r$ **then**
  | | | **if** $p \in l$ **then**
  | | | | print(p);
  | | | **end**
  | | **end**
 | **end**
end

Algorithm 3. Recommendation algorithms

4 Discussion

To estimate the effectiveness of the proposed system, we give an example for our recommendation system. The system parameters are shown in Fig. 3. For instance, the distance between Node 1 and Node 2 is 7 km, and the car transfers on this way with speed 40 km/h at that time. To estimate correctly, we assume at least one taxi driving between nodes at that time (in case more taxi driving in the same route, we will compute by their averaged speed).

By get information from taxi driving reports, we are able to compute the time to transfer among nodes (1,2,3,4....11) based on their speed and distance between nodes as shown in Fig. 4. Notice that these traffic information has few minutes delay, we treat these information as the approximate real-time traffic condition.

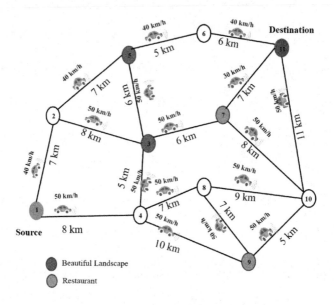

Fig. 3. System model for example

Node	1	2	3	4	5	6	7	8	9	10	11
1	0	0.18	0	0.16	0	0	0	0	0	0	0
2	0.18	0	0,18	0	0,16	0	0	0	0	0	0
3	0	0.16	0	0.1	0.18	0	0.12	0	0	0	0
4	0	0	0.1	0	0	0	0	0.14	0.2	0	0
5	0,16	0.18	0	0	0	0.13	0	0	0	0	0
6	0	0	0.12	0	0.13	0	0	0	0	0	0.15
7	0	0	0.12	0	0	0	0	0	0	0.16	0.2
8	0	0	0	0.14	0	0	0	0	0.14	0.18	0
9	0	0	0	0.2	0	0	0	0.14	0	0.1	0
10	0	0	0	0	0	0	0.16	0.18	0.1	0	0.22
11	0	0	0	0	0	0.15	0.2	0	0	0.22	0

Fig. 4. Example: estimate the time (h) between neighboring nodes

After using phase 1, search algorithm will find out as much as possible the paths from source to destination as well as their data as shown in Table 1. It is up to the context of users, the Recommendation List shows the suitable paths to recommend for users. In this paper, we assume the contexts of users are the shortest-time driving, the famous landscapes and the restaurants.

Table 1. Example: the data of paths from source to destination

Path	Total time	Famous Landscapes	Restaurants
1-2-3-4-8-9-10-7-11	1.2086	3	7;9
1-2-3-4-8-9-10-11	1.035	3	7
1-2-3-4-8-10-7-11	1.128	3	7
1-2-3-4-9-8-10-7-11	1.108	3	7;9
1-2-3-4-9-10-7-11	0.935	3	7;9
1-2-3-5-6-11	0.73	3;5	
1-2-3-7-10-11	0.835	3	7
1-2-3-7-11	0.688	3	7
1-2-5-3-4-8-9-10-7-11	1.343	3;5	7;9
1-2-5-3-4-8-9-10-11	1.17	3	9
1-2-5-3-4-8-10-7-11	1.238	3	7
1-2-5-3-4-9-8-10-7-11	1.483	3;5	7;9
1-2-5-3-4-9-10-7-11	1.263	3;5	7;9
1-2-5-3-4-9-10-11	1.09	3;5	9
1-2-5-3-7-10-11	0.97	3;5	7
1-2-5-3-7-11	0.823	3;5	7
1-2-5-6-11	0.625	5	
1-4-3-2-5-6-11	0.87	3;5	
1-4-3-5-6-11	0.655	3;5	
1-4-3-7-10-11	0.76	3	7
1-4-3-7-11	0.613	3	7
1-4-8-9-10-7-3-2-5-6-11	1.43	3;5	7;9
1-4-8-9-10-7-3-5-6-11	1.195	3;5	7;9
1-4-8-9-10-7-11	0.933		7;9
1-4-8-9-10-11	0.76		4;9
1-4-8-9-10-11	0.76		4;9
1-4-8-10-7-3-2-5-6-11	1.37	3;5	7
1-4-8-10-7-3-5-6-11	1.155	3;5	7;9
1-4-8-10-7-11	0.873		7
1-4-8-10-11	0.7		
1-4-9-8-10-7-3-2-5-6-11	1.57	3;5	7;9
1-4-9-8-10-7-3-5-6-11	1.355	3;5	7;9
1-4-9-8-10-7-11	0.993		7;9
1-4-9-8-10-11	0.82		9
1-4-9-10-7-3-2-5-6-11	1.35	3;5	7;9
1-4-9-10-7-3-5-6-11	1.135	3;5	7;9
1-4-9-10-7-11	0.853		7;9
1-4-9-10-11	0.68		9

Table 2. Example: recommendation list for user

Route	Path	Total time (h)	Distance (km)
1	1-4-3-7-11	0.613	26
2	1-2-5-6-11	0.625	25
3	1-4-3-5-6-11	0.655	30
4	1-4-9-10-11	0.68	34
5	1-4-9-10-7-11	0.853	38

As result which is showed in Table 2, the system will recommend a list of paths which based on the context of users transferring in the road network. For instance, the routes are the path with the shortest-time, the paths obtain place names such as landscapes and restaurants with short-time driving, respectively.

5   Conclusion and Future Work

Recent years, the flow traffic problem become more serious because of the potential growth of vehicles. In this paper, we introduce a context-based traffic real-time recommendation system based on wireless sensor network. First, we estimates the real-time of user which is able to take for their route. Then, we recommend for user the recommend list paths which suitable for their demands by using graph coloring algorithm. This system will bring more benefit for user since it is not only recommend the paths which saving their time, but also introduce the paths which meets their specific preferences.

In this study, we give an example to estimate the effective of the proposed system. The implementation as an experiment environment and evaluated through real participants are considered as future work. Moreover, the context of users could be added more information such as weather, period to recommend more effective to users.

Acknowledgement. This work was supported by the National Research Foundation of Korea (NRF) grant funded by the Korea government (MSIP) (NRF-2014R1A2A2A05007154). Also, this research was supported by the MSIP Ministry of Science, ICT and Future Planning), Korea, under the ITRC(Information Technology Research Center) support program (IITP-2015-H8501-15-1018) supervised by the IITP(Institute for Information and communications Technology Promotion).

References

1. Daponte, P., De Vito, L., Picariello, F., Rapuano, S., Tudosa, I.: Wireless sensor network for traffic safety. In: 2012 IEEE Workshop on Environmental Energy and Structural Monitoring Systems (EESMS), pp. 42–49. IEEE, Perugia (2012)
2. Liang, B.J.: Traffic flow detection based on wireless sensor network. J. Netw. 8(8), 1859–1865 (2013)

3. Li, X., Shu, W., Li, M.L., Huang, H.Y., Luo, P.E., Wu, M.Y.: Performance evaluation of vehicle-based mobile sensor networks for traffic monitoring. In: IEEE Transactions on Environmental Energy and Structural Monitoring Systems (EESMS), 2012 IEEE Workshop, vol. 58, no. 4, pp. 1647–1653. IEEE (2009)

4. Francesco, R., Lior, R., Bracha, S.: Introduction to recommender systems handbook. In: Francesco, R., Lior, R., Bracha, S., Paul, B.K. (eds.) Recommender Systems Handbook, pp. 1–35. Springer, New York (2011)

5. Phanich, M., Pholkul, P., Phimoltares, S.: Food recommendation system using clustering analysis for diabetic patients. In: 2010 International Conference on Information Science and Applications (ICISA), pp. 1–8. IEEE, Seoul, April 2010

6. Soo-Hyun, C., Young-Hak, K., Jae-Bum, P.: Music recommendation system for public places based on sensor network. IJCSNS Int. J. Comput. Sci. Netw. Secur. 7(8), 172–180 (2007)

7. Wang, H., Li, G.L., Hu, H.Q., Chen, S., Shen, B.W., Wu, H., Li, W.S., Tan, K.L.: R3: a real-time route recommendation system. In: 40th International Conference on Very Large Data Bases, pp. 1549–1552. IEEE, Hangzhou (2014)

8. Liu, L., Xu, J., Liao, S.S., Chen, H.: A real-time personalized route recommendation system for self-drive tourists based on vehicle to vehicle communication. J. Expert Syst. Appl. 41(7), 3409–3417 (2014)

9. Meehan, K., Lunney, T., Curran, K., McCaughey, A.: Context-aware intelligent recommendation system for tourism. In: Pervasive Computing and Communications Workshops, pp. 328–331. IEEE, San Diego (2013)

10. Patcharee, S., Anongnart, S.: Personalized Trip Information for E-Tourism Recommendation System Based on Bayes Theorem. Research and Practical Issues of Enterprise Information Systems II, vol. 255, pp. 1271–1275. Springer, New York (2008)

User Timeline and Interest-Based Collaborative Filtering on Social Network

Xuan Hau Pham[1], Jason J. Jung[2(✉)], Bui Khac Hoai Nam[2],
and Tuong Tri Nguyen[3]

[1] Department of Engineering, QuangBinh University, Dong Hoi, Vietnam
pxhauqbu@gmail.com
[2] Department of Computer Engineering, ChungAng University, Seoul, South Korea
j2jung@gmail.com, hoainam.bk2012@gmail.com
[3] Department of Computer Engineering, Yeungnam University, Gyeongsan-si, Korea
tuongtringuyen@gmail.com

Abstract. A lot of users and large amount of information have been posted and shared through on-line systems. User timeline and interest are important features on recommendation systems (e.g., user likes watching action movies in the morning, and likes watching drama movies in the afternoon however he/she likes watching thriller movies in the evening) and also on social network. There are some recommendation applications have been developed on social network to support users selecting what kind of wanted items based on user timeline and interest. However, there is not any approaches based on user timeline and interest have been proposed that user interest have been separated into partitions of user interest. Thus, a recommendation mechanism will be applied on social networks based on extracting user timeline and user interest that is necessary. In this paper, we propose a new approach that user interest will be determined on a set of time partitions.

Keywords: Recommendation systems · Context · User timeline · User interest

1 Introduction

Nowadays, social networking sites (SNS) are good choice to post and share what on their mind is, what they did or their plan to group, community and the world. The data on SNS is growing rapidly as Big Data. There are many applications have been developed on SNS by using social metadata. Recommendation technique is being suitable approach for e-commercial systems. It helps users to overcome the overload information on the web. User is suggested related items that it predicts that they will be interested in. On the social network, these suggestions can be shared to other people who is in the group (e.g., friends, family) or community.

User context contains a set of particular situations that user interact with the system. Context-based recommendation is an approach to improve user satisfaction in particular context. Thus, the context extraction is an important task to

© ICST Institute for Computer Sciences, Social Informatics and Telecommunications Engineering 2016
P.C. Vinh and V. Alagar (Eds.): ICCASA 2015, LNICST 165, pp. 132–140, 2016.
DOI: 10.1007/978-3-319-29236-6_14

understand user activities on the systems. In previous work, we have proposed a context-based recommendation approach based on social context. However, we did not mention about the partitions of time. We just considered time feature as watched history [1].

We consider the following table:

Table 1. User-item model

	Titanic	Ghost rider	Apollo 13	Spider man	Frozen	Lion King
u_1	5	4		3		
u_2	5		3			
u_3				5	5	
u_4					5	4

Table 1 shows user-item model. In traditional collaborative filtering, we just measure the similarity between two users to find potential movies to recommend. However, if considering user watched history as timeline and time is separated into partitions. We have the table as follows:

Table 2. User model in partitions of day

	Morning	Afternoon	Evening
u_1	("Titanic", 5, t_{11})	("Spider man", 3, t_{12})	("Ghost rider", 4, t_{13})
u_2	("Apollo 13", 3, t_{21})		("Titanic", 5, t_{22})
u_3		("Frozen", 5, t_{31})	("Spider man", 5, t_{32})
u_4	("Frozen", 5, t_{41}), ("Lion King", 4, t_{42})		

Table 2 shows a description about user model in partition of day. The day is separated by three partitions, morning, afternoon and evening. Each partition shows a set of movies that each user watched, movie rating and watched time, respectively. Each movie is described by title, a list of genres, director, a list of actors and auxiliary information such as country, language, runtime, and so on. User can rate movie from 1 to 5. Watched time identifies time that user begin watching movie. Making the partition of time will measured by using this parameter. The table has 4 users u_1, u_2, u_3, u_4. In this example, user u_1 has watched three movies in his/her timeline. Based on watched time and partition of day, we separated them into partitions, "Titanic" in the morning, "Spider man" in the afternoon and "Ghost rider" in the evening. The key question is how to apply collaborative filtering in this scenario.

Extracting user interest in a particular context is very necessary for recommending a list of items that user may be interested in at any one moment. There are many approaches to construct user preference. However, user interest may be change over time. Thus, the capturing them is a challenge in recommendation systems. In order to face this problem, in this paper we propose a new approach to determine user interest over time. In our approach, user interest will be determined on a set of time partitions with a set of pair item attribute and value.

Therefore, we focus on two major tasks in this paper:

- Taking into account user interest in partitions of time
- Extending collaborative filtering approach based on them.

The outline of this paper is organized as follows. In Sect. 2, we represent related work. In Sect. 3, we discuss about user timeline and user interest features in social context and in recommendation systems and also present collaborative filtering recommendation approach based on integrated user interest and partition of time. Finally, in Sect. 4, we conclude our proposal and suggest future work.

2   Related Work

Context-based recommendation systems try to improve user interest in particular context [2–6]. The contextual information has been exploited and applied to improve the quality of recommendation systems and discussed by Adomavicius et al. [2]. In [3] they introduced a new context-aware recommendation approach. User profile has been splited into several possibly overlapping sub-profiles as micro-profiling. Each profile represents users in particular contexts. However, they have just focused on calculating the similarity based on user rating. A new approach recommendation systems has been proposed in [5]. Braunhofer et al. [6] has been proposed a new approach for recommendation task by selecting music suited for a place of interest by using emotional tags and developed a mobile application.

User profiling with temporal dynamics has been considered in this approach. Another time-based approach has been proposed in [4,7,8]. Xiang et al. [4] try to capture user preference over time. They focus on explicitly user profiling in long-term and short-term preferences by using implicit datasets. In [7], they proposed a new recommendation method based on time-framed user clustering and association mining.

There are a lot of applications have been developed and posted on social network including recommendation applications. A lot of users and large amount of information have been posted and shared through social networks. The applications will be relied on these information to understand user interest to make more better recommendation. In [9], they investigate the importance and usefulness of tag and time information for predicting users preference on social tagging systems. Abel et al. [10] compare many different strategies for user profiling of personalized recommendations in the social web based on the published Twitter messages and try to understand it changing over time. In [11], a statistical user interest models has been represented in social media.

3   User Timeline and Interest-Based Collaborative Filtering Recommendation Systems

In order to understand our approach, we denote as follows:

- U is a set of users
- I is a set of items
- A is a set of item attributes
- V is a set of attribute values
- R is a set of user ratings

Definition 1 (Recommendation Framework). *Recommendation framework on social network is defined as a tuple:*

$$S = \langle U, I, R, T \rangle$$

where, T is a timeline.

Definition 2 (Partition of Time). *Partition of time is defined as follows:*

$$P = \{(t_1, t_2) | \forall t_1, t_2 : (t_2 - t_1) \geq \lambda\}$$

In our approach, user timeline is separated into partitions of time, denoted P, for example, in Table 2, $P = \{(4 : 00AM, 12 : 00AM), (12 : 01PM, 20 : 00PM), (20 : 01PM, 3 : 59AM)\}$ and we can represent it as follows: $P = \{morning, afternoon, evening\}$. In order to easy represent our example, we denote: $p_1 \longleftarrow morning, p_2 \longleftarrow afternoon, p_3 \longleftarrow evening$. Figure 1 shows an illustration for partition of time.

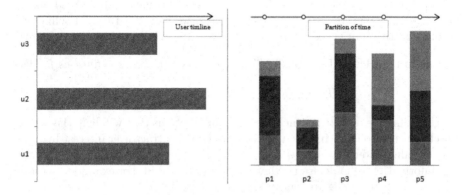

Fig. 1. Partition of time for three users

Depending on each time partition, we collect a set of items for each user on each partition. Each user partition contains a set of items that selected item time belongs to the same time partition.

Definition 3 (Partition of User). *Given user u, the partition of user is defined as follows:*

$$P_u = \{(i, r, t)_p | \forall p \in P, i \in I, r \in R : t \in T\}$$

As Table 2, u_1 watched three movies, each movie is in one partition. We have:
$P_{u_1} = \{(\text{"Titanic"}, 5, t_{11})_{p_1}, (\text{"Spider man"}, 3, t_{12})_{p_2}, (\text{"Ghost rider"}, 4, t_{13})_{p_3}\}$

Therefore, there is a set of items on partition p for all users will expressed as follows:

$$p = \{(u, i, r) | \forall u \in U, i \in I, r \in R : i \in p_u\}$$

For example, in Table 2, we have:

$p_1 = \{(u_1, \text{"Titanic"}, 5), (u_2, \text{"Apollo 13"}, 3), (u_4, \text{"Frozen"}, 5), (u_4, \text{"Lion King"}, 4)\}$

$p_2 = \{(u_1, \text{"Spider man"}, 3), (u_3, \text{"Frozen"}, 5)\}$

$p_3 = \{(u_1, \text{"Ghost rider"}, 4), (u_2, \text{"Titanic"}, 5), (u_3, \text{"Spider man"}, 5)\}$

3.1 User Timeline and User Interest

In the both social network and recommendation systems usually contain important features, user timeline and user interest. Timeline feature is a collection user interactions that is organized the following time feature. It is counted from first login to system to now. It contains a set of time intervals including user contents. For example, on Facebook, user timeline is grouped by year. We can see a set of user events via month highlight. It expresses a lot of related information in that month such as number of friends, number of photos and a list of posted events. Another example on recommendation system as Facebook application is proposed in [1], called my movie history. User timeline is represented one by one for each movie. However, in this approach, we have not taken timeline into account partition of times (i.e., time windows) and integrated interest of user.

Definition 4 (User Timeline). *Timeline of user u, T_u, is defined as follows:*

$$T_u = \{t | t \in T : t_1 < t_2, \forall t_1, t_2 \in T\}$$

User timeline establishes including user interactions that will help the system to refine user profiling. In this approach, we try to extract user interest by using pair of values, item attributes and attribute values. Item description contains rich information to understand what user is interested in. For example, a certain user has high watching frequency on "Steven Spielberg" movies in movie recommendation systems then we can predict that this user want to watch action movies and be directed by this director. Thus, genre (e.g., action) and director (e.g., Steven Spielberg) are dominant item attributes including values in this case, respectively.

Definition 5 (User Interest). *User interest is a representation of dominant values based on a set of item attributes and values. It is defined as follows:*

$$UI = \{(a, v, p) | a \in A, v \in V, p \in P : (a, v) \in Dom(u, I_u)\}$$

where, $Dom(u, I_u)$ is a function to find out which dominant values.

In this paper, user interest will be determined with partitions of time (e.i.,time windows). The size of partition is defined depending on user context. The Algorithm 1 shows process to extract the partition of user.

Algorithm 1. Extracting partition of user

$T = $ user timeline
read λ
$P_u \leftarrow \emptyset$
$P \leftarrow Partition(\lambda)$
for all $t \in T$ **do**
    $t_1 \leftarrow t$
    if $(t - t_1) \leq \lambda$ **then**
        $p \leftarrow (t_1, t)$
        if $p \notin P$ **then**
            $P \leftarrow P \cup p$
        end if
        $P_u \leftarrow P_u \cup (i, r, t)_p$
    end if
end for
return P_u

3.2 Collaborative Filtering Approach

In this section, we will explain our approach based on user timeline and user interest. In traditional collaborative filtering, the similarity between two users is computed based on entire items of two users to make recommendation at current time. However, the similarity on period of time may be different in some cases. Thus, the accurately predicted results is not closed to user interest. In order to apply collaborative filtering method to our model, we have to measure similarity between two users based on partitions of user including user interest.

Definition 6 (User Similarity). *Given two users u_1, u_2, a set of partitions P and user interest UI, the similarity between two users is computed as follows:*

$$sim(u_1, u_2) = \frac{\sum\limits_{p \in P} sim(u_1, u_2)_p}{card(P)} \tag{1}$$

where,

$$sim(u_1, u_2)_p = \frac{\sum\limits_{v \in V_{u_1 u_2}} card(v_{u_1}) card(v_{u_2})}{\sqrt{\sum\limits_{v \in V_{u_1 u_2}} card(v_{u_1})} \sqrt{\sum\limits_{v \in V_{u_1 u_2}} card(v_{u_2})}} \quad (2)$$

Depending on density of selected items of users, we separate in many different time such as day (e.g., morning, afternoon,evening), month (e.g., weeks), year (e.g., seasons). The current time will consider to decide which is the best choice for final recommendation results. For example, we consider the similarity between two users on their time, $sim(u_1, u_2) = 0.85$, $sim(u_1, u_3) = 0.6$, it means that they have the high similarity. However, if we consider them in certain partition of time (current time belongs to this partition), denoted p, we have: $sim(u_1, u_2)_p = 0.2$, $sim(u_1, u_3)_p = 0.8$. It leads to the final recommendation results are different and not accurate.

The similarity is computed based on frequency of attribute values on a set of items that users have already selected. The value vectors will be defined to compute the similarity. We have the partition of user algorithm based on a set of partitions for each user in Algorithm 1. Next, we present our algorithm of collaborative filtering method.

Algorithm 2. User timeline and interest-based collaborative filtering

---

$User\ u_1$
$Extracting\ P_{u_1}$
$Dom(u_1, I_{u_1})_{P_{u_1}}$
for all $u_2 \in U$ **do**
   $Extracting\ P_{u_2}$
   $Dom(u_2, I_{u_2})_{P_{u_2}}$
   for all $p \in P_{u_1, u_2}$ **do**
     $Sim(u_1, u_2)_{p_{u_1, u_2}}$
   end for
   $Sim(u_1, u_2)$
end for
$L \leftarrow Rec(u, I')$
return L

In this approach, the number of computed similarities among users will be decreased. Instead of computation all candidates, we will focus on the partition that current time belongs to.

4   Concluding Remarks

Context-based recommendation systems is an approach for dynamic scenario recommendation to bring more satisfied to users. There are many context features in recommendation systems and social networks. In this paper, we have focused on partitioning user timeline and user interest. User interest is considered with time feature in each partition. In this approach, a user interest model on partitions of time have been built based on a set of attribute values and dominant values. An collaborative filtering recommendation algorithm has been proposed to find out a set of items for recommendation.

In future work, we will present our experimental results by using our collected data and datasets [12] and our dataset. Also we have comparison with other approaches.

Acknowledgment. This research is funded by QuangBinh University. This work was supported by the National Research Foundation of Korea (NRF) grant funded by the Korea government (MSIP) (NRF-2014R1A2A2A05007154). Also, this research was supported by the MSIP(Ministry of Science, ICT and Future Planning), Korea, under the ITRC(Information Technology Research Center) support program (IITP-2015-H8501-15-1018) supervised by the IITP(Institute for Information &communications Technology Promotion).

References

1. Pham, X.H., Jung, J.J., Vu, L.A., Park, S.B.: Exploiting social contexts for movie recommendation. Malaysian J. Comput. Sci. **27**(2), 138–155 (2014)
2. Adomavicius, G., Tuzhilin, A.: Context-aware recommender systems. In: Ricci, F., Rokach, L., Shapira, B., Kantor, P.B. (eds.) Recommender Systems Handbook, pp. 217–253. Springer, New York (2011)
3. Baltrunas, L., Amatriain, X.: Towards time-dependant recommendation based on implicit feedback. In: Proceedings of the Workshop on Context-Aware Systems (CARS-2009) (2009)
4. Xiang, L., Yuan, Q., Zhao, S., Chen, L., Zhang, X., Yang, Q., Sun, J.: Temporal recommendation on graphs via long-and short-term preference fusion. In: Proceedings of the 16th ACM SIGKDD International Conference on Knowledge Discovery and Data Mining, pp. 723–732. ACM (2010)
5. Koren, Y.: Collaborative filtering with temporal dynamics. Commun. ACM **53**(4), 89–97 (2010)
6. Braunhofer, M., Kaminskas, M., Ricci, F.: Recommending music for places of interest in a mobile travel guide. In: Proceedings of the Fifth ACM Conference on Recommender Systems, RecSys 2011, pp. 253–256. ACM, New York, NY, USA (2011)
7. Wang, F.H., Shao, H.M.: Effective personalized recommendation based on time-framed navigation clustering and association mining. Expert Syst. Appl. **27**(3), 365–377 (2004)
8. Lauw, H.W., Lim, E.P., Pang, H., Tan, T.T.: Social network discovery by mining spatio-temporal events. Comput. Math.Organ. Theory **11**(2), 97–118 (2005)
9. Zheng, N., Li, Q.: A recommender system based on tag and time information for social tagging systems. Expert Syst. Appl. **38**(4), 4575–4587 (2011)
10. Abel, F., Gao, Q., Houben, G.J., Tao, K.: Analyzing temporal dynamics in twitter profiles for personalized recommendations in the social web. In: Proceedings of the 3rd International Web Science Conference, p. 2. ACM (2011)

11. Tang, X., Yang, C.C.: Tut: a statistical model for detecting trends, topics and user interests in social media. In: Proceedings of the 21st ACM International Conference on Information and Knowledge Management, pp. 972–981. ACM (2012)
12. Lewis, K., Kaufman, J., Gonzalez, M., Wimmer, A., Christakis, N.: Tastes, ties, and time: a new social network dataset using facebook. com. Social Netw. **30**(4), 330–342 (2008)

Community Centrality-Based Greedy Approach for Identifying Top-K Influencers in Social Networks

Bundit Manaskasemsak$^{(\boxtimes)}$, Nattawut Dejkajonwuth, and Arnon Rungsawang

Massive Information and Knowledge Engineering Laboratory,
Department of Computer Engineering, Faculty of Engineering,
Kasetsart University, Bangkok 10900, Thailand
{un,arnon}@mikelab.net, nattawut.d@ku.th

Abstract. Online social network today is an effective media to share and disperse tons of information, especially for advertizing and marketing. However, with limited budgets, commercial companies make hard efforts to determine a set of source persons who can highly diffuse information of their products, implying that more benefits will be received. In this paper, we propose an algorithm, called community centrality-based greedy algorithm, for the problem of finding top-k influencers in social networks. The algorithm is composed of four main processes. First, a social network is partitioned into communities using the Markov clustering algorithm. Second, nodes with highest centrality values are extracted from each community. Third, some communities are combined; and last, top-k influencers are determined from a set of highest centrality nodes based on the independent cascade model. We conduct experiments on a publicly available Higgs Twitter dataset. Experimental results show that the proposed algorithm executes much faster than the state-of-the-art greedy one, while still maximized nearly the same influence spread.

Keywords: Social network · Community detection · Node centrality · Influence maximization · Influencer

1 Introduction

During the past decade, social network has played an important role as a virtual community where people with common interests can connect to share information, ideas, or even their thoughts. Though this network, commercial companies can gain a lot of benefit by a mechanism of spreading information about their products (or services) from one person to others, called *word-of-mouth* marketing. However, with the limited budget (say, k pieces of the sample product), the companies need to make an attempt to determine a set of source persons who can diffuse information to their friends in a social network as many as possible, so that the number of persons adopting the product is maximized. This effort has been introduced as the *influence maximization* problem [5], and those source persons are called the *influencers*.

© ICST Institute for Computer Sciences, Social Informatics and Telecommunications Engineering 2016
P.C. Vinh and V. Alagar (Eds.): ICCASA 2015, LNICST 165, pp. 141–150, 2016.
DOI: 10.1007/978-3-319-29236-6_15

To simulate the mechanism of influence propagation, two models are formally introduced according to a stochastic cascade model [8], named the *independent cascade model* (ICM) and the *linear threshold model* (LTM). Since a social network, by nature, is very large, developing an efficient algorithm to find top-k influencers is not trivial. Kempe *et al.* [8] have proven that the optimization of influence maximization is NP-Hard. They then suggest applying the greedy approach and have shown that the optimal solution can be approximated. However, their algorithm still takes much time. Recent studies have been proposed algorithms for efficiently maximizing influence in several ways, for instance, by enhancing the naive greedy version [1,11], by employing the centrality heuristics [1,2,9], and by applying graph clustering or community-based detection [3,6,10,12].

In this paper, we propose an algorithm applying community detection technique (i.e., the Markov clustering [14]) before determining top-k influential nodes in social networks. The key contributions of our approach are as follows.

- We define a social network as a *weighted* directed graph constructed from a combination of topological graph (i.e., relationship such as friendship in case of Facebook or following in case of Twitter) and interaction one (e.g., wall posting, user tagging, commenting, liking, and sharing in case of Facebook; or tweeting, mentioning, replying, favoriting, and retweeting in case of Twitter). The difference from other community-based approaches is that those existing ones concentrate on the former type of graph only.
- We employ various *node centrality* heuristics: in-degree, out-degree, betweenness, and closeness, in the analysis.

The remainder of this paper is organized as follows. Section 2 briefly mentions to some studies related to ours. Section 3 details the proposed community centrality-based greedy algorithm. Section 4 reports performance evaluation. Finally, Sect. 5 concludes the paper.

2   Related Work

Motivated by marketing applications, the influence maximization problem in social networks is first investigated by Domingos and Richardson [5]. Later, Kempe *et al.* [8] formulate it as a discrete optimization problem. They show that the optimal solution is NP-hard, and present a greedy algorithm (GA) that guarantees the influence spread within $(1 - \frac{1}{e})$ of the optimal solution. However, their algorithm is very slow in practice and not scalable with the network size. Leskovec *et al.* [11] and Goyal *et al.* [7] propose *CELF* and *CELF++* algorithms, respectively. Both are relied on the lazy-forward optimization that uses the submodularity property to reduce the number of evaluations on the influence spread of nodes. Although the algorithms significantly speed up the greedy, they still cannot scale to very large networks. Chen *et al.* [1] propose two faster greedy-based algorithms: *NewGreedy* and *MixedGreedy*. The main idea behind the former is to reduce the original social graph into a smaller one by removing edges that tend to have no contribution on information propagation, while the latter is a combination of *NewGreedy* and *CELF*. That is, its iterative computation employs *NewGreedy* at the first round and *CELF* for the rest rounds.

Centrality heuristics also have been proven to be an efficient alternative for maximizing influence spread in social networks. The most classic approach is the degree centrality heuristic [16]. The key concept is that a user having a lot of connections (i.e., friends) tends to highly influence others and thus should be selected as an influential candidate seed. Based on such intuition, the degree centrality heuristic selects k nodes that have the highest degree. Chen *et al.* [1] propose the degree discount heuristic based on general idea that if one node is considered as seed, then the links connecting with the node will not be counted as a degree of the other nodes. Thus, when considering the next influential node, a node with the highest degree after the discount is selected as a member of the seed set. This procedure will be repeated until the first k highest degree seeds are selected. Lastly, Chen *et al.* [2] use the eigenvector centrality heuristic to select influential nodes based on their PageRank value [13]. That is, when a social network is represented as a transitional matrix, a PageRank value for each node is first calculated. Then, the k nodes with the highest PageRank values are selected as seeds.

Recently, community-based greedy approaches are introduced in several studies; but, we will mention to some of them here. Most algorithms formally consist of two phases: a graph partitioning and an influence examining on each partition. Wang *et al.* [15] propose the community-based greedy algorithm (*CGA*) which first detects communities in a social network by taking into account information diffusion. Then, top-k influential nodes are selected and examined from those communities using a dynamic programming to speed up the computation. Kim *et al.* [10] propose the variations of a Markov clustering-based algorithm that first partition a network and consider most k influential candidates in those communities. Afterwards, an attractor identification procedure is performed again to find the influencers. Similar to their work, based on the community structure of the network, our community centrality-based greedy algorithm proposed in this paper also employs the Markov clustering. However, the main differences are that (1) top-k candidates are selected from each community using several node centrality heuristics, and (2) a community combination is performed by grouping some very small and dispersed communities to produce more proper ones.

3   Community Centrality-Based Greedy Algorithm

Given a social data—Twitter in our case study, the network is represented by a weighted directed graph $\mathcal{G} = (\mathcal{V}, \mathcal{E}, \mathcal{W})$, where $\mathcal{V}$ is a set of nodes, denoted individuals. $\mathcal{E}$ is a set of edges, referred to reverse direction of followings, identical direction of interactions, or both; for example, if a person v has followed a person u, then an edge $e(u, v)$ is defined. $\mathcal{W}$ is a set of normalized weights assigned on each edge, determined by both topological structure and interactions. Let r_{uv} be a topological indicator, assigned to either 1 if v has followed u, or 0 otherwise;

and let i_{uv} be the number of interactions that u has acted to v. Then, a weight w_{uv} assigned on $e(u, v)$ is defined as:

$$w_{uv} = \omega \frac{r_{uv}}{\sum_{\forall x \in \mathcal{V}} r_{xv}} + (1 - \omega) \frac{i_{uv}}{\sum_{\forall x \in \mathcal{V}} i_{ux}},$$

where ω is a pre-defined coefficient determining the effect of topological graph and interaction one. For example, suppose that a person v has followed three persons, including u; whereas the person u has two followers in total, i.e., v and x. If u has publicly tweeted thrice and also directly mentioned to v twice, implying that the actions from u may influence v and x with five and three attempts, respectively. Then, a weight value of $\omega(\frac{1}{3}) + (1 - \omega)(\frac{5}{5+3})$ is assigned on the edge $e(u, v)$. Note that, in our experiments, we simply set ω by a uniform value (i.e., 0.5).

First of all, an important concept employed in most greedy-based approaches for the independent cascade model is that a node u is said to influence a node v if the node u attempts to activate the node v so that v becomes active from inactive. This activation must be success at least $\mathcal{R}/2$ times out of $\mathcal{R}$ simulations of the diffusion process. In addition, the ability that the node u can influence the node v depends on the weight from u to v.

We now propose the community centrality-based greedy algorithm ($CCGA$). The algorithm workflow, depicted in Fig. 1, is composed of 4 main modules: community detection, centrality analysis, community combination, and influencer identification, respectively.

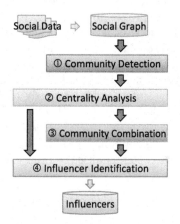

Fig. 1. The community centrality-based greedy workflow.

(1) *Community Detection:* The main idea of our method is to first partition a large network into communities, and then a number of influential candidates are examined from each community. Fortunately, most community detection algorithms rely on the intrinsic property of social networks, i.e., individuals grouped

together into a community will interact with each other more frequently than with those outside the community. So that, within a community, they are more likely to influence each other, in contrast to individuals across communities. This property suggests a good approximation task for choosing and examining influencers only within communities instead of the entire network, in order to reduce the computational time.

In *CCGA*, the original social network is partitioned based on the topological structure into several communities, referred to $\mathcal{C} = \{\mathcal{C}_1, \mathcal{C}_2, \ldots, \mathcal{C}_n\}$, using the Markov clustering [14]. Markov clustering (MCL) is an attractive algorithm adopted in many domains since it divides the network without requiring the number of communities as an input parameter. The algorithm assumes that there exist communities in a network, and takes a random walk approach to clustering. That is, a random walk through the network will result in longer time spent walking within a community, and less time spent traveling along edges joining two different communities. Thus, MCL uses such intuition and groups nodes whose random walker stops at the same node.

(2) *Centrality Analysis:* In the graph theory, node centrality can heuristically be identified as the most important vertices in a graph. We then apply this centrality concept in a social network to determine a number of individuals with the highest centrality values (i.e., top-k) from each community, and mark them as the influential candidates. Furthermore, four criterions of centrality analysis are employed in this paper, including:

- *In-degree centrality* – A simplest analysis measures a node importance by counting the number of ties directed to that node. In other words, the in-degree centrality can be interpreted as a form of node popularity. Suppose a node u belongs to a community $\mathcal{C}_i$. Then, the in-degree centrality of u is defined as:
$$\varphi_I(u) = |\{(v, u) : \forall v \in \mathcal{C}_i\}|.$$

- *Out-degree Centrality* – In contrast to in-degree, the out-degree analysis measure a node importance by counting the number of ties that the node directs to others. Thus, the out-degree centrality can be interpreted as a form of node socialness. Similarly, if a node u belongs to a community $\mathcal{C}_i$ then the out-degree centrality of u is defined as:
$$\varphi_O(u) = |\{(u, v) : \forall v \in \mathcal{C}_i\}|.$$

- *Betweenness Centrality* – A betweenness of a node is defined as the number of pairs of individuals would have to go through that node in order to reach one another with the minimum number of hops. Consider a community $\mathcal{C}_i$, if we let σ_{st} be total number of shortest paths from a node s to a node t within $\mathcal{C}_i$, and $\sigma_{st}(u)$ be the number of those paths that pass through the node u. Then, the betweenness of u is defined as:
$$\varphi_B(u) = \sum_{\forall s, t \in \mathcal{C}_i : s \neq t \neq u} \frac{\sigma_{st}(u)}{\sigma_{st}}.$$

- *Closeness Centrality* – A closeness of a node is defined as the length of the average shortest path between that node and all others in a connected network. Thus, the more central a node is, the lower its total distance from all other nodes. Let $d(u, v)$ be the distance from a node u to a node v within a community C_i. Then, the closeness of u is defined as:

$$\varphi_C(u) = \left(\frac{\sum_{\forall v \in C_i : v \neq u} d(u, v)}{|C_i| - 1} \right)^{-1},$$

where $|C_i|$ denotes the number of nodes existing in C_i.

(3) *Community Combination:* Since the MCL algorithm sometimes generates too many small and dispersed communities, finding influential nodes within those small communities may lead to get useless results. To avoid this problem, the community combination module is introduced to merge some communities in order to produce more proper ones.

Suppose that we have already partitioned a network into n communities, and top-k influential candidates are chosen from each community. Here, we hypothesize that if any two candidates belonging to two different communities are connected (i.e., via either topological structure, interaction, or both), then those communities should be merged together. Mathematically, we let $\mathcal{I}_i$ and $\mathcal{I}_j$ be a set of k candidates with the highest centrality values extracted from individual communities C_i and C_j, respectively. Both C_i and C_j will be further combined if an edge $e(u, v)$ or $e(v, u)$ exists in the social network $\mathcal{G}$, where $u \in \mathcal{I}_i$ and $v \in \mathcal{I}_j$. Recall that the node centrality value can be defined as one of the above four criterions.

(4) *Influencer Identification:* After we obtain the final communities, the influencer identification module aims to find top-k influential nodes over the entire network. More precisely, the top-k candidates are chosen again from each community using the same centrality criterion, and later collected them together as a candidate set $\mathcal{D}$. Then, we employ the independent cascade model (ICM) [8] to simulate the influence propagation. Based on the iterative greedy-based computation, the number of activated nodes (i.e., influence spread) is obtained by examining each combination of candidates in $\mathcal{D}$. Finally, a combination of k candidates with most corresponding influence spread is returned from the algorithm as the first k influencers.

The proposed *CCGA* is outlined in Fig. 2. The algorithm first detects communities using MCL (line 1). Then, some communities are combined with respect to connections between centrality nodes (line 2). At lines 3–7, all top-k influential candidates are collected from each community obtained after the combination process. Statements at lines 8–18 perform the greedy-based ICM for finding the most k influential nodes from all candidates. Given a random process $RanCas()$, in each round i, the algorithm selects a node v (line 10) such that this node together with the previously selected ones in the set S maximizes the influence spread (line 17). In other words, the node v is selected and further included in S as it can maximize the incremental influence spread in this round.

Algorithm: *CCGA*

Input: network $\mathcal{G} = (\mathcal{V}, \mathcal{E}, \mathcal{W})$, size of results k
Output: set $\mathcal{S}$ denoted the top-*k* influencers

1: $\mathcal{C} \leftarrow CommunityDetection(\mathcal{G})$
2: $\mathcal{C}' \leftarrow CommunityCombination(\mathcal{C}, k)$
3: $\mathcal{D} = \emptyset$
4: **for** $i = 1$ to $|\mathcal{C}'|$ **do**
5:      $\mathcal{I}_i \leftarrow CentralityDetection(\mathcal{C}'_i, k)$
6:      $\mathcal{D} = \mathcal{D} \cup \mathcal{I}_i$
7: **end for**
8: $\mathcal{S} = \emptyset, \mathcal{R} = 20000$
9: **for** $i = 1$ to k **do**
10:     **for each** node $v \in \mathcal{D} \setminus \mathcal{S}$ **do**
11:         $s_v = 0$
12:         **for** $j = 1$ to $\mathcal{R}$ **do**
13:             $s_v + = |RanCas(\mathcal{S} \cup \{v\})|$
14:         **end for**
15:         $s_v = s_v / \mathcal{R}$
16:     **end for**
17:     $\mathcal{S} = \mathcal{S} \cup \{\mathrm{argmax}_{v \in \mathcal{D} \setminus \mathcal{S}}(s_v)\}$
18: **end for**
19: **return** $\mathcal{S}$

Fig. 2. The community centrality-based greedy algorithm.

However, to ensure the influence spread of $\mathcal{S} \cup \{v\}$, the *RanCas*() process is repeated $\mathcal{R}$ times, and the values of those spreads are then averaged (lines 11–15). Finally, the algorithm is terminated by returning k selected influencers in $\mathcal{S}$ at line 19.

4 Experiments

4.1 Experimental Setup

We conducted experiments to evaluate the effectiveness and efficiency of the proposed *CCGA*, compared with the state-of-the-art greedy algorithm (*GA*) [8] and *NewGreedy* [1]. We used a dataset excerpted from the publicly available Higgs Twitter dataset [4], which contains 19,483 individuals and 393,136 connections including topological relationships and interactions.

All the experiments were conducted on a server with 2.4 GHz Intel Xeon 8-Core CPU and 32 GB main memory, running Centos/7.0 operating system. The programs were coded using JAVA language.

4.2 Evaluation Metrics

We evaluate the effectiveness of an algorithm in term of the *influence degree*, i.e., the proportion of active nodes to the entire ones in a network. Let $\mathcal{S}$ be the initial set of influencers, and $\mathcal{V}_\mathcal{S}$ be the set of nodes influenced by $\mathcal{S}$ during the information diffusion process. Then, the influence degree of set $\mathcal{S}$ is calculated as:

$$\mathcal{A}(\mathcal{S}) = \frac{|\mathcal{V}_\mathcal{S}|}{|\mathcal{V}|}.$$

To evaluate an efficiency of the algorithms, we measure it in term of the running time spent during the information diffusion process. However, for fairness comparisons, we therefore report the time consumed by *CCGA* in total, including all four processes as described in Sect. 3.

4.3   Results

Figures 3 and 4 report experimental performances in term of the influence degree and the running time for each individual parameter k, respectively. Notice that,

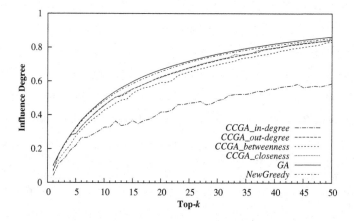

Fig. 3. Influence degree of different algorithms.

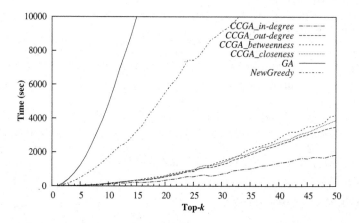

Fig. 4. Running times of different algorithms.

in Fig. 4, we excerpt the curves to show only at most 10,000 s for clear comparison reason.

As it can be seen from the results, all variations of *CCGA* (except *CCGA_in-degree*) can produce the influence degree closed to *GA* and *NewGreedy* while consume significantly lower time, indicating that they are quite effective and indeed efficient. Although *CCGA_in-degree* tents to spend the lowest time as *k* increases, it results the lowest influence degree. Consequently, *CCGA_out-degree* seems to be the best one since it can produce quite high influence degree and takes the second lowest time.

5   Conclusion

In this paper, we investigate the problem of influence maximization. We propose four variations of community centrality-based greedy algorithm. The experimental results show that our algorithms not only can execute much faster than the state-of-the-art greedy and *NewGreedy* algorithms but also still provide nearly the same effectiveness in influence spread.

For the future work, we anticipate to explore other graph-based clustering algorithms to detect the communities. We also interest to experiment with other social network datasets derived from Facebook, Google+, etc. To accelerate the running time of influence maximization, we plan to extend our algorithm in a parallel computing environment.

References

1. Chen, W., Wang, Y., Yang, S.: Efficient influence maximization in social networks. In: Proceedings of the 15th ACM SIGKDD International Conference on Knowledge Discovery and Data Mining, pp. 199–208 (2009)
2. Chen, W., Yuan, Y., Zhang, L.: Scalable influence maximization in social networks under the linear threshold model. In: Proceedings of the IEEE International Conference on Data Mining, pp. 88–97 (2010)
3. Chen, Y.C., Zhu, W.Y., Peng, W.C., Lee, W.C., Lee, S.Y.: CIM: community-based influence maximization in social networks. ACM Trans. Intell. Syst. Technol. **5**(2), 25:1–25:31 (2014)
4. De Domenico, M., Lima, A., Mougel, P., Musolesi, M.: The anatomy of a scientific rumor. Scientific Reports 3(2980) (2013)
5. Domingos, P., Richardson, M.: Mining the network value of customers. In: Proceedings of the 7th ACM SIGKDD International Conference on Knowledge Discovery and Data Mining, pp. 57–66 (2001)
6. Galstyan, A., Musoyan, V.L., Cohen, P.R.: Maximizing influence propagation in networks with community structure. Phys. Rev. E. **79**(5), 056102 (2009)
7. Goyal, A., Lu, W., Lakshmanan, L.V.S.: CELF++: Optimizing the greedy algorithm for influence maximization in social networks. In: Proceedings of the 20th International Conference on World Wide Web (Companion Volume), pp. 47–48 (2011)

8. Kempe, D., Kleinberg, J.M., Tardos, É.: Maximizing the spread of influence through a social network. In: Proceedings of the 9th ACM SIGKDD International Conference on Knowledge Discovery and Data Mining, pp. 137–146 (2003)
9. Kempe, D., Kleinberg, J.M., Tardos, É.: Influential nodes in a diffusion model for social networks. In: Caires, L., Italiano, G.F., Monteiro, L., Palamidessi, C., Yung, M. (eds.) ICALP 2005. LNCS, vol. 3580, pp. 1127–1138. Springer, Heidelberg (2005)
10. Kim, C., Lee, S., Park, S., Lee, S.: Influence maximization algorithm using markov clustering. In: Hong, B., Meng, X., Chen, L., Winiwarter, W., Song, W. (eds.) DASFAA Workshops 2013. LNCS, vol. 7827, pp. 112–126. Springer, Heidelberg (2013)
11. Leskovec, J., Krause, A., Guestrin, C., Faloutsos, C., VanBriesen, J., Glance, N.: Cost-effective outbreak detection in networks. In: Proceedings of the 13th ACM SIGKDD International Conference on Knowledge Discovery and Data Mining, pp. 420–429 (2007)
12. Mehmood, Y., Barbieri, N., Bonchi, F., Ukkonen, A.: CSI: community-level social influence analysis. In: Blockeel, H., Kersting, K., Nijssen, S., Železný, F. (eds.) ECML PKDD 2013, Part II. LNCS, vol. 8189, pp. 48–63. Springer, Heidelberg (2013)
13. Page, L., Brin, S., Motwani, R., Winograd, T.: The pagerank citation ranking: bringing order to the web. Technical report, Stanford Digital Libraries (1999)
14. Van Dongen, S.: Graph clustering via a discrete uncoupling process. SIAM J. Matrix Anal. Appl. 30(1), 121–141 (2008)
15. Wang, Y., Cong, G., Song, G., Xie, K.: Community-based greedy algorithm for mining top-K influential nodes in mobile social networks. In: Proceedings of the 16th ACM SIGKDD International Conference on Knowledge Discovery and Data Mining, pp. 1039–1048 (2008)
16. Wasserman, S., Faust, K.: Social Network Analysis: Methods and Applications. Structural Analysis in the Social Sciences. Cambridge University Press, New York (1994)

Context-Based Service Identification in the Museum Environment

Preeti Khanwalkar and Pallapa Venkataram$^{(\boxtimes)}$

Protocol Engineering and Technology Unit, Department of Electrical
Communication Engineering, Indian Institute of Science, Bangalore, India
{pkhanwalkar,pallapa}@ece.iisc.ernet.in

Abstract. The substantial growth in technology with multi-featured devices, wireless networks and interacting computing infrastructure has increased the demand of ubiquitous services. A ubiquitous service, unlike other service is decided by the system without user requests or interventions. The system uses different contexts such as user context, device context, network context, and many others to decide accurate services for the user. In this work, we design a technique to identify the required services for the visitors in the museum environment by considering the context of the visitors and their surrounding environment. The technique acquires the required context information and formulates *Composite Context (CC)* which leads to *Essential Context-derived Reasons (ECR)*. We use these *ECR* to identify the visitor's required service. The designed technique has been tested in the museum environment with variety of exhibits and services. The experimental results demonstrate the effectiveness of the technique.

Keywords: Context information · Essential Context-derived Reasons · Service identification · Ubiquitous museum-guide services

1 Introduction

The technological advancements in the multi-featured handheld devices, wearables, sensors, storage systems, wireless networks, and interacting computing infrastructure have brought Weiser's concept of ubiquitous computing into reality [1]. The notion of ubiquitous computing is to offer ubiquitous services to the users without their requests or interventions. To facilitate such ubiquitous services, context awareness i.e., understanding the situation of the users and their surrounding environment has been recognized as one of the prerequisite requirement [2,3]. The context of the user such as location, time, type of devices, networks and professional qualifications enable the system to anticipate the user's requirements for providing ubiquitous services [4]. Since last two decades, the needs and benefits of ubiquitous services have been explored in various applications such as museum and tourist guides, health care, learning, and several others.

© ICST Institute for Computer Sciences, Social Informatics and Telecommunications Engineering 2016
P.C. Vinh and V. Alagar (Eds.): ICCASA 2015, LNICST 165, pp. 151–164, 2016.
DOI: 10.1007/978-3-319-29236-6_16

In the museum environment with large area containing variety of exhibits and several other facilities, it is time consuming and exhausting for the visitors to find suitable services as per their requirements. Also, visitors in the museum have different professional backgrounds and hence they have different perspective towards exhibits. The ubiquitous service is considered to be useful in the museum environment to solve many such purposes. For instance, by means of ubiquitous service the system triggers intuitive services to the visitors based on their change of context, provides exhibit information to the visitors according to their perceptions, provides transparent adaptive services without any location and time constraints, and executes many such tasks. However, from the large number of existing services in the museum environment, the identification of the most relevant service is a challenging task. Thus, according to the visitor's context and his/her service requirements which have been previously analyzed by the system, the system identifies the request without visitor's intervention [5]. The use of context provides a promising way to assist/guide the visitors with relevant ubiquitous services and to enhance the museum visiting experience.

In this work, we propose a technique to identify the required Ubiquitous Museum-guide Services (UMS) by considering the *Context Information (CI)* of the visitors, their surrounding system and physical environment. We acquire the required *CI* and combined them to formulate *Composite Context (CC)* which further leads to *Essential Context-derived Reasons (ECR)*. These *ECR* are used to identify the required service for the visitor. Also, based on the variation in *ECR*, the proposed system decides the suitable service configuration. We demonstrate the application of the proposed technique through different case studies in the museum environment.

The rest of the paper is organized as follows. Section 2 describes some of the related works. The overview of the museum environment is illustrated in Sect. 3. The procedure of context information acquisition and analysis is presented in Sect. 4. The system architecture is discussed in Sect. 5 by describing each module functionality. The application of the proposed technique is described in Sect. 6. We discuss the implementation of the system with experimental results in Sect. 7, followed by the conclusion and future works in Sect. 8.

2   Related Work

In the literature, several works have utilized the context information to provide services in the museum environment with different purposes [6–9]. For context-aware mobile applications in the museum, authors in [6] have described the theoretical framework considering different dimensions of the context and discussed the importance of context affecting the visitors and the museum interaction. The context aware museum system iMuseum [7] has proposed to provide customized relic information. They have utilized a 2 sets 3 layers context model based on the ontology and hierarchical model and discussed applications to provide nearby and visitor's interested relic information.

In [10], a context aware framework using mobile agents has been described. They have used location sensing systems to guide the groups of visitors and to

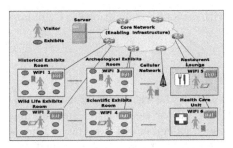

Fig. 1. An overview of the museum environment

Table 1. Some examples of services in the museum environment

Examples of Available Services
1. Location of Registration Service;
2. Exhibit Information Service;
3. Path of Next Exhibit of Interests Service;
4. Restaurant Service;
5. Rest Room Facility Service;
6. Transportation Service;
7. Emergency Exit Service;
8. Infant/Child Care Facility Service;
9. Path to Kids Play Area Service;
10. Antique Items Shopping Service;

provide services on the computers screens that are close to visitors locations. Ubi-Cicero [11], a location aware support with multi-device museum guide services has proposed to provide context dependent museum information and associated games on multiple devices such as mobiles and large screens at nearby locations of the visitors. Authors in [12] has proposed the Context-Information Observation Belief (C-IOB) model with an application of the museum environment in which service requests have been generated based on the acquired context by formulating a set of beliefs combined with the personalization parameters of the visitors. However, unlike other approaches our technique focuses on the identification of the required ubiquitous service in the museum environment without visitor's requests. The proposed system has utilized the record of the set of services in different context availed by the visitors over the past few years. The system correlates and match the context of these services with the formulated context of various combinations of the acquired context to dynamically identify the required services with more accuracy.

3   Museum Environment

An overview of the museum environment is depicted in Fig. 1. The museum environment is enriched with many embedded, sensing and intelligent computing devices to acquire the dynamic context of the visitors. The proposed system functions in the museum environment to offer a wide variety of UMS to the visitors, i.e. information regarding the available exhibits, restaurants/food courts, emergency exits, and several others. Some of the examples of available services are given in the Table 1. With the change in service requirements due to the variation of context such as location, time, activity, network, devices, etc., automatically the relevant UMS is triggered to the visitors.

4   Context Information Analysis

In this section, we first explain different categories of context information related to the visitor in the museum environment and the procedure to acquire them.

Next, we analyze the context information with various combinations to formulate *CC* and *ECR*.

4.1   Context Information *(CI)*

CI is the primitive set of information related to the visitor while using UMS. Different *CI* are acquired by considering the visitor and his/her surrounding environment by using a variety of sources such as embedded, sensing and intelligent computing devices, databases [13]. The *CI* of the visitor is classified and considered to be the set of three categories of information which is given as *CI* = {*PECI, VCI, SCI*}. Each one of these categories of *CI* are described as follows:

Physical Environment Context Information (PECI): It specifies the information related to the local surroundings of the visitor. For example, visitor location: geographic location co-ordinates, near or far from the exhibit, specific region; Time: time at which visitor use the service, time duration for which the service is used, etc.

Visitor's Context Information (VCI): It refers to the information specific to the visitors and their present state of operation. For instance, it includes visitor's educational qualifications: professional, college student, preliminary school student; Visitor activity: standing, walking, sitting, etc.

System Context Information (SCI): It provides the information regarding both the device on which the ubiquitous service is running and the network being used by the visitor. For example, it includes the device context such as Type of device: laptop, smart phone, and others; Device battery strength: low, moderate, or high, and network context such as type of network: 2G/3G, WiFi, etc.; network delay: low, moderate, or high.

4.2   CI Acquisition

The *CI* of the visitors are acquired from the various sources by adopting the procedure of *CI-Constructs* followed in [14]. The *CI-Constructs* represent the multiway data structure with each construct used to acquire related pre-defined *CI*. Different *CI-Constructs* are utilized to collect the complete set of *CI* in a well-defined manner. Some examples of the *CI-Constructs* are:

- *What*: To collect the information related to an object/entity, e.g., visitors activity, visitors schedule, etc.;
- *When*: To get the information regarding time, instant, duration, day of occurrence of an event/occasion;
- *Where*: To obtain the information about location and place of the visitors;
- *Who*: To acquire the information specific to a person or group;
- *Which*: To collect the information about the devices, networks, etc.;

However, these acquired individual primitive *CI* do not convey the significant information about the visitor's situation [15]. Consequently, *CI* are further combined together in different possible combinations which provide more realistic aspects about the situation of the visitor. We analyzed different *CI* combinations which are formulated as *CC* and further leads to the *ECR*. For the analysis we dynamically designed the definite structures of different combinations depending on the application specific services. The further analysis of *CI* is discussed in the following sections.

4.3   Composite Context (CC)

The individual *CI* in different combinations will lead to define high level *CC* which are more realistically useful for identifying the required services. The *CI* are combined together in the combinations of two's, three's, four's and so on, which result into comprehensive number of *CC*. On matching with the definite structures of combinations of *CI* the appropriate valid *CC* can be obtained. Consider the case, if for the visitor the museum environment the system has acquired 8 context parameters from the different categories of *CI* such as:

PECI = { *Visitor/Device Location, Time of Service, Time Duration*};

VCI = { *Visitor Activity, Educational Qualifications*};

SCI = { *Type of Device, Battery Strength, Access Network Delay*};

For instance, two's combinations of *CI* using these 8 context parameters results into total of 28 ($^{8}C_2$) combinations of *CC*. However, based on the definite structures of *CI* combinations the system formulates 25 valid *CC*. Likewise, three's, four's and other possible *CI* combinations results into total 247 *CC*, among which 60 valid *CC* are formulated. The examples of *CC* formation from the two's and three's *CI* combinations are depicted in the Fig. 2. The procedure of *CC* formulation is given in Algorithm 1.

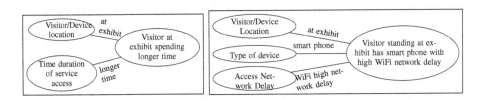

Fig. 2. Examples of *CC* formation

4.4   Essential Context-Derived Reasons (ECR)

The *ECR* are deduced over the different combinations of the *CC*. The formulated *ECR* realizes the visitor's service requirement and enables the system to accurately identify the required service. For instance, suppose that at particular

---

Algorithm 1. Algorithm for CC formulation

Input: CI parameters; **Output:** A set of 'm' formulated CC;
while *Change in CI observed* **do**
    Acquire $CI=\{PECI, VCI, SCI\}$ using associated $CI\text{-}Constructs$ respectively;
    Get total 'n' number of CI;
    Initialize y=1 (* y = number of valid cc *);
    for $x = 2$ *to* n **do**
        Generate 'k' combinations of CI such that $k = \frac{n*(n-1)*\cdots*(n-r-1)}{1*2*\cdots*r}$ with $r=x$;
        for $i = 1$ *to* k **do**
            for $j = i$ *to* k **do**
                if *Matched with CI Combinations in the Context Structures Storage*
                then
                    Formulate valid $cc_y = CI(i,j+1) \cup \cdots \cup CI(i,j=k)$ with 'r'
                    combinations of the CI;
                    y=y+1;
    Obtain a set of valid CC;

---

instant the system obtains 60 CC (mentioned in the previous section). These CC are further combined in two's, three's, four's, and all possible combinations which results into enormous number of ECR. However, on matching with the definite structures of combinations of CC the system obtains 400 valid ECR. These exhaustive set of formulated ECR provides more realistic information about the visitor's service requirement. The examples of ECR formulation with two's and three's combinations of CC are depicted in Fig. 3. The procedure of ECR formulation is given in Algorithm 2.

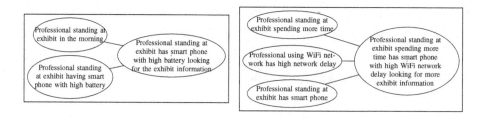

Fig. 3. Examples of ECR formation

5   UMS Identification System

The *UMS Identification System* identifies the required services for visitors in the museum environment without their requests. Figure 4 illustrates the architecture of the *UMS Identification System*. It consists of three modules: (1) *Context Analyzer Module* (2) *Service Identification Module* and (3) *UMS Identification Main Module*. The functionality of each module is discussed as follows.

Algorithm 2. Algorithm for *ECR* formulation

Input: 'm' number of *CC*; **Output:** A set of 'n' valid *ECR*;
while *Change in CC observed* **do**
    Obtain 'm' number of *CC*;
    Initialize y=1 (* y = number of valid ecr *);
    for $x = 2$ to m **do**
        Generate 'k' combinations of *CC* such that $k = \frac{m*(m-1)*\cdots*(m-r-1)}{1*2*\cdots*r}$ with $r=x$;
        for $i = 1$ to k **do**
            for $j = i$ to k **do**
                if *Matched with CC Combinations in the Context Structures Storage*
                then
                    Deduce valid $ecr_y = CC(i,j+1) \cup \cdots \cup CC(i,j=k)$ with 'r'
                    combinations of the *CC*;
                    y=y+1;

    Obtain a set of valid formulated *ECR*;

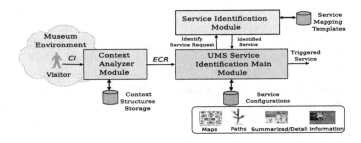

Fig. 4. Ubiquitous museum-guide service identification system architecture

Context Analyzer Module

It is responsible for formulating the *ECR* from the acquired *CI*. As and when the acquired *CI* instances are concurred with the available structures of combinations in the *Context Structures Storage*, accordingly it formulates an exhaustive set of *ECR*. Further, it sends the formulated *ECR* to the *UMS Identification Main Module*.

Context Structures Storage

A persistent storage in the form of the *Context Structures* is used to store dynamically designed definite structures of *CI* combinations based on the application specific services. These predefined structures of different combinations of *CI* enable the system to yield more realistic *CC* and further *ECR* respectively.

Service Mapping Templates

A dynamic storage of service mapping templates is maintained by the system. The system designs and stores the templates based on the set of services in different contexts availed by the visitors over the past few years. The implicit information contained in the templates are potentially found useful to identify the service. Formally, templates define two tuple hypothetical information $\langle ECR, s_j \rangle$ as given in the Table 2, that maps a set of *ECR* to a specific category of the service. A particular template can be chosen using the set of formulated *ECR* to obtain the related service.

Table 2. Examples of service mapping templates

ECR	Exhibit information service in different categories (s_j)
{*Professional scientist standing at the exhibit spending longer time, Professional looking towards exhibit waiting for the information, Professional standing at exhibit with smart phone waiting for the information, · · · , Professional looking at exhibit has smart phone with high battery, Professional standing at the exhibit has smart phone with high WiFi network delay*}	s_1: At higher level for professionals with summarized information;
{*College student standing at the exhibit spending longer time, College student looking at exhibit has smart phone with high battery, Student looking towards exhibit waiting for the information, · · · , Student standing at exhibit with smart phone, College student standing at the exhibit has smart phone with high battery and low WiFi network delay*}	s_2: At average level for college student with detail information;
{*Preliminary school kid standing at the exhibit spending longer time, Preliminary school kid looking towards exhibit waiting for information, · · · , Kid standing at the exhibit with smart phone waiting for the information, Preliminary school kid looking at the exhibit has smart phone with high battery, Kid standing at the exhibit has smart phone with high battery and high WiFi network delay*}	s_3: At lower level for elementary school kids with summarized information;

Service Identification Module

It identifies the visitor's required service according to the formulated *ECR*. The *Service Identification Module* correlates the formulated set of *ECR* with the information available in the *Service Mapping Templates*. Depending on the matched template it obtains the mapping of $ECR \longmapsto s_j$, i.e., a set of formulated *ECR* associated against the available service. Further, it sends the identified service to the *UMS Identification Main Module*. The working of the *Service Identification Module* is explained in Algorithm 3.

Algorithm 3. *Working of Service Identification Module*

Input: A set of formulated *ECR*; A set of different categories of services $S = \{s_1, s_2, \cdots, s_k\}$;
Output: Identified Service $s_j \in S$;
while *Visitor is interacting with the system* **do**
  Get a set of formulated *ECR* from the *UMS Identification Main Module*;
  Correlate the formulated *ECR* and match $\langle ECR, s_j \rangle$ in the *Service Mapping Templates*;
  Map the $ECR \longmapsto s_j$ in the template and select the relevant s_j;
  Send the identified s_j to the *UMS Identification Main Module*;

UMS Identification Main Module

It acts as an intermediary module of the system. Based on the dynamic variations in the *CI*, it obtains a set of *ECR* from the *Context Analyzer Module*. It forwards *ECR* to the *Service Identification Module* and gets the identified service. Finally, according to the requirements, it fetches the *URL* of the relevant configuration of the identified service from the *Service Configurations Database* and triggers the required service. Algorithm 4 explains the working of the *UMS Identification Main Module*.

Service Configurations

The *Service Configurations Database* consists of the *URLs* of the transcoding proxy servers providing different configuration of the services. Several proxy servers are

Algorithm 4. Working of the *UMS Identification Main Module*

Input: A set of formulated *ECR*; Identified Service s_j; **Output:** Triggered s_j;
while *Visitor is interacting with the system* **do**
   if *Change in the CI is Observed* **then**
      Obtain a set of *ECR* from the *Context Analyzer Module*;
      Forward the formulated *ECR* to the *Service Identification Module*;
      Get the identified service s_j from the *Service Identification Module*;
      Select the relevant configuration of the s_j with service lookup in the *Service Configurations Database*;
      Trigger the relevant configuration of s_j to the visitor;

distributed in the museum environment to provide the variety of service configurations such as filtered information at summarized and detailed levels, different adaptable formats, different modalities, and many other forms [16]. Also, periodically the *Service Configurations Database* is updated subject to service availability. Table 3 indicates some of the configurations of available services in the museum environment.

6 Application of Proposed Technique in the Museum Environment

We demonstrate the application of the proposed technique with different case studies in the museum environment. As and when their will be change of *CI* accordingly *ECR* are formulated. The following cases demonstrate the decision of the system to identify the visitor's required services depending on a set of formulated *ECR*.

Case 1: Exhibit information service. When a professional scientist is standing at the exhibit, he is spending longer time waiting for the exhibit information, and has a smart phone with high battery and high network delay. The system maps these formulated set of *ECR* to the exhibit information service at a professional level. Due to high network delay, according to the requirement the system provides the relevant service configuration containing the summarized exhibit information with the necessary details based on the knowledge level of scientist.

Case 2: Path to next exhibit of interests service. When the visitor standing at the exhibit and has spent adequate time, also visitor is looking at other exhibits with the constraint of limited available time, and has a smart phone with moderate battery and low WiFi network delay. Using these set of *ECR* the system identifies service as the path to next exhibit of interests. With limited available time and low network delay, the system provides the detailed information containing map and optimal paths to the exhibits of visitor's interests.

Case 3: Restaurant information service. During the afternoon around 1:00 pm, when the visitor has spent adequate time in the museum, sitting on the bench using a laptop with high battery and low WiFi network delay waiting for

Table 3. Examples of configurations of services

Available Services	Configurations of the Services (s_j)	URLs
Exhibit information service	At higher level I for professionals with summarized/detail information;	exhiinfo_l1@pet.iisc.in
	At average level II for students with summarized/detail information;	exhiinfo_l2@pet.iisc.in
	At lower level III for preliminary school kids with summarized/detail information;	exhiinfo_l3@pet.iisc.in
Path to next exhibit of interests service	Paths to different exhibits with summarized/detail information;	exhipath_l1@pet.iisc.in
	Optimal path to visitor interested exhibits with summarized/detail information;	exhipath_l2@pet.iisc.in
	Shortest path for visitor in hurry with summarized/detail information;	exhipath_l3@pet.iisc.in
Restaurant service	Breakfast menu with summarized/detail information of path and seat availability status;	restser_l1@pet.iisc.in
	Lunch menu with summarized/detail information of path to reach and seat availability status;	restser_l2@pet.iisc.in
	Snacks menu with summarized/detail information of path to reach and seat availability status;	restser_l3@pet.iisc.in
Emergency exit service	Optimal route to emergency exits, location of fire extinguishers, etc. with summarized/detail information;	emerexi_l1@pet.iisc.in
	Shortest route to emergency exits, emergency contact numbers, ambulance facility for critical conditions with summarized/detail information;	emerexi_l2@pet.iisc.in
Transportation facility service	Information regarding different types of transports with summarized/detail information of routes;	transinfo_l1@pet.iisc.in
	Transportation routes according to the budget with summarized/detail information;	transinfo_l2@pet.iisc.in

the information. The system maps these set of *ECR* and identifies the restaurant service. Based on the visitor's requirements determined from the *ECR*, the system provides the relevant configuration of the restaurant service containing summarized information of lunch menu along with the path to reach the restaurant.

Figure 5 depicts the various sequences of events taken place in the museum environment and accordingly the visitor's required services triggered by the system.

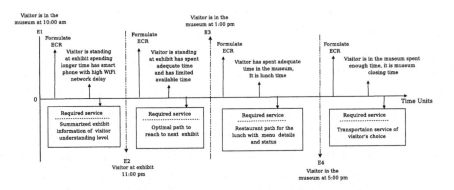

Fig. 5. Event sequence diagram of different cases

7   System Implementation

To explain the functioning of the system, the museum environment is considered with three to four WiFi units and one 2G/3G network unit. Different visitors are considered according to their educational qualifications. On registration for each visitors unique-Id has been assigned. We have considered ten different services depending on the generally used services in the museum environment. A context structure storage has been fed with the definite structures of different combinations of *CI* to formulate the *ECR* depending on the application specific services. Based on the set of services in different contexts availed by the visitors over the past few years, the service mapping templates are created and maintained by the system. Additionally, we have taken the services in different configurations to offer the visitor's required service.

7.1   Results and Discussion

We have conducted series of experiments in the museum environment for different visitors with their variety of acquired *CI*. We have periodically collected *CI* of the visitors consisting of eight different context parameters based on which

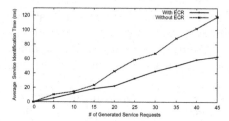

Fig. 6. Average service identification time vs. number of generated service requests

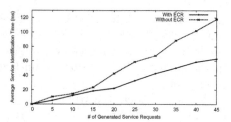

Fig. 7. Precision of the identified service with and without considering ECR

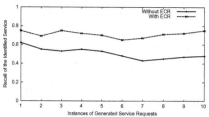

Fig. 8. Recall of the identified service with and without considering ECR

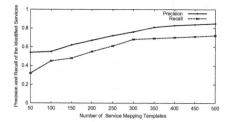

Fig. 9. Precision and recall of the identified service with available templates

ECR are formulated. We have measured the system performance by considering the service identification time, precision and recall of the identified services. During the experiments we found that using an exhaustive set of formulated *ECR*, the system is able to correlate and match quickly with the information in the service mapping templates. Accordingly, using formulated *ECR* the average time required to identify the service is reduced as shown in the Fig. 6 when compared to without *ECR*, i.e. without analyzing different combinations of *CC*.

Further, the system performance is measured by considering the precision and recall of the identified services based on the *ECR*. Precision determines fraction of the identified relevant services among total services retrieved by the system. Recall denotes fraction of the identified services which are expected to be relevant visitor's required services. Precision and Recall are given by Eqs. 1 and 2.

$$Precision = \frac{|\,\{Identified\ Services \cap Retrieved\ Services\}\,|}{|\,\{Retrieved\ Services\}\,|}; \quad (1)$$

$$Recall = \frac{|\,\{Identified\ Services \cap Retrieved\ Services\}\,|}{|\,\{Identified\ Services\}\,|}; \quad (2)$$

As indicated in the Fig. 7 for several instance of generated service requests using an exhaustive set of *ECR*, the system identified more relevent set of services among the existing services. This indicates that, *ECR* enables the system to accurately decide the required services and hence improves the precision. Also, as shown in the Fig. 8, the recall of services are improved using the *ECR* with identified the most relevent services.

Also, we have measured the precision and recall of the identified service depending on the number of service mapping templates. As shown in the Fig. 9 with more number of available service mapping templates based on the ECR the system retrieves more relevant services and improves the precision and recall of the identified service.

8   Conclusion and Future Works

This paper has presented a novel technique to identify the ubiquitous museum-guide services for the visitors in the museum environment without their requests. The proposed system has identified the required services based on the acquired context by formulating an exhaustive set of ECR. The formulated ECR were correlated and matched on to the service mapping templates which were potentially found useful to identify the ubiquitous services. The experimental results have shown that by considering the an exhaustive set of formulated ECR the precision and recall of the identified service has improved. In addition to the museum environment, the proposed technique can also be applied in several applications such as tourist guides, smart homes, ubiquitous commerce and like others. In future works, we are intended to consider the certainty of the required service according to dynamic variation in the context information. Also, we incorporate the visitor's personal interests to identify the required service as per individual requirements. Additionally, we emphasize on the design of content adaptation mechanism to provide the optimal services to the visitors.

References

1. Weiser, M.: The computer of the 21st century. In: ACM SIGMOBILE Mobile Computing and Communications, pp. 3–11, July 1999
2. Dey, A.K.: Dey.: understanding and using context. Pers. Ubiquit. Comput. **5**(1), 4–7 (2001)
3. Geihs, K., Wagner, M.: Context-awareness for self-adaptive applications in ubiquitous computing environments. In: Vinh, P.C., Hung, N.M., Tung, N.T., Suzuki, J. (eds.) ICCASA 2012. LNICST, vol. 109, pp. 108–120. Springer, Heidelberg (2013)
4. Zhou, L., Naixue, X., Shu, L., Vasilakos, A., Yeo, S.S.: Context-aware middleware for multimedia services in heterogeneous networks. IEEE Intell. Syst. **25**(2), 40–47 (2010)
5. Chen, N., Chen, A.: Integrating context-aware computing in decision support system. In: Proceedings of the International MultiConference of Engineers and Computer Scientists (IMECS), vol. I, March 2010
6. Raptis, D., Tselios, N., Avouris, N.: Context-based design of mobile applications for museums: a survey of existing practices. In: Proceedings of the 7th International Conference on MobileHCI, pp. 153–160. ACM (2005)
7. Yu, Z., Zhou, X., Yu, Z., Park, J.H., Ma, J.: iMuseum: a scalable context-aware intelligent museum system. Comput. Commun. **31**(18), 4376–4382 (2008)
8. Abowd, G.D., Atkeson, C.G., Hong, J., Long, S., Kooper, R., Pinkerton, M.: Cyberguide: A mobile contextaware tour guide. Wireless Netw. **3**(5), 421–433 (1997)

9. Oppermann, R., Specht, M., Jaceniak, I.: Hippie: a nomadic information system. In: Gellersen, H.-W. (ed.) HUC 1999. LNCS, vol. 1707, pp. 330–333. Springer, Heidelberg (1999)

10. Satoh, I.: Context-aware deployment of services in public spaces. In: Brinkschulte, U., Givargis, T., Russo, S. (eds.) SEUS 2008. LNCS, vol. 5287, pp. 221–232. Springer, Heidelberg (2008)

11. Ghiani, G., Patern, F., Santoro, C., Spano, L.D.: UbiCicero: a location-aware, multi-device museum guide. Interact. Comput. **21**(4), 288–303 (2009)

12. Venkataram, P., Bharath, M.: Context based service discovery for ubiquitous applications. In: International Conference on Information Networking (ICOIN), pp. 311–316, January 2011

13. Baldauf, M., Dustdar, S., Rosenberg, F.: A survey on context-aware systems. Int. J. Ad Hoc Ubiquitous Comput. **2**(4), 263–277 (2007)

14. Venkataram, P., Bharath, M.: A method of context-based services discovery in ubiquitous environment. In: Vinh, P.C., Alagar, V., Vassev, E., Khare, A. (eds.) ICCASA 2013. LNICST, vol. 128, pp. 260–270. Springer, Heidelberg (2014)

15. Buchholz, T., Krause, M., Linnhoff-Popien, C., Schiffers, M.: CoCo: dynamic composition of context information. In: The First Annual International Conference on Mobile and Ubiquitous Systems: Networking and Services, MOBIQUITOUS, pp. 335–343, August 2004

16. Berhe, G., Brunie, L., Pierson, J.M.: Modeling service-based multimedia content adaptation in pervasive computing. In: Proceedings of the 1st Conference on Computing Frontiers, pp. 60–69 (2004)

A Federated Approach for Simulations in Cyber-Physical Systems

Hoang Van Tran[1(✉)], Tuyen Phong Truong[1], Khoa Thanh Nguyen[1],
Hiep Xuan Huynh[2], and Bernard Pottier[1]

[1] Université de Bretagne Occidentale, Brest, France
tvhoang75@gmail.com, tptuyen@gmail.com, ngthanhkhoa@gmail.com,
pottier@univ-brest.fr
[2] Can Tho University, Can Tho, Vietnam
hxhiep@ctu.edu.vn

Abstract. In this paper, we propose a new approach to federate simulations for cyber-physical systems. A federation is a combination of simulations being able to interact with each other upon a standard of communication. In addition, mixed simulations are defined as several parallel simulations that are taken place in a common time progress. These simulations run on the models of physical systems, which are built based on cellular automata. The experimental results are performed on a typical federation of three simulations for forest fire spread, river pollution diffusion and wireless sensor network. The obtained results can be used to predict as well as observe the behavior of physical systems in their interactions.

Keywords: Cyber-Physical System (CPS) · Cellular Automata (CA) · Federation · High Level Architecture (HLA) · Mixed simulations

1 Introduction

In recent years, more and more researches focus on the cyber-physical system (CPS) [1], which is defined as an integration of computation with the physical systems. Taking advantage of Wireless sensor network (WSN) [12], sensing ability of CPS is significantly considered over the last years. This ability allows CPSs to be able to sense data from the physical world by the facilitation of sensor networks.

Simulating the sensing ability before real implementations will highly reduce cost and effort of development of CPSs. However, due to uncertain interactions of complex physical systems, simulating this type of system is much more complicated compared to the traditional computing systems. One of critical challenges is the involvement of the interoperability in the models.

Several solutions were suggested to confront with that issue over the last years [5,6,20]. But, they do not consider on federating physical systems instead of integrating exiting tools and languages. Furthermore, those approaches are

© ICST Institute for Computer Sciences, Social Informatics and Telecommunications Engineering 2016
P.C. Vinh and V. Alagar (Eds.): ICCASA 2015, LNICST 165, pp. 165–176, 2016.
DOI: 10.1007/978-3-319-29236-6_17

almost targeting embedded systems. This leads to challenges due to the needs of modeling various kinds of physical systems in the sensing process, natural systems as examples.

Cellular automata (CA) [2,3] model has emerged as a very promising technique for dealing with complex physical systems [4]. A typical CA consists of two components: cellular space and transition rule. The cellular space component presents a lattice of cells, each with an identical pattern of local connection to other cells (neighborhood pattern). In addition, each cell consist of a set of states. Meanwhile, the other component indicates how one cell achieves the new states (at time t+1) according to the current local states and states of its neighborhood (at time t).

In this paper, we propose a new approach for federating simulations. This enables to coordinate several parallel simulations as a distributed simulation system, so-called mixed simulation. To achieve it, we at first present a method to model physical systems in accordance with the CA [2,3] model. Then, the parallelism is used to accelerate large scale simulations. A federation of several parallel simulations is conducted according to high level architecture (HLA) [19] standard.

The remainder of this paper is organized as follows. In Sect. 2, we introduce related work. Section 3 describes mixed simulations in the context of CA. A federation of mixed simulations and related discussions are presented in Sect. 4. Section 5 gives some experiments of running a federation. The conclusion of this work will be expressed in Sect. 6.

2 Related Work

In the last decade, several researches have focused on handling challenges of interoperability of various components in CPSs [1].

An approach about coordinating data communication and time synchronization between simulation frameworks is considered. Some practical works following that track are presented in [5,23]. These solutions allow to federate several simulations, however, the issues related to synchronization time are not taken into account.

Likewise, [22] presents a framework for exchanging data and time synchronization by integrating two available tools. This work aims to facilitate design and evaluation of networked control and cyber-physical system (NCCPS) [22] in CPSs.

There are no work replying on applying the CA model for representing physical systems in the context of CPSs. Modeling phenomena and natural systems as well as their interactions in space and time are not taken into account in almost situations.

3 Mixed Simulations

3.1 Modeling Physical Systems Based on Cellular Automata

A physical system is considered as a region which may be monitored by sensor networks such as river, ocean, forest, or road system. However, since their complex behavior and large size, modeling this type of system confronts with many issues. Cellular automata (CA) [2,3] is feasible to handle those issues [4].

In order to model physical systems, a definition of cell system is considered. It consists of a collection of cells. Each cell holds its local states (namely pollution density, insect population), and connections to surrounding cells (neighboring cells), as presented in Fig. 1. We also suppose to use two common types of neighborhood patterns Von neumann 1 (4 neighbor) and Moore 1 (8 neighbor) [2] in this study.

Figure 2 depicts a process of developing physical simulations in terms of the cell systems. Initially, geographic data are processed to generate a cell system, which is associated with definitions of states and transition rules make up a complete model. Physical simulations are achieved by the model executions.

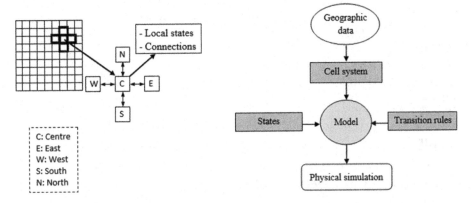

Fig. 1. Illustrating a cell system structure with the Von neumann 1 pattern.

Fig. 2. A process of developing physical simulations from cell systems.

Two models of physical systems are suggested in the next sections: forest fire spread model and river pollution diffusion model. We also suppose that a WSN [12] is deployed to monitor fire in the forest, and its model is thus presented.

3.2   River Pollution Diffusion Model

River pollution diffusion model is built based on the method in the previous section. In the context of pollution, it is possible to think of various potential situations such as chemical, oil, or contaminant. Generally, the diffusion significantly depends on the pollution density. Therefore, pollution density is chosen as cell states

- *state:* The cell state holds a value of the pollution density.
- *transition rules:* Updating the pollution density at $cell_i$ at time t+1, termed as $S(i)_{t+1}$.

$S(i)_{t+1} \leftarrow S(i)_t/2$
for *(j in neighbor of cell$_i$)*
    $S(i)_{t+1} \leftarrow S(i)_{t+1} + S(j)_t$ */ (2 * number of neighbor of cell$_j$)*
end for

3.3   Forest Fire Spread Model

The fire spread model is defined for simulating the fire spread in the forest. For the sake of simplicity, cell state is represented by one of the four values: tree, fire, ash, and empty.

- *state:* tree, fire, ash, and empty.
- *transition rules:* Updating the new state of *cell$_i$* at time t+1, termed as $S(i)_{t+1}$.

if *($S(i)_t$ is TREE **and** at least one of its neighbor is FIRE)*
    $S(i)_{t+1} \leftarrow FIRE$
end if
if *($S(i)_t$ is FIRE)*
    $S(i)_{t+1} \leftarrow ASH$
end if
if *($S(i)_t$ is ASH)*
    $S(i)_{t+1} \leftarrow EMPTY$
end if

3.4   Wireless Sensor Network Model

To represent a sensing component of CPSs, wireless sensor network (WSN) is also taken into account. It regularly collect raw data from the forest, processes those data, and raises emergency alerts in the case of the fire detected. To carry it out, a collection of sensors will first be deployed to monitor the forest. In this case, each sensor node is considered as a cell in cell system. The connectivity of the model is formed by radio links among sensors. And sensing data can be viewed as cell states of the model.

- *state:* The cell state holds a value of sensed data collected from the forest. Thus, its value should be fire or normal.
- *transition rule:* Every simulation cycle, *cell$_i$* checks the sensed data. Signals will be emitted as the fire is detected.

3.5   Parallel Simulations

The simplicity of the CA models actually brings about several benefits in computations. However, since huge sizes and complicated behavior of the physical systems, simulating them poses a challenge to existing simulator, especially in the case of several simulations working together. The parallelism mechanism is thus employed to deal with that in our work.

To implement it, we propose to use the Graphic Processing Unit (GPU) [7,8]. This architecture comes with a set of threads running in parallel. As a result, the computations of cells are easy to be executed simultaneously.

3.6 Mixed Simulations

A mixed simulation is considered as a collection of parallel simulations that are capable of communicating with each other while running concurrently as a distributed system. It is expected that the mixed simulations are able to imitate not only behavior of real systems, but also interactions between them. A central component is responsible for controlling that interoperability, as shown in Fig. 3.

For instance, considering on interactions between the river and the forest system, as shown in Fig. 4. Ashes produced by fire in the forest can pollute the river at the frontier between them. Otherwise, evaporation will also affects fired spread in the forest. These physical interactions are regarded in this type of simulation.

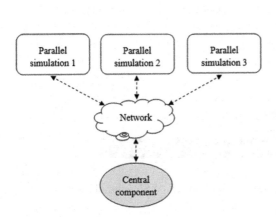

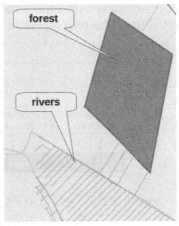

Fig. 3. A general architecture of mixed simulations.

Fig. 4. An example for describing interactions can be happened between river and forest. (data source: OpenStreetMap [16]).

4 Federation of Simulations

As mentioned earlier, a mixed simulation consists of several parallel simulations that concurrently run on different hosts and are connected via a network system. Thus, a federation approach is required to make those parallel simulations working together as a synchronous system. To do that, a model designed in accordance with the High Level Architecture (HLA) [13,14,19] is applied.

In HLA terminology, the entire system is considered as a *federation* which contains several *federates* connected via the central component *Run-Time Infrastructure (RTI)* [19]. The HLA is formally defined by three components.

1. A set of rules describes the responsibilities of federates and their relationship with RTI. An example is that *all exchange of data among federates should occur via the RTI during a federation execution.*
2. An interface specification provides services for managing federates and interactions. For example, it indicates how a federate join or leave a federation.
3. An Object Model Template [15] defines how information is communicated between federates, and how the federates and federation have to be documented (using Federation Object Model FOM) [15]. FOM defines the shared objects, attributes, and interactions for a whole federation.

We assume that some interactions occur between the three systems. Firstly, as fires of the forest approach to the river, ashes produced by the fires will pollute the river. Secondly, the evolution of the physical environment results in the changing of WSN's behavior, emitting signals as soon as the fire is detected.

The overall architecture of the proposed federation is presented in Fig. 5. It is noted that *Observer*, a passive federate, used to visualize the federation.

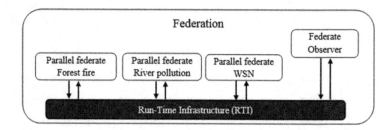

Fig. 5. A federation of four federates: River, forest, WSN, and observer.

4.1 Exchanging Data

Exchanging data between federates is an obligation to the proposed model. To deal with that, a publish-subscribe mechanism is used. This enables subscribers may automatically receive updates from publishers. Thus, federates have to declare what information they publish and subscribe to the central component before the execution of the federation, as shown in Table 1.

The communications are taken place at the end of simulation cycles. This means that the new states are simultaneously computed on the GPUs of the federates which are independently run on their host. Then, data are copied to the CPUs to serve interactions. Thus, the states of publishers at time t may be involved in the evolution of other subscribers at time t+1, as depicted in Fig. 6.

Table 1. Describing publishers and subscribers of shared data between the four federates: forest, river, WSN, and observer.

Object Class	Attributes	Published by	Subscribed by
ForestNode	State, Position	ForestNode	River, WSN, Observer
RiverNode	Pollution density, Position	RiverNode	Observer
WSNNode	State, Position	WSNNode	Obsever

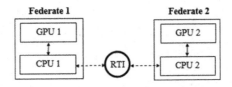

Fig. 6. The model of exchanging data in the federation with two federates.

Clearly, this approach enables to make of an environment of several parallel simulations running at the same time. Although, it costs a little of time for copying data, it significant benefits in the case of several complex and large systems.

4.2   Time Management

Time management is a mechanism for controlling the advancement of each federate in simulation time. This enables federates in the federation to be able to synchronize their local logical time together to ensure the causality. In this case, each federate owns its logical time that will be associated with the sending data, so-called time-stamp. Upon that information, the central component is capable of synchronizing federates as a synchronous system.

This mechanism comes up with two properties, constrained and regulating. The former ensures the federates to be able to send updates. Meanwhile, the latter allows the federates to receive updates from the central component. Therefore, both of them are often enabled for all federates, and only the constrained property is assigned to the observer federate since it is designed without any sending. Table 2 shows time policies proposed for the proposed federation.

Time stepped federates will calculate values based on a point in time and process all data being sent up to the next point in time (current time + time step). Thus, to advance logical time for the time-stepped simulation, each federate has to send its request to the central component. Then, all receive data, which have been sent from federates, with the time-stamp less than or equal to the time requested will be released from the central component. After those data have been received by federates, a time grant is returned to the requesting federate. And then, the federate is able to advance its logical time. In addition, Fig. 7 illustrates how to initialize the synchronizing point for all federates.

Table 2. Time management of the four federates.

Federate	Time constrained	Time regulating	Time advance
Forest	Yes	Yes	Time stepped
River	Yes	Yes	Time stepped
WSN	Yes	Yes	Time stepped
Observer	Yes	Yes/No	Time stepped

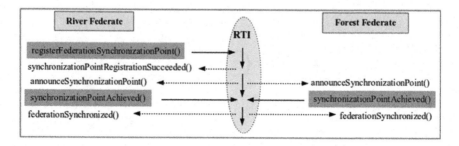

Fig. 7. Federate synchronization for the river and the forest federate.

Therefore, for the proposed federation, the time synchronization of the four federates can be obtained via the following steps.

1. All federates connect to the federation initialized earlier.
2. The federates are put into a common time progress by requesting synchronization point services, as demonstrated in Fig. 7.
3. The federates update the new states, and then send the updates to the central component if they are publishers.
4. Each federate sends an advance time request to the central component.
5. For each federate, it needs to wait until all data on the central component with the time stamps are less than or equal to its requested time are received by subscribers, then it is able to advance its logical time.

5   Experiment

5.1   Data Used

Data used in this study was taken from OpenStreetMap [16]. In which, we considered on a small area located in the Mekong Delta of Vietnam as a study region 4. Those data were used to generate cell system of river, forest, and WSN. The pattern neighborhood were 8, 4, and 4 neighbor, respectively. Since our current focus is the federation of mixed simulation, input data were randomly created for simulations.

5.2 FEMIS Tool

We have developed the FEMIS (FEderation of MIxed Simulation) tool by using C/C++ language. It enables to develop parallel simulations and federate them as distributed simulations from outputs of the PickCell tool [11]. The framework CERTI [17,18] was used in this project as role of RTI. Meanwhile, the X Window System [24] was employed to provide a GUI (Graphical User Interface) environment for displaying simulation results and interacting with users.

5.3 Scenario 1 - The Parallel Simulation of Pollution Diffusion in the River

We used the river model for pollution diffusion that presented in Sect. 3.2. Initially, two polluted points were randomly created in the river. After 4 steps the diffusion of pollution is shown in Fig. 8. The darker regions implied the larger density of pollution, and vice versa.

Fig. 8. The parallel simulation of diffusing pollution in a river. This is initialized with two polluted points (dark points).

5.4 Scenario 2 - The Interactions Between the Forest and the River Federate

Regarding to simulate the interactions of physical systems in CPSs. We lunched a federation of a mixed simulation with three federates: river, forest, and observer. In which, the two first ones run on the GPUs.

In this case, the river federate created and joined the federation on the RTI-CERTI. It waited for the forest federates to enter. The river federate sent a request to others to achieve a synchronization point in the federation. And then the synchronization point was achieved.

Figure 9 showed that the ashes (brown points) formed by the fire (red points) polluted the river from the step 4 as they spread close to the river. This also shows that models based on the CA can work together in the common time progress.

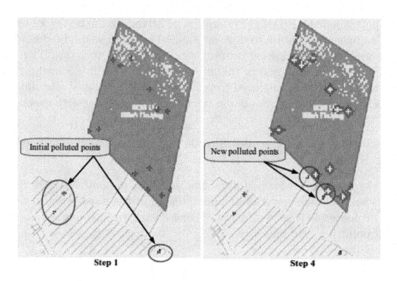

Fig. 9. The screen shoot was taken from the observer federate. It shows the data exchange between the river and forest federate in the federation. Two regions marked the small red circles represent the new polluted points created by the ashes, which are formed from the forest fire after 4 steps (Color figure online).

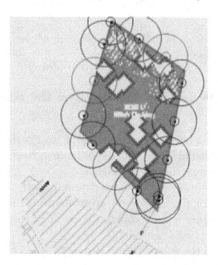

Fig. 10. The interoperability of four federates under the context of the mixed simulation: river, forest, WSN, and observer. The sensors changed to red color since the fire was detected close to them (Color figure online).

5.5 Scenario 3 - The Federation of Mixed Simulation with the Four Federates: River, Forest, WSN, and Observer

The models were presented in Sect. 3.6. The sensors nodes were represented by black points in the forest. They appeared with the sensing ranges (small circles) and communication ranges (large circles).

As the previous case, the four federates first need to achieved a synchronous point. At each step, these federates exchange data together via the RTI.

Figure 10 presents the results captured from the observer federate. In this scenarios, due to no fire close to the river, until step 4, there were no new polluted points created in the river. Meanwhile, since a sensor recognizes that the fire appeared within its sensing range (smaller circle), it will change its color, sensing and communication range (larger circle) to red color.

6 Conclusion

In context of modeling and simulating for cyber-physical systems, we have described a new approach on the federation for simulations. The models of physical systems are based on cellular automata. In this method, they must have at least two components: cell system and transition rules. The FEMIS tool has developed in order to simulate those models in parallel and perform the federations of the those simulations. The parallel computations on the GPU aim to reduce the simulating time for large and complex models. The experimental results were obtained by federating the three parallel simulations for forest fire spread, river pollution diffusion and wireless sensor network. By using federated simulations, the behavior of physical systems with their interactions could be observed in simulation progress.

References

1. Lee, E.A.: CPS foundations. In: Proceedings of the 47th Design Automation Conference (DAC), pp. 737–742. ACM (2010)
2. Wolfram, S.: Computation theory of cellular automata. Commun. Math. Phys. **96**(1), 15–57 (1984)
3. Hoekstra, A.G., Kroc, J., Sloot, P.M.A.: Simulating Complex Systems by Cellular Automata, chap. 1. Springer-Verlag, Berlin and Heidelberg (2010)
4. Wolfram, S.: Cellular automata: a model of complexity. Nature **31**, 419–424 (1984)
5. Riley, D., Eyisi, E., Bai, J., Koutsoukos, X., Xue, Y., Sztipanovits, J.: Networked control system wind tunnel (NCSWT)- an evaluation tool for networked multi-agent systems. In: The Fourth International Conference on Simulation Tools and Techniques (SIMUTools), Barcelona, Spain, p. 918 (2011)
6. Branicky, M.S., Liberatore, V., Al-Hammouri, A.T.: Co-simulation tools for networked control systems. In: Egerstedt, M., Mishra, B. (eds.) HSCC 2008. LNCS, vol. 4981, pp. 16–29. Springer, Heidelberg (2008)
7. Li, D., Li, X., Liu, X., Chen, Y.M., Li, S.Y., Liu, K., Qiao, J.G., Zheng, Y.Z., Zhang, Y.H., Lao, C.H.: GPU-CA model for large-scale land-use change simulation. Chin. Sci. Bull. **57**(19), 2442–2452 (2012). SP Science China Press

8. Liang, Q., Xia, Y., Du, J.: Parallel simulation based on GPU-acceleration. In: Xiao, T., Zhang, L., Fei, M. (eds.) AsiaSim 2012, Part II. CCIS, vol. 324, pp. 355–362. Springer, Heidelberg (2012)

9. Blecic, I., Cecchini, A., Trunfio, G.A.: Cellular automata simulation of urban dynamics through GPGPU. J. Supercomput. **6**(2), 614–629 (2013). Springer, US

10. Gulati, K., Khatri, S.P.: GPU Architecture and the CUDA Programming Model. Hardware Acceleration of EDA Algorithms, chap. 3. Springer, US (2010)

11. Pottier, B., Lucas, P.-Y.: Dynamic networks NetGen: objectives, installation, use, and programming. Université de Bretagne Occidentale (2014)

12. Oliveira, L.M.L., Rodrigues, J.J.P.C.: Wireless sensor networks: a survey on environmental monitoring. J. Commun. **6**(2), 143–151 (2011)

13. IEEE: IEEE Standard for Modeling and Simulation (M&S) High Level Architecture (HLA) - Framework and Rules. IEEE Std 1516TM-2010, pp. 1–38 (2010)

14. IEEE: IEEE Standard for Modeling and Simulation (M&S) High Level Architecture (HLA) - Federate Interface Specification. IEEE Std 1516TM-2010, pp. 1–378 (2010)

15. IEEE: IEEE standard for Modeling and Simulation (M&S) High Level Architecture (HLA) - Object Model Template (omt) Specification. IEEE Std 1516.2TM-2010, pp. 1–110 (2010)

16. Mekong Delta Region, South of Vietnam. https://www.openstreetmap.org

17. Noulard, E., Rousselot, J.-Y., Siron, P.: CERTI, an open source RTI, why and how. Spring Simulation Interoperability Workshop (2009)

18. d'Ausbourg, B., Siron, P., Noulard, E.: Running real time distributed simulations under linux and CERTI. In: 2008 Euro Simulation Interoperability Workshop Proceedings, 08E-SIW-061 (2008)

19. Alvarado, J.R., Osuna, R.V., Tuokko, R.: Distributed simulation in manufacturing using high level architecture. In: Ratchev, S., Koelemeijer, S. (eds.) Micro-Assembly Technologies and Applications. International Federation for Information Processing, vol. 260, pp. 121–156. Springer, US (2008)

20. Lasnier, G., Cardoso, J., Siron, P., Pagetti, C., Derler, P.: Distributed simulation of heterogeneous and real-time systems. In: Proceedings of IEEE International Symposium on Distributed Simulation and Real-Time Applications, pp. 55–62 (2003)

21. Kyoung-Soo, W., Jong-Chan, K., Chang-Gun, L.: A novel simulation framework for supporting real-time cyber-physical interactions. In: The Fifth IEEE International Conference on Service-Oriented Computing and Applications (SOCA), pp. 1–3 (2011)

22. Wu, G., Wu, Y., Xu, J., Lin, J.: NCCPIS: a co-simulation tool for networked control and cyber-physical system evaluation. In: Park, J.J., Zomaya, A., Yeo, S.-S., Sahni, S. (eds.) NPC 2012. LNCS, vol. 7513, pp. 85–93. Springer, Heidelberg (2012)

23. ForwardSim Inc., Simulation and Technologies: HLA Toolbox for MATLAB - HLA Blockset for Simulink (2013). http://www.forwardsim.com

24. Scheifler, R.W., Gettys, J.: The X window system. ACM Trans. Graph. **5**(2), 79–109 (1986)

25. Zhou, F., Li, S., Hou, X.: Development method of simulation and test system for vehicle body CAN bus based on CANoe. In: The 7th World Congress on Intelligent Control and Automation (WCICA), pp. 7515–7519. IEEE (2008)

Forecasting the Brown Plant Hopper Infection Levels Using Set-Valued Decision Rules

Hiep Xuan Huynh, Tai Tan Phan, Lan Phuong Phan[(⌧)],
and Son Truong Nguyen

Can Tho University, Can Tho City, Viet Nam
{hxhiep,pttai,pplan}@ctu.edu.vn,
truongsontukg@gmail.com

Abstract. This study introduces a new approach in forecasting the brown plant hopper (BPH) infection levels using the set-valued decision rules. The experiment was conducted in two scenarios, and was supported by the tool SSBPH – the tool is developed by authors. The experimental results help the agricultural managers process information on BPH, forecast the infection of BPH, and give the recommendation to farmers.

Keywords: Brown plant hopper · Set-valued decision rule · Infection level

1 Introduction

Brown plant hopper*s (BPH)* cling to the stem of rice to absorb the sap. In addition, BPH also cause the yellow dwarf disease - an extremely dangerous disease for rice. The life cycle of BPH is 25–28 days. In each month, the peak period that the mature BPH fly into light traps is 5–7 days [3]. BPH not only spread in the local scope, but also migrate from one region to another [2]. Therefore, forecasting the BPH infection levels help the agricultural managers give the recommendation to farmers. The agricultural managers use the number of mature BPH flying into light traps and other influential factors such as the wind direction, the wind speed, the rainfall, the humidity, etc. to conduct the forecast of BPH.

Some studies on warning BPH are presented in [2, 13, 15, 16]. In [15], simulating the BPH density based on the interpolation technique and the multi-agents system supports the managers in observing the distribution of BPH populations on rice fields. In [13], simulating the spread of BPH in the Mekong River delta is based on the life cycle of BPH and the wind direction. In [2], monitoring the cultivated area, the used rice varieties as well as the development stages of the rice are used in order to prevent BPH. In [16], the linear correlation between the areas cultivated by the BHP resistance varieties and the areas infected by BHP, and the linear regression equation was used to delineate the map of the BHP infected areas. However, all these studies are the single-valued approaches.

This paper proposes a new approach to forecast the BPH infection level using the set-valued decision rule. This rule is formed by many factors such as the number of BPH flying into the light traps, the wind speed, the wind direction, the temperature, and

© ICST Institute for Computer Sciences, Social Informatics and Telecommunications Engineering 2016
P.C. Vinh and V. Alagar (Eds.): ICCASA 2015, LNICST 165, pp. 177–186, 2016.
DOI: 10.1007/978-3-319-29236-6_18

the rainfall. In addition, the peak period must also be selected. This approach will specify the BPH infection level in a region; thereby build the plans for the BPH warning on the immigration levels and the propagation directions in scenarios.

The paper is organized into 5 sections. The first section introduces the context and the approach for solving the problem. The second section focuses on some definitions of set-valued decision information system. The third section proposes the model, forms the set-valued decision rules to warn BPH. The fourth section introduces data and the tool SISBPH used for experiments, and some scenarios for warning BPH. The final section is the conclusion.

2 Set-Valued Decision Rules

2.1 Set-Valued Decision Information System

The set-valued decision information system is defined as as a collection of 4 elements [18] $<U, Q_1 \cup \{d\}, V, f>$, where U is a nonempty finite set of N objects $\{x_1, x_2, \ldots, x_N\}$; Q_1 is a finite set of the condition attributes; d is a decision attribute; $Q = Q_1 \cup \{d\}$, $Q_1 \cap \{d\} = \emptyset$; $V = V_{Q_1} \cup V_d$, where V_{Q_1} is a set of the condition attribute values and V_d is a set of the decision attribute value; f is a mapping from $Ux(Q_1 \cup \{d\})$ to V, that is $f : UxQ_1 \rightarrow 2^{V_{Q_1}}$ is a set-valued mapping and $f : Ux\{d\} \rightarrow V_d$ is a single-valued mapping.

For example, Table 1 presents a set-valued decision information system of 10 objects $= \{x_1, x_2, \ldots, x_{10}\}$, each object has 1 decision attribute $\{d\}$ and 5 condition attributes $Q_1 = \{q_1, q_2, q_3, q_4, q_5\}$.

Table 1. A set-valued decision information system of 10 objects.

U	q_1	q_2	q_3	q_4	q_5	d
x_1	{1}	{0,1}	{0}	{1,2}	{2}	3
x_2	{0,1}	{2}	{1,2}	{0}	{0}	1
x_3	{0}	{1,2}	{1}	{0,1}	{0}	1
x_4	{0}	{1}	{1}	{1}	{0,2}	2
x_5	{2}	{1}	{0,1}	{0}	{1}	2
x_6	{0,2}	{1}	{0,1}	{0}	{1}	2
x_7	{1}	{0,2}	{0,1}	{1}	{2}	3
x_8	{0}	{2}	{1}	{0}	{0,1}	1
x_9	{1}	{0,1}	{0,2}	{1}	{2}	3
x_{10}	{1}	{1}	{2}	{0,1}	{2}	2

2.2 Maximal Tolerance Class

Given a set-valued decision information system $<U, Q_1 \cup \{d\}, V, f>$, a tolerance class of $x \in U$ based on set of the condition attributes $B \subseteq Q_1$ is defined as the following [18]: $T_B(x) = \{y/y \in U, \forall b \in B : b(x) \cap b(y) \neq \emptyset\} = \cap_{b \in B} T_b(x)$.

For example, using Table 1 and if $B = Q_1 = \{q_1, q_2, q_3, q_4, q_5\}$, we have $T_B(x_1) = T_B(x_7) = \{x_1, x_7, x_9\}$, $T_B(x_2) = T_B(x_8) = \{x_2, x_3, x_8\}$, $T_B(x_3) = \{x_2, x_3, x_4, x_8\}$, $T_B(x_4) = \{x_3, x_4\}$, $T_B(x_5) = T_B(x_6) = \{x_5, x_6\}$, $T_B(x_9) = \{x_1, x_7, x_9, x_{10}\}$, $T_B(x_{10}) = \{x_9, x_{10}\}$.

Classifying the set of objects U using the concept of the tolerance class can lead to two cases: (1) the objects of $T_Q(x)$ may not possess any common attribute values; (2) with $x \neq y$; $x, y \in U$, there exist the inclusion relation between $T_Q(x)$ and $T_Q(y)$. In the above example, the inclusion relation is $T_B(x_2) \in T_B(x_3)$.

The maximal tolerance class is the maximal set of objects which are tolerant with each other. For example, using Table 1, the maximal tolerance classes are presented in Table 2.

Table 2. The maximal tolerance classes.

Maximal tolerance class	Tolerance value
$\{x_1, x_7, x_9\}$	(1, 0, 0, 1, 2)
$\{x_2, x_3, x_8\}$	(0, 2, 1, 0, 0)
$\{x_3, x_4\}$	(0, 1, 1, 1, 0)
$\{x_5, x_6\}$	(2, 1, {0, 1}, 0, 1)
$\{x_9, x_{10}\}$	(1, 1, 2, 1, 2)

2.3   Set-Valued Decision Rules

Given a set-valued decision information system $< U, Q_1 \cup \{d\}, V, f >$, and $B \subseteq Q_1$, K^B (K^P) is called the set of maximal tolerance classes on B (P). $desK^B$ is the set of tolerance values of K^B. The decision rule defined by K^B is [18]:

$$desK^B \rightarrow \vee_{i \in d(K^B)}(d, i) where\ d(K^B) = \{i | \exists x \in K^B, d(x) = i\}$$

(i) if $d(K^B) = \{i\}$, $des(K^B) \rightarrow (d, i)$ is called the finite set-valued rule;
(ii) if $i \in d(K^B)$ and $d(K^B) - \{i\} \neq \emptyset$, $des(K^B) \rightarrow (d, i)$ is called the infinite set-valued rule.

Table 3. An example of the decision rules (*: the finite decision rule; **: the infinite decision rule).

K_i^B	$des(K_i^B)$	The decision rule
$K_1^B = \{x_1, x_7, x_9\}$	(1, 0, 0, 1, 2)	(1, 0, 0, 1, 2) → (d,3)*
$K_2^B = \{x_2, x_3, x_8\}$	(0, 2, 1, 0, 0)	(0, 2, 1, 0, 0) → (d,1)*
$K_3^B = \{x_3, x_4\}$	(0, 1, 1, 1, 0)	(0, 1, 1, 1, 0) → (d,1)∨(d,2)**
$K_4^B = \{x_5, x_6\}$	(2, 1, {0, 1}, 0, 1)	(2, 1, {0, 1}, 0, 1) → (d,2)*
$K_5^B = \{x_9, x_{10}\}$	(1, 1, 2, 1, 2)	(1, 1, 2, 1, 2) → (d,2)∨(d,3)**

For example, using Table 1 and if $B = Q_1 = \{q_1, q_2, q_3, q_4, q_5\}$, we have the results as follows (Table 3).

3 Forecasting the BPH Infection Level Using the Set-Valued Decision Rules

3.1 The Set-Valued Decision Information System of the BPH Forecast

The set-valued decision information system is defined as a collection of 4 elements $<U, Q, V, f>$. U is a nonempty finite set of N objects which are the light traps $U = \{b_1, b_2, \ldots, b_N\}$. Q is the set of 5 condition attributes which are the number of BPH, the wind direction, the wind speed, the temperature, and the rainfall $Q = \{q_1, q_2, q_3, q_4, q_5\}$; and 1 decision atrribute. To solve the problem using the set-valued decision information system, some conventions are proposed as follows.

The number of BPH (q1): this attribute is the number of BPH flying into a light trap, and is described in Table 4.

The wind direction (q₂): Vietnam has the tropical monsoon climate with two seasons annually (the dry season and the rainy season); and two main wind directions: southwest from January to July and northeast from late July to December. Therefore, in

Table 4. The convention on the number of BPH flying into a light trap (unit: individual).

The number of BPH (r)	Value of q_1 (the migration level of BPH)
0	0
$0 < r \le 200$	1
$200 < r \le 600$	2
$600 < r \le 900$	3
$900 < r \le 1200$	4
$1200 < r$	5

Table 5. The description of the set-valued decision rules.

d	Explanation
0	At present, the place of a light trap and its neighbours do not have BPH.
1.1	At present, the migration level and the propagation direction at the place of a light trap and its neighbours is 1 and 1 respectively.
1.2	The migration level and the propagation direction are 1 and 2 respectively.
2.1	The migration level and the propagation direction are 2 and 1 respectively.
2.2	The migration level and the propagation direction are 2 and 2 respectively.
3.1	The migration level and the propagation direction are 3 and 1 respectively.
3.2	The migration level and the propagation direction are 3 and 2 respectively.
4.1	The migration level and the propagation direction are 4 and 1 respectively.
4.2	The migration level and the propagation direction are 4 and 2 respectively.
5.1	The migration level and the propagation direction is 5 and 1 respectively.
5.2	The migration level and the propagation direction is 5 and 2 respectively.

the proposed model, information on the wind direction at a light trap is assigned one of two values: 1 (southwest) and 2 (northeast).

The wind speed, the temperature, and the rainfall (q_3, q_4, q_5): are assigned the measured values in the reality (unit of wind speed is m/s, unit of temperature is °C, and unit of rainfall is mm).

The decision attribute (d): is defined as Table 5.

For example, data collected at 3 light traps and on 5 constitutive days is shown in Table 6. The value f of the light trap b_i and the attribute q_j is a set of 5 values corresponding to 5 days.

Table 6. A set-valued decision information system collected at 3 light traps and on 5 constitutive days.

U	q_1	q_2	q_3	q_4	q_5	d
b_1	{1,1,1,1,1}	{1,1,1,1,1}	{2.3,3,4,4,2,3.6}	{27,28,28,28,29}	{4,3,0,0,0}	1.1
b_2	{1,1,2,1,1}	{1,1,1,1,1}	{2.3,3,4,4,2,3.5}	{27,28,28,28,29}	{3,1,0,0,0}	2.1
b_3	{3,1,1,1,1}	{1,1,1,1,1}	{2.3,3,4,4,2,3.6}	{27,28,28,28,29}	{4,3,0,0,0}	3.2

3.2   Forecasting the Migration of BPH – Scenario 1

At the nymphal period of the life cycle (7–10 days), BPH can move from this rice field to other rice fields. The migration of BPH will outbreak when the density is greater than 10000 individual/m^2 or the food is depleted (rice at the pre-harvest stage). When BPH migrate to a particular area, after 5 to 7 days, they will spawn. In the suitable environmental conditions, the proportion of female: male is 3: 1; each female can lay 150–250 eggs, and the hatching time is about 1 week, therefore there are the overlap generations [14].

The objective of the scenario is to identify locations where BPH migrate to and the propagation direction of BPH.

The decision rules
$f(q_{1i})$ is called the value from day 1 to day i, *n.k* is called the decision value. If $\exists f(q_{1i}) = n$ *and* $n = \max(f(q_{1i}))$*then* $d = n.k$. Suppose that the value of wind direction q_2 is 1, and attributes q_3, q_4, q_5 are suitable for the development and the migration of BPH, we define the decision rules as follows.

$$\{q_{1i} = 1, q_2 = 1, q_3, q_4, q_5\} \rightarrow (d, 1.1);$$
$$\{q_{1i} = 2, q_2 = 1, q_3, q_4, q_5\} \rightarrow (d, 2.1);$$
$$\{q_{1i} = 3, q_2 = 1, q_3, q_4, q_5\} \rightarrow (d, 3.1);$$
$$\{q_{1i} = 4, q_2 = 1, q_3, q_4, q_5\} \rightarrow (d, 4.1);$$
$$\{q_{1i} = 5, q_2 = 1, q_3, q_4, q_5\} \rightarrow (d, 1.1).$$

The propagation direction of BPH

If BPH migrate, they mainly move by jumping from this rice leaf to other leaf. Only individual with the long wing can move far. The migration of BPH is based on wind, therefore determining the wind direction and the wind speed is very important [11].

Suppose that the condition attributes q_3, q_4, q_5 are suitable for the development and the migration of BPH, and the value of q_1 is 3, the decision rules corresponding to the wind directions are:

$$\{q_1 = 3, q_2 = 1, q_3, q_4, q_5\} \rightarrow (d, 3.1);$$
$$\{q_1 = 3, q_2 = 2, q_3, q_4, q_5\} \rightarrow (d, 3.2).$$

We call R to be the propagation radius $R = V_{wind} x T_{wind}(1)$ where V_{wind} is the wind speed, T_{wind} is the moving time. The spread area is the circular sector with an angle β. Its area is calculated by $S = \frac{1}{2}R^2\beta(2)$. BPH can migrate to regions of this area.

3.3   Forecasting the Migration of BPH – Scenario 2

The objective of the scenario is to identify locations where BPH do not migrate. The mature BPH tend to fly into the light traps strongly [3]. Therefore,

– If a light trap does not collect any BPH, there are three cases: (1) at present, the migration of BPH does not occur at the place of that light trap and its neighbors; (2) at present, BPH is not yet mature; (3) both of the above cases. The decision rule will be $\{q_1 = 0, q_2, q_3, q_4, q_5\} \rightarrow (d, 0)$.
– If a light trap has BPH, the food (rice) is copious, and the BPH density in the rice field <10000 individual/m^2; then the decision rule will be
– $\{q_1 \neq 0, q_2, q_3, q_4, q_5\} \rightarrow (d, 0)$.

4   Experiment

4.1   Experimental Data

Experimental data is collected at 7 places locating 7 light traps $\{b_1, b_2, \ldots, b_7\}$ on 5 constitutive days from 02/10/2014 to 02/14/2014. For each place, data is stored in the table as the follow (Table 7).

Table 7. The collected data of the first place (b_1) on 5 constitutive days.

	The number of BPH	Wind direction	Wind speed	Temperature	Rainfall
Day 1	0	Southwest	2.3	27	30
Day 2	0	Southwest	3.4	28	3
Day 3	0	Southwest	4	28	0
Day 4	0	Southwest	2	28	0
Day 5	0	Southwest	3.4	29	0

4.2   Tool SSBPH

Tool SSBPH (Set valued decision Information System - warning Brown Plant Hopper) is implemented by using Smalltalk [10], and integrated into Netgen framework [9]. This tool support users the functions: (i) read and store data into a template; (ii) standardize the single-valued data to store into a set-valued decision information systems; (iii) build the tolerance classes; (iv) define the maximal tolerance classes; (v) create the set-valued decision rules; (vi) display the migration level and the propagation direction of BPH on the map; (vii) produce the reports, the charts, and the support plans on warning BPH (Fig. 1).

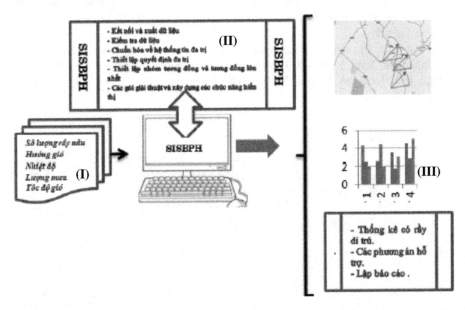

Fig. 1. The tool SISBPH: (I) is the input data – information collected from the places locating the light traps are the number of BPH, the wind direction, the wind speed, the temperature, the rainfall; (II) is the list of functions of this tool; and (III) is the output such as the chart, the report, and the support plans.

4.3   Identifying the Migration of BPH – Scenario 1

The objective of the scenario is to identify locations where BPH migrate to and the propagation direction of BPH for 7 locations $\{b_1, b_2, b_3, b_4, b_5, b_6, b_7\}$.

Using the tool SISBPH and empirical data collected from 7 light traps, the obtained results are the follows.

The maximal tolerance classes are $K_1 = \{b_1, b_3\}; K_2 = \{b_2, b_6\}; K_3 = \{b_4, b_5, b_7\}$
The decision rules are

$$desK_1 = (0, 1, \{2.3, 3.4, 4\}, \{27, 28, 29\}, \{30, 3, 0\}) \rightarrow (d, 0)$$
$$desK_2 = (\{1, 2\}, 1, \{2.3, 4, 2\}, \{27, 28, 29\}, \{3, 0\}) \rightarrow (d, 1) \vee (d, 2)$$
$$desK_3 = (\{2, 3\}, 1, 2, \{28\}, \{3, 1, 0\}) \rightarrow (d, 2) \vee (d, 3)$$

Because of $(\{q_1 > 0\}, q_2, q_3, q_4, q_5) \rightarrow (d, a)$ *and* $a > 0$, the decision rules created by K_2 and K_3 are used for identifying the migration of BPH. For K_2, we choose $d_2 = \max(d_{2i}) = 2(2.1)$; For K_3, we choose $d_3 = \max(d_{3i}) = 3(3.1)$. Therefore, the migration level of BPH at locations $K_2 = \{b_2, b_6\}$ is level 2, and at locations $K_3 = \{b_4, b_5, b_7\}$ is level 3.

The propagation direction. At locations $(\{b_2, b_6\}, \{b_4, b_5, b_7\})$, given the moving time $T_{wind} = 2$ h and $\beta = 30°$, using formulae (1) and (2), the propagation radius R and the area of the circular sector S are R = 19.92 km and S = 597.6 km². The result is shown in Fig. 2.

At that time, the mature BPH flying into the light traps is in level 2 (200–600 individuals) and level 3 (600–900 individuals), we propose the following plans.

Plan 1: at locations K_2 and K_3, rice planted at the propagation regions is very young (seedlings).

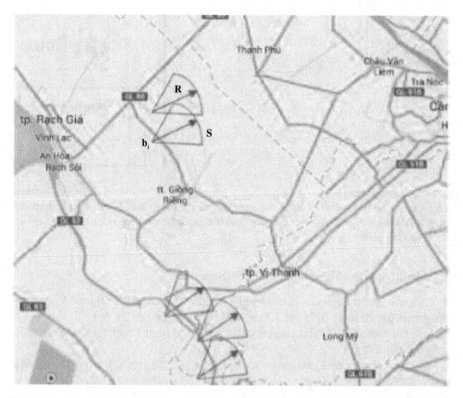

Fig. 2. The map displaying the propagation of BPH at locations K_2 and K_3 with the propagation radius R = 19.92 km and the propagation area S = 597.6 km².

The farmers should let the rice sprout to be flooded in water at night (from 5 pm to 7 am the next morning), and outcropped the water at daytime; this work is maintained in 3–4 days; until the farmers do not see the mature BPH flying the light traps, the water will be managed under the normal method.

Plan 2: at locations K_2 and K_3, rice planted at the propagation regions is less than 20 days old.

Plan 1 can be applied. However, if the density of migration of BPH is high, the farmers should spray the pesticide to keep the natural enemies system on the rice fields. The best time to spray is the time that the number of BPH flying into the light traps is the largest.

Plan 3: at locations K_2 and K_3, rice planted at the propagation regions is greater than 20 days old.

If on the rice field, the BPH is at the age of 1-3, or the number of mature BPH is equal or greater than 3 individuals/strand, the farmers should spray the pesticide.

Plan 4: at locations K_2 and K_3, the propagation regions are prepared for sowing.

The number of BPH flying into the light traps is still collected in next days, if this number decreases, the farmers should prepare seeds and sow them.

4.4   Identifying the Migration of BPH – Scenario 2

The objective of the scenario is to identify locations where BPH do not migrate for 7 locations $\{b_1, b_2, b_3, b_4, b_5, b_6, b_7\}$.

Similar to scenario 1, the tool SISBPH and empirical data collected from 7 light traps are also used. The maximal tolerance classes K_1, K_2, K_3 and the decision rules of both scenarios are the same. Because of $desK_1 \rightarrow (d, 0)$, there is no BPH at locations $K_1 = \{b_1, b_3\}$ and its neighbors. In this case, we do not calculate the radius R and identify the propagation direction.

Plan 1: b_1, b_3 are the propagation regions.

The farmers should visit the rice fields regularly; specify the age of BPH; continue to monitor the light traps every day. When there is the migration of BPH, scenario 1 will be used.

Plan 2: b_1, b_3 are not the propagation regions.

The farmers should visit the rice fields regularly; specify the density of BPH; follow the recommendations of experts on using rice varieties, the pesticide, etc.

5   Conclusion

The paper presents the set-valued decision information system and the basis for establishing the set-valued decision rules. Based on the presented theory, this paper proposes a model to warn the migration of BPH.

In this study, the tool SISBPH is developed to support the experts on warning BPH. This tool process the collected data, established the set-valued decision rules, identify the locations where BPH migrate to as well as the infection levels. The experiment is conducted at seven locations in the Mekong Delta; from this experiment the plans are proposed.

References

1. Otuka, A.: A migration analysis of the rice planthopper Nilaparvata lugens from the Philippines to East Asia with three-dimensional computer simulations. Soc. Popul. Ecol. **47**, 143–150 (2005). doi:10.1007/s10144-005-0216-1
2. Otuka, A.: Migration of rice planthoppers and simulation techniques. In: Heong, K.L., Hardy, B. (eds.) Planthoppers: New Threats to the Sustainability of Intensive Rice Production Systems in Asia, pp. 343–356. International Rice Research Institute, Los Baños (2009)
3. Bong, B.B., et al.: The guide to prevent brown plant hopper. Ministry Agric. Rural Dev. (2006). (Vietnamese)
4. Cios, K.J., Pedrycz, W., Swiniarski, R.W.: Rough Sets: Data Mining: Methods for Knowledge Discovery, pp. 27–45. Kluwer Academic Publishers, Boston (1998)
5. Susanti, E., Ramadhani, F., June, T., Amiena, L.I.: Utilization of climate information for development of early warning system for Brown Plant Hopper attack on rice. Donesian J. Agric. **3**(1), 17–25 (2010)
6. Bierkens, F.P., Finke, P.A., de Willigen, P.: Upscaling and Downscaling Methods for Environmental Research. Kluwer Academic Publishers, Dordrecht (2000). ISBN-10: 0792363396
7. Valacich, J.S., George, J.F., Hoffer, J.A.: Modern System Analysis & Design. Prentice Hall, Pearson Education, Upper Saddle River (2009)
8. Heong, K.L., Hardy, B.: Planthoppers: new threats to the sustainability of intensive rice production systems in Asia. International Rice Research Institute, Los Baños (2009)
9. NetGen website, A generator of concurrent systems. http://wsn.univ-brest.fr/NetGen/
10. Goldberg, A., Robson, D.: Smalltalk-80 the Language, pp. 31–75. Addison Wesley, Reading (1989)
11. Chau, L.M.: State of insecticide resistance of Brown Plant Hopper in Mekong Delta. Cuu Long Delta Rice Research Institute, Omonrice Press, Vietnam, pp. 185–190 (2007)
12. Tai, P.T., et al.: Academic advising undergraduate groups based on the approach of maximal tolerance class of set-valued information system. J. Sci. Can Tho Univ. (Spec. Issue: Inf. Technol.), 123–133 (2013). (Vietnamese)
13. Phan, C.H., Huynh, H.X., Drogoul, A.: An agent-based approach to the simulation of Brown Plant Hopper (BPH) invasions in the Mekong Delta. In: IEEE RIVF 2010, Proceedings of the 8th IEEE International Conference on Computer Sciences: Research & Innovation – Vision for the Future, pp. 43–49. Ville de Hanoi, Vietnam (2010)
14. Van Kim, P.: Principles of Plant Diseases. Can Tho University, Vietnam (2004). (Vietnamese)
15. Huynh, V.K., et al.: Simulating the distribution of BPH in Dongthap province based on inverse distance weight interpolation technique and multi-agent system. Dong Thap University, Cao Lãnh (2010). (Vietnamese)
16. Nguyen, V.G.N., Huynh, H.X.: Toward an agent-based multi-scale recommendation system for Brown Plant Hopper control. In: UKSim-AMSS 6th European Modelling Symposium (2012)
17. Quang, T.T., et al.: Application of GIS in predicting medium term of rice infected by Brown plant hopper – a case study in Dong thap province. J. Sci. Can Tho Univ. **17a**, 103–109 (2011). (Vietnamese)
18. Guan, Y.-Y., Wang, H.-K.: Set-valued information systems. Inf. Sci. **176**(17), 2507–2525 (2006)

The Coverage Model
for the Forest Fire Detection Based
on the Wireless Sensor Network

Hiep Xuan Huynh, Tai Tan Phan, Lan Phuong Phan[(✉)],
and Nguyen Tran Trinh

Can Tho University, Can Tho City, Vietnam
{hxhiep,pttai,pplan}@ctu.edu.vn,
pplan@cit.ctu.edu.vn,
trinhnguyen88@gmail.com

Abstract. Wireless sensor networks are being effectively applied in the forest fire detection. Building a model of sensors covering the entire area of the forest is the important problem. This paper proposes the coverage model using the new approach to decrease the number of sensors. With this approach, the sensors are classified into several groups; and those groups work in the alternative way but meet the complete coverage. Experimental results on the map of the forest in Dong Thap province shows that the model works well and meets the complete coverage.

Keywords: Wireless sensor networks · Coverage model · Forest fire detection

1   Introduction

Wireless sensor networks [8] when deployed have to cover the targets (subjects to be observed and tracked), that is the targets must always lie within the scope for monitoring and tracking sensors. Guaranteeing the coverage is the most important requirement for a sensor network [1, 7] and identifying the coverage area is the task to be studied firstly before sensor networks are deployed. The coverage also helps overcome the limitations of a sensor network such as supporting for routing protocol and MAC protocol [4], or addressing the strict requirement of energy and increasing the lifetime of the network [2, 3]. Therefore, the coverage is an important problem for wireless sensor networks and the problem for identifying the coverage has posed many challenges.

Two approaches related to the use of wireless sensor networks for the forest fire detection are interested in [5, 6]. The first approach studies and improves the collected data processing methods in order to make more accurate forecasts. The second approach optimizes the coverage problem of a sensor network. In the first approach, the theory of Type-2 Fuzzy System, the theory of Dempster-Shafer and the threshold method, the probability and the simulated model, and SVM machine learning are used in [9, 10, 11, 12] respectively. All of those methods identify the forest fires based on collected data sets of wireless sensor networks. The second approach builds the algorithms to optimize the coverage problem in a sensor network. The distribution

© ICST Institute for Computer Sciences, Social Informatics and Telecommunications Engineering 2016
P.C. Vinh and V. Alagar (Eds.): ICCASA 2015, LNICST 165, pp. 187–197, 2016.
DOI: 10.1007/978-3-319-29236-6_19

algorithm PEAS, the algorithm evaluating the redundant nodes, the Clifford algebra, the coverage algorithm for related multi-targets MTACA, K-coverage algorithm are used in [13–16] respectively. Overall, many algorithms were proposed but there are many problems in the algorithms [5–7], and especially, the research on the complete coverage problem for wireless sensor networks of the forest fire detection has not yet investigated.

In this paper, we propose a new approach in specifying the forest area is covered by a wireless sensor network based on a coverage graph. With this approach, the wireless sensor network is seen as an undirected graph, each sensor is a node of the graph, and the communication connection between sensors is a graph edge. The professional knowledge base is the opinions of experts and the specialized information resources in forestry. The research results provide a basis for building the forest fire detection model using the wireless sensor network, a new method to determine the coverage area and to implement the group to subnets to increase the lifetime of the network.

This paper is divided into four parts. The first section presents the importance of the coverage problem for wireless sensor networks, the recent researches for solving the coverage problem and the new approaches for building the coverage model of a wireless sensor network for the forest fire detection. The second section presents the modeling of the forest coverage problem and the method of specifying the coverage of the built model. The third section describes the experimental data and the tool CGFNET, and describes three scenarios: defining the forest areas that are not covered by the wireless sensor network, defining the forest areas that are covered by the sensor network, and defining the minimum coverage groups. The last section is the conclusion.

2 The Forest Coverage Problem

2.1 Modeling the Coverage Problem

Consider a sensor network consisting of n sensors s_i, $i = 1.., n$. Set r_i and R_i to be the sensing scope and communication scope of a sensor s_i respectively. The sensing area of sensor s_i is the plate where s_i is located at the center and r_i is the radius (similarity to the communication scope). There are some problems as the follows (Figs. 1 and 2).

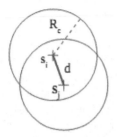

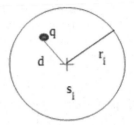

Fig. 1. The connection between the sensor s_i and the sensor s_j.

Fig. 2. The target coverage.

The target coverage: for the target q and the sensor s_i, d is called the Euclidean distance between q and s_i. The target q is covered by sensor s_i if and only if $d(q, s_i)r_i$

The coverage (the area coverage): an area A is covered by sensor s_i if and only if the target q is located in the area A with $d(q, s_i)r_i$. From the coverage problem, the area A is covered by a sensor network S if and only if every point q in A must be covered by at least one sensor s_i belonging S. Two sensors s_i, s_j are connected to each other directly when $d(s_i, s_j)R_C$ where d is the Euclidean distance between s_i and s_j; R_C is the communication scope of s_i and s_j, it means each sensor must be within their communication scope.

The communication graph: given a sensor network of n sensors, the communication graph of the network is the undirected graph $G = (V, E)$ in which V is the set of sensors, and E is the set of edges connecting two sensors that can communicate directly.

The coverage connection: given a sensor network of n sensors, and the observed area A, S is called the coverage connection of A if it meets two conditions: (1) the area A is covered by S; (2) the communication graph created by S is connected.

2.2 The Coverage Graph Based on the Wireless Sensor Network

With convention mentioned in Sect. 2.1, the coverage graph of a wireless sensor network for the forest fire detection is created as follows. Given a wireless sensor network of n sensor and the forest area A, if there is at least 01 sensor of S for 01 location in A, then the network S has the undirected graph $G = (V, E)$ in which $V = \{s_1, s_2, \ldots, s_n\}$ is a set of vertices of the sensors, E is a set of edges between two sensors which its Euclidean distance is within their communication scope.

For example, Fig. 3 presents a network of 5 sensors $\{P1, P2, P3, P4, P5\}$ with the communication radius (the communication scope) R_C. The distances $d(P1, P2)$, $d(P1, P3), d(P2, P3), d(P4, P5) < R_C$ and $d(P1, P4), d(P1, P5), d(P2, P4), d(P2, P5)$, $d(P3, P4), d(P3, P5) > R_C$. Therefore, the respective coverage graph of the network consists of 2 sub-networks: $G1 = (V1, E1)$ where $V1 = \{P1, P2, P3\}, E1 = \{P1.P2; P3.P1; P2.P3; P2.P1; P1.P3; P3.P2\}$ and $G2 = (V2, E2)$ where $V1 = \{P4, P5\}$, $E1 = \{P4.P5; P5.P4\}$.

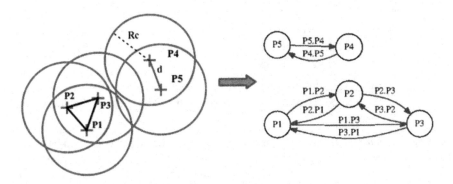

Fig. 3. The coverage graph of the sensor network (5 sensors)

The coverage graph fully reflects the statuses of the deployed sensor network, the cases can occur as follows:

(i)   The sensor network for the forest fire detection S if it satisfies the coverage connection, the coverage graph created using S is connected, corresponding to the forest covered by the deployed network.

(ii) The communication graph of the unconnected network, i.e. the network is discontinued or there are the isolated nodes. The corresponding coverage graph consists of the sub-graphs, or is the single graph with the number of vertices less than the number of nodes of the sensor network. For example, in Fig. 3, $d(P1, P4), d(P1, P5), d(P2, P4), d(P2, P5), d(P3, P4), d(P3, P5) > R_C$, or $P4$, $P5$ are not communicated to $P1, P2, P3$, therefore, the coverage graph has 2 sub-graphs G_1 and G_2.

(iii) The network that does not satisfy the coverage, i.e. there are areas that have not yet been put sensors.

2.3   Defining the Coverage Area

The distance between 02 points that have coordinates (latitude and longitude) is calculated by the Haversine formula [23].

$$a = sin^2(\Delta\varphi/2) + cos\varphi_1 \, cos\varphi_2 \, sin^2(\Delta\lambda/2)$$
$$c = 2.atan2(\sqrt{(a)}, \sqrt{(1-a)})$$

(1)

$$d = R.c$$

where φ is the latitude, λ is the longitude, $\Delta\varphi = \varphi_2 - \varphi_1$, $\Delta\lambda = \lambda_1 - \lambda_1$, and $R = 6.371$ km.

According to geographic coordinate system, the adjacent coordinates separates 01 s in latitude or longitude.

For example, Fig. 4 shows the *coordinate(latitude, longitude)* of x_i $(h_t^0 m_t' s_t''; h_l^0 m_l' s_l'')$ where ^{0} is the degree, $'$ is the minute, and $''$ is the second. 4 adjacent coordinates of x_i are: $x_b(h_t^0 m_t'(s_t + 1)''; h_l^0 m_l' s_l'')$, $x_n(h_t^0 m_t'(s_t - 1)''; h_l^0 m_l' s_l'')$, $x_d(h_t^0 m_t' s_t''; h_l^0 m_l'(s_l + 1)'')$, $x_t(h_t^0 m_t' s_t''; h_l^0 m_l'(s_l - 1)'')$. Using the formula (1), the distance between x_i and x_b is $d(x_i, x_b) \approx 30.9$ m, and the distance between x_i and x_d is $d(x_i, x_d) \approx 30.3$ m. Therefore, the area of x_i is $S_{x_i} = 30.9 \times 30.3 = 936.27$ m^2.

The forest area: given the forest A; Q_A is a set of coordinates x_i, $i = 1, .., n$ $Q_A = \{x_i, i = 1, .., n\}$. S_{x_i} is called the area of x_i, then the area of the forest A is $S_A = \sum_{i=1}^{n} S_{x_i}$ where $x_i Q_A$.

The coverage of a sensor: given a sensor w with the coordinate t (the location where the sensor w is located), and the communication radius R_w. The set Q_w of coordinates x_i, $i = 1, .., n$ is called the coverage of the sensor w if $d(t, x_i) R_w$, or $Q_w = \{x_i | d(t, x_i) R_w, i = 1, .., n\}$.

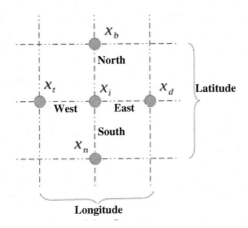

Fig. 4. Locations of the adjacent coordinates

The coverage area of a sensor: given a sensor w with the coverage $Q_w = \{x_i | d(t, x_i) R_w, i = 1, .., n\}$, then the coverage area of the sensor w is calculated as the following. $S_w = \sum_{i=1}^{n} S_{x_i}$ where $x_i Q_w$.

The coverage of a sensor network: given a sensor network W of m sensors, $w_1, w_2, \ldots, w_m$; and $Q_{w_1}, Q_{w_2}, \ldots, Q_{w_m}$ are the coverage of each sensor respectively. Q_C is called the coverage of the sensor network if $Q_C = Q_{w_1} \cup Q_{w_2} \cup \ldots \cup Q_{w_m}$, or $Q_C = \{ x_i | x_i \in Q_{w_i}, i = 1, .., n; j = 1, .., m \}$.

The coverage area of a sensor network: given a sensor network W with the coverage $Q_C = \{x_i | x_i \in Q_{w_i}, i = 1, .., n; j = 1, .., m\}$, then the coverage area of the sensor network Q_C is calculated the follow: $S_c = \sum_{i=1}^{n} S_{x_i}$ where $x_i \in Q_C$.

The complete coverage: given a forest A with the set of coordinates Q_A, and a sensor network W with the coverage Q_C. The forest A is covered completely by the sensor network W if and only if $Q_A \backslash Q_C = \emptyset$, or all coordinates of Q_A have to belong Q_C.

2.4 Defining the Minimum Coverage Groups

The minimum coverage group: given a sensor network W of m sensors $w_1 w_2, \ldots, w_m$, $Q_{w_1}, Q_{w_2}, \ldots, Q_{w_m}$ are the coverage of each sensor respectively. The coverage of that sensor network is $Q_C = \{x_i | x_i \in Q_{w_i}, i = 1, .., n; j = 1, .., m\}$. With a group of k sensors $G = w_1, w_2, \ldots, w_k$ and $k \leq m$, the coverage of that group is called Q_G. G is called the minimum coverage group of the sensor network W if and only if $Q_G \equiv Q_C$, or all coordinates of Q_G and Q_C are the same.

The method for defining the minimum coverage group: given a forest A with n coordinates x_i, $i = 1, .., n$, and a sensor network S with m sensors $s_j, j = 1, .., m$. Q_{w_i} is the coverage of s_j. The following steps are implemented.

Step 1: create a Descartes table $m \times n$ where columns are sensors s_j and rows are coordinates x_i, $(x_i, s_j) = 1$ if $x_i \in Q_j$ and $(x_i, s_j) = 0$ if $x_i \notin Q_j$.

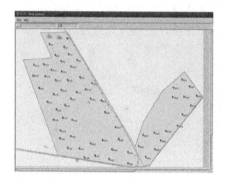

Fig. 5. The representation of 67 sensing locations on the map

Step 2: create a set of equations using the table Descartes. For each equation, its left side equals 1, and its right side is the "collection" of s_j if $(s_j, x_i) = 1$.

Step 3: solve that set of equations; its results are the minimum coverage groups.

For a sensor network of n minimal coverage groups, the lifetime of the network can be increased if the groups work in the alternative way, and the sensors of the groups that do not work at a specific time is in the sleep status [2].

3 Experiments

3.1 Experimental Data

The Forest of Tam Nong district, Dong Thap province was chosen to pilot and assess the empirical results. The input data consists of 02 datasets: the first dataset contains the coordinates (latitude, longitude) of 67 sensors to be deployed; the second dataset contains 81,301 coordinates (latitude, longitude) corresponding to the locations and 7,612 hectares of the forest in Tam Nong. The communication radius of the sensor is 1.2 km. The locations of those sensors are provided by experts (Fig. 5).

3.2 CGFNET Tool

Tools CGFNET (Coverage Graphs of Wireless Sensor Network for Forest Fire Detection) is created by ourselves. This tool is built on the Smalltalk language [24] and integrated into the platform NetGen [22]. CGFNET contains the following main functions: (i) processing the original data - including the locations of the map, the coordinates, and the sensing radius - refining input data, and storing data in the database. (ii) identifying the set of coordinates of the forest, the set of coordinates in the coverage of the sensor network. (iii) calculating the distance between the coordinates. (iv) defining the forest areas that are covered and not covered by the sensor network. (v) calculating the covered area and non-covered area. (vi) constructing the coverage graph of the sensor network. (vii) defining the minimum coverage groups. (viii) displaying the results on a map (Fig. 6).

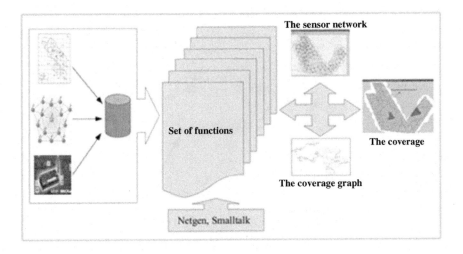

Fig. 6. Tool CGFNET

3.3 Scenarios

Scenario 1: defining the forest areas that are not covered

This scenario must identify the coordinates of all locations that are not covered by the sensor network, and calculate the area that is not covered. The set of identified coordinates are stored in a file.

The sensor network of 67 sensors with the radius 1.2 km deployed in Tam Nong forest is represented as Fig. 7. Figure 8 shows the coverage graph of this network. The constructed graph has 67 nodes, and 197 edges. The result of scenario 1 is displayed in Fig. 9. There are 1,076 locations (with the area 1,007,426.52 m^2) that are not covered by the sensor network. This result is consistent with the opinion of experts, because the locations that have not been covered are lakes, rivers, swamps unnecessary to arrange sensors. The locations - that are not covered by the sensor network - are marked the gray on the map.

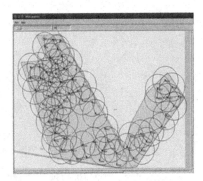

Fig. 7. The network of 67 sensors with the radius 1.2 km

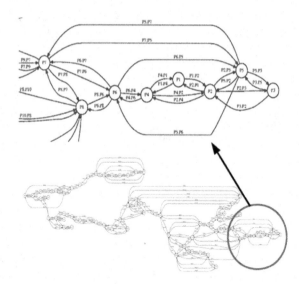

Fig. 8. The representation of the coverage graph (the network of 67 sensors with the radius 1.2 km)

Scenario 2: defining the forest areas that are covered
This scenario must identify the coordinates of all locations that are covered by the sensor network, and calculate the coverage area. The set of identified coordinates are also stored in a file.

The sensor network of 67 sensors and the coverage graph of this network are presented in Figs. 7 and 8 respectively. The result of scenario 2 - the coverage area is marked by the diagonal lines - is displayed in Fig. 10. There are 80,225 locations (with the area 75,112,260.75 m^2) that are covered by the sensor network. For the sensor network to be deployed, this result is suitable with the requirement of experts.

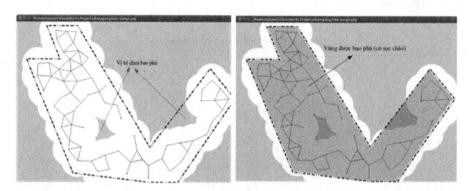

Fig. 9. The representation of the areas that are not covered by the sensor network (1)

Fig. 10. The representation of the areas that are covered by the sensor network (2)

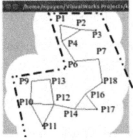

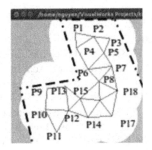

Fig. 11. The coverage of 18 sensors   **Fig. 12.** The minimum coverage group

Scenario 3: defining the minimum coverage groups
This scenario must identify the minimum coverage groups. The return result of scenario 3 is the set of locations of those groups stored in a file, and displays the coverage of groups on the map. With a network of 18 sensors in Fig. 11, we can find 01 minimum coverage group of 15 sensors {P1, P2, P3, P4, P6, P7, P9, P10, P11, P12, P13, P14, P16, P17, P18} as Fig. 12. The group of 15 sensors and the network of 18 sensors have the same coverage.

4   Conclusion

On the basic of the coverage problem for the wireless sensor network and the related issues such as specifying the distance between the coordinates of the geographic coordinate system, finding the minimal coverage, ..., the model of the coverage graph is built to define and calculate the coverage area. This model (i) presents a wireless sensor network as a graph; (ii) evaluates the coverage; (iii) develops a method for defining the coverage and calculating the coverage area by using the tool CGFNET.

The coverage problem is modeled to help the experts the support tool in defining and calculating the coverage area. The scenarios - in which the forest area, the locations and the communication radius of the wireless sensor network are provided by experts - are tested. They (i) define the locations and calculate the area that has not been covered; (ii) define the locations and calculate the area that has been covered; (iii) define the minimum coverage groups. The results of those scenarios are verified and validated by the experts.

References

1. Huang, C.F., Tseng, Y.C.: The coverage problem in a wireless sensor networks. In: Proceedings of the ACM International Workshop on Wireless Sensor Networks and Applications, pp. 115–121 (2003)
2. Luqiao, Z., Qinxin, Z., Juan, W.: Adaptive clustering for maximizing network lifetime and maintaining coverage. J. Netw. 8(3), 616–622 (2013)

3. Yulong, X., Fang, J.-A., Zhu, W.: Cui W (2013) Differential evolution for lifetime maximization of heterogeneous wireless sensor networks. Math. Probl. Eng. **172783**, 1–12 (2013)
4. He, T.C., Cao, W.M., Xie, W.-X.: Coverage analyses of plane target in sensor networks based on Clifford algebra. Acta Electron. Sin. **37**(8), 1681–1685 (2009)
5. Liang, J., Liu, M., Kui, X.: A survey of coverage problems in wireless sensor networks. Sens. Transducers **163**(1), 240–246 (2014)
6. Dagar, A., Saroha, V.: An efficient coverage scheme for wireless sensor network. Int. J. Adv. Res. Comput. Sci. Softw. Eng. **3**(4), 557–563 (2013)
7. Thai, M.T., Wang, F., Du, D.-Z.: Coverage problems in wireless sensor networks: designs and analysis. Int. J. Sens. Netw. Arch. **3**(3), 191–200 (2008)
8. Li, Y., Thai, M.T., Wu, W.: Wireless Sensor Networks and Applications. Signals and Communication Technology. Springer, Heidelberg (2008)
9. Singh, A.K., Singh, H.: Forest fire detection through wireless sensor network using type-2 fuzzy system. Int. J. Comput. Appl. **52**, 19 (2012)
10. Arnoldo, D.-R., et al.: Wireless sensor networks and fusion information methods for forest fire detection. In: The 2012 Iberoamerican Conference on Electronics Engineering and Computer Science, Procedia Technology, vol. 3, pp. 69–79 (2012)
11. Elleuch, M., et al.: Formal probabilistic analysis of a wireless sensor network for forest fire detection. In: Symbolic Computation in Software Science 2012 (SCSS2012), EPTCS 122, pp. 1–9 (2013)
12. Sathik, M.M., Mohamed, M.S., Balasubramanian, A.: Fire detection using support vector machine in wireless sensor network and rescue using pervasive devices. Int. J. Adv. Netw. Appl. **2**(2), 636 (2010)
13. Ye, F., Zhong, G., Lu, S., Zhang, L.: PEAS: a robust energy conserving protocol for long lived sensor networks. In: Proceedings of 10 th IEEE International Conference on Network Protocols (ICNP 2002), Paris, France, pp. 200–201 (2002)
14. Tian, D., Georganas, N.D.: A node scheduling scheme for energy conservation in large wireless sensor networks. Wireless Commun. Mobile Comput. **3**(2), 271–290 (2003)
15. Ping, L.L., Qiang, Z., Sun, Y.-G.: Multiple targets associated coverage algorithm in wireless sensor network. J. Tianjin Univ. **32**(6), 483–489 (2002)
16. Wang, X., Xing, G., Zhang, Y., Lu, C., Pless, R., Gill, C.D.: Integrated coverage and connectivity configuration in wireless sensor networks. In: 1st ACM Conference on Embedded Networked Sensor Systems (2003)
17. Zhou, Z., Das, S., Gupta, H.: Connected k-coverage problem in sensor networks. In: ICCCN (2004)
18. Bai, X., et al.: Optimal patterns for four-connectivity and full coverage in wireless sensor networks. IEEE Trans. Mob. Comput. **9**(3), 435–448 (2010)
19. Ostovari, P., Dehghan, M., Wu, J.: Connected point coverage in wireless sensor networks using robust spanning trees. In: 2011 31st International Conference on Distributed Computing Systems Workshops (ICDCSW), pp. 287–293 (2011)
20. Han, K., Xiang, L., Luo, J., Liu, Y.: Minimum-energy connected coverage in wireless sensor networks with omni-directional and directional features. In: Proceedings of the Thirteenth ACM International Symposium on Mobile Ad Hoc Networking and Computing, pp. 85–94 (2012)
21. Mini, S., Udgata, S.K., Sabat, S.L.: M-connected coverage problem in wireless sensor networks. Int. Sch. Res. Netw. ISRN Sens. Netw. **2012**(858021), 1–9 (2012)

22. NetGen website, a generator of concurrent systems. http://wsn.univ-brest.fr/NetGen/
23. Sinnott, R.W.: Virtues of the haversine. Sky Telescope **68**(2), 159 (1984)
24. Goldberg, A., David, R.: Smalltalk-80 the Language, pp. 31–75. Addison Wesley, Reading (1989)

Information Systems Success: The Project Management Information System for ERP Projects

Thanh D. Nguyen[1,2(✉)], Dat T. Nguyen[2], and Tuan M. Nguyen[2]

[1] Banking University of Ho Chi Minh City, Ho Chi Minh City, Vietnam
thanhnd@buh.edu.vn
[2] HCMC University of Technology, Ho Chi Minh City, Vietnam
ntdat@live.com, n.m.tuan@hcmut.edu.vn

Abstract. Project Management Information System (PMIS) is a core stone for organizations to plan and implement successfully their projects. Hence, PMIS success is also a central topic for both academicians and practitioners. Based on well–known Information Systems Success model (DeLone & McLean), highly cited Technology Acceptance Model (TAM), and the related works, a success model of PMIS for ERP projects is proposed and validated. A survey study with path analysis of 160 participants who have used the PMIS for the ERP projects at FPT Information System – a member of the FPT Group that shows all hypotheses empirically supported. The findings indicate that ERP project's success is determined by PMIS user satisfaction that in turn is influenced by user ease of use, system quality, functional–information quality, and support–service quality.

Keywords: ERP · Information systems · PMIS · Project success

1 Introduction

Globalization and the internationalization of markets have increased competitive pressures on business enterprises [42]. PMIS are widely regarded as an important building block in project management [3, 49]. In the IT industry, Gartner provides that 75 % of projects managed with the support of the PMIS will succeed, while 75 % of projects without such support will fail [27]. The nature and role of a PMIS within a project management system, have been characterized as fundamentally "*subservient to the attainment of project goals and the implementation of project strategies*" [42]. Using PMIS to manage projects, while not sufficient to insure project success, has thus become a necessity [6, 42]. DeLone and McLean [9–11] models refer back to research conducted in the model theoretical foundation of Shannon and Weaver [46] communication theory as well as Mason [29] communication systems approach. However, several researchers had referenced the original model and made suggestions for improvement (e.g., Rai et al. [39]; Seddon [44, 45]). Consequently, the studies on the IS success are essential, it is evidenced by different research that several models have been proposed to determine and measure the IS success (e.g., DeLone and McLean

© ICST Institute for Computer Sciences, Social Informatics and Telecommunications Engineering 2016
P.C. Vinh and V. Alagar (Eds.): ICCASA 2015, LNICST 165, pp. 198–211, 2016.
DOI: 10.1007/978-3-319-29236-6_20

[9, 11]; Seddon [44]; Nguyen [30]). Besides, there are several kinds of studies on PMIS (e.g., Ali et al. [4]; Raymond and Bergeron [42]; Kaiser and Ahlemann [23]). However, these studies are not entirely appropriate for measuring ERP project's success for several reasons, namely specificities, characteristics, implementation complexity [16].

Based on DeLone and McLean [9–11], TAM [8], and the related works (e.g., Seddon [44]; Kaiser and Ahlemann [23]; DeToni et al. [12]; Nwankpa [35] …), this work validates a model of the success of PMIS for ERP projects at FPT Information System (FPT IS). FPT IS is a member of the FPT Group. It includes 10 subsidiaries and a joint venture. FPT IS employs more than 2,700 engineers with in–depth expertise in application, IT and ERP services, systems integration, business process outsourcing, IT equipment provision [15]. This study addresses the following objectives: improving the understanding of the impacts of PMIS on performance for ERP projects. Specifically, one intends to ascertain the success of ERP systems (e.g., information quality, system quality, user satisfaction). The other one will also ascertain to what extent PMIS contribute to the successful completion of ERP projects through the individual and organizational impacts. Besides, verifying if user satisfaction is related to qualities (e.g., service quality, ease of use), and also influence on the ERP project's success. Accordingly, this work is structured as follows: (1) introduction indicates research problem. (2) Research model shows literature review and theoretical framework, including hypotheses, and research methods. (3) Research results provide data, and these analysis results with reliability analysis, exploratory factor analysis, regression analysis, path analysis, and result discussions. (4) Conclusions and future work.

2   Research Model

2.1   Literature Review

Project Management Information System. The theoretical and practical importance of PMIS to the project management field [42], there have been as of yet few studies on the actual use and impacts of these systems. Therefore, highlighting the need to extend project management theory with the developing practice [50]. The PMIS empirical works have been mostly limited to describing the project management software usage characteristics [26] and to evaluating specific applications of these systems to support project management tasks. For example, planning [5], managing risks [22], scheduling [19], estimating and controlling costs [28], managing documents [5]. Project management software usage has also been found to have many drawbacks and limitations, both in theory when compared to an ideal PMIS by scholars and in practice as perceived by project managers [22, 49].

There are several kinds of studies on PMIS. For instance, algorithms for operational problems related to project management [42]; new types of functionality [25]; project management software usage [23]. Besides, PMIS adoption and success have been worked by Ali et al. [4] provided the impact of organizational and project factors on the PMIS adoption and discovered that higher project complexity and the level of information quality explain PMIS usage. Raymond and Bergeron [42] confirmed the role of the information quality. Furthermore, these authors showed that positive impacts on the project manager will lead to higher project success [23]. Specifically, one intends to ascertain the success of these systems as determined by the PMIS quality and the information quality that provide. One will also determine to what extent PMIS contribute to the success of projects through their individual and organizational impacts [42].

Information Systems Success. In 1980, Keen [24] referred to the lack of the scientific basis in IS research and argued that mandatory variables (e.g., user satisfaction, usage) would continue to mislead researchers and dodge the information theory issue. In searching for the IS success, there are many studies have been shown. This is understandable when considers as "information", an output of IS or a message in communication systems, can be viewed at different levels (e.g., technical level, semantic level, and effectiveness level) [9]. In communication context, Shannon and Weaver [46] defined technical level as the propriety and efficiency of the system that effectiveness the information, semantic level as the intended the information in promulgate the intended meaning, and effectiveness level as the effect of the information to the receiver. Based on this basis, Mason [29] considered "*effectiveness*" as "*influence*" and defined information influence level as "*hierarchy of events which take place at the receiving end of an information system which may be used to identify the various approaches that might be used to measure output at the influence level*" [29, p. 227]. According to DeLone and McLean [9], the influence events include the receipt of the information, and the application of the information, leading to a change in recipient behavior and a change in system performance.

After the publication of the first IS success model [9], some scholars claimed that the IS success is incomplete and suggested that more dimensions should be included in the model or proposed the other models. For example, Seddon [44] argued that the IS success model gaps comprehensiveness and further respecified the original IS success model by differentiating actual and expected impacts, as well as by incorporating the additional perceived usefulness in TAM [8]. Then, Rai et al. [39] showed that both original D&M model and Seddon [44]'s model are adequately explained IS success. Therefore, DeLone and McLean [10, 11] added service quality in an updated IS success model. After that, several authors tried to test this model empirically. For example, Gable et al. [16] re–conceptualized the DeLone and McLean model and suggested new IS success model. Additionally, Sabherwal et al. [43] conducted a comprehensive analysis to validate the D&M model and highlighted the importance of contextual attributes in IS success. However, Gable et al. [16] evaluated that many measures in D&M model were inappropriate to measure the ERP success. Thus, Gable et al. [16] removed user satisfaction and proposed another model, including system quality, information quality, individual impact, and organizational impact. This model was also considered as a base for the IS success model [41]. After that, Petter et al. [37] reviewed research published from 1992 to 2007 and identified the variables that potentially can influence on IS success. Furthermore, other domains have been tested using the D&M model that integrated with technology adoption model, including ERP [14, 20, 21, 41], social network [32], cloud–based e–learning [33, 34], e–banking [31, 38], etc.

Moreover, technology adoption is examined extensively in IS research. First, TRA was investigated in psychosocial perspective to identify elements of the trend conscious behavior [2]. Then, TPB proposed from the TRA and add perceived behavioral control dimension [1]. Next, TAM based on the theoretical foundation of the TRA to establish relationships among variables to explain behavior regarding acceptance of IS [8]. The most extended of TAM (e.g., TAM2, TAM3) can be best understood by exploring the determinants to perceived usefulness and perceived ease of use [33, 34].

2.2   Theoretical Framework

According to DeLone and McLean [9–11], TAM [8], and the related studies. The conceptual model and measurement have been proposed that there are five independent variables – such as information quality [9, 11, 16, 23, 42]; system quality [7–11, 13, 16, 42]; service quality [11, 20, 23, 44, 45]; functional quality [23, 25]; ease of use [8, 12, 23]. One intermediate variable – called PMIS user satisfaction [7, 11, 13, 23, 27]. And one dependent variable, namely ERP project's success [11, 17, 21, 23, 40].

Similar to other IS, a successful PMIS should have individual impacts in terms of user satisfaction [7]. The success dimension PMIS for ERP projects should have organizational impacts (e.g., cost, schedule, time [42], quality [11]), and also satisfaction. The success dimension *PMIS user satisfaction* (PUS) constitutes the satisfaction level of the user when utilizing PMIS for ERP projects [11]. It is considered as one of the most important IS success measurement. Widely used user satisfaction instruments are the ones by Doll et al. [13]. However, these instruments also contain quality factors (system, information, and service) rather than measuring user satisfaction. Accordingly, other items have been developed to measure exclusively user satisfaction with an IS [47]. This dimension is referred by the D&M model of DeLone and McLean [10, 11]; research on PMIS on decision making of Caniels and Bakens [7], measuring PMIS success of Doll et al. [13]; Kaiser and Ahlemann [23], research on ERP success by Hsu et al. [20]; Nwankpa [35].

The success dimension *information quality* (INQ) constitutes the desirable characteristics of an IS's output [9, 11]. It subsumes measures the information quality that the system produces and its usefulness for the user [47]. Information quality is seen as a key antecedent of user satisfaction [16]. This dimension is referred by the D&M model of DeLone and McLean [10, 11], research on the extension of the D&M model of IS success of Seddon [44, 45], measuring PMIS success of Kaiser and Ahlemann [23], research on ERP success by Gupta and Naqvi [17]; Hsu et al. [20]; Ifinedo and Olsen [21]. Thus, with PMIS for ERP Projects, it hypothesizes that:

– *H1: Information quality has a positive effect on PMIS user satisfaction.*

The success dimension *system quality* (SYQ) constitutes the desirable characteristics of an IS and subsumes measures of the IS itself [9–11]. These measures typically focus on usability aspects and performance characteristics of the system under examination [47]. This dimension is referred by the D&M model of DeLone and McLean [9–11], TAM by Davis [8]; research on re–conceptualizing IS success of Gable et al. [16], PMIS on project performance of Raymond and Bergeron [42], research on ERP success by DeToni et al. [12]; Hsu et al. [20]; Ifinedo and Olsen [21]. Thus, with PMIS for ERP projects, it hypothesizes that:

- *H2: System quality has a positive effect on PMIS user satisfaction.*

The success dimension *service quality* (SEQ) represents the quality of the support that the users receive from the IS department and IT support personnel [10, 11]. This construct is an enhancement of the updated D&M model that was not part of the original model [47]. The inclusion of this success dimension is not indisputable since system quality is not seen as an important quality measure of a single system [44, 45]. In the PMIS context, this dimension covers the aspects responsiveness, reliability, empathy and competence [23, 48]. This dimension is referred by the D&M model of DeLone and McLean [10, 11]; research on the extension of the DeLone and McLean model of IS success of Seddon [44, 45], measuring PMIS success of Kaiser and Ahlemann [23], research on ERP success by Hsu et al. [20]. Thus, with PMIS for ERP projects, it hypothesizes that:

- *H3: Service quality has a positive effect on PMIS user satisfaction.*

The success dimension *functional quality* (FUQ) consist of measures describing the alignment of the PMIS functionality with the user requirements [23]. This construct is an exaltation of Kaiser and Ahlemann [23] that was not part of the D&M model. High functional quality means that the users find the functionality supports in project management [25]. This dimension is referred by research on measuring PMIS success of Kaiser and Ahlemann [23], the software project management system of Kurbel [25], research on ERP success by DeToni et al. [12]; Ifinedo and Olsen [21]; Nwankpa [35]. Thus, with PMIS for ERP projects, it hypothesizes that:

- *H4: Functional quality has a positive effect on PMIS user satisfaction.*

The success dimension *ease of use* (EOU) is defined as the degree to which customers believe that using PMIS for ERP projects do not require much effort [8]. A common measure is perceived ease of use caused by several of research related to the TAM [8]. This dimension is referred by TAM of Davis [8]; research on measuring PMIS success of Kaiser and Ahlemann [23], research on ERP success by DeToni et al. [12]. Thus, with PMIS for ERP projects, it hypothesizes that:

- *H5: Ease of use has a positive effect on PMIS user satisfaction.*

Besides, PMIS are increasingly used by project managers in all project types that contribute to ERP project's success [42]. In this research, *ERP project's success* is referred by the D&M model of DeLone and McLean [10, 11]; research on measuring PMIS success by Kaiser and Ahlemann [23], PMIS on project performance by Raymond and Bergeron [42], offshore IS project success by Rai et al. [40], research on ERP success by Gupta and Naqvi [17]; DeToni et al. [12]; Hsu et al. [20]; Ifinedo and Olsen [21]; Ravasan et al. [41]; Nwankpa [35]. Hence, the effecting of *PMIS user satisfaction* on *ERP project's success* is hypothesized that:

- *H6: PMIS user satisfaction has a positive effect on ERP project's success.*

2.3   Methodology

Multiple–item scales, closely following previous studies, were used to measure each construct. Data was collected by a survey using convenient sampling. The question-naires were delivered using *Google docs* and hard copies to respondents who have been the members of project teams, and who have used the PMIS for ERP projects at FPT IS in Vietnam. A total of 175 respondents was obtained, 160 was finally usable (15 invalid respondents). All scales were scored on a 5–point Likert scale anchored with strongly disagree (1) and strongly agree (5), with 31 indicators. The data were then analyzed by reliability analysis (Cronbach alpha), exploratory factor analysis (EFA), and regression analysis with the *SPSS* application. Finally, the results of two–phase regression analysis are used for path analysis.

3   Research Results

3.1   Project Characteristics

(1) *Gender*: there is a sizable difference between 71.8 % male and 29.2 % female because most of the people who are members of project teams and PMIS users being male. (2) *Job position*: the majority of the respondents are users who have used the PMIS for ERP projects 30.4 %; then, the members of project teams: functional con-sultant accounted for 29.2 %, team leader 15.5 %, project manager or project director 12.5 %, technical consultant 9.3 %, only 3.1 % respondent is quality assurance. (3) *Experience*: as regards the more than 10–year experience, more than 6–year to 10–year, more than 3–year to 6–year, and 1–year to 3–year is by far the highest at roughly 38.5 %, followed by the latter at 28 %, 18 %, and 15.5 % respectively. (4) *ERP product*: SAP amounted to the highest percentage 38.1 %, Oracle amounted to 31.1 %, Oracle & SAP 9.3 %, others 3.1 %… The detail of project characteristics is presented in Table 1.

3.2   Model and Hypotheses Testing

Exploratory Factor Analysis. After eliminating 2 items that are INQ3 of *information quality* (INQ) and PUS2 of *PMIS user satisfaction* (PUS) dominants in reliability analysis (Cronbach alpha) due to the correlation–item of each factor < 0.60 [18]. The Cronbach alpha of constructs ranges between 0.723 and 0.933. Next, the exploratory factor analysis (EFA) with 29 indicators which are divided into groups of factors in a rotated component matrix according to each factor. There are 2 factors have been loaded from the other observed variations: (i) INQ and *functional quality* (FUQ) dominants group to a factor, thus, the authors propose a new name for this factor called "*functional–information quality*" (F–IQ), and (ii) SYQ4 of *system quality* (SYQ) dominant and *service quality* (SEQ) dominant group to a factor, thus, the authors propose a new name for this factor called "*support–service quality*" (S–SQ). For those reasons, *functional–information quality* and *support–service quality*

Table 1. Project characteristics

Characteristics	Frequency (n = 160)	Percentage (%)
Gender		
– Male	115	71.8
– Female	45	29.2
Job position		
– Functional consultant	46	29.2
– Project manager/Project director	20	12.5
– Quality assurance	5	3.1
– Team leader	25	15.5
– Technical consultant	15	9.3
– Other users	49	30.4
Experience		
– 1–year to 3–year	28	18.0
– More than 3–year to 6–year	25	15.5
– More than 6–year to 10–year	45	28.0
– More than 10–year	62	38.5
ERP product		
– Oracle	49	31.1
– SAP	91	38.1
– Oracle & SAP	15	9.3
– Others	5	3.1

components mean that the impact on *PMIS user satisfaction* (PUS). Then, the Cronbach alpha coefficients for all items of F–IQ and S–SQ included in official measures are satisfactory, implying that they are proper measures with F–IQ (0.785) and S–SQ (0.818). The reliability analysis and EFA are presented in Table 2.

Consequently, these hypotheses *H1, H3,* and *H4* are restated:

– *H1.$_4$: Functional–information quality has a positive effect on user satisfaction.*
– *H3.$_2$: Support–service quality has a positive effect on user satisfaction.*

Besides, Kaiser–Meyer–Olkin (KMO) measure and Bartlett's test with the coefficient KMO equal 0.794 (level of statistical significance, *p–value* = 0.000), implying that EFA of the independent components is appropriate. Total variance extracted (VE) of variables are 71.378 % where these components have eigenvalues > 1 (Table 2), which implies that they can explain 71.378 % of variation in data. Furthermore, with the coefficient KMO equal 0.865 (*p–value* = 0.000) and the VE of 79.275 %, *ERP project's success* (EPS) component can explain the variation in the data rather well. Hence, after EFA, the final measurement scales of the adjusted model include 6 components: F–IQ, S–SQ, SYQ, EOU, PUS, and EPS with 29 observed variables.

Table 2. The summary of reliability and exploratory factor analysis

Factors/Indicatiors			Analysis results		
			EFA loading	Cronbach alpha	Eigenvalues
F-IQ	*Functional–information quality*			0.785	8.377
	— FUQ1	Planning	0.834		
	— FUQ3	Auditing	0.814		
	— INQ1	Availability	0.793		
	— INQ2	Understandability	0.743		
	— FUQ4	Reporting	0.702		
	— FUQ2	Controlling	0.694		
	— INQ5	Security	0.661		
	— INQ4	Comprehensiveness	0.656		
	— FUQ5	Customizing	0.596		
S–SQ	*Support–service quality*			0.818	4.062
	— SEQ4	Empathy	0.883		
	— SEQ2	Responsiveness	0.858		
	— SEQ3	Assurance	0.844		
	— SYQ4	Maintainability	0.690		
	— SEQ1	Tangible	0.673		
SYQ	*System quality*			0.723	1.404
	— SYQ2	Adaptability	0.724		
	— SYQ1	Reliability	0.715		
	— SYQ3	Credibility	0.613		
EOU	*Ease of use*			0.826	1.148
	— EOU3	Overall	0.874		
	— EOU1	Ease of study	0.865		
	— EOU2	Self–efficiency	0.778		
PUS	*PMIS user satisfaction*			0.907	3.669
	— PUS5	Enjoyment	0.873		
	— PUS3	Effectiveness	0.858		
	— PUS4	User survey	0.851		
	— PUS1	Repeat use	0.850		
EPS	*ERP project's success*			0.933	3.964
	— EPS3	Quality	0.951		
	— EPS1	Schedule	0.911		
	— EPS5	Satisfaction	0.881		
	— EPS4	Scope	0.875		
	— EPS2	Cost	0.838		

Regression Analysis. The regression equation representing the relationship between the independent components and *PMIS user satisfaction* (PUS) is written by the following formula:

$$Y_{pus} = \beta_{p0} + \beta_{p1}X_{p1} + \beta_{p2}X_{p2} + \beta_{p3}X_{p3} + \beta_{p4}X_{p4} + \varepsilon_{pus} \qquad (1)$$

Y_{pus}: PUS value; X_{pi}: F–IQ, S–SQ, SYQ, EOU; β_{pi}: regression coefficient; ε_{pus}: random error.

The regression equation representing the relationship between PUS and *ERP project's success* (EPS) is written by the following formula:

$$Y_{eps} = \beta_{e0} + \beta_{e1}X_{e1} + \varepsilon_{eps} \tag{2}$$

Y_{eps}: EPS value; X_{e1}: PUS; β_{ej}: regression coefficient; ε_{eps}: random error.

The regression analysis results are presented in Table 3, with variable values of indicators based on point factor that is scored from EFA. According to Table 3. and formula (1), the regression analysis results show that these factors F–IQ, S–SQ, SYQ, and EOU have positive effect on PUS, with β equaling 0.716 (level of statistical significance, *p–value* = 0.000), 0.416 (*p–value* = 0.000), 0.177 (*p–value* = 0.000), and 0.364 (*p–value* = 0.000) respectively. Hence, *H1.4*, *H3.2*, *H2* and *H5* are supported. Hence, regression equation of PUS is written by the following:

$$PUS = 0.716(F - IQ) + 0.416(S - SQ) + 0.177(SYQ) + 0.364(EOU) + \varepsilon_{pus} \tag{3}$$

Table 3. The summary of regression analysis and hypothesis testing results

Model			β	SE	t	*p–value*	Result
(1)	*H1.4*	F–IQ → PUS	0.716	0.031	23.111	***	*Supported*
	H3.2	S–SQ → PUS	0.416	0.031	13.411	***	*Supported*
	H2	SYQ → PUS	0.177	0.031	5.715	***	*Supported*
	H5	EOU → PUS	0.364	0.031	11.751	***	*Supported*
(2)	*H6*	PUS → EPS	0.818	0.046	17.945	***	*Supported*

$R^2_{pus} = 0.850$; $R^2_{eps} = 0.669$

*** $p = 0.000$

According to Table 3 and formula (2), the regression analysis results show that PUS has a positive effect on *ERP project's success* (EPS) with $\beta = 0.818$ (*p–value* = 0.000), leading to support of *H6*. Thus, regression equation of EPS is written by the following:

$$EPS = 0.818(PUS) + \varepsilon_{eps} \tag{4}$$

In addition, t test of PUS and EPS components are qualified (level of statistical significance, *p–value* = 0.000). The determination coefficient – adjusted R square of PUS (R^2_{pus}) and EPS (R^2_{eps}) are 0.850 and 0.669 respectively. F test with level statistically significant *p–value* = 0.000, so the regression equations, formulas (3) and (4), conform to the data that can be used. The adjusted model to explain the success of PMIS for ERP projects is depicted in Fig. 1.

Path Analysis. According to Pedhazur [36], path analysis is an extension of multivariate regression analysis, total determination coefficient – adjusted R square (R^2) of the model is calculated by following formula:

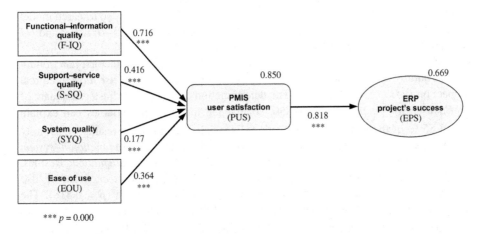

Fig. 1. The success of PMIS for ERP projects – adjusted model

$$R^2 = 1 - \left(1 - R_{pus}^2\right)\left(1 - R_{eps}^2\right) \tag{5}$$

Consequently, according to Table 3 and formula (5), path analysis result:

$$R^2 = 1 - (1 - 0.850)(1 - 0.669) = 0.950 \tag{6}$$

According to the formula (6), the path analysis result provides that total determination coefficient $R^2 = 0.950$, which means that the independent variables (F–IQ, S–SQ, SYQ, EOU) and the intermediate variable (PUS) can explain about 95 % of the variation in the dependent variable (EPS).

These factors, *functional–information quality* (F–IQ), *support–service quality* (S–SQ), *system quality* (SYQ), and *ease of use* (EOU) have impacts on *PMIS user satisfaction* (PUS). Specifically, the strongest influence is from F–IQ, the weakest one is from SYQ, and impact from S–SQ and EOU on PUS. *ERP project's success* (EPS) has been signed by PUS. Generally, the research results provide that five hypotheses (*H1.$_4$*, *H3.$_2$*, *H2*, *H5*, and *H6*) are supported. In summary, Fig. 1 demonstrates the adjusted model for the success of PMIS for ERP projects, the presentation of all paths of the model, and also all hypothesis testing results.

3.3   Discussions

The research results accommodate that all scales of independent variables, *PMIS user satisfaction*, and *ERP project's success* stabilize reliability. The EFA provides two elements, called *system quality*, and *ease of use* are extracted in accordance following the proposed model. Additionally, *information quality, service quality, functional quality elements,* and one item of *system quality* are extracted into two factors, which have been named *functional–system quality, support–service quality,* so research model is changed to adjust model, also changed and reduced the hypotheses – *H1, H3,* and *H4* are restated to *H1.$_4$* and *H3.$_2$*.

Interestingly, the regression analysis results indicate that these factors, *functional–system quality, support–service quality, system quality,* and *ease of use have* the direct impact on *PMIS user satisfaction.* The determination coefficient – adjusted R square of *PMIS user satisfaction* R^2_{pus} = 0.850, so that the independent variables can explain about 85 % of the PMIS user satisfaction. Especially, it shows the results by strongly supporting the relationships between the quality factors (β = 0.716 of *functional–system quality;* β = 0.416 of *support–service quality*) and *PMIS user satisfaction.* Besides, *PMIS user satisfaction* has a positive effect on *ERP project's success,* and it also provides a result strongly supporting the relationship among them (β = 0.818). The determination coefficient – adjusted R square of *ERP project's success* R^2_{eps} = 0.699, so that the intermediate variable can explain roughly 69.9 % of the ERP project's success. Overall, total determination coefficient R^2 = 0.950 in the path analysis result, which means that the independent variables and the intermediate variable can explain about 95 % of the variation in the success of PMIS for ERP projects.

Some empirical studies exploring the DeLone and McLean [9–11] models have been provided in the literature and extended in the IS success models (e.g., Gable et al. [16]; Seddon [44, 45]), and the related works (e.g., Kaiser and Ahlemann [23]; DeToni et al. [12]; Nwankpa [35]). This study continues to contribute to the body of knowledge exploring the predictors of the IS success models, especially the success of PMIS for ERP projects. Besides, a common measure is perceived *ease of use* of the TAM [8] has been added to the research model. Generally, the research model explains about the ERP project's success being tantamount with Ravasan et al. [41], and better than some related works (e.g., DeToni et al. [12]; Ifinedo and Olsen [21]; Nwankpa [35]). Which is harmonized to the context of IS projects.

4   Conclusions and Future Work

Based on well–known IS success model, highly cited TAM, and the related works, a success model of PMIS for ERP projects is proposed. The findings indicate that ERP project's success is determined by the PMIS user satisfaction that in turn is influenced by the user ease of use, system quality, functional–information quality, and support–service quality. The research model was empirically tested and mainly supported. Moreover, the path analysis result also means that the independent variables and the PMIS user satisfaction can explain roughly 95 % of the variation in the success of PMIS for ERP projects. This study continues to contribute to the body of knowledge exploring the predictors of the IS success models, especially the success of PMIS for ERP projects. Interestingly, the research model explains the ERP project's success being tantamount with Ravasan et al. [41], and better than some related works (e.g., DeToni et al. [12]; Ifinedo and Olsen [21]; Nwankpa [35]). Which is harmonized to the context of IS project's success.

In the future work, the authors will work out for the combined effect of the factors, and also expand the research scope and object, add more variables and relationships among the elements of the research model. The measures will be revised more appropriate than with the development situation of the PMIS and the ERP project. Structural equation modeling (SEM) will be used for data analysis.

Acknowledgment. The authors would like to say thank to four anonymous reviewers for their helpful comments on this research.

References

1. Ajzen, I.: From intentions to action: a theory of planned behavior. In: Kuhl, J., Beckmann, J. (eds.) Action Control, pp. 11–39. Springer, Heidelberg (1985)
2. Ajzen, I., Fishbein, M.: Understanding Attitudes and Predicting Social Behavior. Prentice Hall, Englewood Cliffs (1980)
3. Ahlemann, F.: Towards a conceptual reference model for project management information systems. Int. J. Project Manage. 27(1), 19–30 (2009)
4. Ali, A., Anbari, F., Money, W.: Impact of organizational and project factors on acceptance and usage of project management software and perceived project success. Project Manage. J. 39(2), 5–33 (2008)
5. Amami, M., Beghini, G., La Manna, M.: Use of project–management information system for planning information–systems development projects. Int. J. Project Manage. 11(1), 21–28 (1993)
6. Braglia, M., Frosolini, M.: An integrated approach to implement project management information systems within the extended enterprise. Int. J. Project Manage. 32(1), 18–29 (2014)
7. Caniels, M.C., Bakens, R.J.: The effects of project management information systems on decision making in a multi project environment. Int. J. Project Manage. 30(2), 162–175 (2012)
8. Davis, F.D.: Perceived usefulness, perceived ease of use, and user acceptance of information technology. MIS Q. 13(3), 319–340 (1989)
9. DeLone, W.H., McLean, E.R.: Information systems success: The quest for the dependent variable. Inf. Syst. Res. 3(1), 60–95 (1992)
10. DeLone, W.H., McLean, E.R.: Information systems success revisited. In: Proceedings of the HICSS. IEEE (2002)
11. DeLone, W.H., McLean, E.R.: The DeLone and McLean model of information systems success: a ten–year update. J. Manage. Inf. Syst. 19(4), 9–30 (2003)
12. DeToni, A.F., Fornasier, A., Nonino, F.: The impact of implementation process on the perception of enterprise resource planning success. Bus. Process Manage. J. 21(2), 332–352 (2015)
13. Doll, W., Deng, X., Raghunathan, T., Torkzadeh, G., Xia, W.: The meaning and measurement of user satisfaction: A multigroup invariance analysis of the end–user computing satisfaction instrument. J. Manage. Inf. Syst. 21(1), 227–262 (2004)
14. Floropoulos, J., Spathis, C., Halvatzis, D., Tsipouridou, M.: Measuring the success of the Greek taxation information system. Int. J. Inf. Manage. 30(1), 47–56 (2010)
15. FPT IS: Corporate Profile – FPT Information System (2014). http://fis.com.vn

16. Gable, G., Sedera, D., Chan, T.: Re–conceptualizing information system success: The IS–impact measurement model. J. Assoc. Inf. Syst. **9**(7), 377–408 (2008)
17. Gupta, R., Naqvi, S.K.: A framework for applying critical success factors to ERP implementation projects. Int. J. Bus. Inf. Syst. **17**(4), 469–490 (2014)
18. Hair, J., Black, W., Babin, B., Anderson, R., Tatham, R.: Multivariate Data Analysis. Pearson, Upper Saddle River (2014)
19. Herroelen, W.: Project scheduling – Theory and practice. Prod. Oper. Manage. **14**(4), 413–432 (2005)
20. Hsu, P.F., Yen, H.R., Chung, J.C.: Assessing ERP post–implementation success at the individual level: Revisiting the role of service quality. Inf. Manage. **52**(8), 925–942 (2015). In Press
21. Ifinedo, P., Olsen, D.H.: An empirical research on the impacts of organisational decisions' locus, tasks structure rules, knowledge, and IT function's value on ERP system success. Int. J. Prod. Res. **53**(8), 2554–2568 (2015)
22. Jaafari, A.: Time and priority allocation scheduling technique for projects. Int. J. Project Manage. **14**(5), 289–299 (1996)
23. Kaiser, M.G., Ahlemann, F.: Measuring project management information systems success: Towards a conceptual model and survey instrument. In: European Conference on Information Systems (2010)
24. Keen, P.G.: MIS research: Reference disciplines and a cumulative tradition. In: Proceedings of the ICIS, Philadelphia (1980)
25. Kurbel, K.: Groupware extension for a software project management system. Int. J. Project Manage. **12**(4), 222–229 (1994)
26. Liberatore, M.J., Johnson, B.P.: Factors influencing the usage and selection of project management software. IEEE Trans. Eng. Manage. **50**(2), 164–174 (2003)
27. Light, M., Rosser, B., Hayward, S.: Realizing the benefits of project and portfolio management. Gartner (2005)
28. Mahaney, R.C., Lederer, A.L.: The role of monitoring and shirking in information systems project management. Int. J. Project Manage. **28**(1), 14–25 (2010)
29. Mason, R.O.: Measuring information output: A communication systems approach. Inf. Manag. **1**(4), 219–234 (1978)
30. Nguyen, T.D.: A structural model for the success of information systems projects. J. Sci. Technol. Dev. **18**(2Q), 109–120 (2015)
31. Nguyen, T.D., Cao, T.H.: Structural model for adoption and usage of e–banking in Vietnam. Econ. Dev. J. **220**, 116–135 (2014)
32. Nguyen, T.D., Cao, T.H., Tran, N.D.: Structural model for the adoption of online advertising on social network in Vietnam. In: ICACCI, pp. 38–43. IEEE (2014)
33. Nguyen, T.D., Nguyen, D.T., Cao, T.H.: Acceptance and use of information system: E-learning based on cloud computing in Vietnam. In: Linawati, Mahendra, M.S., Neuhold, E.J., Tjoa, A.M., You, I. (eds.) ICT-EurAsia 2014. LNCS, vol. 8407, pp. 139–149. Springer, Heidelberg (2014)
34. Nguyen, T.D., Nguyen, T.M., Pham, Q.-T., Misra, S.: Acceptance and use of e-learning based on cloud computing: the role of consumer innovativeness. In: Murgante, B., Misra, S., Rocha, A.M.A., Torre, C., Rocha, J.G., Falcão, M.I., Taniar, D., Apduhan, B.O., Gervasi, O. (eds.) ICCSA 2014, Part V. LNCS, vol. 8583, pp. 159–174. Springer, Heidelberg (2014)
35. Nwankpa, J.K.: ERP system usage and benefit: A model of antecedents and outcomes. Comput. Hum. Behav. **45**, 335–344 (2015)
36. Pedhazur, E.J.: Structural equation models with observed variables: Path analysis. In: Multiple Regression in Behavioral Research: Explanation and Prediction, pp. 765–840 (1997)

37. Petter, S., DeLone, W., McLean, E.: Measuring information systems success: models, dimensions, measures, and interrelationships. Eur. J. Inf. Syst. **17**(3), 236–263 (2008)
38. Pham, L., Cao, N.Y., Nguyen, T.D., Tran, P.T.: Structural models for e–banking adoption in Vietnam. Int. J. Enterp. Inf. Syst. **9**(1), 31–48 (2013)
39. Rai, A., Lang, S.S., Welker, R.B.: Assessing the validity of IS success models: An empirical test and theoretical analysis. Inf. Syst. Res. **13**(1), 50–69 (2002)
40. Rai, A., Maruping, L.M., Venkatesh, V.: Offshore information systems project success: The Role of social embeddedness and cultural characteristics. MIS Q. **33**(3), 617–641 (2009)
41. Ravasan, A., Nabavi, A., Mansouri, T.: Can organizational structure influence ERP success? Int. J. Inf. Syst. Supply Chain Manage. **8**(1), 39–59 (2015)
42. Raymond, L., Bergeron, F.: Impact of project management information systems on project performance. In: Schwindt, C., Zimmermann, J. (eds.) Handbook on Project Management and Scheduling, vol. 2, pp. 1339–1354. Springer, Heidelberg (2015)
43. Sabherwal, R., Jeyaraj, A., Chowa, C.: Information system success: Individual and organizational determinants. Manage. Sci. **52**(12), 1849–1864 (2006)
44. Seddon, P.B.: A respecification and extension of the DeLone and McLean model of IS success. Inf. Syst. Res. **8**(3), 240–253 (1997)
45. Seddon, P.B.: Implications for strategic IS research of the resource–based theory of the firm: A reflection. J. Strateg. Inf. Syst. **23**(4), 257–269 (2014)
46. Shannon, C., Weaver, W.: Recent contributions to the mathematical theory of communication. In: Mathematical Theory of Communications, pp. 1–28 (1949)
47. Urbach, N., Muller, B.: The updated DeLone and McLean model of information systems success. In: Dwivedi, Y.K., Wade, M.R., Schneberger, S.L. (eds.) Information Systems Theory, pp. 1–18. Springer, New York (2012)
48. Urbach, N., Smolnik, S. Riempp, G.: Development and validation of a model for assessing the success of employee portals. In: ECIS Proceedings (2009)
49. White, D., Fortune, J.: Current practice in project management – An empirical study. Int. J. Project Manage. **20**(1), 1–11 (2002)
50. Winter, M., Smith, C., Morris, P., Cicmil, S.: Directions for future research in project management: The main findings of a UK government–funded research network. Int. J. Project Manage. **24**(8), 638–649 (2006)

Human Object Classification Based on Nonsubsampled Contourlet Transform Combined with Zernike Moment

Luu The Phuong and Nguyen Thanh Binh[✉]

Faculty of Computer Science and Engineering,
Ho Chi Minh City University of Technology, VNU-HCM, Vietnam
phuong7410@gmail.com, ntbinh@hcmut.edu.vn

Abstract. The surveillance systems are more and more popular because of the security needs, but the traditional ones do not meet human's expectation. This paper proposes the algorithm to classify objects mainly based on their contour property which are represented by the amplitude of zernike moment on non-subsampled contourlet transform of a binary contour image. This feature shows promising results by just a simple association with the aspect ratio but gives high accuracy. The aspect ratio helps contour feature in case that the image is too blurred to extract the object's contour. It also plays as a weak filter with nearly no more computational cost except for a division to support contour feature when applying gentle boost algorithm.

Keywords: Object classification · Zernike moment · Nonsubsampled contourlet transform

1 Introduction

Nowadays, the surveillance systems are more and more popular because of the security needs, but the traditional ones do not meet human's expectation. Human must spend money not only on such devices as cameras, monitoring rooms but also on those who sit in front of the monitors and check every second if something happens. That's why we need the intelligent surveillance systems, which can automatically do monitoring tasks. In that tendency, many researchers focus on image and video processing to answer that question. Building an intelligent surveillance system can be split into four main challenges: moving object detection, object classification, object tracking and event or behavior recognition.

Object classification can be applied in many purposes such as security surveillance systems for airports, train stations, schools, or buildings of government etc.; or traffic control systems like automatic traffic signal systems, street-crossing safety systems, traffic density statistics systems etc. Object classification brings the class information of objects for a system to assess the situation. For example, if a situation in which an object moves fast toward another one happens, even you cannot guess what it means without their class information. If that's a man and an airplane, it may be a late coming. If that's a car and a crossing human, it may potentially be a traffic accident. Many expected jobs of

© ICST Institute for Computer Sciences, Social Informatics and Telecommunications Engineering 2016
P.C. Vinh and V. Alagar (Eds.): ICCASA 2015, LNICST 165, pp. 212–222, 2016.
DOI: 10.1007/978-3-319-29236-6_21

the intelligent surveillance systems just cannot be done without object classification problem solved.

The overview of object classification has three stages: moving object detection, feature extraction and classification. A lot of research can be found in recent years such as Setitra [1] and Karasulu [2] some of which are to review about proposed methods for each stage, and their strong and weak points. The successive research will improve and/or merge one or more methods to reach better results. For the moving object detection, Lin [3] use Gaussian Mixture Model (GMM) and Elhoseiny [4] use non-parametric Kernel Density Estimation (KDE), which are both quite old now (more than ten years). GMM is quite fast that it can meet real time requirement for outdoor scenes, but it's not robust to many types of noise like illumination changes, removed object – ghost effect. KDE is quite complex with many sub algorithms for each step that brings it robustness for many types of noise like illumination changes, occlusion, shadow of object etc., and the slow speed, too. The proposal uses the recently proposed algorithm FTSG which is shown better than many state-of-the-art algorithms in [5]. It gives a medium speed (10 fps for a 320×240 video) and the robustness to many types of noise mentioned.

For feature extraction and classification, Lin [3] use four features like: speed, width, RMI and CAR. The speed and RMI features are more complex because of requiring tracks of previous frames for calculating. The classification algorithm bases on thresholds, which may be less accurate in case of different video resolution, camera distance, and perspective. Vishnyakov [6] bases on statistics and Logistic Regression training algorithm, which is tested with a large number. The high accuracy is quite promising but the algorithm uses only statistics as feature so it does not exploit much information from the object image. Elhoseiny [4] uses many features which exploit much information from the object image, so it gives a better result with the support of Adaboost algorithm. But many features cost high computation and the result shows that it requires a lot of training (80 % dataset), which may be scene-dependent. It may be less accurate for completely new scene. In this paper, we proposed a new method for object classification. The proposed method uses contour property as the main feature, which is quite robust to video resolution, distance or perspective because the object can be rotated and characterized the shape of its contour to make training data. This main feature is associated with the aspect ratio to build a better classifier with gentle boost, which is simple and promising to be effective to classify objects. The rest of the paper is organized as follows: we described the background of selecting a new generation wavelet transform and zernike moment in Sect. 2; the proposed method is shown in Sect. 3; the result and conclusion of the paper are presented in Sects. 4 and 5 respectively.

2 Background

2.1 Select a New Generation Wavelet Transform

The wavelet transform (WT) is a good tool to provide time - frequency representation of the signal, so its applications appear in many fields. But WT is not really perfect; it's only good at representing point singularities. If they are lines, edges or textures, WT has a lot of redundant coefficients and is computationally expensive. Ridgelet transform [9] is proposed with better representation for linear singularities. But most of the real world applications do not show straight - line singularities, especially the object's contour. Curvelet transform [10] takes its place to solve the problem by partitioning the image then applying Ridgelet to each part. The idea is a curve split into many parts which correspond to lines. But curvelet also has two drawbacks: first, not optimal for sparse approximation of curve beyond C^2 singularities and second, highly redundant. Contourlet transform [11] is built from a discrete domain first, then extend to the continuous domain, it has lower redundancy and a faster discrete implementation version than curvelet. But contourlet is just multidirectional and multi-scale but not shift - invariant, which causes pseudo-Gibbs phenomena visible on the decoded image by high compression ratio. Nonsubsampled Contourlet transform (NSCT) [12] brings shift - invariance for contourlet with the trade-off of more redundancy. As NSCT is used for contour detection, this redundancy is not a drawback but even gives better results.

The important feature of the proposal bases on object's contour and NSCT is chosen to extract the object's contour. NSCT belongs to the family of the new generation wavelet transform. The NSCT development through its main predecessors may start at wavelet transform (WT) [7] as in [8].

NSCT comprises two parts: a Nonsubsampled Pyramid structure (NSP) which gives multi-scale property and a Nonsubsampled Directional Filter Bank (NSDFB) structure that brings directional property. Both of them are shift - invariant due to Nonsubsampled filter banks. NSP comprises four filters: $H_0(z)$ and $H_1(z)$ are low and high pass decomposition filters, and $G_0(z)$ and $G_1(z)$ are low and high pass reconstruction filters. In an ideal case, the passband supported by low filter at the jth stage is $[(-\pi/2^j), (\pi/2^j)]^2$ and the corresponding high filter supports the complement region $[(-\pi/2^{j-1}), (\pi/2^{j-1})]^2 \setminus [(-\pi/2^j), (\pi/2^j)]^2$. The filters of first stage are upsampled to obtain filters for next stages, so it gives multi-scale property without any more filter design. NSDFB has filters constructed from fan filter banks. The upsampled fan filters of the second stage supports checker-board frequency, when combined with first stage filters will give the four directions in frequency decomposition. The properties of NSCT like multi-scale, multi-direction, shift-invariant make it very suitable for contour detection.

2.2   Zernike Moment

In image processing, moments can be used as object recognition feature which is invariant under translate, scale and/or rotation. There are many types of moments, which can be categorized in two groups [13]:

Non orthogonal moments: Cartesian moments, rotational moments and complex moments are some of this type. This moment type has non orthogonal basis, so as the high redundancy. The invariance is up to the specific moments.

Orthogonal moments: legendre moments, zernike moments and pseudo - zernike moments are some examples. With orthogonal basis, they have no redundancy between moments. Legendre moments are highly sensitive to noise. Zernike moments have better reconstructed image than other moments like Cartesian Moments with same computational accuracy. It is easier to choose the order of moments based on the contribution of each moment due to orthogonality. This property also brings better performance. Zernike is only rotationally invariant, so it will need to be normalized by another moment to be invariant under translation and scale too.

Pseudo - zernike moments are an improved version of Zernike with most of the advantages of Zernike and a higher noisy tolerance, but they are not popular because of high computational cost.

3 Object Classification Based on NSCT Combined with Zernike Moment

In this section, we proposed the method for object classification based on NSCT combined with zernike moment. The overall of the proposed method is presented as Fig. 1.

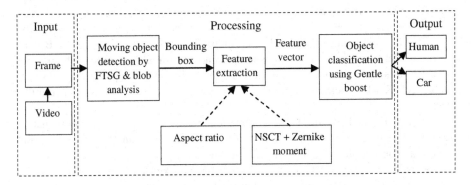

Fig. 1. The overall of the proposed method.

The proposed method has three stages: moving object detection, features extraction and object classification. The input data are videos which have the same serial frames. The outputs are classification of a human or car.

3.1 Moving Object Detection

In this stage, we use Flux Tensor with Split Gaussian models (FTSG) combined with blob analysis for moving object detection. The FTSG algorithm has three main steps: (i) Flux Tensor (FT) and Split Gaussian Model (SG), (ii) Fusion of FT and SG, (iii) Stopped and removed objects classification. Most of detailed implementation can be found in [5].

Flux Tensor is a temporal variation of optical flow field in a local 3D spatiotemporal image volume. It can classify pixels as foreground or background based on temporal gradient changes information incorporated at each step without calculating eigenvalue. Detailed implementation can be found in [14, 15].

Split Gaussian Model is based on GMM [16], but has the model with variable K Gaussian for background and a separated model with one Gaussian only for foreground. This separation prevents background from corrupted by foreground pixels, brings better adaption for complex background environment (static and dynamic). Some not mentioned default values can be used from [16]. In [5], the parameter σ_t^2 is the variance at the time t and defined as:

$$\sigma_t^2 = (1 - \alpha)M\sigma_{t-1}^2 + M\alpha(I_t - \mu_t)^T\alpha(I_t - \mu_t). \tag{1}$$

In here, we defined

$$\sigma_t^2 = (1 - \alpha)M\sigma_{t-1}^2 + M\alpha(I_t - \mu_t)^2. \tag{2}$$

This variance plays as standard to check if a pixel value is considered to be matched to the model or not. T in (1) is from [16], which is the minimum proportion of data that should be accounted for the model. Higher T allows multi-modal distribution to adapt to small motions like leaves, grass or flags in the wind. α is the learning rate at each time a new pixel is updated to the model. Here the proposal chooses to use the version in (2). This is equivalent to T = 1 and just α multiplied to variance of the pixel. By this way, the model adapts to small motions more than just a small portion at each time like in (1). But this way also means that we completely lie on α to update this variance. A value of 0.004 for background and 0.5 for foreground is small enough to avoid this defect.

Fusion of FT and SG in step 2 is complementary. FT is robust to illumination changes, but fails to detect stopped objects. SG is sensitive to illumination changes, but can handle stopped objects due to its background model.

The last step is to help SG to recognize revealed background pixels to incorporate into its model after object moving to another location. By chamfer matching [17] the contour of input image and background model image of SG with foreground mask, it can detect the old object in background model image and foreground mask but not input image.

The algorithm to get moving objects as a bounding box from foreground mask is from Matlab's vision blob analysis [18]. This built-in class will return bounding box information (x, y, width, height) of moving objects and ignore small blobs which are false alarm if any.

3.2 Feature Extraction

Each bounding boxed object will be calculated two values as feature vector: Aspect ratio and Zernike NSCT value. Aspect ratio (AR) is:

$$AR = W/H \tag{3}$$

where W, H are width and height of the bounding box.

AR feature is very simple but quite efficient. The rule of it is that the bounding box of human usually has less in width than height, and the opposite for car. That assumption is usually correct in outdoor scenes, because human usually appears in the standing pose like walking, running. For the car, most cars in real world are more in width than in height, and they appear in one pose only. This feature may fail in cases that human sits down and his height is just a half of the standing pose. Or poses with two raising arms may increase the width of the bounding box and break the assumption. For the car, that is the perspective of the camera. If the camera view is in the same line of a moving car, it will show the longer dimension in height not width. But many of the outdoor cases, the assumption are true.

AR feature is chosen to associate with main feature – contour because it is fast and its nature is completely different so that the union of failed case set of them is smaller. When the AR fails by the human pose or car's perspective, the contour fills in the gap with the training of many poses and perspective of object. And if the contour is blurred because of surrounding color, or bad contour detection algorithm, AR does the job.

Zernike NSCT value is a value that represents the contour property of objects and used to differentiate between a human and a car. It is calculated as the amplitude of Zernike moment on contour binary image of the bounding boxed object as followings: first, the bounding boxed object image is contour detected by applying NSCT [12] decomposition on it. The n levels parameter is [0, 1, 3]. This parameter is has 3 numbers, means using 3 pyramidal levels (from coarser to finer scale). The first number – zero means at level 1 of pyramid, the level of directional filter bank decomposition will be 2 exponent zero to 1. It is the contour image received which is synthesized from two next levels. The second level of pyramid is 2 exponents 1 to 2. It's $\pi/2^1$ so we may see it like the two images with horizontal and vertical ways of energy. Similarly, third level is $\pi/2^3$, which is 8 images with rotation of energy. The synthesis of from third through second and to first level gives us contour image with energy at all ways keeping. The number of levels and direction number at each level is chosen to be computationally efficient and good enough to reflex the contour of object. In our experiment, NSCT is quite slow, but three levels are also enough to do the job. Not all contour images are perfectly detected but it is good enough for the classification result. Detailed implementation of NSCT can be found in [12].

Second, the contour image is converted to binary image based on threshold which is just simply the mean of the pixel values in image. This is just a preparatory step for Zernike, which is done due to [19] that the binary image with just contour point is faster and more accurate than the original image for Zernike.

Third, the binary image is passed through Zernike moment to get amplitude [20]. Zernike moment is rotationally invariant, so it is suitable for characterizing contour of object, which may be changed because of the various activities and this property reduces effort in training many poses which are just the rotations of another. Detailed implementation of Zernike and its amplitude can be found in [12].

3.3   Object Classification

Classifier of the proposal uses Gentle Boost (or Gentle AdaBoost) algorithm [21]. First, the classifier is trained with labeled-by-human-eyes data. Then, it will be used to classify based on object's feature vector.

The training stage is as follows: N objects in training data give us N feature vectors which are merged into a matrix called X with N rows and two columns (each vector has two numbers as in Sect. 3.2). N class values of these objects which are classified by human-eyes are merged into a matrix called Y with N rows and one column. Gentle Boost implementation in Matlab [22] will take X and Y matrixes as parameters to initialize and train the classifier. Three more parameters required by the classifier are (i) method, which is filled by "GentleBoost", (ii) nlearn, which is 2, and (iii) learners which is "Tree".

Boost algorithm family is used because of better performance than SVM [23], and the ability to associate two weak classifiers (two features in Sect. 3.2) to a better classifier that show better accuracy for recognizing objects [4]. The defect of Boost is sensitive to noise in training data, but there is no problem with our labeled-by-human-eye training data. Gentle Boost is chosen from many Boost candidates because of its better performance than Real AdaBoost and LogitBoost [21] and *gentle* property. By using weighted least-squares regression to update, Gentle Boost does not cause large update like Real AdaBoost and LogitBoost when a weak learner shows a perfect classification.

Learners parameter is an array of weak learner templates. The proposal chooses only one template for better performance (the less templates, the less work) and the "Tree" template because in [22], two other options are (i) KNN, which is just for Subspace ensemble and (ii) Discriminant, which requires an assumption about Gaussian distributions to ensure its accuracy that may be not the case for our data.

Nlearn parameter is the number of times that each weak leaner will be trained for every template in Learners. The value of 2 means that two weak learners corresponding to two feature values. By experiment, it also shows high accuracy and speed.

The classification stage is just simple that the feature vector is passed to the predicted method of classifier to get the class value, 0 for human and 1 for car in the proposal. Gentle Boost just aggregates results from weak learners for each class as scores. The class with higher score is returned.

4   Experiments and Results

Experiments are developed in Matlab 2013a and carried out on computer of Intel i7 4700MQ 2.4 GHz CPU and 16 GB DDR3 memory. The proposal focuses on the outdoor scenes so PETS 2001 [24] is chosen. Videos are at the resolution of 768×576 and the rate of 25 frames per second. Dataset 1, 2 and 3 are used which include testing and training videos in different folders. Training data comprise 4710 human and 2714 car objects. Testing data contain 5830 human and 2093 car objects. Some test scene images and sample bounding boxed images of human and car are shown in Figs. 2 and 3.

Fig. 2. Scenes in test dataset. (a) and (b) are scenes in test dataset 1. (c) and (d) are scenes in test dataset 2. (e) and (f) are scenes in test dataset 3.

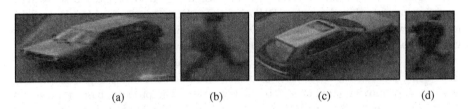

Fig. 3. Sample images. (a) A car in training data. (b) A human in training data. (c) A car in test data. (d) A human in test data.

For the accuracy assessment, the overall result is affected a lot by moving detection stage and compared with human eyes' result for classification. So, missed or wrong (not moving or bounding box bigger than twice of width or height of objects) objects by moving detection stage and objects unrecognizable even by human eyes without the whole frame are ignored. In each frame of videos, each bounding box is counted as an instance of its class. The proposal uses the contour of object as feature, so the object with changing poses will need to be reclassified. The speed is per object and calculated for feature extracting and classification stage only (single threaded), so if each frame has more than one object, the speed per frame will be slower. Certainly, the size of each bounding boxed object image also affects this speed. Table 1 is the experimental results.

The table shows the classification result for test data. There are 5685 correct and 145 incorrect (which are classified as car) results for total 5830 human images and for 2093 car images, they are 1981 correct and 112 incorrect (which are classified as human) images. The overall accuracy of both human and car classification is 96.8 % at 2.0 object per second speed. The proposal fails when objects appear with just a part of them because of stepping in or out of the scene, occlusion by something or bad

Table 1. The overall experimental result.

	Human	Car	Accuracy per class
Human (5,830)	5,685	145	97.5 %
Car (2,093)	112	1,981	94.6 %
Average speed	2.0 object/s	Overall accuracy	96.8 %

Table 2. The overall accuracy comparison on PETS 2001 (dataset 1 to 3).

	The proposal	Somasundaram [25]
Overall accuracy	96.8 %	95.7 %

bounding box (redundant or not enough). But this result is quite good with just a simple association of two features. The limitation on speed of NSCT prevents the experiment from more dataset but it is enough to show the promising of the proposal when compared to the proposal of Somasundaram et al. [25]. Table 2 shows the comparison.

Somasundaram et al. [25] uses area, velocity, DHOG and DCOV features which are combined by a Naive Bayes classifier. These features are also simple and show high accuracy when combined together. DHOG changes HOG to reflex rigid and non rigid motion between vehicles and humans. DCOV uses color, first order and second order gradients to differentiate human from vehicles. Somasundaram's approach bases much on object's appearance; this is a drawback because traffic videos are usually recorded from an average or far view. This results in low resolution of moving object images and less details of moving arms or legs or clothes colors. The proposal bases on contour which is less dependent on resolution than details inside the contour of the object. The more far view, the less details but the whole contour is usually still clear. That's why the proposal can reach a higher accuracy.

5   Conclusion

Object classification can be applied in many purposes such as security surveillance systems for airports, train stations, schools, or buildings of government etc. This task is not easy because they depend on context and environment. This paper proposes the algorithm to classify objects mainly based on their contour property which are represented by the amplitude of Zernike moment on NSCT binary contour image. This feature shows promising results by just a simple association with aspect ratio but gives high accuracy 96.8 %. The speed of NSCT is a bottle neck point for the whole algorithm which needs to be improved in the future to test on more data. And more object classes like scooter, bus, van or group of people, cars, etc. can be added to the experiment to exploit the effectiveness of the main feature in characterizing objects.

Acknowledgments. This research is funded by Ho Chi Minh City University of Technology, VNU-HCM under grant number TSĐH-2015-KHMT-07

References

1. Setitra, I.: Object classification in videos - an overview. J. Autom. Control Eng. **1**(1), 106–109 (2013)
2. Karasulu, B., Korukoglu, S.: Moving object detection and tracking by using annealed background subtraction method in videos: performance optimization. J. Expert Syst. Appl. **39**(1), 33–43 (2012)
3. Lin, D.T., Chen, Y.T.: Pedestrian and vehicle classification surveillance system for street-crossing safety. In: The 2011 International Conference on Image Processing, Computer Vision, and Pattern Recognition, pp. 564–570 (2011)
4. Elhoseiny, M., Bakry, A., Elgammal, A.: MultiClass object classification in video surveillance systems - experimental study. In: Proceedings of the 2013 IEEE Conference on Computer Vision and Pattern Recognition Workshops, pp. 788–793 (2013)
5. Wang, R., Bunyak, F., Seetharaman, G., Palaniappan, K.: Static and moving object detection using flux tensor with split gaussian models. In: Proceedings of IEEE Workshop on Change Detection, pp. 420–424 (2014)
6. Vishnyakov, B.V., Malin, I.K., Vizilter, Y.V., Huang, S.C., Kuo, S.Y.: Fast human/car classification methods in the computer vision tasks. In: Proceedings of SPIE – The International Society for Optics and Photonics (2013)
7. Graps, A.: An introduction to wavelets. IEEE Comput. Sci. Eng. **2**(2), 50–61 (1995)
8. Ma, J., Plonka, G.: The curvelet transform a review of recent applications. IEEE Sig. Process. Mag. **27**(2), 118–133 (2010)
9. Candès, E.J., Donoho, D.L.: Ridgelets: a key to higher- dimensional intermittency? Philos. Trans. R. Soc. A: Math. Phys. Eng. Sci. **357**(1760), 2495–2509 (1999)
10. Candès, E.J., Donoho, D.L.: Curvelets - a surprisingly effective nonadaptive representation for objects with edges. In: Cohen, A., Rabut, C., Larry, L. (eds.) Curves and Surface Fitting: Saint-Malo 1999, pp. 105–120. Vanderbilt University Press, Nashville (2000)
11. Do, M.N., Vetterli, M.: The contourlet transform: an efficient directional multiresolution image representation. IEEE Trans. Image Process. **14**(12), 2091–2106 (2005)
12. Cunha, L.D., Zhou, J., Do, M.N.: The nonsubsampled contourlet transform: theory, design, and applications. IEEE Trans. Image Process. **15**(10), 3089–3101 (2006)
13. Prokop, R.J., Reeves, A.P.: A Survey of moment-based techniques for unoccluded object representation and recognition. CVGIP. Graph. Models Image Process. **54**(5), 438–460 (1992)
14. Bunyak, F., Palaniappan, K., Nath, S.K.: Flux tensor constrained geodesic active contours with sensor fusion for persistent object tracking. J. Multimedia **2**(4), 20–33 (2007)
15. Palaniappan, K., Ersoy, I., Seetharaman, G., Davis, S.R., Kumar, P., Rao, R.M., Linderman, R.: Parallel flux tensor analysis for efficient moving object detection. In: Proceedings of the 14th International Conference on Information Fusion, pp. 1–8 (2011)
16. Stauffer, C., Grimson, W.E.L.: Adaptive background mixture models for real-time tracking. IEEE Comput. Soc. Conf. Comput. Vis. Pattern Recogn. **2**, 246–252 (1999)
17. Barrow, H.G., Tenenbaum, J.M., Bolles, R.C., Wolf, H.C.: Parametric correspondence and chamfer matching: two new techniques for image matching. In: Proceedings of the 5th International Joint Conference on Artificial Intelligence, pp. 659–663 (1977)
18. http://www.mathworks.com/help/vision/ref/vision.blobanalysis-class.html. Accessed 1 August 2015
19. Mukundan, R.: A contour integration method for the computation of zernike moments of a binary image. In: USM-Penang: National Conference on Research and Development in Computer Science and Applications – REDECS 1997, pp. 188–192 (1997)

20. Tahmasbi, A., Saki, F., Shokouhi, S.B.: Classification of benign and malignant masses based on zernike moments. Int. J. Comput. Biol. Med. **41**(8), 726–735 (2011)
21. Friedman, J., Hastie, T., Tibshirani, R.: Additive logistic regression: a statistical view of boosting. J. Ann. Stat. **28**(2), 337–407 (2000)
22. http://www.mathworks.com/help/stats/ensemble-methods.html. Accessed 1 August 2015
23. Cortes, C., Vapnik, V.: Support-vector networks. J. Mach. Learn. **20**(3), 273–297 (1995)
24. ftp.cs.rdg.ac.uk/pub/PETS2001. Accessed 1 August 2015
25. Somasundaram, G., Morellas, V., Papanikolopoulos, N., Bedros, S.: Object classification in traffic scenes using multiple spatio-temporal features. In: The 2012 20th Mediterranean Conference on Control and Automation (MED), pp. 1536–1541 (2012)

Efficient Brain Tumor Segmentation in Magnetic Resonance Image Using Region-Growing Combined with Level Set

Nguyen Mong Hien and Nguyen Thanh Binh[⊠]

Faculty of Computer Science and Engineering,
Ho Chi Minh City University of Technology,
VNU-HCM, Ho Chi Minh City, Vietnam
hientvu@tvu.edu.vn,
ntbinh@hcmut.edu.vn

Abstract. Medical image segmentation plays a great role in image processing because it can help human to extract some suspicious regions from a medical image especially brain images. Brain tumor is one of the huge medical problems. It has an influence on our lives. In this paper, we proposed a method for brain tumor segmentation and detection in magnetic resonance image (MRI). The contrast of MRI is enhanced by using histogram equalization and the tumor region is labeled by using the region-growing technique combined with the level set method to create the exact boundary of tumor region and return the segmentation result. The proposed method is better than the other recent methods based on compared results.

Keywords: Tumor · Magnetic resonance · Segmentation · Region-growing · Level set

1 Introduction

In the modern life, MRI is very useful for doctors in diagnosing and determining medical problems. With the support of MRI, doctors can detect brain tumors to treat as soon as possible in order to reduce the mortality rate in the world. However, detection all regions in MRI is not easy if we use pure MRI. Because the brain consists of various tissues such as gray matters (GM), cerebrospinal fluid (CSF), white matter (WM) and other abnormal tissues. In the brain, old cells will be replaced by new cells. If the process runs wrong, new cells will be created while these cells are not required by the body. And old or spoiled cells do not disappear as they should. A mass of tissue is called a tumor that is created by the increase of extra cells.

Recently, a lot of methods are proposed to segment tumors in MRI. Researchers have combined some algorithms together in order to build new better methods. They however cannot solve some special cases, particularly, when the tumor is small and has low sensitivity. Bing [1] and Chuang [2] proposed a method that is combined spatial fuzzy clustering with the level set method to segment medical images. This method is successful in general but its result is not the best because the result of level set method

© ICST Institute for Computer Sciences, Social Informatics and Telecommunications Engineering 2016
P.C. Vinh and V. Alagar (Eds.): ICCASA 2015, LNICST 165, pp. 223–232, 2016.
DOI: 10.1007/978-3-319-29236-6_22

depends on the output of Fuzzy C-mean algorithm which may contain more segmented region than the ones of the region-growing technique. In other words, the result of region-growing only contains tumor regions. Salvakumar [3] used K-mean clustering and Fuzzy C-mean algorithm to segment and compute the area of the tumor in MRI. This technique determines a threshold [18] based on intensity values to separate pixels in various classes into two groups. The first group includes the pixels having their intensity value greater than the threshold. And the second one is remained pixels. The technique images can present two colors in black and white. Therefore, it will ignore tumor cells. Kalaiselve [4] proposed a method that is better than Fuzzy c-means because this method bases on intensity values to choose the centroids. Its result however depends on how to set the value for the initial centroid of the regions in gray image. Chenyang [5] formulated a new variation level set. It provides a new kind of level set evolution named distance regularized level set evolution (DRLSE). The DRLSE formulation is effective for image segmentation. Particularly, it is applied to an edge-based active contour model. Chunming [6] presented a framework of level set to segment as well as bias correction of image with intensity in homogeneities. In [6], a minimized energy function is proposed to combine segmentation and bias field estimation. Tran [7] proposed an efficient pancreas segmentation method. Histogram equalization is used to enhance the quality of input images and then the region-growing technique is also applied to segment pancreas. Kailash [8] proposed efficient segmentation methods for tumor detection in MRI images, in which some clustering methods and segmentation algorithms are combined together in order to improve the result. Gopal [9] proposed a method to build an intelligent system which can be used to diagnose brain tumor via MRI by using image processing clustering algorithms. Jichuan [10] proposed a novel local threshold segmentation algorithm with shape information to improve quality. This method is useful for the case, in which, many objects with a similar shape locate in an image. Because most of local threshold algorithms often use intensity value to analyze. Nabizadeh [11] proposed a method to detect and segment brain tumors in MR images. This method shows that statistical features are better than Gabor wavelet features. The result of method however depends on the threshold for the number of mutual information. It has a detectable influence on the size of the tumors. Halder [12] used K-means and Object labeling method to detect tumor in MR images. But the accuracy of the approach is depended on the result of K-means method. Koley [13] used region growing technique to identify the infected regions in brain MR images and then contour detection algorithm is applied to create accurate boundaries of the regions. However, most of these methods are complex.

In this paper, we have proposed an approach to segment tumor in brain MRI using histogram equalization to enhance images and the region growing technique to segment tumor regions if present and then using the level set method to make the exact contour of tumor region based on the previous result. The rest of the paper is organized as follows: we described the background of Jaccard index, the region-based segmentation and level set method in Sect. 2; the proposed method is shown in Sect. 3; the result and conclusion of the paper are presented in Sects. 4 and 5 respectively.

2 Background

2.1 Jaccard Index (J.I)

The similarity between two operational taxonomic units (OTUs) is considered by Jaccard's similarity index. Jaccard's index [19] can be introduced in various ways. One of the popular ways is:

$$J = \frac{C}{A + B - C} \tag{1}$$

where A and B are the amount of attributes present in OTU a and OTU b respectively and C is the amount of attributes present in both OTU a and OTU b.

Jaccard's index can also be introduced by:

$$J = \frac{C}{A + B + C} \tag{2}$$

in which A is the amount of attributes present in OTU a and absent in OTU b, B is the amount of attributes present in OTU b and absent in OTU a, and the role of C is the same in Eq. (1).

Another approach of introducing Jaccard's index is:

$$J = \frac{C}{N} \tag{3}$$

where C holds the role as in Eq. (2) and N is the total amount of attributes found in both OTUs together.

2.2 Region-Based Segmentation

The aim of region-based segmentation is to try to split or group regions based on common image characteristics [16]. The characteristics of images include intensity values, textures and spectral profiles.

In region-growing algorithm, intensity value is considered as a property. Combining the seeding and region-growing method to segment pixels set that is made by initially choosing one or more pixels in the image (named the seed points). Those seeds are made by interacting between users and beginning from the growing regions by appending to each seed with its neighbor pixels which satisfy the conditions. In this algorithm, the segmented pixels set will be added by all the pixels which are r-connected to the initial seed pixel and fall the limits of threshold. To be r-connected to another, two pixels must share at least r corner points. The segmented pixel set is added recursively by all the pixels which are connected to the current members of the pixel set. Region growth will stop if no more pixels satisfy the condition for inclusion in that region.

Let: $f(x, y)$ means an array of input image; $S(x, y)$ means a seed array containing two values (1 and 0), the value at the locations of seed points is 1s and 0s elsewhere; and Q means a predication to be applied for each location (x, y). The size of arrays f and S are assumed to be equal. The core of region-growing algorithm based on 8-connectivity should be followed by:

(i)   Find all connected components in $S(x, y)$ and erode each one to a pixel and label all pixels found as 1. The other ones in S are assigned 0.
(ii) Build an image f_Q such that, with each pair of coordinates (x, y), if the given predication Q is satisfied at those coordinates then $f_Q(x, y)$ is set to 1; in contrast, it is set to 0.
(iii) Adding to each seed point in S all 1-valued points in f_Q that are 8-connected to the seed point in order to form an image g.
(iv) Various region label is assigned to each connected component in g. The obtaining segmented image is region growing.

And then, a predication must be specified and add all the pixels to each seed. Those pixels are not only k-connected to the seed but also similar to it. Various intensities are used as a measure of similarity, the predication used at each location (x, y) is Q. Q = true if the absolute difference of the intensities between the seed and the pixel at (x, y) is $\leq$ T where T is a specified threshold. Otherwise, Q = false.

2.3   Level Set Method

The level set method [14, 17] is simple and useful for calculating and analyzing the motion of an interface Γ in two or three dimensions. A region Ω is bounded by the Γ. Its aim is to calculate and analyze the next motion of Γ under a velocity field v. The velocity can be affected by the geometry of the interface, the external physics, time and position. This interface is for the next time as this zero level set of a smooth function $\varphi(x, t)$. It means that $\Gamma(t) = \{x|\ \varphi(x, t) = 0\}$, φ is positive inside Ω, negative outside Ω, and is zero on $\Gamma(t)$.

The function (φ) of level set includes some properties below:

$$\varphi(x, t) > 0 \ \text{for} \ x \in \Omega$$
$$\varphi(x, t) < 0 \ \text{for} \ x \notin \overline{\Omega} \qquad (4)$$
$$\varphi(x, t) = 0 \ \text{for} \ x \in \partial\Omega = \Gamma(t)$$

3   Efficient Brain Tumor Segmentation in MRI

In this section, we propose an efficient brain tumor segmentation in magnetic resonance that is based on region-growing combined with level set method. The generalized block diagram of the proposed method is given in Fig. 1. The proposed method includes three stages: histogram processing, region-growing segmentation and level set. The stages will be explained in the following subsections.

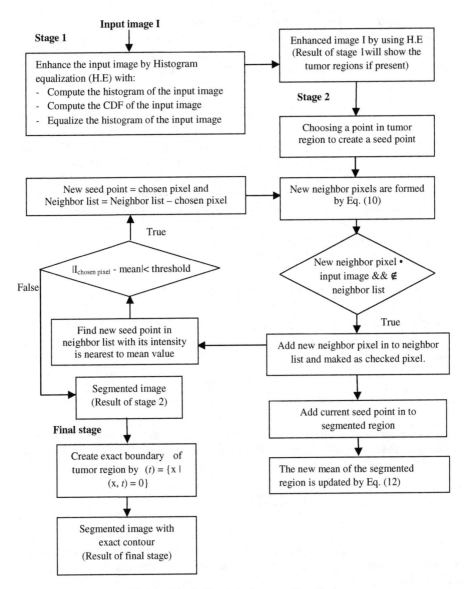

Fig. 1. Block diagram of proposed method.

3.1   Histogram Processing

In the first stage, we apply histogram equalization method to enhance the input image. This task should be done because the real medical image usually has low contrast. With the support of the method, the contrast of output image is improved significantly. As a result, it is easier to recognize the subjects in the image. Especially, the subjects are tumors with low contrast as well as strange shapes. It can be described as follows:

3.1.1   Compute the Histogram of the Input Image

Histogram is a basic processing method in spatial domain. The information can be gotten directly from an image by statistics. The image can be enhanced easily by histogram. The histogram [15] with intensity levels in the range [0, L−1] of an image is a discrete function

$$h(r_k) = n_k \tag{5}$$

where r_k is the kth value of intensity, n^k is the amount of pixels in the range of intensity r_k and L is the amount of intensity levels. With r is a discrete random variable showing intensity values in the range [0, L−1] and with $p(r_k)$ is the normalized histogram component corresponding to value r_k, and it is considered as an estimate of the probability that intensity r_k happens in the image base on that the histogram is obtained.

3.1.2   Compute the CDF of the Input Image

In a given image the probability $p(r_k)$ of intensity level r_k is computed as

$$p(r_k) = \frac{n_k}{MN} \quad k = 0, 1, 2, \ldots, L-1 \tag{6}$$

where MN is the total amount of pixels.

A function of transformation of special importance in image processing follows the form

$$s = T(r) = (L-1) \int_0^r p_r(w)dw \tag{7}$$

with w is an integration dummy variable. The equation right side is recognized as the Cumulative Distribution Function (CDF) of random variable r. The discrete form of the above transformation follows by:

$$s_k = T(r_k) = (L-1) \sum_{j=0}^{k} p_r(r_j) \quad k = 0, 1, 2, \ldots, L-1 \tag{8}$$

Therefore, a result image is that each pixel in the input image maps with intensity r_k into a corresponding pixel with level s_k in the result image. This transformation $T(r_k)$ is named a histogram equalization.

3.1.3   The Histogram of the Input Image

is equalized by

$$I_p = T(I_p) \tag{9}$$

Where I_p is intensity value of pixel in the input image.

3.2 Region-Growing Segmentation

In the second stage, the result image of the first stage is used as the input image. This result is very useful for choosing a point on the tumor region being a seed point (x, y) because the contrast of among regions in the image becomes higher. We can find out where tumor regions easily. Moreover, the result of region-growing technique is also more accurate because the nature of this technique is based on intensity value of neighbor pixels. The region-growing technique will segment tumor regions. The stage can be described as follows:

(i)   The neighbors of each pixel (x, y) are formed by

$$(x+1, \ y), \ (x-1, \ y), \ (x, \ y+1), \ (x, \ y-1) \tag{10}$$

If neighbor pixel $\in$ input image and not belong the neighbor list then this neighbor pixel will be added to the neighbor list and marked as checked pixels.

(ii)   The current seed point will be added in to segmented region.

(iii)   In the next iteration the new seed point will be chosen by finding the pixel with intensity nearest to mean value of segmented region. The minimum distance depends on the chosen pixel and means value of intensity:

$$min_{distance} = \min_{i=1..n} |I_i - m_{mean}| \tag{11}$$

where I_i is an intensity of pixel p_i in neighbor list, m_{mean} is mean of the segmented region which is computed by:

$$m_{mean} = (m_{mean} * |R| + I_p)/(|R| + 1) \tag{12}$$

where $|R|$ is size of segmented region

(iv)   The new mean of the segmented region is updated by Eq. (12) and then the neighbor list = neighbor list\chosen pixel.

(v)   While (distance between region and possible new pixels $\leq$ the certain threshold) do the above processes.

Proposed algorithm will return the segmented region as a logical matrix that contains brain tumor region which has the same properties to seed point.

3.3 Level Set Method

In the final stage, this process needs to use the result of the second stage because this result is the image with intensity homogeneity. In real world, it is not easy for us to get images with intensity homogeneity because of different factors. As a consequence, it causes many problems in image processing. It is considered as hard work for image segmentation especially images with intensity inhomogeneity because of the over-laps among the ranges of the intensities in the regions. It cannot identify the regions based on the pixel intensity value. Meanwhile, the level set method will give a good segmentation result if input data is an image with intensity homogeneity. That is why the region-growing technique is required in the proposed method. Osher [14] gave the level set way to hold topology changes of curves. In the paper, the initial segmentation is run by region-growing technique that makes approximated boundary. The level set method is applied to make the exact boundary. A demonstration of the level set method is when the surface intersects with zero planes to give the curve that depends on the changes of surface. To see the evolution of boundary by tracking the zero level set implicitly with Eq. (4).

4   Experiments and Evaluation

In this section, we implemented the proposed approach in Sect. 3. We applied the proposed method for MRI data that obtained from many cases. We use the Jaccard index (J.I) between an extracted region and a true one [19].

The index ranges from 0 to 100 %, with higher values representing better performance. The resolution of tested images is 512 × 512. The threshold used in experiments ranges from 0.04 to 0.08. We have experimented on image dataset collected from many resources. Here, we report the results of some cases as Fig. 2.

In Fig. 2, the results of the proposed method are better than the other method. The region-growing technique and the method of [3] are based on the threshold to segment brain tumor region. It is not easy to set an ideal threshold value for these methods. If this value is too low the segmented region will lack the pixels which belong to the tumor region. Because the intensity distance between those pixels and mean value is

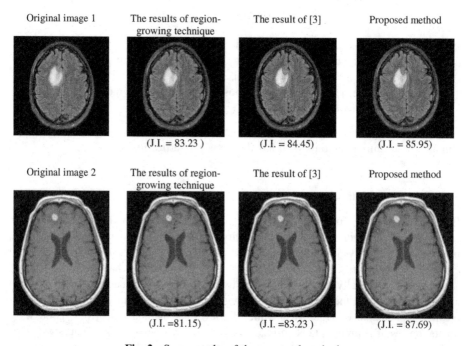

Original image 1	The results of region-growing technique	The result of [3]	Proposed method
	(J.I. = 83.23)	(J.I. = 84.45)	(J.I. = 85.95)
Original image 2	The results of region-growing technique	The result of [3]	Proposed method
	(J.I. =81.15)	(J.I. =83.23)	(J.I. = 87.69)

Fig. 2. Some results of the proposed method

higher than the threshold value. In contrast, if the value is too high the segmented region will contain the pixels which belong to other regions. Because the intensity distance between those pixels and mean value is lower than the threshold value. That is reason why those proposed methods need to be improved.

Our method has solved the problem. It means that our results are more exact than the ones of these methods thanks to using the level set method to improve the result of the region-growing technique. The level set method is simple and useful for calculating and analyzing the motion of an interface Γ in two or three dimensions. The tumor region is bounded by the Γ. The method supports to calculate and analyze the next motion of Γ under a velocity field v. The tumor region is get for next time as this zero level set of a smooth function $\varphi(x, t)$. It means that $\Gamma(t) = \{x \mid \varphi(x, t) = 0\}$. The speaking above explains why the result of our method which is evaluated by J.I tool is better than other methods in Fig. 2.

5   Conclusion

Brain tumor segmentation helps the doctors during diagnosis. This is hard work because the brain cells usually have a small size. Therefore, algorithm segmentation must be high. This paper shows an efficient brain tumor segmentation method from MRI. Histogram equalization is applied to improve the contrast of MRI in which a brain tumor region is labeled by using the region-growing technique. And then, the level set method is used to create the exact boundary of the brain tumor region which is labeled in the previous stage. The proposed method performs better because it is easy for us to find out tumor regions thanks to the histogram equalization technique. And only tumor regions are labeled by using the region-growing technique. Finally, the level set method is applied to the output result of the previous stage to create the exact boundary of tumor region. As a result, the proposed method gives a good result which presents segmented tumor regions with the exact contour.

Acknowledgments. This research is funded by Ho Chi Minh City University of Technology, VNU-HCM under grant number TNCS - KHMT - 2015 – 23.

References

1. Li, B.N., Chui, C.K., Chang, S., Ong, S.H.: Integrating spatial fuzzy clustering with level set methods for automated medical image segmentation. Comput. Biol. Med. **41**, 1–10 (2011)
2. Chuang, K.-S., Tzeng, H.-L., Chen, S., Wu, J., Chen, T.-J.: Fuzzy c-means clustering with information for image segmentation. J. Comput. Med. Imaging Graph. **30**, 9–15 (2005)
3. Salvakumar, J., Lakshmi, A., Arivoli, T.: Brain tumor segmentation and its area calculation in brain MR images using K-mean clustering and Fuzzy C-mean algorithm. In: International Conference on Advances in Engineering Science and Management, pp. 186–190 (2012)
4. Thiruvenkadam, K., Karuppanagounder, S.: Fuzzy C-means technique with histogram based centroid initialization for brain tissue segmentation in MRI of head scan. In: International Symposium on Humanities, Science and Engineering Research, pp. 149–150 (2011)

5. Xu, C., Li, C., Gui, C., Fox, M.D.: Distance regularized level set evolution and its application to image segmentation. IEEE Trans. Image Process. **19**, 3243–3254 (2010)

6. Li, C., Huang, R., Ding, Z., Gatenby, J.C., Metaxas, D.N.: A level set method for image segmentation in the presence of intensity in homogeneities with application to MRI. IEEE Trans. Image Process. **20**, 2007–2016 (2011)

7. Tam, T.D., Binh, N.T.: Efficient pancreas segmentation in computed tomography based on region-growing. In: Vinh, P.C., Vassev, E., Hinchey, M. (eds.) ICTCC 2014. LNICST, vol. 144, pp. 332–340. Springer, Heidelberg (2015)

8. Sinha, K., Sinha, G.R.: Efficient segmentation methods for tumor detection in MRI images. In: IEEE Student's Conference on Electrical, Electronics and Computer Science, pp. 1–6 (2014)

9. Gopal, N.N., Karnan, M.: Diagnose brain tumor through MRI using image processing clustering algorithm such as Fuzz C means along with intelligent optimization techniques. In: IEEE International Conference on Computational Intelligence and Computing Research, vol. 2, pp. 1–4 (2010)

10. Shi, J., Zhang, H.: Adaptive local threshold with shape information and its application to object segmentation. In: IEEE International Conference, pp. 1123–1128 (2009)

11. Nabizadeh, N., Kubat, M.: Brain tumors detection and segmentation in MR images: Gabor wavelet vs. statistical features. Comput. Electr. Eng. **45**, 286–301 (2015)

12. Halder, A., Giri, C., Halder, A.: Brain tumor detection using segmentation based object labeling algorithm. In: IEEE International Conference on Electronics, Communication and Instrumentation, pp. 1–4 (2014)

13. Koley, S., Pal, K., Ghosh, G., Bhattacharya, M.: GUI based brain tumor identification system by detecting infected region through a combination of region growing, cryptography, and digital watermarking technique. In: IEEE Fourth International Conference on Communication Systems and Network Technologies, pp. 756–761 (2014)

14. Osher, S., Fedkiw, R.P.: Level set methods: an overview and some recent results. J. Comput. Phys. **169**, 463–502 (2001)

15. Jin, Y., Fayad, L., Laine, A.: Contrast enhancement by multi-scale adaptive histogram equalization. In: Wavelet: Application in Signal and Image Processing IX, Proceedings of SPIE, vol. 4478, pp. 206–213 (2001)

16. Gonzalez, R.C., Woods, R.E.: Digital Image Processing, 3rd edn. Prentice Hall, Upper Saddle River (2002)

17. Abdalla, Z., Neveenm, I.G., Ella, H.A., Hesham, A.H.: Level set based CT liver image segmentation with watershed and artifiacial neural networks. In: 12th International Conference on Hybrid Intelligent Systems, pp. 96–102 (2012)

18. Chowdhury, M.H., Little, W.D.: Image thresholding techniques. In: IEEE Pacific Rim Conference on Communication, Computers, and Signal Processing, pp. 585–589 (1995)

19. Real, R., Varga, J.M.: The probabilistic basis of Jaccard's index of similarity. Syst. Biol. **45**, 380–385 (1996)

Burn Image Classification Using One-Class Support Vector Machine

Hai Tran[1]([✉]), Triet Le[1], Thai Le[2], and Thuy Nguyen[3]

[1] Informatics Technology Faculty,
University of Pedagogy, HCMC, Vietnam
{haits, trietlm}@hcmup.edu.vn
[2] Computer Science Department,
University of Science, HCMC, Vietnam
lhthai@fit.hcmus.edu.vn
[3] University of Engineering and Technology,
Ha Noi, Vietnam
nguyenthanhthuy@vnu.edu.vn

Abstract. Burn image classification is critical and attempted problems in medical image processing. This paper proposes the image classification model applied for burn images. The proposal model use one-class Support Vector Machine with color features for burn image classification. The aim of this model is to identify automatically the degrees of burns in three levels: II, III, and IV. The skin burn color images are used as inputs to the model. Then, we apply the multi-color channels extraction and binary based on adaptive threshold for Support Vector Machine classifier. The proposal model uses One- class Support Vector Machine instead of kernel Support Vector Machine because of unbalance degrees of burns images database. The experiments are conducted with the real-life image provided by Cho Ray hospital with the precision 77.78 %. The validation process shows that our main results and the feasibility of our proposal model are stated (Fig. 1) .

Keywords: Burn image classification · Support Vector Machine (SVM) · Multi- color channels

1 Introduction

Medical image processing has a variety of potential applications in the recent years. There were many research results applying image processing for medical in both general applicable theory and specific applications. Computer-aided diagnostic processing has already become a significant part of clinical routine. The aim of this research is to develop the computer-aided system for burn image classification.

Burns, commonly caused by fire, can also result from chemicals, electricity, and other heat accidents. Burns are classified based on how much of the skin's thickness is involved [1]. The purpose of burn image classification is to identify automatically the burning degree of patients based on the color images of burning regions.

© ICST Institute for Computer Sciences, Social Informatics and Telecommunications Engineering 2016
P.C. Vinh and V. Alagar (Eds.): ICCASA 2015, LNICST 165, pp. 233–242, 2016.
DOI: 10.1007/978-3-319-29236-6_23

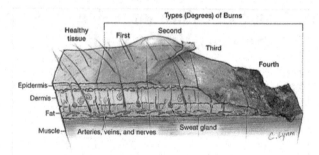

Fig. 1. Degrees of burn [1]. This shows a figure consisting of four types of burns relating to the depths of skin. The more into the depths, higher degree of burn, for example, as the fourth degree, the burn wounds are into the muscle depth.

1.1   Medical Image Processing

The historical study of medical imaging has been very long. This is an interesting research problem [2]. In recent years, the more developing of computer vision, the more integration of computer vision system and medical image process system:

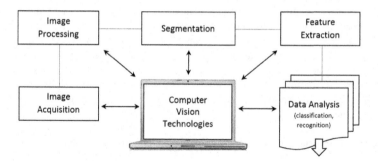

Fig. 2. Computer vision applies for medical image processing in almost phase such as image acquisition, segmentation extraction, processing and classification or recognition.

In the above Fig. 2, the computer vision technology can apply for almost phases in the medical imaging system, especially, some artificial intelligent tools are very useful for data analysis such as pattern recognition, classification.

In the medical imaging topic, automatic burn image classification is the open problem. In this research, we try to apply computer vision processing and machine learning for identifying the degrees of burns. In the clinical burning patient diagnosing code, the doctor need to identify the degrees of burn: Degrees I, Degrees II, Degrees III, and Degrees IV based on the depth of levels of burns and scalds and some clinical diagnosis and diagnosis related groups. Degree I of burns involves only the top layer of the skin. Degree II of burns injures deeper into the skin and cause blistering.

Degree III of burns involves all the layers of the skin, including the nerves. Degree IV of burns extends into the muscle.

1.2   Medical Image Classification

The medical test in the medical diagnosis often uses laboratory analysis, bio signal analysis (ECG, EEEG...) and image analysis. Burn image classification is a kind of image classification with the lower number classes in the medical imaging focusing on the image analysis. Thus, we must use the image processing techniques for image feature extraction. The feature extraction techniques common used for medical imaging is Fourier transform, 2D function for monochrome image, image brightness profiles, or RGB color component profiles.

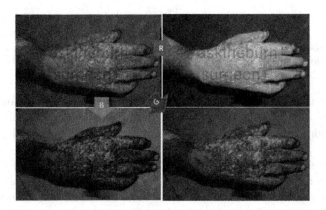

Fig. 3. An example of multi-color channels. The top-left is the original burn image. The top-right is the red channel extracting from the original image. The bottom-left is the blue channel extracting from the original image. The bottom-right is the green channel extracting from the original image.

In the burn images process, the Red channel is the most significant channel. There is a little difference between the Blue and the Green channel. For the above burn image example in Fig. 3, Degree II and Degree IV have the same form in the Blue and the Green channel, but the Red channel of Degree II and Degree IV are not the same.

1.3   Classifier Based on Machine Learning

The image classification model using machine-learning technique often has two phases: training phase and classifying phase. In the training phase, the system uses machine-learning algorithm to update the parameter of classifier model. For example, SVM computes the coefficient of hyperplanes in the training. After that, SVM uses the hyperplanes to classify the image in the testing phase. The common architecture of image classification using machine-learning system is below:

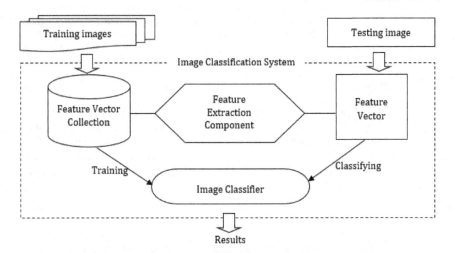

Fig. 4. Image classification architecture using machine learning. The feature extraction component is used in both training and classifying phases. The feature vectors of images are used as inputs to the image classifier.

There are many kinds of classifiers applied for medical classification: some use expert system and some use learning from data. They often use machine learning Neural Network, Support Vector Machine... with the suitable learning algorithm (Fig. 4).

Some popular learning algorithms are unsupervised learning, supervised learning, semi-supervisor learning, or active learning. In the burn image classification, most of burn image data from the hospital labeled. Given the data with annotation by the doctors, either supervised or unsupervised learning approaches could apply for burn image classification. The burn images dataset is small and pre-labeled. Thus, we uses supervised learning approaches.

There is very little burn image classification systems suggested by some researchers. For example, M. Survana [3] has applied Template Matching, k-NN and SVM classification methods for skin burn images with their own collection dataset with only 120 images in 3 types of burns (superficial dermal, partial thickness and full thickness). This experimental results show that SVM is more suitable classifier for burn images than k-NN and Template Matching. Besides, B. Acha [4] also proposed the classification of burn wounds using SVM by color and texture information of burn images. That is the reason why we suggest using SVM for burn images of classification. To the best of our knowledge, there is not any image classification model for identifying the degrees of burns based on machine learning in Vietnam. The aim of this paper is to build a burning classification system for Vietnamese patients (Fig. 5).

The digital color burn image will be drop and segmentation before it is extracted color feature. The color features of burn images are used as inputs to the SVM classifier. The out of SVM classifier are the degrees of burn. The remainder of this paper is organized as follows. Section 2 deals with the preprocessing and feature extraction from burn images. Section 3 provides a detailed exposition of the proposal model

Fig. 5. SVM classifier applies for burn image. This figure shows diagram of SVM burn image classification from the burn image input to the degrees of burn output.

applying for burn image classification. Section 4 is devoted to the study and discussion of the experimental results. Conclusion and future works are mentioned in the Sect. 5.

In some cases, it is the Contact Volume Editor that checks all the pdfs. In such cases, the authors are not involved in the checking phase (Fig. 6).

2   Burn Image Feature Extraction

Firstly, we normalize the burn images in a standard size with the rate 4:3 for removing un-burned region of images. The dropped images will be segmented based on color information by B. Acha [4].

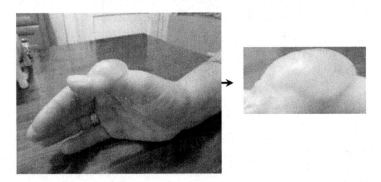

Fig. 6. Burn image size standardization for segmentation. The original burn image is on the left and the dropped image removing some unrelated burning background objects is on the right.

Due to the requirement of the processing speed is real time, this paper suggested to use the fast feature extraction based on multi-color channels Red, Green, Blue and Gray. In order to improve the performance of machine learning, the multi-color channels will be binary to 0 or 1 (Fig. 7).

3   Burn Image Classification Model

The overview of burn image classification model includes four stages: image acquisition, image pre-processing, feature extraction and classification. It is presented in the below diagram:

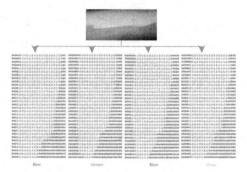

Fig. 7. Multi-color channels extraction. The burn image is extracted into Red, Green, Blue and Gray color channels (color figure online).

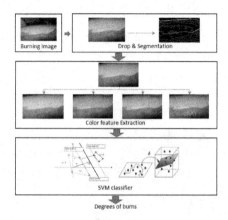

Fig. 8. Burn image classification model. The figure shows the overview of our burn image classification using SVM.

The burn images have been collected and supplied from the Cho Ray hospital, Vietnam and published in http://fit.hcmup.edu.vn/medical_image_project/. The burn image will be standardize and segmentation before inputting the feature extraction component. The output burn image features are the multi-color binary channels, which are used as inputs to the SVM classifier (Fig. 8).

4   Experimental Results

We have built images databases from Cho Ray hospital consisting 396 burn images in the 4 degrees of burn II, III and IV. We do not classify the degrees I of burn because it is minor level and might cause from the sun sight. This is also the reason why many Vietnamese people do not care about the degrees I of burns at this time. The degree II of burns has 180 images, the degree III of burns has 192 and the degree IV of burns has

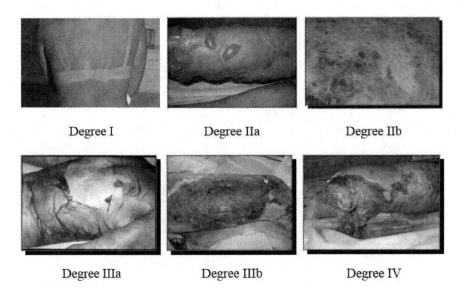

| Degree I | Degree IIa | Degree IIb |

| Degree IIIa | Degree IIIb | Degree IV |

Fig. 9. Illustration for degrees of burn images. The degrees from I to IV display from top-left to bottom-right.

24 images. There are very little images of the degrees IV of burns because this is high level of burn and the patients maybe die before inpatient entrance (Fig. 9).

We create two folders: a half images in training and a half images in testing like two-folded cross validation scheme to divide the database. Some images in training folder and in testing folder are below:

The precision, false acceptance rate (FAR) and false reject rate is the common criterion to evaluate the classification rate, simplify given by:

$$
\begin{aligned}
\text{Precision} &= \frac{\#\text{correctly classified images}}{\#\text{ total images}} \\
FAR &= \frac{\#\text{False classified images}}{\text{classified images}} \\
\text{FRR} &= \frac{\#\text{False classified images}}{\text{rejected images}}
\end{aligned}
\tag{1}
$$

The experimental results in the precision, FAR and FRR will help us to analysis the root cause of classification errors and improve the suggested model. The experimental results with multiple SVM kernels are presented in the below Table 1 in order to identify the suitable SVM kernel for burn image classification (Fig. 10).

The results show that the One-Class SVM (OC-SVM) [5] is suitable in this classification problem because of the unbalance data. It shows that our main aims are stated and proved. OC-SVM if compared to SVM has the higher accuracy of burn image classification. However, OC-SVM required the trade of computing time to the accuracy in the case using the simple binary features (Table 2).

Table 1. Burn image classification detail results using SVM

Degrees	#image for training	#image for testing	#image classified correctly using Gauss kernel	Precision classification using Gauss kernel	#image classified correctly using Polynomial	Precision classification using Polynomial
II	90	90	63	70 %	68	76 %
III	96	96	72	75 %	72	75 %
IV	12	12	7	58 %	6	50 %

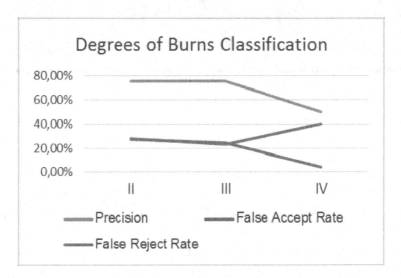

Fig. 10. Precision and FAR- FRR on Degrees of Burn Identification results. the FAR of Degrees IV is high and the FRR of Degrees IV is low because of unbalance burn image of Degrees IV image is too low due to the number of burn inpatient in this level. To improve upon this unbalance data shortcoming, we suggest using One Class SVM instead of traditional SVM.

Table 2. Classification results using one-class SVM vs. traditional SVM

Methods	#training images	#testing images	Precision classification using Gauss kernel	Precision classification using Polynomial
SVM	198	198	71.71 %	73.73 %
One-class SVMIV	198	198	73.23 %	77.78 %

From experimental results of SVM classification method using Polynomial kernel is more accuracy than Gauss kernel. It maybe cause from the distributed of burn image data is 48 % in the degrees II of burn and 47 % in the degrees III of burns. The rest distributes under 5 %. The wrong classification is focus on the Degrees IV of burn.

The number of images of this degree is too lower than the Degrees II and III. Due to this unbalance in the training, we try to use one-class SVM instead of traditional SVM. It has been improve the accuracy of classification.

The overall precision is less than 80 % because we have not yet combined local feature extraction method, for example, Local Binary Pattern (LBP) with multi-color channels feature. Besides, the training and testing images are very difference in the same Degree. For example, the burning Degree II patient is on the hand used for training and another one is on the leg used for testing. These burn images are only similar in some local features, but they are very difference in general view.

5 Conclusion and Future Works

This paper introduces an approach using one-class SVM with color feature for burn image classification. This paper proposes the classification model for burn image to identify automatically the degrees of burns in three levels for Vietnamese patients. The proposal model uses the multi-color channels extraction and binary based on adaptive threshold. Because of the unbalance degrees of burns data, we suggest use one-class SVM instead of traditional SVM. The experiments were conducted with the real-life image provided by Cho Ray hospital with the precision 77.78 %. The experimental results show the feasibility of the proposal model in the starting researching phase.

The expectation of improving the accuracy and the real time processing are opening challenges of this problem. We cannot trade off the classification time because its requirement is real time in the diagnosis degrees of burns phase of treatment process. However, we can trade off the training time to improve the precision of classification. So that in the future work, we can use a big data for training phase and use some improved SVM such Fuzzy SVM or another complex training model in order to increase the classifying accuracy.

Acknowledgments. The author is greatly indebted to Doctor Vo Van Phuc and his colleges in the burn department of Cho Ray hospital for his helping, guidance, understanding, and most importantly, his expertise during this study.

References

1. Janet, M., Torpy, M.D.: Burn injuries. the Journal of the American Medical Association (JAMA), Vol. 302, No. 16 (2009). doi:10.1001/jama.302.16.1828
2. Michał, S.: Introduction to Medical Imaging, Biomedical Engineering, IFE (2013)
3. Survana, M., Sivakumar Niranjan, U.C.: Classification methods of skin burn images. In: IJCSIT (2013)
4. Acha, B., Serrano, C., Laura M.R: Segmentation and classification of burn images by color and texture information. J. biomed. opt. 10(3) (2005)
5. Guerbai, Y., Youcef, C., Bilal, H.: The effective use of the one-class SVM classifier for handwritten signature verification based on writer-independent parameters. Pattern Recogn. (2014)

6. Chebira, A., Kovačević, J.: Multiresolution techniques for the classification of bioimage and biometric datasets. In: Optical Engineering + Applications, International Society for Optics and Photonics, p. 67010G (2007)
7. Tam, Tran Duc, Binh, Nguyen Thanh: Efficient pancreas segmentation in computed tomography based on region-growing. In: Vinh, Phan Cong, Vassev, Emil, Hinchey, Mike (eds.) ICTCC 2014. LNICST, vol. 144, pp. 332–340. Springer, Heidelberg (2015)
8. Bao, P.T.: Fast multi-face detection using facial component based validation by fuzzy logic. In: Proceedings of the International conference on Image Processing and Computer Vision (IPCV 2006), Las Vergas, Nevada (2006)
9. Thai, L.H., Hai, T.S., Thuy, N.T.: Image classification using support vector machine and artificial neural network. I. J. Inf. Technol. Comput. Sci. 5(4), 32–38 (2012). doi:10.5815/ijitcs.2012.05.05
10. Van, H.T., Tat, P.Q., Le, T.H.: Palmprint verification using GridPCA for Gabor features. In: Proceedings of the Second Symposium on Information and Communication Technology, pp. 217–225. ACM (2011)

Discriminative Semi-supervised Learning
in Manifold Subspace for Face Recognition

Tue-Minh Dinh Vo, Hung Phuoc Truong, and Thai Hoang Le[✉]

Faculty of Information Technology,
University of Science, VNU-HCM, Ho Chi Minh City, Vietnam
1112190@student.hcmus.edu.vn,
{tphung,lhthai}@fit.hcmus.edu.vn

Abstract. Linear Discriminant Analysis (LDA) is a commonly used method for dimensionality reduction, which preserves class separability. Despite its successes, it has limitations under some situations, including the small sample size problem. In practice, when the training data set is small, the covariance matrix of each class may not be accurately estimated. Moreover, LDA doesn't handle unlabeled data. In this paper, we propose a semi-supervised method called Discriminative Semi-supervised Learning in Manifold subspace (DSLM), which aims at overcoming all these limitations. The proposed method is designed to explore the discriminative information of labeled data and to preserve the intrinsic geometric structure of the data. We empirically compare our method with several related methods on face databases. Results are obtained from the experiments showing the effectiveness of our proposed method .

Keywords: Face recognition · Manifold · Semi-supervised

1 Introduction

In many areas of artificial intelligence, information retrieval, and data mining, one is often confronted with intrinsically low-dimensional data lying in a very high-dimensional space. This leads one to consider methods of dimensionality reduction that allow one to represent the data in a lower dimensional space. Two of the most popular techniques for this purpose are Principal Component Analysis (PCA) and Linear Discriminant Analysis (LDA).

PCA is an unsupervised and an eigenvector method designed to model linear variation in high-dimensional data. PCA is guaranteed to discover the dimensionality of the subspace and produces a compact representation when the data is embedded in a linear subspace.

LDA is a supervised method. LDA searches for the project axes on which the data points of different classes are far from each other while requiring data points of the same class to be close to each other. LDA encodes discriminating information in a linear separable space using bases are not necessarily orthogonal. When label information available, *e.g.* for classification task, LDA can achieve significant better performance than PCA. However, recent work [4] shows that when the training dataset is small, PCA can outperform LDA. The reason is covariance matrix of each class in

© ICST Institute for Computer Sciences, Social Informatics and Telecommunications Engineering 2016
P.C. Vinh and V. Alagar (Eds.): ICCASA 2015, LNICST 165, pp. 243–253, 2016.
DOI: 10.1007/978-3-319-29236-6_24

LDA may not be accurately estimated. There are a lot of approaches that try to improve the performance of PCA and LDA, which are [1–3].

Recently, a number of research efforts have shown that the face images possibly reside on a nonlinear manifold [6, 10, 11, 16–18, 20–22]. Both PCA and LDA fail to discover the underlying structure when the face images lie on a manifold since they effectively see only the Euclidean structure. There has been some interest in the problem of developing low dimensional representations through kernel based techniques for face recognition [14,15]. These methods can discover the nonlinear structure of the face images. However, they are computationally expensive, and none of them explicitly considers the structure of the manifold on which the face images possibly reside. In the meantime, some nonlinear techniques have been proposed to discover the nonlinear structure of manifold, *e.g.* ISOMAP [13], LLE [6], Laplacian Eigenmap [12]. However, these nonlinear manifold learning techniques might not be suitable for face recognition since they do not generally provide a functional mapping between the high and low dimensional spaces that are valid both on and off the training data. There are a lot of approaches that try to address this issue by explicitly requiring an embedding function either linear or in reproducing kernel Hilbert space when minimizing the objective function [16–18]. One of the major limitations of these methods is that they fail to characterize the manifold structure of data when there are insufficient training samples. To solve this problem, many techniques have been proposed [19, 20] which have significantly improved the face recognition performance. However, these recognition algorithms struggle in achieving a reliable performance under more practical environments, where facial appearances are of large variations in illumination, expression, pose. An approach based on deep neural network has been proposed [5] to learn a nonlinear embedding from a high-dimensional data space to a low-dimensional space. However, this technique is computationally expensive and hard to determine the parameters.

In reality, we usually have small part of input data labeled, along with a large number of unlabeled data. Thus, semi-supervised learning has attracted an increasing amount of attention. Two well-known algorithms are extension of Support Vector Machine [21] and graph-based learning [10, 22]. Despite of their performance, it is unclear to determine the *good* graph.

In this paper, we propose a new semi-supervised dimensionality reduction algorithm, called Semi-supervised Learning in Manifold subspace (DSLM). Our proposed algorithm aims to find a projection which captures not only the discriminant structure inferred from the labeled data but also the intrinsic geometrical structure inferred from the whole training data. Specifically, the training data is used to build a graph incorporating neighborhood information in which each data point is represented as a linear combination of the neighboring data points. The graph provides a discrete approximation to the local geometry of the data manifold. In this way, DSLM can optimally preserves the manifold structure.

The rest of this paper is organized as follows: The Semi-supervised Learning in Manifold subspace (DSLM) algorithm is described in Sect. 2. A variety of experimental results are presented in Sect. 3. Section 4 discusses the effectiveness of our proposed algorithm. Finally, we provide some concluding remarks and suggestions for future work in Sect. 5.

2 Semi-supervised Learning in Manifold Subspace (DSLM)

2.1 The Objective Function

Suppose we have a set of n sample $X = \{x_i\}_{i=1}^n, x_i \in \mathbb{R}^D$ belonging to c classes. The basic idea of Linear Discriminant Analysis (LDA) is to seek directions on which the data points of different classes are far from each other while requiring data points of the same class to be close to each other. The objective function of LDA is as follow:

$$a_{opt} = \arg\max_a \frac{a^T S_b a}{a^T S_w a}. \tag{1}$$

where S_w is called the within-class scatter matrix and S_b is called the between-class scatter matrix. Define the total scatter matrix $S_t = S_W + S_b$:

$$S_t = \sum_{i=1}^n (x_i - \mu)(x_i - \mu)^T. \tag{2}$$

where μ is the total sample mean vector, n_k is the number of samples in the k-th class, $\mu^{(k)}$ is the average vector of the k-th class, $x_i^{(k)}$ is the i-th sample of the k-th class. Then the object function of LDA in Eq. (1) is equivalent to

$$a_{opt} = \arg\max_a \frac{a^T S_b a}{a^T S_t a}. \tag{3}$$

We denote the matrix $X = [X^{(1)}, \ldots, X^{(c)}]$ and the matrix W_{LDA} as

$$W_{LDA} = \begin{bmatrix} W^{(1)} & 0 & \cdots & 0 \\ 0 & W^{(2)} & \cdots & 0 \\ \vdots & \vdots & \ddots & \vdots \\ 0 & 0 & \cdots & W^{(c)} \end{bmatrix}. \tag{4}$$

where $W^{(k)}$ is a $n_k \times n_k$ matrix with all elements equal to $\frac{1}{n_k}$ and $X^{(k)}$ is the data matrix of k-th class. The object function of LDA in Eq. (3) can be rewritten as [10]:

$$a_{opt} = \arg\max_a \frac{a^T X W_{LDA} X^T a}{a^T X X^T a}. \tag{5}$$

When there is only one sample, LDA may be an ill-posed problem. When there is a small training set, overfitting may occur. The technique to solve those problem is regularization by introducing additional information. The optimization problem of regularized version of LDA can be written as follows [9]:

$$\max_a \frac{a^T S_b a}{a^T S_t a + \alpha J(a)}. \tag{6}$$

where $J(a)$ controls the learning complexity of the hypothesis family, and the coefficient α controls balance between the model complexity and the empirical loss. The regularizer term $J(a)$ provides us the flexibility to incorporate our prior knowledge on some particular applications. The key to semi-supervised learning algorithm is the prior assumption of consistency. For classification, it means nearby points are likely to have the same label [7]. For dimensionally reduction, it means nearby points will have similar low-dimensional representations. Motivated by this intuition, we take advantage of the geometric properties of manifold patches. Specifically, if the data points lying on the same patch are likely to have the same label, which can be seen as Fig. 1.

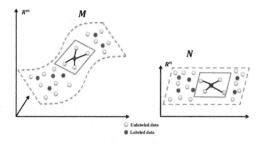

Fig. 1. Data points lie on same patch

Suppose X is from a smooth underlying manifold of dimensionality $d \ll D$. Each data points can be reconstructed from its neighbors with appropriate weights and these weights should be the same in low-dimensional space. Let $y_1, \ldots, y_n \in \mathbb{R}^d$ be the corresponded mapped data. We have the cost function of a *good* map [6] under appropriate constraints as:

$$\Phi(y) = \sum_i \left(y_i - \sum_j W_{ij} y_j \right)^2. \tag{8}$$

which adds up the squared distances between all the data points and their reconstructions. W_i reveals the layout of the point around x_i. Suppose the transformation is linear, that is, $y_i = f(x_i) = a^T x_i$. We define

$$z = y - Wy = (I - W)y. \tag{9}$$

The cost function in Eq. (8) can be reduced to

$$\Phi(y) = \sum_i \left(y_i - \sum_j W_{ij} y_j \right)^2 = \sum_i (z_i)^2 = a^T X M X^T a. \tag{10}$$

where $M = (I - W)^T (I - W)$

Finally, we apply the approach of LDA and use the preserving local patches cost function as a regularizer term to make the objective function of DSLM:

$$\max_a \frac{a^T S_b a}{a^T S_t a + \alpha J(a)} = \max_a \frac{a^T S_b a}{a^T (S_t + \alpha X M X^T) a}. \tag{11}$$

Without loss of generality, we assume that the first n data points are labeled and ordered according to their labels. We use $X_l = [x_1, \ldots, x_l]$ to denote the labeled data matrix. We define the weight matrix $W \in \mathbb{R}^{n \times n}$ as

$$W = \begin{bmatrix} W_{LDA} & 0 \\ 0 & 0 \end{bmatrix}, \tilde{I} = \begin{bmatrix} I & 0 \\ 0 & 0 \end{bmatrix}.$$

where $W_{LDA} \in \mathbb{R}^{l \times l}$ is defined in Eq. (4), I is an identity matrix of size $l \times l$. We have

$$S_b = X_l W_{LDA} X_l^T = X W X^T. \tag{12}$$

$$S_t = X_l X_l^T = X \tilde{I} X^T. \tag{13}$$

Then the objective function of DSLM in Eq. (11) can be rewritten as

$$\max_a \frac{a X W X^T a}{a^T X (\tilde{I} + \alpha M) X^T a}. \tag{14}$$

2.2   The Algorithm

Given data set $X = \{x_i\}_{i=1}^n$ includes labeled set $X_l = \{x_i, y_i\}_{i=1}^l$ belonging to c classes and ordered according to their labels, and unlabeled set $X_u = \{x_i\}_{i=l+1}^n$. The k-th class have l_k samples, $\sum_{i=1}^c l_k = l$.

1. Construct the adjacency graph:
   In this step, we construct the adjacency graph G of all data set X by using the k-nearest neighbors method.
2. Compute the weights:
   In this step, we compute the weights on the edges of G. Let W be the weight matrix with W_{ij} having the weight of the edge from node i to node j, and 0 if there is no such edge. We define $M = (I - W)^T (I - W)$ where I is the identity matrix of size $n \times n$.
   Please see [6] for details about how to compute W.

3. Construct the graph for labeled data:

In this step, we construct the weight matrix $\tilde{W} \in \mathbb{R}^{n \times n}$ for labeled data

$$\tilde{W} = \begin{bmatrix} W_l & 0 \\ 0 & 0 \end{bmatrix}, \tilde{I} = \begin{bmatrix} I & 0 \\ 0 & 0 \end{bmatrix}.$$

where $W_l \in \mathbb{R}^{l \times l}$ is defined in Eq. (9), I is an identity matrix of size $l \times l$.

4. Computing the projections:

In this step, we compute the linear projections by solving the following generalized eigenvector problem

$$X\tilde{W}X^T a = \lambda X(\tilde{I} + \alpha M)X^T a \tag{16}$$

It is easy to check that $\tilde{W}$ is of rank c and we will have c eigenvectors with respect to non-zero eigenvalue [8]. Let $A = [a_0, a_1, \ldots, a_{c-1}]$ be the solution of Eq. (16), ordered according to their eigenvalues, $\lambda_0 \geq \lambda_1 \geq \ldots \geq \lambda_{c-1} > 0$. A is a $n \times c$ matrix. The mapping subspace is as follows

$$\mathbf{x} \rightarrow \mathbf{z} = A^T \mathbf{x}$$

3 Experimental Results

In this section, we investigate the use of our proposed approach for face recognition. We compare our DSLM algorithm with several representative dimension reduction algorithms, which include PCA, LDA, SDA [10]. PCA and LDA are the two most widely used subspace learning techniques for face recognition. SDA is the algorithm with high accuracy on semi-supervised face recognition [10].

3.1 Dataset Descriptions

The YALE face database contains 165 grayscale images of size 320×243 of 15 people (11 samples for person). The images demonstrate variations in lighting condition (left-light, center-light, right-light), facial expression (normal, happy, sad, sleepy, surprised and wink), and with/without glasses.

The ORL face database contains 400 gray images of size 92×112 of 40 people (10 samples for person). The images were captured at different times and have different variation including expressions (open or closed eyes, smiling or non-smiling) and face details (glasses or no glasses). The images were taken with a tolerance for some tilting and rotation of face up to 20 degrees.

3.2 Data Preparation and Experimental Settings

In all the experiments, preprocessing to locate the faces was applying. Original images were normalized (in scale and orientation) such that the two eyes were aligned at the same position. Then the facial areas were cropped into the final image for matching. The size of each cropped image in all the experiment is 32×32 pixels, with 256 gray levels per pixel. Thus, each image can be represented by 1024-dimesional vector in image space. No further preprocessing is done. 10 images of a person in YALE and 10 images of a person in ORL are displayed in Fig. 2.

 (a) YALE face database   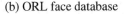 (b) ORL face database

 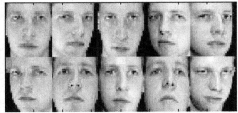

Fig. 2. Samples from YALE face database and ORL face database with different facial expression and details.

We use the semi-supervised setting for our experiments. That is, the available training set during the training phase contains both labeled and unlabeled examples, and the testing set is not available during the training phase. In this paper, we apply nearest-neighbor classifier for its simplicity. For each person in dataset, n images are randomly selected as the training set. Among these n images, l images are randomly selected and labeled which leaves other $n - l$ images unlabeled. We average the result over 25 random split. The recognition performance is measured by the accuracy:

$$Acc = \frac{Number\ of\ correctly\ classificated\ test\ samples}{Number\ of\ test\ samples} \times 100\%$$

3.3 Face Recognition with Different Dimensions

In this experiment, we fix $\alpha = 0.1$ for two methods SDA and DSLM. The number of nearest neighbors k is between 2 and 4, the recognition is carried out then. In general, the accuracy rates varies with the dimension of the face subspace. Figure 3 shows the plots of accuracy rates versus dimensionality reduction for the PCA, LDA, SDA and DSLM. The best result obtained in the optimal subspace and the corresponding dimensionality for each method are shown in Table 1. Note that the upper bound of dimensionality of SDA and DSLM is c where c is the number of classes. When there is a single labeled training image per class, LDA cannot be applied since the within-class

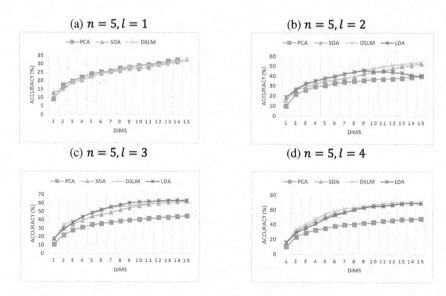

Fig. 3. Accuracy rates vs. dimensionality reduction on the YALE face database.

Table 1. Performance comparisons on the YALE face database

Method		PCA	LDA	SDA	DSLM
$n = 5$	$l = 1$	32.6 (14)	–	**32.8 (15)**	**32.8 (15)**
	$l = 2$	43.5 (29)	45.8 (9)5454	52.5 (15)	**54.2 (15)**
	$l = 3$	50.4 (44)	63.6 (14)	62.1 (15)	**64.6 (15)**
	$l = 4$	54.4 (59)	69.1 (14)	69.7 (15)	**71.6 (15)**

scatter matrix is the zero matrix. As can be seen, our DSLM algorithm performed the best for all the cases. Moreover, the optimal dimensionality obtained by DSLM, SDA and LDA is much lower than that obtained by PCA.

3.4   Face Recognition with Different k-Nearest Neighbors

The most important parameter in all of the manifold approaches which make use of the manifold structure is k-nearest neighbors. We test and compare two methods SDA and DSLM with different values of k. In this experiment, we use the ORL face database and fix $n = 7, l = 3, \alpha = 0.1$; k is chosen between 2 and 6; the recognition is carried out then. Figure 4 shows the plots of accuracy rates versus number nearest of neighbor. Table 2 shows the performance comparison of those. As can be seen, our DSLM algorithm performed better result. Moreover, the accuracy of our DSLM algorithm is stable with varying value of parameter k. It is shown that our DSLM algorithm is stability with varying size of patches on manifold.

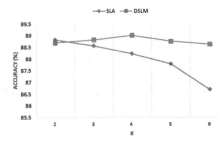

Table 2. Performance comparison on ORL face database

k	SDA	DSLM
2	**88.83**	88.70
3	88.57	88.83
4	88.23	**89.02**
5	87.80	88.77
6	86.70	88.64

Fig. 4. Accuracy rates vs. k-nearest neighbor

4   Discussion

It is worthwhile to high light several aspects of the proposed approach here:

1. Our proposed algorithm DSLM shares some similar properties with Semi-supervised Discriminant Analysis [10] algorithm. Both of them aim to find the optimal projection of the discriminative power of the labeled data and of the locality preserving power of manifold. However, their graphs which discover manifold structure are totally different. Thus, their objective functions are different.
2. Some manifold learning algorithms like ISOMAP, LLE, Laplacian eigenmaps are defined only on the training data points and it is unclear how to evaluate the map for new test points. DSLM can find the optimal linear projection. Thus, this makes it fast and suitable for practical applications, e.g. face recognition.
3. DSLM can be performed and product significant results in small datasets which cannot be achieved by LDA, which can be seen as experimental results.

5   Conclusion

In this paper, we proposed a new linear dimensionality reduction algorithm called Discriminative Semi-supervised Learning in Manifold subspace. By using a graph which characterizes the locality structure of manifold data and taking advance of discriminative power of LDA method, our algorithm can make use of both labeled data and unlabeled data points to find optimal projection. Experimental results on face recognition have demonstrated the effectiveness of our algorithm.

For future works, we are interested in applying the proposed method to other graphs which characterize better the geometric properties of the dataset. On the other hand, the algorithm should be investigated in supervised mode.

Acknowledgements. This research is supported by research funding from Science Research funding (T-2015.21) and Honors Program, University of Science, Vietnam National University - Ho Chi Minh City.

References

1. Truong, H., Le, T.: Fusion of bidirectional image matrices and 2D-LDA: an efficient approach for face recognition. In: Proceedings of Third Symposium on Information and Communication Technology, pp. 142–148. ACM, New York (2012)
2. Le, T., Truong, H., Do, H., Vo, D.: On approaching 2D-FPCA technique to improve image representation in frequency domain. In: Proceedings of Fourth Symposium on Information and Communication Technology, pp. 172–180. ACM, New York (2013)
3. Le, D.K., Truong, H., Le, T.: Facial expression recognition using statistical subspace. In: IEEE International Conference on Image Processing, pp. 5981–5985. IEEE (2014)
4. Martinez, A.M., Kak, A.C.: PCA versus LDA. IEEE Trans. Pattern Anal. Mach. Intell. **23** (2), 228–233 (2001)
5. Huang, Y., Wang, W., Wang, L., Tan, T.: A general nonlinear embedding framework based on deep neural network. In: ICPR, pp. 732–737 (2014)
6. Roweis, S., Saul, L.K.: Nonlinear dimensionality reduction by locally linear embedding. Science **290**, 2323–2326 (2000)
7. Zhou, D., Bousquet, O., Lal, T., Weston, J., Schölkopf, B.: Learning with local and global consistency. In: Advances in Neural Information Processing Systems, vol. 16 (2003)
8. Golub, G.H., Loan, C.F.V.: Matrix computations. Johns Hopkins University Press, Maryland (1996)
9. Friedman, J.H.: Regularized discriminant analysis. J. Am. Stat. Assoc. **84**(405), 165–175 (1989)
10. Cai, D., He, X., Han, J.: Semi-supervised discriminant analysis. In: International Conference on Pattern Recognition, pp. 1–7 (2007)
11. Chang, Y., Hu, C., Turk, M.: Manifold of facial expression. In: Proceedings of IEEE International Workshop on Analysis and Modeling of Faces and Gestures. France (2003)
12. Belkin, M., Niyogi, P.: Laplacian eigenmaps and spectral techniques for embedding and clustering. In: Advances in Neural Information Processing System, vol. 15. Canada (2001)
13. Tenenbaum, J.B., de Silva, V., Langford, J.C.: A global geometric framework for nonlinear dimensionality reduction. Science **290**, 2319–2323 (2000)
14. Liu, Q., Huang, R., Lu, H., Ma, S.: Face recognition using kernel based fisher discriminant analysis. In: 5th FG. Washington, D.C. (2002)
15. Roweis, S., Saul, L., Hinton, G.: Global coordination of local linear models. In: Advances in Neural Information Processing System, vol. 14 (2001)
16. Yan, S., Xu, D., Zhang, B., Zhang, H.-J., Yang, Q., Lin, S.: Graph embedding and extension: a general framework for dimensionality reduction. IEEE Trans. Pattern Anal. Mach. Intell. **29**(1), 40–51 (2007)
17. He, X., Niyogi, P.: Locality preserving projections. In: Advances in Neural Information Processing Systems, vol. 16. MIT Press, Cambridge (2003)
18. Chen, X., Wei, J., Li, J., Zhang, X.: Integrating local and global manifold structures for unsupervised dimensionality reduction. In: IJCNN. China (2014)
19. Lu, J., Tan, Y.P.: Cost-sensitive subspace learning for face recognition. In: The IEEE Conference on Computer Vision and Pattern Recognition, pp. 2661–2666 (2010)
20. Lu, J., Tan, Y.P., Wang, G.: Discriminative multi-manifold analysis for face recognition from a single training sample per person. In: ICCV, pp. 1943–1950 (2011)

21. Belkin, M., Niyogi, P., Sindhwani, V.: Manifold regularization: a geometric framework for learning from examples. J. Mach. Learn. Res. **7**, 2399–2434 (2006)
22. Goldberg, A.B., Li, M., Zhu, X.: Online manifold regularization: a new learning setting and empirical study. In: Proceedings of 19th European Conference on Machine Learning, pp. 393–407. Belgium (2008)

Context-Aware Handwritten and Optical Character Recognition Using a Combination of Wavelet Transform, PCA and Neural Networks

Ngoc Hoang Phan[(✉)] and Thi Thu Trang Bui

Faculty of Information Technology, Ba Ria-Vung Tau University,
Truong van Bang Street 01, Vung Tau city, Ba Ria-Vung Tau province, Vietnam
{hoangpn285, trangbt.084}@gmail.com

Abstract. This paper proposes a novel context-aware handwritten and optical character recognition algorithm using a combination of wavelet transform, PCA and neural networks. At first, the features of character are extracted using combination of wavelet transform and PCA. Then multi-layer feed-forward neural networks will be used to classify these extracted features. In this algorithm, we use one neural network for each training character. This neural network is used to determine whether an input character is training character or not. The paper experimental results show that the proposed algorithm gives an effective performance of character recognition on noisy images and competes with state-of-the-art algorithms.

Keywords: Character recognition · Wavelet transform · PCA · Neural network · Image processing

1 Introduction

In recent years, pattern recognition problem is one of the most widely studied tasks in the field of image processing. The solution of pattern recognition is demanded in various areas of modern society. In addition, character recognition is one of the urgent pattern recognition tasks. The solution of this task can be used to solve other tasks, such as license plate recognition, text recognition and so on.

Wavelet transform is an effective method used to extract image features. By using wavelet transform, we will obtain the necessary information about the image. In addition, the wavelet transform is also quickly enough to be calculated. In the algorithms [1–6], wavelet transform is used to solve problem of image classification. The experimental results of these algorithms show that image features extracted by using wavelet transform give 76–99.7 % accuracy rate of image classification.

In addition, the experimental results of the algorithms [7–12] show that wavelet transform is effectively used to solve the pattern recognition tasks, in particular face recognition task on noisy images. Accuracy rate of face recognition in this case is 90–98.5 %.

© ICST Institute for Computer Sciences, Social Informatics and Telecommunications Engineering 2016
P.C. Vinh and V. Alagar (Eds.): ICCASA 2015, LNICST 165, pp. 254–263, 2016.
DOI: 10.1007/978-3-319-29236-6_25

Thus, using wavelet transform is perspective way for development of novel context-aware character recognition algorithm. In this paper we propose a novel context-aware algorithm for character recognition based on combination of wavelet transform, PCA and neural networks. In case of image processing, context is any information about an image such as: image pixel, contour, noise and so on.

2   Proposed Algorithm

The proposed algorithm for character recognition consists of two main steps. The first step is training neural networks. In the second one character is recognized by using trained neural networks. The proposed character recognition algorithm works as follows.

Step 1: Training neural networks

1.1. Using wavelet transform to extract features of characters of training set.
1.2. Using PCA to reduce dimension of vectors of extracted feature.
1.3. Using obtained feature vectors to train neural networks.

Step 2: Recognizing character

2.1. Using wavelet transform to extract features of testing character.
2.2. Using PCA to reduce dimension of vector of extracted feature.
2.3. Using obtained vector and trained neural networks to recognize character.

2.1   Character Feature Extraction

Extracting feature of character using wavelet transform works as follows. Firstly, the image of character is resized to 64 × 64 pixels. Then wavelet transform is applied to obtained image and the low-frequency wavelet coefficients are extracted. In the result, we have matrix that consists of 32 × 32 low-frequency wavelet coefficients.

In order to extract local features of character, the image of character is divided to 12 parts with the same size 32 × 32 pixels (Fig. 1). Then wavelet transform is applied to each part and the low-frequency wavelet coefficients are extracted. In the result we have 12 matrixes, each of which consists of 16 × 16 low-frequency wavelet coefficients.

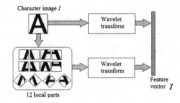

Fig. 1. Example of feature extraction of character "A".

Finally, character feature vector is formed using low-frequency wavelet coefficients obtained in the previous steps. In the result we have character feature vector that consists of $32 \times 32 + 12 \times 32 \times 32 = 4096$ elements (Fig. 1).

2.2   Dimension Reduction

Before submission to the inputs of neural networks, dimension of feature vector is reduced. In order to solve this problem we use PCA. At first, we create eigenspace for characters (eigencharacter) using M images of characters. Creation of character eigenspace is carried out as follows.

At first, extraction feature process is applied to each of M images. In the result we have a set of $\vec{I}_1, \ldots, \vec{I}_M$. feature vectors. Then we form the mean vector, the value of each element of which is calculated by the formula (1):

$$\vec{I}_{avg} = \frac{1}{M} \sum_{n=1}^{M} \vec{I}_n. \tag{1}$$

Then each of the M feature vectors is subtracted mean vector by formula (2):

$$\vec{\Phi}_n = \vec{I}_n - \vec{I}_{cp}, \; n = 1, \ldots, M. \tag{2}$$

After that we create the eigenspace consisting of K eigenvectors of the covariance matrix C (3), that in the best way describe the distribution of M feature vectors ($K < M$).

$$C = \frac{1}{M} \sum_{n=1}^{M} \vec{\Phi}_n \vec{\Phi}_n^T = AA^T, \quad A = \left\{ \vec{\Phi}_1, \ldots, \vec{\Phi}_M \right\}. \tag{3}$$

In this case k-th vector $\vec{u}_k$ satisfies maximization of the following (4):

$$\lambda_k = \frac{1}{M} \sum_{n=1}^{M} \left(\vec{u}_k^T \vec{\Phi}_n \right)^2. \tag{4}$$

and an orthogonality condition (5):

$$\vec{u}_l^T \vec{u}_k = \begin{cases} 1, & l = k \\ 0, & \text{otherwise} \end{cases}. \tag{5}$$

Vectors $\vec{u}_k$ and values λ_k are eigenvectors and eigenvalues of covariance matrix C.

In order to create this eigenspace, at first, we calculate M eigenvectors $\vec{u}_l$ of covariance matrix C by using eigenvectors of other matrix $L = A^T A$. Each vector $\vec{u}_l$ is calculated by the following formula (6):

$$\vec{u}_l = \frac{1}{M} \sum_{k=1}^{M} v_{lk} \Phi_k, l = 1, \ldots, M. \tag{6}$$

Then we select K eigenvectors with the largest eigenvalues from M obtained eigenvectors. The eigenspace is the set of K selected eigenvectors (Fig. 2).

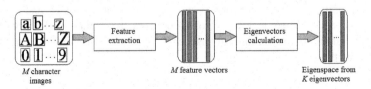

Fig. 2. Creation of character eigenspace.

After the character eigenspace is created, reducing of dimension of character feature vector $\vec{I}_{in}$ is carried out as follows.

At first, the character feature vector is decomposed on K eigenvectors $\vec{u}_i$ and corresponding decomposition coefficients are calculated by the following formula (7):

$$w_i = \vec{u}_i^T (\vec{I}_{in} - \vec{I}_{avg}), \; i = 1, \ldots, K. \tag{7}$$

Then we obtain a vector (8):

$$\vec{\Omega}^T = \{w_1, \ldots, w_K\}. \tag{8}$$

This vector describes the distribution of each eigenvectors in presentation of character feature vector. In the result of dimension reduction we have a new character feature vector $\vec{\Omega}$ consisting of K elements. In this case $K < {<}4096$ (Fig. 3).

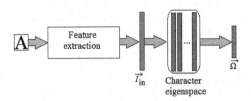

Fig. 3. Reducing of dimension of character feature vector.

2.3 Character Recognition

Back-propagation feed-forward neural networks are used for classifying character based on obtained feature vectors. In this proposed algorithm we create one multi-layered feed-forward neural network for each character of training set. These neural networks are trained by back propagation method. The input of these neural networks is the character feature vector $\overrightarrow{\Omega}$ (8), that consists of K elements. The output layer of these neural networks has one neuron, which returns a value from 0 to 1. Using one neural network for each character of training set can speed up the process of neural network training.

Each neural network determines the similarity between input character and the only one character of training set. The input character is recognized by neural networks as follows. At first, we extract feature vector of the input character and reduce its dimension. Then obtained feature vector is used as the input of all trained neural networks. Input character is recognized as a character of training set, neural network of which returns the largest value (Fig. 4.).

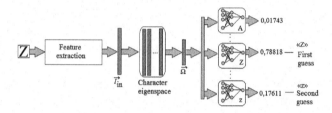

Fig. 4. Recognizing character by neural networks.

Besides, using one neural network for each character of training set allows us to include the second guess in recognition result. The second guess is a character of training set, neural network of which returns the second largest value. Using the second guess has an advantage when recognizing characters, that similarly written, such as {c, C}, {o, O}, {p, P}, {s, S}, {u, U}, {v, V}, {w, W}, {x, X} и {z, Z} (Fig. 4).

3   Experimetal Results

The proposed algorithm was tested using handwritten character and printed character images. All experiments were performed on a laptop with the processor Intel Core Duo P7350 2.0 GHz and 2.0 GB of RAM.

3.1   Handwritten Character Recognition

In the first experiment the proposed algorithm was tested on handwritten character recognition task. In order to carry out this experiment we use the known data set of handwritten digits MNIST [13, 14]. This data set consists of 60000 images for training and 10000 images for testing. All images have the same size 28 × 28 pixels and all digits are centered within the images.

In this experiment we created additional test data set by adding to images of original test set MNIST "salt and pepper" noise with probation 5, 10, 15, 20, 25, 30 %.

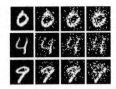

Fig. 5. Examples of test images of handwritten digits.

Examples of using images are shown in Fig. 5 (from left to right: images of handwritten digit with 10, 20 and 30 % noise).

The recognition results of handwritten digits MNIST depending on dimension of feature vector are shown in Fig. 6. Handwritten digits recognition accuracy (δ, %) is presented on vertical axis, and number of features (K) – on horizontal axis. It is shown that the recognition accuracy depends on dimension of character feature vector. When using more number of features, the recognition accuracy is higher. The recognition accuracy becomes stable and ranges 97–97.5 % (*1st guess*) and 98.8–99 % (*2nd guess*) when number of features is more than 37. The highest recognition accuracy 97.5 % (*1st guess*) and 99 % (*2nd guess*) is obtained when using the vector of 49 features. So the vector of 49 features will be used for testing with noisy data set.

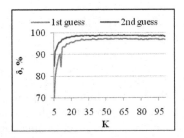

Fig. 6. Results of recognition of handwritten digits MNIST.

Table 1. Comparison of proposed algorithm and HTM network.

Processor	Algorithm	δ, %	Trainning time	Testing time
Intel coreTM 3.47 GHz	HTM network (Greedy)	97.3	05:34:12	01:38:43
	HTM network (AHC)	97.6	05:15:17	01:30:56
	HTM network (MTC)	98.5	05:21:47	01:32:35
Intel core Duo P3750 2.0 GHz	Proposed algorithm (1st guess)	97.5	00:24:36	00:06:08
	Proposed algorithm (2nd guess)	99.0	00:24:36	00:06:08

Recognition results of handwritten digits MNIST by proposed algorithm and *Hierarchical Temporary Memory* (HTM) network are shown in Table 1. In this case HTM network was trained by various algorithms, such as *Greedy*, *Aglomerative Hierarchical Clustering* (AHC) и *Maximum Temporal Connection* (MTC).

It is shown that proposed algorithm is 13 times trained and 15 times performs more rapidly, than HTM network. The highest recognition accuracy 99 % obtained by using proposed algorithm (*2nd guess*).

The obtained results were also compared with the results of other algorithms tested on the handwritten digits data set MNIST [13, 14]. The comparison results of different algorithms are shown in Table 2. It is shown that the recognition accuracy of proposed algorithm is comparable with other recognition algorithms.

Table 2. Recognition results of different algorithms tested on MNIST data set.

Algorithm	Minimum error, %	Maximum error, %
Linear clssifiers	7.6	12
Non-linear classifier	3.3	3.6
HTM network	1.5	1.5
Boosted stumps	0.87	7.7
K-nearest neighbors	0.63	5
SVMs	0.56	1.4
Neural nets	0.35	4.7
Convolutional nets	0.23	1.7
Proposed algorithm (1st guess)	2.5	3
Proposed algorithm (2nd guess)	1	1.2

In this experiment the proposed algorithm was also tested with noisy images of handwritten digits using vector of 49 features. The testing results are shown in Fig. 7. It is shown that the proposed algorithm allows recognizing handwritten digits on noisy images. The recognition accuracy considerably decreases when the noise level exceeds 20 %.

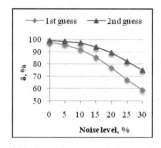

Fig. 7. Results of recognition of handwritten digits MNIST on noisy images.

3.2   Optical Printed Character Recognition

In this experiment the proposed algorithm was tested with printed characters. In order to train the proposed algorithm we created the training set consisting of 1488 images of 10 digits (0–9) and 52 characters (a–z, A–Z). Each character was presented by two fonts Times New Roman and Arial with bold and normal styles, and 16, 18, 20, 22, 24 and 26 sizes. In this case each character of training set has 24 images.

In order to test the proposed algorithm we used images of printed characters of 8 popular fonts: 4 serif fonts – Times New Roman, Garamond, Courier New and Bookman Old Style, 4 sans-serif fonts – Arial, Lucida Sans, Tahoma and Verdana. For each font we created one test set consisting 2480 images of 10 digits (0–9) and 52 characters (a–z, A–Z). Each character was presented with bold and normal styles, and 12, 14, 16, 18, 20, 22, 24, 26, 28 and 36 sizes.

Figure 8 shows the recognition results of printed characters of different fonts depending on the dimensionality of feature vector. The vertical axis is recognition accuracy (δ, %), and the horizontal axis is the number of features (K).

The experiment results show that the propose algorithm, that trained by only characters of two fonts, may recognize characters of other fonts. It is shown that the recognition accuracy of proposed algorithm for all fonts is acceptable when the number of features is between 20 and 60. The recognition accuracy of sans-serif fonts is better and more stable than the recognition results of serif fonts. The best recognition result for most fonts obtained using vector of 27 features. So this feature vector is being used to test proposed algorithm with printed characters on noisy images.

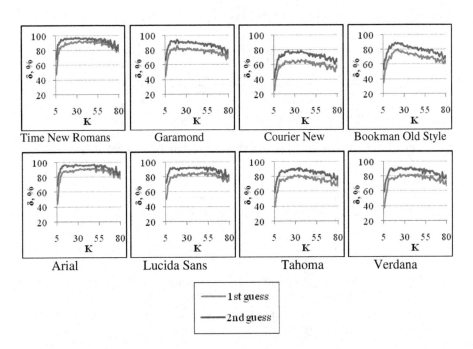

Fig. 8. Results of recognition of printed characters.

0 0 0 0
A A A A

Fig. 9. Examples of optical printed character images.

For each font we created additional test set by adding 5, 10, 15, 20, 25 and 30 % of salt and pepper noise to images of existing test sample. Examples of printed character image and his noisy images with level 10, 20, and 30 % are shown in Fig. 9 from left to right.

The results of recognition printed character on noisy images are presented in Fig. 10. It is shown that the proposed algorithm is able to effectively recognize printed character of different fonts on noisy images. Recognition accuracy depends on the noise level.

The comparison results of proposed algorithm and systems ABBYY FineReader 11 and Tesseract OCR on recognition of printed character with two fonts Times New Roman and Arial on noisy images are shown in Fig. 11.

It is shown that when noise level is increased the recognition accuracy of systems FineReader 11 and Tesseract OCR significantly decreased, but the recognition accuracy

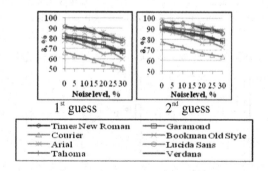

Fig. 10. Results of optical printed character recognition on noisy images.

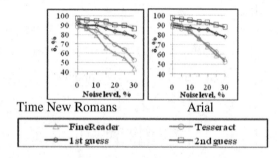

Fig. 11. Comparision results of printed character recognition on noisy images.

of proposed algorithm is more slowly decreased. The proposed algorithm more effectively recognize printed character on noisy images than systems FineReader 11 and Tesseract OCR. When the noise level is more than 15 %, the difference between their recognition results becomes more noticeable.

4 Conclusion

In this paper we developed a novel algorithm for handwritten and printed character recognition based on wavelet transform, principal component analysis and neural networks. Developed algorithm allows effectively recognizing handwritten and printed on noisy images.

References

1. Mehdi, L., Solimani, A., Dargazany, A.: Combining wavelet transforms and neural networks for image classification. In: 41st Southeasten Symposium on System Theory, Tullahoma, TN, USA, pp. 44–48 (2009)
2. Weibao, Z., Li, Y.: Image classification using wavelet coefficients in low-pass bands. In: Proceedings of International Joint Conference on Neural Networks, Orlando, Florida, USA, pp. 114–118 (2007)
3. Chang, T., Jay, K.: Texture analysis and classification with tree-structured wavelet transform. IEEE Trans. Image Process. 2(4), 429–440 (1993)
4. Daniel, M.R.S., Shanmugam, A.: ANN and SVM based war scence classification using wavelet features: a comparative study. J. Comput. Inf. Syst. 7(5), 1402–1411 (2011)
5. Park, S.B., Lee, J.W., Kim, S.K.: Content-based image classification using a neural network. Pattern Recogn. Lett. 25(3), 287–300 (2004)
6. Riveron, E.M.F., Sossa, J.H., Gonzalez, A.C., Pogrebnyak, O.: Histograms, wavelets and neural networks applied to image retrieval. In: Gelbukh, A., Reyes-Garcia, C.A. (eds.) MICAI 2006. LNCS (LNAI), vol. 4293, pp. 820–827. Springer, Heidelberg (2006)
7. Lai, J.H., Yuen, P.C., Feng, G.C.: Face recognition using holistic Fourier invariant features. Pattern Recogn. 34, 95–109 (2001)
8. Kakarwal, S., Dsehmuhk, R.: Wavelet transform based feature extraction for face recognition. Informatica 15(2), 243–250 (2004)
9. Zhang, B.-L., Zhang, H.: Face recognition by applying wavelet subband representation and kernel assosiative memory. IEEE Trans. Image Process. 4(11), 1549–1560 (1995)
10. Gumus, E., Kilic, N., Sertbas, A., Ucan, O.N.: Evulation of face recognition techniques using PCA, wavelets and SVM. Expert Syst. Appl. 37, 6404–6408 (2010)
11. Wadkar, P.D., Wankhade, M.: Face recognition using discrete wavelet transform. Int. J. Adv. Eng. Technol. III(I), 239–242 (2012)
12. Mazloom, M., Kasaei, K.: Face recognition using PCA, wavelets and neural networks. In: Proceeding of the First International Conference on Modeling, Simulation and Applied Optimization, Sharjah, UAE, pp. 1–6, 1-3 February (2005)
13. LeCun, Y., Bottou, L., Bengio, Y., Haffner, P.: Gradient based learning applied to document recognition. Proc. IEEE 86(11), 2278–2324 (1998)
14. LeCun, Y., Kavukcuoglu, K., Farabet, C.: Convolutional networks and applications in vision. In: International Symposium on Circuits and Systems, Paris, pp. 253-256 (2010)

Enhancing Wearable Systems by Introducing Context-Awareness and FCA

Alaa Alsaig[1,2,3], Mubarak Mohammad[1,2,3], and Ammar Alsaig[1,2,3]([✉])

[1] Effat University, Jeddah, Kingdom of Saudi Arabia
aalsaig@effatuniversity.edu.sa,
mubarak.sami@gmail.com, aasaig@uqu.edu.sa
[2] Concordia University, Montreal, Canada
[3] Umm Al-Qura University, Mecca, Kingdom of Saudi Arabia

Abstract. Data collected from wearable devices form basis for assessment, analysis, and predictions. It is used in various fields of study such as health and education to improve status, define goals, and measure progress. Currently, there is no formal model used to define relationships among goals in a particular wearable system. Therefore, this paper proposes a novel approach based on context information and Formal Concept Analysis theory for modeling an entire problem domain using lattice theory. The resulted model shows the conceptual structure, different layers of abstractions, and hierarchical relations between wearable devices, collected data, defined goals, and predicted results. The structure is prerequisite for any further analysis.

Keywords: Context · Wearable system · Model · Formal Concept Analysis FCA · Lattice tree

1 Introduction

Wearable devices comprise built-in sensors to gather data about human's body. They can track different health metrics such as burned calories, sleeping habits and activities pattern during the day [3]. Moreover, some wearable devices can be used as health cards for their users, where users can define other inputs such as blood sugar, blood pressure and oxygen saturation [4].

Users of healthcare wearable devices aim to achieve healthy goals. The way of reaching these healthy goals can be different based on the healthy goal to be reached, the user data sensed by the wearable device, and the proper technique to reach the goal.

Wearable device continuously collect huge amount of information to track health metrics. This information is collected to update the users of their progress on reaching their set goals. However, this huge amount of contextual information is not used more than to update the users of their status. The current architecture of wearable devices does not allow this data to be analyzed. The collected data about the user is only used to track their progress on a set goal. Furthermore, there is no model that can make full use of the history of the collected data, or allow for further data analysis.

Due to the absence of a model to manage and analyze this amount of data many problems appear. People are slowly losing interest in wearable devices.

© ICST Institute for Computer Sciences, Social Informatics and Telecommunications Engineering 2016
P.C. Vinh and V. Alagar (Eds.): ICCASA 2015, LNICST 165, pp. 264–271, 2016.
DOI: 10.1007/978-3-319-29236-6_26

"Consumers indicated less interest in buying smart watches (35 %), smart (sensor-equipped) clothing (20 %), smart glasses (19 %) or people tracking devices (13 %)" [5]. The main reason mentioned is that users do not feel involved. "Dean Hovey, CEO of Digifit, an online ecosystem for health trackers, said the challenge is understanding each user and hooking the people who could benefit most". There is a need for a formal model that can hook the different information together and pave the road for further analysis to solve the mentioned consumers' problems. That is, the current wearable applications[1] collect data to monitor information about different goals such as sleeping quality and burned calories. However, why does the device collect information about these goals? Does one goal affect another one? The answers for these questions help users to be more engaged and more motivated to accomplish their goals. The definition for relationships among two or more goals must be based on logical trustable theory. Hence, the use of a formal model to define the relationships among goals of a particular system is essential.

In this paper, we provide a new architecture for wearable devices. In this architecture, we consider the context and context history of the user. Moreover, we propose a formal model based on Formal Concept Analysis (FCA) theory that can define the data and its interrelationship. Our proposed solution allow for this huge amount of information to be analyzed. Our contributions in this work are listed hereunder:

1. Propose a data model for wearable systems.
2. Use Formal Context Analysis Theory to define a formal relationship among data components of wearable system.

2 Data of Wearable Systems

Users of wearable devices aim to achieve health goals by working on one or set of health metrics. We will refer to health goals as goals and health metrics as attributes.

In wearable systems, data is collected by different methodologies. Based on this, data is classified into three different data types explained as follows:

a. Sensed Data: user data gathered by sensors of wearable systems such as heart rate.
b. Entered Data: data entered manually by user such as height.
c. Generated Data: data that is automatically calculated using sensed or entered data such as age from date of birth.

The above mentioned data types are structured in the following manner Fig. 1:

1. **Attribute:** A health metric that is sensed by the wearable device or entered by the user. This metric affect one or more goals.
2. **Goal:** A high level definition of the health goal that the user aims to achieve.
3. **Technique:** A node that includes one or set of attributes. Every technique can influence one or more goals. A list of these goals is also included in the techinique.

---

[1] GymGoal2, Jawbone UP, Google Fit, 7 Minute Workout, MyFitnessPal, Amwell, MyNetDiary, Diet Assistant, Endomondo, Fitness Body, Fitoracy, Fooducate, JEFIT workout, Instant Heart Rate, Run Keeper, Ideal Weight, Daily Burn, Charge HR, Nike + Running, Weight Watcher Mobile.

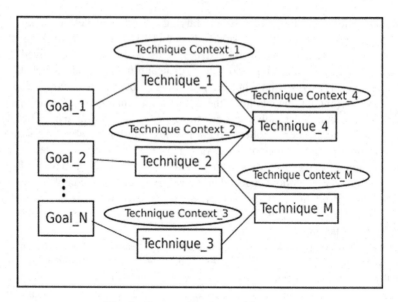

Fig. 1. Data model of wearable system

The distribution of these techniques and their relationships are based on the FCA analysis that is discussed in Sect. 3.

4. **Context:** Context is set of attributes and their values Fig. 2. This notion of context is formally defined by WAN [7]. In this paper, we propose two types of contexts;

Attributes	Values
Attribute 1	Value 1
Attribute 2	Value 2
Attribute N	Value N

Fig. 2. Context component structure

a. **User Context:** The user context defined by a set of attributes that are relevant to the user and their values.

b. **Technique Context:** The technique context includes the values of the attributes defined in the technique. The technique context and the user context have some attributes in common. The difference in the values of these attributes let users know how far they are from achieving their goals.

Whenever the data is collected, the user context is constructed by mapping each attribute of user context to its mutual attribute of the collected data Fig. 3.

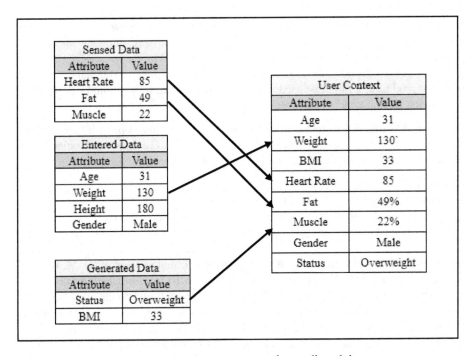

Fig. 3. Constructing user context from collected data

By now, we have introduced the data components that we will use in our work. Given these different categories of data and the huge amount of contextual information gathered by wearable device, we need a formal model that defines the relationship among different data components. This will allow the users to be aware of goals that are enhanced or affected by attributes they are working on. For example, if a user is using a wearable system to lose weight, he will work on every part that helps them to achieve their goal. However, many users do not know that decreasing weight of body is related to sleeping habits [8], which is a different health goal. Current solutions do not capture this information. However, the formal model provided in this paper, allows the user to be aware that sleeping habits will be enhanced too. Considering formalism in modeling data of wearable systems is a building block for further analysis.

The following sections, we will introduce the FCA theory and then our solution will be explained.

3   Formal Concept Analysis (FCA)

Formal Concept Analysis (FCA) *"is a method mainly used for the analysis of data, i.e. for deriving implicit relationships between objects described through a set of attributes on the one hand and these attributes on the other. The data are structured into units which are formal abstractions of concepts of human thought, allowing meaningful comprehensible interpretation (Ganter & Wille, 1999)"* [1].

Thus, as FCA supports the abstract concept by providing the intentional description or data it produces, it might be used as a clustering method. In addition, FCA provides a definition for the concept of <u>context</u>*[2]:

Definition 1 (Formal <u>Context</u>): A triple (G, M, I) is a formal <u>context</u> if G and M are sets and $I \subseteq G \times M$ is a binary relation between G and M. G elements are objects, and M elements are attributes and I is the incidence of the <u>context</u>.

For $A \subseteq G$, A': = {m ∈ M| $\forall g \in A$: (g,m) ∈ I}
For $B \subseteq M$: B': = {g ∈ G | $\forall m \in B$: (g,m) ∈ I}
A' is the set that includes all attributes common to objects of A
B' is the set that includes all objects that have all attributes in B [1]

Definition 2 (Formal Concept): "A pair (A, B) is a formal concept of (G, M, I) if and only if $A \subseteq G$; $B \subseteq M$, A' = B and A = B'. That is, (A,B) is a formal concept if the set of all attributes shared by the objects of A is identical with B and on the other hand A is also the set of all objects that have all attributes in B. A is then called the extent and B the intent of the formal concept (A, B). The formal concepts of a given <u>context</u> are naturally ordered by the subconcept-superconcept relation as defined by:

(A1, B1) ≤ (A2, B2) ⇔ $A1 \subseteq A2$ (⇔ $B2 \subseteq B1$)" [1, 2]
Extent and Intent Formula
Concepts Extent = Ext (X, Y, I) = {A ∈ 2x | (A, B) ∈ B (X, Y, I) for some B}
Concepts Intent = Int (X, Y, I) = {B ∈ 2y | (A, B) ∈ B (X, Y, I) for some A} [6]

Definition 3 (Lattice Tree): Concept lattice is a classification system, which is an output of formal concept analysis. Generally, a concept lattice might not need to be a tree as it is possible to include overlapping clusters. On the other hand, tree-like structures are appealing and many methods of classification produce this tree as an output [6].

4   Modeling Based on FCA Theory – Lattice Tree

Based on the FCA, we want to define the relation among specific goals and their defined attributes. Therefore, we used Lattice Miner software to create a table that defines four health goals and mapped to all or a subset of five defined attributes Fig. 4.

---

[2] The underlined context is an FCA terminology and it is different from the one stated in the rest of the paper.

Before we explain the model, we need to map the FCA terminologies to our data components Table 1:

Table 1. Mapping FCA to wearable system model

FCA terminology	Data component
Object	Goal
Attribute	Attribute
Tree Node	Technique

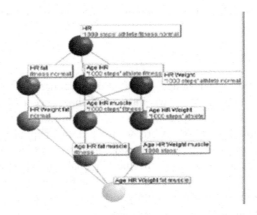

Fig. 4. Table include object and attributes sets

Then, the lattice tree is generated from the defined table Fig. 5.

Fig. 5. Generated Lattice Tree from created table.

In the lattice tree Fig. 5, the techniques are ordered sub-concept- super-concept top to bottom techniques. Every technique includes attributes and goals influenced by these attributes. That is, the least upper bound (join) has the fewest number of attributes and is a subset of the three techniques in the second layer. If we take any possible path of a goal starting from the join down to the greatest lower bound (meet). We find the following remarks:

- The number of attributes increases as we go down the lattice tree, which is resulting from the natural relationship between the layers such that the attributes in the upper layer is a subset of the attributes set in the lower layer.
- The number of goals decreases as we travel down the lattice tree. This means that the lower we go, the more focused we are on a specific goal.
- Reaching the lowest level means reaching the ultimate improvement for a specific goal.
- The higher the technique on the lattice tree, the more goals are influenced.

5 Overall Observation

Using this model Fig. 1 in practical case will solve some existing problems such as lack of user engagement and the poor utilization of wearable systems data.

When data of user is gathered, he will be able to pick up one of the health goals provided by the wearable device. Once he starts working on a particular goal, he will be aware of influences he is making on other goals. With the help of our model, he will also be able to know information such as the techniques that affect the maximum number of goals and the ultimate level he can reach for a certain goal. More importantly, with the comparison between technique context and user context, user can know how far he is from reaching a specific technique.

The details the model provides make the user more engaged and motivated to keep working to reach their health goals. Moreover, the work done on data categorization and inclusion of context information made a better use of the gathered data.

6 Conclusion

Context-awareness and formal modeling should be introduced to wearable devices to take them to the next level. We have introduced the concept of user context and technique context for wearable system. Also, we have introduced a new classification for data of the wearable system. Afterward, we use a formal approach, i.e. lattice tree to provide a formal model goals and techniques defining relationships among them. This formal concept allows the user to be informed of goal influenced in each technique he/she passes through. The novelty of our approach is focused on the formal modeling of the whole domain problem. Thus, in this work we provided the first building block to a smarter, formal, and practical wearable systems.

References

1. Cimiano, P., Hotho, A., Staab, S.: Learning concept hierarchies from text corpora using formal concept analysis. J. Artif. Intell. Res. (JAIR) **24**, 305–339 (2005)
2. Godin, R., Valtchev, P.: Formal concept analysis-based class hierarchy design in object-oriented software development. In: Ganter, B., Stumme, G., Wille, R. (eds.) Formal Concept Analysis. LNCS (LNAI), vol. 3626, pp. 304–323. Springer, Heidelberg (2005)

3. Pantelopoulos, A., Bourbakis, N.G.: A survey on wearable sensor-based systems for health monitoring and prognosis. IEEE Trans. Syst. Man Cybern. Part C Appl. Rev. **40**(1), 1–12 (2010)
4. Gurman, M.: This is Healthbook, Apple's major first step into health & fitness tracking (2014). http://9to5mac.com/2014/03/17/this-is-healthbook-apples-first-major-step-into-health-fitness-tracking/. Accessed 17 March 2014
5. Barnes, K., Kauffman, V., Connolly, C. (n.d.).: Health wearables: Early days (2014). http://www.pwc.com/en_US/us/health-industries/top-health-industry-issues/assets/pwc-hri-wearable-devices.pdf. Accessed 1 June 2014
6. Wormuth, B., Becker, P.: Introduction to formal concept analysis. In: 2nd International Conference of Formal Concept Analysis, vol. 23, February 2004
7. Wan, K.: Lucx: Lucid enriched with context (Doctoral dissertation, Concordia University) (2006)
8. Schmid, S.M., Hallschmid, M., Jauch-Chara, K., Born, J., Schultes, B.: A single night of sleep deprivation increases ghrelin levels and feelings of hunger in normal-weight healthy men. J. Sleep Res. **17**(3), 331–334 (2008)

Applying PNZ Model in Reliability Prediction of Component-Based Systems and Fault Tolerance Structures Technique

Pham Binh[1]([⊠]), Huynh Quyet-Thang[1], Nguyen Thanh-Hung[1], and Nguyen Hung-Cuong[2]

[1] Department of Software Engineering, School of Information and Communication Technology, Hanoi University of Science and Technology, Hanoi, Vietnam
binh.pham92@gmail.com, {thanghq,hungnt}@soict.hust.edu.vn
[2] Math - Technology Faculty, Hung Vuong University, Viet Tri, Vietnam
cuongnh@hvu.edu.vn

Abstract. Reliability is the chief quality that one wishes for in anything. Reliability is also the main issue with computer systems. One of the purposes of system reliability analysis is to identify the weakness in a system and to quantify the impact of component failures. However, existing reliability prediction approaches for component-based software systems are limited in their applicability because they either neglect or do not support modeling explicitly several factors like error propagation, software fault tolerance mechanisms. In this paper, we evaluate reliability prediction of component-based system and fault tolerance structures technique by applying Pham Nordmann Zhang (PNZ) model, one of the best models based on non homogeneous Poisson process. Our approach uses a reliability modeling schema whose models are automatically transformed by a reliability prediction tool into PNZ models for reliability predictions and sensitivity analyses. Via these our case studies, we demonstrate its applicability and introduce how much reliability of software system can be improved by using fault tolerance structures technique.

Keywords: Software reliability prediction · Software reliability growth model

1 Introduction

Software reliability is one of eight main quality characteristics of software system [1]. This measure has a big number of applications in many phases of software life cycle: analysis, design, coding and testing. There are two approaches to work with this characteristic: evaluating [2–4] and predicting [5–7]. Trung et al. [7] introduced prediction scenario for component-based architecture, a modern technique of software engineering, with six steps.

Software reliability modelling is a mathematics model to evaluate some reliability properties of software system. There are more than hundred introduced

© ICST Institute for Computer Sciences, Social Informatics and Telecommunications Engineering 2016
P.C. Vinh and V. Alagar (Eds.): ICCASA 2015, LNICST 165, pp. 272–281, 2016.
DOI: 10.1007/978-3-319-29236-6_27

models based on many mathematics techniques and work with many areas of project resources. One of the most developed group based on non-homogeneous Poisson process (NHPP) to build a time dependent function to present expected number of faults detected by time t. From this function, a practitioner can calculate some reliability measures of system as: the total number of errors, the predicted time of next failure. Pham [8] shows that Pham Nordman Zhang (PNZ) model is one of the best models in this group.

Fault tolerance structures technique (FTS) is a part of Software Fault Tolerance Mechanisms (FTMs). Avizienis et al. [9] describe in detail the principle of FTMs, and Trung et al. [7] introduced some basic concept of FTS. FTMs are often included in a software system and constitute an important means to improve the system reliability. FTMs mask faults in systems, prevent them from leading to failures, and can be applied on different abstraction levels (e.g. source code level with exception handling, architecture level with replication) [10]. FTS only provides RetryStructure and MultiTryCatchStructure. Because in an FTMs, error detection is a prerequisite for error handling and not all detected errors can be handled. Therefore, at most, a RetryStructure or a MultiTryCatchStructure can provide error handling only for signaled failures, which are consequences of errors that can be detected and signaled by error detection.

Based on a good evaluation of PNZ model in NHPP group, we try to apply it into reliability prediction of component-based system and fault tolerance structures technique. Our study is organised as follows: after this introduction section, next section presents about software reliability modelling and PNZ model, the used model. Section 3 presents a reliability-prediction scenario to component based system and Sect. 4 introduces fault tolerance structures to improve software reliability. The last section shows some experimental results when apply those theoretical methods in real system.

2   Software Reliability Modelling and PNZ Model

Let's use some functions to describe characteristic of system when model it by non-homogeneous Poisson process in Table 1.

By time t, a system has $a(t)$ faults and $m(t)$ faults have been detected so we have $a(t) - m(t)$ remaining faults. With detection rate is $b(t)$, we have a relationship among number of faults detected in period Δt, total remaining faults of system and fault detection rate:

Table 1. Characteristic functions of software system

$a(t)$	Total number of faults
$b(t)$	Fault detection rate
$m(t)$	Expected number of fault detected by time t (mean value function)
$\lambda(t)$	Failure intensity

$$m(t + \Delta t) - m(t) = b(t)[a(t) - m(t)]\Delta t + o(\Delta t) \tag{1}$$

where $o(\Delta t)$ is infinitesimal value with Δt: $\lim_{\Delta t \to 0} \frac{o(\Delta t)}{\Delta t} = 0$. Let $\Delta t \to 0$:

$$\frac{\partial}{\partial t} m(t) = b(t)[a(t) - m(t)] \tag{2}$$

If t_0 is the starting time of testing process, with initial conditions $m(t_0) = m_0$ and $\lim_{t \to \infty} m(t) = a(t)$, Pham shows that general solution of (2) is [11]:

$$m(t) = e^{-B(t)} \left[m_0 + \int_{t_0}^{t} a(\tau)b(\tau)e^{B(\tau)} d\tau \right] \tag{3}$$

where

$$B(t) = \int_{t_0}^{t} b(s) ds \tag{4}$$

Pham et al. [11] introduce a Non-homogeneous Poisson process (NHPP) software reliability modeling (SRM) with time dependent functions:

$$a(t) = a(1 + \alpha t) \tag{5}$$

$$b(t) = \frac{b}{1 + \beta e^{-bt}} \tag{6}$$

So:

$$m(t) = \frac{a}{1 + \beta e^{-bt}} [(1 - e^{-bt})(1 - \frac{a}{\beta}) + at] \tag{7}$$

Existing publications show that PNZ model is one of the best model in NHPP sub-group.

3   Reliability Prediction for Component-Based System

3.1   Prediction Scenario

Our approach follows repetitively six steps [7] as depicted in Fig. 1.

3.2   Applying PNZ Model in Prediction Scenario

In step 3 of prediction scenario for component-based software system which has been shown in 3.1. After software architects create a system reliability model, the resulting model should be transformed into some kinds of model that can execute reliability, in this paper we use PNZ models.

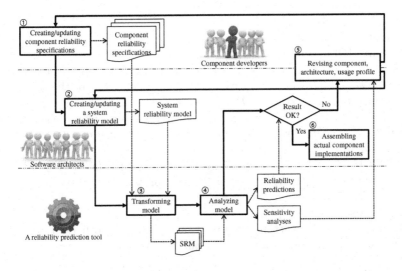

Fig. 1. Prediction scenario for component-based software system

In RetryStructure. For each possible input $I \in$ AIOS (Set of All sets of failure types) of a RetryStructure, the transformation instead of building a PNZ model like original from RMPI tool, we build a PNZ model that reflects all the possible execution paths of the RetryStructure with the input I and their corresponding probabilities, and then build up the failure model for the equivalent IA from this PNZ model.

Step 1: The transformation builds a PNZ block for each retry. The PNZ Block for the ith retry ($\mathrm{MB}(I, RP_i)$) reflects its possible execution paths for signaled failures (Fig. 2). It includes a state labeled "I, RP_i" ($[I, RP_i]$, for short) as an initial state, states $[RP_i, F]$ for all $F \in$ AFS as states of signaled failures. The probability of reaching state $[RP_i, F]$ from state $[I, RP_i]$ is $\mathrm{Pr}_{RP}(I, F) \; \forall F \in$ AFS.

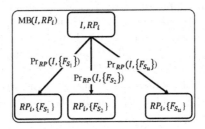

Fig. 2. PNZ block for i^{th} retry

Step 2: The transformation assembles these PNZ blocks into a single PNZ model that reflects all the possible execution paths of the RetryStructure with the input $I \in$ AIOS as follows:

- Add a state $[I, \text{START}]$.
- Add states $[F]$ for all $F \in \text{AFS}$.
- Add states $[O]$ for all $O \in \text{AIOS}$.
- Add a transition from state $[I, \text{START}]$ to state $[I, RP_0]$ with probability 1.0.
- For all PNZ block $\text{MB}(I, RP_i)$ with $i \in \{0, 1, \cdots, rc\}$, let rc be the retry count, add transitions from state $[I, RP_i]$ to state $[O]$ with probability $\text{Pr}_{PR}(I, O)$ for all $O \in \text{AIOS}$. This is because a correct (resp. erroneous) output of the RetryPart's execution leads to a correct (resp. erroneous) output of the whole RetryStructure.
- For PNZ block $\text{MB}(I, RP_{rc})$ (i.e. the PNZ block of the last retry), add transitions from state $[RP_{rc}, F]$ to state $[F]$ with probability 1.0 for all $F \in \text{AFS}$.
- For other PNZ blocks, i.e. $\text{MB}(I, RP_i)$ with $i \in \{0, 1, \cdots, rc - 1\}$, add transitions from state $[RP_i, F]$ to
  (1) state $[I, RP_{i+1}]$ with probability 1.0 if $F \in F_H$, or otherwise to
  (2) state $[F]$ with probability 1.0 for all $F \in \text{AFS}$.

Step 3: After the transformation generated the PNZ model, the failure model for the equivalent IA is built up as follows:

- For all $F \in \text{AFS}$: $\text{Pr}_{IA}(I, F)$ is the probability of reaching absorbing state $[F]$ from transient state $[I, \text{START}]$.
- For all $O \in \text{AIOS}$: $\text{Pr}_{IA}(I, O)$ is the probability of reaching absorbing state $[O]$ from transient state $[I, \text{START}]$.

The transition matrix for the generated chain of PNZ blocks has the following format:

$$P = \begin{pmatrix} Q & R \\ O & I \end{pmatrix} \tag{8}$$

where the upper left transition matrix Q is a square matrix representing one-step transitions between transient states $[I, \text{START}]$, $[I, RPi]$, and $[RPi, F]$ for all $F \in \text{AFS}$ (with $i \in \{0, 1, \cdots, rc\}$), the upper right transition matrix R represents one-step transitions from the transient states to absorbing states $[F]$ for all $F \in \text{AFS}$ and $[O]$ for all $O \in \text{AIOS}$, I is an identify matrix with the size equal to the number of the absorbing states. Let $B = (I - Q)^{-1}R$ be the matrix computed from the matrices I, Q and R. Because this is an absorbing chain of PNZ Blocks, the entry b_{ij} of the matrix B is the probability that the chain will be absorbed in the absorbing state s_j if it starts in the transient state s_i. Thus, the failure model of the equivalent IA can be obtained from the matrix B.

In MultiTryCastStructure. Similar to the case of RetryStructures, for each possible input $I \in \text{AIOS}$ of a MultiTryCatchStructure, the transformation builds a PNZ model that reflects all the possible execution paths of the MultiTryCatch-Structure with the input I and their corresponding probabilities, and then builds up the failure model for the equivalent IA from this PNZ model.

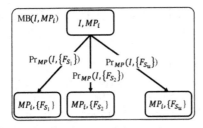

Fig. 3. PNZ block for MultiTryCatchPart i

Step 1: The transformation builds a PNZ block for each MultiTryCatchPart. The PNZ Block for the MultiTryCatchPart i (MB(I, MP_i)) reflects its possible execution paths for signaled failures (Fig. 3). It includes a state $[I, MP_i]$ as an initial state, states $[MP_i, F]$ for all $F \in$ AFS as states of signaled failures. The probability of reaching state $[MP_i, F]$ from state $[I, MP_i]$ is $\Pr_{MP_i}(I, F)$ for all $F \in$ AFS.

Step 2: The transformation assembles these PNZ blocks into a single PNZ model that reflects all the possible execution paths of the MultiTryCatchStructure with the input $I \in$ AIOS as follows:

- Add a state $[I, \mathrm{START}]$.
- Add states $[F]$ for all $F \in$ AFS.
- Add states $[O]$ for all $O \in$ AIOS.
- Add a transition from state $[I, \mathrm{START}]$ to state $[I, MP_i]$ with probability 1.0.
- For all PNZ blocks MB(I, MP_i) with $i \in \{1, 2, \cdots, n\}$, let n be the number of MultiTryCatchParts, add transitions from state $[I, MP_i]$ to state $[O]$ with probability $\Pr_{MP_i}(I, O)$ for all $O \in$ AIOS. This is because a correct (resp. erroneous) output of a MultiTryCatchPart's execution leads to a correct (resp. erroneous) output of the whole MultiTryCatchStructure.
- For PNZ block MB(I, MP_n) (i.e. the PNZ block of the last MultiTryCatch-Part), add transitions from state $[MP_n, F]$ to state $[F]$ with probability 1.0 for all $F \in$ AFS.
- For other PNZ blocks, i.e. MB(I, MP_i) with $i \in \{1, 2, \cdots, n-1\}$, add transitions from state $[MP_i, F]$ to
  (1) state $[I, MP_x]$ with probability 1.0 where $x \in \{i+1, i+2, \cdots, n\}$ is the lowest index satisfying $F \in F_{Hx}$, or to
  (2) state $[F]$ with probability 1.0 if no such index $x \in \{i+1, i+2, \cdots, n\}$ satisfying $F \in F_{Hx}$ for all $F \in$ AFS.

Step 3: Because the resulting PNZ model is an absorbing chain of PNZ blocks, the failure model for the equivalent IA is built up as follows. For all $F \in$ AFS, $\Pr_{IA}(I, F)$ is the probability of reaching absorbing state $[F]$ from transient state $[I, \mathrm{START}]$. For all $O \in$ AIOS, $\Pr_{IA}(I, O)$ is the probability of reaching absorbing state $[O]$ from transient state $[I, \mathrm{START}]$.

4   Improving Reliability of Software System by Fault Tolerance Structures

Avizienis et al. [9] describe in detail the principle of Software Fault Tolerance Mechanisms (FTMs). An FTM is carried out via error detection and system recovery. Error detection is to identify the presence of an error. Error handling followed by fault handling together form system recovery. Error handling is to eliminate errors from the system state, e.g. by bringing the system back to a saved state that existed prior to error occurrence. Fault handling is to prevent faults from being activated again, e.g. by either switching in spare components or reassigning tasks among non-failed components.

To support modeling FTMs, our reliability modeling schema provides Fault Tolerance Structures (FTSs) [12], namely RetryStructure and MultiTryCatchStructure. Because in an FTM, error detection is a prerequisite for error handling and not all detected errors can be handled. Therefore, at most, a RetryStructure or a MultiTryCatchStructure can provide error handling only for signaled failures, which are consequences of errors that can be detected and signaled by error detection.

RetryStructure. An effective technique to handle transient failures is service re-execution. A RetryStructure is taking ideas from this technique. The structure contains a single RetryPart which, in turn, can contain different activity types, structure types, and even a nested RetryStructure. The first execution of the RetryPart models normal service execution while the following executions of the RetryPart model the service re-executions.

MultiTryCatchStructure. A MultiTryCatchStructure is taking ideas from the exception handling in object-oriented programming. The structure consists of two or more MultiTryCatchParts. Each MultiTryCatchPart can contain different activity types, structure types, and even a nested MultiTryCatchStructure. Similar to try and catch blocks in exception handling, the first MultiTryCatchPart models the normal service execution while the following MultiTryCatchParts handle certain failures of stopping failure types and launch alternative activities.

After obtaining the results of system reliability, as well as the rate of occurrence of the error by using the tools RMPI. We will determine the type of error that has the highest rate of appearance and then follow the 3 steps below to reduce the possibility that errors occur and thereby improve the overall reliability of the entire system.

In system reliability model that system architects have designed from the beginning, we will add a module called fault-tolerant module, this module will be built right before the module that contains the error rates appear most which been identified above. We follow 3 steps:

Step 1. Model the component Fault-Tolerance.
Step 2. Create an instance of this component.
Step 3. Redefine some component connectors.

5   Experimental Results of WebScan Sub-system

5.1   Preparing Reliability Prediction Scenario

We take following steps to build reliability model.

Step 1: modeling services, components and service implementations.

Sub-step 1.1: first of all, we model all the services, here we have six services:

1. serveClientRequest.
2. configureScanSettings.
3. scan.
4. createNewDocument.
5. addPageToDocument.
6. saveDocument.

Sub-step 1.2: after that, we model three components.

Sub-step 1.3: then, we model service implementations for provided services of components.

Step 2: modeling failure models. We model all kinds of failure models include: propagating failure type and stopping failure types.

1. For propagating failure type:
   – ContentPropagatingFailure $\leftrightarrow F_{P1}$.
2. For stopping failure types:
   – ServingRequestFailure $\leftrightarrow F_{S1}$.
   – ConfiguringScanFailure $\leftrightarrow F_{S2}$.
   – ScanningFailure $\leftrightarrow F_{S3}$.
   – CreatingDocumentFailure $\leftrightarrow F_{S4}$.
   – AddingPageFailure $\leftrightarrow F_{S5}$.
   – SavingDocumentFailure $\leftrightarrow F_{S6}$.

Step 3: modeling system architecture and usage profile

Sub-step 3.1: first, we define architecure of the whole system.

Sub-step 3.2: then, we define component instances:

   – ClientInteraction $\leftrightarrow$ clientInteraction
   – WebScanControl $\leftrightarrow$ webScanControl
   – DocumentManager $\leftrightarrow$ documentManager

Sub-step 3.3: after that, we define component connectors.

Sub-step 3.4: we define user interface(s). For WebScan sub-system, we only have one user interface corresponding to serverClientRequest service and called as webScanUI.

Step 4: using tool RMPI to predict WebScan sub-systems reliability. From this, failure F_{S2} "ConfiguringScanFailure" is the most frequent failure type. This failure occurred between 2 modules is "WebScanControl" model and "Document-Manager" model and its corresponding with" configureScanSettings" service.

5.2   Applying Fault Tolerance Structures Method

Follow 3 steps outlined in Sect. 4, we have

Step 1: model the component Fault-Tolerance.

Step 2: create an instance of this component WebScanControlFaultTolerance $\leftrightarrow$ webScanControlFaultTolerance

Step 3: redefine some component connectors.

5.3   Reliability Comparison

After we have completed the structural changes in the system like above, we use RMPI tool to compare results (before and after changing happened) by:

```
java -jar RMPITool.jar -p WebScan_WithFTS.xml Output.txt
```

Comparing the results of the reliability and rate of occurrence of system failures before and after Webscan sub-system have added fault-tolerant components FTS, we have the following result in Table 2. From this result:

- The predicted reliability has increased 0.042277 %.
- The predicted failure probability for "ConfiguringScanFailure" has decreased 99.84899954 %.

Table 2. Result after applying fault tolenrance structures method

	WebScan	WebScan_WithFTS
Reliability	0.9981865558446795	0.9986085685485016
CreatingDocumentFailure	1.5764455152E-4	1.5764455152E-4
ConfiguringScanFailure	4.22706018E-4	6.382880502600001E-7
ServingRequestFailure	2.25E-4	2.25E-4
AddingPageFailure	2.9063232776269386E-4	2.9063232776269386E-4
SavingDocumentFailure	1.5098630021824724E-4	1.5098630021824724E-4
ScanningFailure	3.085747310766729E-4	3.085747310766729E-4
ContentPropagatingFailure	2.5790022674295393E-4	2.5795525287075817E-4

6   Conclusions and Future Works

The article evaluates reliability prediction of component-based system and fault tolerance structures technique by applying PNZ model based on good evaluation of PNZ model in NHPP group. We presented prediction scenario for component-based architecture, a modern technique of software engineering, with six steps. We also introduced PNZ model and how to apply this model into reliability prediction of component-based system.

To apply our approach, component developers create component reliability specifications and software architects create a system reliability model using provide reliability modeling schema. Then, these artifacts are transformed automatically to PNZ models for reliability predictions and sensitivity analyses by our reliability prediction tool. After all, to improve reliability of software system by FTS, component developers can revise the components and/or software architects can revise the system architecture and the usage profile. Via case studies, we demonstrated the applicability of our approach, also shown how much reliability of software system can be improved. This kind of helps can lead to more reliable software systems in a cost-effective way because potentially high costs for late life-cycle changes for reliability improvements can be avoided.

We plan to extend our approach with more complex error propagation for concurrent executions, to include more software FTSs, and to validate further our approach. We also plan to continue developing our reliability modeling schema and prediction tool to help component developers automatically provide component reliability specifications. Those future works was sketched and will further increase the applicability of our approach.

Acknowledgement. This research was supported by The National Foundation for Science and Technology Development (NAFOSTED) under Grant 102.03-2013.39: Automated verification and error localization methods for component-based software.

References

1. ISO/IEC-25010:2011: Systems and software quality requirements and evaluation (square) system and software quality models (square) (2011)
2. Rana, R.: Defect prediction & prevention in automotive software development (2013)
3. Roshandel, R.: Calculating architectural reliability via modeling and analysis. Ph.D. thesis, University of Southern California (2006)
4. Chengjie, X.: Availability and Reliability Analysis of Computer Software Systems Considering Maintenance and Security Issues. Ph.D. thesis (2011)
5. Brosch, F.: Integrated Software Architecture-Based Reliability Prediction for IT Systems, vol. 9. KIT Scientific Publishing, Karlsruhe (2012)
6. Larsson, M.: Predicting quality attributes in component-based software systems. Mälardalen University (2004)
7. Pham, T.-T., Defago, X.: Reliability prediction for component-based software systems with architectural-level fault tolerance mechanisms. In: Eighth International Conference on Availability, Reliability and Security, pp. 11–20. IEEE (2013)
8. Pham, H.: System Software Reliability. Springer, Heidelberg (2006)
9. Avizienis, A., Laprie, J.-C., Randell, B., Landwehr, C.: Basic concepts and taxonomy of dependable and secure computing. IEEE Trans. Dependable Secure Comput. **1**(1), 11–33 (2004)
10. Pullum, L.L.: Software Fault Tolerance Techniques and Implementation. Artech House, Norwood (2001)
11. Pham, H., Nordmann, L., Zhang, Z.: A general imperfect-software-debugging model with s-shaped fault-detection rate. IEEE Trans. Reliab. **48**(2), 169–175 (1999)
12. Avizienis, A.: Fault-tolerance and fault-intolerance: complementary approaches to reliable computing. In: ACM SIGPLAN Notices, vol. 10, pp. 458–464 (1975)

The Performance of TimeER Model
by Description Logics

Nguyen Viet Chanh[✉] and Hoang Quang

Faculty of Information Technology – College of Sciences, Hue University, 77
Nguyen Hue Street, Hue City, Vietnam
chanhkhmt@gmail.com, hquang@hueuni.edu.vn

Abstract. The relationship between Description Logic (DL) and database is
quite close. Indeed, the needs for the building of the systems that can manage
both the database and the knowledge representation are really necessary. A de-
scription-logic based on the knowledge representation system not only allows
the knowledge management, but also provides a standard framework which is
considered to be very close to the language used to represent the
Entity-Relationship model (ER model). On the other hand, the temporal ER
model is used to model the time aspects of the conceptual database schema.
Thus, the problem of the use of description logic to express temporal ER models
is really useful for modeling the conceptual data models. Based on the temporal
DL, Alessandro Artale et al. (2011) presented temporal ER schemas and
integrity constraints in the form of complex inclusion dependencies. The paper
approaches the representation method of Alessandro Artale and proposes
mapping multi-valued attributes in the temporal ER model to DL. Description
logic application in TimeER modeling

Keywords: ER model · Temporal ER model · Description logic · Temporal
description logic

1 Introduction

In recent years, Description Logic has usually been mentioned as an effective
knowledge representation method. Description Logic is applied in varied fields, it is
considered as languages representing knowledge and inference. In particular applications, they can use description logic, the application domain's knowledge specified by
the concepts and relationships.

During the past time, the description logic has been used in many fields such as:
software technology, configuration setting, electronic library systems, information
system, semantic web, natural language processing, and database administration…

Description logic has a quite close relationship with database. In fact, it is really
necessary to build a system that is able to represent description logic knowledge while
it still allows database administration. Database administration systems resolve date
integrity issue and administers a large amount of data, while description logic
knowledge base representation system manages knowledge. In addition, description

© ICST Institute for Computer Sciences, Social Informatics and Telecommunications Engineering 2016
P.C. Vinh and V. Alagar (Eds.): ICCASA 2015, LNICST 165, pp. 282–297, 2016.
DOI: 10.1007/978-3-319-29236-6_28

logic provides a standard frame considered to be close to the languages is used to model data as Entity– Relationship model.

In temporal database, it has launched many different data models, each model has its certain advantages and disadvantages. Temporal ER model (Entity model– Relationship with time factor) is a model using for modeling temporal database in the concept That temporal ER model is performed as diagrams (Figs. 1 and 4) and has developed the time factor in the database schema, that is valid time and transaction time, makes us easily see the change of data at different times. Temporal ER models has been researched such as: TERM, RAKE, MOTAR, TEER, STEER, ERT, TimeER,....

In the other side, Entity– Relationship (ER) model has temporal component used to model temporal aspects of the conceptual database schema, such as valid time– a time that event happens is right in practice, and transaction time– a time that event is stored in database. Temporal ER model has two main approaches proposed by researchers are: Implicit approach (Fig. 1) and explicit approach (Fig. 4), which are used to support modeling temporal ER models, then to represent temporal integrity constraints. Different versions of ER model have been proposed to model temporal concepts of models at concept level. This modeling has provided some formalization methods and expansions in temporal ER model. However, there are some complex constraints which can not be represented in temporal ER model, and temporal ER model has many different versions which have some inconsistent representation symbols, they causes many difficulties for designers in designing database.

Based on description logic with temporal factor, Alessandro Artale and partners [1] have represented temporal ER schemes and integrity constraints by formalizing inclusion dependencies with inclusion axioms. This study, in addition to the introduction of a method performed by the authors, we would like to propose multi-valued attributes representation on temporal ER models by representation logic. In this paper, we present a method of performing the ER models representation by describing the logic time with the temporal factor and indicate the result through modeling temporal ER model with description logic. Finally, this is the conclusion.

2   Modeling Temporal ER Model by Description Logic

Representing a temporal ER model in the description logic is performed through defining a conversion function Φ from temporal ER model to knowledge base ALCQIT.

Modeling is performed as the following. All the names of entities and relationships in temporal ER scheme are switched in correspondence with the names of the concepts in ALCQIT. The names of the domains are corresponding with additional concepts in separated pair. The attributes of entity sets and the role of relationships in corresponding ER model are names of roles in ALCQIT and with limited number to clear that the attribute is single-valued, in case of the multi-valued attributes, this limited number will be removed. IS-A relationship among entity sets or relationships is modeled by using term axioms. Number version constraints in temporal ER model are represented by number of words in ALCQIT. Natures of temporal in ER model are represented in correspondence with temporal operators in ALCQIT [2].

As mentioned above, there are two approaches in building a temporal ER model: implicit approach and explicit approach. Therefore, in order to model temporal ER models, we need to perform this representation on each particular approach. However, this research only focuses on modeling with implicit ER model.

Firstly, we consider switching an ER model (regardless of integrity constraints) to ALCQIT knowledge base as the following.

2.1   Modeling Implicit Temporal ER Model

2.1.1   Switch Implicit Temporal ER Model to Knowledge Base

Consider temporal ER model in implicit approach as the following Fig. 1

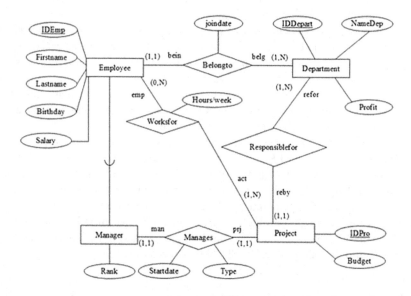

Fig. 1. A temporal ER model by implicit approach.

Given an ER model $\mathcal{D}$. Then, knowledge base Σ is called a switch from scheme $\mathcal{D}$ through the function $\Phi(\mathcal{D})$, if Σ contains 3 following sets:

- Set of elementary concepts $\Phi(A)$ corresponding with each range name, entity name and relationship name A in ER model $\mathcal{D}$;
- Set of elementary concepts $\Phi(P)$ corresponding with attributes name and roles name of a relationship P in ER model $\mathcal{D}$;
- Set of term axioms of Σ includes the following components:
  - Each IS-A relationship between two sets of entities E_1, E_2 (or two corresponding relationships R_1, R_2) with E_1 *Isa* E_2 (or R_1 *Isa* R_2) in $\mathcal{D}$ then we have the following term axiom:

$$\Phi(E_1) \sqsubseteq \Phi(E_2) \text{ (or } \Phi(R_1) \sqsubseteq \Phi(R_2))$$

- Each set of entities E with attributes $A_1,...,A_h$ corresponding with value range $D_1,...,D_h$ then term axiom:

$$\Phi(E) \sqsubseteq \forall\Phi(A_1).\Phi(D_1) \sqcap ... \sqcap \forall\Phi(A_h).\Phi(D_h) \sqcap$$
$$(= 1\Phi(A_1)) \sqcap ... \sqcap (= 1\Phi(A_h))$$

- Each relationship R with attributes $A_1,...,A_h$ corresponding with value range $D_1,...,D_h$ then we have the following term axiom:

$$\Phi(R) \sqsubseteq \forall\Phi(A_1).\Phi(D_1) \sqcap ... \sqcap \forall\Phi(A_h).\Phi(D_h) \sqcap$$
$$(= 1\Phi(A_1)) \sqcap ... \sqcap (= 1\Phi(A_h))$$

- Each relationship R level k between sets of entities $E_1,...,E_k$ with R is connected by k roles $U_1,...,U_k$ then we have following term axiom:

$$\Phi(R) \sqsubseteq \forall\Phi(U_1).\Phi(E_1) \sqcap ... \sqcap = \forall\Phi(U_k).\Phi(E_k) \sqcap$$
$$(= 1\Phi(U_1)) \sqcap ... \sqcap (= 1\Phi(U_k))$$

- To the value n, m corresponding with the value (min, max) in number version constraint, on the role U connecting relationship R and set of entities E, and:
  - If $n \neq 0$ then we have the following term axiom:

$$\Phi(E) \sqsubseteq (\geq n(\Phi(U_i))^-.\Phi(R)) \text{ with } i \in \{1,...,k\}, k \text{ is level.}$$

  - If $m \neq \infty$ then we have the following term axiom:

$$\Phi(E) \sqsubseteq (\leq m(\Phi(U_i))^-.\Phi(R)) \text{ with } i \in \{1,...,k\}, k \text{ islevel.}$$

- Each pair of symbol X_1, X_2 that:
  - $X_1 \in D; X_2 \in E \cup D; X_1 \neq X_2$, or:
  - $X_1 \in R; X_2 \in E \cup R; X_1$ và X_2 with different levels, then we have the following term axiom: $\Phi(X_1) \sqsubseteq \neg\Phi(X_2)$, with D is the name of value range; R is set of relationships name and E is set of enities name.

$$\Phi(E) \sqsubseteq (= 1 \sim {}^*\Phi(A))$$
$$\top \sqsubseteq (\leq 1(\Phi(A))^-.\Phi(E)$$

- To each attribute A which is a key attribute of entity set E then we have the following term axiom:

$$\Phi(\text{E}) \sqsubseteq (= 1 \sim {}^*\Phi(A))$$
$$\top \sqsubseteq (\leq 1(\Phi(A))^-.\Phi(\text{E})$$

- If the entity set E is the generalization of separate entity sets $E_1, ..., E_n$ then it can be switched to the following term axiom:

$$\Phi(E) \sqsubseteq \Phi(E_1) \sqcup ... \sqcup \Phi(E_n)$$
$$\Phi(E_1) \sqsubseteq \Phi(E) \sqcap \neg\Phi(E_2) \sqcap \neg\Phi(E_3) \sqcap ... \sqcap \neg\Phi(E_n)$$
$$\Phi(E_2) \sqsubseteq \Phi(E) \sqcap \neg\Phi(E_3) \sqcap \neg\Phi(E_4) \sqcap ... \sqcap \neg\Phi(E_n)$$
$$\Phi(E_{n-1}) \sqsubseteq \Phi(E) \sqcap \neg\Phi(E_n)$$
$$\Phi(E_n) \sqsubseteq \Phi(E)$$

- Each entity set E with attribute $A_1, ..., A_p, A_{p+1}, ..., A_h$ corresponding with value ranges $D_1, ..., D_p, D_{p+1}, ..., D_h$, in which $A_1, .., A_p$ are single-valued attributes and $A_{p+1}, ..., A_h$ are multi-valued attributes, then we have the following axiom:

$$\Phi(E) \sqsubseteq \forall\Phi(A_1).\Phi(D_1) \sqcap ... \sqcap \forall\Phi(A_p).\Phi(D_p) \sqcap$$
$$\left(\geq 1\Phi(A_{p+1}).\Phi(D_{p+1})\right) \sqcap ... \sqcap \left(\geq 1\Phi(A_h).\Phi(D_h)\right) \sqcap \left(= 1\Phi(A_1)\right) \sqcap ...$$
$$\sqcap \left(= 1\Phi(A_p)\right) \sqcap \left(\neg \geq 1\Phi(A_{p+1}).\neg\Phi(D_{p+1})\right) \sqcap ... \sqcap \left(\neg \geq 1\Phi(A_h).\neg\Phi(D_h)\right)$$

- If an entity set E with attribute A which is a compound attribute with components $A_1, ..., A_p$ then we have the term axiom for representation as following:

$$\Phi(E) \sqsubseteq \forall\Phi(A).\left(\forall\Phi(A_1).\Phi(D_1) \sqcap ... \sqcap \forall\Phi(A_p).\Phi(D_p) \sqcap\right.$$
$$\left(= 1\Phi(A_1)\right) \sqcap ... \sqcap \left(= 1\Phi(A_p)\right)) \sqcap \left(= 1\Phi(A)\right)$$

Example 1.

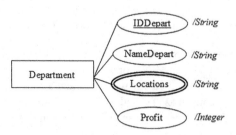

Fig. 2. Example of multi-valued attribute

In the above example, entity set *Department* with attribute *Locations* is multi-valued attribute, we have the representing term axiom:

$$Department \sqsubseteq \forall IDDepart.String \sqcap \forall NameDepart.String \sqcap$$
$$\left(\geq 1Locations.String\right) \sqcap \forall Profit.Integer \sqcap \left(= 1IDDepart\right) \sqcap$$
$$\left(= 1NameDepart\right) \sqcap \left(=1Profit\right)) \sqcap \left(\neg \geq 1Locations.\neg String\right)$$

Example 2.

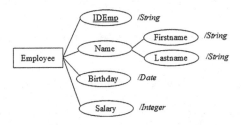

Fig. 3. Example of compound attribute

In Fig. 3 the entity set *Employee* with the attribute *Name* has a compound attribute containing two elementary attributes *FirstName* and *LastName*, we will have a representation term axiom:

$$Employee \sqsubseteq IDEmp.String \sqcap \forall Name.(\forall Firstname.String \sqcap$$
$$Lastname.String \sqcap (= 1Firstname) \sqcap (= 1Lastname)) \sqcap$$
$$\forall Birthday.Date \sqcap \forall Salary.Integer \sqcap (= 1IDEmp) \sqcap$$
$$(= 1Name) \sqcap (= 1Birthday) \sqcap (= 1Salary)$$

In addition, this constraint of temporal integrity is represented in description logic by adding term axioms in .... A term axiom represents an inclusion among the concepts. Therefore, a integrity constraint is an inclusive dependence form represented in temporal description logic ALCQIT.

2.1.2 Inclusive Dependence

An integrity constraint for an ER model $\mathcal{D}$ is an inclusive dependence that can be represented in a knowledge base in correspondence with Σ by a term axiom in a form of $C \sqsubseteq D$, in which elementary concept appears in C, D corresponding with the name of the domain, entity set or relationship in $\mathcal{D}$.

There is a correspondence in switching between valid database status of $\mathcal{D}$ and models of deduced knowledge base. The appearance of this correspondence drags on correspondence between solutions for checking a nature in ER model and corresponding deduction in description logic and vice versa. Thus, it can use deduction operations in description logic to check a nature of ER schema [4].

Example 3. Consider the example shown in Fig. 2, coding integrity constraints is represented by term axioms in a knowledge base Σ_{IC} as following:

$$Manager \sqsubseteq Qualified\ \mathcal{S}\ (Employee \sqcap \neg Manager)$$

The above constraint shows that all of managers are eligible after a period of being a staff.

In fact, integrity constraints are logical deductions from $\Sigma_{ER} \cup \Sigma_{IC}$, for example:

$$\Sigma_{ER} \cup \Sigma_{IC} \vDash Project \sqsubseteq \exists(act^- \circ emp).\neg Manager$$

The above constraint shows that each project exists a staff who is not a manager working for it.

$$\Sigma_{ER} \cup \Sigma_{IC} \vDash Manager \sqsubseteq {}^-\exists(emp^- \circ act).Project$$

The above constraint represents that a manager needs to have a temporal of the work in the past for a project (maybe another project).

2.2   Modeling Explicit Temporal ER Model

As we know, temporal ER model with explicit approach remains non-temporal semantic meaning for normal ER models, in the other side, it also implements new structures which allow to represent entity sets, temporal relationships and temporal dependences between them.

In this part, we propose a formalization approach to model explicit temporal ER model by using simple constraints to define temporal and non-temporal structures, thus it remains upward compatibility. Temporal description logic ALCQIT can represent explicit ER model, at first by applying switching principles in the previous part (modeling explicit temporal ER model) and then adding axioms to distinguish temporal and non-temporal structures. Below are some presentations of additional axioms for coding this model.

2.2.1   Entity Set and Temporal and Non-Temporal Relationship

As stated above, for an explicit temporal ER model, entity sets and relationships include non-temporal structure and temporal structure. Therefore, when modeling, we have more additional axioms to clear the following structure:

- Each non-temporal entity set E is represented by the following axiom:

$$\Phi(E) \sqsubseteq (\sim {}^+\Phi(E)) \sqcap (\sim {}^-\Phi(E)), \text{ that means } \Phi(E) \equiv \sim {}^*\Phi(E)$$

The above axiom shows that entity set is right whenever that entity set must be right at any point in the past and the future. Indeed, non-temporal entity sets have an overall living temporal.

- In the other side, if the entity set E is a temporal entity set, it will be represented:

$$\Phi(E) \sqsubseteq ({}^+\neg\Phi(E)) \sqcup ({}^-\neg\Phi(E))$$

The axiom represents that there is a point in the past or in the future when entities exist. Indeed, temporal entity sets have a limit of living temporal of entity set.

Similar to entity sets, the relationships also have axioms to distinguish temporal and non-temporal structures.

- Each non-temporal relationship R level k between entity sets $E_1,...,E_k$ that R is connected by k roles $U_1,...,U_k$ is represented by the following term axioms:

$$\Phi(R) \sqsubseteq (\sim{}^+\Phi(R)) \sqcap (\sim{}^-\Phi(R)) - \text{ that means } \Phi(R) \equiv \sim{}^*\Phi(R);$$
$$\Phi(R) \sqsubseteq (= 1 \sim{}^*\Phi(U_1)) \sqcap ... \sqcap (= 1 \sim{}^*\Phi(U_k))$$

- If the relationship R is a temporal relationship, it will be distinguished by the following term axiom:

$$\Phi(R) \sqsubseteq ({}^+\neg\Phi(R)) \sqcup ({}^-\neg\Phi(R)) \sqcup \neg((= 1 \sim{}^*\Phi(U_1)) \sqcap ... \sqcap (= 1 \sim{}^*\Phi(U_k)))$$

Example 4. Consider temporal ER model in Fig. 4.

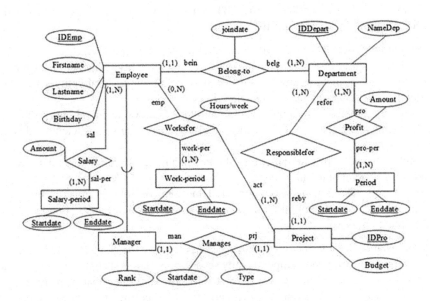

Fig. 4. An example of temporal ER model [4]

In Fig. 4. The entity set *Department* can be considered as a non-temporal entity set because organizational structure of the business does not change over temporal, while the entity set *Manager* can be considered as a temporal entity set because the manager can change over temporal. Thus we have the distinguishing axiom which is temporal or non-temporal entity set added when representing the entity set *Department* and *Manager* as following:

$$Department \sqsubseteq (\sim{}^+ Department) \sqcap (\sim{}^- Department)$$
$$Manager \sqsubseteq ({}^+\neg Manager) \sqcup ({}^-\neg Manager)$$

With considered example in Figs. 1 and 4; the relationship *Worksfor* is a temporal relationship, the relationship *Responsiblefor* is a non-temporal relationship, therefore we have the following distinguishing axioms:

– Non-temporal relationship *Responsiblefor*

$$Responsiblefor \sqsubseteq (\sim {}^+Responsiblefor) \sqcap (\sim {}^-Responsiblefor);$$
$$Responsiblefor \sqsubseteq (= 1 \sim {}^*reby) \sqcap (= 1 \sim {}^*refor)$$

– Temporal relationship *Worksfor*

$$Worksfor \sqsubseteq ({}^+ \neg Worksfor) \sqcup ({}^- \neg Worksfor) \sqcup$$
$$\neg((= 1 \sim {}^*act) \sqcap (= 1 \sim {}^*emp))$$

Using of deduction ability of ALCQIT can support database designer to identify matching natures with temporal ER scheme:

– An entity subset of a temporal entity set is a temporal entity set.
– An entity subset of a non-temporal entity set and an entity father-set of a temporal entity set or implicit temporal entity set may be a non-temporal entity set or temporal entity set or implicit temporal entity set.
– An entity father-set of a non-temporal entity set is a non-temporal entity set.
– A schema is inconsistent if one entity set of all separate subsets is a temporal entity set.
– Entity sets taking part in non-temporal relationships can be non-temporal entity sets or implicit temporal entity sets.
– Entity sets taking part in temporal relationships or implicit relationships with temporal factor can be non-temporal entity sets or implicit temporal entity sets or temporal entity sets.

For instance, we consider the following example to see the correction of the scheme organization for using both temporal entity set and non-temporal entity set, we consider the interactive between entity sets by IS-A relations. Assuming that there is an IS-A relation between a time less entity set E_1 and a temporal entity set E_2. The temporal ER model switched to the following knowledge base is not satisfied:

$$\Phi(E_1) \sqsubseteq (\sim {}^+ \Phi(E_1)) \sqcap (\sim {}^- \Phi(E_1))$$
$$\Phi(E_2) \sqsubseteq ({}^+ \neg \Phi(E_2)) \sqcup ({}^- \neg \Phi(E_2))$$
$$\Phi(E_1) \sqsubseteq \Phi(E_2)$$

Thus, a non-temporal entity set cannot be a subset of a temporal entity set, this is always true with taxonomic relation included in temporal ER model. This can be explained by an observation: if the relation IS-A has a representation called a, for example: a is representation of E_1 and E_2 at a certain instance t_0- is represented by the following symbol set: $\{a : E_1, a : E_2\}_{t_0}$. According to the statement of temporal axiom for E_2, at an instance of $t1$, the representation a is not E_2 - $\{a : \neg E_2\}_{t_1}$. In the other side, because E_1 is a non-temporal entity set, the representation a is E_1 at any instance, and especially at the instance of t_1 - $\{a : \neg E_2, a : E_1\}_{t_1}$. According to layer relation, it will be shown that a is E_2 at t_1 - $\{a : \neg E_2, a : E_1, a : E_2\}_{t_1}$. This shows that both a of E_2 and a are not E_2 at t_1, this is a contradiction.

Based on those comments, it is easy to understand the reasons of the following consequences:

$$\Phi(E_2) \sqsubseteq \{(^+ \neg \Phi(E_2)) \sqcup (^- \neg \Phi(E_2)), \Phi(E_1) \sqsubseteq \Phi(E_2)\} \vDash \Phi(E_1) \sqsubseteq$$
$$(^+ \neg \Phi(E_1)) \sqcup (^- \neg \Phi(E_1))$$

$$\Phi(E_1) \sqsubseteq \{(\sim{}^+ \Phi(E_1)) \sqcap (\sim{}^- \Phi(E_1)), \Phi(E_1) \sqsubseteq \Phi(E_2)\} \vDash \Phi(E_2) \sqsubseteq$$
$$(\sim{}^+ \Phi(E_2)) \sqcap (\sim{}^- \Phi(E_2))$$

that means, all entity subsets of temporal entity set are temporal entity sets and an entity father-set of a non-temporal entity set is a non-temporal entity set [4].

2.2.2 Attributes with Time Factor

At different instances, an entity set may have different values for the same attribute. These attributes are combined by a valid time, in other words, they are attributes with time factor. Therefore, so as to model attributes with time factor, there are some more term axioms to distinguish attributes with and without time factor besides applying switching principles for attribute given in the part of modeling a model.

An entity set E (corresponding with R) with attributes $A_1, ..., A_h$ and with:

- Each attribute A_i (so that $A_i \in \{A_1, ..., A_h\}$) is a non-temporal attribute of the entity set E (corresponding with the relationship R) then the term axiom is added as following:

$$\Phi(E) \sqsubseteq (= 1 \sim{}^* \Phi(A_i))$$
equal to $\quad \Phi(R) \sqsubseteq (= 1 \sim{}^* \Phi(A_i))$

- Each attribute A_i (so that $A_i \in \{A_1, ..., A_h\}$) is a temporal attribute of the entity attribute E (corresponding with the relationship R) then the term axiom is added as following:

$$\Phi(E) \sqsubseteq \neg(= 1 \sim{}^* \Phi(A_i))$$
equal to $\quad \Phi(R) \sqsubseteq \neg(= 1 \sim{}^* \Phi(A_i))$

Example 5. In the entity set *Employee* in Figs. 1 and 4, we see that attributes *First-Name*, *LastName*, *Birthday* are non-temporal attributes, *Salary* is temporal attribute, so we have the distinguishing axioms as following:

$$Employee \sqsubseteq (= 1 \sim {}^*FirstName);$$
$$Employee \sqsubseteq (= 1 \sim {}^*LastName);$$
$$Employee \sqsubseteq (= 1 \sim {}^*Birthday);$$
$$Employee \sqsubseteq \neg (= 1 \sim {}^*Salary)$$

2.2.3   Coding Time Number Version Constraint

For temporal ER model with explicit approach, besides number versions constraint *(min, max)* assigned a role to limit number of entity of an entity set that is allowed to take part in through roles of relationship, there is also a constraint of living temporal of entity set with relationship represented by the pair of number version *(minL, maxL)* on the role from entity set to relationship. With the meaning that during the time of the exist of an entity, each entity $e \in E$ will have relationship with minimum of *minL* element and maximum of *maxL* element of relationship R.

Assuming that the values n, m are corresponding with the values *(minL, maxL)* in number version constraint of living temporal of entity set to relationship, and:

- If n $\neq$ 0 then we have the following term axiom:

$$\Phi(E) \sqsubseteq (\geq n(\Phi(U_i))^- . {}^*\Phi(R) \text{ with } i \in \{1, \ldots, k\} \text{ and } k \text{ is the level.}$$

- If m $\neq \infty$ then we have the following term axiom:

$$\Phi(E) \sqsubseteq (\leq m(\Phi(U_i))^- . {}^*\Phi(R)) \text{ with } i \in \{1, \ldots, k\} \text{ and } k \text{ is level.}$$

Example 6. Assuming that during exist the manager has managed 1 project at minimum and 5 projects at maximum. With this constraint of living temporal we have the following representation:

$$Manager \sqsubseteq (\geq 1man^- . {}^*Manages) \sqcap (\leq 5man^- . {}^*Manages)$$

3   Application of Description Logic in Modeling TimeER Model

In this part, the paper will proceed modeling TimeER model with description logic. As above introduction, TimeER model (Fig. 5) is a temporal ER model in explicit approach. Therefore, in order to model this model we need to use switching principles for explicit temporal ER model, in other words, we have to apply both switch definition in 2.1 and implement axioms to distinguish temporal and non-temporal structures in 2.2 (Table 1).

Considering temporal ER model represented in Fig. 4. If we represent this model with TimeER model, we have the following scheme:

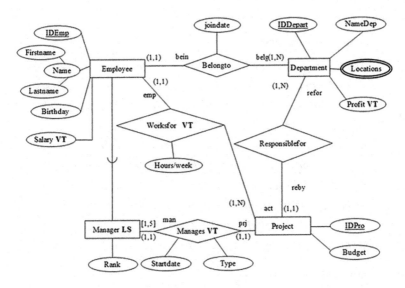

Fig. 5. An example of TimeER model

With TimeER model in Fig. 5, assuming that attributes of entity sets and relationships in this model are corresponding with the domains as following:

Modeling TimeER model (Fig. 5) by switching function Φ from TimeER model to knowledge base Σ. We have knowledge base received from this switch including:

Table 1. Corresponding domains for attribute in Fig. 5

Entity set or relationship	Attribute and corresponding domain
Employee	*{IDEmp: String, FirstName: String, LastName: String, Birthday: Date, Salary: Integer}*
Manager	*{Rank: String}*
Department	*{IDDepart: String, NameDep: String, Locations: String, Profit: Integer}*
Project	*{IDPro: String, Budget: Integer}*
Belongto	*{joindate: Date}*
Worksfor	*{Hours/week: String}*
Manages	*{Startdate: Date, Type: String}*

Set of elementary concepts Φ(*A*) = {*String, Integer, Date, Employee, Manager, Department, Project, Belongto, Worksfor, Responsiblefor, Manages*}

Set of elementary roles Φ(*P*) = {*IDEmp, FirstName, LastName, Name, Birthday, Salary, joindate, IDDepart, NameDep, Locations, Profit, Hours/week, IDPro, Budget, Startdate, Type, Rank, emp, act, bein, belg, refor, reby, man, prj*}

Set of term axioms of Σ as the following:

- Entity sets and their attributes

$$Employee \sqsubseteq \forall IDEmp.String \sqcap \forall Name.(\forall Firstname.String \sqcap$$
$$\forall Lastname.String \sqcap (= 1Firstname) \sqcap (= 1Lastname)) \sqcap$$
$$\forall Birthday.Date \sqcap \forall Salary.Integer \sqcap (= 1IDEmp) \sqcap$$
$$(= 1Name) \sqcap (= 1Birthday) \sqcap (= 1Salary)$$
$$Department \sqsubseteq \forall IDDepart.String \sqcap \forall NameDepart.String \sqcap$$
$$(\geq 1Locations.String) \sqcap \forall Profit.Integer \sqcap (= 1IDDepart) \sqcap$$
$$(= 1NameDepart) \sqcap (= 1Profit)) \sqcap (\neg \geq 1Locations.\neg String)$$
$$Project \sqsubseteq \forall IDPro.String \sqcap \forall Budget.Integer \sqcap$$
$$(= 1IDPro) \sqcap (= 1Budget)$$
$$Manager \sqsubseteq Employee \sqcap \forall Rank.String \sqcap (= 1Rank)$$

- Relationships and their attributes

$$Belongto \sqsubseteq \forall joindate.Date \sqcap (= 1joindate)$$
$$Worksfor \sqsubseteq \forall Hours/week.String \sqcap (= 1Hours/week)$$
$$Manages \sqsubseteq \forall Startdate.Date \sqcap \forall Type.String \sqcap$$
$$(= 1Startdate) \sqcap (= 1Type)$$

- Relationships with connecting role between these relationships and entity sets

$$Belongto \sqsubseteq \forall bein.Employee \sqcap \forall belg.Department \sqcap$$
$$(= 1bein) \sqcap (= 1belg)$$
$$Workfor \sqsubseteq \forall emp.Employee \sqcap \forall act.Project \sqcap (= 1emp) \sqcap (= 1act)$$
$$Responsiblefor \sqsubseteq \forall refor.Department \sqcap \forall reby.Project \sqcap$$
$$(= 1refor) \sqcap (= 1reby)$$
$$Manages \sqsubseteq \forall man.Manager \sqcap \forall prj.Project \sqcap (= 1man) \sqcap (= 1prj)$$

- Non-temporal constraints

$$Employee \sqsubseteq (= 1bein^-.Belongto) \sqcap (= 1emp^-.Worksfor)$$
$$Project \sqsubseteq (= 1prj^-.Manages) \sqcap (= 1reby^-.Responsiblefor) \sqcap$$
$$(\geq 1act^-.Worksfor)$$
$$Department \sqsubseteq (\geq 1belg^-.Belongto) \sqcap (\geq 1refor^-.Responsiblefor)$$
$$Manager \sqsubseteq (= 1man^-.Manages)$$

- Keys of entity sets

$$Employee \sqsubseteq (= 1^* IDEmp)$$
$$\top \sqsubseteq (\leq 1 IDEmp^-.Employee)$$
$$Department \sqsubseteq (= 1^* IDDepart)$$
$$\top \sqsubseteq (\leq 1 IDDepart^-.Department)$$
$$Project \sqsubseteq (= 1^* IDPro)$$
$$\top \sqsubseteq (\leq 1 IDPro^-.Project)$$

- Distinguishing temporal and non-temporal entity sets

$$Employee \sqsubseteq (\sim^+ Employee) \sqcap (\sim^- Employee)$$
$$Project \sqsubseteq (\sim^+ Project) \sqcap (\sim^- Project)$$
$$Department \sqsubseteq (\sim^+ Department) \sqcap (\sim^- Department)$$
$$Manager \sqsubseteq (^+\neg Manager) \sqcup (^-\neg Manager)$$

- Distinguishing temporal and non-temporal relationships

$$Belongto \sqsubseteq (\sim^+ Belongto) \sqcap (\sim^- Belongto)$$
$$Belongto \sqsubseteq (= 1 \sim^* bein) \sqcap (= 1 \sim^* belg)$$
$$Responsiblefor \sqsubseteq (\sim^+ Responsiblefor) \sqcap (\sim^- Responsiblefor)$$
$$Responsiblefor \sqsubseteq (= 1 \sim^* reby) \sqcap (= 1 \sim^* refor)$$
$$Workfor \sqsubseteq (^+\neg Workfor) \sqcup (^-\neg Workfor) \sqcup$$
$$\neg ((= 1^* act) \sqcap (= 1^* emp))$$
$$Manages \sqsubseteq (^+\neg Manages) \sqcup (^-\neg Manages) \sqcup$$
$$\neg ((= 1 \sim^* man) \sqcap (= 1 \sim^* prj))$$

- Attributes with and without time factor

$$Employee \sqsubseteq (= 1 \sim^* Name).((= 1 \sim^* FirstName) \sqcap$$
$$(= 1 \sim^* LastName)) \sqcap (= 1 \sim^* Birthday)$$
$$Employee \sqsubseteq \neg (= 1 \sim^* Salary)$$
$$Department \sqsubseteq (= 1 \sim^* NameDep) \sqcap (= 1 \sim^* Locations)$$
$$Department \sqsubseteq \neg (= 1 \sim^* Profit)$$
$$Project \sqsubseteq (= 1 \sim^* Budget)$$
$$Manager \sqsubseteq (= 1 \sim^* Rank)$$
$$Belongto \sqsubseteq (= 1 \sim^* joindate)$$
$$Worksfor \sqsubseteq (= 1 \sim^* Hours/week)$$
$$Manages \sqsubseteq (= 1 \sim^* Startdate) \sqcap (= 1 \sim^* Type)$$

- Constraint of living time

$$Manager \sqsubseteq (\geq 1man^-.{}^*Manages) \sqcap (\leq 5man^-.{}^*Manages)$$

4 Conclusion

In this paper, we have shown the representation of implicit and explicit TimeER models with temporal description logic. In addition, we have implemented representation multi-valued and compound attribute on TimeER models with inclusive axioms in description logic. The paper will also present an application of description logic in modeling TimeER model with the above approaches.

Besides, in practice there are still many extending issues in theory of description logic and its applications in the field of the database. Therefore, according to this research, we will continue to use description logic to perform database models having the time factor, which are relational database model and object-oriented database model.

References

1. Artale, A., Kontchakov, R., Ryzhikov, V., Zakharyaschev, M.: Tailoring temporal description logics for reasoning over temporal conceptual models. In: Tinelli, C., Sofronie-Stokkermans, V. (eds.) FroCoS 2011. LNCS, vol. 6989, pp. 1–11. Springer, Heidelberg (2011)
2. Artale, A., Franconi, E., Wolter, F., Zakharyaschev, M.: Reasoning over conceptual schemas and queries in temporal database. In: Proceedings of the 9th Italian Database Conference (2002)
3. Artale, A., Franconi, E.: Reasoning with enhanced temporal entity-relationship models. In: Proceedings of the International Workshop on Spatio-Temporal Data Models and Languages. IEEE Computer Society Press, Also in Proceedings of the 6th International Workshop on Knowledge Representation meets Databases (KRDB 1999), and in Proceedings of the 1999 International Workshop on Description Logics (DL 1999) (1999)
4. Calvanes, D., Lenzerini, M., Nardi, D.: Description logics for conceptual data modeling. In: Chomicki, J., Saake, G. (eds.) Logics for Databases and Information Systems. Kluwer Academic Publisher (1998)
5. Artale, A., Franconi, E.: Temporal ER modelling with description logics. In: Akoka, J., Bouzeghoub, M., Comyn-Wattiau, I., Métais, E. (eds.) ER 1999. LNCS, vol. 1728, pp. 81–95. Springer, Heidelberg (1999)
6. Artale, A., Franconi, E., Mandreoli, F.: Description logics for modelling dynamic information. In: Chomicki, J., van der Meyden, R., Saake, G. (eds.) Logics for Emerging Applications of Databases. LNCS, pp. 239–275. Springer, Heidelberg (2003)
7. Baader, F., Calvanese, D., McGuinness, D., Nardi, D., Patel-Shneiter, P.F.: The Description Logic Handbook: Theory, Implementation and Applications, 2nd edn. Cambridge University Press, Cambridge (2007)

8. Artale, A., Franconi, E.: Foundations of temporal conceptual data models. In: Borgida, A.T., Chaudhri, V.K., Giorgini, P., Yu, E.S. (eds.) Conceptual Modeling: Foundations and Applications. LNCS, vol. 5600, pp. 10–35. Springer, Heidelberg (2009)
9. Rudolph, S.: Foundations of Description Logics. Karlsruhe Institute of Technology, Germany (2011)
10. Hoang, Q., Van Nguyen, T.: Extraction of a temporal conceptual model from a relational database. Int. J. Intell. Inf. Database Syst. **7**(4), 340–355 (2013)

Querying Object-Oriented Databases Based on Signature File Hierarchy and Signature Graph

Tran Minh Bao[✉] and Truong Cong Tuan

College of Science, Hue University,
77 Nguyen Hue Street, Hue City, Viet Nam
tmbaovn@gmail.com, tctuan_it_dept@yahoo.com

Abstract. Chen and his partners [2] proposed an approach which combines nested signature file hierarchy and signature graph as follow: (1) all files containing signatures are organized in a hierarchy for a quick filter of unsuitable data; (2) Each signature file is stored in a graph structure (called signature graph) to speed up signature scanning. This technique reduces significantly searching space, so it improves significantly query time complexity. In this paper, we improve query algorithm on signature graph based on the approach proposed by Chen and his partners, to improve query time on signature graph.

Keywords: Object-oriented query · Object signature · Signature file · Signature graph

1 Introduction

Study of indexing technique is always an important issue in effective information searching from databases. For object-oriented databases, direct query on objects has a large time cost. There are many database indexing techniques to process query on object-oriented databases in which signature file approach has been widely acknowledged and been an effective approach in processing query on object-oriented databases. For this approach, objects of a class are coded into object signatures by using hash function and stored in a signature file. However, query on signature file has a disadvantage which is high cost due to scanning the whole file. Some other indexing methods try to overcome this and can be found in many researches [1–3, 8, 9].

In this paper, we propose improvement of query algorithm on signature graph which can be used to improve query time. Firstly, we organize sequential signature files in nested signature file hierarchy to reduce searching space during querying. Then we store each signature file in signature graph to speed up signature file scanning. The larger signature file is, the more time can be saved by using this approach.

This paper is organized as follows. In part 2, we provide background. Part 3 proposes an improved approach of algorithm on signature graph. Part 4 proposes an approach combining signature file hierarchy and signature graph. Finally, part 5 gives out a conclusion.

© ICST Institute for Computer Sciences, Social Informatics and Telecommunications Engineering 2016
P.C. Vinh and V. Alagar (Eds.): ICCASA 2015, LNICST 165, pp. 298–308, 2016.
DOI: 10.1007/978-3-319-29236-6_29

2   Background

This part only presents some basic concepts related to object signatures, signature files. Further information can be found in [1, 2].

2.1   Attribute Signature

In an object-oriented database, each object is presented by a set of attribute values. Signature of an attribute value is a sequence of hashed-code bits. Given an attribute value, for example the word "student", we decompose it into a string of three-letter sets as follow: "stu", "tud", "ude", "den" and "ent". Then, using hash function h, we map a triplet to an integer k which means kth bit in a string assigned value 1. For example, assuming that we have h(stu) = 2, h(tud) = 7, h(ude) = 10, h(den) = 5 and h(ent) = 11. Then we create a bit string: 010 010 100 110 which is signature of the word.

2.2   Attribute Signature, Signature File

Object signature is constructed by logical OR algorithm for all signatures of attribute values of the object. Below is an example of an attribute signature:

Example 1. Consider an object which has attribute values of "student", "12345678", "professor". Suppose that signature of these attributes is:

$$
\begin{array}{cccc}
010 & 010 & 100 & 110 \\
100 & 010 & 010 & 100 \\
110 & 100 & 011 & 000
\end{array}
$$

In this case, object signature is 110 110 111 110, generated from attribute signatures by using logical OR algorithm. Object signatures of a class are stored in a file, called object signature file.

2.3   Query Signature

An object query will be encoded into a query signature together with hash function applied to objects. When a query needs to be executed, object signatures will be scanned and unmatched objects will be excluded. Then query signature is compared with object signatures of signature file. There are three possibilities:

(i)   The object matches with the query, i.e., for every bit in query signature s_q, corresponding bit in object signature s is the same, i.e., $s_q \wedge s = s_q$, a real object of query.
(ii) The object does not match with the query, i.e., $s_q \wedge s \neq s_q$;
(iii) Signatures are compared and matching one is found but its object does not match with searching condition of the query. To eliminate this case, objects must be checked after object signatures are matched.

Example 2. This example illustrates the query for object signature in Example 1:

Query :	Query signature :				Result :
student	010	000	100	110	successful
john	011	000	100	100	unsuccessful
11223344	110	100	100	000	false drop

Comment: comparing query signature s_q object signature s is incorrect comparison. That means, query signature s_q matches with signature s if for any 1 bit in s_q, the corresponding bit in s is also 1 bit. However, for any 0 bit in s_q, the corresponding bit in s can be 0 or 1.

2.4   Querying Object-Oriented Databases

In object-oriented CSDL system, an entity displayed according to object type including methods and properties. Objects have similar methods and properties gathered in the same layer. If the C layer has a complex property with domain C', so we shall create relation between C and C'. This relation is general relation. When using arrow to connect layers for displaying general relation, need to create general hierarchy for displaying nested structure of layers.

Example 3. This is an example about nested object hierarchy system illustrated like this:

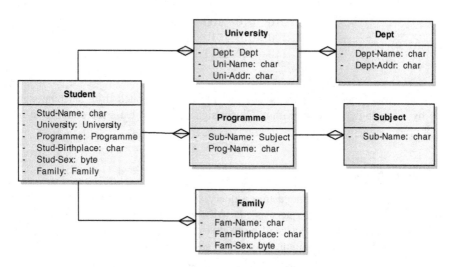

Fig. 1. An example of a nested object hierarchy

Object o referenced is a property of object o', then object o considered as nested with each other in o', and o' considered as 'father-object' of o.

In object-oriented CSDL, condition found in query collected in a collection of properties. This property is a nested property of target layers.

Example 4. The query "retrieve all students born in *Ben Tre* of dept *information technology*" can be expressed as:

```
Select Student
Where Student.Stud-Birthplace = "Ben Tre"
And   Student.University.Dept.Dept-Name  =  "information
technology"
```

Without indexing structures, the above query can be evaluated in a top-down manner as follows. First, the system has to retrieve all of the objects in the class Student and single out those who were born in *Ben Tre*. Then, the system retrieves the University objects referenced by the Student born in *Ben Tre* and checks the Dept-Name of the Dept. Finally, those Students born in *Ben Tre* by a University that has Dept *information technology* are returned.

2.5   Signature File Hierarchy and Query Algorithm

2.5.1   Signature File Hierarchy

Purpose of using signature file: remove unconditional objects, it means if we have a signature is not suitable with query signature so the object related with this signature surely ignored. So therefore we do not need to access to these objects.

Example 5. Signature and signature file hierarchy:

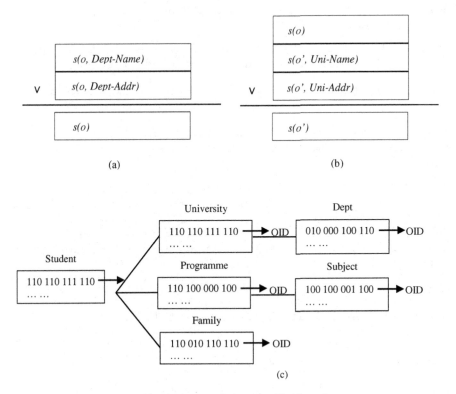

Fig. 2. Signature and signature file hierarchy

Considering Dept layer in 0 hierarchy of complex properties in Fig. 1. Signature of o object can be created by method in Fig. 2(a), each $s(o, x)$ signature symbol created for property value x of o and $s(o)$ signature symbol o. To layers of complex properties, signature of objects can be created with the same method, like layer of original properties. Difference: signature of complex property is signature of referenced object illustrated in Fig. 2(b). In Fig. 2(b), o' marked object of University layer. And o object of Dept layer is Dept's property value of o'. Hierarchy of signature file is used for creating databases displayed in Fig. 1 also illustrated in Fig. 2(c).

2.5.2   Query Algorithm Based on Signature File

We use query signature-tree to decrease searching-space. In this method, we need two *stack* structures to control prioritize scanning according to depth of tree structures: $stack_q$ to $Q(s, t)$ and $stack_c$ to class hierarchy. In $stack_q$, each component is a signature, meanwhile in $stack_c$, each component is a collection of objects belong to the same layer can be approached by scanning class-hierarchy.

Algorithm 1. [4] top-down-hierarchy-retrieval;

Input: an object query Q;

Output: a set of OIDs whose texts satisfy the query.

Method:

Step 1. Compute the query signature hierarchy $Q_{(s,t)}$ for the query Q.

Step 2. Push the root signature of $Q_{(s,t)}$ into $stack_q$; push the set of object OID of the target class into $stack_c$.

Step 3. If $stack_q$ is not empty, s_q←pop $stack_q$; else go to (7).

Step 4. S←pop $stack_c$; for each oid_i E S, if its signature $osig_i$ does not compare s_q, remove it from S; put S in S_{result}.

Step 5. Let C be the class to which the objects of S belong; let C_1, ..., C_k be the subclasses of C; then partition the OID set of the objects referenced by the objects of S into S_1, ..., S_k such that S_i belongs to C_i; push S_1, ..., S_k into $stack_c$; push the child nodes of s_q into $stack_q$.

Step 6. Go to (3).

Step 7. For each leaf object, check false drops.

This technique helps for optimization when we implement step (4). In this step, some objects selected by using corresponding signature in query signature tree. In step (5), referenced objects and son-node's signatures of query signature tree is added to $stack_c$ and $stack_q$. In step (7), we will conduct inspection on errors.

Example 6. Assuming we have a part of signature file hierarchy is created for a CSDL based on a diagram in Fig. 1 belongs to type described in Fig. 3:

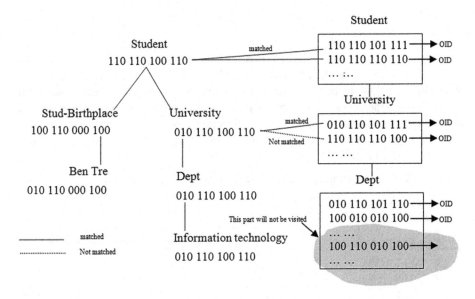

Fig. 3. Illustration of query evaluation

When the first signatures of signature-file for Student is suitable with signature in query signature tree, signatures are referenced by themselves in signature file for University need to have additional inspection. Assuming we have the first signature of University is referenced by the first signature in Student meanwhile the second signature in University is referenced by the second signature in Student. We can see that the second signature in University is not suitable with corresponding signature in query signature tree. Therefore, all signatures of Dept object is referenced by Dept object won't be inspected (watching grey illustration in Fig. 3). This method is optimal method when comparing with "searching from top to bottom" because in "searching from top to bottom" must inspect all Dept's object-signatures.

2.6   Signature Graph

2.6.1   Construction of Signature Graph
To find a matching signature, a signature file has to be scanned. If it is large, the amount of time elapsed for searching such a file becomes significant. The first idea to

improve this process is to sort the signature file and then employ a binary searching. Unfortunately, this does not work due to the fact that a signature file is only an inexact filter. The following example helps for illustration.

Example 7. Consider a sorted signature file containing only three signatures:

$$010 \quad 000 \quad 100 \quad 110$$
$$010 \quad 100 \quad 011 \quad 000$$
$$100 \quad 010 \quad 010 \quad 100$$

Assume that the query signature s_q is equal to 000 010 010 100. It matches 100 010 010 100. However, if we use a binary search, 100 010 010 100 cannot be found. On the other side, there might be the same signatures in the signature file that match with objects having the same content, query processing needs to find out all locations of suitable objects. Due to this reason, we will organize signature file in a graph, called signature graph, to store signature list and allow reverse query for location of corresponding data. We have the following definition:

Example 8. Consider the signature file and signature graph (Fig. 4):

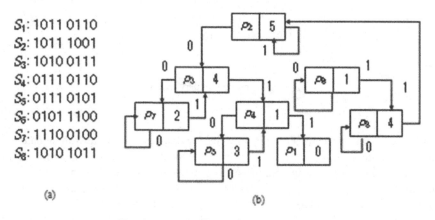

Fig. 4. Signature file and signature graph

3 Improved Algorithm

In this part, we propose improvement of query algorithm on signature graph [3] which can be used to improve query time as follows:

3.1 Improved Algorithm for Signature Graph Search

Algorithm 2 signature-graphs-search

Input: a query signature Sq;

Output: set of signatures which survive the checking;

Method:

Step 1. Compute the Signature weight for the query signature.

Step 2. Set←∅

Step 3. Push the root of the signature tree into stack$_p$.

Step 4. If stack$_p$ is not empty, v←pop(stack$_p$); else return (Set).

Step 5. If v is not a marked node and skip ≠ 0, i←skip(v); mark v;

If S_q=0, push C_r and C_l into stack$_p$; (where C_r and C_l are v's right and left child, respectively) otherwise, put only C_r into stack$_p$.

Step 6. If signature weight is smaller than 50% then search the query signature in the signature nodes for the unset bits.

Step 7. Else search the query signature in the signature nodes for the set bits

Step 8. Compare S_q with the signature pointed by p(v).

(p(v) pointer to a signature)

If S_q matches, Set ← Set ∪ {p(v)}.

Step 9. Go to (3).

3.2 Time Complexity

From [3], query time complexity on signature graph is $O(N/2^l)$, where N is the number of signatures in the signature file and l is the number of bit 1 put in query signature S_q.

If query signature weight is higher than 50 % then the number of bit 1 is larger than the number of bit 0 in S_q. Let k be the number of bit 0 put in query signature S_q, then we have $O(N/2^l) > O(N/2^k)$. Otherwise, $O(N/2^l) < O(N/2^k)$.

The above analysis shows that if signature weight is higher than 50 %, comparison between query signature and signature of signature file will be based on bit 1. Otherwise, it will be based on bit 0, this way can improve query time on signature graph.

4 Approach Combining Signature File Hierarchy and Signature Graph

4.1 Query Data Structure Model

To improve query time on databases, we need to describe data structure in a more simple way and build a corresponding data structure to reduce searching space during implementing query while ensuring query of necessary objects by using signature graph. From [3], to make query more optimized, we need to combine signature file hierarchy and signature graph, this issue has been proved to improve query time better. From Algorithm 3, query time complexity on signature graph is smaller than query time complexity of Algorithm 2. Thus, we still use signature file hierarchy as in [3], but replace Algorithm 2 with Algorithm 3 to improve query time better.

Base on theoretical basis and suggested algorithm, the paper proposes improved approach for query algorithm on signature graph combining signature file hierarchy as follows: (1) Each signature file is stored in signature graph structure to speed up signature file scanning; (2) All of signature files are organized in hierarchy to facilitate implementing step by step filter technique.

Example 9. Construction of signature graph is illustrated as below (Fig. 5):

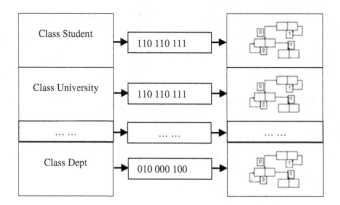

Fig. 5. Construction signature graph

Example 10. Combination of signature file hierarchy and signature graph is illustrated as follow (Fig. 6):

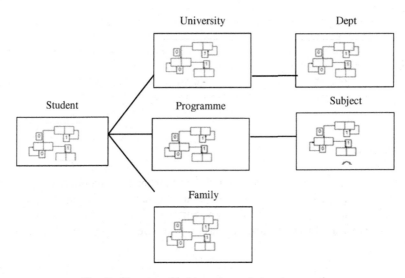

Fig. 6. Signature file hierarchy and signature graph

Data structure is totally stored in the main memory, in this case, inserting or deleting a signature on a signature graph can be done easily. However, files are very large in databases, so database structure cannot store in the main memory but in the external memory. For object-oriented databases, they will be stored and implemented on the external memory. An object-oriented database has many classes, each class has many objects. There is a signature graph structure corresponding with each class, also each object will form an object signature. The entire object-oriented database is partitioned in a hash table structure including object's signatures to implement query process.

4.2   Object-Oriented Query Processing

To execute a query of an object in an object-oriented database, firstly we have to change an object-oriented database into data structure as above, we do:

```
Step 1. Attribute of the object is hashed into binary
signatures and attributes which form object signatures.
Step 2. Object signatures in a same layer will form
signature graphs.
Step 3. Create signature file hierarchy where each file
is a signature graph.
```

After having data structure for query, we execute object query process on object-oriented databases as follow:

```
Step 1. Encode key words which need to be retrieved into
binary signature.
Step 2. Execute key word signature query to determine
classes which need to be searched.
Step 3. Execute key word signature query on signature
graphs corresponding with determined classes.
```

5 Conclusion

In this paper, we propose a query algorithm improvement on signature graph. Signature graph structure is built on signature file for a class and help improve significantly signature file searching. Signature files are built up to a hierarchy with structure of nested classes in an object-oriented database to improve significantly query time.

References

1. Chen, Y., Chen, Y.: On the signature tree construction and analysis. IEEE Trans. Knowl. Data Eng. **18**(9), 1207–1224 (2006)
2. Chen, Y.: Building signature trees into OODBs. J. Inf. Sci. Eng. **20**(2), 275–304 (2004)
3. Chen, Y., Chen, Y.: Signature file hierarchies and signature graphs: a new index method for object-oriented databases. In: Proceedings of the 2004 ACM Symposium on Applied Computing, Nicosia, Cyprus, pp. 724–728, 14–17 March, 2004
4. Dervos, D., Manolopulos, Y., Linardis, P.: Comparison of signature file models with superimposed coding. J. Inf. Proc. Lett. **65**, 101–106 (1998)
5. Faloutsos, C.: Signature files: design and performance comparaison of some signature extraction methods. ACM Sigmod Rec. **14**(4), 63–82 (1985)
6. Lee, D.L., Kim, Y.M., Patel, G.: Efficient signature file methods for text retrieval. IEEE Trans. Knowl. Data Eng. **7**(3), 423–435 (1995)
7. Lee, W.C., Lee, D.L.: Signature file methods for indexing object-oriented database systems. In: Proceedings of the 2nd International Computer Science Conference, Hong Kong, pp. 616–622 (1992)
8. Mahatthanapiwat, P.: Flexible searching for graph aggregation hierarchy. In: Proceedings of the World Congress on Engineering, London, UK, pp. 405–409, June 30–July 2, 2010
9. Tousidoua, E., Bozanis, P., Manolopoulos, Y.: Signature-based structures for objects with set-valued attributes. Elsevier Sci. Inf. Syst. **27**(2), 93–121 (2002)

Query Optimization in Object Oriented Databases Based on Signature File Hierarchy and SD-Tree

Tran Minh Bao[(⊠)] and Truong Cong Tuan

College of Science, Hue University, 77 Nguyen Hue Street, Hue City, Viet Nam
tmbaovn@gmail.com, tctuan_it_dept@yahoo.com

Abstract. Direct query on objects in object-oriented databases costs a lot of data storage during query processing and time to execute query on real data systems. Recently, there are many researches focusing on resolving that problem by indexing on single classes, class hierarchies or nested objects hierarchies. In this paper, we propose a new indexing approach. This approach is based on the technique of using signature files and SD-Trees where signature files are in hierarchical organization to quickly filter irrelevant data and each signature file is stored in the similar structure with SD-Tree to fasten signatures scanning. This technique helps reduce significantly searching space, hence improves significantly time complexity of query.

Keywords: Object-oriented database system · Index · Signature file · SD-Tree · Object-oriented query

1 Introduction

Direct query on objects in object-oriented databases costs a lot of data storage during processing query and time to execute query on real data system. The problem is to describe data system in a more simple way and construct a corresponding data structure to reduce searching space during executing query while necessary objects are ensured to be searched.

To reduce space of data query, proposed indexing techniques used to evaluate query in databases [6] have been developed based on binary tree balancing mechanism which was added some special characteristics to reduce tree balance or minimize accesses to data files. These techniques have been developed to increase query speed in object-oriented databases [10–12]. The main idea is that each SD-Tree on a class in hierarchy is remained but indexes are nested by relation of subclass–target class. Besides indexes in inherited hierarchy structure, many indexing approaches used for nested characteristic query have been proposed [1–3, 7, 9]. Instead of concentrating on inherited hierarchy of classes, researchers have discovered general hierarchy of classes and proposed different index structures following nested characteristics [1, 2, 7, 9] … Signature file storage structures will reduce searching space and optimize data query process.

© ICST Institute for Computer Sciences, Social Informatics and Telecommunications Engineering 2016
P.C. Vinh and V. Alagar (Eds.): ICCASA 2015, LNICST 165, pp. 309–321, 2016.
DOI: 10.1007/978-3-319-29236-6_30

It is necessary to construct a data structure for signature file storage to improve searching. These signature file storage structures can be in form of sequential signature files, sliced signature files, signature tree structure, signature graph structure... where the cost of sliced signature file storage is double of sequential signature files and triple of sequential signature files or more [8]. The main advantage of this approach is its effect in processing new insert and query to parts of word. However, when comparing with indexing based on tree structure, using sequential signature files has 2 disadvantages: (1) they cannot be used to evaluate range query; (2) for each processed query, entire signature files need to be scanned, it makes I/O processing cost increase.

In this paper, we try to improve the second problem to a certain point. Firstly, we organize sequential signature files in hierarchical structure to reduce searching space during query evaluating process. Next, we store signature files in form of a SD-Tree to execute scanning only one single signature file. If signature file size is large, time saved by this approach is really significant. In fact, this is a B^+-tree constructed by signature files. Therefore, it can speed up the process of identifying signature position in a signature file. However, in a signature tree, each path is corresponding with one signature identification which can be used to determine its only corresponding signature in signature file. This way helps quickly find out a set of corresponding signatures with query signature.

The remaining of this paper is presented as follows. In Part 2, we provide background. Part 3 proposes an approach combining signature files and SD-Tree hierarchy. Finally, Part 4 gives the conclusion.

2   Background

2.1   Characteristic Signature

In an object-oriented database, each object is presented by a set of characteristic values. Signature of an characteristic value is a sequence of hashed-code bits. Given an characteristic value, for example the word "student", we decompose it into a string of three-letter sets as follow: "stu", "tud", "ude", "den" and "ent". Then, using hash function h, we map a triplet to an integer k which means kth bit in a string assigned value 1. For example, assuming that we have h(stu) = 2, h(tud) = 7, h(ude) = 10, h (den) = 5 and h(ent) = 11. Then we create a bit string: 010 010 100 110 which is signature of the word.

2.2   Characteristic Signature, Signature File

Object signature is constructed by logical OR algorithm for all signatures of characteristic values of the object. Below is an example of an characteristic signature:

Example 1. Consider an object which has characteristic values of "student", "12345678", "professor". Suppose that signature of these characteristic is:

$$
\begin{array}{cccc}
010 & 010 & 100 & 110 \\
100 & 010 & 010 & 100 \\
110 & 100 & 011 & 000
\end{array}
$$

In this case, object signature is 110 110 111 110, generated from characteristic signatures by using logical OR algorithm. Object signatures of a class are stored in a file, called object signature file.

2.3   Query Signature

An object query will be encoded into a query signature together with hash function applied to objects. When a query needs to be executed, object signatures will be scanned and unmatched objects will be excluded. Then query signature is compared with object signatures of signature file. There are three possibilities:

(i)   The object matches with the query, i.e., for every bit in query signature s_q, corresponding bit in object signature s is the same, i.e., $s_q \wedge s = s_q$, a real object of query.
(ii) The object does not match with the query, i.e., $s_q \wedge s \neq s_q$;
(iii) Signatures are compared and matching one is found but its object does not match with searching condition of the query. To eliminate this case, objects must be checked after object signatures are matched.

Example 2. This example illustrates the query for object signature in Example 1:

Query :	Query signature :				Result :
student	010	000	100	110	successful
john	011	000	100	100	unsuccessful
11223344	110	100	100	000	false drop

Comment: comparing query signature s_q to object signature s is incorrect comparison. That means, query signature s_q matches with signature s if for any 1 bit in s_q, the corresponding bit in s is also 1 bit. However, for any 0 bit in s_q, the corresponding bit in s can be 0 or 1.

2.4   Querying Object-Oriented Databases

In object-oriented CSDL system, an entity displayed according to object type including methods and properties. Objects have similar methods and properties gathered in the same layer. If the C layer has a complex property with domain C', so we shall create relation between C and C'. This relation is a general relation. When using arrows to connect layers for displaying general relation, have to create general hierarchies for displaying nested structure of layers.

Example 3. An example for nested object hierarchy system illustrated such as follows:

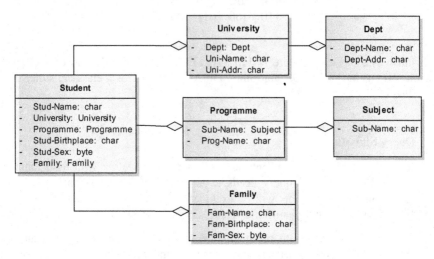

Fig. 1. An example of a nested object hierarchy

Object *o* referenced is a property of object *o'*, then object *o* considered as nested in *o'*, and *o'* considered as 'father-object' of *o*.

In object-oriented CSDL system, condition found in query collected in a properties collection. This property is nested property of target layers.

Example 4. The query "retrieve all students born in *Ben Tre* of dept *information technology*" can be expressed as:

```
Select Student
Where Student.Stud-Birthplace = "Ben Tre"
And   Student.University.Dept.Dept-Name  =  "information
technology"
```

Without indexing structures, the above query can be evaluated in a top-down manner as follows. First, the system has to retrieve all of the objects in the class Student and single out those who were born in *Ben Tre*. Then, the system retrieves the University objects referenced by the Student born in *Ben Tre* and checks the Dept-Name of the Dept. Finally, those Students born in *Ben Tre* by a University that has Dept *information technology* are returned.

2.5   Signature File Hierarchy and Query Algorithm

2.5.1   Signature File Hierarchy

Purpose of using signature file: remove unconditional objects, means if a signature is not suitable with query signature so the object related with this signature surely ignored. So therefore we do not need to access to these objects.

Example 5. Signature and signature file hierarchy:

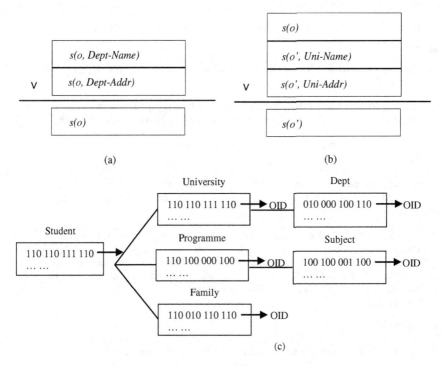

(a)   (b)

(c)

Fig. 2. Signature and signature file hierarchy

Considering Dept layer in 0 hierarchy of complex properties in Fig. 1. Signature of o object can be created by method in Fig. 2(a), each $s(o, x)$ signature symbol created for property value x of o and $s(o)$ signature symbol o. To layers of complex properties, signature of objects can be created with the same method, like layer of original properties. Difference: signature of complex property is signature of referenced object illustrated in Fig. 2(b). In Fig. 2(b), o' marked object of University layer. And o object of Dept layer is property value of Dept of o'. Hierarchy of signature file can be used for building database displayed in Fig. 1 also illustrated in Fig. 2(c).

2.5.2   Query Algorithm Based on Signature File

Using query signature tree to decrease searching space. This method, we need two *stack* structures to control prioritize scanning according to depth of tree structures: $stack_q$ to $Q(s, t)$ and $stack_c$ to class hierarchy. In $stack_q$, each component is a signature, meanwhile in $stack_c$, each component is a collection of objects belong to the same layer can be approached by scanning class hierarchy.

Algorithm 1. [4] top-down-hierarchy-retrieval;

Input: an object query Q;

Output: a set of OIDs whose texts satisfy the query.

Method:

Step 1. Compute the query signature hierarchy $Q_{(s,t)}$ for the query Q.

Step 2. Push the root signature of $Q_{(s,t)}$ into $stack_q$; push the set of object OID of the target class into $stack_c$.

Step 3. If $stack_q$ is not empty, $s_q \leftarrow$ pop $stack_q$; else go to (7).

Step 4. $S \leftarrow$ pop $stack_c$; for each oid_i E S, if its signature $osig_i$ does not compare s_q, remove it from S; put S in S_{result}.

Step 5. Let C be the class to which the objects of S belong; let C_1, ..., C_k be the subclasses of C; then partition the OID set of the objects referenced by the objects of S into S_1, ..., S_k such that S_i belongs to C_i; push S_1, ..., S_k into $stack_c$; push the child nodes of s_q into $stack_q$.

Step 6.Go to (3).

Step 7. For each leaf object, check false drops.

This technique helps for optimization when implementing step (4). In this step, some objects selected by using corresponding signature in query signature tree. In step (5), referenced objects and son node's signatures of query signature tree is added to $stack_c$ and $stack_q$. In step (7), conduct inspection on errors.

Example 6. Assuming a part of signature file hierarchy created for a CSDL according to a diagram in Fig. 1 belongs to type described in Fig. 3:

When the first signatures of signature file for Student suitable with signature in query signature tree, signatures are referenced by themselves in signature file for University need to have additional inspection. Assuming the first signature of University is referenced by the first signature in Student meanwhile the second signature in University is referenced by the second signature in Student. We can see that the second signature in University is not suitable with corresponding signature in query signature tree. Therefore all signatures of Dept object is referenced by Dept object won't be inspected (watching grey illustration in Fig. 3). This method is optimal method when comparing with "searching from top to bottom" because in "searching from top to bottom" must inspect all object signatures of Dept.

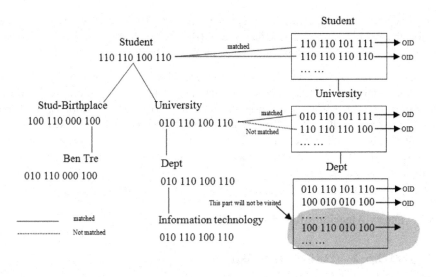

Fig. 3. Illustration of query evaluation

2.6   SD-Tree

2.6.1   Overall Structure of SD-Tree

Technique on creating index in Object-Oriented CSDL system using dynamic balance method of B^+-tree called SD-Tree (Signature Declustering). In this implementation, positions of bit 1 in signature is overall via collection of leaf node. Using this method for an available query signature, so all matched signatures can be queried accumulated in a single-node. Querying, optimal searching method is considered to boost speed of total progress.

Example 7. Overall structure of SD-Tree (Fig. 4):

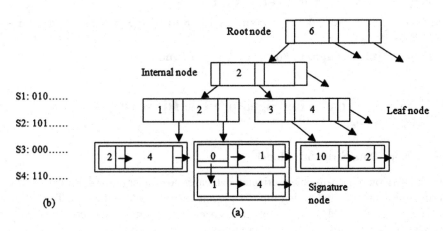

Fig. 4. Overall structure of SD-Tree [13]

Processing a query signature S_q, final appearance of bit 1 at position i in S_q is found out together with creating intermediate prefix (B). Then signature node of leaf node i accessed from root and all signatures with queried prefix B.

Example 8. Give $S_q = 011001000110$. To search all matched signatures S_q, SD-Tree considered well from root and node values compared with bit's position of S_q. Final appearance of 1 in S_q stay at position 11. Binary prefixes is created for S_q by using position of bit 1 such 0110010001. A node with key-value is 11 accessed in saved signature list bit 1 with collection type and all signatures in signatures list are inspected prefix value 0110010001. Therefore, except bit sample of S_q, all matched signatures are returned in a single-access.

2.6.2   Query Algorithm Based on SD-Tree

```
Algorithm 2. [14] Search(S_q)

Input: The (query) signature to search.

Output: The list of signatures matching the given
signature.

Method:
Step 1. Compute the Signature weight for the query
signature.

Step 2. If signature weight is greater than 50% then
search the query signature in the leaf nodes for the
unset bits.

Step 3. Else search the query signature in the leaf nodes
for the set bits.

Step 4. Access leaf node.

Step 5. Compare the prefix of Sq.

Step 6. If Found () then read and output the list of
signatures.

Step 7. Else report "no matching signatures".
```

3   Approach Combining Signature File Hierarchy and SD-Tree

3.1   Query Data Structure Model

Direct query on objects in object-oriented databases costs a large space for data storage during query process and a long time to execute query on real databases. To improve this problem, we need to represent data system more simply and construct corresponding data structure to reduce searching space during query executing process while necessary objects are still retrieved by using signature tree. From [4], to optimize the query we need to combine signature file hierarchy with signature tree. This has been shown to improve query time. From [13], query time complexity on SD-Tree is much smaller than signature tree's query time complexity. Therefore, we still use signature file hierarchy as in [4] but replace signature tree with SD-Tree to improve query time. Base on theory and suggested algorithms, this paper proposes an approach which combines signature file hierarchy with SD-Tree as follows: (1) all of signature files are organized in hierarchical structure to make it easier for executing stepwise filtering technique; (2) each signature file is stored in form of SD-Tree structure to speed up signature file scanning.

In an object-oriented database, each object is presented by a set of characteristic values. Signature of an characteristic is a string of hash-encoded bits. Object signature is constructed by overlapping all of characteristic signatures of the object. Object signatures of a class are stored in a file, called signature file. Signature files form SD-Tree.

Example 9. Construction of SD-Tree is illustrated as below (Fig. 5):

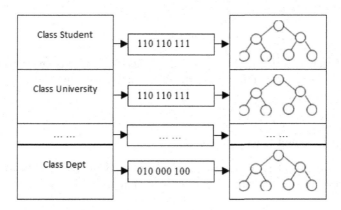

Fig. 5. SD-Tree construction

On an object-oriented database, if a class C has an characteristic that is composite with domain C', relation between C and C' will be created. This relation is called general relation. When connecting these classes by using arrows to present general relation, a general hierarchy is built to present nested structure of classes. Classes are encoded into signature files and signature files form signature file hierarchy. Each signature file forms a SD-Tree.

Example 10. Combination of signature file hierarchy and SD-Tree is illustrated as follow (Fig. 6):

Data structure is stored entirely in the main memory. In this case, inserting and deleting a signature on SD-Tree is executed easily. However, files in databases are usually very big. Therefore, data structure cannot be stored in the main memory but external memory. For object-oriented databases, they will be stored and executed in external memory. An object-oriented database has many classes, each class has many objects. A SD-Tree structure will be constructed corresponding with each class, in the

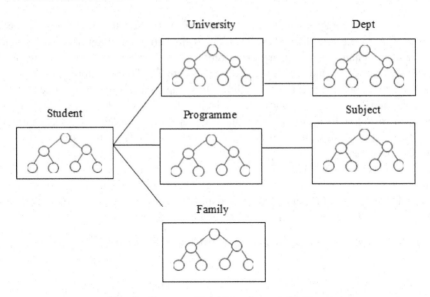

Fig. 6. Signature files hierarchy and SD-Tree

same time, each object will form an object signature. The entire object-oriented database will be organized in form of hash table structure including object signatures to execute queries.

3.2   Object-Oriented Query Processing

To execute a query of an object in an object-oriented database, firstly we have to change an object-oriented database into data structure as above. We do:

```
Step 1. Attribute of the object is hashed into binary
signatures and attributes which form object signatures.
Step 2. Object signatures in a same layer will form SD-
tree.
Step 3. Create signature file hierarchy where each file
is a SD-tree.
```

After having data structure for query, we execute object query process on object-oriented databases as follow:

```
Step 1. Encode key words which need to be retrieved into
binary signature.
Step 2. Execute key word signature query to determine
classes which need to be searched.
Step 3. Execute key word signature query on SD-tree
corresponding with determined classes.
```

3.3   Time Complexity

3.3.1   Comparison of Searching Between Young's Method and Signature File Hierarchy

In [4], to estimate objects accessed in a query using two different methods: (1) Yong method is recommended in [15]; (2) searching according to hierarchy from top to bottom.

(i) *Yong's method*

Yong method, signature of the referenced object will be saved in referenced objects. Then, we can inspect first-order logic on signatures of them before accessing. In this way, we do not need to implement too much mathematical methods I/O.

(ii) *Top down hierarchy retrieval*

This method helps us to select stronger than Yong's method. Because of inspection on a node in query signature hierarchy, not only first-order logic related to current node but also other first-order logics, their effects will be added into links leading to that node. Using query signature hierarchy, has objects in target layer will be removed by inspecting matched signature files, helps to decrease effectively accessed objects.

In [4], we can see that we can get high performance by using hierarchy search method from top to bottom from abstract perspective, query signature hierarchy is a "*general*" filter meanwhile cloning techniques developed by Yong is a "*internal*" filter. These two methods help to decrease accessed objects.

3.3.2   Comparison of Time Complexity Between Signature Tree and SD-Tree

(i) *Signature tree method*

In [13], complexity of time to insert into signature tree is $O(nF)$, n is amount of signatures of files and F is length of signature including bit 0 and bit 1. To signature tree, height of signature tree is limited: $O(\log_2 n)$, n is amount of leaf node. Costs used for searching signature tree normally is $O(\lambda.\log_2 n)$, λ is amount of ways passed.

(ii) *SD-Tree method*

In [13], SD-Tree used according to indexing structure for big data collection, F value is small, time used for creating SD-Tree will be decreased. Complexity of time to insert is limited: $O(n.m)$, n is amount of signatures in files and m is amount of bit 1 in available signature. Another useful characteristic of SD-Tree: with higher F value, by changing p value, h value, height of signature tree can be remained in low-level to boost speed of searching faster limited is $O(\log_p(F/p-1))$. Search time is used for a query with a collection of bit at i position, finally is total accessed time on leaf node (T_{li}) and time is used for searching signature node (T_{si}) is calculated like this:

$$T_s = T_{li} + T_{si}.$$

We can see that T_{li} doesn't change for all leaf nodes for a dynamic balance structure such as SD-Tree and T_{si} will be increased when the value of i is increased. Therefore, search time is limited is $O(T_{li} + 2^{i-1})$.

Comparing search time's complexity of signature tree is $O(\lambda.\log_2 n)$ and SD-Tree is $O(T_{li} + 2^{i-1})$, we can see that T_{li} value is very small comparing with λ value, that's a good point of SD-Tree.

4 Conclusion

In this paper, we propose a new indexing technique. This approach is a combination of signature file and SD-Tree hierarchy. To optimize scanning objects hierarchy, we base on signature file hierarchy to reduce number of sub-trees. However, because signature file only works as an incorrect filter, it cannot be ordered or binary searched, thus cannot be used to speed up signature scanning process. Hence, we propose construction of a SD-Tree on the file where signature appears as a node of signature file hierarchy. This technique can avoid sequential searching, thus help reduce time needed for searching on signature file.

References

1. Bertino, E.: Optimization of queries using nested indices. In: Proceedings of International Conference on Extending Database Technology, pp. 44–59 (1990)
2. Bertino, E., Guglielmani, C.: Optimization of object-oriented queries using path indices. In: 2nd International Workshop on Research Issues on Data Engineering: Transaction and Query Processing, pp. 140–149 (1992)
3. Choenni, S., Bertino, E., Blanken, H.M., Chang, T.: On the selection of optimal index configuration in OO databases. In: Proceedings of 10th International Conference on Data Engineering, pp. 526–537 (1994)
4. Chen, Y.: Building signature trees into OODBs. J. Inf. Sci. Eng. 20(2), 275–304 (2004)
5. Dervos, D., Manolopoulos, Y., Linardis, P.: Comparison of signature file models with superimposed coding. J. Inf. Proc. Lett. 65, 101–106 (1998)
6. Elmasri, R., Navathe, S.B.: Fundamentals of Database Systems. Benjamin Cumming, California (1989)
7. Fotouhi, F., Lee, T.G., Grosky, W.I.: The generalized index model for object-oriented database systems. In: 10th Annual International Phoenix Conference on Computers and Communication, pp. 302–308 (1991)
8. Ishikawa, Y., Kitagawa, H., Ohbo, N.: Evaluation of signature files as set access facilities in OODBs. In: Proceedings of ACM SIGMOD International Conference on Management of Data, pp. 247–256 (1993)
9. Kim, W., Kim, K.C., Dale, A.: Indexing Techniques for Object Oriented Databases, pp. 371–394. Addison Wesley, Reading (1989)
10. Kemper, A., Moerkotte, G.: Access support relations: an indexing method for object bases. Inf. Syst. 17, 117–145 (1992)

11. Low, C.C., Ooi, B.C., Lu, H.: H-trees: a dynamic associative search index for OODB. In: Proceedings of 1992 ACM SIGMOD Conference on the Management of Data, pp. 134–143 (1992)
12. Sreenath, B., Seshadri, S.: The hcC-tree: an efficient index structure for object oriented database. In: Proceedings of International Conference on Very Large Database, pp. 203–213 (1994)
13. Shanthi, I.E., Nadarajan, R.: Applying SD-tree for object-oriented query processing. Informatica (Slovenia) **33**(2), 169–179 (2009)
14. Thakur, A., Chauhan, M.: Optimizing search for fast query retrieval in object oriented databases using signature declustering. Int. J. Eng. Res. Dev. 46–50 (2012)
15. Yong, S., Lee, S., Kim, H.J.: Applying signatures for forward traversal query processing in object-oriented databases. In: Proceedings of 10th International Conference on Data Engineering, pp. 518–525 (1994)

Indexing Based on Topic Modeling and MATHML for Building Vietnamese Technical Document Retrieval Effectively

Tuan Cao Xuan[1], Linh Bui Khanh[2], Hung Vo Trung[3],
Ha Nguyen Thi Thu[2(✉)], and Tinh Dao Thanh[4]

[1] Vietnam Ministry of Education and Training, Hanoi, Vietnam
cxtuan@moet.edu.vn
[2] Information Technology Faculty, Electric Power University, Hanoi, Vietnam
{linhbk,hantt}@epu.edu.vn
[3] Danang University, Da Nang, Vietnam
vthung@dut.udn.vn, nmhung@yahoo.com
[4] Information Technology Faculty, Le Quy Don Technical University,
Hanoi, Vietnam
tinhdt@mta.edu.vn

Abstract. The grow of data on the Internet has brought to people many information and it also opened some important problem in Information retrieval…Along with it, some search engines have developed for user's purpose. User can retrieve information by content, keyword or anything what they need. However, data on the Internet is too huge, the results feedback is often millions or hundreds millions for each query. Therefore, with the narrow field, we will meet a difficult to find related information, especially technical information that contain formulas. In this paper, we present a method for building Vietnamese technical text based on topic modeling and MathML for indexing. System has built and tested with over 500 Vietnamese technical text shown that, this system satisfied users' requires in accuracy and speed.

Keywords: Mathml · Topic modeling · Vietnamese technical text · Search engine · Information retrieval

1 Introduction

Big data is a very widespread concept in life today when data sources on the Internet become popular. The huge amounts of data share online every day brings convenience to seek information consistent with user's purpose, but also difficulties to find financing specialty information, especially is technical documents contain multiple formulations, special notation: π, Ω, $\frac{-b \pm \sqrt{b^2-4ac}}{2a}$, $(x+a)^n = \sum_{k=0}^{n} \binom{n}{k} x^k a^{n-k}$ [3, 8]. These popular search engines Google Search, Yahoo Search, Live Search,... not allow type and identify the formula naturally, so search results usually are not matched with user's requires. Therefore, should have a search engine for searching mathematical formula that have shared on the Internet [7, 8].

© ICST Institute for Computer Sciences, Social Informatics and Telecommunications Engineering 2016
P.C. Vinh and V. Alagar (Eds.): ICCASA 2015, LNICST 165, pp. 322–332, 2016.
DOI: 10.1007/978-3-319-29236-6_31

There are many search engines that can search formulas developed. Egomath allow searches mathematical formulas on Wikipedia.org [18], LatexSearch support the mathematical formula that using LaTeX markup language [15]. But these search engines didn't support formula typing frame so the user feel very difficult when they want to find documents that contain flexibility formula and they can't search for particular language or specific major.

There isn't any similar system for Vietnamese technical document because it is seem difficult to Vietnamese. In this paper, we present our research on building, developing and result of experimental with Vietnamese technical text retrieval by using topic modeling and MathML to indexing formula solution, It has a frame for typing formula based on WIRIS open source [19] and topic modeling is the way to optimize retrieval technical text, easy to search, matched with user's query better than other general search engines.

The rest of the paper structured as follows: Sect. 2 introduce some related works, our method in the Sect. 3, the results and experimental in Sect. 4 and Sect. 5 is conclusion.

2   Related Works

For advantage some function of popular search engines: Google, Yahoo search, Live search in searching mathematical documents, some search engines have been built. MathWebSearch is a mathematical engine based on expression semantic. Mathematic Expressions are stored by data tree. Each node on these tree called substitution that corresponds to a function. A mathematic expression can be represented from root along path on the tree. With this, there are many mathematic expression represented on a tree, and the searching become easier. MathWebSearch can process and index expressions encoded with content MathML or OpenMath [6, 9, 11].

LeActiveMath index OMDoc documents, in this, mathematical formulas processed by OpenMath. User can search text or formulas via this system. With each document, LeActiveMath index title, content and formulas. Like some other search engines, documents will be rank by similarity score of queries. LeActiveMath is developed based on Lucene, documents stored in database [20] (Fig. 1).

Egomath has been developed by Charles University in Prague. It can search mathematical formulas that wrote in LaTeX or MathML and simple document, the search results display along with quotations that contain matches the queries. From the search interface, users can enter queries through two data fields. A field to enter the plain text and the rest to enter mathematical formulas [18].

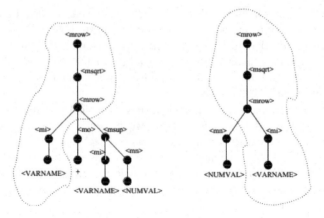

Fig. 1. Representation of $\sqrt{x+x^2}$ and $\sqrt{2x}$

3 Indexing Method Effectively for Building Vietnamese Technical Document Retrieval System

3.1 Topic Modeling

Vietnamese is a single syllable language, one of the Asian languages have single word and compound of word. These words in Vietnamese no distinction based on white spaces, so when mine Vietnamese text, the traditional methods commonly used word processing tool kit to solve the problem of Vietnamese as: text summary, text extraction, information retrieval, text classification... With this approach, always need so much times for processing, and effective is not high in Fig. 2.

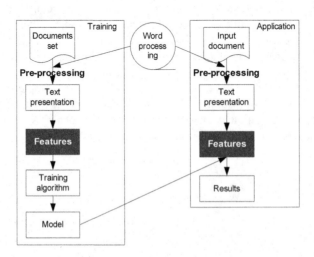

Fig. 2. Vietnamese text mining system.

For text classification problem, large of features are extracted from text and then use one of machine learning methods: SVM, Naïve Bayes, Decision tree, K-nearest neighbor… to classify or identify what category it belong is. With this approach, need high cost and time to process with a large amount of texts and features (Fig. 3).

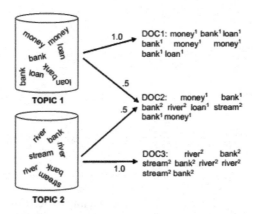

Fig. 3. Topic modeling in text classification.

Topic modeling developed by Blei [1], there are many approach for text mining have been proposed, and proven it's really effective in text mining field by reducing features in text. It helps text mining systems become faster and more accuracy [2, 5, 10].

In this paper, we use the topic modeling to identify Vietnamese technical documents automatic. With topic modeling, very easy to recognize Vietnamese texts in the large database with multiple languages. We can reduce time for processing, identify Vietnamese technical documents more correctly, and improve retrieval process by reduced large number of features.

3.2   Indexing and Store Database with MathML

MathML (Mathematical Markup Language) is an extension language based on XML to present symbols and mathematical formulas. MathML's purpose is to display mathematic communication methods on the computer and the World Wide Web. For display on websites, structure of MathML is not concise like TeX, but it is easy analyzed by the browser, immediate display of mathematical formulas, and transmit to calculating applications. MathML is supported by the office software like Microsoft Word, OpenOffice.org, and other calculation software like Maple, Mathematica and MathCad and on the difference operating systems like Linux, Windows [13, 16].

We can present a + b^2 formula can be written in MatML.

```
<math       xmlns="http://www.w3.org/1998/Math/MathML">
            <mrow>
             <mi>a</mi>
             <mo>+</mo>
             <msup>
              <mi>b</mi>
              <mn>2</mn>
             </msup>
            </mrow>
</math>
```

After that, it convert to

```
math(mrow(mi(a)mo(+)msup(mi(b)mn(2))))
```

3.3   Methodology of Vietnamese Technical Document Retrieval

Based on topic modeling and MathML for indexing and storing Vietnamese technical document in the database, we present a solution for building Vietnamese technical document retrieval system through some steps:

- Step 1: Collect training set with n Vietnamese technical documents $D = \{d_1, d_2, \ldots, d_n\}$ automatic by classify documents based on topic modeling [5].
- Step 2: Store terms in Technical field that extract from topic modeling.
- Step 3: Identify formulas from training set by Infty Reader. And use MathML to store formulas in database by tree indexing.
- Step 4: Feature representation of each document with probabilistic.

Four steps can be present like Fig. 4 below.

4   Experimental

4.1   Functions of Vietnamese Technical Documents Retrieval System

We built a system for searching Vietnamese technical documents that contains mathematical formulas by entering formula visually on the input box. Here is some functions of system:

- Allow searching PDF, .Doc, .docx and XHTML format type.
- User can enter formula from input box.
- User can enter text from input box.
- Searching document based on content or formula. (User can enter: "Pythagoras", all documents contain formula: $a^2 + b^2 = c^2$ or content: Pythagoras will be appearance in the interface of system).
- Results are ranked by user's queries.

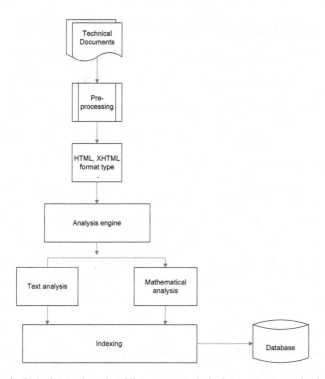

Fig. 4. Indexing and storing Vietnamese technical documents on database.

4.2 Integrate Formula Input Box

On the interface of system, user can type mathematical formulas directly on the search box by integrating mathematical formulas tool called WIRIS. WIRIS is an open source that wrote by JavaScript helps users enter and edit formulas, it is a visual formulas editor like equation tool in Microsoft word. Users select format of formula and then they edit its to complete form.

WIRIS can display all web browsers: Firefox, Internet Explorer, Chrome, Safari,… and anything of operators Windows, Linux, Mac,…It is integrated in the web application like a plugin. Responds of results are stored MathML and we use it for indexing (Fig. 5).

Here is the interface of WIRIS

4.3 Ranking

Ranking equivalent with two searching ways: based on text query and based on visual formula. For formulas searching, we used similarity score between input formula and documents in database that contain formula indexed by tree graph. For example: when users enter a^2, the first document contain independent a^2, and from the second

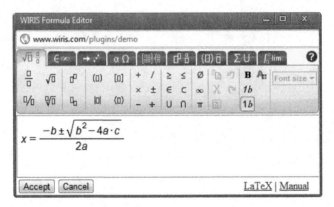

Fig. 5. Formulas input frame - WIRIS

document can contain formulas that deployment from a^2. With queries, the results rank by frequency of terms that occurred on queries and documents.

4.4 Results

Typically, a search engine includes three components: Crawl, index creation and search. Our corpus has been built from many source: Internet, library of Danang University, and corpus includes: articles, technical reports, scientific projects, e-books,... The table below is the description of the corpus (Table 1).

Index creator is a function of administrator when we developed this system. Administrator can create new indexes or delete. Figure below is the index creator what we use indexing with documents and then store it in the database of system (Fig. 6).

Table 1. Corpus

Sources	Library of Danang university, Online material, Offline material, ...
Quantity	50 files collected manually from library of Danang university: articles, reports, scientific projects, e- books,... 530 files collected from Internet by Vietnamese text classification system based on topic modeling [5]
Format type	.doc, .docx, .pdf, .html, .latex
Number of formulas after indexing	694

Formulas are converted to MathML form after indexing and stored in the SQL Server Database (Fig. 7).

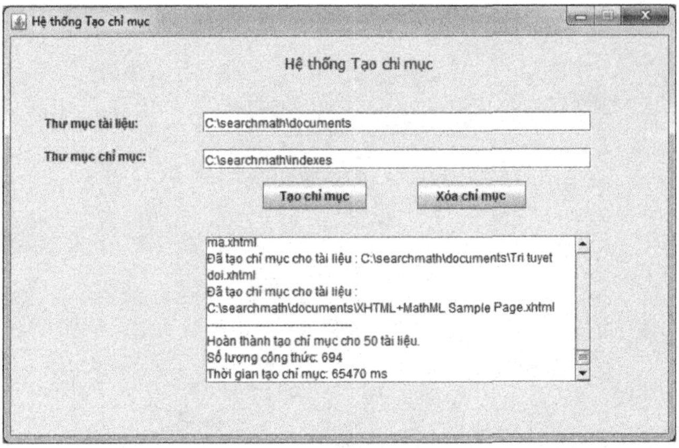

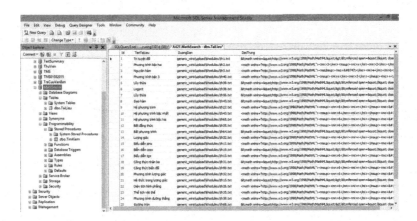

Fig. 6. Indexing creator

Fig. 7. Stored formulas in the database

The Vietnamese technical document retrieval engine has been built and developed by web technology. Searching interface of system includes input box that allow user enter text or formula. Visual formula frame has been integrated in it (Fig. 8).

After users enter mathematical formulas or any query and then click Search button, the system will find related documents. Results displayed and ranked on the interface:

- Name of document.
- Quote part document that contains formula or terms that user entered on the input box.
- Query execution time.

Vietnamese technical document retrieval system hasn't built before. Therefore, it is difficult to compare our method with others. In this paper, we have to evaluate the results that generated by system by Precision and Recall (Fig. 9).

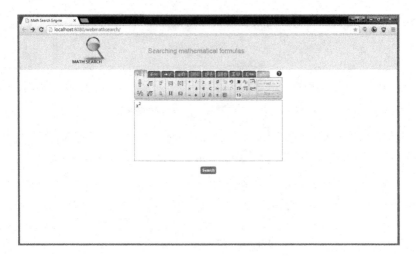

Fig. 8. Searching interface

Fig. 9. Results interface

We tested based on 580 Vietnamese technical documents

- Mathematical major: 210 documents.
- Physic major: 17 documents.
- Information technology major: 140 documents.
- Electric engineering, electronic and automation major: 152 documents.
- Others: 61 documents.

On the other documents have $\sim 70\ \%$ documents isn't contain in its. Experimental were performed two searching methods: by query and by formula. Formulas entered from WIRIS that integrated on system.

Results of experimental are display on the Table 2.

Table 2. Results of experimental.

Retrieval results by content of text		Retrieval results by formulas	
Precision	Recall	Precision	Recall
0.84	0.233	0.96	0.35

5 Conclusion

The convenient search engine on the Internet allows users find their purpose's relatedly documents very easily. However, when the amount of information is too much, the results returned to hundreds of millions of documents with each query, it become difficult to find documents in a narrow field.

In this paper, we presented our research and solutions for Vietnamese technical documents retrieval. It can help for Scientists, technicians search technical documents contain formulas through enter formulas from visualization input box and system display related documents contain formulas that user entered.

We have carried out to build system and evaluated results of the system based on precision and recall measure. Its results shown that, our method and solution is really effectively and high accuracy with each queries. In the future, we will develop our system to online and receive any feedback from users to improve Vietnamese technical document retrieval system.

References

1. Blei, D., Ng, A., Jordan, M.: Latent Dirichlet allocation. J. Mach. Learn. Res. **3**, 993–1022 (2003)
2. Vulic, I., De Smet, W., Moens, M.F.: Cross language information retrieval models based on latent topic models traned with document aligned comparable corpora. Inf. Retrieval **16**(3), 331–368. Springer (2013)

3. Mišutka, J., Galamboš, L.: Extending full text search engine for mathematical content. Charles University in Prague, Ke Karlovu 3, 121 16 Prague, Czech Republic (2008)

4. Lau, J.H., Newman, D., Karimi, S., Baldwin, T.: Best topic word selection for topic labelling. In: Coling 2010: Posters, pp. 605–613 (2010)

5. Thu, H.N.T., Thanh, T.D., Hai, T.N., Ngoc, V.H.: Building Vietnamese topic modeling based on core terms and applying in text classification. In: Proceedings of the Fifth IEEE International Conference on Communication Systems and Network Technologies, pp. 1284–1288 (2015). doi: 10.1109/CSNT.2015.22

6. Kohlhase, M., Prodescu, C.: MathWebSearch: low-latency unification-based search. Center for Advanced Systems Engineering, Jacobs University Bremen, Germany, NTCIR-10 (2013)

7. Růžička, M.: Maths information retrieval for digital libraries. Technical report, Brno University (2013)

8. Adeel, M., Cheung, H.S., Khiyal, S.H.: Math go! Prototype of a content based mathematical formula search engine. J. Appl. Theor. Inf. Technol. JATIT 4(10), 1002 (2008)

9. Kohlhase, M.: An open markup format for mathematical documents. Technical report, Computer Science, International University Bremen (2009)

10. Moens, M.-F., Vulić, I.: Monolingual and cross-lingual probabilistic topic models and their applications in information retrieval. In: Serdyukov, P., Braslavski, P., Kuznetsov, S.O., Kamps, J., Rüger, S., Agichtein, E., Segalovich, I., Yilmaz, E. (eds.) ECIR 2013. LNCS, vol. 7814, pp. 874–877. Springer, Heidelberg (2013)

11. Caprotti, O., Cohen, A.M., Cuypers, H., Sterk, H.: OpenMath technology for interactive mathematical documents. Technical report, Department of Mathematics and Computing Science, Eindhoven University of Technology, P.O. Box 513, NL-5600 MB Eindhoven, The Netherlands (2002)

12. Sojka, P., Líška, M.: Indexing and searching mathematics in digital libraries. Masaryk University, Faculty of Informatics, Botanická 68a, 602 00 Brno, Czech Republic (2011)

13. Ion, P.D.F.: MathML: a key to math on the web. Mathematical Reviews, P.O. Box 8604, Ann Arbor, MI 48107, USA (1999)

14. Anca, S., Kohlhase, M.: MaTeSearch, a combined math and text search engine. Jacobs University (2007)

15. Oetiker, T., Partl, H., Hyna, I., Schlegl, E.: The not so short introduction to LATEX. Version 5.04 (2014)

16. Trung Hung, V., Tuan, C.X.: MathML for the management of mathematical formula in text editor. Int. J. Eng. Res. Technol. 4(05) (2015)

17. Trung Hung, V., Tuan, C.X.: VM-SEMWEB: a semantic web for vietnamese mathematical documents. Int. J. Eng. Res. Technol. 4(05) (2015)

18. https://en.wikipedia.org/wiki/Egomath

19. http://www.wiris.com/

20. http://www.leactivemath.org/

Ambiguous Antecedents Resolution in Summarization of Vietnamese Sentences Formed by Identical Relationship with Copula "LÀ"

Trung Tran[(✉)] and Dang Tuan Nguyen

Faculty of Computer Science, University of Information Technology,
Vietnam National University - Ho Chi Minh City, Ho Chi Minh City, Vietnam
ttrung@nlke-group.net, dangnt@uit.edu.vn

Abstract. We deal with two main issues in this article for the contexts of Vietnamese paragraphs composing two simple sentences having the main feature: the first sentence has two identical objects connected by copula "là"; the second sentence has one anaphoric pronoun indicating human. As the special context, between two identical objects at the first sentence there is only one is actually referred to by the pronoun at the second sentence. At the first issue, we express the mechanism for determining exact antecedents of anaphoric human pronouns and building the meaning representation structure for each sentential pair. We continue to present techniques for analyzing this structure for the issue which is to determine main contents and relationships. Then, we propose the method to generate a new complete Vietnamese sentence having the content which summarizes the meaning of the original pair of sentences.

Keywords: Anaphoric pronoun · Referent resolution · Meaning representation · Meaning summarization · Sentence generation

1 Introduction

In our new approach for summarizing the meaning of pairs of simple Vietnamese sentences, an important step is to resolve the ambiguous problem in determining antecedents of anaphoric pronouns. Firstly, we proposed in [13] a new approach which is the combination of ideas and techniques belonging to two research fields are Natural Language Generation (cf. [3]) and Text Summarization (cf. [1, 2, 5–7]). At the first phase, we proposed the solution to understand the meaning of the input pair with two processes: resolve anaphoric pronouns and build a meaning representation structure for the paragraph. Next, we proposed the solution for generating the new meaning-summarizing Vietnamese sentence with three processes: determine and model relationship factors from the above structure; generate the syntactic structure; combine the lexical set to complete the new sentence. However, in [13] we only applied the new approach in the contexts of four pair types having the general characteristic: the first sentence has one transitive verb relating to two objects which are not identical; the second sentence has one pronoun indicating human, standing with demonstrative

P.C. Vinh and V. Alagar (Eds.): ICCASA 2015, LNICST 165, pp. 333–343, 2016.
DOI: 10.1007/978-3-319-29236-6_32

adjective ["ta" / "ấy" / "này"] and relating to the object at the first sentence taking the object role of the transitive verb. We only presented in [13] steps for implementing processes at the second phase, and we applied techniques in [12] to implement processes at the first phase.

Expanding the research, in [14] we considered the others contexts of four types in which there is the appearance of pronoun "nó" at the second sentence. This is a special pronoun in Vietnamese, can indicate human, animated or non-animated object depending on the actual context and content of the paragraph. Therefore, an important issue is to resolve the ambiguous problem in determining the object at the first sentence which is referred to by pronoun "nó". We applied techniques in [12] and proposed some improvements in describing lexical structure to determine the exact referent and build the meaning representation structure. Next, we analyze this structure, identify relationships. Finally we proposed the algorithm for generating the syntactic structure and combined with the built lexical set to complete the new sentence.

Based on the new approach, the considered contexts here are pairs of simple Vietnamese sentences having characteristic: the first sentence has two identical objects are connected by copula "là" (is) and has the structure as in Table 1; the second sentence has one pronoun indicating human and has the structure as in Table 2. With these types, although two objects at the first sentence are identical but there is only one object is mentioned and referred to by the pronoun at the second sentence. To handle this problem, we propose some improvements in comparison with [12]:

- Propose the new strategy to find the antecedent at the first sentence.
- Add appropriate information in technique of describing the lexical characteristics.
- Adjust the technique that implements the referent finding algorithm.

At the next phase, we analyze the meaning representation structure to determine: the main content of the paragraph; relationships between found object with the next verb or adjective. Then, we propose new general algorithm for generating the syntactic structure of the new sentence and combine with the lexical set to complete.

Table 1. The structure of the first sentence

Type	Characteristic
1	• The object which is represented by a proper noun stands at the subject position of verb "là". Example 1: *"Nhân là người thanh niên."* (English: *"Nhân is a young man."*)
2	• The object which is represented by a proper noun stands at the object position of verb "là". Example 2: *"Người đàn ông là Nghĩa."* (English: *"The guy is Nghĩa."*)
3	• Two objects are represented by two proper nouns. Example 3: *"Lễ là ông Trí."* (English: *"Lễ is Mr Trí."*)
4	• Two objects are represented by two common nouns. Example 4: *"Người đàn ông là giám đốc."* (English: *"The guy is the chairman."*)

Table 2. The structure of the second sentence

Type	Characteristic
1	• The pronoun stands at the subject role of verb "là". Example 5: "*Anh là bác sĩ.*" (English: "*He is a doctor.*")
2	• The pronoun stands at the object role of verb "là". Example 6: "*Bác sĩ là anh.*" (English: "*The doctor is him.*")
3	• The pronoun stands at the subject role of adjective. Example 7: "*Anh đẹp trai.*" (English: "*He is handsome.*")
4	• The pronoun stands at the subject role of intransitive verb. Example 8: "*Anh mỉm cười.*" (English: "*He smiles.*")
5	• The pronoun stands at the subject role of transitive verb. Example 9: "*Anh giúp Nghĩa.*" (English: "*He helps Nghĩa.*")
6	• The pronoun stands at the object role of transitive verb. Example 10: "*Tín nói chuyện với anh.*" (English: "*Tín talks to him.*")

2 Determine the Referent of Anaphoric Human Pronoun

In this section, we present some improvements from the method in [12] to determine the exact antecedent and build the appropriate meaning representation structure.

Based on framework Graph Unification Logic Programming (GULP) [8], our method of resolving anaphoric pronouns and building the meaning representation structure in [12] included steps: (i) analyzed the paragraph into two separated sentences and described position information; (ii) analyzed the syntactic structure of each sentence and described the appropriate characteristic information; (iii) described the characteristic of each lexicon; (iv) in turn built each component of the meaning representation structure; (v) determine the referent for each pronoun. These steps were implemented based on information transferring mechanism in the syntactic tree of theory Unification-Based Grammar [8]. In our approach, we apply Discourse Representation Theory (DRT [4, 9–11]) in which the semantic of a paragraph is represented by a structure called Discourse Representation Structure (DRS) which is a tuple of two ordered lists: (i) the first contains unique indexes indicating each object in the paragraph and denoted as U; (ii) the second contains predicates (in the sense of theory DRT) represent conditions which objects have to satisfy and denoted as Con.

With considered paragraphs in this study, we propose the new referent finding strategy. The main idea is based on the experiences in actual contexts: a main object will normally be referred to first or described by a proper noun. The general strategy:

- If the first sentence has proper noun:
  - If the first sentence has one proper noun: The referent is the object which is described by this proper noun.
  - If the first sentence has two proper nouns: The referent is either the first or the second object. We choose the object standing at the object role of copula "là".

- If the first sentence does not have proper noun: The referent is the object which is described by the noun standing at the subject role of copula "là".

To realize this strategy, firstly we identify the information for finding the referent: position of the object in the paragraph (at the first or second sentence); sub-class of category (proper or common noun); role of verb or adjective (subject or object role). Then, we implement improvements from techniques in [12] as follows:

- Describe additional feature flag_role describing the role of the object in relationship with copula "là" in analyzing structure of the sentence which has the structure in Table 1. This feature takes value [subject] for the object taking the subject role, [object] for the object taking the object role (Fig. 1).

```
s(S,H1,H3) -->  {
        S = syn~flag_position~FP,
        NP1 = syn~flag_position~FP,      NP2 = syn~flag_position~FP,
        NP1 = syn~flag_role~[subject],   NP2 = syn~flag_role~[object],
        S = sem~A,
        NP1 = sem~A,                     NP2 = sem~B,
        NP1 = sem~scope~B,
        NP1 = syn~flag_index~I1,         NP2 = syn~flag_index~I2,
        NP2 = sem~scope~ (in~ [drs(U,Con)|Super] ..
                          out~ [drs(U,[(I1=I2)|Con])|Super])
}, np(NP1,H1,H2), [là], np(NP2,H2,H3).
```

Fig. 1. Analyze the structure of the sentence in Table 1 (based on framework GULP [8])

- Describe additional feature flag_proper and predicate f_proper in describing lexical characteristics. This feature and predicate take value [proper] if the lexicon is proper noun, [common] if the lexicon is common noun. Predicate f_proper is added to the DRS structure and helps for determining the referent in the technique that resolves the anaphoric pronoun (Fig. 2).

When meet a pronoun at the second sentence, we in turn resolve according to two algorithms: the first algorithm finds the proper noun (Fig. 3), the second algorithm finds the noun standing at the subject role of copula "là" (Fig. 4).

Algorithm 1: Find the proper noun.

```
Consider DRS at the time considering the current anaphoric pronoun;
While index I is in list U
  While predicate associated with I is in list Con
    If (position(I) takes value [first]) && (species(I) takes value
[human]) && (f_proper(I) takes value [proper]) Then
          Index of Referent = I;
      End If
    End While
  End While
```

```
n(N) --> [nhân],{
   append([position(I,FP),role(I,FR), species(I,FS),f_proper(I,FPR),
        named(I,[nhân],noun,proper)], Con,NewCon),
   unique_integer(I), FS = [human], FPR = [proper],
   N = syn~(flag_index~I ..    flag_position~FP ..
             flag_role~FR .. flag_species~FS ..
             flag_proper~FPR) ..
        sem~(in~  DRSList .. out~ NewDRSList),
   add_to_topmost_drs(I,[position(I,FP),role(I,FR),species(I,FS),
f_proper(I,FPR),
        named(I,[nhân],noun,proper)], DRSList,NewDRSList) }.
```

Fig. 2. Describe the characteristics of proper noun "Nhân" (based on framework GULP [8])

```
np(NP,H,H) -->  ([anh]),{
   NP=sem~in~DrsList,
   member(drs(U,Con),DrsList),member(Index,U),
   member(position(Index2,[first]),Con),
      member(species(Index2,[human]),Con),
      member(f_proper(Index2,[proper]),Con),
      Index == Index2,
   NP=syn~flag_index~Index,
   NP=sem~scope~in~DrsList, NP=sem~scope~out~DrsOut,
   NP=sem~out~DrsOut }.
```

Fig. 3. Implement Algorithm 1 (based on framework GULP [8])

Algorithm 2: Find the noun standing at the subject role of copula "là".

```
Consider DRS at the time considering the current anaphoric pronoun;
While index I is in list U
  While predicate associated with I is in list Con
    If (position(I) takes value [first]) && (species(I) takes value
[human]) && (role(I) takes value [subject]) Then
          Index of Referent = I;
    End If
  End While
End While
```

The final result of this first phase is a DRS structure representing the meaning of the paragraph. As an example, the DRS structure of the pair of Vietnamese sentences *"Tín là nhà thơ. Anh nhạy cảm."* (English: *"Tín is a poet. He is sensitive."*) (Fig. 5):

3   Generate the New Vietnamese Sentence

The main content of this section is to present determining main contents and relationships in the paragraph through analyzing the DRS structure. Thence, we propose the algorithm for generating the syntactic structure and complete the new sentence.

```
np(NP,H,H) --> ([anh]),{
    NP=sem~in~DrsList,
    member(drs(U,Con),DrsList),member(Index,U),
    member(position(Index2,[first]),Con),
        member(species(Index2,[human]),Con),
        member(role(Index2,[subject]),Con),
        Index == Index2,
    NP=syn~flag_index~Index,
    NP=sem~scope~in~DrsList, NP=sem~scope~out~DrsOut,
    NP=sem~out~DrsOut }.
```

Fig. 4. Implement Algorithm 2 (based on framework GULP [8])

3.1   Determine Main Contents and Relationships

At the first analyzing step, we determine that contents of the paragraph is described by main predicates in list Con of the DRS. These are predicates describing semantic of noun, verb, adjective and in turn indicate object, action or property. With the considered sentential pairs, the content indicating two identical objects is described by a special predicate form which we call identical predicate. This predicate form has structure "I1 = I2" in which I1 is unique index indicating the first object and I2 is unique index indicating the second object. Consider the DRS in Fig. 5, we build three ordered lists containing indexes and predicates which describe main contents:

```
[1,2]
named(1,[tín],noun,proper)
f_proper(1,[proper])
species(1,[human])
role(1,[subject])
position(1,[first])
nhà_thơ(2,[nhà,thơ],noun,common)
f_proper(2,[common])
species(2,[human])
role(2,[object])
position(2,[first])
1=2
nhạy_cảm(1,[nhạy,cảm],adjective)
```

Fig. 5. The DRS structure of paragraph *"Tín là nhà thơ. Anh nhạy cảm."*

- mapIndexObjects: contain indexes indicating each object in the paragraph: 1 – indicates object "Tín"; 2 – indicates object "nhà thơ".
- mapPredicateObjects: contain predicates describing semantic of nouns:
  - named(1,[tín],noun,proper) – describe the semantic of proper noun "Tín".
  - nhà_thơ(2,[nhà,thơ],noun,common) – describe the semantic of common noun "nhà thơ".
- mapPredicateBehaviors: contain predicates describing semantic of verb, adjective and identical predicates:
  - 1 = 2 – describes object "Tín" is identical with object "nhà thơ".

– nhạy_cảm(1, [nhạy, cảm], adjective, property)   – describe the semantic of adjective "nhạy cảm".

We determine relationships when analyzing predicates in mapPredicateBehaviors. These predicates contain the information about indexes associating to objects which have the relationship with each other and with action or property. Generally, we model in Table 3 predicates describing semantic of verb, adjective or identical.

3.2   Generate the New Meaning-Summarizing Vietnamese Sentence

Based on predicate structures in Table 3, we determine considered pairs of sentences are represented by pairs of predicates in which the first predicate has the structure form 4 and the second predicate has the structure 1, 2, 3, 4. We propose the algorithm for generating the syntactic structure of the new sentence: in turn adds predicates describing semantic of lexicons into appropriate positions in the syntactic structure.

Algorithm 3: Generate the syntactic structure of the new Vietnamese sentence.

```
(i) Step 1: Consider index I1 or I2 appearing in both predicate.
If is I1 Then
     Add predicate object associated with I1;        Add "là" (is);
     Add predicate object associated with I2;
Else If is I2 Then
     Add predicate object associated with I2;        Add "là";
     Add predicate object associated with I1;
End If
Add "và" (and);
(ii) Step 2: Consider second predicate.
If is predicate of intransitive or adjective Then
    If I1 taking subject role Then
       Add predicate object associated with I1; Add second predicate;
    Else If I2 taking subject role Then
       Add predicate object associated with I1; Add second predicate;
Else If is predicate of transitive Then
    If I1 or I2 taking subject role Then
       Add second predicate; Add predicate object associated with I3;
    Else If I1 or I2 taking object role Then
       Add "được" (is - passive voice);      Add second predicate;
       Add "bởi" (by);      Add predicate object associated with I3;
    End If
Else If is identical predicate Then
    Add "là" (is);   Add predicate object associated with I3;
End If
```

Table 3. Modeled structure of semantic predicates of verb, adjective, identical

Form	Structure
1	• `p_transitive(I1, I2, content, verb, transitive)` ➔ Relationships: `I1` is the subject of transitive verb `p_transitive`; `I2` is the object of transitive verb `p_transitive`.
2	• `p_intransitive(I, content, verb, intransitive)` ➔ Relationships: `I` is the subject of intransitive verb `p_intransitive`.
3	• `p_adjective(I, content, adjective)` ➔ Relationships: `I` is the subject of adjective `p_adjective`.
4	• `I1 = I2` ➔ Relationships: `I1` and `I2` are identical.

In Table 4, we synthesize pairs of predicates and general syntactic structures of new Vietnamese sentences when applying Algorithm 3. We use the notation [I] to indicate the semantic predicate of the object associating to index I.

Applying the algorithm in [14] about replacing each component in the syntactic structure by the appropriate Vietnamese lexicon, we complete the new meaning-summarizing Vietnamese sentence. Ad an example, consider the paragraph having the DRS structure in Fig. 5, determined main predicates in Sect. 3.1, the syntactic structure and new complete Vietnamese sentence:

- The syntactic structure: `named(1,[tín],noun,proper)` + "là" + nhà_thơ `(2,[nhà,thơ],noun,common)` + "và" + nhạy_cảm`(1,[nhạy,cảm],ad-jective,property)`
- The complete Vietnamese sentence: *"Tín là nhà thơ và nhạy cảm"* (English: *"Tín is a poet and is sensitive."*)

4 Experiment and Discussions

For testing, we collected 120 paragraphs in which the first sentence has the structure as in Table 1 and the second sentence has the structure as in Table 2. The experiment is performed through two phases: the first phase is to test determining the antecedent of the anaphoric pronoun and build the semantic representation structure; the second phase is to test generating the new meaning-summarizing Vietnamese sentence.

At the first experiment phase, the system determines antecedents for anaphoric pronouns and builds DRS structures for all 120 paragraphs. Analyzing the results, due to there is no impaction of external factors of time or space, so the pronoun resolution for these paragraphs is suitable for proposed strategies in Sect. 2. There is a problem here with some pairs of sentences in which the first sentence does not have proper noun, and the proposed strategy in Sect. 2 is finding the object which is described by the noun standing at the subject role of copula "là" and is commonly accepted in reality. However, if the sentence structure is more complex and there are addition factors then the result may be not correct.

Table 4. Pairs of Predicates and Syntactic Structures of the New Sentences

Type	Pair of predicates
1	➜ Structure form of each predicate: I1 = I2; p_transitive(I1, I3) ➜ Syntactic structure of the new Vietnamese sentence: [I1] + "là" + [I2] + "và" + p_transitive(I1, I3) + [I3]
2	➜ Structure form of each predicate: I1 = I2; p_transitive(I3, I1) ➜ Syntactic structure of the new Vietnamese sentence: [I1] + "là" + [I2] + "và" + "được" + p_transitive(I1, I3) + "bởi" + [I3]
3	➜ Structure form of each predicate: I1 = I2; p_transitive(I2, I3) ➜ Syntactic structure of the new Vietnamese sentence: [I2] + "là" + [I1] + "và" + p_transitive(I2, I3) + [I3]
4	➜ Structure form of each predicate: I1 = I2; p_transitive(I3, I2) ➜ Syntactic structure of the new Vietnamese sentence: [I2] + "là" + [I1] + "và" + "được" + p_transitive(I3, I2) + "bởi" + [I3]
5	➜ Structure form of each predicate: I1 = I2; p_intransitive(I1) ➜ Syntactic structure of the new Vietnamese sentence: [I1] + "là" + [I2] + "và" + p_intransitive(I1)
6	➜ Structure form of each predicate: I1 = I2; p_intransitive(I2) ➜ Syntactic structure of the new Vietnamese sentence: [I2] + "là" + [I1] + "và" + p_intransitive(I2)
7	➜ Structure form of each predicate: I1 = I2; p_adjective(I1) ➜ Syntactic structure of the new Vietnamese sentence: [I1] + "là" + [I2] + "và" + p_adjective(I1)
8	➜ Structure form of each predicate: I1 = I2; p_adjective(I2) ➜ Syntactic structure of the new Vietnamese sentence: [I2] + "là" + [I1] + "và" + p_adjective(I2)
9	➜ Structure form of each predicate: I1 = I2; I1 = I3 ➜ Syntactic structure of the new Vietnamese sentence: [I1] + "là" + [I2] + "và" + "là" + [I3]
10	➜ Structure form of each predicate: I1 = I2; I2 = I3 ➜ Syntactic structure of the new Vietnamese sentence: [I2] + "là" + [I1] + "và" + "là" + [I3]

At the second experiment phase, the system generates 120 new Vietnamese sentences for 120 DRS structures. Analyzing the results, these new Vietnamese sentences satisfy two main requirements: having the grammatically correct structure in Vietnamese; and having the content that summarizes the meaning of the original paragraph. However, we point out that there are two issues here:

- Following the new approach, the new Vietnamese sentence is generated based on the DRS structure which is built from the source pair of Vietnamese sentences. This leads to if the anaphoric pronoun resolution is not totally correct and thus the DRS structure does not exactly represent the meaning of the paragraph, then the new Vietnamese sentence does not have accurate content.

- With Algorithm 3 generating the syntactic structure, there are some generated Vietnamese sentences are not totally natural, in the sense of commonly using, in the common Vietnamese communication.

Moreover, we see that can continue to extend the research to apply for paragraphs having more complex structure or composing more than two sentences.

5 Conclusion

We presented in this paper some changes and improvements in comparison with [12] to resolve some ambiguity in determining antecedents for anaphoric human pronouns in paragraphs composing two Vietnamese sentences which have the structure presented in section Introduction. We also presented steps in the phase that generates the new meaning-summarizing Vietnamese sentences with modeling the structure of pairs of predicates corresponding to each sentential pair and the general syntactic structure of each form of new Vietnamese sentence.

The experiment shows that with presented techniques based on the new approach, the generated Vietnamese sentences satisfied the given requirements. We also pointed out some limitations. These limitations will be objectives in our next researches.

References

1. Das, D., Martins, A.F.T.: A survey on automatic text summarization. Language Technologies Institute, Carnegie Mellon University (2007)
2. Lloret, E.: Text summarization: an overview, paper supported by the Spanish Government under the project TEXT-MESS (TIN2006-15265-C06-01) (2008)
3. Reiter, E., Dale, R.: Building Natural Language Generation System. Cambridge University Press, Cambridge (1997)
4. Kamp, H.: A theory of truth and semantic representation. In: Groenendijk, J., Janssen, T.M. V., Stokhof, M. (eds.) Formal Methods in the Study of Language, Part 1, pp. 277–322. Mathematical Centre Tracts, Amsterdam (1981)
5. Mani, I., Maybury, M.T.: Advances in Automatic Text Summarization. MIT Press, Cambridge (1999)
6. Jezek, K., Steinberger, J.: Automatic text summarization. In: Snasel, V. (ed.): Znalosti 2008, FIIT STU Brarislava, Ustav Informatiky a softveroveho inzinierstva, pp. 1–12 (2008). ISBN 978-80-227-2827-0
7. Jones, K.S.: Automatic summarising: a review and discussion of the state of the art, Technical Report 679, Computer Laboratory, University of Cambridge (2007)
8. Covington, M.A.: GULP 4: An Extension of Prolog for Unification Based Grammar. Research Report number: AI-1994-06. USA: Artificial Intelligence Center, The University of Georgia (2007)

9. Covington, M.A., Schmitz, N.: An Implementation of Discourse Representation Theory. ACMC Research Report number: 01-0023. Advanced Computational Methods Center, The University of Georgia (1989)

10. Covington, M.A., Nute, D., Schmitz, N., Goodman, D.: From English to Prolog via Discourse Representation Theory. ACMC Research Report number: 01-0024. Advanced Computational Methods Center, University of Georgia (1988)

11. Blackburn, P., Bos, J.: Representation and Inference for Natural Language. Working with Discourse Representation Structures, vol. II. Department of Computational Linguistics, University of Saarland, Germany (1999)

12. Tran, T., Nguyen, D.T.: A solution for resolving inter-sentential anaphoric pronouns for vietnamese paragraphs composing two single sentences. In: Proceedings of the 5th International Conference of Soft Computing and Pattern Recognition (SoCPaR 2013), Hanoi, Vietnam, pp. 172–177 (2013)

13. Tran, T., Nguyen, D.T.: Merging two vietnamese sentences related by inter-sentential anaphoric pronouns for summarizing. In: Proceedings of The 1st NAFOSTED Conference on Information and Computer Science, Hanoi, Vietnam, pp. 371–381 (2014)

14. Tran, T., Nguyen, D.T.: Semantic predicative analysis for resolving some cases of ambiguous referents of pronoun "Nó" in summarizing meaning of two vietnamese sentences. In: Proceedings of UKSim-AMSS 17th International Conference on Computer Modelling and Simulation (UKSim2015), Cambridge, UK, pp. 340–345 (2015)

Referent Disambiguation for Anaphoric Human Pronouns in Contexts of Pairs of Vietnamese Sentences Using Affecting and Communicating Verbs

Trung Tran[✉] and Dang Tuan Nguyen

Faculty of Computer Science, University of Information Technology,
Vietnam National University - Ho Chi Minh City, Ho Chi Minh City, Vietnam
ttrung@nlke-group.net, dangnt@uit.edu.vn

Abstract. In Vietnamese paragraphs, there are two types of personal pronoun which are often used simultaneously in the sentences: type (i) – personal pronouns which stand alone; type (ii) – personal pronouns standing with demonstrative adjectives. This paper considers the contexts of pairs of simple Vietnamese sentences in which there are the simultaneous appearances of two personal pronouns belonging to these above types at the second sentence. The objectives of this research have the following characteristics: the first sentence has one transitive verb having the relationship with two different human objects; the second sentence has one transitive verb having the relationship with two different pronouns, in which the one belonging to type (ii) takes the subject role and the other belonging to type (i) takes the object role. To determine the object in the first sentence which is referred to by each pronoun at the second sentence, we propose a presupposition about the relationship contexts between two verbs. The proposed strategy is based on the idea: the transitive verbs are classified according to two properties which is "affect" and "communication", then specify the pair of properties of two transitive verbs to determine the antecedent for each pronoun.

Keywords: Anaphoric human pronoun · Ambiguous referent · Verbal relationship context · Discourse representation structure · Semantic representation

1 Introduction

In general, to understand and represent the semantics of a paragraph is an important research section in "abstractive" approach in text summarization field [2, 4, 5, 6, 10, 11, 16]. Especially, the most important part which has to be resolved when doing this study is to determine the exact relationship of a personal pronoun appearing at a sentence and its antecedent appearing at the preceding sentence in some appropriate contexts of the paragraph. To handle this problem, many authors proposed different strategies and methods based on the foundations: Discourse Representation Theory [8, 13, 14, 15, 17], WordNet Ontology [19], Centering Theory [1, 3], and others [7, 9].

Studying the pairs of Vietnamese sentences, which are considered as simplest paragraphs, we initially proposed in [20] the basic strategies and mechanism to perform

© ICST Institute for Computer Sciences, Social Informatics and Telecommunications Engineering 2016
P.C. Vinh and V. Alagar (Eds.): ICCASA 2015, LNICST 165, pp. 344–353, 2016.
DOI: 10.1007/978-3-319-29236-6_33

these strategies with framework Graph Unification Logic Programming (GULP – [12]) combining between Discourse Representation Theory (DRT – [8, 13, 14, 17]) and Unification-Based Grammar (UBG – [18]). The performing mechanism was proposed with the main phases: (a) analyze the syntactic structure of the paragraph into two separated sentences and set the position for each sentence; (b) analyze the syntactic tree of each sentence and set the appropriate informational characteristics; (c) describe the grammatical characteristics of each lexicon and build the Discourse Representation Structure (DRS) – the central structure of DRT theory which help for representing the relationship between the anaphoric pronoun and its antecedent in the context of each sentence and from this representing the meaning of the paragraph; (d) find the antecedent for each pronoun according to the strategies based on the components of the DRS structure which had been built before.

Based on performing mechanism in [20], we considered in [22, 23] the sentential pairs having the special characteristics with the contexts in which there are the appearances of pronoun "nó" – a special pronoun in Vietnamese – and the contexts in which using relative clauses. We established the strategies for resolving the pronouns which were more detail than as in [20] with the priority orders: (i) determine that pronoun "nó" refers to animate or non-animated object at the first sentence; (ii) determine pronoun "nó" refers to object having smaller age in the identified context; (iii) determine the only pronoun indicating person standing with demonstrative adjective ["ta"/"ấy"/"này"] refers to the human object taking the object role at the first sentence. With these strategies, we improved the performing mechanism: added some characteristics in analyzing the syntactic tree of the sentence; added some grammatical characteristics of lexicon; adjusted the antecedent finding algorithm.

In this research, we consider the following contexts of pairs of sentences: the first sentence has one transitive verb having the relationships with two different persons; the second sentence has one transitive verb having the relationship with two different pronouns indicating person, in which the pronoun belonging to type (ii) takes the subject role and the pronoun belonging to type (i) takes the object role. In this context, we focus on two types of pronouns indicating person: type (i) are pronouns ["anh"/ "cô"/"chị"/"ông"/"bà"/"bạn"/"em"] standing alone; and type (ii) are these pronouns standing with demonstrative adjective ["ta"/"ấy"/"này"]. We establish a presupposition based on reality experience in using Vietnamese: a transitive verb often has one of two properties "affect" and "communication" in the context of sentence. Then, we classify the considered sentential pairs into four groups according to concrete context:

- Group A: the first transitive verb has property "affect"; the second transitive verb has property "affect". Example 1: *"Nhân chăm sóc em trai. Anh ta dạy dỗ anh."* (English: *"Nhân cares for the brother. He teaches him."*)
- Group B: the first transitive verb has property "affect"; the second transitive verb has property "communication". Example 2: *"Nhân giúp đỡ Nghĩa. Anh ta cảm ơn anh."* (English: *"Nhân helps Nghĩa. He thanks him."*)
- Group C: the first transitive verb has property "communication"; the second transitive verb has property "affect". Example 3: *"Nhân gặp bác sĩ. Ông ta khám cho anh."* (English: *"Nhân meets the doctor. He examines him."*)

- Group D: the first transitive verb has property "communication"; the second transitive verb has property "communication". Example 4: *"Huấn luyện viên gặp Nhân. Ông ấy hướng dẫn anh."* (English: *"The coach meets Nhân. He guides him."*)

With the contexts of these groups, the main idea of strategies for resolving each pronoun is: determine the antecedent is one of two human objects at the first sentence satisfying the appropriate characteristics about the position in the paragraph, relationship role with the first transitive verb, and property of each verb.

To perform these strategies, we propose some improvements in the techniques and algorithm of resolving anaphoric pronouns in [20] with some main points:

- Add the appropriate information in describing characteristics of transitive verb.
- Add the appropriate information in describing characteristics of noun.
- Adjust the characteristic description in analyzing verb phrase.
- Adjust the technique to perform the algorithm for each pair.

The result of the process of determining the antecedent for pronouns at the second sentence is the meaning representation structure of the original pair.

2 The Resolving Process

2.1 The Strategies for Finding the Antecedents

As presented in Section Introduction, in this research, we establish a presupposition based on the reality experience in Vietnamese communication: in the sentence at a concrete context, an action which is expressed by a transitive verb often has one of two properties are "affect" or "communication". With this presupposition, applying to the considered pairs of sentences, we have the comments:

- The first comment: If two consecutive "affect" or "communication" actions are performed, commonly both actions are done by one object.
- The second comment: If one "affect" action is performed then other "communication" action is performed or vice versa, commonly the pronoun standing alone relates to the object taking the subject role of the first action, the pronoun standing with demonstrative adjective relates to the object taking the object role of the first action. According to above comments, we propose the strategies for resolving pronouns:
- For the context of pairs of sentences belonging to group A

The antecedent finding strategy: because the transitive verb at the first and second sentence both have property "affect" then according to the first comment, in the context of the relationship between two verbs, these verbs are performed by one object.

Therefore we detemine rthe antecedents:

- The pronoun standing with demonstrative adjective taking the subject role refers to the object taking the subject role at the first sentence.
- The pronoun standing alone taking the object role refers to the object taking the object role at the first sentence.

- For the context of pairs of sentences belonging to group B

  The antecedent finding strategy: because the transitive verb at the first sentence has property "affect" and the transitive verb at the second sentence has property "communication" then according to the second comment, in the context of the relationship between two verbs, these verbs are performed by different objects. Therefore we determine the antecedents:

- The pronoun standing with demonstrative adjective taking the subject role refers to the object taking the object role at the first sentence.
- The pronoun standing alone taking the subject role refers to the object taking the subject role at the first sentence.

- For the context of pairs of sentences belonging to group C

  The antecedent finding strategy: because the transitive verb at the first sentence has property "communication" and the transitive verb at the second sentence has property "affect" then according to the second comment, in the context of the relationship between two verbs, these verbs are performed by different objects. Therefore we determine the antecedents:

- The pronoun standing with demonstrative adjective taking the subject role refers to the object taking the object role at the first sentence.
- The pronoun standing alone taking the subject role refers to the object taking the subject role at the first sentence.

- For the context of pairs of sentences belonging to group D

  The antecedent finding strategy: because the transitive verb at the first and second sentence both have property "communication" then according to the first comment, in the context of the relationship between two verbs, these verbs are performed by one object. Therefore we determine the antecedents:

- The pronoun standing with demonstrative adjective taking the subject role refers to the object taking the subject role at the first sentence.
- The pronoun standing with demonstrative adjective taking the subject role refers to the object taking the subject role at the first sentence.

2.2 Improve the Techniques in Mechanism for Implementing the Strategies

To implement the proposed strategies in Sect. 2.1, we apply and propose some improvements in the performing mechanism in [20] as follows:

- In describing grammatical characteristics of transitive verb:

- Define additional characteristic `flag_property_of_verb`. This characteristic takes value `[affect]` if the verb has property "affect", take value `[communication]` if the verb has property "communication".
- Define additional predicate `property_of_verb`. This predicate will be added to the predicate list of DRS structure. This predicate has two arguments: The first

argument take value [first] or [second] corresponding to the position of the verb at the first or second sentence – this information is transferred down in the syntactic tree when analyzing the paragraph into two separated sentences; the second argument takes value [affect] or [communication] corresponding to the property of the verb (Fig. 1).

```
p(P) --> [khám], {
    append([property_of_verb(FP,FPOV),
           đóng(Arg1,Arg2,CO,CAT,FCLASS,FPOV)],
           Con,NewCon),
    CO = [khám],
    CAT = [action],
    FCLASS = [transitive],
    FPOV = [affect],
    P = syn~(flag_arg1~Arg1 ..
             flag_arg2~Arg2 ..
             flag_position~FP ..
             flag_property_of_verb~FPOV) ..
         sem~(in~ [drs(U,Con)|Super] ..
              out~ [drs(U,NewCon)|Super])
}.
```

Fig. 1. Describe transitive verb "khám" in Example 3 with framework GULP [12]. Characteristic property_of_verb takes value [affect]. Predicate property_of_verb has two arguments: the first argument takes value FP is the position information will be transferred down in the syntactic tree, the second argument takes value [affect].

- In describing grammatical characteristics of noun:

- Define additional characteristic flag_property_of_verb. The characteristic shows that the noun or pronoun has the relationship with the verb having what property. This characteristic takes value [affect] if the verb has property "affect", takes value [communication] if the verb has property "communication".
- Define additional characteristic flag_index_other. We notice that two different pronouns relate to two different objects, we propose a technique in which when determine the antecedent for one pronoun then simultaneously determine the remaining object as the antecedent for the other pronoun. This characteristic takes value as the unique index of the object which is determined as the antecedent of the remaining pronoun. This value is different from the value of characteristic flag_index (Fig. 2).

- In analyzing verb phrase into verb and noun phrase:

- Add the mechanism for transferring value F of characteristic flag_property_of_verb of the verb to the noun phrase. This value is transferred down in the syntactic tree to characteristic flag_property_of_verb of the noun.
- Add the mechanism for transferring value G of characteristic flag_index_other of the noun phrase to the first argument flag_arg1 of the transitive verb. The value of characteristic flag_index and flag_index_other corresponding to the indexes of two antecedents of the second and first pronoun. These two indexes will be determined when implementing the antecedent finding algorithm (Fig. 3).

```
n(N) --> [nhân],{
   append([position(I,FP), role(I,FR),species(I,FCLASS),
            nhân(I,CO,CAT,FCLASS)],
         Con,NewCon),
   unique_integer(I),
   CO = [nhân],
   CAT = [object],
   FCLASS = [human],
   N = syn~(flag_index~I ..
            flag_position~FP ..
            flag_property_of_verb~FPOV ..
            flag_index_other~FIO ..
            flag_role~FR) ..
         sem~(in~ [drs(U,Con)|Super] ..
            out~ [drs([I|U],NewCon)|Super])
}.
```

Fig. 2. Describe characteristics of noun "nhân" in Example 3 with framework GULP [12].

- Propose the algorithm for implementing the antecedent finding strategies. With the notice that when improving describing characteristics of noun, we determine the index of the antecedent for the pronoun standing alone – corresponding to the second pronoun taking the object role of the second transitive verb. This index becomes the value for characteristic flag_index of noun. The index of the remaining object will becomes the value for characteristic flag_index_other of noun – corresponding to the antecedent of the remaining pronoun. The general algorithm:

Algorithm 1: Determine the antecendents for pronouns.

Consider DRS structure at current time;

Step 1: Check property of second verb
  - o Express by value of feature flag_property_of_verb of second pronoun.

Step 2: Check property of first verb
  - o Express by value of predicate property_of_verb() of first verb.

Step 3: Check object having index I and value of predicate position(I), species(I), role(I)
  - o If group A then these values are [first], [human], [goal] respectively.
  - o If group B then these values are [first], [human], [agent] respectively.
  - o If group C then these values are [first], [human], [agent] respectively.
  - o If group D then these values are [first], [human], [goal] respectively.

Step 4: The antecedence of the second pronoun is object having index I
  - o Set feature flag_index of second pronoun value I;
  - o Transfer this value to feature flag_arg2 of the second verb;

Step 5: Check object having index I_other and
  - o I_other is different from I

Step 6: The antecedence of the first pronoun is object having index I_other
  - o Set feature flag_index_other of second pronoun value I_other;
  - o Transfer this value to feature flag_arg1 of the second verb;

```
pp(PP,H1,H2) -->        {
    PP = syn~flag_position~E,
    NP = syn~flag_position~E,
    P = syn~flag_position~E,
    P = syn~D,
    PP = syn~D,
    NP = sem~A,
    PP = sem~A,
    NP = syn~flag_index~C,
    PP = syn~flag_arg2~C,
    NP = syn~flag_index_other~G,
    PP = syn~flag_arg1~G,
    NP = syn~flag_role~[goal],
    PP = syn~flag_property_of_verb~F,
    NP = syn~flag_property_of_verb~F,
    P = sem~B,
    NP = sem~scope~B
},
p(P), np(NP,H1,H2).
```

Fig. 3. Analyze the syntactic of verb phrase with framework GULP [12].

After performing the above improvements, we determine the antecedents for pronouns at the second sentence and complete the DRS structure. Consider the pair of sentences in Example 3, we have the result

– A list contains indexes: index 1 expresses object "nhân"; index 2 expresses object "bác sĩ".

```
np(NP,H,H) -->    ([anh]; [cô]; [chị]; [ông]; [bà]; [bạn]; [em]),{
    NP=sem~in~DrsList,
    NP=syn~flag_property_of_verb~FPOV,
    FPOV == [affect],
    member(drs(U,Con),DrsList),
    member(property_of_verb([first],[affect]),Con),
    member(Index,U),
        member(position(Index2,[first]),Con),
        member(species(Index2,[human]),Con),
        member(role(Index2,[goal]),Con),
        Index == Index2,
    NP=syn~flag_index~Index,
    member(Index_Other,U),
        Index_Other \= Index2,
    NP=syn~flag_index_other~Index_Other,
    NP=sem~scope~in~DrsList,
    NP=sem~scope~out~DrsOut,
    NP=sem~out~DrsOut
}.
```

Fig. 4. Implement Algorithm 1 with framework GULP [12].

– A list contains predicates:

– Express information about the object having index 1:
   • nhân(1,[nhân],[object],[human])
   • species(1,[human])

- role(1,[agent])
- position(1,[first])
- Express information about the object having index 2:
  - bác_sĩ(2,[bác,sĩ],[object],[human])
  - species(2,[human])
  - role(2,[goal])
  - position(2,[first])
- Express information about the first transitive verb:
  - gặp(1,2,[gặp],[action],[transitive],[communication])
  - property_of_verb([first],[communication])
- Express information about the second transitive verb:
  - khám(2,1,[khám],[action],[transitive],[affect])
  - property_of_verb([second],[affect])

3 Experiment and Discussions

For testing, we collected 200 pairs of Vietnamese sentences having characteristics which are suitable for the research objective and are classified as: group A has 45 pairs, group B has 47 pairs, group C has 48 pairs, and group D has 60 pairs. The testing results:

- Determine correctly the antecedents and build the DRS structures for 29 pairs of group A. The successful rate is 64.44 %.
- Determine correctly the antecedents and build the DRS structures for 41 pairs of group B. The successful rate is 87.23 %.
- Determine correctly the antecedents and build the DRS structures for 37 pairs of group C. The successful rate is 77.08 %.
- Determine correctly the antecedents and build the DRS structures for 51 pairs of group D. The successful rate is 85 %.

The testing results show that, the system determined the exact antecedents for pairs of pronouns at the major of tested pairs of sentences. Analyzing deeper, we notice some points:

- With sentential pairs of group A, in which there are two "affect" actions are performed consecutively, in some cases the second action is performed by the second object. This situation also happened commonly in reality because the second object will react against the previous action of the first object.
- With sentential pairs of the other groups, because there is lack of some additional factors such as time or space which affect the context, therefore the results maybe not correct.

Besides, we see that the techniques in this research are applied for specific types of pairs of sentences. This requires more improvements so that we can apply for pairs of sentences having more complex characteristics.

4   Conclusion

In this research, we presented strategies and techniques for determining the antecedents for each pairs of pronouns belonging to two types: type (i) are pronouns indicating person standing alone; type (ii) are these pronouns standing with demonstrative adjective. With the classification of pairs of sentences into groups based on two properties "affect" and "communication" of transitive verbs at two sentences, we proposed the appropriate resolving strategies.

The testing results show that the antecedent finding strategies and algorithm are suitable for the major of tested pairs of sentences. We also pointed out some points that need to be improved so that can apply for more complex pairs of sentences.

References

1. Joshi, A.K., Weinstein, S.: "Control of inference: role of some aspects of discourse structure centering". In: Proceedings of the International Joint Conference on Artificial Intelligence (IJCAI 1981), pp. 385–387 (1981)
2. Khan, A., Salim, N.: A Review on Abstractive Summarization Methods. J. Theor. Appl. Inf. Technol. **59**(1), 64–72 (2014)
3. Grosz, B.J., Joshi, A.K., Weinstein, S.: Centering: a framework for modeling the local coherence of discourse. Comput. Linguist. **21**(2), 203–225 (1995)
4. Saranyamol, C.S., Sindhu, L.: A survey on automatic text summarization. Int. J. Comput. Sci. Inf. Technol. **5**(6), 7889–7893 (2014)
5. Das, D., Martins, A.F.T.: A survey on automatic text summarization. Language Technologies Institute, Carnegie Mellon University (2007)
6. Lloret, E.: "Text summarization: an overview", paper supported by the Spanish Government under the project TEXT-MESS (TIN2006-15265-C06-01) (2008)
7. Cornish, F.: Inter-sentential anaphora and coherence relations in discourse: a perfect match. Lang. Sci. **31**(5), 572–592 (2009)
8. Kamp, H.: A theory of truth and semantic representation. In: Jeroen, A.G.G., Janssen, T.M. V., Stokhof, M.B.J. (eds.) Formal Methods in the Study of Language, Part 1. Mathematical Centre Tracts, pp. 277–322 (1981)
9. Carbonell, J.G., Brown, R.D.: Anaphora resolution: a multi-strategy approach. In: Proceedings of the 12th International Conference on Computational Linguistics, pp. 96–101 (1988)
10. Jezek, K., Steinberger, J.: Automatic text summarization. In: Snasel, V. (Ed.): Znalosti 2008, ISBN 978-80-227-2827-0, FIIT STU Brarislava, Ustav Informatiky a softveroveho inzinierstva, pp. 1–12 (2008)
11. Jones, K.S.: "Automatic summarising: a review and discussion of the state of the art", Technical report 679. University of Cambridge, Computer Laboratory (2007)
12. Covington, M.A.: "GULP 4: An Extension of Prolog for Unification Based Grammar", Research Report number: AI-1994-06. Artificial Intelligence Center, The University of Georgia, USA (2007)
13. Covington, M.A., Schmitz, N.: "An Implementation of Discourse Representation Theory", ACMC Research Report number: 01-0023. The University of Georgia, Advanced Computational Methods Center (1989)

14. Covington, M.A., Nute, D., Schmitz, N., Goodman, D.: "From English to Prolog via Discourse Representation Theory", ACMC Research Report number: 01-0024. University of Georgia, Advanced Computational Methods Center (1988)
15. Johnson, M., Klein, E.: "Discourse, anaphora and parsing", Report number: CSLI-86-63. Center for the Study of Language and Information, Stanford University, USA (1986)
16. Kasture, N.R., Yargal, N., Singh, N.N., Kulkarni, N., Mathur, V.: A survey on methods of abstractive text summarization. Int. J. Res. Merging Sci. Technol. 1(6), 53–57 (2014)
17. Blackburn, P., Bos, J.: Representation and inference for natural language – volume ii: working with discourse representation structures. Department of Computational Linguistics, University of Saarland (1999)
18. Shieber, S.M.: An Introduction to Unification-Based Approaches to Grammar. Microtome Publishing Brookline, Massachusetts (2003)
19. Liang, T., Wu, D.S.: Automatic pronominal anaphora resolution in english texts. Comput. Linguist. Chin. Lang. Process. 9(1), 21–40 (2004)
20. Tran, T., Nguyen, D.T.: A solution for resolving inter-sentential anaphoric pronouns for vietnamese paragraphs composing two single sentences. In: Proceedings of the 5th International Conference of Soft Computing and Pattern Recognition (SoCPaR 2013), Hanoi, Vietnam, pp. 172–177 (2013)
21. Tran, T., Nguyen, D.T.: "Merging two vietnamese sentences related by inter-sentential anaphoric pronouns for summarizing. In: Proceedings of the 1st NAFOSTED Conference on Information and Computer Science, Hanoi, Vietnam, pp. 371–381 (2014)
22. Tran, T., Nguyen, D.T.: Semantic predicative analysis for resolving some cases of ambiguous referents of pronoun "Nó" in summarizing meaning of two vietnamese sentences. In: Proceedings of the UKSim-AMSS 17th International Conference on Computer Modelling and Simulation (UKSim 2015), pp. 340–345. Cambridge, United Kingdom (2015)
23. Tran, T., Nguyen, D. T.: Combined method of analyzing anaphoric pronouns and inter-sentential relationships between transitive verbs for enhancing pairs of sentences summarization. In: Silhavy, R., et al. (eds.) Proceedings of the 4th Computer Science On-line Conference (CSOC2015) – Vol 1: Artificial Intelligence Perspectives and Applications, Advances in Intelligent Systems and Computing – Vol. 347, Faculty of Applied Informatics, Tomas Bata University in Zlin, Czech Republic, pp. 67–77 (2015)

Building Multiple Multicast Trees with Guarranteed QOS for Service Based Routing Using Artificial Algorithms

Nguyen Thanh Long[1(✉)], Nguyen Duc Thuy[2],
and Pham Huy Hoang[3]

[1] Software Development Division III,
Informatics Center of Hanoi Telecommunications,
Hoan Kiem, Hanoi, Vietnam
Ntlptpml@yahoo.com
[2] Center for Applied Research and Technology Development,
Research Institute of Posts and Telecommunications, Hanoi, Vietnam
Nguyenducthuy07@gmail.com
[3] Information Technology Institute, Ha Noi University of Science Technology,
Hanoi, Vietnam
Hoangph@soict.hut.edu.vn

Abstract. In Service Based Routing (SBR), data is transmitted from a source node to destination nodes are not depended on destination addresses. Hence, it is comfortable with new advanced technology as cloud computing and also flexible and reliable. Multicast routing is advanced technique to deliver data simultaneously from one source node to multiple destination nodes with QOS (quality of service). In this paper, we introduce a technique that is extended from multicast technique with multiple multicast trees that are conformed quality of service routing. This technique is based on Greedy, Ant Colony Optimization, and fuzzy logic to get optimal routes to transmit data from one source to multiple destination node very effectively. The usage of the ANT Colony optimization, Greedy, fuzzy logic algorithms to find cyclic or multiple paths routes on each trunk by multiple criterions to transmit data effectively.

Keywords: MANET · Service · Routing · Multi-paths · Bandwidth · Cluster · ANT · Tree · Multicast · Colony · Optimization · Greedy · QOS · MST

1 Basical Concepts

In order to model a general network in common by a graph in discrete mathematics. In which denote V is the set of vertics that are nodes in the network, E is the set of the edges that are links to connect each pair of nodes in the graph. The routing problem is to make optimization routes from routing table. The inputs of the routing table are collected by routing process. The routing process consists of several minor detail processes: In the reactive or on-demand routing protocol: (i) Broadcast packets over network to find routes; (ii) Collecting reply packets to build optimal routes; in proactive protocol it usually collects network information through flooding HELLO messages.

© ICST Institute for Computer Sciences, Social Informatics and Telecommunications Engineering 2016
P.C. Vinh and V. Alagar (Eds.): ICCASA 2015, LNICST 165, pp. 354–369, 2016.
DOI: 10.1007/978-3-319-29236-6_34

On receiving HELLO packets, network node updates the routing table to use to find routes as introducing in the next section. HELLO messages are effective to collect network information.

2 Artificial Algorithms

2.1 Fuzzy Logic

The fuzzy logic is a branch of logical field of mathematic [1] based on the probabilistic of the related factors. It uses inference regulation to make decision based on fuzzy inputs. It may also use some formulas to calculate fuzzy outputs based on weights assigned to fuzzy inputs. We all know that in reality every thing also has a level of true, especially in MANET, all nodes continuous move with changing velocity and very limited energy. So applying this kind of logic to assess the metrics of MANET is very comfortable. For example, GOOGLE are building many automatically system to coordinate vehicle system such as satellite system, planet, astronaut, so every thing can be apply this theory. So MANET routing is granted an important role in these systems. In the moving using GREEDY and ACO algorithms is very comfortable to assess the velocity and orbital motion of moving objects. In particular, the coordination of moving system can be tracked by GPS system and these can be put into artificial system to optimize. IOT is short for Internet of thing that is a trend to connect all the things of the Planet. So from living tools to astronaut all connected by Global Internet. For example, on the move we can connect to operate our work.

2.2 Greedy Algorithm

The greedy algorithm is very popular in vehicle routing. That may be effective in MANET routing because in this routing all nodes are usually to move randomly. So in this paper will focus on these algorithms to make multiple paths routing with quality of service [2]. The Greedy algorithm executes based on heuristic principle, that continuously find local optimal solution in each step of the total operation until global optimal solution found or a predefined processing steps.

2.3 Ant Colony Optimization

The ACO and Greedy algorithms are two artificial algorithms, which choose routes based on probability of each connection between each pair of nodes. The probability of each connection is assigned by fuzzy logic introduced above. When the detecting process operates, that assigns each connection found a weight. This weight is used to calculated probability for choosing the route. The probability may be calculates by some methods, for example using RREQ messages that emitting from a node and the replied RREP messages. RREP contains information to measure connection probability. Beside, in proactive routing, it is based on nodes' received HELLOs information to assess probability of connection: $Prob(Connection(i, j)) = F(M\_1, M\_2,..., M\_n)$, $M\_1, M2, ..., M\_i$ are some metrics to assess connection.

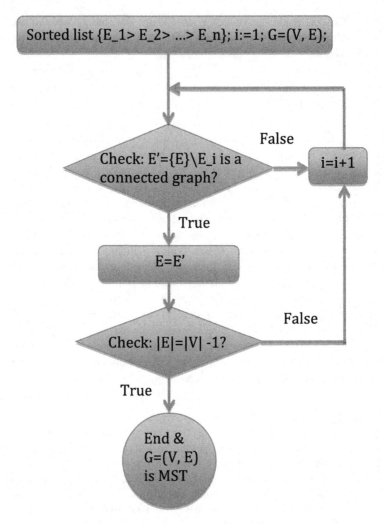

Fig. 1. The flow diagram of algorithm to find a MST tree.

Prob(Route) = $\prod$(Prob(Connection(i, j)))|, (i, j) is connection of this route (Fig. 1).

3 Build Multicast Tree

3.1 Use Greedy Algorithm

3.1.1 Find Minimum Spanning Tree (MST)

(i) Using three above algorithms [1, 2] to find and assign weight for each edge of
the graph.

$$\text{Cost}(E(v\_1, v\_2)) = \text{FZY}|\text{GRD}|\text{ACO}(E(v\_1, v\_2)) \qquad (1)$$

(ii)   At first making minimum spanning tree, then regulating this tree to get multicast tree.

Sorting the edges of the graph in descending order;

(iii) Remove edges beginning from the first element of this sorted list individually with the condition that this process doesn't divide this graph into two disjoint components;

(iv)   Check the number of edges of the graph, if it is equal to number of vertices minus one. If the condition is true then the algorithm ends to get the tree.

$$\text{Count}(\text{edges}) = \text{Count}(\text{vertices}) - 1. \qquad (2)$$

3.1.2   Find Multicast Tree

We denote multicast tree by: $(S, \{D\_1, D\_2, ..., D\_n\})$, s is source node, $D = \{D\_1, D\_2, ..., D\_n\}$ is the destination set. Choose the root of the tree, which is the source node to the tree, $D = \{\varnothing\}$, scanned edges set $SC = \{\varnothing\}$. Tracing the tree from this source node to the destination nodes individually by all directions following the edges that are not in SC: $S \rightarrow \{C\_1, C\_2, ..., C\_n\}$. For each C_i: (i) check whether C_i is in SC, if not: (ii) check whether C_i is destination node, if true: $D = D \cup C\_i$; (iii) $SC = SC \cup (S, C\_i)$; (iv) scan C_i by above (i), (ii), (iii) steps. To each destination node, if it continues connecting to another nodes, using GEN/BEE/ACO algorithms to find optimal path for remaining nodes. Otherwise using the next steps to get the optimal solution (Fig. 2).

The alg. ends when all destination nodes are added to the tree. All branches of the tree that don't end with a destination node are being cut.

3.1.3   Assessing This Algorithm

The MST finding algorithm has complexity close to $O(\log(|V|) + (|\text{edges}|\text{-}|V|))$.

3.2   Use KrusKal Algorithm

This algorithm picks edges for MST depends on the principle:

(i)   Sort the edge set in ascending order: $\{E\_1, E\_2, ..., E\_n\}$.

(ii) Make for each vertex v a set of vertices V that are all connected to V. At first assign: $V = \{v\}$. Assume i is the current edge picked, $E\_i = (v\_k, v\_h)$, if v_k and v_h are belonged to two disjoint sets of vertices (that have no common vertices: $V\_k \cap V\_h = \varnothing$), add E_i to the MST, We update:

MST = MST $\cup$ E_i, merge V_k and V_h into V_k:

$$V\_k = V\_k \cup V\_h. \qquad (3)$$

Until the number of elements of MST equal to $|V|-1$ (Fig. 3).

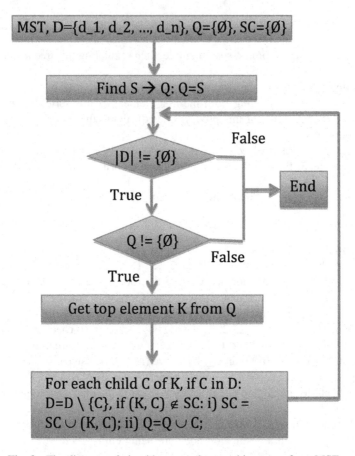

Fig. 2. The diagram of algorithm to make a multicast tree from MST.

At that time all vertices are in one common connected graph with total minimum distance between these vertices. That also means all disjoint vertices sets are merged into one component. The complexity of this algorithm is less than above introduced algorithm. Because the complexity of this algorithms is reduced after each round. The number of disjoint sets is reduced by one after a edge is added to the MST. Only when number of element of MST is equal to number of vertices minus one then the algorithm ends:

$$O(Alg.) = |V| * (|V| - 1)/2. \tag{4}$$

So it is very good for the network with number of nodes is not large.

4   Make Qos Routes from Multiple Multicast Tree

We continuously apply the above algorithm to find some multicast trees. After finding out one tree, in the next step of finding using the edges minus all the edges of the found trees. So this algorithm converses fast. Until the remaining set of edges contains

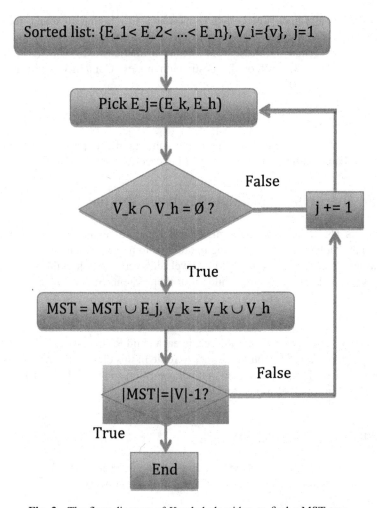

Fig. 3. The flow diagram of Kruskal algorithm to find a MST tree.

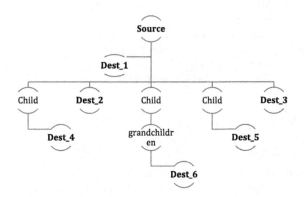

Fig. 4. The multicast tree from a source node to six destination nodes.

number of edges less than |Vertices|−1 then ending. Combining all found trees to get multiple path of each branch of the tree to make QOS routes (Fig. 4).

When joining found multicast trees, denote a multicast MST(S, S(D)), S is the source node, S(D) is the set of the destination nodes. Combined multicast tree is denoted by: MBT(S, S(D)).

$$MBT(S, \ S(D)) \ = \ Combine(MST(S, \ S(D))) \tag{5}$$

So each route is multiplied by combining some gradients paths from these MST trees. So the bandwidth of route is easily to increase to meet the demand.

5 Build Hierarchical Multiple Multicast Routing

In the papers [1, 2, 6, 7] we have mentioned some strategies to make hierarchical routing. In the global network, applying the R^+ tree to manage the network. Assume, at a level in this tree, R is the vertex at this level, this vertex has n child vertices {C_1, C_2, ..., C_n}, which are R^+ tree children of their parent. So we have:

$$R^+ \ = \ R^+(C\_1) \cup R^+(C\_2) \cup \ldots \cup R^+(C\_n) \tag{6}$$

In which, C_i is root of a child R^+ tree, in each child R^+ tree, we use the introduced algorithms to make multiple multicast trees to route in this cluster of whole network. In each multicast tree, it may be used an optimal algorithm such as GEN or BEE or ACO [1–3, 7, 8] to find optimal routes for data transmission.

6 Algorithms' Simulations

In order to simulate above analyzed algorithms, we have to setup data structures to store the sets of vertices and edges of the graph of the network.

a) *The vertex class:*

```
1.  public class cVertice
2.    {
3.        public int V { get; set; }
4.        public double Probability { get; set; }
5.  public List<cVertice> children_nodes { get; set; }
6.        public cVertice parent { get; set; }
7.        public cVertice(int v_id, double p_prob_exist)
8.        {
9.            v_id = V;
10.           Probability = p_prob_exist;
11.       }
12. }
```

The Probability property for assessing the probability the node is belonged to the current network class. So it can use the artificial Neuron network to validate to increase the correctness and reliability. The parent node property stores a pointer to this node in the hierarchical model. The property children_nodes stores the link list of nodes of the next level in this model, these nodes are managed by this current node.

b) Edge class:
```
1.  public class cEdge
2.     {
3.         public int fVertice { get; set; }
4.         public int eVertice { get; set; }
5.         public double Probability { get; set; }
6.         public cEdge(int fV, int eV, double c, double p)
7.         {
8.            fVertice = fV;
9.            eVertice = eV;
10.           cost = c;
11.           Probability = p;
12.        }
   }
```

The fVertice property stores beginning vertex of the current edge, the property eVertice stores the ending vertex of this edge. The cost property stores cost metric of the edge to validate the QOS of routes that pass this hop.

c) The minimum skeleton tree
```
public class cMST
{
    public List<cVertice> MsTree { get; set; }
    public cMST()
    {
        MsTree = new List<cVertice>();
    }

    public cVertice find_MCstTr(int snd, List<int> lst_dnd)
    {
        cVertice mctr = null;
        for (int i = 0; i < MsTree.Count; i++)
        {
            mctr = find_mcs_root(MsTree[i], snd);
            if (mctr != null)
                break;
        }

        return mctr;
    }

    cVertice find_mcs_root(cVertice fnd, int snd)
    {
        List<cVertice> lst_nde = new List<cVertice>();
        cVertice root_mcs = null;
        lst_nde.Add(fnd);
        while (lst_nde.Count > 0)
        {
            root_mcs = lst_nde[0];
            if (snd == root_mcs.V)
            {
                break;
```

```
        }
        else
        {
           lst_nde.AddRange(root_mcs.parents);
                    lst_nde.remove(root_mcs);
        }
     }
     return root_mcs;
   }
}
```

In order to find the multicast tree, the routers have to find all MST trees. This kind of tree is made by the above algorithm.

d) *The multicast tree class*

```
public class cMT
    {
        public List<cVertice> s_n { get; set; }
        public int root { get; set; }
        public List<cVertice> d_lst { get; set; }
        public List<List<cVertice>> r_lst = new List<List<cVertice>>();
        public cMST mst { get; set; }
        public cMT()
        {
        cVertice c_v = null, c_v1 = null;
        s_n = new List<cVertice>();
        List<cVertice> c_vertls = new List<cVertice>();
        for (int i = 0; i < mst.MsTree.Count; i++)
        {
           c_vertls.Clear();
           c_vertls.Add(mst.MsTree[i]);
           while (c_vertls.Count > 0)
           {
              c_v = c_vertls[0];
              if (c_v.V == root)
              {
                 s_n.Add(c_v);
                 break;
              }
```

```
        else
        {
           c_vertls.AddRange(c_v.parents);
           c_vertls.Remove(c_v);
        }
      }
    }
    if (s_n != null)
    {
       for (int i = 0; i < s_n.Count; i++)
       {
         c_v = s_n[i];
         while (c_v.child_node != null)
         {
           c_v1 = c_v.child_node;
           c_v.parents.Add(c_v1);
           c_v.child_node = null;
           c_v = c_v1;
         }
       }
    }
  }
}

public List<cVertice> find_route(cVertice root, List<cVertice> dest_lst)
{
  List<cVertice> stack = new List<cVertice>();
  List<cVertice> route = new List<cVertice>();
  cVertice tmp = null, tmp_1 = null, tmp_2 = null, tmp_3 = null;
  stack.Add(root);
  while (stack.Count > 0)
  {
    tmp = stack[0];
    for (int i = 0; i < tmp.parents.Count; i++)
    {
       route.Add(tmp.parents[i]);
       tmp_1 = dest_lst.Find(n => n.V == tmp.parents[i].V);
       if (tmp_1 != null)
       {
         tmp_2 = new cVertice(root.V, 1, 1);
         route.Add(tmp_2);
         for (int k = 1; k < route.Count; k++)
         {
```

This class stores some methods to make some multicast trees from the founded MSTs. This class has the property root that stores some information (ex. Identifier and coordinates) about the source node of the tree. The property s_n is the set of vertices that are roots of the founded multicast trees. The destination nodes are stored in the list d_lst, this class has some methods to find immediate nodes to add to the result tree.

```
                    tmp_3 = new cVertice(route[k].V, 1, 1);
                    tmp_2.parents.Add(tmp_3);
                    tmp_2 = tmp_3;
                }
            }
        }
        stack.RemoveAt(0);
    }
    return route;
    }
}
```

e) The algorithm for finding MST

```
public class cKruskal
{
    public List<cVertice> Vertices { get; set; }
    public List<cEdge> Edges {get; set;}
    public int iSo_dinh { get; set; }
    public int[][] routing_table { get; set; }
    cVertice vtc;
    cEdge cEdg;
    cVertice cVtc, cVtc_1;
    bool bIn_V = false;
    List<int> edges_add;

    int[][] get_weight(string f_name)
    {
        int[][] k_q;
        List<List<string>> lSt_val = new List<List<string>>();
        List<string> ar_val = new List<string>();
        string lVal = null;
        string[] vArr = null;
        StreamReader rd = new StreamReader(f_name);
        while (!rd.EndOfStream)
        {
            lVal = rd.ReadLine();
            vArr = lVal.Split(new char[] { ' ' });
            ar_val = new List<string>(lVal.Split(new char[] { ' ' }));
            lSt_val.Add(ar_val);
        }
        k_q = new int[lSt_val.Count][];
        for (int i = 0; i < lSt_val.Count; i++)
        {
            k_q[i] = new int[lSt_val[i].Count];
            for (int j = 0; j < lSt_val[i].Count; j++)
            {
                k_q[i][j] = Convert.ToInt32(lSt_val[i][j]);
            }
        }
        return k_q;
    }
```

```
public cKruskal(string f_name)
{
   init_alg(f_name);
}

int init_alg(string f_name)
{
   int k_q = 0;
   List<cVertice> q_verts;
   try
   {
      routing_table = get_weight(f_name);
      Edges = new List<cEdge>();
      q_verts = new List<cVertice>();
      iSo_dinh = routing_table.Length;
      Vertices = new List<cVertice>();
      edges_add = new List<int>();
      for (int i = 0; i < routing_table.Length; i++)
      {
         for (int j = 0; j < routing_table[i].Length; j++)
         {
            if (routing_table[i][j] != 0)
            {
               cEdg = new cEdge(i, j, routing_table[i][j]);
               Edges.Add(cEdg);
            }
         }
      }
      Edges.Sort(delegate(cEdge e1, cEdge e2)
      {
         return e1.weight.CompareTo(e2.weight);
      });
   }
   catch
   {
      k_q = -1;
   }
   return k_q;
}
```

```
public cMST find_MST()
{
  List<int> edges_add = new List<int>();
  int edg_count, iRoot, iRoot_1;
  edg_count = 0;
  List<cVertice> MST = new List<cVertice>();
  cMST mt = new cMST();
  iRoot = 0;
  iRoot_1 = 0;
  for (int i = 0; i < Edges.Count; i++)
  {
    bIn_V = false;
    iRoot = -1;
    cVtc = find_Edge(Edges[i].fVertice, MST, ref bIn_V, ref iRoot);
    if (!bIn_V)
    {
      vtc = new cVertice(i, 1, Edges[i].weight);
      MST.Add(vtc);
      edg_count++;
      edges_add.Add(i);
    }
    else
    {
      if (cVtc != null)
      {
        cVtc_1 = find_Edge(Edges[i].eVertice, MST, ref bIn_V, ref iRoot_1);
        if (cVtc_1 != null)
        {
          if (iRoot != iRoot_1)
          {
            cVtc.parents.Add(cVtc_1);
            cVtc_1.child_node = cVtc;
            edg_count++;
            edges_add.Add(i);
          }
        }
      }
```

```
            tmp_v = q_verts[0];
            if (tmp_v.V == V)
            {
               iRoot = tmp_v.V;
               in_V = true;
               break;
            }
            q_verts.RemoveAt(0);
            if (tmp_v.parents != null)
            {
               q_verts.AddRange(tmp_v.parents);
            }
         }
      }
      if (!in_V)
         iRoot = 0;
      return tmp_v;
   }

   public cMT find_MT(int sr_n, List<int> ds_set, cMST Mst)
   {
      cMT Mt = new cMT();


      return Mt;
   }
}
```

```
      tmp_v = q_verts[0];
      if (tmp_v.V == V)
      {
         iRoot = tmp_v.V;
         in_V = true;
         break;
      }
      q_verts.RemoveAt(0);
      if (tmp_v.parents != null)
      {
         q_verts.AddRange(tmp_v.parents);
      }
   }
}
if (!in_V)
   iRoot = 0;
return tmp_v;
}

public cMT find_MT(int sr_n, List<int> ds_set, cMST Mst)
{
   cMT Mt = new cMT();


   return Mt;
}
}
```

This class uses the MST finding algorithm by the principles of KrusKal Alg. to accept properly vertices to the result set. This algorithm is effective when the number of vertices of the graph is not large. By the above analysis the number of the edges is more than the number of vertices one. This Alg. finds more than one MST tree until the number of remaining vertices is not enough for one properly MST or there is no founded MST.

The next is the diagram to test the performance of the MST making Alg. that the given graph has less than or equal to 10000 nodes. The number of times to simulate is 1000. The time to execute from 100 up to 170 ms. The cost of each edge is generated randomly with the given graph is full connected, the number of edges is: $|V|*(|V|-1)/2 = 500000$ (Fig. 5).

This diagram finds MST when number of nodes of the given graph is changed. The Alg. to find the multicast tree is rather simple as above introduction. Sometimes the time to execute the Alg. is not increased when the number of nodes of the graph is increasing.

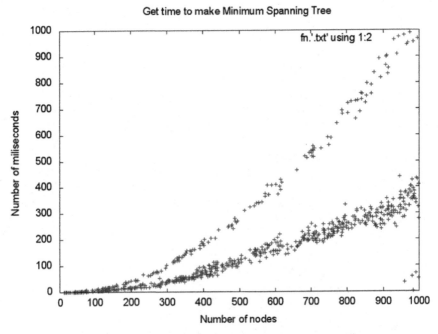

Fig. 5. The graph visualizes the processes to make MSTs.

7 Conclusions

Normal network node can use proactive or reactive or on-demand routing protocol based on network situation and mobile rate of nodes. So applying above algorithms to find multiple paths routes with QOS guaranteed is very effectively and the capability to scale to large networks. When the number of nodes increases, we may use the above-introduced R^+ tree to make hierarchical multicast routing. The purpose of hierarchical multicast routing is mainly aimed to reduce overhead in large network routing. The algorithms that are used for finding multiple multicast trees are both very comfortable for from small to large networks with guaranteed QOS.

References

1. Long, N.T., Thuy, N.D., Hoang, P.H.: Research on applying hierachical clustered based routing technique using artificial intelligence algorithms for quality of service of service based routing, internet of things and cloud computing. Spec. Issue Qual. Serv. Serv. Based Routing **3**(6–1), 1–8 (2015). doi:10.11648/j.iotcc.s.2015030601.11
2. Long, N.T., Thuy, N.D., Hoang, P.H.: Research on innovating and applying evolutionary algorithms based hierarchical clustering and multiple paths routing for guaranteed quality of service on service based routing, internet of things and cloud computing. Spec. Issue Qual. Serv. Serv. Based Routing **3**(6–1), 9–15 (2015). doi:10.11648/j.iotcc.s.2015030601.12
3. Srungaram, K., Krishna Prasad, M.H.M.: Enhanced Cluster Based Routing Protocol for Manets
4. Ferreira, C.: Gene Expression Programming: A New Adaptive Algorithm for Solving Problems
5. Roy, B.: Ant Colony based Routing for Mobile Ad-Hoc Networks towards Improved Quality of Services
6. Long, N.T., Thuy, N.D., Hoang, P.H., Chien, T.D.: Innovating R tree to create summary filter for message forwarding technique in service-based routing. In: Qian, H., Kang, K. (eds.) WICON 2013. LNICST, vol. 121, pp. 178–188. Springer, Heidelberg (2013). ISBN: 978-3-642-41773-3
7. Long, N.T., Tam, N.T., Chien, T., Thuy, N.D.: Research on innovating, applying multiple paths routing technique based on fuzzy logic and genetic algorithm for routing messages in service - oriented routing. J. Scalable Inf. Syst. EAI
8. Chen, K.-T., Fan, K., Dai, Y., Baba, T.: A Particle Swarm Optimization with Adaptive Multi-Swarm Strategy for Capacitated Vehicle Routing Problem
9. Bano, T., Singhai, J.: Probabilistic: a fuzzy logic-based distance broadcasting scheme for mobile ad hoc networks. Int. J. Adv. Comput. Sci. Appl. (IJACSA) **3**(9), 124–129 (2012)
10. Roy, B.: Ant Colony based Routing for Mobile Ad-Hoc Networks towards Improved Quality of Services

Innovating R Tree and Multicast Routing to Make QOS Multiple Paths for Service Based Routing

Nguyen Thanh Long[1(✉)], Nguyen Duc Thuy[2], and Pham Huy Hoang[3]

[1] Software Development Division III, Informatics Center of Hanoi Telecommunications,
Hoan Kiem, Hanoi, Vietnam
Ntlptpm1@yahoo.com
[2] Center for Applied Research and Technology Development,
Research Institute of Posts and Telecommunications, Hanoi, Vietnam
Nguyenducthuy07@gmail.com
[3] Information Technology Institute, Ha Noi University of Science Technology, Hanoi, Vietnam
Hoangph@soict.hut.edu.vn

Abstract. In the advanced routing of new networks communication and network technologies, it not only operates on some lower levels of a network protocol. But it also operates on some upper layers such as the application layer the highest-level layer in network protocol stack of OSI model. The routing process can be known by a more abstract concept. It can process on many layers on network's stack of OSI model. So this kind of routing may be called the upper layer routing protocol. As the content based routing, in the service based routing protocol, the information can be classified by categories or service classes. Subscribers and publishers can communicate with each other but they don't know other's address. So it is more dynamical in processing and more comfortable for ad-hoc network. However the upper routing must be based on lower layers to make routing decisions. But normal routing protocols are used for most static network or rather small wireless networks or not high mobility networks. In mobile ad-hoc networks, nodes move very often and fast, so bandwidth of connection between them may be reduced. Therefore the transmission delay may be increased. The paper aims at purpose to increase QOS of routing by hierarchical clustering routing by using R^+ tree in addition with some advanced techniques multicast routing, multiple paths, use GEN/ BEE/ ANT to optimize routes to transmit data. In R^+ tree model, the network's nodes are managed by Bottom-Up model from leaf nodes to root of the tree. All the leaf nodes, inner nodes and root of this tree are used for two roles: (i) Manage a cluster that consists all nodes that have direct connections with this node; (ii) Operate as a normal node. The paper mentions: (i) Setup hierarchical clustering network by using R tree structure. (ii) Making multicast tree from some cluster heads for fast routing. (iii) Making optimized route by Ant Colony Optimization.

Keywords: MANET · R^+ · Service · Routing · Multi-paths · Bandwidth · Cluster · Tree · Multicast · QOS · Overhead · Ant · ACO

© ICST Institute for Computer Sciences, Social Informatics and Telecommunications Engineering 2016
P.C. Vinh and V. Alagar (Eds.): ICCASA 2015, LNICST 165, pp. 370–379, 2016.
DOI: 10.1007/978-3-319-29236-6_35

1   Basic Concepts

R tree is also the same as another tree, such as it has root, branches, and leaves. However it always keeps balance in its structure that is after each insert, update, delete operations it has to regulate its structure to remain each node has number of its children in the predefined range.

The routing protocol in MANET is very popular in recently communication and computer technologies. In particular, routing protocol for service based routing is emerging in some recent years. In this paper, we analyze the R^+ to organize the network topology in hierarchical clustering model. The R^+ tree is rather simple to use for programming and design (Fig. 1). The R^+ can be expressed by the formula:

$$R^+ = R^+ \left(C_1 \right) \, U \, R^+ \left(C_2 \right) \, U \, ... \, U \, R^+ \left(C_n \right). \tag{1}$$

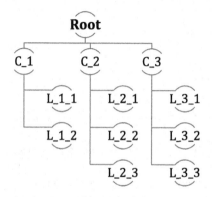

Fig. 1. A R^+ tree with two levels and node range [2, 3].

We assume R^+ tree has n children C_1, C_2, ..., C_n. In turn, each C_i is a child that connects directly to the root of R^+ tree. Each R^+ child tree, that has some children as its parent. In R^+ tree, each inner node has a number of children that is in a predefined range [m, M], in which m, M are two bounds of this range. The lower bound m is belonged to the range $[0, \lfloor M/2 \rfloor]$. In a network, the nodes usually connect to each other to establish a network topology. This topology may be RING, STAR, BUS ... But when the number of nodes is increased and the space that occupies very large. The normal topologies are not very comfortable, it must to innovate these traditional topologies that in the recent time the multicast topology is usually used, to the larger network we may use hierarchical clustering model to organize the network topology. In this paper, we apply R^+ tree to organize the network in hierarchical clustering model. So multiple levels from the root of the tree to its leaves distribute the network. In the tree, the network nodes in a level and belonged to a local root that are called a cluster or group. In a cluster or small group, the nodes usually have some more common characteristics with a cluster head, this is main node of a cluster. The cluster head manages all important tasks in this cluster.

The cluster head is usually has much energy and operational capacity, that can operate continuously to communicate with each node in its cluster and some other cluster heads. The network of some cluster heads may establish the framework for the upper level of cluster (Fig. 2).

$$\text{NETWORK}\left(U\left(CH_i\right)\right) = CH_1 U\, CH_2 U\, CH_3 U\, \ldots\, U\, CH_n. \qquad (2)$$

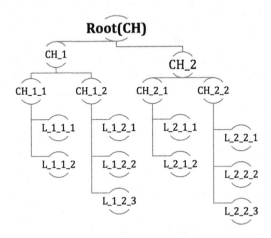

Fig. 2. R^+ tree with cluster hierarchical model.

This NETWORK(U(CH$_i$)) is established that called a next level of cluster, that also has a cluster head. In this way, up to the root we have the root of the tree is cluster head of the highest level of the whole network. Therefore, it is very easy to realize that in the first level there are some n basic clusters, $n \in [m, M]$, in which each cluster has some nodes that in fact are network nodes, that has this root of this cluster is cluster head. The cluster head is a leaf node of the main R tree. So these nodes communicate with this cluster head for controlling and data communication in this cluster and outside networks. In the next levels, the roots of lower level establish the upper level, and they vote one of these nodes is cluster head. Therefore, it is easy to realize that the root of an upper level manages all nodes of all branches that connect to this local root. Then it is also the cluster head of this upper level of some cluster heads of one level lower some clusters.

2 R^+ Tree Advantages for Hierarchical Cluster Routing

The algorithms are used to make R^+ tree is introduced in our previous papers rather deeply. In this paper will introduce some more details on using this tree to make hierarchical clustered routing. R tree can be expressed by a four items tuple:

$$R = \{m, M, root, \{F\}\} \qquad (3)$$

{F} is the set of functions to insert, update, delete and regulate the tree.

We define R^+ tree by recursive formula:

$$\mathbf{R^+\,(Root)\ =\ R^+\left(Child_1\right)\ U\,R^+\left(Child_2\right)\ U\ ...\ U\,R^+\left(child_n\right).} \tag{4}$$

In that, Root is root of the R^+ tree, so it is the most important node of the whole network, is the cluster head of top level cluster. Root often transmits control messages to their children members to coordinate its one level lower clusters. In turn these children members also manage their clusters by sending controlling messages. So overhead on control messages is:

$$\mathbf{OverHead\,(Control)\ =\ n_1{}^*n_2{}^*\,...{}^*\,n_m.} \tag{5}$$

For every leaf node can be operate. In that n_1 is number of children nodes in level 1 of R^+ tree, n_2 is average number of children nodes of each cluster in level 2... As mention above, $n_i \in [m, M]$, with the level of this tree m usually not large. Especially controlling messages are sending simultaneously from a cluster head to all its children nodes. So its delay is guaranteed as QOS request. Normally controlling messages are flooding on network, so it very fast causes network congestion. Especially it reduces network or route bandwidth (B) very fast for data transmission because almost B is used for controlling network. The configuration of each cluster is operated in low-level service of cluster head by Operating System. When a node is covered by a cluster head with satisfied bandwidth, it may join this cluster by invitation message of this cluster head. Then this network local change is transmitted to network by multicast tree of some clusters. At first, this control message (M) is transmitted to the cluster head (CH) of parent cluster (PC) of the cluster head of current cluster. The cluster head of PC transmits this M to all members of PC and to CH of its cluster. By this way, this change of network configuration is very fast to be updated on all CHs. All child nodes of network leaf nodes don't need to receive this information, so it reduces much of bandwidth. The number of leaf nodes is:

$$n_1{}^*n_2{}^*\,...{}^*\,n_m = \prod_{i=1}^{m} n_i. \tag{6}$$

with m level of network. Because the tree always is balanced so this number is rather stable. So each cluster has to store two main kinds of connections: (i) one to the cluster head of cluster that it belonged; (ii) one to all its cluster members. This number of connections is near to:

$$n_i + 1. \tag{7}$$

Hence it is very good for storage management in each cluster head. In each child node of a leaf node of tree that needs to store only one connection to its cluster head.

The algorithm to choose cluster head as introduced by our previous papers [1, 2, 6, 7]. In fact, a node can be belonged to some clusters simultaneously because all connections to these clusters also satisfy bandwidth demand. At the time to join network with very high density of nodes. For instance, many upper levels of cluster may accept this node at closed time. If this node stores all connections to these cluster heads then the time to update network topology is reduced by multicast tree from this node to all these CHs. With this way the root of R^+ can be connected to some another trees easily. It establishes a daisy chain R^+ trees. Because this model of networks can avoid the constraint of [m, M] in each level of R^+.

3 Find Optimized Route by Multiple Paths and Multicast Routing

The temporary backbone of network of R^+ daisy chain can be established some multicast trees or meshes of cluster heads of some clusters of this network for data transmission. Hence it avoids R^+ structure in some critical circumstances to directly transmitting data from a source node to many destinations. This concept is very comfortable to upper layer routing in advanced networks. The algorithms to establish multiple multicasts and multiple paths with optimized routes that are found by GEN/BEE/ACO are introduced in [3, 4].

4 The Procedures to Accept a Node

As any normal protocol, when a node wants to join a network, it has to make HELLO message to broadcast it over network. When a cluster head receives this message, it checks some conditions. If these conditions such as node's energy, strength of signal, CH will make a join request to send to this node. This node will send this CH its authentication information to join this cluster. As introduced in [6], this node information is processed and it will be propagate to a basically cluster from this cluster. When the properly cluster accepts this node, all changes needed will be operated from this cluster to the root of R^+ tree. So it may happen the new node can be cluster head based on its capability and the procedures to vote new cluster for this cluster is processed. Hence at first it will be cluster of current cluster. The some cluster heads with the same level with this cluster head will vote new cluster head for the next level of clusters. The new node may be root of R^+ tree, if it satisfies the conditions.

4.1 Accepting Node Procedure

When a node is invited to join R^+ tree or the root of a R^+ that can be a branch of the large R^+ to receïve the HELLO of this node. The node's information is propagating back to the root of the R^+ tree. The node's information is processed to choose the child (branch) of the root node to accept this node. The function to assess a node to decide the child of a CH to accept a node is operated based on some parameters. These parameters are fuzzed to put to a fuzzy logic controller to get the fuzzed output result to make the decision. The process is propagate to the leaf node of the R^+ tree to add to one basically cluster.

4.2 Voting Cluster Head Procedure

The procedure to vote cluster head depends on some metrics of nodes in each cluster. When a cluster is established, some neuron network or fuzzy logic controller chooses the cluster head or a range of some cluster heads. Then the network of cluster heads of R^+ tree is optimized by GEN algorithm.

5 Using Ant Colony Optimization to Find Stable Multiple Path QOS Route

QOS route is satisfied for communication demands of many kinds of applications, it utilizes network resources very efficiently. QoS consists of some metrics: end-to-end delay, available bandwidth, cost, loss probability. ACO [14] supports some QoS features: (i) Multiple paths routing, (ii) Traffic adaptive routing, (iii) Do not decide based on local estimates, (iv) Find optimal paths based on many criteria to load balancing.

The paper introduces an algorithm to find QOS routes based on ACO which consists of two phases: (i) route discovery; (ii) route maintenance. In the discovery phase, it uses two kinds of packets like route request and route reply of DSR protocol which are Ant_Route_Request and Ant_Route_Reply. Some QOS demands are stored in Ant_Route_Request in combination with visited node's list field, this field stores nodes that are visited by this packet. So this packet contains: source address, destination address, hop count, bandwidth, visited node list initialized with source node.

5.1 Basic Concepts

Pheromone evaporation is some condition to choose the route. On the route to find food, an ant uses some pheromone evaporations to mask good routes. So other ants easy to find and go to the food source.

Establish to assess preference probability to choose a route based on: bandwidth of each link on the route, valid time remaining of links of route, total delay of all links, the hop count of this route by the formula:

Denote $G = (V, E)$ that represents the graph of the network, V is the set of vertices, E is the set of edges. Assume R is route found that consists of n links: $R = \{(V_1, V_2),$ $(V_2, V_3), \ldots, (V_{n-1}, V_n)\}$. Hence, bandwidth of R is calculated by:

$$B_R = \text{Min}_{i \in \overline{1,n-1}} B(V_i, V_{i+1}) \tag{8}$$

The valid time is remained of R that is defined by:

$$T(R) = \text{Min}_{i \in \overline{1,n-1}} T(V_i, V_{i+1}) \tag{9}$$

Total delay of R is:

$$D(R) = \sum_{i=1}^{n-1} D(V_i, V_{i+1}) \tag{10}$$

The hop count of R is:

$$H(R) = n - 1 \tag{11}$$

Each parameter has a weight factor: β_B, β_T, β_D and β_H for B_R, T(R), D(R), H(R) respectively.

Hence the route's quality is the same on each link of the route which is calculated by the formula:

$$QOS(R) = \frac{B(R)^{\beta_B} + T(R)^{\beta_T}}{D(R)^{\beta_D} + H(R)^{\beta_H}} \tag{12}$$

The quality of each link is defined as the visibility of the ant by the formula:

$$\eta_{i \to i+1} = \frac{B(V_i, V_{i+1})^{\alpha_B} + T(V_i, V_{i+1})^{\alpha_T}}{D(V_i, V_{i+1})^{\alpha_D} + H(V_i, V_{i+1})^{\alpha_H}} \tag{13}$$

5.2   Discovery Phase

Ant_Route_Request is broadcasted to 1-hop neighbors of the source node like a HELLO packet of OLSR. In each neighbor node: (i) node has to maintain its link quality table $\{L_{i \to j}\}$ of 1-hop distance nodes based on the accessing pheromone evaporation, it calculates the preference probability (P_{pref}) of each link based on information of routing table on this node. If P_{pref} is more than predefined threshold preference probability, then this link is chosen for forwarding Ant_Route_Request next into the network; (ii) Choose a 1-hop distance node among 1-hop distance nodes that is MPR, that has connections to almost 2-hop distance nodes of this node. So in choosing MPR is the next hop for the route to the destination. Now MPR functions as source node, it carries the same functions: broadcast Ant_Route_Request to its 1-hop distance nodes. When packet to find a route arrives at the destination node. Destination immediately creates Ant_Route_Reply to transfer back to the source node. In Ant_Route_Reply stores route has been detected, it is transferred by the unicast protocol to the source.

5.3   Maintenance Phase

Some routes can be detected in one discovery phase, but choose the optimal route by Genetic algorithm to transfer data. The remaining routes will be cached in the buffer of the source for multiple path routing, backup route in the case of main route hasn't existed by topology changes. But these routes are periodically checked for existence state.

6   Simulations

6.1   Establish R⁺ Tree for Hierarchical Network Clustering

The algorithms for establishing, updating R⁺ to hierarchically cluster network as the algorithms in [6] for building R⁺ to manage service based routing table.

Some Modifications: (i) A leaf node N_L stores n components $(C_1, C_2, ..., C_n)$, each component C_i stores a pointer P to an indexed item and a summary filter FS of its child node. Each indexed item stores a pair of two elements node identifier and its filter. Leaf node stores a summary filter of its components and cluster head's ID of its group. So each leaf node give information about one basic group of the network; (ii) Similarly, each inner or root node stores information about an upper group of the network. That is a cluster head's ID of its group, some components that have pointers to its child nodes and their summary filters; (iii) Condition for inserting a node N to a child group GC of a current group G is: check each components of G, calculate the formula: $FT = |(F \vee F_G)\backslash F|$, F_G is FS of GC, F is the filter of the inserted node. Put N to GC that gives FT is minimum or maximum result based on real condition. Starting this algorithm at root node of R to a leaf node, at the leaf node actually insert N to this basic group and regulate the R tree to the root node for satisfying condition: number of elements of each group in the range [m, M].

6.2   Simulate These Algorithms of Applying R⁺ Tree to Cluster Network

Execute the process to insert node to the network until there are 1000 nodes. Perform this process by the regulation: when adding enough 10 nodes, then remove 1 node. Measure time in ms needed to add or remove a node, then collect the results to make a below graph (Fig. 3):

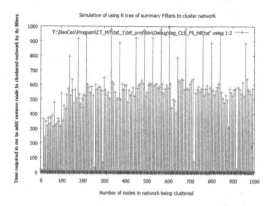

Fig. 3. Simulation results of applying R⁺ tree to insert/remove node of clustered network.

As the graph shows that the time required to execute does not increase when the number of nodes increases. It is approximate one milli second. Sometimes this time increases for regulating R^+ tree, but it is lower than one second. The time is rather high in the whole tree building process.

7 Assessment and Future Research

All above analysis are introduced in our previous papers, so they have very good performance. In the future, we have to research some compression techniques and encode data. It may help to reduce requested bandwidth and increase network security for data transmission. We may develop hierarchical clustering routing by using GPS to detect position of nodes with some techniques to estimate this position based on orbit of moving and velocity of node with some weighting model to assess these metrics to get correct node position to cluster network.

References

1. Long, N.T., Thuy, N.D., Hoang, P.H.: Research on applying hierachical clustered based routing technique using artificial intelligence algorithms for quality of service of service based routing. Internet Things Cloud Comput. 3(6–1), 1–8 (2015). doi:10.11648/j.iotcc.s. 2015030601.11. Special Issue:Quality of Service of Service Based Routing
2. Long, N.T., Thuy, N.D., Hoang, P.H.: Research on innovating and applying evolutionary algorithms based hierarchical clustering and multiple paths routing for guaranteed quality of service on service based routing. Internet Things Cloud Comput. 3(6–1), 9–15 (2015). doi: 10.11648/j.iotcc.s.2015030601.12. Special Issue:Quality of Service of Service Based Routing
3. Srungaram, K., Prasad, M.H.M.K.: Department of Information Technology, JNTUK-UCEV, Vizianagaram, A.P, India, Enhanced Cluster Based Routing Protocol for MANETS
4. Ferreira, C.: Departamento de Ciências Agrárias, Universidade dos Açores, 9701–851 Terra-Chã, Angra do Heroísmo, Portugal, "Gene Expression Programming: A New Adaptive Algorithm for Solving Problems"
5. Roy, B.: Tripura Institute of Technology, Narsingarh, Tripura, India, Ant Colony based Routing for Mobile Ad-Hoc Networks towards Improved Quality of Services
6. Hoang, P.H., Chien, T.D., Long, N.T., Thuy, N.D.: Innovating R tree to create summary filter for message forwarding technique in service-based routing. In: Qian, H., Kang, K. (eds.) WICON 2013. LNICST, vol. 121, pp. 178–188. Springer, Heidelberg (2013). ISBN: 978-3-642-41773-3
7. Long, N.T., Thuy, N.D., Hoang, P.H.: Research on innovating, applying multiple paths routing technique based on fuzzy logic and genetic algorithm for routing messages in service - oriented routing. J. Scalable Inf. Syst. EAI
8. Chen, K.-T., Fan, K., Dai, Y., Baba, T.: A particle swarm optimization with adaptive multi-swarm strategy for capacitated vehicle routing problem. Research Center and Graduate School of Information, Production and Systems, Waseda University, 2–7 Hibikino, Kitakyushu, Fukuoka, Japan
9. Roy, B.: Tripura Institute of Technology, Narsingarh, Tripura, India, Ant Colony based Routing for Mobile Ad-Hoc Networks towards Improved Quality of Services

10. Thuy, N.D., Long, N.T., Hoang, P.H.: Research on innovating, evaluating and applying multicast routing technique for routing messages in service-oriented routing. In: Vinh, P.C., Hung, N.M., Tung, N.T., Suzuki, J. (eds.) ICCASA 2012. LNICST, vol. 109, pp. 212–228. Springer, Heidelberg (2013). ISBN: 978-1-936968-65-7

Optimizing the Connection Time for LEO Satellite Based on Dynamic Sensor Field

Tuyen Phong Truong[1]([⊠]), Hoang Van Tran[1], Hiep Xuan Huynh[2], and Bernard Pottier[1]

[1] Université de Bretagne Occidentale, Brest, France
{phong-tuyen.truong,pottier}@univ-brest.fr, tvhoang@ctu.edu.vn
[2] Can Tho University, Can Tho, Vietnam
hxhiep@ctu.edu.vn

Abstract. In this paper, we propose a new approach to optimize the connection time for Low Earth Orbit (LEO) satellite based on dynamic sensor field. A dynamic sensor field is a long range sensor network that is able to redefine the gateway for extension communication time with LEO satellite to adapt with the shift of the satellite's ground track at each revolution. The model for optimization comprises the parameters of both ground and space segment. The experimental results are performed on two sensor field deployments which aim at optimizing the connection time for successful communication.

Keywords: Connection time · LEO satellite · Satellite communications · Satellite orbit · Sensor field

1 Introduction

Wireless Sensor Network (WSN) [2] is known as a network of sensors cooperatively operating in order to surveillance or collect the environmental parameters. In addition, a sensor field is included a number of devices that can interact with one another and also to the environment. Most of existing wireless technique aims at short range application in aspect of smart cities such as parking allocation, home services, and so on [1,4]. Although the short transmission range can be compensated by applying a mesh topology, it would be economically infeasible to deploy in large geographic areas or behind obstacles (mountains, oceans, ...). To overcome these disadvantages, a long range wireless sensor network is proposed as a field of nodes (sensors or/and actuators) networking wirelessly in a far distance.

LEO satellites are classified into Sun synchronized [19]. Due to the Earth's rotation, the orbit of LEO satellite is shifted in westward direction around the polar axis at each revolution, as shown in Fig. 1 [1]. It leads to the meeting points of a gateway on the Earth's surface and the LEO satellite will be changed over time. Moreover, gateways can only communicate with LEO satellites when the satellites in their visibility region, generally in a short time approximately

© ICST Institute for Computer Sciences, Social Informatics and Telecommunications Engineering 2016
P.C. Vinh and V. Alagar (Eds.): ICCASA 2015, LNICST 165, pp. 380–394, 2016.
DOI: 10.1007/978-3-319-29236-6_36

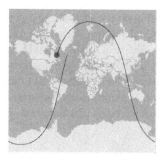

Fig. 1. LEO satellite's trajectory westward shifts because of the Earth's rotation [1].

5–10 min [5]. With a static sensor field, it can be occasionally unsuccessful in communication with the LEO satellite because the meeting time do not enough for data exchange.

A dynamic sensor field, which has the ability to redetermine its gateway to adapt with the shifts of LEO satellite's paths, is suitable to improve the connection time. To optimize the connection time, it is necessary to choose proper gateways for the longest length of connection time. Therefore, the connections between a LEO satellite and a dynamic sensor field is presented by graph-based model because it is convenient to observe and apply the optimization algorithms. In this paper, we propose a new approach based on dynamic sensor field to optimize connection time for LEO satellites.

The remainder of this paper is organized as follows. In Sect. 2, we overview related works. Section 3 presents a dynamic sensor field model. How to optimize the connection time between a sensor field and a LEO satellite based on dynamic sensor field is presented in Sect. 4. Section 5 gives two experiments of optimizing the connection time before a conclusion is drawn.

2 Related Work

In the last decade, researches on communication services provided by LEO satellites have focused on several main directions as follows.

Almost studies in LEO satellite design aim at optimizing the design the mechanics, interconnections, electric circuits, power supply to increase the lifetime of satellites [4,18].

Besides, many papers present about orbit design work, for example [5,20,21]. These researches focus on design satellites' trajectory, handover traffic and constellation for better operations in missions. Some of surveys also address the related issues of cooperating and optimizing the positions of ground stations in order to improve the durations of communications, as can be seen in [3,13].

On another approach, many surveys show the research topics in the optimization of communications that attracts so many researchers. They work on protocols, radio frequencies, onboard transceivers and antenna designs to enhance the quality of communication services with a low power consumption which were introduced in so many technical papers such as [6,16,17].

The LEO satellite communication can be used in mobile satellite communications, surveillance the Earth surface, geological surveys, so on [4]. However, the direct radio links between sensor fields and LEO satellites are not considered in literature. In recent years, it emerges as an attractive topic because of the current innovation solutions such as LoRa Semtech and solutions from vendors QB50 [1,8].

3   Dynamic Sensor Field

3.1   Sensor Field

A sensor field (SF) [7] is presented by a graph G(V, E) with a set of vertices $V = \{v_1, v_2, ..., v_n\}$ and a set of edges $E = \{e_1, e_2, ..., e_m\}$ with $e_k = e(v_i, v_j)$, $k = 1..m$, $i = 1..n$, $j = 1..m$, $m = 2^n$. The weights of these edges are defined by $W = \{w_1, w_2, ..., w_m\}$ where the value of each w_k is given by function $f_1()$, $w_k = f_1()$ (Fig. 2).

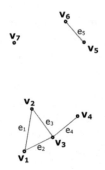

Fig. 2. A graph of a sensor field with 7 vertices (nodes) $V = \{v_1, v_2, v_3, v_4, v_5, v_6, v_7\}$ and 5 edges $E = \{e_1 = e(v_1, v_2), e_2 = e(v_1, v_3), e_3 = e(v_2, v_3), e_4 = e(v_3, v_4), e_5 = e(v_5, v_6)\}$.

Each node of SF has a maximum communication range that is indicated by a circle with radius r. In order to define the conditions to exist an edge, we introduce two following definitions:

Definition 1 (Established Edge). An edge is established if and only if the distance between a pair of vertices is less or equal to the minimum value of their radii, $d_{(v_i, v_j)} \leq \min(r_i, r_j)$.

Definition 2 (Not Established Edge). An edge is not established if the distance between a pair of vertices is greater than the minimum value of their radii, $d_{(v_i, v_j)} > \min(r_i, r_j)$.

As can be seen in Fig. 3, a pair of vertices (v_5, v_6) have the same maximum communication range that is indicated by two solid red circles with radius r.

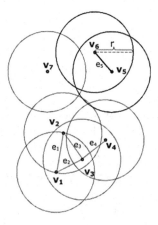

Fig. 3. The graph of a sensor field. The maximum communication range of nodes that is indicated by two solid red circles with radius

Because the distance between v_5 and v_6 is less than r, $d(v_5, v_6) < r$, based on Definition 1 there exists an edge e_5 connecting them. Similarly, the others edges of this graph namely $e_1 = e(v_1, v_2), e_2 = e(v_1, v_3), e_3 = e(v_2, v_3), e_4 = e(v_3, v_4)$ could be established. There are $2^n - 5$ edges between a pair of vertices of this graph that are not existed due to adequacy of Definition 2. Note that vertex v_7 is isolated because all distance values between it and the other vertices are inadequate to the Definition 1.

3.2   Extended Sensor Field

An extended sensor field (ESF) is used to describe a sensor field in the connection with a LEO satellite. When a LEO satellite connects with a sensor field, its sub-point on the ground (sub-satellite point) is considered as a center vertex, s, of the graph. Consequently, the graph consists of $n + 1$ vertices $P = \{V, s\} = \{v_1, v_2, ..., v_n, s\}$. In addition, the number edges of the graph are $m + n$ by adding

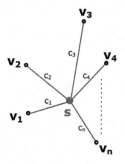

Fig. 4. A star graph of the connections between center vertex s (a sub-satellite point) and other vertices $\{v_1, v_2, ..., v_n\}$ (nodes of a sensor field).

n new edges $C = \{c_1, c_2, ..., c_n\}$ with $c_i = c(s, v_i)$, $i = 1..n$. The weights of the n new edges are defined by $Z = \{z_1, z_2, ..., z_n\}$ where the value of each z_i is given by function $f_2()$, $z_i = f_2()$. Hence, in this case the set of edges is $R = \{E, C\} = \{e_1, e_2, ..., e_m, c_1, c_2, ..., c_n\}$ and the set of corresponding weights is $Q = \{W, Z\} = \{\{w_k\}, \{z_i\}\}$ with $k = 1..m$, $i = 1..n$. As a result, the ESF is presented by a graph G(P,R).

Figure 4 illustrates a star graph of the connections between a center vertex s (a sub-satellite point on the Earth's surface) and a set of n vertices, $V = \{v_1, v_2, ..., v_n\}$ (nodes of a SF). It is noted that sub-satellite point, s, is where on the ground the straight line connecting the center of the Earth and the satellite meets the Earth's surface. If the satellite and any node can communicate with each other, there exists an edge between them. Thus, n direct connections between s and the set of vertices are indicated by a set of n edges $C = \{c_1, c_2, ..., c_n\}$.

3.3   Dynamic Sensor Field

To describe a dynamic sensor field (DSF) in connections with a LEO satellite, we propose two definitions as follows:

Definition 3 (Connection Vector). Connection vector is a vector which stores vertices in set $V = \{v_1, v_2, ..., v_n\}$ connecting with center vertex s in chronological order.

Definition 4 (Time Vector). Time vector is a vector which stores time of the corresponding connections in *Vector connection*.

In a dynamic sensor field, only one vertex (node) in set $V = \{v_1, v_2, ..., v_n\}$ is chosen to connect with the center vertex (sub-satellite point), s, at a time. Generally, different nodes could be chosen based on the set of weights at different times. The name of chosen node is stored in *Connection vector* and the corresponding time is stored in *Time vector*.

Connection number	1	2	3	...
Connection vector	v_1	v_4	v_2	...
Time vector	t_1	t_2	t_3	...

Fig. 5. An example of satellite connection data with three rows: *Connection number*, *Connection vector* and *Time vector*.

Figure 5 shows that in *connection 1*, center vertex s establishes the connection with v_1 at time t_1. In a similar way, in *connection 2* at time t_2 and *connection 3* at time t_3, v_4 and v_2 are chosen to connect with s respectively.

Three graphs of the dynamic sensor field in three different connections with the center vertex, s, at different times t_1, t_2 and t_3 are shown in Fig. 6. At time t_1 (see Fig. 6(a)), vertex v_1 is chosen and edge c_1 is established. Similarly, in Fig. 6(b) and (c) vertex v_4, v_2 are chosen that leads to c_4, c_2 are established at time t_2 and t_3 respectively.

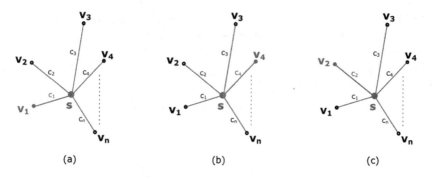

Fig. 6. The graph of a dynamic sensor field with three different connections (solid red lines) at time t_1, t_2 and t_3.

4   Connection Optimization

4.1   Compute the Connection Time

In this section, we describe the way to calculate connection time, f_2, between a LEO satellite and a gateway of DSF, v_i [19,22]. Similarly, the calculation could be applied for all other nodes. Note that every node of the sensor field is assumed as a gateway for the connection with the satellite in calculating the values of connection time.

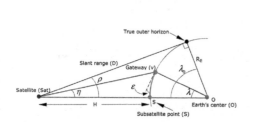

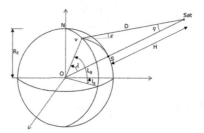

Fig. 7. Gateway of sensor field geometry [19].   **Fig. 8.** Geometrical relation between sub-satellite point (S) in coordinate frame [19].

First, it is necessary to define the angles and related distances between satellite, a gateway on the ground and the Earth's center. The parameters are indicated on Figs. 7 and 8. For angular radius of the spherical Earth, ρ_i, can be found from relation

$$\sin(\rho_i) = \frac{R_E}{R_E + H} \qquad (1)$$

where $R_E = 6378.14\,\mathrm{km}$ is the Earth's radius and H is the altitude of the satellite above the Earth's surface.

In this work, we assume that connection duration is the amount of time when a gateway is still under the access area of LEO satellite with $\varepsilon_i \geq 5\ deg$, therefore $\varepsilon_{i_{min}} = 5\ deg$. With the value of $\varepsilon_{i_{min}}$, the values of *maximum Earth central angle*, $\lambda_{i_{max}}$, *maximum nadir angle*, $\eta_{i_{max}}$, and *maximum slant range*, $D_{i_{max}}$, can be computed by the following equations:

$$\sin(\eta_{i_{max}}) = \sin(\rho_i)\cos(\varepsilon_{i_{min}}) \tag{2}$$

$$\lambda_{i_{max}} = 90\ deg - \varepsilon_{i_{min}} - \eta_{i_{max}} \tag{3}$$

$$D_{i_{max}} = R_E\frac{\sin(\lambda_{i_{min}})}{\sin(\eta_{i_{max}})} \tag{4}$$

The maximum Earth central angle, $\lambda_{i_{max}}$ is defined as the radius of the access area. The double of $\lambda_{i_{max}}$ value is the ground track's swath width. From Fig. 9, the maximum value of the instantaneous access area, $IAA_{i_{max}}$, of a gateway on the Earth's surface will be defined by

$$IAA_{i_{max}} = 2\pi R_E^2(1 - \cos(\lambda_{i_{max}})) \tag{5}$$

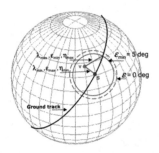

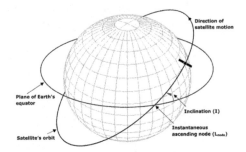

Fig. 9. Determination of the coverage for LEO satellite [19].

Fig. 10. A LEO satellite on its orbit [19].

As can be seen on Fig. 10, the orbit of a LEO satellite is specified by two main parameters namely the inclination angle, I, and longitude, L_{node}, of the instantaneous ascending node. In Earth geometry, these parameters often expressed in terms of the pole of the orbit plane with coordinates as

$$lat_{pole} = 90\ deg - I \tag{6}$$

$$long_{pole} = L_{node} - 90\ deg \tag{7}$$

From the geometry of Fig. 8, knowing the latitude and longitude of both the orbit pole and the gateway the value $\lambda_{i_{min}}$ can be found from

$$\sin(\lambda_{i_{min}}) = \sin(lat_{pole})\sin(lat_{g_i}) + \cos(lat_{pole})\cos(lat_{g_i})\cos(\Delta long_i) \tag{8}$$

where $\Delta long_i$ is the longitude difference between the gateway and the orbit pole. Consider the satellite in a circular orbit, the *orbit period* in minutes, P, is related to altitude, H, in kilometers by

$$P = 1.658669 \times 10^{-4} \times (6,378.14 + H)^{3/2} \tag{9}$$

Finally, the *connection time*, f_{2_i}, is given by

$$f_{2_i} = (\frac{P}{180 \ deg}) \arccos(\frac{\cos(\lambda_{i_{max}})}{\cos(\lambda_{i_{min}})}) \tag{10}$$

4.2   Define the Operation Modes of DSF

In order to describe the behaviors of a dynamic sensor field, we propose two definitions as follows:

Definition 5 (Passive Mode). Passive mode of a dynamic sensor field is established when a dynamic sensor field automatically collects and prepares the environmental data to sent before visiting a LEO satellite. Each time the satellite is perceived, the gateway of sensor field will establish the connection and then send the data. All processes of a dynamic sensor field are programmed and repeated systematically.

Definition 6 (Active Mode). Active mode of a dynamic sensor field is established when a dynamic sensor field has the ability to response satellite's commands before the end of a contact. In this mode, a LEO satellite visits a dynamic sensor field and establishes a connection with a gateway. The satellite then sends a command to gateway for control purposes and/or collecting environmental data from DSF. After a certain period of time, it expects to receive the feedback data also via a gateway. Hence, there is a pair of gateways: *Input gateway* for receiving satellite's command at the starting time and *Output gateway* for sending data to satellite before the satellite leaving.

4.3   Constraint

The altitude of a LEO satellite must be in range from 275 km to 1400 km due to atmosphere drag and Van Allen radiation effects [3,19]. Besides, the experimental results were announced by High Altitude Society in United Kingdom that LoRa SemTech transceivers can communicate in distance up to 600 km in environment without any obstacle and 20–40 km in urban area [8]. Based on these factors, maximum communication range for all nodes in long range sensor fields is 40 km in this work. LEO's satellites are chosen in our experiments must have the orbit altitude less than 600 km. Furthermore, the satellite's relative speed over a fixed point on the Earth's surface must be around 7.5–8.0 km/sec [19]. The speed of the satellite is calculated by

$$v = \sqrt{\frac{Gm_E}{R_E + H}} \tag{11}$$

Equation 11 shows that the speed of the satellite in orbit is in inverse proportion of its altitude [19]. Where G is universal gravitational constant ($G = 6.67 \times 10^{-11}$ Nm^2/kg^2) and m_E is the mass of the Earth ($m_E = 5.98 \times 10^{24}$ kg). With orbit altitude of satellite in range 300–600 km, the speed of satellite on orbit must be in range 7.56–7.73 km/sec.

4.4 Optimization Method

In order to present the method of optimization for connection time, we introduce two following definitions:

Definition 7 (Sensorset). A sensorset is created whenever one or more nodes appear and/or disappear in a subset of nodes.

Let a DSF with n nodes, $V = \{v_i\}$, $i = 1..n$, and an extended node, s, which is the sub-satellite point of a LEO satellite. The problem is how to optimize the connection time between the DSF with a satellite. A sensorset $A_k = \{v_j\}$, $j = 1..m$ with $m \leq n$, is several nodes that the satellite can connect at a time. A_k is a subset of V so that the union of all subsets A_k in the period of time, $T = t_k$, $k = 1..p$ is set V, $V = A_1 \cup A_2.. \cup A_p$. It is necessary to find out a set of proper nodes that provides the longest length of time for the connection. This leads to two following sub-problems:

Problem 1: Consider a sensorset, which node provides the longest connection duration time.

The connection times of all nodes are calculated and then sorted in a descending list. To obtain maximum connection time, the node corresponding to the value at the top of this list is selected to connect with the satellite.

The algorithm for selecting the gateways of the DSF is briefly presented as follows:

```
//Calculate connection durations
for i = 1 to n
    f2ᵢ = Time4Con(Nodei.Position, SubSat.Position);
//Find the maximum value of connection durations
MaxVal = max{f2};
//Node, which has the maximum value of connection durations, will
become a gateway
if (f2ᵢ = MaxVal) then
    UpdateConnectionData(i,Nodeᵢ,t);
```

Problem 2: Consider all nodes of a DSF, which set of nodes provide total of connection times which is the longest.

To select a proper set of nodes, the *association analysis algorithm* [23] is applied. If a DSF V has n nodes, there are $2^n - 1$ connection items, $G = \{g_l\}$, $l=1..(2^n - 1)$. The DSF is represented in a binary format, where each row corresponds to a connection item and each column corresponds to a node. A node value is one if the node appears in a connection item and zero otherwise. Weight of a connection item determines how often a connection item is applicable to a set of connection items. The weight of a connection item, $g_i \in G$, can be defined as follows:

$$w(g_i) =\mid \{g_l \mid g_i \subseteq g_l, g_l \in G\} \mid \tag{12}$$

where the symbol $\mid . \mid$ denotes the number of elements in a set.

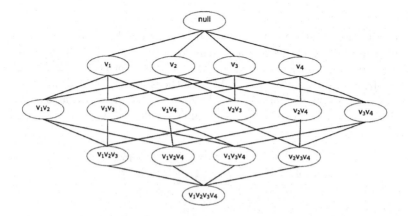

Fig. 11. A sensors lattice for a DSF $V = \{v_1, v_2, v_3, v_4\}$.

A lattice structure is used to enumerate the list of all possible connection items. In Fig. 11, a connection item lattice for a DSF $V = \{v_1, v_2, v_3, v_4\}$ is depicted. Connection item corresponding to the highest weight is chosen aim at achieving the longest length of connection time.

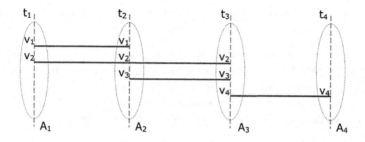

Fig. 12. The connections between a 4-node DSF with a LEO satellite.

For example, in Fig. 12 a DSF with 4 nodes, $V = \{v_1, v_2, v_3, v_4\}$. There are 4 sensorsets $A_1 = \{v_1, v_2\}$, $A_2 = \{v_1, v_2, v_3\}$, $A_3 = \{v_2, v_3, v_4\}$ and $A_4 = \{v_4\}$.

Connection items	Weights
(v_1, v_2, v_4)	1
(v_1, v_3, v_4)	1
(v_2, v_4)	3
(v_2, v_3, v_4)	1

Fig. 13. The weights of connection items in a DSF with 4 nodes.

The weights of connection items are presented in Fig. 13. Because the weight of connection item (v_2, v_4) is highest, this connection is chosen.

5 Experiment

5.1 Data Used

For experiments, there are two abstract structure of the long-range sensor fields for fire forest surveillance were generated by using NetGen [9]. Figure 14 shows the first dynamic sensor field consists of 50 sensor nodes (DSF50) that is stretched from South Central Coastal to Southeast and extended up to Mekong River Delta in Vietnam. The second dynamic sensor field contains 110 nodes (DSF110) that was deployed along Vietnam's border.

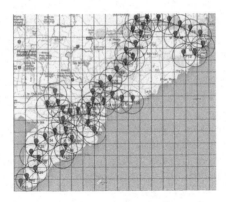

Fig. 14. A dynamic sensor field with 50 nodes (DSF50) was deployed by using NetGen.

According to the constraints about the satellite's orbit altitude as discussed in Sect. 4.3, BEESAT-3 [12] was chosen in this experiment. Thirty data orbits of BEESAT-3 were used as input data of optimization process (see Fig. 15). The data are stored in plain text (.txt files) that are used as input data. Figure 16 presents the structure of a orbit data (orbit 12794) after reforming.

12794	12795	12801	12802	12809	12810	12816	12817	12824	12825
12831	12832	12839	12840	12846	12847	12854	12855	12861	12862
12869	12870	12876	12877	12884	12885	12891	12899	12900	12906

Fig. 15. Thirty orbits of BEESAT-3 from 17 to 25 August 2015.

Time	Lat	Lon
17/08/2015 15:58:24	-9.81	117.00
17/08/2015 15:58:34	-9.24	117.23
...	...	...

Fig. 16. The orbit 12794 of BEESAT-3 after reforming.

5.2 DYNSEN Tool

We have developed the DYNSEN tool by Octave [14], that enables to optimize the connection time between a dynamic sensor field with a LEO satellite. GPredict [10] is used to provide the information about satellite path. Besides, NetGen tool [9] is utilized to generate the abstract network of two dynamic sensor fields from geographic data provided by Google maps service. The obtained result is nodes of the DSFs which should be configured as gateways for the best connection duration times.

5.3 Scenario 1: The Dynamic Sensor Field in Passive Mode

Thirty sensorsets are created with each satellite's orbit, during the period of time the BEESAT-3 visits the DSF50. With each sensorset, a subset of connections is established. The weights of each connection in subset are then computed. A set of connection items is created by combining these subsets. The best connection is chosen based on the weights of connection items. For instance, with orbit 12974 and 12795 node v_{08} and v_{44} are chosen corresponding to the connection time 6.5691 and 9.9812 min, respectively.

Orbit	Static Sensor Field		Dynamic Sensor Field	
	Gateway (lat, long)	Connection time (minutes)	Gateway (lat, long)	Connection time (minutes)
12794	V30 (10.04, 105.74)	4.5182	V08 (11.75, 109.10)	6.5691
12795	V30 (10.04, 105.74)	9.9145	V44 (10.40, 105.37)	9.9812

Fig. 17. The connection times of DSF50 in two BEESAT-3's orbits (12794, 12795) on August 17, 2015.

The gateways of DSF50 in two BEESAT-3's orbits (12794 and 12795) on August 17, 2015 are shown in Fig. 17. From the experimental results with the thirty different orbits of BEESAT-3, the dynamic gateway gives the longer length of time for connection than the static one.

The chart in Fig. 18 presents the average connection duration of the DSF50 in thirty orbits of BEESAT-3 and the corresponding the value of DSF110. It is obvious that in case of applying a dynamic gateway, the connection times are 8.16 and 8.41 min for DSF50, DSF110 respectively that are better than the values with a static gateway, 7.04 min. Consequently, the increment in connection duration is around 65–80 s which is equivalent to an increase of 15–20 %.

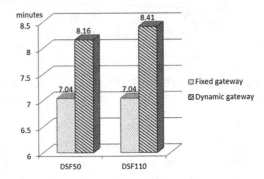

Fig. 18. The average of connection times of DSF50 and DSF110 over thirty different orbits of BEESAT-3.

5.4   Scenario 2: The Dynamic Sensor Field in Active Mode

In this scenario, the dynamic sensor field with 110 nodes is used in our experiments. We also use the information about ground track of two BEESAT-3's orbits (12794 and 12795) on August 17, 2015 as input data. The similar process as described in scenarios 1 is utilized, but in this case a pair of nodes must be chosen as *Input gateway* and *Output gateway* for the best connection time with each satellite's orbit.

Orbit	Input gateway (lat, long)	Output gateway (lat, long)
12794	V81 (11.70, 109.12)	V13 (20.31, 105.59)
12795	V109 (10.37, 104.80)	V03 (22.08, 104.06)

Fig. 19. Two pairs of *(Input gateway, Output gateway)* are chosen corresponding to two BEESAT-3's orbits (12794 and 12795) in August 17, 2015.

Figure 19 shows pairs of *(Input gateway, Output gateway)* for two BEESAT-3's orbits. With orbit 12794, v_{81} was selected as *Input gateway* and v_{13} was selected as *Output gateway*. However, with orbit 12795 (v_{109}, v_{03}) was a chosen as pair of *(Input gateway, Output gateway)*.

6   Conclusion

Based on the dynamic structure of a sensor field, we have described a new approach in order to optimize the connection time for LEO satellites. The distances between the sub-satellite point and each node of the sensor field is utilised for determination a pair of gateways to adapt with different satellite path. The experimental results were obtained by performing DYNSEN in two different scenarios in which the dynamic sensor field was optimized to adapt with the shifts of satellite paths. With dynamic sensor field approach, the amount of time for communication could be improved in long-range sensor field applications using satellite connections to monitor, control and collect environmental data.

Acknowledgment. The author gratefully acknowledges the MOET-VIED (Ministry of Education and Training - Vietnam International Education Development) of the Vietnam Government for awarding a scholarship to the first author of this research.

References

1. Lucas, P.-Y., Van Long, N.H., Truong, T.P., Pottier, B.: Wire-less sensor networks and satellite simulation. In: 7th EAI International Conference onWireless and Satellite Systems (WiSATS 2015), Bradford, United Kingdom (2015)
2. Àlvarez, C., Duch, A., Gabarro, J., Serna, M.: Sensor field: a computational model. In: Dolev, S. (ed.) ALGOSENSORS 2009. LNCS, vol. 5804, pp. 3–14. Springer, Heidelberg (2009)
3. Cakaj, S., Fischer, M., Scholtz, A.L.: Practical horizon plane for low earth orbiting (LEO) satellite ground stations. In: TELE-INFO 2009 Proceedings of the 8th WSEAS International Conference on Telecommunications and Informatics, pp. 62–67. ACM Digital Library (2009)
4. Celandroni, N., et al.: A survey of architectures and scenarios in satellite-based wireless sensor networks: system design aspects. Int. J. Satell. Commun. Network. **31**(1), 1–38 (2013). Wiley
5. Cakaj, S., Kamo, B., Lala, A., Rakipi, A.: The coverage analysis for low earth orbiting satellites at low elevation. Int. J. Adv. Comput. Sci. Appl.(ijacsa), **5**(6) (2014)
6. Cakaj, Sh., Keim, W., Malaric, K.: Communication duration with low earth orbiting satellites. In: Proceedings of IEEE, IASTED, 4th International Conference on Antennas, Radar and Wave Propagation, Montreal, pp. 85–88 (2007)
7. Bayat, D., Habibi, D., Ahmad, I.: Development of a wireless sensor node for environmental monitoring. In: The Sixth International Conference on Sensor Technologies and Applications (SENSORCOMM), pp. 1–5. International Academy, Research, and Industry Association (IARIA) (2012)
8. UK High Altitude Society. http://www.instructables.com/id/Introducing-LoRa-/step19/LoRa-receiver-links/
9. Pottier, B., Lucas, P.-Y.: Dynamic networks NetGen: objectives, installation, use, and programming. Technical report, Universit de Bretagne Occidentale, France (2014)
10. Alexandru Csete, GPredict project. http://gpredict.oz9aec.net/
11. Google Maps services, the map of Vietnam. https://www.google.fr/maps/place/Vietnam/@15.9030623,105.8066791,6z/data=!3m1!4b1!4m2!3m1!1s0x31157a4d736a1e5f:0xb03bb0c9e2fe62be
12. Berlin Experimental and Educational Satellite-2 and -3. https://directory.eoportal.org/web/eoportal/satellite-missions/b/beesat-2-3
13. Cakaj, S.: Elevation variation with low earth orbiting search and rescue satellites for the station implemented in kosovo. Univers. J. Commun. Netw. **1**, 32–37 (2013). Horizon Research Publishing

14. Eaton, J.W.: GNU Octave 4.0.0. (2015). https://www.gnu.org/software/octave/
15. Dosiere, F., Zein, T., Maral, G., Boutes, J.P.: A model for the handover traffic in
    . low earth-orbiting (LEO) satellite networks for personal communications. Int. J.
    Satell. Commun. pp. 574–578 (1993)
16. Fernandez Del Rio, J.E., Nubla, A., Bustamante, L., Van't Klooster, K: SOPERA:
    a new antenna concept for low Earth orbit satellites. In: Antennas and Propagation
    Society International Symposium, pp. 688–691. IEEE Press (1999)
17. Sreeja, T.K., Arun, A., Jaya Kumari, J.: An: S-Band Micro-strip Patch Array
    Antenna for nano-satellite applications. In: International Conference on Green
    Technologies (ICGT), pp. 325–328 (2012)
18. Abdi, B., Alimardani, A., Ghasemi, R., Mirtalaei, S.M.M.: Energy storage selection
    for LEO satellites. Int. J. Mach. Learn. Comput. 3(3), 287–290 (2013)
19. Larson, W.J., Wertz, J.R.: Chapter 5: Space Mission Geometry. Space Mission
    Analysis and Design, 3rd edn, pp. 95–230. Microcosm Press, El Segundo (2003)
20. Muri, P., McNair, J.: A survey of communication sub-systems for intersatellite
    linked systems and CubeSat missions. J. Commun. 7(4), 290–308 (2012)
21. Chowdhury, P.K., Atiquzzaman, M., Ivancic, W.: Handover Schemes in Satellite
    Networks: State-of-the-Art and Future Research Directions. Communications Sur-
    veys & Tutorials, 8(4). IEEE express (2006) Signal Processing and Communica-
    tions Perspectives, pp. 277–309. John Wiley & Sons Ltd (2207)
22. Capderou, M.: Chapter 8- Ground track of a statellite. Handbook of satellite orbits
    from Kepler to GPS, pp. 301–338. Springer International Publishing Switzerland
    (2014)
23. Tan, P.-N., Steinbach, M., Kumar, V.: Chapter 6 Association Analysis: Basic Con-
    cepts and Algorithms. Introduction to Data Mining, pp. 327–413. Addison-Wesley
    Longman Publishing Co., Inc., Boston (2005)

Extraction of Chondromalacia Knee Cartilage Using Multi Slice Thresholding Method

Jan Kubicek[✉], Jan Valosek, Marek Penhaker, and Iveta Bryjova

The Department of Cybernetics and Biomedical Engineering, FEI, VSB-TU
Ostrava, 17. listopadu 15, 70833 Ostrava-Poruba, The Czech Republic
{jan.kubicek,jan.valosek.st,marek.penhaker,
iveta.bryjova}@vsb.cz

Abstract. The paper deals with design of segmentation method for extraction special types of pathological changes of knee cartilage. Those changes are called chondromalacia of knee cartilage. These pathological changes unfavorable influence cartilage's surface and significantly deteriorate their structure. Knee cartilage is typically investigated by Magnetic resonance imaging (MRI). MRI is very effective method which is able to differentiate individual knee structures. On the other hand some tiny tissue's changes are not clearly recognizable because MRI generates image outputs in shade gray levels. Chondromalacia in early stage is manifested by weak contrast compared to its surroundings and therefore it is very complicated to recognize and locate spots where this change is. The proposed segmentation method is able to precisely differentiate individual cartilage structures and perform extraction of cartilage structure and adjacent pathological changes. Furthermore the proposed segmentation method transform MRI data to contrasting color map which is more effective approach then gray shade levels. The proposed algorithm is being tested on sample 30 patient's records and results are discussed with radiological experts.

Keywords: Multi slice thresholding · Image segmentation · MRI · Chondromalacia · Articular cartilage · MATLAB

1 The Structure of Articular Cartilage

Covering the surface of bone in all joints is articular cartilage. Articular cartilage is smooth white and glistening. This type of cartilage is very specialized and has several functions. One of the most important functions is force distribution. If a load is placed on the joint the cartilage spreads the load out so that it is distributed over a large surface area. This protects the bone and makes it so that the underlying bone is not subjected to large forces. Normal cartilage also is very smooth and slippery. A joint is able to bend and straighten with very little resistance because of the low coefficient of friction of articular cartilage which is less than that of ice. Lastly the shape of the bone and cartilage surface provides stability to the joint.

The composition of articular cartilage is very complex and is made up of collagen (protein in skin and nails), water and various other proteins. These proteins and water are in a compressed state and because of this balance are able to resist load. When a

© ICST Institute for Computer Sciences, Social Informatics and Telecommunications Engineering 2016
P.C. Vinh and V. Alagar (Eds.): ICCASA 2015, LNICST 165, pp. 395–403, 2016.
DOI: 10.1007/978-3-319-29236-6_37

load is placed on the joint the cartilage surface will compress and the water and protein will be pushed closer together. Water and protein have opposite charges (positive and negative) and repel each other as they are compressed and therefore resist load. The load is also spread out over a large area to dissipate the force. This is the way that articular cartilage is able to decrease the load on the underlying bone and protect it. The most frequent used sequences for examination of articular cartilages are spin-echo sequence (Fig. 1) and fast spin echo sequence with fat saturation (Fig. 2) [1–6].

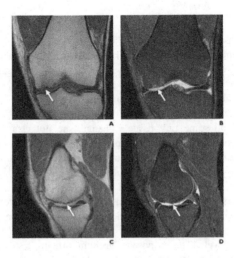

Fig. 1. Multiple planes of fast spin-echo (FSE) images show cartilage damage in 54-year-old man

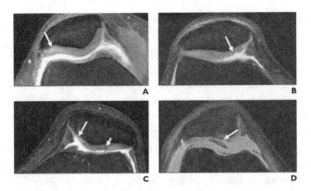

Fig. 2. Axial fast spin-echo (FSE) images with fat saturation of cartilage damage

2   The Design of Multi Slice Segmentation Algorithm

After loading input image it is necessary defining region of interest (RoI). This step is needed for localization area where cartilage structure should be. By this procedure it is increased analyzed area, there is a disadvantage because it is focused smaller part of image which contains less pixels. Therefore it is needed to perform pixel's interpolation for achieving better image contrast. For this task, linear interpolation method is used.

The core of segmentation method is based on the Otsu method. Otsu method normally uses just one thresholding. Segmentation method with only one thresholding is not suitable for processing of medical images. In this area, it is much better to use which is based on the multi slice thresholding approach, which increases sensitivity of recognition individual structures in cartilage images. Furthermore segmentation procedure transforms shade level pixels to contrasting color map with high level of contrast scale.

Proposed thresholding method finds specific levels for a image based on the histogram distribution into equally large areas. Specific thresholding level is used for each area. The analyzed image is consequently segmented according to all thresholding levels.

Individual pixels with different shade levels are labeled as L with range: $[0,1,...,L]$. Number of thresholding levels is given as p. The size of one segmented area is given by equation:

$$a = \frac{L}{p} \tag{1}$$

Between class variance σ^2 is calculated similarly as Otsu method:

$$\sigma^2 = W_0 * W_1 * (\mu_0 - \mu_1)^2 \tag{2}$$

The number of divided regions of the histogram is equal to the number of thresholding levels p. Optimal thresholding levels for individual areas are given:

$$P_p = max_p(\sigma^2) \tag{3}$$

For the validity of the above formulas is necessary that the number of pixels in different shades of gray L is equal to $256 * j$. Number of thresholding levels p must be from set: $[2*j, 4*j, 8*j]$, where j belongs to set: $[1,2,...,\infty]$. According to practical results, it is recommended to use set: $[1,2,...,8]$.

The segmentation output would be normally generated by shade gray levels. This way is it not appropriate because gray scale is not obviously recognizable. Due this fact transformation to color spectrum is performed. Each output segmentation class is coded by one number which represents individual structure. This transformation assigns to each class unique color. By this procedure is achieved contrasting map when individual colors reflect detected structures. [7–9] (Fig. 3)

The proposed algorithm for chondromalacia extraction is described by following diagram: [10–12]

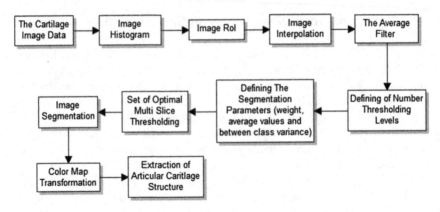

Fig. 3. The block diagram of multi slice algorithm for chondromalacia extraction

3   Data Analysis and Segmentation Results

The proposed algorithm has been tested on the sample of 30 patient's records. For examination of articular cartilage are normally used two types of MRI sequences: spin-echo sequence and fast spin echo sequence with fat saturation. There are four stages of chondromalacia:

- Degree 0 – physiological cartilage.
- Degree I – cartilage with swelling and softening.
- Degree II – partial rupture with a crack on the surface that does not interfere with the subchondral bone.
- Degree III – a crack extending to the subchondral bone with a diameter of up to 1.5 cm.
- Degree IV – exposed subchondral bone.

Physiological cartilage is normally represented by single colour spectrum (usually by white color but it depends which imaging sequence is used). If some color changes are registered on cartilage surface, it indicates pathological lesions. In Terms of image processing Degrees II – IV are not so interesting because those disorders are manifested by significant contrasting changes. Degree I is usually manifested by weaker change of color spectrum in comparison with adjacent structures. Those changes are badly recognizable by human eye. Therefore is for clinical practice really needed image processing tool for automatic recognizing areas of pathological spots. Significant advantage of the proposed software solution is expanding of interesting area to maximum size for better view (Fig. 4).

The proposed algorithm has been tested on sample image data which contain cartilage structure. Cartilage is corrupted by chondromalacia of first degree. At the first view those pathological changes are not clearly visible.

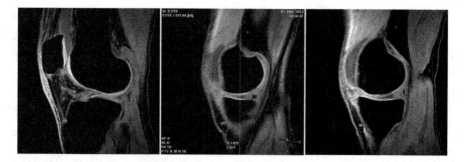

Fig. 4. Example of analyzed data

- Case 1

The articular cartilage is represented by darker-white color. Physiological cartilage would have been shown by white color. At the first view it is not obvious any changes on cartilage surface. After detailed investigation it is a little viewed weaker contrasting change on the cartilage surface. It is indicated first degree of chondromalacia. It is going to loss (delamination) of cartilage's dorsal part medial condyle of femur. In the square window area of interest is focused. Segmentation results create color map which differentiate individual tissue's structures (Fig. 5. left image). Physiological cartilage is represented by red color. It is obvious interruption on cartilage's surface (Fig. 5. right image).

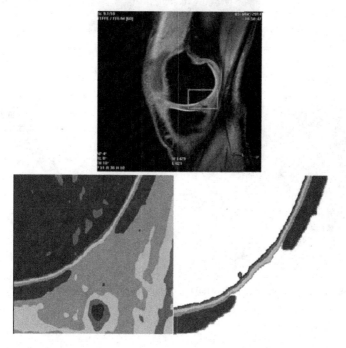

Fig. 5. Original MRI image data (up), segmentation results (left) and detected cartilage's surface with pathological interruption (right)

- Case 2

There are two images of articular cartilage which is suffered from chondromalacia of first degree. It is again needed to perform extraction of articular cartilage and pathological interruptions (Figs. 6, 7 and 8).

- Case 3

The third case deals with detection of inhomogeneity on cartilage of medial condyle's femur and tibia. These changes are very difficult recognizable in standard shade levels imagining. In segmentation output it is obvious changes of cartilage's structure. Those changes are accompanied by color changes from yellow to lightly blue color spectrum (Fig. 9).

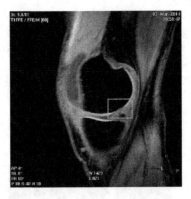

Fig. 6. Original image data with RoI

Fig. 7. Segmentation results (left), cartilage surface with interruption (right)

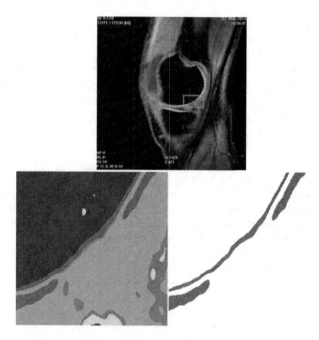

Fig. 8. Original MRI image data (up), segmentation results (left) and detected cartilage's surface with pathological interruption (right)

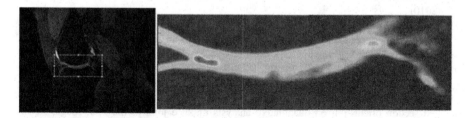

Fig. 9. Original MRI image (left) and segmentation output (right) (Color figure online)

4 Conclusion

The Article deals with design and testing of multi slice thresholding method for chondromalacia detection. The proposed algorithm is able to perform color mapping of individual structures from MRI images. The significant benefit is separation those structures to isolated classes and consequent selection interested structures. By described procedure it is possible to extract specific tissues from original MRI data. Benefit of proposed solution is deep sensitivity of classification even for the structures which are accompanied by badly visible contrast. This feature is needed especially for extraction of early stage chondromalacia. This disorder is manifested by weak contrast changes and therefore it is practically impossible to recognize and locate those pathological areas. On the base segmentation procedure articular cartilage is represented by single color spectrum (usually red color) and pathological interruptions are clearly indicated unlike from native MRI images. In clinical practice, there is no any other alternative for assessing articular cartilages. Those structures are assessed by human's eyes. This process is influenced by relative significant subjective error. The proposed software solution has been tested on the sample real patient's data and for now gives satisfactory results because it is able to reliably separate physiological cartilage and chondromalacia's changes. It is very favorable assumption for using it in clinical practice.

Acknowledgement. This article has been supported by financial support of TA ČR PRE SEED: TG01010137 GAMA PP1. The work and the contributions were supported by the project SP2015/179 'Biomedicínské inženýrské systémy XI' and This work is partially supported by the Science and Research Fund 2014 of the Moravia-Silesian Region, Czech Republic and this paper has been elaborated in the framework of the project "Support research and development in the Moravian-Silesian Region 2014 DT 1 - Research Teams" (RRC/07/2014). Financed from the budget of the Moravian-Silesian Region.

References

1. Otsu, N.: A threshold selection method from gray-scale histogram. IEEE Trans. Syst. Man Cybern. **9**(1), 62–66 (1979)
2. Fernández, S., et al.: Soft tresholding for medical image segmentation. In: IEEE EMBS (2010)
3. Graichen, H., Al Shamari, D., Hinterwimmer, S., Eisenhart-Rothe, R., Vogl, T., Eckstein, F.: Accuracy of quantitative magnetic resonance imaging in the detection of ex vivo focal cartilage defects. Ann. Rheum. Dis. **64**, 1120–1125 (2005)
4. Alparslan, L., Winalski, C.S., Boutin, R.D., Minas, T.: Postoperative magnetic resonance imaging of articular cartilage repair. Semin. Musculoskel Radiol. **5**, 345–363 (2001)
5. Eckstein, F., Stammberger, T., Priebsch, J., Englmeier, K.H., Reiser, M.: Effect of gradient and section orientation on quantitative analysis of knee joint cartilage. J. Magn. Reson. Imaging **11**, 161–167 (2000)
6. Disler, D.G., McCauley, T.R., Kelman, C.G., Fuchs, M.D., Ratner, L.M., Wirth, C.R., et al.: Fat-suppressed three-dimensional spoiled gradient-echo MR imaging of hyaline cartilage defects in the knee: comparison with standard MR imaging and arthroscopy. AJR Am. J. Roentgenol. **167**, 127–132 (1996)
7. Kubicek, J., et al.: Segmentation of MRI data to extract the blood vessels based on fuzzy thresholding. In: Barbucha, D., Nguyen, N.T., Batubara, J. (eds.) New Trends in Intelligent Information and Database Systems, pp. 43–52. Springer International Publishing, Switzerland (2015)
8. Kubicek, J., Penhaker, M.: Fuzzy algorithm for segmentation of images in extraction of objects from MRI. In: 2014 International Conference on Advances in Computing, Communications and Informatics (ICACCI). IEEE (2014)
9. Penhaker, M., Kodaj, M., Kubicek, J., Bryjova, I.: Articular cartilage defect detection based on image segmentation with colour mapping. In: Hwang, D., Jung, J.J., Nguyen, N.-T. (eds.) ICCCI 2014. LNCS, vol. 8733, pp. 214–222. Springer, Heidelberg (2014)

10. Kubicek, J., Valosek, J., Selamat, A., Penhaker, M., Bryjova, I., Grepl, J.: Extraction of blood vessels using multilevel thresholding with color coding. In: The 2nd International Conference on Communication and Computer Engineering, 9–11 June 2015, Phuket, Thailand (2015)
11. Kubicek, J., Penhaker, M., Feltl, D., Cvek, J.: Guidelines for modelling BED in simultaneous radiotherapy of two volumes: tpv(1) and tpv(2). IEEE (2013)
12. Pustkova, R., Kutalek, F., Penhaker, M., Novak, V.: Measurement and calculation of cerebrospinal fluid in proportion to the skull (2010)

Determining the State of Cardiovascular System Using Non-invasive Multichannel Photoplethysmography

Lukas Peter[1(✉)], Ivo Vorek[1], Bertrand Massot[2], and Jan Kubicek[1]

[1] FEECS, Department of Cybernetics and Biomedical Engineering,
VSB – Technical University of Ostrava, 17. listopadu 15,
70833 Ostrava, Czech Republic
{lukas.peter,jan.kubicek,jan.kubicek}@vsb.cz
[2] INL, UMR5270 CNRS-INSA Lyon, University of Lyon,
69621 Villeurbanne Cedex, France
bertrand.massot@insa-lyon.fr

Abstract. The cardiovascular system is one of the most important system in human body and it is necessary to oversee its right function. Clinicians would benefit from the evaluation of the state of the cardiovascular system without using invasive entrance and to have information about state of all main parts of cardiovascular system. Pulse wave measurement could be one possibility of how to noninvasively evaluate the state of cardiovascular system and its individual parts. The paper introduces methodology of pulse wave measurement from several sites on the human body and the ECG signal simultaneously. Hardware and software materials developed for the solution are described and preliminary results are presented.

Keywords: ECG · Multichannel photoplethysmography · State of cardiovascular system · PWV · Labview

1 Introduction

Cardiovascular diseases are the most frequent causes of death in the world. This is very known and discussed problem, and yet many people underestimate risks connected to the formation of these diseases. Clinicians, together with engineers, try to find some reliable and noninvasive methods which help to evaluate the rate of cardiovascular problems. One of possible methods could be pulse wave measurement.

Parameters of pulse wave provide relevant information about heart rate and also about the good functioning of heart thanks to the information about start and end of systole and, what is very important, information about pulse wave velocity. Pulse wave velocity could be used for the evaluation of the stiffness of blood vessel or for the evaluation of blood pressure which is a complex indicator about state of cardiovascular system [1, 2].

Pulse wave results from the work of the left part of heart. From this part, the blood is ejected into the aorta, and the heart provides energy to make the blood circulate. A single pulse wave is generated during each cardio cycle, defined by the interval

© ICST Institute for Computer Sciences, Social Informatics and Telecommunications Engineering 2016
P.C. Vinh and V. Alagar (Eds.): ICCASA 2015, LNICST 165, pp. 404–412, 2016.
DOI: 10.1007/978-3-319-29236-6_38

between two successive systoles. Each pulse wave consists from a forward wave and a backward wave, the latter arising arises thanks to reflection of forward wave from the division of artery, and its shape is affected by elasticity of blood vessel. Decrease of stiffness of artery makes the forward wave smaller and backward wave bigger and vice versa [3, 4] (Fig. 1).

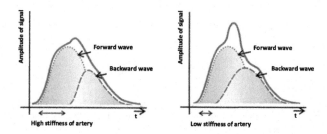

Fig. 1. Comparison of the shape of pulse wave based on stiffness of artery. High stiffness leads to faster waves and backward wave makes blood pressure higher. Low stiffness leads to a slower backward and positively affects blood flow.

Most of the time, Pulse wave is measured from periphery like fingertip or from places showing good blood perfusion like ear lobe, nose or forehead. This measurement is noninvasive and relatively comfortable for the patient. This is why the diagnostic methods based on processing of pulse wave could end up being a good candidate for the prevention of cardiovascular failure.

2 Problem Definition

Both pulse wave velocity and pulse transmit time depend on the properties of blood vessels and from heart mechanisms. Thus it is possible to evaluate non-invasively the state of cardiovascular system. From pulse wave it is also possible to evaluate the right functioning of heart because of its anacrotic and catacrotic parts. Anacrotic part is the increasing part of pulse wave which is produced by systole and catacrotic part is the slowly decreasing part which captures moving of artery wall during diastole.

Pulse waves which are measured on different places of human body has different properties. Differences of state of cardiovascular segments can then be identified (Fig. 2).

Pulse wave is affected by arterial stiffness which is also the reason why its shape is different on different places. The pulse wave velocity increases along with arterial stiffness for both forward and backward wave. In this case backward wave can affect the next forward wave already in anacrotic part which causes increasing of blood pressure [4–6].

It is possible to measure the pulse wave as a pressure wave, thanks to invasive pressure sensor, or as a volume wave, thanks to plethysmography. From plethysmography measurement, it is possible to obtain relevant information about shape and properties of pulse wave while this non-invasive method remains comfortable for the patient [7, 8]. Clinicians would from the use of a noninvasive system to help them with the evaluation

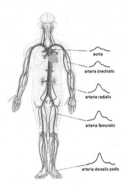

Fig. 2. Different shape of pulse wave based on location of measurement. For diagnosis not only the changes in shape of the wave are important, but also the time delay of pulse wave propagation from heart to the periphery.

of the state of cardiovascular system. The assessment of pulse waves from different parts of human body seems to be a relevant indicator. For the monitoring of cardiovascular system, it is necessary to use an accurate multichannel photoplethysmograph which can provide more complex information [9].

3   Implementation of New Solution

Our main objective was to develop a measurement device which would be able to non-invasively measure pulse wave from several parts of human body simultaneously and synchronously. Our solution consists from two parts; hardware part for analog prepro-cessing of measured signal and for AD conversion, and a software user interface for the display of measured signal and digital signal processing.

The hardware designed includes 6 channels for PPG measurement one channel for ECG measurement and an AD convertor. Software part includes digital filtering of measured signals and signal processing which is needed for evaluation of state of cardi-ovascular system.

3.1   Measurement Device

The whole hardware was developed as an independent device for the measurement of biological signals. For our purpose, it was mandatory to ensure a proper synchronous measurement between the channels in order to avoid time delay between the samples, and also a higher sampling rate than usual was required (Fig. 3).

PPG and ECG signals were preprocessed by an analog frontend for better conversion to digital form.

We used standard reflexive and transmission PPG sensors. All of these sensors were photoplethysmography sensors so they included one IR LED as transmitter and one photodiode as receiver, from which a small current is measured through a transimpe-dance amplifier to provide a voltage that can be converted by the ADC. Directly after

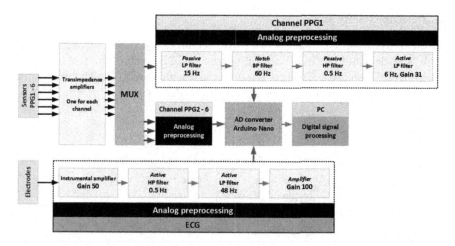

Fig. 3. Block scheme of the hardware part developed. The device includes six PPG channels and one ECG channel. Signal from each channel is processed analogically for better digital conversion. A software-controlled multiplexor enables to connect the output of the same amplifier to all channels to evaluate the delay between samples of different channels.

this amplifier the signals are sent through a multiplexor. This multiplexor enables to connect the output of one transimpedance amplifier to all measurement channels, while disconnecting other amplifiers. Having the same signal on every channel enables the evaluation of time delay between the different channel after analog processing and analog to digital conversion. A software compensation is then applied to cancel the delay during future measurements.

The analog preprocessing chain for PPG sensors consists of a series of filter for the removal of undesirable frequency components of the signal. Active and passive filters are used to preserve the 0.5 Hz–6 Hz frequency band which contains the relevant variations of the signal.

An Arduino Nano was used for digital conversion. This module includes a microcontroller which provides an 8-channel, 10-bit ADC. This microcontroller is also used to synchronously control the multiplexor using PWM.

The device is connected and powered by a host computer using USB (Fig. 4).

Fig. 4. Multichannel photoplethysmography device with three connectors for ECG electrodes. ECG in this device is used for time synchronization of all of pulse wave during one cardiac cycle.

3.2   Developed Software

The software developed consists of two parts. Acquiring and visualization of measured signals is made with LabView (National Instruments Corporation) for real time measurement. Digital signal processing of signals is made with Matlab (The Mathworks, Inc.) with the implementation of online processing tools (Fig. 5).

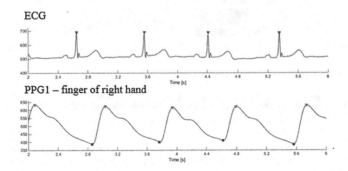

Fig. 5. Detection of significant points on signals measured. R-peak of ECG is detected as point of heart's systole, and subsequent valley and peak of pulse wave are detected on each channel. All of these point are used for statistical analysis and evaluation of relationship between parameters of pulse wave and state of cardiovascular system.

It is supposed that heart's systole can be determine as R wave from ECG. It means that for processing of ECG signal, an algorithm for detection of R waves based on adaptive threshold was implemented to determine which peak should be taken.

Digital processing of measured signals is focused on the computation of main parameters of PPG signals. Parameters evaluated are: the length of anacrotic and catacrotic part, and the length of each pulse wave and time delay between heart's systole and arriving of pulse wave at periphery. For the determination of these values it is necessary to determine peak and valley of each pulse wave. This detection is based on first derivation of the PPG signal [5].

4   Signal Analysis

Preliminary tests were conducted on a group of 6 individuals. The group was composed of men and women from three categories of age. The youngest category was composed of two healthy sportsmen without any chronic disease. The second category was composed of middle-age man and woman with adequate body. The woman has been treating hypertension for a long time. During the tests, measurements have shown that the man was also subject to hypertension. The oldest category of patients were two people with cardiac problems. The man has been subject to heart attacks and received twice bypass surgery. The woman did also have heart attack and she has a stent in coronary venous (Table 1).

Table 1. Group of measured patients.

Gender	Age	Smoker	BP	bpm
Male	24	No	121/80	74
Female	22	No	117/77	64
Male	52	Occasional	210/134	84
Female	51	Yes	134/81	80
Male	66	No	134/81	80
Female	67	Yes	103/63	61

All measurements were made at rest. Each subject was sitting on a chair and at the same time wasn't measured only pulse wave and ECG signal but also noninvasive blood pressure was measured by standard automatic tonometer.

Pulse waves were measured from index finger of right hand (PPG1); index finger of left hand (PPG2); second finger of right foot (PPG3); second finger of left foot (PPG4); right temporal bone (PPG5); left temporal bone (PPG6).

The length of anacrotic part of pulse wave was determined as the time duration between valley and peak of pulse wave; the length of catacrotic part was determined as the time duration between peak of one wave and valley from next wave. The duration of the whole pulse wave, and the time delay (PTT) between pulse wave and R wave from ECG were also measured. The Pulse wave velocity is calculated thanks to equation [6]:

$$PWV = \frac{D}{PTT} \tag{1}$$

Where D is the distance between heart and the place where the pulse wave was measured. This distance was measured by tape.

The expandability of blood vessels was also evaluated thanks to equation [6]:

$$Expandability = \left(\frac{3.57}{PWV} \right)^2 \tag{2}$$

After the evaluation all of parameters, a statistical analysis was made based on linear regression. Length of anacrotic part of pulse wave and age of patients were compared (Fig. 6).

It can be seen that anacrotic phase duration increases with age of. It can be interpreted as an effect of stiffness of blood vessel and also of heart mechanisms.

Another analysis was made on the relationship between expandability of blood vessel and age of patient (Fig. 7).

It can be seen that with increasing of age of patient, the expandability of blood vessel decreases.

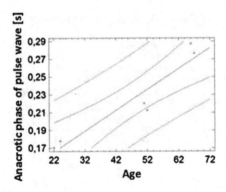

Fig. 6. Relationship between anacrotic phase of pulse wave, which corresponds to systole of heart, and age of patient. With increasing of age of patient; time of anacrotic phase of pulse wave decreases. Picture shows analysis which was made on signals from PPG1 (index finger of right hand).

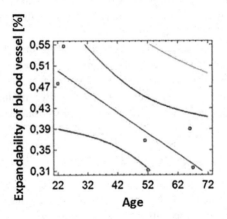

Fig. 7. Relationship between expandability of blood vessel and age of patient. With increasing of age; expandability of blood vessel decreases. Picture shows analysis which was made on signal from PPG1 (index finger of right hand).

Expandability of blood vessel and duration of the anacrotic part of pulse wave can be relevant of the actual state of cardiovascular system. These parameters affects blood pressure and heart's function. Table 2 shows comparison between all of these parameters all of patients. Interestingly, the third patient had hypertension during measurement. These preliminary results tends to confirm that stiffness of blood vessels has strong effect on blood pressure.

Table 2. Group of measured patients. Comparison between all of patient and main evaluating parameters.

PPG1				
Gender	Age	Expandability [%]	Anacrotic part [ms]	BP [mmHg]
Male	24	0.63	0.18	121/80
Female	22	0.61	0.17	117/77
Male	**52**	**0.38**	**0.21**	**210/134**
Female	51	0.52	0.22	134/81
Male	66	0.50	0.29	131/85
Female	67	0.48	0.28	103/63

5   Conclusion and Summary

It is very important to monitor state of cardiovascular system. There are many parameters which can bring significant information about its condition. A relevant indicator is the value of blood pressure. This value gives global information about state of cardiovascular system but many times it is more useful to know information about each part of cardiovascular system. A possibility to evaluate parameters of each parts is to measure pulse wave which gives information about state of blood vessel reflecting state of cardiovascular system.

Our main objective was to develop a system which could be used for evaluation of each part of cardiovascular system and gives complex information about state of cardiovascular system. This system should be accurate and comfortable for patient because of possibility of continuous long time monitoring.

Our measurements were made using a developed multichannel photoplethysmograph which was tested on group of six people. Six photoplethysmography signals from different places on human body were measured and analysis of these signals were conducted to study the impact of age on the duration of anacronic part of pulse wave and the expandability of blood vessels. Moreover the study has confirmed that this expendability has a direct impact on blood pressure.

Our device and methodology have thus shown promising results. This has been tested in laboratory conditions and now and the next step will be to integrate testing within clinical trials. Indeed for the validation of this method it is necessary to confirm the preliminary results obtained on a bigger group of patients and compare them to standard methods for evaluation stiffness of blood vessels or blood pressure.

Multichannel photoplethysmography is thus a promising method for long time monitoring of state of cardiovascular system which will bring better information about treatment of this system and it could prevent heart failure or; in the worst case, premature death.

Acknowledgments. This article has been supported by financial support of TA ČR PRE SEED: TG01010137 GAMA PP1. The work and the contributions were supported by the project SP2015/179 'Biomedicínské inženýrské systémy XI' and This work is partially supported by the Science and Research Fund 2014 of the Moravia-Silesian Region, Czech Republic and this paper has been elaborated in the framework of the project "Support research and development in the Moravian-Silesian Region 2014 DT 1 - Research Teams" (RRC/07/2014). Financed from the budget of the Moravian-Silesian Region.

References

1. Nichols, W., O'Rourke, M., Vlachopoulos, C.: McDonald's Blood Flow in Arteries: Theoretical, Experimental, and Clinical Principles, 6th edn. Hodder Arnold, London (2011). ISBN 978-0-340-98501-4, vol. xiv, 755
2. Peter, L., Noury, N., Cerny, M.: A review of methods for non-invasive and continuous blood pressure monitoring: pulse transit time method is promising? IRBM **35**(5), 271–282 (2014)
3. Peter, L., Foltyn, J., Cerny, M.: Pulse wave velocity measurement; developing process of new measuring device. In: 2015 IEEE 13th International Symposium on Applied Machine Intelligence and Informatics (SAMI), pp. 59–62. IEEE (2015)
4. Prutchi, D., Norris, M.: Design and Development of Medical Electronic Instrumentation: A Practical Perspective of the Design, Construction, and Test of Medical Devices. Wiley-Interscience, Hoboken (2005). ISBN 0471676233, vol. xv, 461
5. Pilt, K.: New Photoplethysmographic Signal Analysis Algorithm for Arterial Stiffness Estimation. Hindawi Publishing Corporation, Cairo (2013)
6. Salvi, P.: Pulse Waves: How Vascular Hemodynamics Affects Blood Pressure. Springer, New York (2012). ISBN: 978-884-7024-380
7. Augustynek, M., Semkovic, J., Penhakerova, P., Penhaker, M., Cerny, M.: Measurement and diagnosis assessment of plethysmographycal record. In: Abu Osman, N.A., Abas, W.A.W., Abdul Wahab, A.K., Ting, H.-N. (eds.) 5th Kuala Lumpur International Conference on Biomedical Engineering 2011. IFMBE Proceedings, vol. 35, pp. 320–323. Springer, Heidelberg (2011)
8. Collet, J., Cerny, M., Delporte, L., Noury, N.: Objective evaluation of body displacements during activities using the wearable inertial system ActimedARM. In: Engineering in Medicine and Biology Society EMBC 2014, 36th Annual International Conference of the IEEE, Chicago, United States, 26–30 August 2014
9. Cerny, M., Penhaker, M.: Wireless body sensor network in health maintenance systems. Elektronika Ir Elektrotechnika (9), 113–116 (2011). doi: 10.5755/j01.eee.115.9.762

Multichannel Photoplethysmography: Developing of Precise Measuring Device for Analysis of Cardiovascular System

Lukas Peter[1(✉)], Ivo Vorek[1], Bertrand Massot[2], and Jan Kubicek[1]

[1] Department of Cybernetics and Biomedical Engineering, FEECS,
VSB – Technical University of Ostrava, 17. listopadu 15, 70833 Ostrava, Czech Republic
{lukas.peter,ivo.vorek,jan.kubicek}@vsb.cz
[2] Lyon Institute of Nanotechnology, UMR CNRS 5270 INL-INSA Lyon,
University of Lyon, 69621 Villeurbanne Cedex, France
bertrand.massot@insa-lyon.fr

Abstract. State of cardiovascular system is possible to evaluate noninvasively thanks to analysis of pulse wave. Pulse wave is produced by heart which squirts blood to artery during systole. It is effect of changing in volume of blood vessels during propagation of blood. Pulse wave is affected by properties of blood vessel, as stiffness and diameter, and heart's work. Thanks to shape and time properties of pulse wave it is possible to evaluate state of cardiovascular system. Measurement of pulse waves from different parts of human body could bring complex information about state of cardiovascular system in whole human body. For such a measurement it is necessary to develop precise device which will be able to measure several pulse waves simultaneously without time delay between measuring channels. Paper describes developing of such device which also includes one channel for ECG measurement as time synchronization. For precise measurement was also developed measuring software for displaying of measured signals and their analysis.

Keywords: ECG · Multichannel photoplethysmography · State of cardiovascular system · PWV · LabView

1 Introduction

Diseases of the cardiovascular system is one of the most important diseases in the World. In Europe, cardiovascular disease is one of the most common causes of death. Medical doctors cooperate with engineers and they try to find to find a reliable, accurate, for patient comfortable and noninvasive method that would help to detect the cardiovascular disease and help to prevent preliminary death or heart's failure [1, 2].

It seems to be promising method noninvasive monitoring of the pulse wave. From the properties and parameters of the pulse wave it is possible to evaluate a variety of information such as heart rate, pulse wave propagation velocity associated with the calculation of elasticity of blood vessels and also blood pressure values [3].

© ICST Institute for Computer Sciences, Social Informatics and Telecommunications Engineering 2016
P.C. Vinh and V. Alagar (Eds.): ICCASA 2015, LNICST 165, pp. 413–419, 2016.
DOI: 10.1007/978-3-319-29236-6_39

The elasticity of the blood vessels can significantly contribute to the overall assessment of the state of the cardiovascular system. Reduced the elasticity of blood vessels can be effect of atherosclerosis or calcification in artery's wall [4, 5] (Fig. 1).

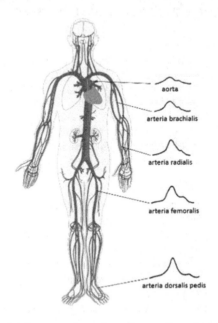

Fig. 1. Different shape of pulse waves in each cardiovascular segments. There is possible also to evaluated time dependency between these signals compare with ECG signal.

Analysis of pulse wave can bring good knowledge about state of cardiovascular system because shape and time properties are affect by state of blood vessel and of course by heart's work. The measuring of pulse waves from several places on human body simultaneously bring complex information about each segment of cardiovascular system [6–8].

2 Problem Definition

For precise measurement of pulse waves from several parts of human body simultaneously; it was necessary to develop multichannel device which included several channels for PPG measurement and also one channel for ECG measurement for time dependency analysis. It was necessary to be focused on some important facts:

- Measuring channels have to measure simultaneously without time delay.
- It is necessary to make calibration all of channels for precise measurement.
- Device has to have low power consumption for possibility of transporting.
- Measurement could be comfortable for patient because of long time monitoring.
- Measurement has to be safe for patient.

This paper describes our main objective to develop such a device and measuring software which helps medical doctor with better diagnosis of problems with cardiovascular system.

3   Implementation of New Solution

Multichannel photoplethysmography device consists from two parts. Hardware part for analogue signal preprocessing for better digital conversion and software part for displaying and digital processing of measured signals.

Thanks to standard Cannon DB9 connector could be used any standard PPG sensor which are connected to device. Device also includes biological calibration which is needed for evaluation of time delay between channels [9–11].

3.1   Measuring Hardware

The device includes six individual channels for measuring the pulse wave. For measurement can be used standard transmission and reflective PPG sensors. Pulse waves were measured simultaneously with one lead of ECG. ECG measurement was used as time synchronization for exact placement each pulse wave to right cardiac cycle and also for evaluation time dependency of pulse waves.

For accurate measurement of the pulse waves circuit contained a calibration. This function was formed by a multiplexer and was used for detecting unwanted time delays between each measuring channels.

For digitalization of the signal, control of multiplexers and communication with the computer was used development board Arduino Nano (Fig. 2).

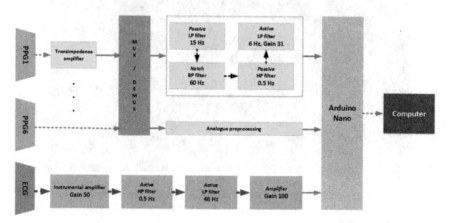

Fig. 2.   Block scheme of measuring hardware. Hardware includes six channel of PPG and one channel of ECG measurement.

Acquiring of signals of pulse waves was made by six identical measurement channels. Output from each trans impedance amplifier is bring to multiplexor which is there used because of calibration. From multiplexor is signal bring to analogue preprocessing where is signal amplified and filtered for better digital conversion.

Pulse wave was measured by sensor which includes infrared LED as transmitter and photodiode as receiver. The photodiode generates a current at its output which is needed to convert to voltage. This is make by trans impedance amplifier with a gain 4.7 M. After conversion of the signal to voltage it is put a series of filters. DPF signal is filtered by the cutoff frequency of 6 Hz, notch filter cut-off frequency of 60 Hz and HPF cutoff frequency of 0.8 Hz. In the last phase of the signal is filtered by an active filter formed OZ type DPF on the cutoff frequency of 6 Hz again and amplified by Gain = 31. In the last part of the circuit is ranked last type DPF filter cutoff frequency of 4.8 Hz. Amplification and filtering is on all six channels of pulse wave measuring identical [3].

Acquisition of ECG signal is made by one lead ECG circuit. Hardware preprocessing of signal consists from instrumental amplifier, analogue active filters and amplification.

For developing of measuring circuit were used rail-to-rail operational amplifiers. As instrumental amplifier was used INA126. Signals from two electrodes come to inputs of INA126. There are subtracted from each other because of their difference is raw ECG signal which is thanks to INA126 also amplify. For better digital conversion of signal was needed to filter signal. It was used active HP filter with cut off frequency 0.5 Hz for removing of slow changing of signal which is produce by breathing. After HP filter was put active LP filter with cut frequency 100 Hz for removing of high frequency of noise. Filtered signal is ready to AD conversion. Whole hardware solution was tested on scope (Fig. 3).

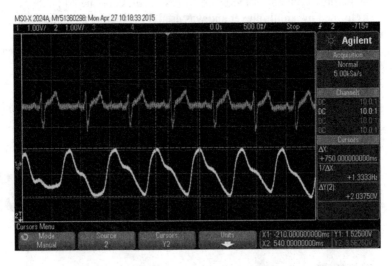

Fig. 3. Synchronous signals from one lead of ECG and one PPG sensor. Signals were measured simultaneously. Yellow curve shows ECG signal and green curve PPG signal from finger of right hand (Color figure online).

To eliminate the time difference between channels of the pulse wave measurement is made by a pair of multiplexers CD74HC4053F. Management of these multiplexers is provided by development board Arduino Nano. Calibration of these channels is made as biological calibration. When calibration mode is set calibration mode; multiplexor switch all of its inputs to one. It is used one sensor which is placed on human body and thanks to multiplexor signal from it comes to analog preprocessing part of all of channels. It is possible to evaluate time delay between channels and also it is possible to adjust amplitude of signal. This biological calibration ensures precise measurement.

The AD conversion and control of multiplexer ensures development board Arduino Nano. This module is a measuring board connected to developed device. The basis of this board is ATMega microcontroller 328. It is an 8-bit microcontroller with advanced RISC architecture. The main advantage of this microcontroller is a 10 bit eight channels of AD converter which ensures the transfer of seven signals to digital form and PWM output which controls multiplexers.

Maximum of sampling rate of this converter is 10000 samples per second for all channels together which means 1400 samples per second for each channel. For this developed device was used 1000 samples per second sampling rate.

Communication between the microcontroller and the computer is provided by USB converter CH340 G; it is a development board unoriginal.

Whole device is powered via USB by nonsymmetrical power supply +5 V and the current consumption is reduced at 500 mA [1] (Fig. 4).

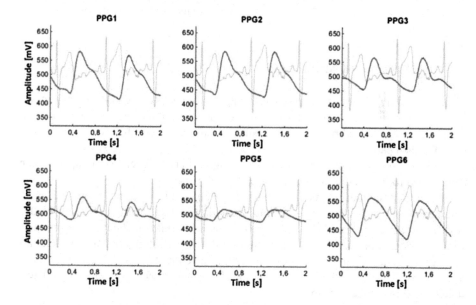

Fig. 4. Synchronous signals from all of six PPG sensors which were measured simultaneously. Signals were measure also simultaneously with ECG which was used as time synchronization of each cardiac cycle. Blue curve shows differences between PPG which were measured on different places on human body (Color figure online).

The circuit board consists of one piece cuprexitu about 15 × 15 cm and is equipped with classical components. The board is also designed for adding of galvanically isolated power supply with stabilized voltage + 5 V. This prototype is; for patient safely; powered by Arduino development board which is connected to computer via USB.

Individual PPG sensors are connected via a standard DB9 connector Cannon. In this nine pin connector are used only four pins. Two are used for supply and two for connecting of infrared diodes and the photodetector. Infrared LEDs are powered by +5 V and their resistance is adjustable via a potentiometer with value of resistor from 47 to 1047 Ω. By controlling this resistance it is possible to vary the intensity of infrared light for improved recording pulse waveform.

The whole device is packaged in a black plastic box with options to connect to a personal computer using the mini USB cable (Fig. 5).

Fig. 5. Multichannel photoplethysmography device with six channels for PPG sensors, potentiometers for adjusting of PPG wave and three connectors for ECG electrodes.

4   Conclusion and Summary

After developing of hardware part of measuring device it was tested in laboratory conditions. It was discovered time delay between each channels and device was calibrated. Thanks to integrated calibration it is possible to calibrate device before each measurement for each patient.

Multichannel plethysmography is improving of standard plethysmography which can be used for evaluation of state of cardiovascular system.

It is very important to monitor state of cardiovascular system. There are many parameters which can bring significant information about its condition. Good indicator is value of blood pressure. This value gives global information about state of cardiovascular system but many times it is more useful to know information about each part of cardiovascular system. Possibility how to evaluated parameters of each parts is to measure pulse wave which gives information about state of blood vessel which reflects state of cardiovascular system.

Our main objective was to developed system which could be used for evaluation of each part of cardiovascular system and gives complex information about state of cardiovascular system. This system should be accurate and comfortable for patient because of possibility of continuous long time monitoring.

Out device and methodology bring us promising results. It was tested in laboratory conditions and now it is ready to use it during clinical test. For validation of this method it is necessary to measure bigger group of patients and results from this measurement to compare with standard method for evaluation stiffness of blood vessels or blood pressure.

Multichannel photoplethysmography is promising method for long time monitoring of state of cardiovascular system which will bring better information about treatment of this system and it could prevent heart failure or; in the worst case, premature death.

Acknowledgment. This article has been supported by financial support of TA ČR PRE SEED: TG01010137 GAMA PP1. The work and the contributions were supported by the project SP2015/179 'Biomedicínské inženýrské systémy XI' and This work is partially supported by the Science and Research Fund 2014 of the Moravia-Silesian Region, Czech Republic and this paper has been elaborated in the framework of the project "Support research and development in the Moravian-Silesian Region 2014 DT 1 - Research Teams" (RRC/07/2014). Financed from the budget of the Moravian-Silesian Region.

References

1. Nichols, W.W., McDonald, D.A.: McDonald's Blood Flow in Arteries: Theoretic, Experimental, and Clinical Principles, 6th edn., xiv, 755 p. Hodder Arnold, London (2011). ISBN: 978-0-340-98501-4
2. Salvi, P.: Pulse Waves: How Vascular Hemodynamics Affects Blood Pressure. New York: Springer (2012). ISBN: 978-884-7024-380
3. Peter, L., Foltyn, J., Cerny, M.: Pulse wave velocity measurement; developing process of new measuring device. In: 2015 IEEE 13th International Symposium on Applied Machine Intelligence and Informatics (SAMI), pp. 59–62. IEEE (2015)
4. Lopez, S., Americas, R.T.A.C.: Pulse oximeter fundamentals and design. Free-scale Semiconductor, Inc., Application Note Document Number: AN4327 Rev 1(09) (2011)
5. Prutchi, D., Norris, M.: Design and Development of Medical Electronic Instrumentation: A Practical Perspective of the Design, Construction, and Test of Medical Devices, xv, 461 p. Wiley-InterScience, Hoboken (2005). ISBN: 0471676233
6. Augustynek, M., Penhaker, M.: Non Invasive measurement and visualizations of blood pressure. Elektronika Ir Elektrotechnika 116(10), 55–58 (2011). doi:10.5755/j01.eee.116.10.880
7. Augustynek, M., Penhaker, M., Semkovic, J., Penhakerova, P., Cerny, M.: Measurement and diagnosis assessment of plethysmographycal record. In: AbuOsman, N.A., Abas, W.A.W., AbdulWahab, A.K., Ting, H.N. (eds.) 5th Kuala Lumpur International Conference on Biomedical Engineering 2011, vol. 35, pp. 320–323 (2011)
8. Augustynek, M., Penhaker, M.: Finger plethysmography classification by orthogonal transformatios. In: Proceedings of the 2010 Second International Conference on Computer Engineering and Applications, ICCEA 2010, vol. 2, pp. 173–177 (2010). doi:10.1109/iccea.2010.188
9. Cerny, M., Penhaker, M.: Wireless body sensor network in health maintenance systems. Elektronika Ir Elektrotechnika 115(9), 113–116 (2011). doi:10.5755/j01.eee.115.9.762
10. Collet, J., Cerny, M., Delporte, L., Noury, N.: Assessment of the motion using the ActimedARM: impact of the sensor placement. In: Proceedings of YBERC 2014, 6th Biomedical Engineering Conference of Young Biomedical Engineers and Researchers, Bratislava, Slovak Republic, 2–4 July 2014
11. Zurek, P., Krejcar, O., Penhaker, M., Cerny, M., Frischer, R.: Continuous noninvasive blood pressure measurement by near infra red CCD camera and pulse transmit time systems. In: Paper Presented at the 2nd International Conference on Computer Engineering and Applications, ICCEA 2010 (2010)

Diagnosis of Vascular Access for Hemodialysis Using Software Application

Martin Augustynek, Jiri Sterba, Josef Cihak, Jan Kubicek,
and Marek Penhaker[✉]

Department of Cybernetics and Biomedical Engineering,
Faculty of Electrical Engineering and Computer Science,
VSB – Technical University of Ostrava, Ostrava, Czech Republic
{martin.augustynek,jan.kubicek,marek.penhaker}@vsb.cz

Abstract. Sufficient blood flow in arteriovenous shunt (AVS) is one of the key parameters for successful and effective hemodialysis treatment. The development flow is monitored using a blood temperature monitor (BTM), which is a module which based on the thermodilution method can measure recirculation in the AVS. From the measured recirculation, then we can calculate the flow rate in AVS. Subsequent calculations and interpretation of measured data has to choose the appropriate type of software that users, and physicians provides a comprehensive picture of the patient's vascular access. Flow measurement in vascular access AVS in the department of chronic hemodialysis has long been monitored by Doppler ultrasound examination, which is considered a basic examination. Flow measurement in AVS using BTM module can be considered as an alternative method of measurement.

Keywords: Arteriovenous shunt · Vascular access · Dialyzer · Hemodialysis · Hemodialysis monitor · Thermodilution · Recirculation

1 Introduction

Hemodialysis is a method of cleansing the blood, carried out by means of hemodialysis monitor acute or chronic renal failure. Dialysis is the transfer of substances through a semipermeable membrane. Blood purification is based on biophysical principles such as diffusion, convection, ultrafiltration, adsorption and osmosis [1, 2].

Hemodialysis monitor consists of a system of extracorporeal blood circulation to enable the safe collection of blood from the vascular access for patients and safe return of blood back to the patient (see Fig. 1). Basic elements of the extracorporeal blood circulation consists of a dialysis needle (or catheter), which are input and output of a patient's blood. The dialysis set, head over blood safety features to the dialyzer and back to cleaning. Taking a dialyzer can be considered as a key element of extracorporeal circulation, since it is used for the purification of blood [3].

© ICST Institute for Computer Sciences, Social Informatics and Telecommunications Engineering 2016
P.C. Vinh and V. Alagar (Eds.): ICCASA 2015, LNICST 165, pp. 420–427, 2016.
DOI: 10.1007/978-3-319-29236-6_40

2   Vascular Access

Surgical creation of arteriovenous connection that is used to re-connect the patient to hemodialysis, one of the basic vascular surgical procedures. By this operation is the creation of arteriovenous shunt, or shunt (AVS) which can be easily cannula and can withstand repeated punctures. Securing adequate blood flow is necessary for efficient operation of the hemodialysis apparatus. Even after surgery perfection but life AVS limited and depends on many factors. We distinguish between temporary and permanent vascular access vascular access [4].

Fig. 1. Monitor fresenius hemodialysis.

Temporary vascular access for aid venous catheter is de-signed for a limited number of performances (one or more) and use it for all patients who require acute perform any of dialysis methods, most hemodialysis. Also, it is used in patients on chronic dialysis program, the permanent vascular access cannot be created [3].

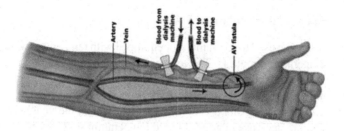

Fig. 2. Vascular access (AV shunt, fistula).

Permanent vascular access is chosen in patients when hemodialysis and its related techniques are repeated at regular intervals (e.g., 2 to 3 times per week) for a period not months but years. Italians Cimino and Brescia in 1966, was first used by native subcutaneous arteriovenous shunt (fistula, shunt) when sewn to the artery vein (see Fig. 2). Most frequently used connection between the radial artery and cephalic v. the non-dominant limb, rarely is then used connection between the brachial artery and cephalic v. or femoral artery and saphenous vein. The resulting "short-vein" to expand the influence of hemodynamic conditions, arches over nivaeu and is then easily accessible to puncture [2, 3].

3   Recirculation

Situation where in the dialyzer together with the non-adjusted blood flows and certain amount of blood that has flowed dialyzer and back into it returns without flow through the organism, the term function (see Fig. 3). Ideally enters the dialyzer from the arterial needle a given amount of blood (QB ml/min), after flowing through the dialyzer returns venous needle set and into the bloodstream. All cleaned blood flows downstream into the central venous system into the dialyzer inflow of new blood falsetto. However, it may happen that part of the already adjusted blood does not flow into the central venous system, but it gets back to the arterial needle and returns to the dialyzer, or recirculated. This situation is referred to as recirculation in the vascular access. Recirculation occurs under two circumstances. Either Exchanged placement of needles or blood flow to the dialyzer exceeds the total blood flow fistulas [5, 13, 15].

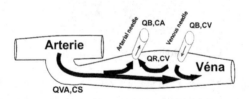

Fig. 3.   Recirculation in AV shunt (free reposted F. Lopot 2012 [6]).

3.1   Measurement of Recirculation

For this purpose, can be used dialysis monitor equipped with temperature monitor blood BTM (blood temperature monitor). The temporary change in temperature of dialysate inflow into the dialyzer is created bolus temperature, which is transferred to the blood side of the dialyzer. Cooling the dialysate for 2 min, the cooling of small volumes of blood, at 35 °C. Thus cooled blood is detected by a sensor in the venous set. Another sensor allows capture decrease in arterial blood temperature set by recirculation. It is a method of "on-line" and the waiting staff very simple. Value recirculation appears on the display for about 2 min at the touch of a button. Thermodilution method can also be used to calculate blood flow fistulas [5, 7–10].

4   Analysis and Results

Evaluation of the development of AVS flows derived from Doppler ultrasound (ultrasound) hemodialysis centres Faculty Hospital in Ostrava. The aim of this study was to determine whether the long-term trend is prevailing development flow AVS increasing or decreasing. Monitoring were 8 patients who underwent regular ultrasound over 6 years. Analyzing the data, it was possible to demonstrate the changing flow of the AVS over the years. Graphic development flow AVS is always interspersed with linear trend, this development follows. The resulting analysis of the data obtained during the reporting period (see Fig. 4) in these patients is the declining flow in AVS during the few years since its inception.

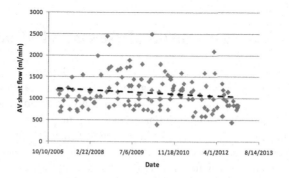

Fig. 4. The final analysis of the development flow.

Were also analyzed results obtained from a hemodialysis center in Vsetin derived from BTM module hemodialysis monitor Fresenius 4008S. From the imposing number of measurements obtained 391 was created histogram showing the distribution of ratings QVA occurrence of flow. Results forms a bell curve, with the highest incidence occurred in the flow range 700–1000 ml/min. Another objective was to determine the long term with the prevailing trend. Due to the diversity of patients aged measured at different intervals were chosen group of patients whose measurements are repeated regularly over the years and whose frequency of occurrence of the selected 391 measurements were highest. Chosen were 7 patients who were regularly at BTM module measurements during 5 years. The resulting trend of the patients again showed a gradually decreasing.

In order to justify the measurement obtained from the BTM module needed its own measurements for evaluating the accuracy with which it can be used during hemodialysis process measured. Measurements were carried out on eleven patients of which 5 women and 6 men. In total, 24 measurements were acquired. The goal was always com-paring measurements obtained from BTM module with the current result obtained using Doppler ultrasound examination. Out of 24 measurements, measuring 19 (79 %) was the difference of 15 % and 5 measurements (21 %) with a difference of more than 15 % compared to ultrasound. Based on the measurement and evaluation of their results, we can say that the AVS for flow measurement in routine clinical practice at the bedside BTM module is sufficiently precise and therefore satisfactory (see Fig. 5).

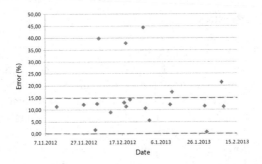

Fig. 5. Analysis of measurement accuracy BTM module.

5   Software for Evaluation of the Measurement Patients

To facilitate control, flow calculation and evaluation of the state of flow in AVS in terms of the time horizon was made program, which has a staff of hemodialysis centers to facilitate its work. With this program, the physician obtains the necessary overview of developments in the vascular access, who may be helpful in assessing its long-term condition. The program has a particular task to calculate the flow rate of the AVS data obtained from BTM module, and the data for a particular patient clearly interpret the doctor whenever he could analyze the results. The program has a simple user interface (see Fig. 6) and the window where the patient enters basic information about the patient, window measurement protocol, which entered data obtained from measurements at BTM module graph of flow in the AV shunt created a database of patients. The data stored for each individual patient can then be retrieved and updated at any time [11, 14].

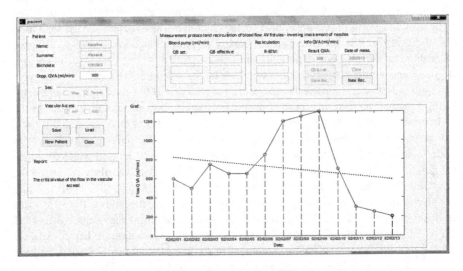

Fig. 6. User interface SW.

After starting the program, the user can establish a new patient or retrieve stored measurements. If the user decides to create a new patient must fill out all data in the protocol called "patient". In this protocol, the user enters the name, surname, date of birth (dd/mm/yyyy) fills the last known result in vascular access flow derived Doppler ultrasound examination, selects gender and type of vascular access AVF (AVS of native vessels) or AVG (AVS artificial material). If the protocol is completely filled with the patient presses the save button [12].

The measurement protocol recirculation user fills in the details of the haemodialysis monitor and blood flow to the pump set and effective (Fig. 7).

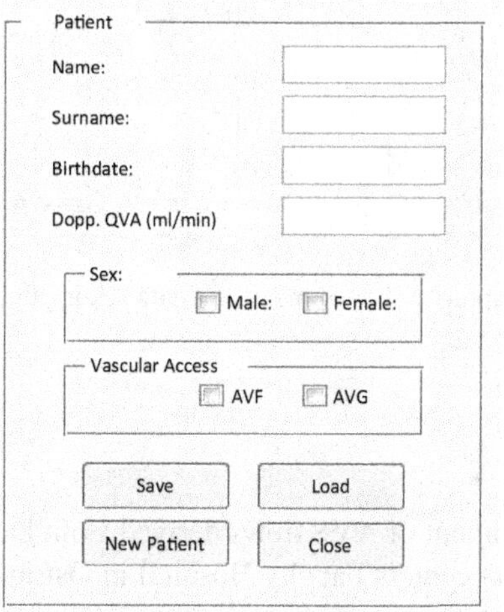

Fig. 7. User interface SW patient.

From module BTM user then logs the recirculation appropriate value (see Fig. 8). When this protocol being fully completed, the user presses the button to calculate QVA. After successful completion of the calculation is displayed in the log info QVA field result QVA. The final step the user fills measurement date (in the format dd/mm/yyyy) Protocol QVA info. Press to save the recording is the result QVA stored along with the date of measurement in graphical form.

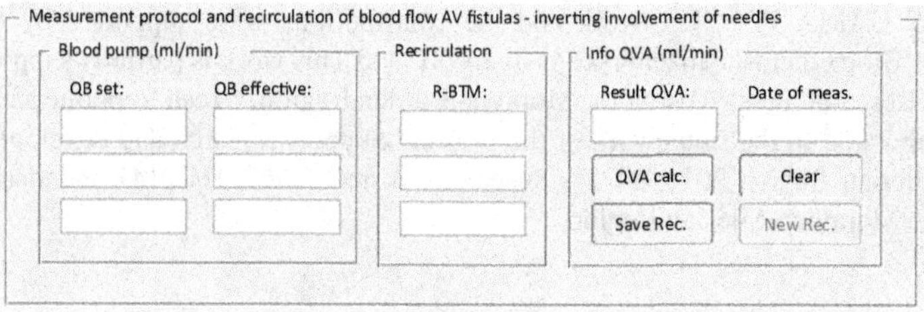

Fig. 8. User interface SW protocol.

In the case that the flow in the AVS will be lower than the limit, the user is notified both in graphic form (Fig. 9) colorfully while announcing the result actually field message. For the stored measurements of a given patient, the user can browse at any time by pressing the Load button. The user selects a patient who wants to explore or continue existing measurements.

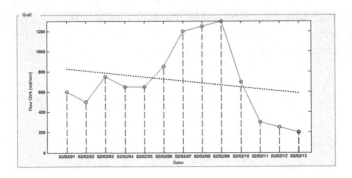

Fig. 9. Graphic design of measured data (Color figure online)

6   Conclusion

Evaluation of the development of AVS flows derived from Doppler ultrasound examination of the hemodialysis centers Faculty Hospital in Ostrava. The resulting analysis of the data obtained during the reporting period, the declining flow in AVS during the few years since its inception. Were also analyzed results obtained from a hemodialysis center in Vsetin derived from BTM module Fresenius hemodialysis monitor. The resulting trend of the patients again showed a gradually decreasing. Furthermore demonstrated the accuracy of measurement BTM module. Based on the measurement and evaluation of their results, we can say that the AVS for flow measurement in routine clinical practice at the bedside BTM module is sufficiently precise and therefore satisfactory. Given the above, it is appropriate to regular check-ups AVS. Designed and described SW is the path could continue interpretation and storage of collected measurement data.

Acknowledgments. This article has been supported by financial support of TA ČR PRE SEED: TG01010137 GAMA PP1. The work and the contributions were supported by the project SP2015/179 'Biomedicínské inženýrské systémy XI' and This work is partially supported by the Science and Research Fund 2014 of the Moravia-Silesian Region, Czech Republic and this paper has been elaborated in the framework of the project "Support research and development in the Moravian-Silesian Region 2014 DT 1 - Research Teams" (RRC/07/2014). Financed from the budget of the Moravian-Silesian Region.

References

1. Lopot, F.: Základy techniky hemodialýzy., Praha (1989)
2. Čihák, J., Augustynek, M.: Infuzní technika a hemodialyzační technika a technologie. VŠB - Technická univerzita Ostrava, Ostrava (2013)
3. Lachmanová, J.: Očišťovací metody krve. 1. Grada, Praha (1999)
4. Janoušek, L.B., Petr: Hemodialyzační arteriovenózní přístupy. Grada, Praha (2008)
5. Cerny, M., Penhaker, M.: Wireless body sensor network in health maintenance systems. Elektronika Ir Elektrotechnika 113–116 (2011)
6. Lopot, F.: Adekvátnost dialýzy pro sestry: Certifiko-vaný kurz – Péče o nemocné léčené eliminačními metoda-mi, část: Hemodialyzační technologie. Praha (2012)
7. Sulková, S.: Hemodialýza. Maxdorf, Praha (2000)
8. Lopot, F., Nejedly, B., Svarova, B., Sulkova, S., Malek, V., Bodlakova, B., Svara, E.: Vascular access monitoring evaluated from automated recirculation measurement. EDTNA ERCA J **27**, 17–22 (2001)
9. Hochman, V., Cihak, J., Augustynek, M.: Interaction of infusion set and volumetric infusion pump and their impact on the quality of treatment. In: Lacković, I., Vasic, D. (eds.) IFMBE Proceedings, pp. 645–648. Springer, Heidelberg (2015)
10. Augustynek, M., Sterba, J., Cihak, J.: Hemodynamic diagnostics shunt for hemodialysis. Biomed. Eng. Environ. Eng. **145**, 163 (2014)
11. Augustynek, M., Penhaker, M.: Non Invasive Measurement and Visualizations of Blood Pressure. Elektronika Ir Elektrotechnika 55–58 (2011)
12. Penhaker, M., Darebnikova, M., Jurek, F., Augustynek, M.: Evaluation of electrocardiographic leads and establishing significance intra-individuality. In: Abraham, A., Krömer, P., Snášel, V. (eds.) Innovations in Bio-Inspired Computing and Applications, pp. 295–303. Springer, Heidelberg (2014)
13. Krejcar, O., Penhaker, M.: Remote measurement and control with sensors via the BT interface. Paper Presented at the IEEE 16th International Conference on Intelligent Engineering Systems, INES 2012, Lisbon (2012)
14. Krejcar, O., Penhaker, M., Janckulik, D., Motalova, L.: Performance test of multiplatform real time processing of biomedical signals. In: 2010 8th IEEE International Conference on Paper Presented at the Industrial Informatics (INDIN) (2010)
15. Peterek, T., Augustynek, M., Zurek, P., Penhaker, M.: Global courseware for visualization and processing biosignals. In: Dossel, O., Schlegel, W.C. (eds.) World Congress on Medical Physics and Biomedical Engineering, vol. 25, Pt 12, pp. 404–407 (2009)

Software Simulation of CT Reconstructions and Artifacts

Jan Kubicek[✉], Tomas Rehacek, Marek Penhaker, and Iveta Bryjova

FEI, VSB – Technical University of Ostrava,
K450, 17. listopadu 15, Ostrava, Poruba, Czech Republic
{jan.kubicek,tomas.rehacek.st,
marek.penhaker,iveta.bryjova}@vsb.cz

Abstract. The paper deals with design of complex simulation environment which is able to simulate on the base of mathematical techniques individual reconstructions methods which are normally used on Computed Tomography (CT). Primary attention is focused on The Single Back Projection technique (SBP) and The Filtered Back Projection (FBP). There is a significant benefit with comparison of normally used mathematical software. This simulation instrument is fully dynamic. Individual transformation methods are generated by form dynamic simulations which graphically explain the process of whole reconstruction procedure. The second part deals with simulation of Beam Hardening artifact. It is special type of artifact which significantly deteriorates CT images. This artifact is created especially on the surround of metal object. This simulation is important especially in term of manifestation of artifact. Simulation is helpful for design of filter for Beam Hardening suppressing as well. The complex simulation environment is performed in software MATLAB.

Keywords: CT reconstructions · Artifacts · MATLAB · Beam hardening · Radon transformation

1 Introduction

The Computed Tomography is based on the same principle as X-ray imagining. We observe decrease X radiation within pass by patient (absorption) between X-ray tube and detector. On the CT, there are also problems with X-ray imagining, where is the main disadvantage the superposition of structures and dispersion of CT beams. The CT produces image of human body as series of tomographic slices (images). The acquisition of image data is performed in consecutive measurement of decrease closely collimated X-radiation within translating and rotating movement of mechanical system X ray tube and detector. Within the translating movement is taken one projection of scene. Consequently is performed the rotating movement of mechanical system X ray tube-detector by angle increment and taking next projection of same scene under different angle [1–5] (Fig. 1).

© ICST Institute for Computer Sciences, Social Informatics and Telecommunications Engineering 2016
P.C. Vinh and V. Alagar (Eds.): ICCASA 2015, LNICST 165, pp. 428–437, 2016.
DOI: 10.1007/978-3-319-29236-6_41

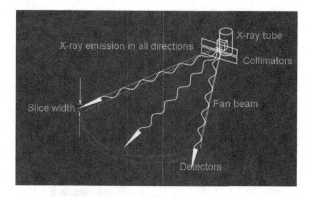

Fig. 1. The principle of CT data acquisition [6]

The cause of metal artifacts consists unwanted blackouts in the images (data become saturated), which might be caused by presence of an object with the highest absorption in the place of scanning. The object absorbs radiation and these results in an artifact. Such object is a standard metal object, for instance, dental materials, clamps or electrodes. The metal artifact is shown as pronounced clear bends which are, often, grouped in a so-called star-like layout [8–10] (Fig. 2).

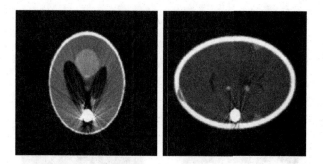

Fig. 2. Manifestation of beam hardening artifact [7]

2   Simulation of Radon Transformation

For creation of Radon transformation we must keep on mind that software MATLAB works with discrete data, therefore within simulation resulting image is summed by certain trajectory. By summing of columns image matrix we obtain projections under one angle. For obtaining system of all projection it is necessary to perform rotation of image. The rotation is taken in certain interval (0°, 180°) and within the rotation it is necessary to perform rotation in steps (iteratively) with stable angle increment. Result of described operation is called sinogram. Sinogram is two dimensional image which is created by sorting of 1D projections under their scanning angle (Figs. 3 and 4).

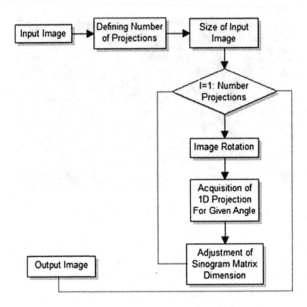

Fig. 3. Block diagram of radon transformation

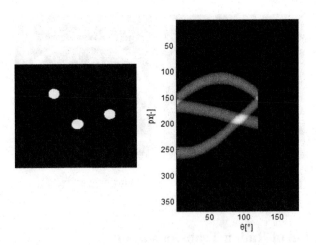

Fig. 4. The illustration of consecutive filling 1D projections to empty matrix, where px[-] is length of projection, θ[°] is angle of individual projection – number of projections: 180

The dynamic animation of sinogram is performed by consecutive sorting of 1D projections under specific angle to empty matrix. The length of x axes is depended on number of projections. The length of y axes is same as the length of projection. In the algorithm input is possible to take number of projections which form whole transformation process (Fig. 5).

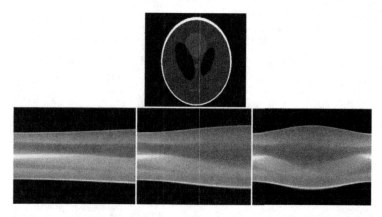

Fig. 5. Testing head phantom (upside), sinogram: number of projections: 1–45 (left), sinogram: number of projections: 1–90 (in the middle), sinogram: number of projections: 1–90 (right)

3   Simulation of Single Back Projection (SBP)

Practical realization is identic as in the case of Radon transformation. After creating sinogram is generated reconstruction matrix. The reconstruction matrix is created as zero matrix. Size of the matrix is same as matrix of reconstructed image. By loop for is consecutively scanned vector which contains information of taken projections and individual projections from sinogram are spread. This matrix is again rotated under same angle, which projection is obtained. By this procedure it is kept size of the matrix. After comparison of sizes spread and reconstructed projection, divided by two and rounding, we get values which are necessary for adding spread and rotated projection to reconstruction matrix under given angle. In the next step overlaps are removed in order to reconstructed image has same size as input image and let him draw [11, 12] (Figs. 6 and 7).

In Fig. 8, there is demonstrated process of reconstruction SBP by form dynamic animation. For individuals outputs have been used 35, 70, 105 and 140 projections. In Fig. 9, there is comparison of reconstruction by using various numbers of projections. These outputs conclusively declare that number of projections significantly influences quality of imaging process (Figs. 8 and 9).

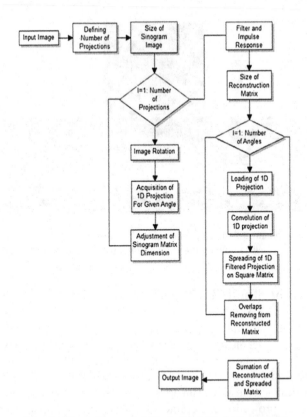

Fig. 6. Block diagram of Single Back Projection (SBP)

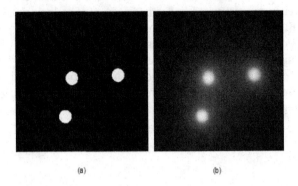

(a)   (b)

Fig. 7. Original image (a) and reconstructed image by method Single Back Projection (b)

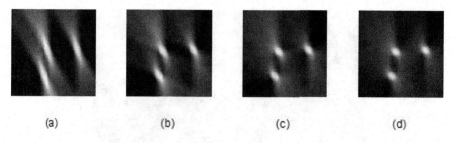

Fig. 8. Partial reconstruction from: 35 projections (a), 70 projections (b), 105 projections (c) and 140 projections (d)

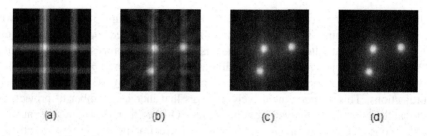

Fig. 9. SBP from various number of projections: 2 projections (a), 10 projections (b), 60 projections (c) and 180 projections (d)

4 Simulation of Filtered Back Projection (FBP)

Practical realization of FBP is quite similar as SBP. After creating sinogram, reconstruction matrix is generated which represents the output image. Individual projections are again spread to this matrix. Impulse response of ramp filter is consequently designed. By loop for are consecutively loaded individual projections from sinogram matrix. These projections are filtered by convolution process. Filtered projections are spread and rotated under angle which was projection taken. After taking correction of size spread and reconstruction projection, we obtain values which are necessary for adding spread and rotated projection to reconstruction matrix under given angle. In the final step all overlaps are removed in order to reconstructed image has same size as input image and let him draw [13] (Fig. 10).

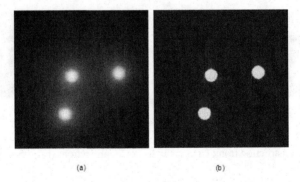

Fig. 10. Original image (a) and reconstructed image by method Filtered Back Projection (b)

It is obvious that reconstructed image by FBP is not so impairs by noise of lower frequencies with comparison of image from SBP. The lower frequencies are filtered out by low pass Ram-Lak filter. In Fig. 11, there is demonstrated process of reconstruction FBP by form dynamic animation. For individual outputs are used 30, 70, 130 and 140 projections. In Fig. 12, there is comparison of reconstructions by using various numbers of projections. This output conclusively declares that increase number of projections significantly influences quality of imaging process. On the other hand increasing number of projections increases computation time of reconstruction process (Figs. 11 and 12).

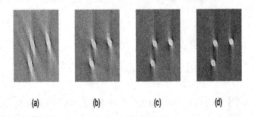

Fig. 11. Partial reconstruction from: 30 projections (a), 70 projections (b), 130 projections (c) and 140 projections (d)

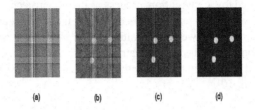

Fig. 12. FBP from various number of projections: 2 projections (a), 10 projections (b), 60 projections (c) and 180 projections (d)

5   Simulation of Beam Hardening Artifact

From theory it is obvious that Beam Hardening artifact is caused by weak attenuation in given voxel. Within the simulation image is loaded where is artifact simulated and image which contains metal object which introduces the source of artifact. In the next step Radon transformation is created from both images. After that output matrix is created where is saved resulted sinogram created by comparison of point values from sinograms. The first dimension of matrix is same as the maximum length of projection created sinogram from image without metal objects. The second matrix dimension is same as number of angles of given projection - 180[px]. By loop for are values of individual points from sinogram of image with metal object compared with zero value. If this value greater than zero, this value will be rewritten by maximum value from sinogram image. Otherwise value of pixels from image sinogram is copied. By described procedure Beam Hardening artifact is appeared in the resulting sinogram matrix. This matrix is consequently reconstructed by inverse Radon transformation. Artifact is appeared in the resulting reconstructed image [7] (Figs. 13 and 14).

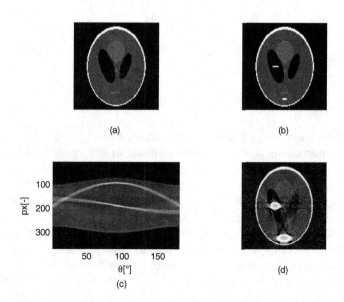

Fig. 13. Original image (a), Image with metal object (b), Radon transformation (c) and simulation of Beam hardening in reconstructed image (d)

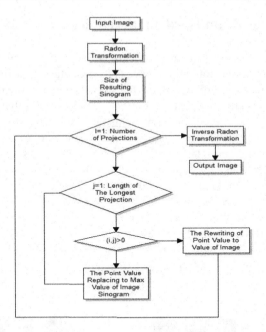

Fig. 14. Block diagram of simulation Beam Hardening artifact

6   Conclusion

The aim of the work is complex graphical user interface which serves as educative portal for studies of mathematical reconstruction methods which are used for image reconstruction from individual projection imaging. The significant benefit of software solution is also generating of artifacts which are created during CT examination and deteriorate resulting images. Simulation methods of artifact consists important base for design and implementation of filtration methods to their elimination. Reconstruction methods on the base of Radon transformation are often contented in mathematical software. The main benefit of proposed solution introduces fully dynamic animations of these methods. These simulations in consecutive iteration steps demonstrate whole process of reconstruction. The quality of output image signal is strongly depended on number of set projections. If we chose lower number of projections, output image would be in worse quality. From this view is better to perform reconstruction form more projections. On the other hand for increase number of projections computation time is also increased. In the coming time we would like to focus our research on simulation of mathematical methods for Algebraic iterative methods. These methods are principally different then SBP and FBP. By these methods is possible partially eliminate Beam Hardening artifact and therefore these methods consist reliable base for suppressing of this unwanted phenomenon.

Acknowledgment. This article has been supported by financial support of TA ČR PRE SEED: TG01010137 GAMA PP1. The work and the contributions were supported by the project SP2015/179 'Biomedicínské inženýrské systémy XI' and This work is partially supported by the Science and Research Fund 2014 of the Moravia-Silesian Region, Czech Republic and this paper has been elaborated in the framework of the project "Support research and development in the Moravian-Silesian Region 2014 DT 1 - Research Teams" (RRC/07/2014). Financed from the budget of the Moravian-Silesian Region.

References

1. Aootaphao, S., Pintavirooj, C., Sotthivirat, S.: Penalized-likelihood reconstruction for metal artifact reduction in cone-beam CT. In: International IEEE EMBS Conference (2008)
2. Youngshin, K., Yoon, S., Yi, J.: Effective sinogram-inpainting for metal artifacts reduction in x-ray CT images. In: International Conference on Image Processing (2010)
3. Seeram, E.: Image Quality. Computed Tomography: Physical Principles, Clinical Applications and Quality Control, 2nd edn., pp. 174–199. Saunders, Philadelphia (2001)
4. Taguchi, K., Aradate, H.: Algorithm for image reconstruction in multi-slice helical CT. Med. Phys. **25**, 550–561 (1998)
5. Kubíček, J.: Creation of the beam hardening artifact. IFMBE Proc. **43**, 196–198 (2014)
6. Kubicek, J., Penhaker, M., Bryjova, I., Kodaj, M.: Articular cartilage defect detection based on image segmentation with colour mapping. In: Jung, J.J., Nguyen, N.-T., Hwang, D. (eds.) ICCCI 2014. LNCS, vol. 8733, pp. 214–222. Springer, Heidelberg (2014)
7. Kubiček, J., Penhaker, M.: Guidelines for modeling BED in simultaneous radiotherapy. IFMBE Proc. **43**, 271–274 (2014)
8. Kubicek, J., Penhaker, M., Feltl, D., Cvek, J.: Guidelines for modeling BED in simultaneous radiotherapy of two volumes: Tpv1 and tpv2. In: SAMI 2013 - Proceedings of the IEEE 11th International Symposium on Applied Machine Intelligence and Informatics, Article no. 6480960, pp. 131–135 (2013)
9. Kasik, V., Penhaker, M., Novák, V., Bridzik, R., Krawiec, J.: User interactive biomedical data web services application. In: Yonazi, J.J., Sedoyeka, E., Ariwa, E., El-Qawasmeh, E. (eds.) ICeND 2011. CCIS, vol. 171, pp. 223–237. Springer, Heidelberg (2011)
10. Kubicek, J., Penhaker, M., Feltl, D., Cvek, J., IEEE: Guidelines for modelling BED in simultaneous radiotherapy of two volumes: tpv(1) and tpv(2) (2013)
11. Pustkova, R., Kutalek, F., Penhaker, M., Novak, V.: Measurement and calculation of cerebrospinal fluid in proportion to the skull (2010)
12. Kasik, V., Penhaker, M., Novak, V., Pustkova, R., Kutalek, F.: Bio-inspired genetic algorithms on fpga evolvable hardware. In: Pan, J.-S., Chen, S.-M., Nguyen, N.T. (eds.) ACIIDS 2012, Part II. LNCS, vol. 7197, pp. 439–447. Springer, Heidelberg (2012)
13. Penhaker, M., Krawiec, J., Krejcar, O., Novak, V., Bridzik, R., Society, I.C.: Web system for electrophysiological data management. In: Proceedings 2010 Second International Conference on Computer Engineering and Applications: ICCEA 2010, vol. 1, pp. 404–407 (2010). doi:10.1109/iccea.2010.85

Macular Lesions Extraction Using Active Appearance Method

Jan Kubicek[✉], Iveta Bryjova, and Marek Penhaker

Department of Cybernetics and Biomedical Engineering,
FEI, VSB-TU Ostrava, 17. Listopadu 15, 708 33 Ostrava-Poruba, The Czech Republic
{jan.kubicek,iveta.bryjova,marek.penhaker}@vsb.cz

Abstract. Age-related macular degeneration (ARMD) is one of the most wide-spread diseases of the eye fundus and is the most common cause of vision loss for those over the age of 60. There are several ways to diagnose ARMD. One of them is the Fundus Autofluorescence (FAF) method, and is one of the modalities of Heidelberg Engineering diagnostic devices. The BluePeakTM modality utilizes the fluorescence of lipofuscin (a pigment in the affected cells) to display the extent of the disease's progression. In clinical practice is often quite complicated to perform assessment of precise parameters macular lesions. The main aim of the article is design of the method which is able to locate and consequently perform extraction of these lesions. The algorithm body is composed of several essential parts: image preprocessing, filtration of interested area and segmentation procedure. In the first step, extraction area of interest is performed. Filtration process should suppress adjacent structures. Final step is segmentation procedure. The main advantage is that the whole process is fully automatic. The result of segmentation is closed curve which is formed iteratively to edges of analyzed object. The resulting curve reflects geometrical parameters of analyzed structure. On the base this fact is quite easy to calculate perimeter and area of analyzed area.

Keywords: Macular degeneration · Optical coherence tomography · Image processing · Active contour · Medical image segmentation · MATLAB · Geometrical parameters · Macular lesions

1 Introduction

Reticular macular lesions, also known as 'reticular macular disease', 'reticular drusen', 'reticular pseudodrusen', or 'subretinal drusenoid deposits', are a pattern of lesions commonly found in age-related macular degeneration and best visualized using at least two imaging techniques in combination. Reticular lesions have four stages of progression observable on spectral domain optical coherence tomography, but they do not show the usual signs of regression of soft drusen (calcification and pigment changes). Furthermore, reticular lesions correlate histologically with subretinal drusenoid deposits localized between the retinal pigment epithelium and the inner segment ellipsoid band. Reticular

© ICST Institute for Computer Sciences, Social Informatics and Telecommunications Engineering 2016
P.C. Vinh and V. Alagar (Eds.): ICCASA 2015, LNICST 165, pp. 438–447, 2016.
DOI: 10.1007/978-3-319-29236-6_42

lesions are most commonly seen in older age groups of female patients with age related macular degeneration and are usually bilateral. They are not clearly associated with known age-related macular degeneration genes and are highly associated with late-stage age-related macular degeneration and an increased mortality rate. They are also associated with alterations in the neural retina and choroid [1–3, 16] (Fig. 1).

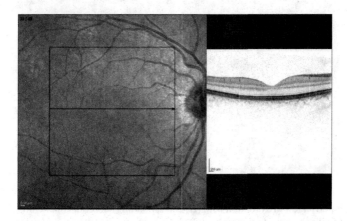

Fig. 1. Cut of area physiological macula with using infrared shootings (left) and OCT cut (right) [1].

2   Age-Related Macular Degeneration

Age-related macular degeneration is a major cause of blindness worldwide. With ageing populations in many countries, more than 20 % might have the disorder. Advanced age-related macular degeneration, including neovascular age-related macular degeneration (wet) and geographic atrophy (late dry), is associated with substantial, progressive visual impairment. Major risk factors include cigarette smoking, nutritional factors, cardio-vascular diseases, and genetic markers, including genes regulating complement, lipid, angiogenic, and extracellular matrix pathways. Some studies have suggested a declining prevalence of age-related macular degeneration, perhaps due to reduced exposure to modifiable risk factors. Accurate diagnosis combines clinical examination and investigations, including retinal photography, angiography, and optical coherence tomography. Dietary anti-oxidant supplementation slows progression of the disease. Treatment for neovascular age-related macular degeneration incorporates intraocular injections of anti-VEGF agents, occasionally combined with other modalities. Evidence suggests that two commonly used anti-VEGF therapies, ranibizumab and bevacizumab, have similar efficacy, but possible differences in systemic safety are difficult to assess. Future treatments include inhibition of other angiogenic factors, and regenerative and topical therapies [1, 2, 4–6] (Fig. 2).

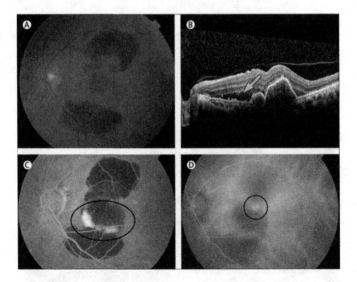

Fig. 2. Patient with polypoidal choroidal vasculopathy. (A) Fundus photograph showing massive subretinal haemorrhage and exudation with (B) corresponding subretinal thickening and elevation (arrow) on optical coherence tomography. (C) Corresponding fluorescein angiogram showing ill-defined "occult" pattern leakage (circled), whereas the indocyanine-green angiogram (D) shows discrete polypoidal lesions under the fovea (circled) [1].

3   Optical Coherence Tomography (OCT)

OCT is a laser device that employs a superluminiscent diode as the source of its coherent beam. This diode emits a beam of a suitable wavelength into the eye structure; the beam is reflected by various layers of the retina and interferes with a second reference beam in a detector. The resulting interference signal is then digitized and used to obtain the final image. For developing a method for automatically calculating macular lesions, we used images acquired by a Spectralis unit from Heidelberg Engineering [8–11].

3.1   Blue Laser Auto Fluorescence

One modality of OCT devices is BluePeakTM, which excites the ocular fundus (fundus oculi) with a blue spectrum laser beam ($\lambda = 488$ nm). This modality is most commonly used for diagnosing macular degeneration due to the presence of lipofuscin, which is a specific source of fluorescence. During the examination, the beam is shot into the patient's eye where it induces lipofuscin fluorescence that is caught by the detector and subsequently analysed. The main advantage is the possibility of comparison with OCT results that provide information on the morphological changes in the retinal pigment epithelium (RPE), while BluePeak^{TM} shows metabolic changes [7, 12–16].

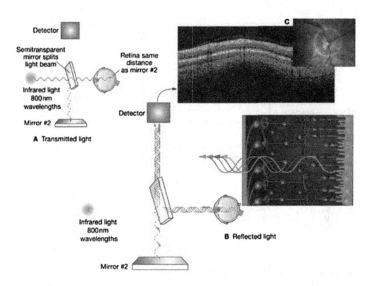

Fig. 3. High-resolution images of the internal retinal structure taken with optical coherence tomography (OCT) [1]

4   The Proposed Solution for Automatic Extraction of Macular Lesions and Geometrical Parameters

As it is mentioned above, analysis of macular lesions is for clinical practice very important. Currently, ophthalmological physicians for many cases must perform analysis and clinical diagnosis of macular lesions only by their eyes. The main intention of proposed software solution is improving and mainly validating of diagnosis macular lesions. In terms of macular lesion diagnosis is the most important extraction of geometrical parameters. Especially it is needed to obtain closed area of macular lesion and consequently area of this contour. At the beginning of algorithm ophthalmologic records are loaded. In the next step it is necessary to perform preprocessing of records. This part includes filtration process by average filter and image resizing. For our purpose is used average filter of dimension 4×4. After that the center of macular lesion is set. Segmentation procedure is done in iterative steps. Using of more iterative steps give the elaborated shape of final contour but on the other hand it increases computational time of whole process. Because of it, it is used compromise of 100 iterative steps which reliably reach contour of macular lesion. In the final step it is computed number of pixels which are placed inside the contour (Fig. 4).

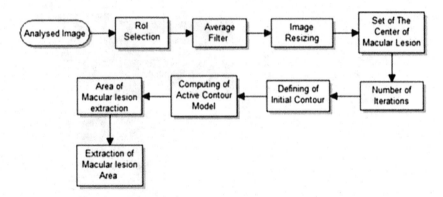

Fig. 4. The proposed algorithm for analyzing of macular lesions

4.1 The Principle of Active Contour Method

Used type of geometrical contour is derived from implicit equation of initial curve. For purposes of our analyses circle with zero shift is used:

$$x^2 + y^2 = r^2 \rightarrow x^2 + y^2 - r^2 = 0 \tag{1}$$

Initialization function is formed in individual iteration steps to shape of macular lesion. On level set method, analyzed image is divided by contour into inside and outside part. Image is composed from three parts: Inside area is consist by negative values (negative values of shortest Euclidean distance of points from contour). Inside area (positive value of the shortest Euclidean distance points from contour) and contour with zero value. The further away from the point of the curve, the larger the resulting value. The result of this procedure is the cone which defines the distance the positive and negative values from zero, and thereby to form level set area. Level set area is defined by level set function Φ which is given by following equation:

$$\Phi(x, y, t) \tag{2}$$

Value range of function Φ is placed to $\mathbb{R}^3$. It is not just curve, but whole domain is defined which is consecutive changed by the time. For the simplest case for defining level set evolution it is necessary to define gradient. Gradient is needed for performing proper evolution of level set area:

$$\nabla\Phi = \left(\frac{\partial\Phi}{\partial x}, \frac{\partial\Phi}{\partial y} \right) \tag{3}$$

Evolution of level set by the time is given by partial derivation level set function Φ by the time $\frac{\partial\Phi}{\partial t}$.

Final contour is formed by the time in the direction of normal when velocity of evolution "c" is being stable.

$$\frac{\partial \Phi}{\partial t} = c.N \tag{4}$$

Normal vector is given by relationship:

$$N = \frac{\nabla \Phi}{|\nabla \Phi|} \tag{5}$$

Direction of normal is determined by gradient. Normal vector is vertical to tangent of contour which is developed in direction of this normal multiplied by constant. Instead of constant velocity we can use function divergence of normal. Divergence function determines when vectors converge to some particular point. In the first step normal and divergences are calculated. Negative divergence denotes on convergence of vectors. Evolution of level set area is performed by this approach. This level set area is independent on image values.

The most frequently used contours are based on principle of minimization of energy functional. Functional is representation which assigns real number. Contour is placed in functional and its size of energy is controlled. If the energy is too large, the contour is gradually deformed into a shape that reduces energy. This procedure is performed until we reach energy minimization. Active contour method is iterative algorithm, which forms final contour in consecutive steps. The key parameter is number of those steps. We must keep perimeter of analyzed object. For our purpose 100 iterations have been used for reaching shape of macular lesions [13, 16–19].

5   Analysis of Macular Lesions

For testing of the designed software, 40 patient's records of macular lesions have been used. Testing has been performed with same requirement and its background suppression and reaching of final contour macular lesion. Segmentation gave satisfactory results for 35 patients. On the rest images we had problems with adjacent blood vessels which we are not able to suppress. This fact causes worse effectivity of detection. Images obtained through the BluePeak modality provide unique information about the condition of macular degeneration and its terminal stage – geographic atrophy. Thanks to these high contrast images, it is possible to determine the geometric parameters of macular lesions. For the subsequent processing of native images, we used the MATLAB® interactive programming environment. The aim was to quantify the area of the ocular fundus of macular lesions. This geometric parameter allows clinicians to clarify and predict the further development of the disease. Emphasis was particularly placed on those segmentation methods that allow for an automated analysis. The geometric active contours driven by local Gaussian distribution fitting energy method – one of the level-set segmentation procedures – proved to be the best. The algorithm is divided into several basic parts. First, the patient's image is loaded into the device and the macular lesion zone is framed; calculation of the macular lesion area follows. The selection of the macular lesion area (in Fig. 3) is indicated using the active contour model (the gradual shaping of contours up to the edge of the object in the image). With zero approximation, the contour is defined as initial circle whose size is consecutively adapted to the size of the lesion. After the contour completes the segmentation, the number of pixels contained therein is calculated. Here we use the properties of level-set methods that divide the image into two parts: the part inside the contour and the part outside the contour. The contour corresponds to zero values. The sum of the number of pixels is defined by a cycle that evaluates all the pixels in the contour as being logical ones. The conversion of the number of pixels per unit area occurs via image resolution. In Heidelberg Spectralis OCT devices, this resolution corresponds to 200 μm. The resulting geometric parameter, i.e. the size of lesion area, is $S = 7.156$ mm^2 in the first case (in Fig. 3c) and $S = 8.9796$ mm^2 in the latter case (in Fig. 3f). A current shortfall of this analysis is the vascular bed, which is one of the most contrasted parts of the ocular fundus and the active contour extends behind it. Further development of this method should focus on subtracting the area of the vascular bed, which will significantly improve the diagnosis of retinal disease [16] (Fig. 5).

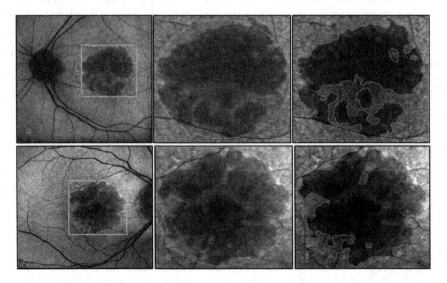

Fig. 5. Selection of macular lesion area (a, d), the contour's initial state before segmentation process (b, e) and resulting segmentation outputs (c, f) [16].

6   The Design of Application GA ANALYSIS

The final result of analysis is function application which is intended for using in clinical practice. The function of application is presented in the following patient's record. 91 years old patient with geographical atrophy, placed in left eye. Infrared image and OCT is shown in Fig. 6. For this particular case it is obtained the fundus diameter 8808 μm. The working environment of OCT Spectralis is shown in Fig. 6. On the infrared image, there are marked spots where OCT cuts are performed. One of them is in the right part of the image. There is also visible the ablation of retinal layers in the area of geographic atrophy (Fig. 7).

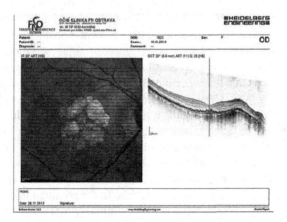

Fig. 6. The working environment of OCT Spectralis. IR image of right eye (left) and OCT cut by disordered macula (right)

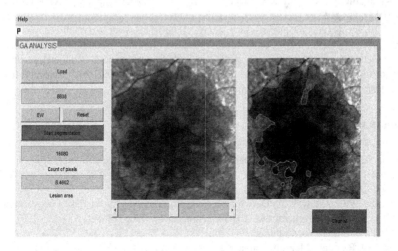

Fig. 7. The working environment of software GA ANALYSIS

7 Conclusion

Analysis of macular lesions is very important task in the field of ophthalmologic. In clinical practice it is important automatic method for assessing of macular lesion area and consequent evaluation of geometrical parameters. The proposed software solution offers appropriate way for automatic extraction of macular lesion and geometrical parameters as well. The proposed software solution has been tested on the sample of 40 patient's records. In the algorithm output image data are loaded. After that segmentation procedure is performed by active contour method. This method is going in iteration steps. For our purposes it is used 100 iterative steps. In the case of using larger number of iterations, we may use the more elaborate shape of analyzed object. On the other hand it would increase computation time of whole segmentation process. The significant problem of detection macular lesion is presence of adjacent blood vessels on the analyzed images. If we did not suppress those structures, active contour would spread out of analyzed object and whole segmentation process would be deteriorated. Due this fact, average filter is used. On the base low pass filtration it is possible to partially suppress adjacent structures and highlight area of macular lesions. In the present time the proposed software is being tested in clinical practice. Software results are being compared with opinions of ophthalmologic physicians from University hospital of Ostrava. There is one unfavorable fact witch deal with adjacent structures of analyzed records. In some cases it is complicated to suppress adjacent blood vessels in order to achieve more precise detection of macular lesion. In the coming time we want to focus on developing model of macular lesion which completely suppress those structures and process of detection will be more effective.

Acknowledgement. This article has been supported by financial support of TA ČR PRE SEED: TG01010137 GAMA PP1. The work and the contributions were supported by the project SP2015/179 'Biomedicínské inženýrské systémy XI' and This work is partially supported by the Science and Research Fund 2014 of the Moravia-Silesian Region, Czech Republic and this paper has been elaborated in the framework of the project "Support research and development in the Moravian-Silesian Region 2014 DT 1 - Research Teams" (RRC/07/2014). Financed from the budget of the Moravian-Silesian Region.

References

1. Wang, Z.L., et al.: Bevacizumab cured age-related macular degeneration (AMD) via down-regulate TLR2 pathway. Cent. Eur. J. Biol. **9**(5), 469–475 (2014). doi:10.2478/s11535-014-0290-5
2. Christen, W.G., Chew, E.Y.: Does long-term aspirin use increase the risk of neovascular age-related macular degeneration? Expert Opin. Drug Saf. **13**(4), 421–429 (2014). doi:10.1517/14740338.2014.889680
3. Pustkova, R., et al.: Measurement and calculation of cerebrospinal fluid in proportion to the skull. In: 2010 9th Roedunet International Conference (RoEduNet) (2010)
4. Cheung, L.K., Eaton, A.: Age-related macular degeneration. Pharmacother. J. Hum. Pharmacol. Drug Ther. **33**(8), 838–855 (2013). doi:10.1002/phar.1264
5. Penhaker, M., Matejka, V.: Image registration in neurology applications. In: 2010 International Conference on Networking and Information Technology (ICNIT) (2010)
6. Tsika, C., Tsilimbaris, M.K., Makridaki, M., Kontadakis, G., Plainis, S., Mos-chandreas, J.: Assessment of macular pigment optical density (MPOD) in patients with unilateral wet age-related macular degeneration (AMD). Acta Ophthalmol. **89**(7), e573–e578 (2011)

7. Besirli, C.G., Comer, G.M.: High-resolution OCT imaging of RPE degeneration in bilateral diffuse uveal melanocytic proliferation. Ophthalmic Surg. Lasers Imaging **41**(6), S96–S100 (2010). doi:10.3928/15428877-20101031-03

8. Stetson, P.F., et al.: OCT Minimum intensity as a predictor of geographic atrophy enlargement. Invest. Ophthalmol. **55**(2), 792–800 (2014). doi:10.1167/iovs.13-13199

9. Alam, S., et al.: Clinical application of rapid serial fourier-domain optical coherence tomography for macular imaging. Ophthalmology **113**(8), 1425–1431 (2006). doi:10.1016/j.ophtha.2006.03.020

10. Kubicek, J., et al.: Segmentation of MRI data to extract the blood vessels based on fuzzy thresholding. In: Barbucha, D., Nguyen, N.T., Batubara, J. (eds.) New Trends in Intelligent Information and Database Systems, pp. 43–52. Springer International Publishing, Heidelberg (2015)

11. Coscas, G., et al.: Optical Coherence Tomography in Age-Related Macular Degeneration: OCT in AMD. Springer, Heidelberg (2009). ISBN: 978-364-2014-680

12. BLUE LASER AUTOFLUORESCENCE. A supplement to Ophthalmology Times Europe: Blue Laser Autofluorescence. Advanstar Communications, Chester, UK [cit. 2013-12-03] (2009). ISSN: 1753-3066

13. Wang, L., et al: Active contour driven by local Gaussian distribution fitting energy. Sig. Process. **89**(12), 2435–2447 (2009). doi:10.1016/j.sigpro.2009.03.014

14. Kubicek, J., Penhaker, M.: Fuzzy algorithm for segmentation of images in extraction of objects from MRI. In: 2014 International Conference on Advances in Computing, Communications and Informatics (ICACCI 2014). IEEE (2014)

15. Kodaj, M., Kubicek, J., Penhaker, M., Bryjova, I.: Articular cartilage defect detection based on image segmentation with colour mapping. In: Hwang, D., Jung, J.J., Nguyen, N.-T. (eds.) ICCCI 2014. LNCS, vol. 8733, pp. 214–222. Springer, Heidelberg (2014)

16. Kubicek, J., Bryjova, I., Penhaker, M., Javurkova, J., Kolarcik, L.: Segmentation of macular lesions using active shape contour method. In: The 1st European-Middle Asian Conference on Computer Modelling, Issyk Kul, Kyrgyzstan, 25–27 August 2015

17. Krawiec, J., Penhaker, M., Novák, V., Bridzik, R., Kasik, V.: User interactive biomedical data web services application. In: Yonazi, J.J., Sedoyeka, E., Ariwa, E., El-Qawasmeh, E. (eds.) ICeND 2011. CCIS, vol. 171, pp. 223–237. Springer, Heidelberg (2011)

18. Kubicek, J., Penhaker, M., Feltl, D., Cvek, J.: Guidelines for modelling BED in simultaneous radiotherapy of two volumes: Tpv1 and Tpv2, 131–135 (2013). doi:10.1109/SAMI.2013.6480960

19. Pustkova, R., Kutalek, F., Penhaker, M., Novak, V.: Measurement and calculation of cerebrospinal fluid in proportion to the skull, 95–99 (2010)

Author Index

Printed in the United States
By Bookmasters